W9-CNJ-763

Criminalization, Representation, Regulation

Criminalization, Representation, Regulation
Thinking Differently about Crime

Edited by
Deborah Brock, Amanda Glasbeek,
and Carmela Murdocca

 UNIVERSITY OF TORONTO PRESS

Copyright © University of Toronto Press Incorporated 2014

Higher Education Division

www.utppublishing.com

All rights reserved. The use of any part of this publication reproduced, transmitted
in any form or by any means, electronic, mechanical, photocopying, recording,
or otherwise, or stored in a retrieval system, without prior written consent of
the publisher—or in the case of photocopying, a licence from Access Copyright
(Canadian Copyright Licensing Agency), One Yonge Street, Suite 1900, Toronto,
Ontario M5E 1E5—is an infringement of the copyright law.

LIBRARY AND ARCHIVES CANADA CATALOGUING IN PUBLICATION

Criminalization, representation, regulation : thinking differently about crime / edited by
    Deborah Brock, Amanda Glasbeek, and Carmela Murdocca.

Includes bibliographical references and index.

Issued in print and electronic formats.

ISBN 978-1-4426-0710-1 (pbk.).—ISBN 978-1-4426-0711-8 (pdf).—
ISBN 978-1-4426-0713-2 (epub)

    1. Crime—Canada.   2. Crime—Social aspects—Canada.   3. Criminal law—
Canada.   I. Brock, Deborah R. (Deborah Rose), 1956–, author, editor   II. Glasbeek,
Amanda, 1967–, author, editor   III. Murdocca, Carmela, 1975–, author, editor

HV6807.C758 2014   364.971   C2014-902006-6
                                       C2014-902007-4

We welcome comments and suggestions regarding any aspect of our publications—
please feel free to contact us at news@utphighereducation.com or visit our Internet site
at www.utppublishing.com.

North America   *UK, Ireland, and continental Europe*
5201 Dufferin Street   NBN International
North York, Ontario, Canada, M3H 5T8   Estover Road, Plymouth, PL6 7PY, UK
                                         ORDERS PHONE: 44 (0) 1752 202301
2250 Military Road   ORDERS FAX: 44 (0) 1752 202333
Tonawanda, New York, USA, 14150   ORDERS E-MAIL: enquiries@nbninternational.com

ORDERS PHONE: 1-800-565-9523
ORDERS FAX: 1-800-221-9985
ORDERS E-MAIL: utpbooks@utpress.utoronto.ca

Every effort has been made to contact copyright holders; in the event of an error or
omission, please notify the publisher.

The University of Toronto Press acknowledges the financial support for its publishing
activities of the Government of Canada through the Canada Book Fund.

For Stuart Hall

Contents

Illustrations

Image Credits: p. 37 © Blair Gable/Reuters/Landov; **p. 66** "Cycles of Exile" from *Prisoners of the War on Drugs*, comic book, by Sabrina Jones, Ellen Miller-Mack, and Lois Ahrens. © 2005 The Real Cost of Prisons Project, www.realcostofprisons.org/comics.html; **p. 71** © 2006 K. Knight, www.kchronicles.com; **p. 112** © E.J. Camp/Corbis; **p. 115** P. Raibmon, *Authentic Indians: Episodes of Encounter from the Late-Nineteenth Century Northwest Coast.* Durham, NC: Duke University Press, 2005, p. 7; **p. 119** © Everett Collection/The Canadian Press; **p. 122** © Monkeybusinessimages/Dreamstime.com/GetStock.com; **p. 123** © Craig Robertson/Toronto Sun/QMI Agency; **p. 124** © Court Handout/QMI Agency; **p. 125** © Gerard Kwiatkowski/The Canadian Press; **p. 127** © Caryn Ceolin/Daily Herald-Tribune/QMI Agency; **p. 145** © HOMITOHIKARU/iStock.com; **p. 149** © floridastock/iStock.com; **p. 153** © a_berent/iStock.com; **p. 178** © Bill Hearne/Newspix/Getty Images; **p. 183** © MARK BLINCH/Reuters/Landov; **p. 184** © Robert Taylor/Edmonton Sun/QMI Agency; p. 201 Courtesy of IKEA Italy and Jacopo Cima (photographer); **p. 210** Courtesy of Deborah Brock; **p. 260** © Jupiterimages/Thickstock; **p. 263** © kodda/iStock.com; **p. 273** Courtesy of Tamara Abdul Hadi.; **p. 286** Created with permission of Canada Border Services Agency; **p. 290** © Courtesy of RCMP; **p. 295** © Chris Roussakis/QMI Agency; **p. 332** United Nations Photo; **p. 346** © Reza Shirmohammadi/AP Photo/The Canadian Press; **p. 348** © JODI BIEBER/EPA/Landov; **p. 360** © Kerry Doubleday/The Canadian Press; **p. 379** © andipantz/iStock.com; **p. 386** © WARREN TODA/EPA/Landov; **p. 406** © Shaney Komulainen/The Canadian Press; **p. 411** © David Maracle.

Acknowledgments

We have dedicated this book to Stuart Hall (1932–2014), whose influence on each of our own scholarly development cannot be measured. From his work on "policing the crisis" (a conjunctural analysis of the rise of the New Right in 1970s England that connected economic and class politics with the racialization of crime) to his later work on the politics of representation and his final work on challenging neoliberalism, Stuart Hall broke conventional boundaries and made scholarly pursuits exciting. He will be missed.

We want to thank the many hundreds of students who have taken our courses in sociolegal studies, criminology, and social, sexual, and moral regulation over the years. They have been our guides in instructing us about what is required to produce scholarship that is relevant, accessible, and useful—and moreover, how to teach it.

Amanda Glasbeek and Carmela Murdocca wish to express their gratitude and thanks to their co-editor, Deborah Brock, for her unflagging support and mentorship, not only on this project but in our professional endeavours generally. She has been an exemplary colleague and we would not have been able to undertake this project without her inspiration.

Carmela would also like to thank her past teaching assistants (without whom teaching a course of 200+ would be impossible) for their commitment to the distinct approach of the course "Sociology of Crime and Social Regulation," which inspired this textbook. In particular, Anke Allspach, Fenn Stewart, and Shaira Vadasaria engaged thoroughly with the course for a number of years. Carmela also extends thanks to her parents for their support and encouragement.

Amanda Glasbeek offers her thanks to the students and teaching assistants in criminology who have taught her many things about justice. Amanda also extends her appreciation to the faculty in the Department of Social Science for their much needed and always respectful collegial support. Finally, Amanda thanks Phil and Sasha, for everything else.

Deborah Brock extends a bouquet of thanks to Carmela and Amanda for being such first-rate collaborators and terrific scholars and teachers. Thanks also go to the Department of Sociology at York University for allowing us the latitude to rethink what it means to do criminology through our courses, particularly the "Sociology of Crime and Social Regulation." Deborah would also like to thank the International Institute for the Sociology of Law in Oñati, Basque Country, Spain, for many wonderful experiences as a visiting scholar, and Artscape Gibralter Point on Toronto Islands for providing a unique oasis in which to research and write. Special thanks go to Gerard de Witt for the "sunflower room" in Utrecht, The Netherlands. Gezellig!

We extend our deep appreciation and many thanks to our production team at the University of Toronto Press, and, in particular, to our editor Anne Brackenbury. Anne has been solidly behind this project since the early stages, and a great source of support and advice. Finally, a big thank-you to Gaye Chan for the striking cover design. The cover image is of a construction hoarding at Hastings and Main Streets in Vancouver's Downtown East Side. Perhaps no other neighbourhood in Canada has been as closely identified with crime as this one; yet when we peel back the layers of representation, we might think differently about crime.

introduction

Thinking Differently about Crime

DEBORAH BROCK

At some point in time, we all break a law. Usually these transgressions are minor, and we may not even be aware of what we have done, or we may consciously dismiss the transgression with the idea that "everyone does it" or that it was a ridiculous law that deserved to be broken. We typically distance ourselves from "real" crime by associating it with extreme cases such as deliberately taking the life of another—cases that actually constitute a small percentage of the crimes committed. We might also be "suspect" for criminal wrongdoing simply because we inhabit a particular kind of body, or we might be one who implicates certain "others" because of their identity. Criminalization, then, is an intensely social activity that is not as removed from our own actions and our own bodies as we might think.

Criminalization, Representation, Regulation does not situate crime as asocial or atypical phenomena, but rather begins with the recognition that naming what counts as crime, who commits it, and who is implicated in it are social decisions. Our task is to problematize ideas about what crime is and who commits it. Rather than taking crime as an already existing social phenomenon—as a social fact—we explore *criminalization* as an active social process, focusing in particular on how crime and those who commit crimes are constituted. By *constituted* we mean the "making up" (or social production) of people, beliefs, and practices through everyday activities, discourses and ideologies, and the flow of power. Each chapter in this volume explores the dynamic interplay between processes of criminalization and the ways that such processes circulate to both reflect and constitute crime and "justice."

It is not our intention to dismiss the incidence and prevalence of crime or to undermine the potential seriousness of many actions that violate the law. Instead, we mean to open up the analyses of crime in the tradition of critical criminology. We aim to expose the complexity of the issues and the debates surrounding crime, processes of criminalization, and the means of regulation. We unpack crime as a social "fact," and as you will read in Chapter Four, "The Politics of Counting Crime," written by Michael Mopas, we turn a critical eye to the explanation, measurement, and administration of crime.

Thinking beyond "Crime"

A focus on criminalization is only part of what we do. This textbook was designed to situate criminalization within broader relations of regulation that shape subjectivity and action. The beliefs and practices of people, individually and as members of a group, are infused with power relations that influence our will, our interests, what we can know, and how we can know what we know.

Our task is to make the connections between our own knowledge and experience and "the big picture" of social institutions, processes, and power. We will find that the assumptions we may hold about the distinction between the private life of the self and the broader world of politics and power fall away. Who we are, how we see ourselves, and how we regard others are inseparable from power. How we think, what ideas we advocate, and how we live and act come together to reproduce, challenge, and redeploy power. It is not possible to think about criminalization, representation, and regulation, then, without also considering how power is enacted through these processes.

Regulation is a useful umbrella concept in part because it does not imply any one particular theoretical approach, meaning that the concept of regulation is one that can be understood broadly. Here we will explain how we use it in order to make it less unwieldy to understand and to use as you read the chapters that follow. First, we have adopted an understanding of power and regulation that was introduced by Michel Foucault, which has become foundational to the governmentality approach. As you will learn in Carmela Murdocca's chapter "Michel Foucault: Theories and 'Method'" (Chapter One), Foucault productively complicated our understanding of power through his nuanced exploration of the numerous forms that it can take. He identified governmental power as the most pervasive form in contemporary Western liberal democratic societies, but by *government* he specified a flow of power that extended far beyond the political apparatus of the state. This form of power is not limited to the exercise of authority and control *over* individuals and populations—it is distinguished by its relational character and by its entanglement with the production of knowledge. For example, the privileging of certain forms of knowledge as "truth" implies that power relations are already present.

At the same time, power is most effective when it is exercised through the shaping of ideas and beliefs, rather than when it is exercised with a fist, handcuffs, or a prison cell. Governmental power is realized in people's capacity to be self-reflective, to judge, and to act. We are governed through the deployment of knowledge that privileges certain ways of knowing and being, and we actively participate in governmental relations through our own government of others and of ourselves. For these reasons, a broadly Foucauldian approach informs what we do in this book. It is an effective theoretical orientation for undertaking contemporary, historical, and materially grounded research. An approach that draws attention to the social basis of law also allows for more comprehensive attention to the processes of regulation that may be, but are not necessarily, state centred. Our approach to regulation shifts analysis away from the top-down exercise of social control so that we may more easily identify regulation as a range of processes that permeate our everyday lives and activities.

The second direction that we will pursue is to centre an analysis of the politics of representation. This is a crucial vantage point for comprehending how meaning is given and how knowledge and power intersect in dominant explanations of crime, as you will find in Ummni Khan's chapter "The Politics of Representation" (Chapter Three). For now, we want you to think about a typical representation of a criminal. Does the image that comes to mind have a gender? What is the colour of her or his skin? How is he or she dressed? What is she or he doing? Is the body being represented similar to or different from your own?

Much of people's knowledge about crime and criminality is derived not from their own experience but from mainstream media and popular culture. We explore representations of crime and criminality in media and popular culture not only to challenge the myths and stereotypes that surround crime, but also to examine the forms of regulation that inform representations of criminalization. In Chapter Seven, "Women Gone Bad? Women, Criminalization, and Representation," Amanda Glasbeek explores how fact and fiction often blur when women are constructed as criminals, especially when they are accused of violent crimes. You will find that Ruthann Lee's contribution, "Gendering Crime: Men and Masculinities" (Chapter Six), devotes particular attention to representations of racialized masculinities in contemporary mainstream film. You will see how South Asian racialized masculinities are variously represented in relation to crime, albeit in a manner that implicates their racial and ethnic origin in some way. Racism occurs when any action by a person is taken as representative of their ethnic or racial group or, where the actions of a racialized person are seen in a positive light, as a departure from the typical characteristics of their racial or ethnic group.

A notable feature of this textbook is its attention to the interconnections between processes of colonialism and racialization. Tracking these processes provides a framework that links criminalization with the emergence of the white nation-state. You will find ample evidence throughout this book of the importance of historical analyses for exploring processes of racialization and criminalization. In Chapter Two, "History Matters," Amanda Glasbeek explores how the *historicization* of crime can contribute to our critical engagement with processes of representation, criminalization, and regulation. Moreover, given the privileged place of moral reasoning in the formation of law and ethics, in Chapter Two you will learn more about how moral regulation was foundational to the expansion of the Criminal Code from its inception in 1892.

The place of morality in processes of criminalization is not restricted to the past, despite recent efforts in Canadian law to shift from morals-based reasoning to harm-based reasoning. For example, in Chapter Nine, "Crime and Social Classes: Regulating and Representing Public Disorder" Marie-Eve Sylvestre suggests that poverty has been remoralized, pathologized, and de facto criminalized. The treatment of people whose greatest offence was to be born poor is situated in stark contrast to the treatment of corporate crime, which is the topic of Steven Bittle's chapter "Where Are All the Corporate Criminals?" (Chapter Thirteen).

In Chapter Five, "Racialization, Criminalization, Representation," Carmela Murdocca takes aim at uncovering the constitution of race in the history of Canadian nation-building and the formation of Canadian law. You will find that historicizing social processes such as the creation of law grants insight into the patterns of continuity and change and to the dynamics at work in producing what counts as crime. Chapter Five identifies the ongoing significance of these processes for First Nations peoples, for racialized peoples, and for broad sociopolitical relations in which modern states, the international economy, and global culture flourish in ways that marginalize and imperil a significant portion of the world's population.

We have chosen to foreground processes of racialization because of the significance of the invention of "race" for the formation of local and global inequalities. Further, race is pervasive in narratives about crime. Racialization is most fruitfully explored relationally, through its intersections with the constitution of gender, sexualities, class, and citizenship. So, for example, in Chapter Eight, "Sexual Regulation: Sexing Governmentality; Governing Sex," Deborah Brock includes a discussion of the mutual constitution of race and sexuality. We will find here that the simultaneous racialization and sexualization of particular bodies (for example, the Black slave body, the indigenous body, the "oriental" body) has constituted those bodies as sites of governance. We also note the particular ways in which racialized bodies are marked bodies, targeted through surveillance, through racial profiling, and through border policing. These issues are taken up in Chapter Ten, "Profiles and Profiling Technology: Stereotypes, Surveillance, and Governmentality," by Martin French and Simone Browne and in Chapter Eleven, "Wanted by the Canada Border Services Agency," by Anna Pratt.

What about global human rights? Increasingly, we look to human rights to acknowledge if not to rectify past injustices. You will find in Marcia Oliver's chapter "In the Name of Human Rights: Governing and Representing Non-Western Lives in Post-9/11" (Chapter Twelve) that while few have claimed that human rights are a panacea for global inequalities, their effectiveness in confronting inequalities facing indigenous and racialized peoples are highly questionable. How can we continue to speak of human rights in the context of ongoing state-organized violence, the violation of peoples and their environments, and suffering on a global scale?

Criminalization, Representation, Regulation is a text that explores and challenges mainstream approaches to crime and criminality, and the critical analysis undertaken is motivated by a specific interest in social justice. This textbook encourages the development of critical analytic thought toward the pragmatic consideration of social issues and problems and how to resolve them more effectively. Tia Dafnos's chapter "Social Movements and Critical Resistance: Policing Colonial Capitalist Order" (Chapter Fourteen) was placed as the final chapter of this text to underscore that criminal injustice is a pervasive feature of criminalization, representation, and regulation and to emphasize the need for social action. Chapter Fourteen gives special attention to the criminalization of protest and dissent by focusing on the policing of Aboriginal protests.

Overview of the Book

Criminalization, Representation, Regulation is organized into three thematic sections. Part One, "Thinking Differently about Crime," serves as an introduction to the main objectives and issues of the book and establishes the theoretical and methodological context for the chapters that follow. We turn a critical lens on definitions of crime and criminality and reflect on the origins of information, meaning, and interpretation. This section orients readers to practices of reading, observing, and hearing that are filtered through everyday assumptions and directs them toward a more critical interrogation of representations, discourses, and data.

Part Two, "Intersections," explores the broad social intersections through which criminalization processes, as well as the dynamics of representation of crime, can be concretely examined. The bodies of subjects entangled with the law—whether as victims, suspects, or agents of the law—matter when we look at how legal processes unfold and the ways that crime is understood as a social fact. The ways in which race, gender, sexuality, class, and nation-building intersect with one another and with processes of criminalization are the focus of this section. Together they help the reader to grasp the social bases for criminalization processes, and they demonstrate the importance of understanding the connections between social bases of inequality and the regulation and representation of "crime."

Part Three, "Emerging Issues in Canada and Beyond: Connecting the Global to the Local," explores the social and legal contexts through which processes of criminalization and regulation can be concretely examined. Each chapter addresses a global contemporary context that includes surveillance, national security and borders, crime in an international context, environmental crime, and social movements. These chapters provide readers with an interdisciplinary and critical framework with which to investigate these contemporary social and political issues.

Learning Objectives

This textbook is based on our combined years of experience teaching large and small courses in criminology and sociolegal studies. When thinking about how to develop this book, our students have been our best teachers. We also brought to this project a number of important objectives. The first objective is to encourage students' appreciation of the uses of history and theory for exploring criminalization, representation, and regulation as active social processes. Second, we want students to question taken-for-granted assumptions about crime and criminality and to think about where those assumptions come from. Third, we want to provide students with some tools to become more critical consumers of information. Fourth, we want to encourage students to think together about how to identify and challenge social injustices that are at the root of processes of criminalization.

We hope that the distinctive features of this textbook will provide you with some helpful tools with which to engage with these objectives. These features include the *combined use* of a governmentality approach, the linking of legal regulation to broader forms of social and moral regulation, a focus on the politics of representation, an integration of historical and contemporary research, an engagement with local and global frameworks, and an engagement with the politics of resistance.

It has been our pleasure to work with many hundreds of students who are deeply interested in the issues presented in this book, and whose concern about local and global social inequalities have motivated them to not only produce their own important analyses, but in the words of Mahatma Gandhi, to be part of the change that they wish to see in the world. We are also grateful to have recruited such an impressive collection of contributors who share our enthusiasm for the book and who have provided their expertise and their time toward realizing its objectives.

PART I

Thinking Differently about Crime

This is a book that asks you to identify and challenge your underlying assumptions about crime and criminality. As you will learn in Part One, "Thinking Differently about Crime," our aim is to expose you to the complexity of the issues and the debates surrounding crime; explore the social processes involved in the criminalization of people, identities, and groups; and understand the relationship between criminalization and the broader processes of regulation.

Part One of *Criminalization, Representation, Regulation* introduces readers to the central themes and issues of the book and establishes the theoretical and methodological context for the chapters that follow. You will turn a critical lens on definitions of *crime* and *criminality* and reflect on the origins of their sources of information, meaning, and interpretation. The chapters in Part One identify practices of reading, observing, and hearing that are shaped by everyday assumptions, suggesting the need for a more critical interrogation of representations, discourses, and data.

We begin by outlining an approach to crime, criminalization, and regulation in which these concepts are more than legal definitions and practices, but active social processes whose historical constitution and contemporary representations must be explored. Given the extent of our critique of mainstream criminal justice, it is incumbent on us to suggest how we might begin to reimagine the social organization of crime. While it is not our objective to provide blueprints for social change, we present readers with examples of social movement activism that counter mainstream perspectives, policy, and action. The importance of the politics of resistance and reimagining that is the raison d'être of social movement activism (a matter that we will return to in our conclusion to this collection) is stressed. Our general aim in this part opener is to establish the conceptual framework through which the chapters that follow will be presented, provide an overview of the themes and topics that follow, and present the learning objectives for students who are working with this textbook.

In Chapter One, "Michel Foucault: Theories and 'Method,'" Carmela Murdocca situate the emergence of critical ideas concerning crime, representation, and regulation in the context of Michel Foucault's work on discipline, punishment, and governance. Foucault's key insights have had a significant impact on the related disciplines of criminology and sociolegal studies. You will begin to see how this approach opens up a complex nexus of regulation that inspires many researchers to engage in detailed, localized, and empirically grounded studies. While the Foucauldian approach is commonly associated with poststructuralist theorizing, *Criminalization, Representation, Regulation* aims to present a materially grounded analysis. Murdocca demonstrates how Foucault's insights can enhance political and economic research and analyses of crime and criminalization. This is particularly the case where research is simultaneously informed by anti-racist, postcolonial, feminist, and queer theories. As such, an *intersectional* and *relational* analytic framework is crucial and will be explained in detail.

One of the key features of governmentality scholarship is that it historicizes our assumptions about what crime is (and is not). Chapter Two, "History Matters," by Amanda Glasbeek raises the issue of how the social and geographical character and constitution of crime and criminalization further problematize how they are known. The chapter acquaints students with what it means to undertake a historical and spatial analysis of crime and regulation. It will then identify a key underpinning for definitions of crime and processes of regulation throughout Canadian history—*moral regulation*—the significance of which is linked to governmentality studies. Finally, moral regulation will be explored in relation to the formation of law, nation-building, and colonialism and their significance for contemporary understandings and practices of crime, representation, and regulation. This chapter will compel you to think more about how a historical perspective can assist us in problematizing the notion of crime and, in particular, grasp the significance of moral regulation for definitions of crime and criminality.

Much of our knowledge of the social world is derived not from our own experience but from myth—"common knowledge," popular media, and the like. Even our perceptions of our own experiences are shaped in some way by these external forces and discourses. Chapter Three critiques our ways of knowing by introducing students to "The Politics of Representation." Drawing on the work of Stuart Hall, Ummni Khan chapter explores how meaning is given to things, people, and practices, and thus how knowledge and power intersect. She provides you with some direction for critically viewing images so that their underlying political and regulatory dimensions become more visible. This chapter will provide you with numerous examples of representations of crime and criminality, giving particular attention to the racialization of crime, to demonstrate the significance of the politics of representation for the chapters that follow. We will ask you to think about why an analysis of the politics of representation is so crucial to challenging our assumptions about crime and criminality.

In these first three chapters, readers learn to problematize the notion of crime itself by not only being introduced to the historical constitution of notions of crime, but also to the social and economic context in which crime, processes of criminalization, and regulation occur. Chapter Four, "The Politics of Counting Crime," presents a number of methodological and statistical approaches to the study and measurement of crime, demonstrating some of the flaws and limitations that make crime so difficult to quantify. Here Michael Mopas unpacks crime as a social "fact" and turns a critical eye to the explanation, measurement, and administration of crime. Rather than being an instrument of objective truth-telling, you will see how statistics have an important role in meaning-making and the creation of "truths." This should lead you to further challenge your preexisting notions about crime and criminality by exposing taken-for-granted and "**common sense**" assumptions and incomplete reasoning. Finally, this chapter will explore how methodologists might make best (and provisional) use of data collection methods. Generally, we want to provide you with instruction in how to critique crime-related data, whether the data are derived from police reports, government studies, or popular media. Along the way, the chapter addresses questions such as "What is it incidence and prevalence of crime in Canada?" "Why is it so difficult to measure crime?" "How can one, in effect, 'lie' with statistics?" "What is the best, however provisional, means of giving crime an empirical face?"

one

Michel Foucault:
Theories and "Method"

CARMELA MURDOCCA

Introduction

Michel Foucault was one of the most influential intellectuals of the twentieth century. He began to publish his writing in the 1960s, and his work has influenced sociology, criminology, postcolonial studies, literary and cultural studies, queer theory, women's studies, anthropology, education, and other disciplines. This introductory chapter explores some of the major themes concerning discipline, punishment, and governance advanced in Foucault's writings. Arguably, his writings have had the most significant impact on thinking about questions concerning criminalization and **social regulation**. Foucault's scholarship has allowed researchers to engage in detailed, localized, and empirically grounded studies.

Who Is Michel Foucault?

Michel Foucault was born in 1926 in Poitiers, France, and studied history, philosophy, and psychology. In his lifetime, he was a teacher, professor, and activist. He died at the age of 57 in 1984. Foucault was a prolific writer, lecturer, and public intellectual. He is considered to be part of a philosophi-cal movement called **poststructuralism**. Poststructuralist theories generally "conceive of social space (organizations, institutions, social categories, con-cepts, identities and relationships, etc.) and the world of material objects as discursive in nature ... A second tenet of post-structuralist theory of discourse is that ... meaning is never finally fixed; it is always in an unstable flux."[1] Definitions for *discursive* and *discourse* will become clearer as we pursue an examination of Foucault's work.

Foucault wrote many books, articles, and gave many lectures and inter-views. Some of the more significant of his books include *Madness and Civilization* (1961), *The Birth of the Clinic* (1963), *The Order of Things* (1966), *The Archaeology of Knowledge* (1969), *Discipline and Punish* (1975), *The Use of*

---

1 "Post-Structuralism and Discourse Theory," Universiteit Gent, http://www.english.ugent.be/da/poststructuralisttheory (accessed April 15, 2013).

Pleasure (1984), and *The History of Sexuality, Volume 1* (1978). As the titles of his books suggest, Foucault was an eclectic writer and thinker. His writings examine a range of topics including psychiatry and the development of the medical profession, sexuality, prisons, methodology and the nature of knowledge, and changing state formations. His eclecticism highlights the fact that he is not an easily categorizable scholar. Is Foucault a philosopher? Is Foucault a historical sociologist, a historical psychologist, or a criminologist? Michel Foucault would himself eschew these questions. He might indicate that to answer these questions would be to conform to and confirm the power of social science knowledge to organize, fix, and define meaning for people. Foucault is not interested in fixed categories. He wanted readers of his books (and especially those who interviewed him) to recognize that his ideas change over time and that ways of thinking he might have been attached to early in his career might be ways of thinking that he would or might later come to fiercely contest. When writing about who he is as a thinker and writer, Foucault suggests the following in one of his earlier books: "Do not ask who I am and do not ask me to remain the same: leave it to our bureaucrats and our police to see that our papers are in order. At least spare us their morality when we write."[2]

Foucault did not want his writing to be read as definitive accounts about a particular topic. For example, *Discipline and Punish*, which focuses on the social and philosophical changes in the nature of punishment in the modern era using the French penal system as a case study, should not be understood as a definitive account of punishment and penality in France in the modern era. Instead, his writings offer a set of ideas and guidelines that provide new ways of asking questions and new directions for research. Foucault wanted his books (*Discipline and Punish* in particular) to be read with the following caveat in mind: "I would like my books to be a kind of tool-box which others can rummage through to find a tool which they can use however they wish in their own area ... I would like the little volume that I want to write on disciplinary systems to be useful to an educator, a warden, a magistrate, a conscientious objector. I don't write for an audience, I write for users, not readers."[3]

In the spirit of rummaging through Foucault's work, this chapter identifies some of the tools that he offers for analyzing the relationships between criminalization, regulation, and representation. In particular, the concepts of power, knowledge, discipline, governmentality, and biopolitics are examined.

---

2 Michel Foucault, *The Archaeology of Knowledge*, trans. A.M. Sheridan Smith (New York: Routledge, 2007), 19.

3 Michel Foucault, "Prisons et asiles dans le mécanisme du pouvoir," in *Dits et Ecrits*, vol. 11 (Paris: Gallimard, 1994 [1974]), 523–24. (This passage trans. Clare O'Farrell.)

These concepts are indispensable when undertaking interdisciplinary studies of criminalization, regulation, and representation.

Foucault's "Method"

Although he did not want to be categorized as a particular type of scholar, there were certain themes that remained consistent throughout Foucault's writing. In all of Foucault's more historical works (though not "historical" in the sense of offering a totalizing history about a particular topic), like *Discipline and Punish*, he is interested in (1) the ways in which certain social, political, and legal practices were different from the practices that preceded them in an earlier time or generation, and (2) providing an account of the ways in which these changes may have occurred. To account for social changes, he sometimes fashioned himself as an "archaeologist" mining new social, political, and legal phenomena for answers to the most pressing political questions of a particular generation. As a result, some of Foucault's work can be understood as methodological, in the sense that his writing offers research tools for examining social and political institutions, practices, and formations. He did not seek to advance a "total history" on a particular topic (which he viewed as one of the great limitations of the traditional historical method); instead, the tools for historical analysis he espoused were directed at examining changes, alterations, divergences, vacillations, and transformations in historical, political, and sociological worlds and institutions. How does political change occur? How do social views about a particular crime change over time? As Foucault explains:

> The great problem presented by such historical analyses is not how continuities are established, how a single pattern is formed and preserved, how for so many different, successive minds there is a single horizon ... the problem is no longer one of tradition, of tracing a line, but one of division, of limits; it is no longer one of lasting foundations, but one of transformations that serve as new foundations, the rebuilding of foundations.[4]

Foucault sought to move away from historical analyses of "vast unities like 'periods' or 'centuries'" to examinations that prioritized the "phenomena of rupture, of discontinuity."[5]

---

4 Foucault, *The Archaeology of Knowledge*, 6.
5 Ibid., 4.

Foucault's **archaeological method** used the archive (the archive as a place, a concept, and a metaphor) as the domain in which discontinuities and ruptures can be analyzed in a historical process. Of the archive, Foucault states:

> By this term I do not mean the sum of all texts that a culture has kept upon its person as documents attesting to its own past, or as evidence of continuing identity; nor do I mean the institutions, which, in a given society, make it possible to record and preserve those discourses that one wishes to remember and keep in circulation. On the contrary ... the archive is also that which determines that all these things said do not accumulate endlessly in an amorphous mass, nor are they inscribed in an unbroken linearity ... Archaeology describes discourses and practices specified in the element of the archive.[6]

As Barry Smart explains further: "The object of archaeological analysis is then a description of the archive, literally what may be spoken of in discourse; what statements survive, disappear, get re-used, etc. The ultimate objective of such an analysis of discourse is not to reveal a hidden meaning or deep truth, neither is it to trace the origin of discourse to a particular mind or subject, but to document its conditions of existence and the field in which it is deployed."[7] For Foucault, an archaeological approach means trying to ascertain why certain ways of thinking, why particular kinds of analysis (the kinds of questions we ask), why certain ways of explaining social and political phenomena survive and proliferate in a particular culture. An archaeological approach "constitutes the set of rules which define the limits and forms of expressibility, conservation, memory, reactivation and appropriation in a particular time, culture or institution."[8] An archaeological analysis directs us to examine how certain statements stand in for the "truth," how particular individuals are endowed with the expertise to make "truth claims" about a particular subject, and how these ways of speaking and "truth-making" produce particular forms of knowledge, power, and dominant ways of thinking in a particular culture, society, or institution. In using the example of the institution of medicine and expertise of doctors and medical practitioners, Foucault suggests the following about how one might undertake an archaeological analysis:

> Qualitative descriptions, biographical accounts, the location,
> interpretation, and cross-checking of signs, reasonings by analogy,

---

6 Ibid., 145–47.
7 Barry Smart, *Michel Foucault* (London: Routledge, 2004), 48.
8 Ibid., 48.

deduction, statistical calculations, experimental verifications, and many other forms of statement are to be found in the discourse of nineteenth-century doctors. What is it that links them together? What necessity binds them together? Why these and not others?[9]

These kinds of questions form the basis of Foucault's archaeological "method." In this approach, Foucault has identified that related questions may include

Who is speaking? ... Who is qualified to do so? ... Who derives from it his own special quality, his prestige, and from whom, in return, does he receive if not the assurance, at least the presumption that what he says is true? What is the status of the individuals who—alone—have the right, sanctioned by law or tradition, juridically defined or spontaneously accepted, to proffer such a discourse. The status of doctor involves criteria of competence and knowledge; institutions, systems, pedagogic norms; legal conditions that give the right—though not with laying down certain limitations—to practice and to extend one's knowledge.[10]

As you can tell, Foucault's archaeological method aims to examine the inner workings of bureaucracies, systems, and institutions to ask questions about the relations between people and systems and the forms of knowledge, discourses, processes, and procedures that produce systems and institutions in a given society.

In later work, Foucault refined the archaeological "method" and supplanted (or altered) his approach with the introduction of the concept of **genealogy**.[11] His genealogical method is often described as "a history of the present," in the sense that the approach examines contemporary social phenomena in relation to the histories on which they depend.[12] For example, in *Discipline and Punish*, Foucault did not seek to write a chronological account of punishment in nineteenth-century France. His aim was to account for the profound transformation in ideas about punishment—changes that were not

---

9 Foucault, *The Archaeology of Knowledge*, 6.

10 Ibid., 55–56.

11 Barry Smart suggests that elements of Foucault's archaeological approach remained as a part of the genealogical method. The two methods appear to overlap in their concerns and the kinds of questions they encourage us to ask.

12 Mitchell Dean, "A Genealogy of the Government of Poverty," *Economy and Society* 21, no. 3 (1992): 215–51.

only relegated to the domain of the prison but were accompanied by changes throughout French society. In this work, he is interested in examining what he calls *discontinuities* or *ruptures* in historical processes. In the case of philosophies pertaining to the French penal system (which he tracks in *Discipline and Punish*) and the changes that occurred in ideas about punishment in the modern era, Foucault is interested in asking how ideas about punishment shifted so dramatically in France between 1757 through to the 1840s and later. We will explore these changes in more detail in the next section.

In his famous essay "Nietzsche, Genealogy, History," Foucault begins by describing genealogy in the following manner: "Genealogy is gray, meticulous, and patiently documentary. It operates on a field of entangled and confused parchments, on documents that have been scratched over and recopied many times."[13] The task of the historical, social, and political analyst is to trace the ways in which social, historical, and political relations are constituted in an archive through language and meaning. Barry Smart describes genealogy in the following manner: "[G]enealogy uncovers the eternal play of dominations, the domain of violence, subjugation and struggle."[14]

For now, it is important to appreciate that Foucault's genealogical method requires that we analyze present social, political, and cultural phenomena "based upon their historical establishment"[15] (like contemporary ideas about punishment and criminalization) with a particular focus on contingency (the ways in which the historical past assists with our understanding of the present) and on discursive power. Foucault maintains that a genealogical approach "locate(s) forms of power, the channels it takes, and the discourses it permeates."[16]

Discourse, Power, and Knowledge

Michel Foucault uses the words **discourse**, **power**, and **knowledge** consistently throughout his work. One of the central themes of Foucault's work is the relationship between individuals and power in a given society. Paul Rabinow has described this theme in the following manner: The main

---

13 In this essay, Foucault is attempting to trace the influences of Nietzsche's work in his genealogical approach. Michel Foucault, "Nietzsche, Genealogy, History," in *Michel Foucault: Ethics, Subjectivity, and Truth*, ed. Paul Rabinow, 76–100 (New York: The New Press, 1994).

14 Smart, *Michel Foucault*, 59.

15 Sylvere Lotringer, ed., *Foucault Live: Interviews 1966–1984*, trans. J. Johnson (New York: Semiotexte, 1989), 64.

16 Michel Foucault, *The History of Sexuality*, vol. 2, trans. Robert Hurley (New York: Pantheon, 1978), 11.

objective of Michel Foucault's work was to "create a history of the different modes by which, in our culture, human beings are made subjects."[17]

What does Foucault mean by power? In his own words (and in an often-cited quote), Foucault expressed that he is interested in how power "reaches into the very grain of individuals, touches their bodies and inserts itself into their actions and attitudes, their discourses, learning processes and everyday lives."[18] Foucault examines the reasons why (and the ways in which) individuals conform to the rules of a given society. He is interested in the ways in which rules, procedures, and institutions are organized to enable people to conform to a given system. In this sense, the idea of power that Foucault pursues is not the conventional power of rulers, leaders, prime ministers, and presidents, rather it is the forms of power that operate in mundane and subtle ways in a given society.

As you may have noticed from Foucault's definition of power, power does not exist in isolation. Power is situated among many social practices and is interwoven into our identities and into our behaviour. Power exists within discourse. What, then, is discourse? As Stuart Hall explains,

> [By] "discourse," Foucault meant a "group of statements which provide a language for talking about—a way of representing knowledge about—a particular topic at a particular historical moment ... Discourse is about the production of knowledge through language. But ... since all social practices entail *meaning*, and meanings shape and influence what we do—our conduct—all practices have a discursive aspect.[19]

For Foucault, discourse becomes a dimension of how power relations work between institutions, groups, and individuals.[20] Following Hall's analysis of Foucault, discourse is (1) a "system of representation" and (2) about "language and practice." Discourse is a *group of statements* that provide a language for talking about a particular topic in a particular historical moment. Discourse, Foucault argues, "*constructs* a particular topic.... It defines and produces the objects of our knowledge. It governs the way that a topic can meaningfully be talked about and reasoned about."[21] As Hall explains,

17 Michel Foucault, cited in Paul Rabinow, *The Foucault Reader* (New York: Pantheon, 1984), 7.
18 Michel Foucault, *Power/Knowledge: Selected Interviews & Other Writings 1972–1977*, ed. C. Gordon, trans. C. Gordon, L. Marshal, J. Mepham, and K. Sober (New York: Pantheon Books, 1980), 30.
19 Stuart Hall, "The Work of Representation," in *Representation: Cultural Representation and Signifying Practices*, ed. Stuart Hall (London: Sage, 1992), 72.
20 Teun A. Van Dijk, "Structures of Discourse and Structures of Power," *Communication Yearbook* 12: 18–59.
21 Hall, "The Work of Representation," 72.

Foucault was interested in the *rules and practices* that produce meaningful statements and regulated discourse in different historical periods.[22]

To use a concrete example, criminology is a discourse that invents or produces its own set of ideas and languages about the "criminal" as a subject and object to be studied. And criminology, as a discourse, is backed up by many institutions like prisons, the criminal justice system, courts, criminology courses, criminology programs, and so on. Foucault would refer to these institutions and practices as **discursive formations**—that is, social, political, and historical formations that give rise to discourse. Foucault states that "discourse produces objects of knowledge."[23] Power works its way distinctly through discourse to help shape the whole of society's view of crime and criminality. Knowledge in this way may act as a way of keeping people in control or of regulating individual behaviour. The most important idea about discourse is the question of *meaning*. As Ernesto Laclau and Chantal Mouffe put it, "we use [the term discourse] to emphasize the fact that every social configuration is *meaningful*. The concept of discourse is not about whether things exist but where meaning comes from."[24]

You will notice that in Foucault's idea of discourse, the concepts of power and knowledge play key supporting roles. The social, political, and historical configuration of discourse is intimately connected to the concepts of power and knowledge. *Discourse facilitates, produces, and is constitutive of the relationship between power and knowledge.* In making this connection, Stuart Hall argues that Foucault identified two "radically novel" ideas about power: (1) the connection between knowledge, power, and "truth," and (2) a new conception of power. It is important to address each of these propositions.[25]

Knowledge, Power, and Regimes of "Truth"

Foucault developed important links between knowledge, power, and "truth." He suggests that "knowledge (is) always a form of power."[26] The particular words used by Foucault are important: He is not suggesting that knowledge *is* power. Rather, he argues that knowledge is a mechanism of power—a form of power. As others have explained, "Foucault refutes the idea that he makes the claim 'knowledge is power' and says that he is interested in studying the complex relations between power and knowledge *without saying they are the same*

---

22 Ibid.
23 Ibid.
24 Ibid., 73.
25 Ibid.
26 Ibid., 76.

thing."[27] Thus, Foucault establishes an important connection between particular forms of power and the establishment of fields of knowledge. For example, the social sciences (sociology, criminology, law, history, geography, economics, etc.) represent fields of knowledge that "not only assume the authority of 'the truth' but has the power to *make itself true.*"[28] An important feature of Foucault's ideas about power and knowledge is the realm of specialized knowledge:

> According to Foucault, what we think we "know" in a particular period about, say, crime has a bearing on how we regulate, control and punish criminals. Knowledge does not operate in a void. It is put to work, through certain technologies and strategies of application, in specific situations, historical contexts and institutional regimes. To study punishment, you must study how the combination of discourse and power—power/knowledge—has produced a certain conception of crime and the criminal, has had certain real effects both for the criminal and for the punisher, and how these have been set into practice in certain historically specific prison regimes.[29]

These important connections between specific contexts and sites (e.g., national or local media), institutions (e.g., prisons), and historical contexts together produce what Foucault describes as "regimes of truth." In *Discipline and Punish*, Foucault explains that "each society has its regime of truth, its general politics of truth: that is the types of discourse which it accepts and makes function as true; the mechanisms and instances which enable one to distinguish true and false statements, the means by which each is sanctioned the techniques and procedures accorded value in the acquisition of truth, the status of those who are charged with saying what counts as true."[30]

Productive Power

The second contribution of Foucault's theorizations of power is that power is productive rather than repressive. Typically we view power as something that is repressive and destructive. Even a cursory review of words and phrases that appear in the definition of power in the *Oxford English Dictionary* ("to affect

---

27 Clare O'Farrell, "Michel Foucault: Key Concepts" (2007), http://www.michel-foucault.com/concepts/ (accessed March 19, 2014). Emphasis added.

28 Hall, "The Work of Representation," 76. Emphasis in original.

29 Ibid., 76.

30 Michel Foucault, *Discipline and Punish: The Birth of the Prison* (New York: Vintage Books, 1977), 207.

something strongly," control, authority, dominion, rule, command) reveal this conventional view of power as repressive. Foucault attempted to broaden our definition of power and our understanding of its sociohistorical, political, and institutional dimensions. For Foucault, power is everywhere and it works its way through people and discourses *and* is supported and produced by systems, governments, and institutions. Power is productive because it shapes and guides all social relations. As Foucault explains, power "does not only weigh on us as a force that says no, but ... it traverses and produces things, it induces pleasure, forms of knowledge, produces discourse. It needs to be thought of as a productive network which runs through the whole social body."[31] Power is productive to the extent that it works through all social and discursive formations:

> The punishment system, for example, produces books, treatises, regulations, new strategies of control and resistance, debates in Parliament, conversations, confessions, legal briefs and appeals, training regimes for prison officers, and so on. The efforts to control sexuality, produce a veritable explosion of discourse—talk about sex, television and radio programmes, sermons and legislation, novels, stories and magazine features, medical and counseling advice, essays and articles, learned theses and research programmes, as well as new sexual practices (e.g., "safe" sex) and the pornography industry. Without denying the state, the law, the sovereign or the dominant class may have positions of dominance, Foucault shifts our attention away from the grand, overall strategies of power, toward many localized circuits, tactics, mechanisms and effects through which power circulates—what Foucault calls the "meticulous rituals" or the *"microphysics of power."*[32]

Foucault establishes that power is situated among many social practices and is interwoven into our identities. Discourse is a dimension of how power relations work between institutions, groups, and individuals.

Discipline and Punish

By the time Foucault published *Discipline and Punish* in 1975, he had already established important links between power and knowledge in his scholarship on the genealogy of contemporary society. As he states in *Discipline and Punish*, "there is no power relation without the correlative constitution of a

---

31 Michel Foucault, *Power/Knowledge* (Brighton: Harvester, 1980), 119.
32 Hall, "The Work of Representation." Emphasis added.

field of knowledge, nor any knowledge that does not presuppose and constitute at the same time power relations."[33] Often cited as Foucault's most significant work in the field of social regulation and criminology, *Discipline and Punish* further develops his theory of power and knowledge.[34]

Discipline and Punish begins with a vivid scene of the public execution of Robert-François Damiens, a French domestic servant who was convicted of attempting to assassinate King Louis XV of France in 1757. This was the last public execution in France. In reading Foucault's synopsis of the execution, one is confronted with explicit details concerning the brutality and bodily violence that marked his execution. Foucault describes the execution in the following manner:

> On a scaffold that will be erected ... the flesh will be torn from his breasts, arms, thighs and calves with red hot pincer, his right hand ... burnt with sulphur, and, on those places where the flesh will be torn away, poured molten lead, boiling oil, burning resin, wax and sulphur melted together and then his body drawn and quartered by four horses and his limbs and body consumed by fire, reduced to ashes and thrown to the winds.[35]

The execution of Damiens was directly exercised on his body. The brutal forms of violence were bodily, spectacular, and excessive. In the opening pages of *Discipline and Punish*, the description of the public execution is followed closely by an excerpt from Léon Faucher's (a French politician and economist) book *De la réforme des prisons* (1838) in which he devised a set of rules for a "house of young prisoners" in Paris. An excerpt from his set of rules reads as follows:

> Art. 17. The prisoners' day will begin at six in the morning in winter and at five in the summer ... they will work for nine hours a day ...
>
> Art. 18. Rising. At the first drum-roll, the prisoners must rise and dress in silence ... at the second drum-roll, they must be dressed and make their beds. At the third, they must line up and proceed to the chapel for morning prayer ...
>
> Art. 19. The prayers are conducted by the chaplain and followed by a moral and religious reading. This exercise must not last more than half an hour ...

---

33 Foucault, *Discipline and Punish*, 27.
34 Mariana Valverde, "Specters of Foucault in Law and Society Scholarship," *Annual Review of Law and Social Science* 6 (2010): 45–59.
35 Foucault, *Discipline and Punish*, 27.

Art. 20. Work. At quarter to six in the summer, a quarter to seven in winter, the prisoners go down to the courtyard where they must wash their hands and faces, and receive their first ration of bread.[36]

Importantly, Foucault points out that 80 years separate the public execution of Damiens and Faucher's rules for young prisoners. By describing two radically different *scenes of punishment* separated by 80 years—a public execution and a timetable—Foucault is inviting us to consider two distinct forms of penality and punishment. The dramatic first few pages of *Discipline and Punish* invite us to ask, "As forms of punishment, what is the difference between a public execution and a timetable? Why is it important to examine the difference between a public execution and a timetable?"

In *Discipline and Punish*, Foucault set out to write a book about the history of the prison or what he called the birth of the prison. The timetable serves as an example of some of the "new" approaches to punishment that began to appear at the end of the eighteenth century. Recalling Foucault's genealogical method, Faucher's timetable must be understood as a rupture or discontinuity in the history of punishment and penality in France. The two approaches to punishment invite us to reflect upon the following question: How does it come to be that ideas and practices of punishment shifted so dramatically in 80 years in France? France was not unique in its shifting ideas about punishment among Western European and North American countries. For example, Nicholas Melady, Jr., was the last publicly executed person in Canada. He was hanged in Goderich, Ontario, in 1869 for the murder of his father and stepmother.[37] Arguably, since 1869 Canadian views about public execution have also changed.

Examining how societies change over time motivates Foucault's genealogical method. The public execution and the timetable reveal two dramatically and philosophically different approaches to punishment. The public execution requires brutal and lethal forms of violence directed at the body. The timetable, alternatively, is a model of punishment that is structured, rule-governed, and requires the institutional form of the prison and corresponding practices of surveillance to keep prisoners in line. The difference between these two approaches is consistent with a historical period spanning the sixteenth to eighteenth centuries, which was "characterized by dramatic revolutions in science, philosophy, society and politics; these revolutions swept away the medieval world-view and ushered in our modern western world."[38]

---

36 Foucault, *Discipline and Punish*, 6.
37 John Melady, *Double Trap: The Last Public Hanging in Canada* (Toronto: Dundurn Press, 2005).
38 William Bristow, "Enlightenment," in *Stanford Encyclopedia of Philosophy*, http://plato.stanford .edu/archives/sum2011/entries/enlightenment/ (accessed June 8, 2013).

The historical changes in approaches to punishment that Foucault investigates directly relates to changes consistent with the Enlightenment period. The philosophical characteristics of the Enlightenment, including the centrality of reason; the rise of empiricism and science, universalism, and the search for general laws; the notion that the human condition can be improved; the rise of secularism; the idea of progress and the fundamental belief in freedom are consistent with the shift in the approach to punishment evidenced in the first few pages of *Discipline and Punish*. Foucault's depiction of rational, rule-bound punishment, highlighted by the use of a schedule, is more closely aligned with the hallmarks of Enlightenment thinking than public torture as spectacle.

Some scholars suggest that *Discipline and Punish* explores the transition from a "culture of spectacle" to a "carceral culture" (society's culture of punishment and surveillance): "Whereas in the former punishment was effected on the body in public displays of torture, dismemberment, and obliteration, in the latter punishment and discipline become internalized and was more directed upon the idea to reform a subject or a prisoner—and it was mainly directed on the so-called rehabilitation of certain delinquent subjects."[39] As Foucault observes, by the end of the eighteenth and the beginning of the nineteenth century, "the gloomy festival of punishment was dying out, though here and there it flickered momentarily into life."[40] As Foucault predicts, although *torture as spectacle* gave way to the *punishment as timetable*, the latter did not entirely replace the former. As we explore later in this chapter, these two demonstrations of power assisted in furthering the development of Foucault's theory of power.

The Panopticon

If we follow Foucault's historicization, the "gloomy festival of punishment" gave way to the institutionalization of the prison.[41] The prison is a space of confinement and surveillance where freedom and liberty are curtailed. The timetable reveals that prison is also a place where orderly, disciplined behaviour is indoctrinated. In order to genealogically trace the historical process from a "culture of spectacle" to a "carceral culture," Foucault invoked the architectural structure and conceptual idea of the panopticon.

---

39 Dino Felluga, "Modules on Foucault: II. On Panoptic and Carceral Society," in *Introductory Guide to Critical Theory*, http://www.cla.purdue.edu/english/theory/newhistoricism/modules/foucaultcarceral.html (accessed June 11, 2013).
40 Foucault, *Discipline and Punish*, 6.
41 Ibid., 8.

Figure 1.1 Jeremy Bentham, Panopticon

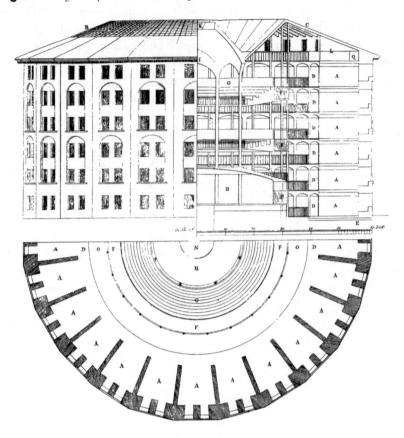

A **panopticon** is foremost an architectural design developed by Jeremy Bentham (1748–1832), a British social reformer and philosopher.[42] In Bentham's own words, he described a panopticon in the following manner:

> A building circular ... The prisoners in their cells, occupying the circumference—The officers in the centre. By blinds and other contrivances, the Inspectors concealed ... from the observation of the prisoners: hence the sentiment of a sort of omnipresence—The whole circuit reviewable with little, or ... without any, change of

---

42 Bentham is a utilitarian philosopher because of his emphasis that "the morally right action is the action that produces the most good." Julia Driver, "The History of Utilitarianism," in *Stanford Encyclopedia of Philosophy*, http://plato.stanford.edu/archives/sum2009/entries/utilitarianism-history/ (accessed June 8, 2013).

place. One station in the inspection part affording the most perfect view of every cell.[43]

Creating an architectural design in which a central tower permits and compels an observer to watch prisoners at all times, a panopticon invokes the idea of being under constant watch and surveillance. As Bentham stated, "the inmate must never know whether he is being looked at any one moment; but he must be sure that he may always be so."[44] In Bentham's design, an ideal prison would be constructed in such a way that prisoners would be subjected to the surveillance of the panoptic tower. This surveillance turned prisoners into "docile bodies."[45] As Dino Felluga explains, the panopticon literally means "'all-seeing' and it was meant to function as a round-the-clock surveillance machine. Its design ensured that no prisoner could ever see the 'inspector' who conducted surveillance from the privileged central location within the radial configuration. The prisoner could never know when he was being surveilled—mental uncertainty that in itself would prove to be a crucial instrument of discipline."[46]

Many scholars conclude that the popularity of the concept of the panopticon today is directly related to Foucault's use of it in *Discipline and Punish*, rather than as a result of Bentham's architectural model. Indeed, Bentham's architectural panopticon was not realized in his own time, though there is much evidence that panoptic characteristics are present in contemporary architectural design. In addition to its utility as an architectural model for an efficient prison, Bentham viewed the panopticon, and the constitutive practices of surveillance and discipline that are central elements of the design, to be paradigmatic of how society should function as a whole. "To maintain order in a democratic and capitalist society, the populace needs to believe that any person could be surveilled at any time," Bentham explained.[47] Supervision, order, regulation, and discipline, therefore, were not only required in prisons but also required in other social institutions like schools, hospitals, and factories. The panopticon, Foucault explains in *Discipline and Punish*, is therefore

> polyvalent in its applications; it serves to reform prisoner, but also to treat patients, to instruct schoolchildren, to confine the insane, to supervise workers, to put beggars and idlers to work. It is a type of location of bodies in space, of distribution of individuals in

---

43 Jeremy Bentham, *Proposal for a New and Less Expensive Mode of Employing and Reforming Convicts* (London, 1798).
44 Bentham, *Proposal for a New and Less Expensive Mode of Employing and Reforming Convicts*.
45 Foucault, *Discipline and Punish*, 6.
46 Felluga, "Modules on Foucault: II. On Panoptic and Carceral Society."
47 Ibid.

relation to one another, of hierarchical organization, of disposition of centres and channels of power, of definition of the instruments and modes of intervention of power, which can be implemented in hospitals, workshops, schools, prisons. Whenever one is dealing with a multiplicity of individuals on whom a task or a particular form of behaviour must be imposed, the panoptic schema may be used.[48]

The panopticon offers a paradigm for how society functions. In the complex quote above, Foucault makes important connections between the school, the prison, and the hospital through the panoptic schema. As Felluga explains, "By carceral culture, Foucault refers to a culture in which the panoptic model of surveillance has been diffused as a principle of social organization, affecting such disparate things as the university classroom; urban planning (organized on a grid structure to facilitate movement but also to discourage concealment); hospital and factory architecture; and so on."[49] In a panoptic formation, power is anchored spatially. As Foucault explains,

> It is an important mechanism, for it automatizes and disindividualizes power. *Power has its principle not so much in a person as in a certain concerted distribution of bodies*, surfaces, lights, gazes; in an arrangement whose internal mechanisms produce the relation in which individuals are caught up. The ceremonies, the rituals, the marks by which the sovereign's surplus power was manifested are useless.[50]

A panopticon *arranges* power in a given society and a given institution. The arrangement of power necessarily gives rise to certain forms of regulation, subjection, and discipline. In addition to architecture (in our own time), the arrangement of power is accomplished and facilitated through surveillance (panoptic) technologies: smartphones, passports, ATMs, credit cards, body scanners, government surveillance, closed-circuit television, and so on.

In the first few pages of *Discipline and Punish*, Foucault traces two ways of exercising powering. Using two different historical periods—and two ways of exercising punishment in those historical periods—Foucault reveals two forms of modern power. The first form of power is sovereign power. **Sovereign power**, demonstrated by the public execution, is power exercised by the sovereign or ruler. Sovereign power is brutal, direct, and exact. The second form of power, invoked by the prisoners' timetable, is disciplinary

---

48 Foucault, *Discipline and Punish*, 6.
49 Felluga, "Modules on Foucault: II. On Panoptic and Carceral Society."
50 Foucault, *Discipline and Punish*, 6. Emphasis added.

power. **Disciplinary power** is ordered, regulatory, and the result of practices of surveillance. "Discipline is a mechanism of power which regulates the behaviour of individuals in the social body. This is done by regulating the organization of space (architecture, etc.), of time (timetables) and people's activity and behaviour (drills, posture, movement) ... Foucault argues that 'disciplinary power' gradually took over from 'sovereign power' in the eighteenth and nineteenth centuries. Even now, however, remnants of sovereign power still remain in tension with disciplinary power."[51]

Disciplinary Society

When Foucault examines the impact of the panopticon on society as a whole, he uses the phrase **disciplinary society**. All institutions in a given society—prisons, schools, the military, the health care system, the justice system—"make up" the component parts of a disciplinary society. Arguably, social institutions function in a manner that resembles Bentham's panopticon. Our social worlds and institutions are structured as disciplinary panoptic machines: We are not only subject to the disciplinary and regulatory techniques of institutions, but our placement, participation, and different social roles within particular institutions facilitate the smooth functioning of those institutions. In effect, we are both the autonomous subjects of power in a given institution and *subjected to* the diffuse nature of power in a social institution. As "docile bodies" in a panoptic and disciplinary society, we internalize, normalize, and ultimately "perform" the rules, systems, and regulations of a given social organization. As we are increasingly "disciplined" and internalize the rules, we begin to "self-discipline."

In fact, the concept of a disciplinary society encourages us to think about the similarities (rather than the differences) in content and form between prisons, schools, the health care system, and the social welfare system. In matters of crime and criminalization, for example, ideas about crime and criminality are a part of all of the systems in a given society rather than simply restricted to the purview of the criminal justice or penal system. In *Discipline and Punish*, Foucault's "genealogy" suggests that the techniques of punishment that emerged in the nineteenth century were translated across all social institutions as general technologies for controlling entire populations (prisoners, students, citizens, etc.). To analyze how a disciplinary society functions and is accomplished, Foucault argued that social sciences, and knowledge production more generally, is integral to the functioning of a disciplinary society. In effect, a disciplinary society is the process through which social and moral regulation is made manifest.

---

51 Clare O'Farrell, *Michel Foucault* (London: Sage Publications, 2005), 132.

In his later work, Foucault became less interested in the general function-ing of the surveillance panoptic machine in a disciplinary society and more concerned with what he called "technologies of the self."[52] Technologies of the self "permit individuals to effect by their own means, or with the help of others, a certain number of operations on their own bodies and souls, thoughts, conduct and way of being, so as to transform themselves in order to attain a certain state of happiness, purity, wisdom, perfection of immortal-ity."[53] Technologies of the self refers to how (and in what ways) individuals *use* knowledge and information available to them in a given society. These technologies include the choices and behaviours that regulate how and what we eat, how we express our sexual selves, and our daily habits and lifestyle patterns, among other practices. A disciplinary society, then, includes the myriad ways that we are governed by state and social institutions (and the plethora of knowledge that is required by the state and social institutions) and, in turn, how we govern ourselves.

Governmentality

If we accept the premise that we live in a disciplinary society, how (as social scientists and theorists) can we track the ways in which a disciplin-ary society works in everyday life? In *Discipline and Punish*, Foucault is interested in showing how power is diffused and dispersed throughout the social body. In examining changing views of punishment, it is no lon-ger the case that the sovereign simply has power over his or her citizens. Rather, rules have become internalized by each one of us; power is produc-tive (rather than repressive) and a range of benevolent institutions (schools, health care organizations, etc.) facilitate processes of self-discipline and self-governance.

In his later work, Foucault suggests that one of the ways that we can track how the disciplinary society works at the level of everyday life is through the idea of governmentality. **Governmentality** refers to the ways in which populations are governed. You will notice that the word *governmentality* is made up of two words: *govern* + *mentality*. In effect, governmentality *is* the governing of mentalities. Thomas Lemke argues that "the semantic linking of governing ('gouverner') and modes of thought ('mentalité') indicates that it is not possible to study the technologies of power without an analysis of the

---

52 Michel Foucault, "Technologies of the Self," in *Michel Foucault: Ethics, Subjectivity, and Truth*, ed. Paul Rabinow (New York: The New Press, 1994).

53 Foucault, "Technologies of the Self," 227.

political rationality underpinning them."[54] Governmentality seeks to understand how the disciplinary forms of power revealed in *Discipline and Punish* work in specific ways (and on specific populations like students, soldiers, prisoners, etc.) to shape the conduct of people. Foucault refers to governmentality as the *"art of government"* (i.e., how governance is accomplished) and as the *"conduct of conduct"* (i.e., how certain behaviours are brought about and any attempt to shape or guide behaviour with specific goals in mind). Given this definition of governmentality, you may be thinking that governmentality is a broad concept that can include a wide range of regulations, **norms**, and rules that shape our behaviours and comportment. Indeed, this broad view of regulation and governance is exactly what Foucault was trying to capture with the introduction of the concept of governmentality.

In highlighting **governmental power**, Foucault highlights forms of power that are not only accomplished through spectacular sovereign acts like state punishment and torture. Rather, he sought to demonstrate that sovereign power emerges with governmental forms of regulation and power. Instead of focusing on the primacy of the state and elected officials to explain power, Foucault's concept of governmentality attempts to capture more mundane, programmatic, and systematic forms of power. As Randy Lippert and Grace Park explain,

> Governance, then, includes, laws, policies and practices of the municipal, provincial, and federal levels of the state but also efforts of countless private authorities and organizations (e.g., private corporations, business organizations, churches, condominium corporations, sports clubs and so on) as well as those who do no easily fit into public or private categories. Governance also encompasses self-governance or the reflection of one's own behaviour that can lead to efforts to change for the better.[55]

Through "governmentality, Foucault endeavors to show how the modern sovereign state and the modern autonomous individual co-determine each other's emergence."[56]

It has been widely shown that the concepts of governmentality and discipline have influenced the social sciences (and criminology in particular)

---

54 Thomas Lemke, "'The Birth of Bio-Politics': Michel Foucault's Lecture at the Collège de France on Neo-Liberal Governmentality," *Economy and Society* 30, no. 2 (2001): 190–207.
55 Randy Lippert and Grace Park, "Governmentality and Criminology," in *Criminology: Critical Canadian Perspectives*, ed. Kirsten Kramer (Toronto: Pearson, 2011), 176.
56 Lemke, "'The Birth of Bio-Politics.'"

the most profoundly.[57] Social science studies have used a governmentality approach to look at nonstate realms of social regulation and governance. Some of these areas include examining the impact of closed-circuit television surveillance on everyday regulation, rehabilitative programs, self-improvement practices, the study of policy and curriculum, examining municipal and administrative law, examining the rules and regulations of a sport, examining on-the-job practices of the police, among others. As Lippert and Park explain, a focus on "three major concepts" defines a governmentaility approach: (1) rationalities (i.e., the underlying logic or "questions" that facilitate forms of governance); (2) programs (i.e., "prescriptions, plans or schema for acting on some element of social conduct"); and (3) technologies (i.e., "the practical features of governance that put rationalities into place and bring programs into effect").[58] To examine the relationship between rationalities, programs, and technologies, studies of governmentality are always sustained by a simultaneous focus on Foucault's concepts of discourse, power, and knowledge. In addition to addressing the forms of knowledge and power that are required to produce, arrange, and organize specific rationalities, programs, and technologies in a given society, Foucault emphasized that it is imperative to examine how the idea of "population" was central to the changing nature of punishment. As Foucault explains, "the transition which takes place in the eighteenth century from ... a regime dominated by structures of sovereignty to one of rule by techniques of government, turns on the theme of population and also on the birth of the political economy."[59]

Biopower

To address the theme and idea of population emerging through systems of power and knowledge, Foucault introduced the concept of **biopower**. He first introduced the concept of biopower in *The History of Sexuality, Volume 1,* where he states "biopower is a political technology that brought life and its mechanisms into the realm of explicit calculations and made knowledge/power an agent of transformation of human life."[60] The concept of biopower is meant to account for the ways in which forms of discipline and governance

---

57 Valverde, "Specters of Foucault in Law and Society Scholarship."
58 Lippert and Park, "Governmentality and Criminology," 176.
59 Michel Foucualt, "Governmentality," in *The Foucault Effect: Studies in Governmentality,* ed. G. Burchell, C. Gordon, and P. Miller (Chicago: University of Chicago Press, 1991), 101.
60 Michel Foucault, *The History of Sexuality,* vol. 1, *An Introduction,* trans. Robert Hurley (New York: Vintage Books, 1990), 143.

require establishing and assessing specific groups of people *as populations.* For example, the concepts of discipline and surveillance in *Discipline and Punish* are made against specific populations (prisoners, students, etc.). How do individual people become constituted as a population? How and why are populations (as units of social analysis and social regulation) central to the functioning of a society? These are the kinds of questions that underpin Foucault's concept of **biopolitics.** In his later work, he reflected on this concept: "By [biopolitics] I meant the endeavor, begun in the eighteenth century by the phenomena characteristic of a group of living human beings constituted as a population: health, sanitation, birthrate, longevity, race ... It seems to be that these problems could not be dissociated from the political rationality within which they appeared."[61]

Foucault introduced the concept of biopower to address the new configurations of power in the nineteenth century that he traced in *Discipline and Punish.* As this chapter has shown, this period saw a shift from sovereign forms of power to disciplinary forms of power that were dispersed throughout the social body and gave rise to the management of the life and death processes of individuals and entire populations. These new forms of power were facilitated by the emergence of a range of sciences and professional discourses that rendered people and populations thinkable, translatable, and manageable to forms of government and political/economic systems. For example, life processes of birth, disease, illness, death, reproduction, and sexuality became sites of biopower. Public health, mortality, health care, biosurveillance—biopower includes all of the ways in which states control and promote a better life among people. The idea of the "population" is an important resource for power and knowledge production.

Biopower functions through state power and is connected to state policies because certain populations can be adjusted in accordance with state processes involved in the process of nation-building.[62] For example, when using race, gender, age, religion, health status, state and nonstate practices and programs can be thought of as invoking a form of biopower. As noted elsewhere, there is a dual process to the operation of biopower: "The dual operation of biopower works through technologies of governance (or governmentality) that bring together both the disciplinary effects of state practices and consequences for individual subjects. First, biopower operates

---

61 Michel Foucault, *Ethics, Subjectivity, Truth,* ed. Paul Rabinow (New York: The New Press, 1994), 73.

62 Carmela Murdocca, *To Right Historical Wrongs: Race, Gender and Sentencing in Canada* (Vancouver: UBC Press, 2013).

directly on the body of the individual/subjects in order to individually classify subjects as a population in accordance with state practice. Second, biopower operates through what Foucault describes as 'technologies of the self' which refers to the range of practices through which individuals constitute themselves within systems of power regulating their bodies, their thoughts, and their conduct."[63]

Conclusion

This chapter is an overview of some of the main concepts that Michel Foucault discusses in his work. Foucault's work assists with tracking shifts in our understanding of crime and punishment. Significantly, Foucault demonstrated the specific ways in which ideas about punishment are part of larger systems of social regulation distributed through all social institutions. The distribution of forms of social and moral regulation assist in examining how (through both everyday and, at times, mundane practices) and through the particular means (surveillance, governance, policing) regulation is accomplished. In revealing the interdependence between power and knowledge production, Foucault reveals not only the disciplinary function of distinct forms of punishment, but also how discipline is one of the preeminent features of contemporary social life.

Study Questions

1. Statement #1: Power produces knowledge and knowledge produces power. Statement: #2: Knowledge is power.

   Explain why Michel Foucault would agree with statement #1 and might disagree with statement #2.

2. What is sovereign power? What is disciplinary power?

3. What is a panopticon and why is it an important concept for understanding contemporary society and modern forms of social regulation?

Exercise

Consider your average daily schedule. Apply a governmentality analysis to your daily schedule. What kinds of rationalities, programs, and technologies underpin the ways in which you progress throughout your day?

---

63 Ibid., 18.

Keywords

social regulation; archaeology; genealogy; discourse; power; knowledge; discipline; disciplinary society; governmentality; norms; governmental power; sovereign power; biopower

Bibliography

Bentham, Jeremy. *Proposal for a New and Less Expensive Mode of Employing and Reforming Convicts*. London, 1798.

Bristow, William. "Enlightenment." In *Stanford Encyclopedia of Philosophy*. http://plato .stanford.edu/archives/sum2011/entries/enlightenment/ (accessed June 8, 2013).

Dean, Mitchell. "A Genealogy of the Government of Poverty." *Economy and Society* 21, no. 3 (1992): 215–51. http://dx.doi.org/10.1080/03085149200000012.

Driver, Julia. "The History of Utilitarianism." In *Stanford Encyclopedia of Philosophy*. http:// plato.stanford.edu/archives/sum2009/entries/utilitarianism-history/ (accessed June 8, 2013).

Felluga, Dino. "Modules on Foucault: II. On Panoptic and Carceral Society." In *Introductory Guide to Critical Theory*. http://www.cla.purdue.edu/english/theory/newhistoricism/ modules/foucaultcarceral.html (accessed June 11, 2013).

Foucault, Michel. *The Archaeology of Knowledge*. Translated by A.M. Sheridan Smith. New York: Routledge, 2007.

Foucault, Michel. *Discipline and Punish*. Translated by A.M. Sheridan. New York: Vintage Books, 1977.

Foucault, Michel. "Nietzche, Genealogy, History." In *Language, Countermemory and Practice: Selected Essays and Interviews*, edited by D. Bouchard, 139–64. Ithaca: Cornell University Press, 1977.

Foucault, Michel. *The History of Sexuality*. Vol. 1, *An Introduction*. Translated by Robert Hurley. New York: Pantheon, 1978.

Foucault, Michel *The History of Sexuality*. Vol. 2. Translated by Robert Hurley. New York: Pantheon, 1978.

Foucault, Michel. *Power/Knowledge*. Brighton: Harvester, 1980.

Foucault, Michel. (1994) [1974]. "Prisons et asiles dans le mécanisme du pouvoir." In *Dits et Ecrits*. Vol. 11. Paris: Gallimard, 523–24.

Foucault, Michel. "Technologies of the Self." In *Michel Foucault: Ethics, Subjectivity, and Truth*, edited by Paul Rabinow. New York: The New Press, 1994.

Foucualt, Michel. "Governmentality." In *The Foucault Effect: Studies in Governmentality*, edited by G. Burchell, C. Gordon, and P. Miller. Chicago: University of Chicago Press, 1991.

Foucault, Michel. *Ethics, Subjectivity, Truth*. Edited by Paul Rabinow. New York: The New Press, 1994.

Hall, Stuart. "The Work of Representation." In *Representation: Cultural Representation and Signifying Practices*, edited by Stuart Hall. London: Sage, 1992.

Lemke, Thomas. "'The Birth of Bio-Politics'—Michel Foucault's Lecture at the Collège de France on Neo-Liberal Governmentality." *Economy and Society* 30, no. 2 (2001): 190–207. http://dx.doi.org/10.1080/03085140120042271.

Lippert, Randy, and Grace Park. "Governmentality and Criminology." In *Criminology: Critical Canadian Perspectives*, edited by Kirsten Kramer. Toronto: Pearson, 2011.

Lotringer, S., ed. *Foucault Live: Interviews 1966–1984*. Translated by J. Johnson. New York: Semiotexte, 1989.

Melady, John. *Double Trap: The Last Public Hanging in Canada*. Toronto: Dundurn Press, 2005.

Murdocca, Carmela. *To Right Historical Wrongs: Race, Gender and Sentencing in Canada*. Vancouver: UBC Press, 2013.

O'Farrell, Clare. *Michel Foucault*. London: Sage Publications, 2005.

O'Farrell, Clare. "Michel Foucault: Key Concepts." http://www.michel-foucault.com/concepts/ (accessed March 19, 2014).

Rabinow, Paul. *The Foucault Reader*. New York: Pantheon, 1984.

Smart, Barry. *Michel Foucault*. London: Routledge, 2004.

Universiteit Gent, "Post-Structuralism and Discourse Theory." http://www.english.ugent.be/da/poststructuralisttheory (accessed April 15, 2013).

Valverde, Mariana. "Specters of Foucault in Law and Society Scholarship." *Annual Review of Law and Social Science* 6, no. 1 (2010): 45–59. http://dx.doi.org/10.1146/annurev-lawsocsci-102209-152951.

Van Dijk, Teun A. "Structures of Discourse and Structures of Power." *Communication Yearbook* 12, 18–59.

two
History Matters

AMANDA GLASBEEK

Introduction

In most cases, criminal acts get represented as immediate, often as crises, and typically as events unto themselves; this is especially true in mainstream media. Yet, as you read in the Introduction to this book, one of our key aims is to think differently about crime—specifically, to think of it as a *process* rather than a discrete moment in time. We seek to connect criminal events to broader social processes and social relations, to practices and forms of regulation and governmentality, and to analyze them through the lenses of power, representation, and historical processes (which is the focus of this chapter). In other words, if we are to fully grasp the significance of how criminalization occurs and the ways in which race, gender, sexuality, class, and nation-building intersect with one another and with processes of criminalization, then we must also recognize that history matters.

This chapter looks expressly at what the **historicization** of crime can contribute to our critical engagement with the processes of criminalization, regulation, and representation. In keeping with the themes of this book, and especially with a view to lessons drawn from Foucault about the entanglement between what gets represented as historical "fact" and the discursive relations of power that produce "truths" about our social world (see Chapter One), this chapter does not seek to provide an authoritative history of crime in Canada. Instead, the focus is on how the ways in which we approach history matter: Whose voices do we listen to? How do we seek connections and discontinuities between the past and the present? What themes relating to power, nation-building, colonialism, and the social relations of gender, class, race, and sexuality become visible through a historical lens? What can be learned from history that can help us to understand the present and imagine change for the future? It is in these kinds of ways that history matters.

There are some obvious reasons why history matters, especially for critical studies of criminalization. Indeed, there is a clear link between being attentive to history and the use of the term *criminalization*. At the most basic level, grounded empirical studies of the past can help us understand where our laws come from and how some things come to be called crimes in different historical moments. One cannot lay a charge of "truancy," for example, unless there already exists a system of compulsory education. (Male) homosexual acts were once criminalized in Canada, but now they are not. In late 2013, Canadian laws relating to prostitution, many of them originally enacted in 1913, were struck down by the Supreme Court of Canada, following a long century of complex *Criminal Code* amendments that have criminalized practices related to prostitution even though the act of prostitution itself has never been a crime in Canada. History, then, shows us that laws are made and unmade and that nothing about our criminal law, the practices of criminalization, or the definitions of crime is inevitable. To the contrary, criminal law is very much the product of the social relations in which it is embedded—knowing this is part of what makes resistance to injustices possible.

Yet, as important as it is to document historical change, it is also important to not treat historical processes as if they exist on a unidimensional, linear path of enlightenment. Sometimes referred to as a **whiggish view of history**, this approach suggests that things get consistently better over time. For instance, we may congratulate ourselves on decriminalizing homosexuality, and treat the fact that it used to be in the *Criminal Code* as a relic of a discriminatory past when people didn't know better or were uninformed or ignorant, from which problematic views we are now free. But while it is undeniably a good thing that same-sex relations have been decriminalized, to view this as evidence of a progressive history of improvement obscures more than it reveals. Such a view masks the role of social movements and protest in making change (see, for example, Chapters Eight and Fourteen) and renders invisible the ongoing forms of intolerance and discrimination faced by LGBTQ (lesbian, gay, bisexual, trans, queer) communities. This kind of triumphalist view—that such injustices are safely in the past and the problem is solved—also misses a key argument of this text, namely that criminalization can shift into new forms of regulation and that there are important links between these. As Stuart Hall noted of the "permissive" period (which lasted roughly from the late 1950s to the early 1970s) in Britain, which similarly saw the decriminalization of homosexuality, the significance of this shift was not that it indicated a full liberalization of social relations, but rather that regulation moved from the public sphere to the private sphere, a move that sharpened the distinction between crime and immorality and that shifted the regulation of sexual acts between men from the public, criminal sphere to the private sphere of civil society.[1] In this shift, homosexuality is transformed

---

1 Stuart Hall, "Reformism and the Legislation of Consent," in *Permissiveness and Control: The Fate of the Sixties Legislation*, ed. National Deviancy Conference, 1–43 (New York: Barnes and Noble, 1980).

from a criminal problem to a medical or social problem, thus rendering it subject to different kinds of regulation rather than no regulation at all. Hall referred to this new form of regulation as **moral regulation**, a concept and a method taken up later in this chapter. For now, however, it is significant to note that we need to be careful about how we treat questions of change and be attentive not just to the content of law, but also to its forms, practices, and links to other forms of regulation in the governance of everyday life.

So how should we think about and approach history? This chapter offers an overview of two key moments in historical methodology—historical materialism and moral regulation—that have helped shape the ways that sociolegal scholars study the history of crime, criminalization, and regulation. As you read in Chapter One, Michel Foucault's influential writings on the nature of power also challenged many traditional models of analysis, especially Marxist-inspired ones. This challenge included a different approach to historical analysis that shifted the focus away from attempts at totalizing narratives and reconfiguring how one imagines not just history but the very documents that are said to be evidence of historical events. As this chapter demonstrates, these challenges have been taken up by critical scholars from a range of disciplines, many of whom adopt different approaches to history, but all of whom begin from the premise that history matters.

Historical Materialism

Historical materialism is a term drawn from the work of Karl Marx and Friedrich Engels and refers to both a philosophy and a method. At its most basic level, historical materialism refers to the Marxian interpretation that "processes of social change are determined primarily (but not exclusively) by economic factors."[2] As explained more fully by Philip Abrams,

> [Marx and Engels] described their work as *historical* because they saw
> human societies as embedded in their own past and thus regarded
> history as the necessary method for any adequate understanding
> of one's own world. And they identified it as historical *materialism*
> because they regarded the processes and relationships of production as
> the essential and defining processes and relationships in the creation
> of human societies.[3]

---

2 *Social Science Dictionary*, "historical materialism," http://www.socialsciencedictionary.com/historical_materialism (accessed June 21, 2013).

3 Philip Abrams, *Historical Sociology* (Ithaca, NY: Cornell University Press, 1982), 35; emphases in original.

This approach to history has been influential in how scholars have undertaken histories of the law, especially criminal law. Perhaps the most famous legal history text in this tradition is *Albion's Fatal Tree*, a collection of essays produced by prominent British historian E.P. Thompson and his students.[4] Thompson and his colleagues were members of the New Left, a movement that arose in the late 1960s that sought, in part, to render academic knowledge relevant to the social movements of the time. One of these scholars, Douglas Hay, contributed an essay entitled "Property, Authority, and the Criminal Law" that exemplifies a historical materialist approach to criminal law.[5] As you will see, Hay drew together history, class analysis, and a critical engagement with power to locate the significance of the law as an instrument of class rule.

Hay's historical interest lay neither in the origins of criminal law nor in its specific content, but rather the larger question of the legitimacy of capitalist law. Looking to the eighteenth century, he asked how a system of criminal law that defended property rights and that was written exclusively by property holders (because there was, in eighteenth-century Britain, a property requirement to vote or hold office) could come to be widely understood as "justice" in the first place. Even more specifically, Hay asked how it came to be that a law known as the "Bloody Code," which created 200 capital (i.e., hanging) offences over 50 years, almost all of them for newly constituted property offences such as poaching or smuggling, be embraced as legitimate? Why did poor people, the principal victims of these new laws, not revolt against what appeared on the surface to be self-serving legal violences that protected the wealthy and penalized the poor (who made up the vast majority of the population)? His answers to these questions fundamentally reshaped our understanding of both history and criminal law.

As Hay and his colleagues demonstrated, there was no question that the modern system of British law (the common law that also came to define the legal systems throughout the British Empire, including Canada and the United States) was a class system. It evolved into its modernly recognizable form at a time when enclosure laws in Britain were being enforced with considerable vigour. While enclosure laws had existed since the thirteenth century (see Chapter Nine), they became particularly important in the economic, political, and social transition to capitalism. Simply put, enclosure laws transformed

---

4 Douglas Hay, Peter Linebaugh, John G. Rule, E.P. Thompson, and Cal Winslow, *Albion's Fatal Tree: Crime and Society in Eighteenth-Century England* (New York: Pantheon Books, 1975).

5 Douglas Hay, "Property, Authority, and the Criminal Law," in Douglas Hay, Peter Linebaugh, John G. Rule, E.P. Thompson, and Cal Winslow, *Albion's Fatal Tree: Crime and Society in Eighteenth-Century England*, 17–63 (New York: Pantheon Books, 1975).

lands that were once considered to be held "in common"—that is, lands that were traditionally held as common grounds from which anyone could collect what they needed, such as firewood, peat moss, fish, and so on to supplement their livelihoods—into private lands that gave the new owners the power to exclude others from using them. Thus, the traditional patterns that people had used to collect firewood, for example, became theft under this new private property regime. These new laws thus also forced people to find new ways to make do and, specifically, forced people into new relationships through which they exchanged their labour power for money that they could use to purchase (from the same property owners) the very things they used to be able to gather for free. Not surprisingly, these new relations gave rise to considerable lawlessness because people resisted these restrictions and continued to hunt, gather, forage, fish, and so on as they had always done. In response, the property owners voted in Parliaments to enact new criminal laws, of trespass, of poaching, of theft, of wrecking (collecting goods from shipwrecks that were floating just off shore), and so on. These became the 200 new property offences that made up the "Bloody Code." There is good reason, then, for Hay to ask how it was that these new laws could be understood as "justice."

In surveying the historical record, Hay points out that although the number of capital offences grew, the number of actual hangings did not. This suggests that there was more going on than merely terror. In fact, Hay says that if it were only terror, the law could never have achieved the level of legitimacy and authority that it did. People may have been afraid of the law, but they would not have seen it as legitimate if it was a pure and simple exercise of repression. So how could a Bloody Code that criminalized activities that had formerly been seen as just come to hold as much authority as it did, and become the tradition upon which our own modern legal system is built? The famous answer proposed by Hay is that the law is about much more than its content. Rather, the criminal law speaks to us ideologically and symbolically, so it is not just an institution but a statement and performance of values that assure us the system is just. Specifically, Hay says the eighteenth-century British Criminal Code embodied three core ideological qualities that overrode its coercive nature: majesty, justice, and mercy.

Majesty

The eighteenth-century Assize Courts that Hay studied were steeped in what he calls *majesty*. By this he meant that they were theatres of spectacle and awe. The Assize Courts were travelling circuit or district courts in which judges rode out as representatives of the King (or the state) to deliver justice to the districts of England. The judges were, of course, selected from the elite class. Each district had a maximum of four Assizes per year, usually one per season, and they might have less. All the indictable cases from that district were heard at these sittings, which could last for several days. As Hay notes, the arrival of the Assize justices was a major event. One observer in 1822 described it as follows:

> Upon their approach they are received by the sheriff, and often by a great part of the wealthiest inhabitants of the county; the latter come in person to meet them, or send their carriages, with their richest liveries, to serve as an escort, and increase the splendour of the occasion. They enter the town with bells ringing and trumpets playing, preceded by the sheriff's men, to the number of 12 or 20, in full dress, armed with javelins. The trumpeters and javelin-men remain in attendance on them during the time of their stay, and escort them every day to the assize-hall, and back again to their apartments.[6]

The arrival of the Assize judges was typically the social event of the season. Wealthy families brought their marriageable daughters into town, it was an opportunity to show off the latest fashions, and usually there were society balls held to celebrate. The specific courtrooms were marked by spectacle as well. The judges wore scarlet robes trimmed with ermine, full wigs, and sat in the highest place in the room so they could look down on everyone as a literal representation of their power. They also used the opportunity to make what Hay calls secular sermons, which were structured at least twice into the proceedings. The first opportunity came when they made their charge to the grand jurors (who would hear the cases); this was an opportunity to remind them of the goodness of the laws of the land and their responsibilities as gentlemen to those laws. The second opportunity was at the pronouncement of sentences, which was done to the most dramatic effect. Judges evoked powerful imagery when they pronounced sentences. For the death penalty, they donned black caps; if they had what was called a maiden docket (no executions) they wore white gloves. They also maintained dramatic arcs by providing the sentences in sequence so that the climax was the pronouncement of death, an emotive buildup that is familiar to us today in most of our media. They would speak of majestic characteristics when they pronounced sentences as well, which offered them the space to comment on

---

6 Ibid., 27.

morality and order being restored. All of these awe-inspiring forms of public theatre or majestic rituals, Hay argues, made the circuit courts "a reminder of the close relationship between law, property, and power."[7]

Justice

But within this spectacle the courts still had to offer justice. It was (and still is) part of the judge's job to ensure that trials be conducted fairly. In other words, judges were charged with the duty of ensuring that even the poorest person was guaranteed justice in the courts. Hay observes a variety of practices that ensured justice was the key appearance of the court. One of these was a strict observance of procedural rules. This was necessary because law, if it is to be called just, must be known and determinant, not capricious. Thus a variety of technicalities could be used to release prisoners. For example, if the word *farmer* appeared under an accused person's occupation rather than the preferred *yeoman*, the prisoner might be released on the logic that the technical charge against him was incorrect and therefore could not proceed. Rather than bring the law into disrepute, Hay suggests that this "absurd formalism"[8] helped legitimize the law by proving that all the rules must be consistently and equally applied, or they could not be applied at all.

A second way that justice was broadcast through the courts was by publicizing the trials of the wealthy. Although it was clearly the case that the vast majority of those tried in the criminal courts and under the Bloody Code were poor, from time to time the wealthy class produced thieves, forgers, poachers, and other offenders. It was, of course, necessary to prove that the law was something more than simply the creation of a ruling class (even though it was their creation). Thus, men of standing were executed when they were found guilty of a capital crime and their executions were widely publicized. Importantly, this contributed to the idea that the justice system was just—that is, equally applied to all rule breakers, regardless of social standing.

Mercy

The final characteristic of the eighteenth-century legal regime that allowed a system based on terror to appear just and to stand as a legitimate form of authority was—perhaps ironically—mercy. This was the discretionary power that judges had to pardon or grant clemency to convicted prisoners. Hay

---

7 Ibid., 31.
8 Ibid., 33.

argues that mercy was also a form of currency: The convicted poor could beseech the wealthy class—that is, those with direct access to the judges and the King—to solicit mercy on their behalf, in exchange for which they offered their gratitude and service. Thus, the discretionary quality of mercy ultimately upheld and strengthened the very unequal and hierarchical class structure in which this system operated. It allowed those with wealth to appear as benevolent and kind, and it ensured a pattern of subordination and deference among those who needed this benevolence. Thus, the class structure retained its authority. This, says Hay, was the "peculiar genius of the law. It allowed the rulers of England to make the courts a selective instrument of class justice, yet simultaneously to proclaim the law's incorruptible impartiality and absolute determinacy ... Discretion ... allowed the class that passed one of the bloodiest penal codes in Europe to congratulate itself on its humanity."[9]

It was through these important qualities that a profoundly unequal legal system based on class and conflicts about class power gained legitimacy and authority as quintessentially just, fair, and equal. Hay refers to this process as a conspiracy of class interests. By this, he does not mean that the wealthy sat around and plotted to trick the rest of the population. On the contrary, the need to do so was obviated by the complexity of the system itself and, in all likelihood, those of the wealthy class believed their own rhetoric. Nonetheless, the effect was the same. Even more importantly, Hay's Marxist approach to criminal law history demonstrates that while the content of the law may change in response to changing ideas about crime and disorder, the fundamental systemic organization of criminal law remains the same.

One might find many parallels in contemporary society to what Hay found evident in the eighteenth century. To this day, we use the language of class to refer to judges: Your Honour, Your Worship, My Lord. Our Supreme Court justices wear robes and sit on high (see Figure 2.1), and their pronouncements continue to be treated as secular sermons. The crimes of the wealthy or famous are treated like important news, which circulates as evidence that everyone is equal in the courts. Many people complain that offenders are let off on technicalities, a practice that continues to be defended as necessary to producing a larger sense of justice.

Clearly, the authority of the law has retained its force throughout the centuries. Hay's class account of the history of criminal law offers important insights into the place of law in our society, including law as a spectacle or as a theatre of power. The influence of this kind of history continues to shape contemporary critical analyses of criminal law.

---

9 Ibid., 48.

Figure 2.1 The Supreme Court Justices of Canada

Moral Regulation and Governance

The concept of moral regulation, and its later incarnation as governance, emerged as something of a productive meeting place between the historical materialism of the Marxist tradition and the genealogies of the Foucauldian approach (see Chapter One). While moral regulation is not a concept that has ever been universally defined—different scholars use and define the term differently—it nonetheless came to represent an important intervention into historical method and has proved to be particularly useful for scholars interested in the intersections between legal and social forms of regulation. As originally conceived by Philip Corrigan, moral regulation referred to the practices of the state.[10] Corrigan was interested in the "forms and norms"[11] by which everyday conduct was regulated. Corrigan's express intention was to understand why people conform to social practices in an unequal social order. Drawing on sociological traditions associated with Émile Durkheim and Karl Marx, and acknowledging the insights of Foucault, Corrigan wanted to find a middle ground that challenged the "general dichotomization between coercion (associated with the state)

---

10 Philip Corrigan, "On Moral Regulation: Some Preliminary Remarks," *Sociological Review* 29, no. 2 (1981): 313–38.
11 Ibid., 321.

and consensus (associated with acculturation and value-systems)."[12] As elaborated in *The Great Arch*, written by Corrigan and Derek Sayer, moral regulation was defined as

> A project of normalizing, rendering natural, taken for granted, in a word "obvious" what are in fact ontological and epistemological premises of a particular and historical form of social order. Moral regulation is coextensive with state formation, and state forms are always animated and legitimated by a particular moral ethos. Centrally, state agencies attempt to give unitary and unifying expression to what are in reality multifaceted and differential historical experiences to groups within society, denying their particularity.[13]

Through this lens, moral regulation scholars focus their attention on the practices through which "normal" is produced.

While Corrigan and Sayer insisted that moral regulation "was coextensive with state formation," other scholars took up the term to investigate practices of regulation and governing beyond the state. Mariana Valverde and Lorna Weir, for example, drew on explicitly Foucauldian and feminist critical tools to argue that moral regulation is a specific type of regulation that is distinct from economic or political forms of regulation.[14] Importantly, Valverde and Weir distinguished between **the state** and **the nation**: "[N]ation-building was not synonymous or even coterminous with state formation: while the state needed citizens, the nation needed moral subjects, subjects with 'character.'"[15] Moral regulation, in this sense, is a particular mode of regulation that focuses on producing "good" subjects in the broader project of nation-building. For some scholars, such as Carolyn Strange and Tina Loo, this means that moral regulation is about the regulation of that which is considered "moral."[16] This includes areas of everyday life such as sexuality, alcohol consumption, dress, and other modes of behaviour that are associated more broadly with normality or respectability. For still others, moral regulation is a project that is about self-formation. Sometimes referred to as *ethical subjectivity*, in this definition

---

12 Ibid., 325.

13 Philip Corrigan and Derek Sayer, *The Great Arch: English State Formation as Cultural Revolution* (London: Basil Blackwell, 1985), 4.

14 Mariana Valverde and Lorna Weir, "The Struggles of the Immoral: Preliminary Remarks on Moral Regulation," *Resources for Feminist Research* 17, no. 3 (1988): 31–34.

15 Ibid., 31.

16 Carolyn Strange and Tina Loo, *Making Good: Law and Moral Regulation in Canada, 1867–1939* (Toronto: University of Toronto Press, 1997).

moral regulation is about the discursive practices and tools—for example, self-help books—through which we regulate our own subjectivities according to norms and (often implicit) rules of conduct.[17] And still others adhere more closely to Corrigan's original proposition—that the state is always a player in moral regulation, even if the state's role is not explicitly evident.[18]

Despite these varying definitions and applications of the term moral regulation, there are some elements of this approach that are common and that can be used to define the field of moral regulation studies. First, moral regulation distinguishes itself from more traditional sociological models of social control in attempting to understand the production of conformity. Rather than seeing the state as a "hammer" that exercises an often-coercive control over a population that is often seen as passive,[19] moral regulation scholars argue that "a central issue of all processes of governing and regulating [is] agency. Who is it that attempts to govern whom and how those targeted respond should be central questions."[20] In addition, as Alan Hunt argues, the processes of governing can come from many directions: from above (e.g., the state), from the middle (e.g., middle-class reform groups), and from below (e.g., local grassroots groups).[21]

Second, moral regulation radically redefines what we mean by "moral." Rather than referring to a (typically conservative) religious mentality, moral regulation scholars treat the moral as a comprehensive politics through which particular forms of behaviour, such as sexuality, become publicly interesting. Thus, rather than treating morality and politics as separate, moral regulation scholars argue that political developments are always moral in nature in the sense that they are always (productive) statements on what constitutes "good" forms of citizenship or behaviour.[22]

Third (and perhaps most importantly), moral regulation scholars have transformed the meaning of regulation. Drawing principally on Foucault, in particular his "simple inversion of commonplace assumptions" about power,[23]

---

17 Mitchell Dean, "'A Social Structure of Many Souls': Moral Regulation, Government and Self-Formation," *Canadian Journal of Sociology* 19, no. 2 (1994): 145–68.

18 Dorothy Chunn and Shelley Gavigan, "Welfare Law, Welfare Fraud, and the Moral Regulation of the 'Never Deserving' Poor," *Social and Legal Studies* 13, no. 2 (2004): 219–43.

19 Dorothy Chunn and Shelley Gavigan, "Social Control: Analytic Tool or Analytic Quagmire?" *Contemporary Crises* 12 (1988): 107–24.

20 Alan Hunt, *Governing Morals: A Social History of Moral Regulation* (Cambridge: Cambridge University Press, 1999), 19.

21 Ibid., 5.

22 Amanda Glasbeek, "Introduction," in *Moral Regulation and Governance in Canada: History, Context, and Critical Issues*, ed. A. Glasbeek, 1–8 (Toronto: Canadian Scholars' Press, 2006).

23 Mindie Lazarus-Black and Susan Hirsch, "Introduction," in *Contested States: Law, Hegemony, and Resistance*, ed. M. Lazarus-Black and S. Hirsch (New York: Routledge, 1994), 3.

moral regulation scholars insist that power is neither wholly monopolized by the state nor exclusively repressive. As Mariana Valverde argued in her ground-breaking moral regulation study of moral reform movements in English Canada at the turn of the twentieth century, what is significant about these reformers was their "vision [that] I will here call 'positive' not because it was necessarily good, but to distinguish it from negativity, from mere prohibition."[24] In other words, it is not that moral reformers were interested in banning certain behaviours, like prostitution, but the "veritable discursive explosion"[25] of new knowledges about gender, sexuality, race, marriage, nation, and citizenship that were encapsulated in the turn-of-the-century anti-prostitution campaigns that constitute the realm of moral regulation.

This approach to social order has proved enormously productive for accounts of regulatory initiatives, and has been especially well employed by social historians (and historical sociologists) of a period of intense nation-building in Canada (generally 1880–1920). From studies of campaigns against venereal diseases aimed at the middle classes,[26] which developed new medical–social knowledges of respectable sexuality,[27] to analyses of the emergence of "homosexuality" as a social problem,[28] to historical accounts of grocery shopping as a moralized activity intimately connected to citizenship,[29] to the history of the regulation of welfare mothers,[30] to name but a few, moral regulation scholars have teased out the connections between regulation, morality, and the production of order in Canadian history.[31]

---

24 Mariana Valverde, *The Age of Light, Soap, and Water: Moral Reform in English Canada, 1885–1925* (Toronto: University of Toronto Press, 1991), 23.

25 Michel Foucault, *The History of Sexuality*, vol. 1, *An Introduction*, trans. R. Hurley (New York: Vingage Books, 1980), 17.

26 Renisa Mawani, "Regulating the 'Respectable' Classes: Venereal Disease, Gender, and Public Health Initiatives in Canada, 1914–35," in *Regulating Lives: Historical Essays on the State, Society, the Individual, and the Law*, ed. John McLaren, Robert Menzies, and Dorothy Chunn, 170–195 (Vancouver: UBC Press 2002).

27 Mary Louise Adams, *The Trouble with Normal: Postwar Youth and the Making of Heterosexuality* (Toronto: University of Toronto Press, 1997).

28 Gary Kinsman, *The Regulation of Desire: Homo and Hetero Sexuality in Canada* (Montreal: Black Rose Books, 1996).

29 Franca Iacovetta, "Recipes for Democracy? Gender, Family, and Making Female Citizens in Cold War Canada," *Canadian Woman Studies* 20, no. 2 (2000): 12–21.

30 Margaret Hillyard Little, *No Car, No Radio, No Liquor Permit: The Moral Regulation of Single Mothers in Ontario, 1920–1997* (Toronto: Oxford University Press, 1998).

31 For overviews, see Mariana Valverde, ed., *Studies in Moral Regulation* (Toronto: Centre for Criminology and Canadian Journal of Sociology, 1994); Deborah Brock, ed., *Making Normal: Social Regulation in Canada* (Toronto: Thomson Nelson, 2003); Amanda Glasbeek, ed., *Moral Regulation and Governance in Canada: History, Context, and Critical Issues* (Toronto: Canadian Scholars' Press, 2006).

Yet, within this rich literature there remains a tension over the role of the state and, even more germane to our studies, of the law. Given that the law is a product of the state, and that criminal law in particular is seen as a repressive instrument that is exclusively monopolized by the state, many moral regulation scholars shifted their attention away from legal regulation. But clearly the law, and especially criminal law, is an important terrain of regulation. Moreover, not all populations are regulated in the same ways. While moral regulation campaigns might be well defined as those that are aimed at the production of "good" citizens, it remains the case that some groups of people will not (or are not able to) meet these definitions of respectability. Thus, temperance campaigns may produce literature about the "rightness" of abstaining from alcohol, but there will always be people who drink—sometimes to excess—even when drinking is rendered an offence by legislation. Similarly, while single young women may have been targeted by early twentieth-century moral regulation campaigns to live virtuous and chaste lives, some women enjoyed hanging out with men, having sex, dancing at the ferry docks, and staying out all night unchaperoned. Many of these people found themselves in courts to answer for such "unrespectable" behaviours.

Rather than treating such responses to moral breaches as outside moral regulation, a number of scholars include the processes of criminalization as linked to, if not part of, moral regulation itself.[32] In other words, criminal law and practices of criminalization are themselves morally regulative activities. As Joan Sangster has argued in her study of the criminalization of girls and women in early twentieth-century Ontario, some women, determined to be in need of moral correction, "experienced a more *repressive* version of regulation."[33]

While such debates were never fully resolved in moral regulation scholarship, it is clear that those using this method for historical inquiry have produced a fruitful field through which to understand a full panoply of interconnected modes of regulatory activities that include, but are not limited to, legal forms. Criminal law can be understood as moralized regulation, while moral regulation is understood as something that can occur outside the state. This form of inquiry thus directs our attention to the ways that strategies and practices of regulation are linked in different times and places, and from which contemporary orderings of "normal" and "deviant" behaviours come to be seen as "obvious." The usefulness of such an approach to analyzing both historical and contemporary instances of criminalization should be clear.

---

32 Amanda Glasbeek, *Feminized Justice: The Toronto Women's Court, 1913–34* (Vancouver: UBC Press, 2009).

33 Joan Sangster, *Regulating Girls and Women: Sexuality, Family, and the Law in Ontario, 1920–1960* (Toronto: Oxford University Press, 2001), 3. Emphasis in original.

Governmentality, Risk, and Histories of the Present

As you read in Chapter One, the concept of **governmentality** is drawn from Foucault and refers most broadly to the "conduct of conduct," or to the political rationalities (or mentalities) of governing. Like moral regulation, governmentality extends our analysis beyond the realm of formal state apparatus to include nonstate agents and, more importantly, power–knowledge centres (e.g., medical knowledge) within the analysis of the governance of everyday life. In addition, governmentality studies draw on Foucault's genealogical method to produce "histories of the present." Governmentality studies have also been intimately linked to the emergence of neoliberal governing technologies and rationales at the turn of the twenty-first century.[34] Perhaps not surprisingly, many of the same scholars who undertook moral regulation analyses of nation-building campaigns in the early twentieth century are those who also conducted governmentality studies of the profound political, economic, moral, and social changes that have occurred as we have entered the twenty-first century.

Central to many of these studies, and especially those that focus on law, order, crime, and conformity, is the concept of **risk**. The shift to **neoliberalism** that began in the late twentieth century was attended by a shift in the way we think about crime.[35] This transformation entailed a move away from a focus on rehabilitation, or the idea that the principal purpose of criminal sanctions was to rehabilitate the offender to become a law-abiding, participating member of society, and toward what has come to be known as *actuarial justice*, which sees crime as a set of predictable, if inevitable, probabilities or risks.[36] Risks require management in advance of their occurrence rather than correction after the fact. The risk society thus produces a new governing strategy that has been characterized by Pat O'Malley as **prudentialism**, which is "a technology of governance that removes the key conception of regulating individuals by collectivist risk management, and throws back upon the individual the responsibility for managing risk."[37] In other words, we all become responsible for managing our own risks of crime, for example, by purchasing home alarm systems or taking a self-defence course.

---

34 Nikolas Rose and Peter Miller, "Political Power beyond the State: Problematics of Government," *The British Journal of Sociology* 43, no. 2 (1992): 173–205.

35 David Garland, *The Culture of Control* (Oxford: Oxford University Press, 2001).

36 Malcolm Feeley and Jonathon Simon, "Actuarial Justice: The Emerging New Criminal Law," in *The Futures of Criminology*, ed. D. Nelken (London: Sage, 1994).

37 Pat O'Malley, "Risk and Responsibility," in *Foucault and Political Reason: Liberalism, Neo-Liberalism and Rationalities of Government*, ed. A. Barry, T. Osborne, and N. Rose (Chicago: University of Chicago Press, 1996), 189.

A key feature of the risk society is that it is endlessly engaged in the production of knowledge about risk itself to enable the responsible, prudent citizen to manage his or her own day-to-day risks.[38]

As Alan Hunt has argued, contemporary risk discourses act as a form of moral regulation in which risk operates as the modern equivalent of nineteenth-century notions of harm in the construction of a universalizing discourse of good and evil.[39] Consider, for example, contemporary anti-obesity campaigns. While the issue of obesity might once have been taken up as an issue of unequal access to good nutrition and accessible health care, in the risk society obesity becomes a personal issue that is indicative of poor conduct and limited self-control. People who are obese are constructed as "irresponsible" and who cost prudent subjects money in health care costs. "Good" or responsible citizens are those who diet, go to the gym, eat natural or unprocessed foods, and who otherwise take care of their own health so that they are not a burden to others. Thus, although campaigns about obesity typically appear as amoral and technical advice to take care of oneself, in fact they are highly moralized campaigns that, through risk discourses, produce good and bad citizens (see Figure 2.2). As Hunt argues, in this link between risk and the moralization of everyday practices (shopping, eating, exercise regimens, etc.), risk is not just a condition to be encountered, avoided, or managed but is itself productive of moralized subjectivities—that is, the "good" citizen who avoids "risky" behaviours.

The governance of risk has become central to contemporary understandings of criminalized behaviours as well (see Figure 2.3). From campaigns against date-rape drugs,[40] to the criminalization of squeegee kids,[41] to drug testing,[42] to the assessment of female prisoners,[43] to the threat of sexual assault,[44] among other issues, contemporary scholars have deployed a history of the present approach to the modern governance of everyday life.

---

38 Richard V. Ericson and Kevin Haggerty, *Policing the Risk Society* (Toronto: University of Toronto Press, 1997).

39 Alan Hunt, "Risk and Moralization," in *Risk and Morality*, ed. R.V. Ericson and A. Doyle, 165–192 (Toronto: University of Toronto Press, 2003).

40 Dawn Moore and Mariana Valverde, "Maidens at Risk: 'Date Rape Drugs' and the Formation of Hybrid Risk Knowledges," *Economy and Society* 29, no. 4 (2000): 514–31.

41 Amanda Glasbeek, "'My Wife Has Endured a Torrent of Abuse': Gender, Safety, and Anti-Squeegee Discourses in Toronto, 1998–2000," *Windsor Yearbook of Access to Justice* 24 (2006): 55–76.

42 Dawn Moore and Kevin Haggerty, "Bring It on Home: Home Drug Testing and the Relocation of the War on Drugs," *Social and Legal Studies* 10, no. 3 (2001): 377–95.

43 Kelly Hannah-Moffat, "Moral Agent or Actuarial Subject: Risk and Canadian Women's Imprisonment," *Theoretical Criminology* 3, no. 1 (1999): 71–94.

44 Elizabeth Stanko, "Safety Talk: Conceptualizing Women's Risk Assessment as a 'Technology of the Soul,'" *Theoretical Criminology* 1, no. 4 (1997): 479–99.

Figure 2.2 Anti-obesity poster

Figure 2.3 "You Are at Risk of Cybercrime" poster

The link between such contemporary campaigns and historical campaigns of moral regulation is significant. In each historical moment, as the political, economic, and social orders undergo major shifts, there are clear anxieties about the future and about the "character" of the nation. While it is overly simplistic to draw a straight line between the past and the present, there are some common themes relating to how respectable citizenship is to be articulated as well as to how it is to be policed. A broader historical view can help make sense of such profound changes and enable us to more fully appreciate the significance of any specific set of changes that aim to produce "order" through regulatory initiatives.

Conclusion

As you read this book, you will find that different chapters offer specific histories of the topics under discussion. Chapter Five, for example, offers a detailed history of the significance of colonialism, while Chapter Eight looks at the origins of our contemporary ideas about sexuality, and Chapter Twelve provides a historical overview of the human rights framework and its emergence as a dominant model for imagining social justice. Other chapters offer different histories as well. None of these histories fits neatly into a single box of historical materialism, genealogy, or moral regulation, but all of them draw in some way and with different emphases on the main thrusts of these different historical approaches. The ability to be flexible in our methods of inquiry is one of the pleasures of conducting interdisciplinary research. Yet you will see that certain themes persist: a focus on power and its shifting locations; an attention to knowledge, discourse, and moral or symbolic meaning-making; and an appreciation of the importance of historical continuity and change in the production and representation of crime and its necessary correlate, order.

As an overview and introduction to historical inquiry, this chapter's aim has been to familiarize you with the approaches that have helped to structure critical sociolegal studies of patterns of criminalization and regulation. It should go without saying, however, that knowing our history is not the same as knowing the ending of the story. In this way, historical inquiry is not just oriented to the past: It is also a way of producing change, so that historical injustices may be resisted and reshaped in the future.

Study Questions

1. Explain Hay's concepts of majesty, justice, and mercy. Do these have relevance for a contemporary analysis of the criminal justice system? Why or why not?

2. What is the difference between a historical materialist approach and a genealogical approach to history? How does a moral regulation approach bridge some of these differences?

Exercise

Find an example of a contemporary risk campaign related to crime or criminal activity (campaigns against gambling, drunk driving, drug use, etc.). How is risk constructed? How is it moralized? How does the campaign relate to historical notions of the nation, citizenship, and "good" and "bad" subjects (or behaviours)? What role does criminal law play in this campaign, and how does a broader historical view of the law help to understand the contemporary issue?

Keywords

historicization; whiggish view of history; moral regulation; historical materialism; the state; the nation; neoliberalism; risk; prudentialism

Bibliography

Abrams, Philip. *Historical Sociology.* Ithaca: Cornell University Press, 1982.

Adams, Mary Louise. *The Trouble with Normal: Postwar Youth and the Making of Heterosexuality.* Toronto: University of Toronto Press, 1997.

Brock, Deborah, ed. *Making Normal: Social Regulation in Canada.* Toronto: Thomson Nelson, 2003.

Chunn, Dorothy, and Shelley Gavigan. "Social Control: Analytic Tool or Analytic Quagmire?" *Contemporary Crises* 12, no. 2 (1988): 107–24. http://dx.doi.org/10.1007/BF00729670.

Chunn, Dorothy, and Shelley Gavigan. "Welfare Law, Welfare Fraud, and the Moral Regulation of the 'Never Deserving' Poor." *Social & Legal Studies* 13, no. 2 (2004): 219–43. http://dx.doi.org/10.1177/0964663904042552.

Corrigan, Philip. "On Moral Regulation: Some Preliminary Remarks." *Sociological Review* 29, no. 2 (1981): 313–37. http://dx.doi.org/10.1111/j.1467-954X.1981.tb00176.x.

Corrigan, Philip, and Derek Sayer. *The Great Arch: English State Formation as Cultural Revolution.* London: Basil Blackwell, 1985.

Dean, Mitchell. "'A Social Structure of Many Souls': Moral Regulation, Government and Self-Formation." *Canadian Journal of Sociology* 19, no. 2 (1994): 145–68. http://dx.doi.org/10.2307/3341342.

Ericson, Richard V., and Kevin Haggerty. *Policing the Risk Society.* Toronto: University of Toronto Press, 1997.

Feeley, Malcolm, and Jonathon Simon. "Actuarial Justice: The Emerging New Criminal Law." In *The Futures of Criminology,* edited by D. Nelken. London: Sage, 1994.

Foucault, Michel. *The History of Sexuality.* Vol. 1, *An Introduction.* Translated by R. Hurley. New York: Vintage Books, 1980.

Garland, David. *The Culture of Control.* Oxford: Oxford University Press, 2001.

Glasbeek, Amanda. *Feminized Justice: The Toronto Women's Court, 1913–34.* Vancouver: UBC Press, 2009.

Glasbeek, Amanda, ed. *Moral Regulation and Governance in Canada: History, Context, and Critical Issues.* Toronto: Canadian Scholars' Press, 2006.

Glasbeek, Amanda. "'My Wife Has Endured a Torrent of Abuse': Gender, Safety, and Anti-Squeegee Discourses in Toronto, 1998–2000." *Windsor Yearbook of Access to Justice* 24 (2006): 55–76.

Hall, Stuart. "Reformism and the Legislation of Consent." In *Permissiveness and Control: The Fate of the Sixties Legislation,* edited by National Deviancy Conference, 1–43. New York: Barnes and Noble, 1980.

Hannah-Moffat, Kelly. "Moral Agent or Actuarial Subject: Risk and Canadian Women's Imprisonment." *Theoretical Criminology* 3, no. 1 (1999): 71–94.

Hay, Douglas. "Property, Authority and the Criminal Law." In *Albion's Fatal Tree: Crime and Society in Eighteenth-Century England,* edited by Douglas Hay, Peter Linebaugh, John G. Rule, E.P. Thompson, and Cal Winslow, 17–63. New York: Pantheon Books, 1975.

Hunt, Alan. *Governing Morals: A Social History of Moral Regulation.* Cambridge: Cambridge University Press, 1999.

Hunt, Alan. "Risk and Moralization." In *Risk and Morality,* edited by R.V. Ericson and A. Doyle, 165–92. Toronto: University of Toronto Press, 2003.

Iacovetta, Franca. "Recipes for Democracy? Gender, Family, and Making Female Citizens in Cold War Canada." *Canadian Women's Studies* 20, no. 2 (2000): 12–21.

Kinsman, Gary. *The Regulation of Desire: Homo and Hetero Sexuality in Canada.* Montreal: Black Rose Books, 1996.

Lazarus-Black, Mindie, and Susan Hirsch, eds. *Contested States: Law, Hegemony, and Resistance.* New York: Routledge, 1994.

Little, Margaret Hillyard. *No Car, No Radio, No Liquor Permit: The Moral Regulation of Single Mothers in Ontario, 1920–1997.* Toronto: Oxford University Press, 1998.

Mawani, Renisa. "Regulating the 'Respectable' Classes: Venereal Disease, Gender, and Public Health Initiatives in Canada, 1914–35." In *Regulating Lives: Historical Essays on the State, Society, the Individual, and the Law,* edited by J. McLaren, R. Menzies, and D. Chunn, 170–95. Vancouver: UBC Press, 2002.

Moore, Dawn, and Kevin Haggerty. "Bring It on Home: Home Drug Testing and the Relocation of the War on Drugs." *Social & Legal Studies* 10, no. 3 (2001): 377–95.

Moore, Dawn, and Mariana Valverde. "Maidens at Risk: 'Date Rape Drugs' and the Formation of Hybrid Risk Knowledges." *Economy and Society* 29, no. 4 (2000): 514–31. http://dx.doi.org/10.1080/03085140050174769.

O'Malley, Patrick. "Risk and Responsibility." In *Foucault and Political Reason: Liberalism, Neo-Liberalism and Rationalities of Government,* edited by A. Barry, T. Osborne and N. Rose. Chicago: University of Chicago Press, 1996.

Rose, Nikolas, and Peter Miller. "Political Power beyond the State: Problematics of Government." *British Journal of Sociology* 43, 2 (1992): 173–205. http://dx.doi.org/10.2307/591464.

Sangster, Joan. *Regulating Girls and Women: Sexuality, Family, and the Law in Ontario, 1920–1960.* Toronto: Oxford University Press, 2001.

Social Science Dictionary, "historical materialism." http://www.socialsciencedictionary.com/historical_materialism.

Stanko, Elizabeth. "Safety Talk: Conceptualizing Women's Risk Assessment as a 'Technology of the Soul.'" *Theoretical Criminology* 1, no. 4 (1997): 479–99. http://dx.doi.org/10.1177/1362480697001004004.

Strange, Carolyn, and Tina Loo. *Making Good: Law and Moral Regulation in Canada, 1867–1939.* Toronto: University of Toronto Press, 1997.

Valverde, Mariana. *The Age of Light, Soap, and Water: Moral Reform in English Canada, 1885–1925.* Toronto: University of Toronto Press, 1991.

Valverde, Mariana, ed. *Studies in Moral Regulation.* Toronto: Centre for Criminology and Canadian Journal of Sociology, 1994.

Valverde, Mariana, and Lorna Weir. "The Struggles of the Immoral: Preliminary Remarks on Moral Regulation." *Resources for Feminist Research* 17, no. 3 (1988): 31–34.

three
The Politics of Representation

UMMNI KHAN

Introduction

The central goal of this chapter is to explore how constructions of criminality are produced and contested through practices of representation. For most people in Canada, knowledge about "criminals" will be based on mediated information. As such, messages about the nature of criminality are mediated through some source of data, for example, media articles, online blogs, television shows, or cinematic renditions. Even our own experiences can be filtered by these external narratives because they provide a context and a language that shape how we interpret our perceptions. This chapter will provide theoretical frameworks and tools to help you learn how to critique representations of crime by addressing how such mediated information informs the **politics of representation.**

What exactly do we mean by *politics of representation?* To answer this question, we will analyze how power, privilege, and identity are interconnected with dominant explanations of crime. There are political stakes involved in representational practices that address core questions: What is deemed a crime? Who commits crime? Where does crime take place? When does crime take place? Why does crime take place? How do we stop crime? Furthermore, this chapter will provide insight into how particular criminal labels attach to certain marginalized identities and personalities, as well as how such representations can be resignified and contested. An analysis of the politics of representation is crucial to challenging our assumptions about crime and criminality.

We will address two main strategies for challenging the truth-value of a particular representation of crime: empirical challenges and constructionist challenges. Empirical challenges use factual data to contest the implicit or explicit truth-claims of a dominant representation of crime. Such data will be based on social science evidence, which can include quantitative data like statistical reports or qualitative data like interview transcripts. Constructionists, on the other hand, reject the notion that there are discernable and objective social facts that exist outside of a cultural context. The constructionist strategy, pioneered by cultural studies critic Stuart Hall, seeks to understand how language—broadly defined—constitutes meaning. Language is thus not a neutral descriptor of reality, but rather a generative enterprise that shapes how we make sense of the material world, both factually and normatively. The task of the cultural critic is to deconstruct the language in a particular area and expose its underlying political and regulatory agenda. While this chapter will focus primarily on the constructionist strategy, it will also provide direction on critical methodology, enabling you to draw on both empirical and constructionist approaches in discerning and challenging the meaning of a criminal representation.

Before we address the politics of criminal representation, it will be helpful to step back and learn some background information about cultural studies and the key theorist who informs this chapter, Stuart Hall.

Stuart Hall and Cultural Studies

Stuart Hall (1932–2014) was a central thinker in the development of **cultural studies**, an interdisciplinary approach that began to flourish in England in the 1960s and has since been adopted by scholars from other regions, including the United States and Canada. Hall's highly influential and prolific scholarship focuses on the political significance of representations as sites of both indoctrination and contestation. Hall argues that through cultural representations, people can be seduced into adopting and supporting policies that are often against their own interests.[1] He has provided ground-breaking analysis on the ways in which racial representations are used in the media and in cultural practices to associate Black and immigrant identity with crime and anti-social behaviour.[2] While much of Hall's work seeks to expose how media representations render particular racialized identities as dangerous and tending toward criminality, he also believes that audience members are not necessarily passive recipients of these racist constructions. People can read representations differently and can exercise agency through oppositional interpretations.

While rooted in both literary theory and sociology, cultural studies stands in contrast to traditional literary hermeneutics and **positivist approaches** to social science. Instead of seeking to define the authentic meaning of a cultural text or to map out universal dynamics in society, cultural studies questions and challenges accepted truths about culture and social processes. The field overlaps with and draws from other critical approaches that concentrate

---

1 Stuart Hall, *Representation: Cultural Representations and Signifying Practices* (Thousand Oaks, CA: Sage in association with the Open University, 1997).

2 Stuart Hall et al., *Policing the Crisis: Mugging, the State, and Law and Order* (London: Macmillan, 1978).

on different axes of identity and injustice. For example, cultural studies is heavily influenced by **Marxist** critiques of unequal class relations, **Black studies'** critiques of racial oppression, and feminist critiques of sex inequality. In addition, because of its rejection of stable truths and fixed meanings, cultural studies is associated with **postmodern** and poststructuralist theory, in particular Foucauldian critiques of knowledge regimes.

It is important to understand that despite its dismissal of the possibility of essential truths, cultural studies does not take a "neutral" stance toward culture. Its affiliation with the aforementioned critical strands—Marxism, Black studies, and feminist theory—positions cultural studies in tension with conventional disciplines because of its unabashedly political agenda. Moreover, in its most radical manifestations, cultural studies is committed to both intellectual inquiry and concrete action. Indeed, Hall denounces what he perceives to be a "liberal" tendency to divorce analysis from action.[3] As an analytical project, cultural studies interrogates cultural artifacts within their sociopolitical context and seeks to uncover how cultural practices, processes, and knowledge systems are related to power and oppression. As a practical project, cultural studies seeks to apply these analyses to restructure and change relations of dominance and subordination.

Semiotics, Discourse, Ideology, and Hegemony

Language and Semiotics

To fully understand cultural studies theory and methodology as it applies to criminology, it is helpful to understand how certain terms are used within the field. The first important term is **language**. In its standard meaning, language refers to a system of words and grammatical structures shared by a group of people within a particular cultural tradition or geographic area. For example, the French language denotes the words used primarily by those living in France and in areas colonized by France after 1500. For cultural critics, however, language refers to any communicative system. Language encompasses not only written and spoken words, but also imagery, fashion, music, body gestures, advertisements, and so on. This broad definition of language is based on **semiotics**, the study of communication through signs.

Rooted in the field of linguistics, semiotics is a variegated, complex, and sometimes controversial theory and interpretive methodology with many different branches. For the purposes of this chapter, we will focus on its

---

3 Hall et al., *Policing the Crisis*, ix.

implications for the study of representation through a constructionist model. The origin of semiotics lies with Swiss linguist Ferdinand de Saussure (1857–1913), who investigated the nature of language as a system of signs.[4] From this perspective, as with the expansive understanding of *language* cited above, basically anything can be a sign (a word, an image, an odour, a flavour, a texture, a musical note, etc.) so long as it expresses an idea or conveys information and refers to something other than itself.

A rich resource for considering the semiotic understanding of signs is the database of clip art graphics, the images offered by word processing programs for possible insertion into documents. Microsoft Office offers one such online library of images,[5] which provides a search box for those needing a visual sign to represent something (such as an idea, feeling, person, object, or concept). If you type the word "justice" in this search box this graphic appears on the first page of images:

Figure 3.1 Scales of justice

4 Ferdinand de Saussure et al., *Course in General Linguistics* (New York: McGraw-Hill, 1966).
5 "Images: Clip Art, Photos, Sound, & Animations," Office.com, http://office.microsoft.com/en-us/images/results.aspx?qu=justice&ex=2 (accessed December 22, 2013).

The title of this image expresses the ideas that the sign is meant to convey: "Lawyer holding a briefcase and scales of justice." The tagged keywords provide further information about the ideas the creators believe the image encapsulates: "government, justice, lawyers, men, occupations, scales, symbols, people." Both the title and the keywords tell us the explicit and intentional meaning of this sign.

But signs can also have implicit, inadvertent, or latent meanings. A semiotic scholar might interpret the implicit meaning of the clip art sign as suggesting that only a professional lawyer can deliver justice. A feminist scholar might further decipher the latent meaning of this sign as indicative of the patriarchal nature of the legal system and the ways that justice is associated with masculine subjectivity. This scholar might then turn to empirical work to support her analysis. For example, content-analysis research has found that clip art graphics more frequently depict white males overall, and also depict white males in more active and desirable roles than members of any other identity group.[6] And yet an opposing scholar might point out that the figure holding the scales of justice is usually gendered female, and because of this the image of a male in this role should be understood as iconoclastic. Indeed, out of the eight images of a person holding the scales of justice provided by Microsoft Office's clip art gallery, five are clearly gendered female, two are ambiguous, and only one, the image shown above, depicts a male figure. This scholar might thus argue that the image of a male figure holding the scales of justice offers a modest counterbalance to the dominant association of justice with femininity.

Yet our original feminist scholar might respond that while feminine figures may act as metaphors for justice, this does not translate into an equitable representation of real women alongside men in higher positions within the legal profession.[7] Signs are thus not only open to different semantic interpretations, but also different political interpretations.

To further nuance an analysis of the nature of signs, Saussure breaks down the components that make up a sign into two parts. The form of the sign, like the cartoon image of the lawyer in Figure 3.1, is called the **signifier**. The actual idea or concept to which the signifier refers, like the concept of justice or the idea of a male lawyer, is called the **signified**.

---

6 Sharon Seidman Milburn, Dana R. Carney, and Aaron M. Ramirez, "Even in Modern Media, the Picture Is Still the Same: A Content Analysis of Clip Art Images," *Sex Roles* 44, no. 5 (2001): 277–94.

7 Fiona M. Kay and Joan Brockman, "Barriers to Gender Equality in the Canadian Legal Establishment," *Feminist Legal Studies* 8, no. 2 (2000): 169–98. Also excerpted in U. Schultz and G. Shaw, *Women in the World's Legal Professions* (Oxford: Hart Publishing, 2003).

While both signifier and signified are integral to the process of representation, there is usually an arbitrary relationship between these two elements. As observed by Juliet Capulet, Shakespeare's famous star-crossed lover, "What's in a name? that which we call a rose / By any other name would smell as sweet; So Romeo would, were he not Romeo call'd, / Retain that dear perfection which he owes / Without that title ..."[8] Juliet aptly describes how the word *rose* and the title *Romeo* have no direct connection to the notion of a rose's sweet smell or the perception of Romeo's dear perfection. This arbitrary relationship is further evidenced by the way different languages have different signifiers for the same signified concept. For example, *dog* in English and *chien* in French are different signifiers for the same signified canine animal. In this way, meaning does not reside in the form of the signifier, but rather in the shared codes of a culture.

The signification process thus allows human subjects to classify and categorize in order to create meaning and communicate ideas. A social space where people are intelligible to one another requires some representational system that makes sense of the infinite number of things in our world—from material objects that we can perceive with our senses to the most rarefied philosophical ideas that exist only in the abstract plane. From the perspective of traditional linguistics then, representation operates through the arbitrary, but culturally specific, connection between signifier and signified, which produces signs that reference the "real" world in some way.[9]

In the context of critical analysis and cultural studies, representation challenges the notion of the "real" world. Etymologically, if we parse the term *represent* into its two main component parts—*re* and *present*—it denotes a sign or a stand-in of an original phenomenon, whether it is a material object, an event, a feeling, or an idea. From this conventional perspective, representation must occur after the phenomenon and can either be a faithful or an inaccurate representation of the original. Hall makes an important intervention here that challenges this simplistic view of representation. He urges us to move away from the idea of an essential truth or a fixed reality that representation can either reflect authentically or distortedly. Instead, we must understand that representation itself constitutes the phenomenon it seeks to stand in for.[10] In this way, it does not exist outside of reality, but rather constructs reality. For example, consider how the label *sex trafficking* in today's political climate conjures up images

---

8 William Shakespeare, *Romeo and Juliet*, 2.2.

9 Hall, *Representation: Cultural Representations and Signifying Practices*, 36.

10 Stuart Hall, *Representation and the Media* (audiovisual) (1997; Massachusetts: Media Education Foundation at Transcript), 7.

of enslaved women and children, brutal traffickers, and rapacious "johns." Such sensationalist and reductionist representations prevent, or at the very least make difficult, any consideration that some forms of cross-border sex work might instead be framed within the context of labour and migrant rights.[11] Representations structure and frame how we are meant to think about a phenomenon. Hall does not deny that a material world exists, but rather emphasizes that we cannot access the meaning of the material world without recourse to language, which necessitates participating in symbolic codes and discourses.

Discourse

Within cultural studies, **discourse**, like *language*, holds a more complex and theoretical meaning than its standard dictionary definition. In common usage, discourse denotes communication through words that are used in a conversation, debate, or formal treatment of a subject in speech or writing. Within the linguistic field and at its most basic level, discourse refers to language that extends beyond a sentence or clause.[12] Critical discourse analysis expands this approach to consider how language is used in relation to social, cultural, and political forces.

As you have learned in preceding chapters, Michel Foucault understood discourse as an ideological practice that systematically organizes knowledge into truth regimes. Those endowed with "expertise" are often at the forefront of producing discourse. For example, from a Foucauldian perspective, psychiatrists do not "discover" pathologies or disorders, but rather construct and catalogue knowledge of mental illness into coherent discourses. In this way, discourse refers to clusters of ideas and representations that do more than delineate a subject. Discourse structures how one should evaluate the subject under study and often suppresses alternative ways of making sense of an issue.

Another example is classic criminological discourse, which structures its theories and findings to construct lawbreakers as deviants who violate fair and just social norms and laws. It follows that the solution toward such deviants is to "fix" the problem, either through punishment, rehabilitation, and deterrent measures or by incapacitation through imprisonment or the death penalty. The notion that the legal and criminal justice system may be

---

11 Laura Maria Agustín, *Sex at the Margins: Migration, Labour Markets and the Rescue Industry* (London: Zed Books, 2007).

12 Adam Jaworski and Nikolas Coupland, eds., *The Discourse Reader* (London: Routledge, 1999).

biased or unfair is rendered unthinkable within this criminological discourse. Discourse is thus linked to wielding the power to create reality.

Foucault's theories of power also help us understand how power works through representations. The standard definition of power denotes control over an individual or groups (e.g., the power of a judge to sentence convicted criminals to prison). While recognizing this blatant form of power, Foucault introduced the notion of more subtle and insidious forms of power, including the idea of power through governmentality. As you learned in Chapter One, the word *governmentality* is a hybrid word that combines *government* with *mentality*. In this sense, it addresses how the process and practice of governing can become a state of mind. Foucault theorized that not only is power exercised explicitly through laws, police enforcement, and military threats, but that governance works most effectively when it is naturalized, internalized, and reproduced. For example, consider how the gender binary of "male" and "female" governs our lives through multiple circuits of power. Explicit government laws and policies demand individuals to fit within this binary through birth certificates, driver's licences, or prison structures. In addition to these governmental processes, signifying practices like popular culture or scientific authority also assume, enforce, and perpetuate the gender binary. In dynamic relationship to these meaning-making arenas, individuals govern themselves in conformity to the gender binary. Gender becomes naturalized and embodied on the micro level as individuals express their male and female identities through dress, grooming, conduct, and even desire. Those who fail to govern themselves in accordance with their assigned gender can be labelled as deviant and even criminalized.

Ideology and Hegemony

To challenge this construction of reality, let's consider how a cultural theorist might engage in a discourse analysis using a Foucauldian and Marxist lens. Such a methodology might seek to expose how the label *deviant* does not objectively signify a category of people, but rather reflects and perpetuates unequal power relations, for example, between the rich and the poor or between gender-conforming and gender-nonconforming individuals. This unequal power issues from blatant sources, such as the ability to incarcerate a transgendered woman in a male prison, and from governmental sources, such as the ability to induce shame of one's deviant status through moral or psychiatric discourse. Yet a conventional theorist might argue that if crime is not deviant, why do most people, including poor and working-class people, fear and despise the criminalized class? And if gender is not natural, then why do most people gladly conform to their assigned gender? Cultural studies uses two intertwining concepts to explain how the populace might be pacified in this regard: ideology and hegemony.

French philosopher Antoine Destutt de Tracy (1754–1836) is usually credited with coining the term **ideology** to convey the idea that a "science of ideas" would help to expose latent biases.[13] Within the field of sociology, the term ideology originates from the philosophy of Karl Marx (1818–83), a historian and social theorist whose highly influential and ground-breaking work provided a radical critique of capitalism and class relations. In classical Marxist theory, ideology denotes the way the ruling class uses doctrines to distort reality and naturalize, justify, and legitimate the subordination of the working class. But recall that cultural theorists generally do not subscribe to this essentialist view of a knowable and describable reality that is falsified through ideological articulations. Instead, ideology—from a nonessentialist perspective—refers to a group of attitudes, assumptions, beliefs, values, moral stances, and political philosophies that frame one's understanding of the world and of humanity. For example, as you will see in some of the chapters that follow, laws that punish street crime more heavily than corporate crime reflect a classist ideology that views poor criminals as more culpable and more dangerous than rich ones.

When the ideological perspective of those who are most privileged is adopted by the majority, including those who are most marginalized, the resulting situation is one of **hegemony**. In cultural studies, the concept of hegemony stems mainly from the work of Antonio Gramsci (1891–1937), an Italian Marxist and political activist. Gramsci theorized that an oppressive state must not rely solely or even primarily on explicit force to ensure social order, but rather must manipulate the population so that the interests of the ruling class will be understood as universal interests. Gramsci highlighted the role culture plays in ensuring this manipulation. The ruling class controls the dominant modes of meaning-making: for example, judicial decisions, mainstream news reports, and popular culture. Through these mediums, those who benefit from the social order foster ways of thinking and interpreting that support the status quo and categorize dissenters as deviants. Hegemony cultivates the population's consent so that force becomes unnecessary. But unlike a strict model of ideological indoctrination, Gramsci insisted that securing hegemonic consent was not a seamless top-down process, but rather a back-and-forth negotiation or struggle between contrasting ideas, understandings, and social forces. To put it another way, people are not robots that can be perfectly programmed and governed, but rather complex agents who can resist and negotiate, as well as internalize, dominant ideologies.

---

13 Antoine Destutt de Tracy and Henri Gouhier, *Éléments D'idéologie* (Paris: J.Vrin, 1970).

Methods of Interpretation

Reception Theories and Their Effects

Let's now consider how media theorists have taken up the concepts of ideology and hegemony. One of the most influential theorists on mass media effects was a communications theorist named George Gerbner (1919–2005) who founded **cultivation theory**. Beginning in the 1960s, Gerbner began to research how television influences viewers' perceptions of social reality, paying specific attention to the ways in which heavy doses of violent television tended to inculcate a negative and fearful impression of the world—a phenomenon dubbed the "Mean World Syndrome."[14] A television viewer who repeatedly watches depictions of extreme violence, whether it be terrorists on the nail-biting *24*, pedophiles on the sensationalist *Law & Order: Special Victims Unit*, or serial killers on the graphically violent *Criminal Minds*, is susceptible to this syndrome, which manifests in a tacit belief that the world is fraught with monstrous figures and that danger lurks behind every bush.

Media and crime research has extended cultivation theory beyond television shows to include other discursive products, most notably the role played by the news media in exaggerating audience perceptions of the current crime rate and in associating certain ethnic identities with crime.[15] One possible impact of this hegemonic construction of a "mean world" is that the viewer is led to support politicians who advance "tough on crime" bills and anti-immigrant policies while sacrificing the due process rights of suspects or accused persons in the name of a safer society.

Beyond the perception-shaping effect of the media, behavioural theorists have examined the imitative impact of media exposure, particularly with regard to violent representations. Numerous studies have been carried out that explore the connection between watching aggression or violence and subsequent behaviour.[16] Often the focus has been on children, who are constructed as more impressionable than adults.[17] The early research in the 1970s targeted television, but more recent studies are concerned with newer forms

---

14 George Gerbner and Michael Morgan, *Against the Mainstream* (New York: Peter Lang, 2002).

15 Ray Surette, *Media, Crime, and Criminal Justice: Images, Realities, and Policies* (Belmont, CA: Wadsworth, 2010).

16 Brad. J. Bushman and L. Rowell Huesmann, "Short-Term and Long-Term Effects of Violent Media on Aggression in Children and Adults," *Archives of Pediatrics and Adolescent Medicine* 160, no. 4 (2006): 348–52.

17 John P. Murray, "Media Violence," *American Behavioral Scientist* 51, no. 8 (2008): 1212–30.

of media like video games.[18] Although many of these studies have established some connection, it is important to distinguish between *correlation* and *causation*.[19] While some scientists insist there is strong evidence that video games cause aggressive or violent behaviour,[20] others counter that the studies only establish correlation, which can have other explanations (e.g., that children who are already violent or aggressive are attracted to such games).[21] From a critical perspective, the "monkey see, monkey do" hypothesis can foster a "moral panic," or more precisely a "media panic"—an intense fear that a new media form threatens core cultural values and societal safety.[22] Thus, while the behavioural impact of representations can be a source of critical insight, you should also be on the lookout for media panics that say more about cultural fears than empirical facts.

In addition to cultivation and imitation theories, some scholars have turned their attention to the relationship media consumers can have (or imagine they have) with a particular figure in a narrative representation. Media theorist Jonathan Cohen provides an overview of the literature, helpfully distinguishing between imitation, the behavioural concept we have just examined, with the more relational concepts of liking, parasocial interaction, and identification.[23]

When a consumer experiences positive feelings toward a character, for example, if she likes the character, she will usually judge the character's actions and feelings as reasonable and understandable. Likewise, if a character is disliked, then his or her actions will generally be condemned. When considering the politics of representation, notice how a narrative can construct a character in ways that elicit such feelings as admiration or disgust within the audience member, and how this might affect one's understanding of crime. For example, if a television cop show depicts the police officer as a likeable, relatable character and the criminal as a bloodthirsty monster, this might

---

18 Douglas A. Gentile, Paul J. Lynch, Jennifer Ruh Linder, and David A. Walsh, "The Effects of Violent Video Game Habits on Adolescent Hostility, Aggressive Behaviors, and School Performance," *Journal of Adolescence* 27, no. 1 (2004): 5–22.

19 Cheryl K. Olson, Lawrence Kutner, and Eugene V. Beresin, "Children and Video Games: How Much Do We Know?" *Psychiatric Times* 24, no. 12 (2007): 1.

20 Craig A. Anderson, "An Update on the Effects of Playing Violent Video Games," *Journal of Adolescence* 27, no. 1 (2004): 113–22.

21 John Grohol, "The Link between Video Games and Violence," *Psych Central* (2008), http://psychcentral.com/blog/archives/2008/05/17/the-link-between-video-games-and-violence/ (accessed September 6, 2012).

22 Kirsten Drotner, "Dangerous Media? Panic Discourses and Dilemmas of Modernity," *Paedagogica Historica* 35, no. 3 (1999): 593–619.

23 Jonathan Cohen, "Defining Identification: A Theoretical Look at the Identification of Audiences with Media Characters," *Mass Communication & Society* 4, no. 3 (2001): 245–64.

cultivate punitive attitudes toward such criminalized people in real life while generating approval for police forces.

Another relational site that should be on the critical scholar's radar is parasocial interaction. The concept refers to a consumer subjectively experiencing friendship or connection with a character or actor. A good example of parasocial interaction is when a media consumer becomes a devoted fan of a particular actor, not only watching all of the movies she stars in, but also following her life's events through celebrity gossip publications. Such a fan may feel intimately connected to the actor and have strong affection for her, but the affective experience is not based on mutuality—it is an entirely one-sided attachment. What might be relevant for the politics of representation are the ways this star appeal can have hegemonic ramifications. For example, when an adored actor stars in a film that supports military solutions to global conflict, the fan may be more likely to support the film's ideology. Furthermore, many actors wield their star power to directly intervene in public debates by supporting political candidates or causes. Such strategies bank on the power of parasocial relationships to convince fans to get on board with the celebrity's political agenda.

Liking a character, or interacting parasocially with a character or actor, both involve external relationships. When this sense of affection or connection gets extended such that the consumer "loses" herself in the character, the result has been described as the most powerful form of positive affect: **identification**. Cohen defines identification as not only liking a character, but also adopting the identity, perspectives, desires, and fears of the character. For the duration of narrative consumption, the reader becomes decreasingly self-aware as she becomes increasingly connected to the character on cognitive and emotional levels.[24] Consider how horror movies can make some people fearful or even scream when the killer jumps out from a hiding place. In this moment the audience member is not merely sympathizing with the character, he is empathizing with her. Identification thus facilitates vicarious experiences through a process of psychological merging.[25] In your analysis of a criminal representation, you may want to investigate if and how a narrative encourages identification with figures like the lawyer, the police officer, the lone vigilante, the victim, or the "bad guy" and theorize what hegemonic or counterhegemonic agenda may be advanced by this identification.

While cultivation, impact, and affect theories provide important frameworks to understand the politics of representation, they should be viewed

---

24 Cohen, "Defining Identification," 251.

25 Keith Oatley, "Meetings of Minds: Dialogue, Sympathy, and Identification in Reading Fiction," *Poetics* 26, no. 5 (1999): 439–54.

as partial theories. After all, if representations could completely structure audience perceptions of social reality or trigger predictable behaviour, there would be no political debate or struggle over meaning. As Gramsci argued, this is clearly not the case: Hegemonic constructions never fully achieve a closure in meaning. Cultural theorists like Stuart Hall have thus further nuanced this perspective by highlighting the semiotic instability of representations. Hall argues that an image does not have a fixed meaning, but rather can support a wide range of meanings, including contradictory meanings. When we seek to determine the meaning of a cultural text, our analysis is always contextualized by our political understandings and our sociohistorical position, as demonstrated by the different ways one can read the clip art image of a male lawyer holding the scales of justice shown in Figure 3.1. This anti-essentialist perspective, which refuses an inherent meaning to a representation, can be described as a poststructuralist approach to the cultural study of crime.

Critics of this poststructuralist perspective have argued that if there is no inherent meaning in a cultural artifact, then how can we convincingly analyze or deconstruct it? And more importantly, how do we mobilize people to resist hegemonic constructions if we reject the notion of an essential truth or a fixed reality? In order to understand Hall's response to these objections, recall his position that there is no way to access the "true" meaning of an event that is outside of discourse. Even those trying to "fight the power" cannot escape the limits of language, nor can they step outside of their own sociohistorical context. Because of this, Hall suggests that when we attempt to analyze a text we do so "without guarantees"—that is, we can never guarantee that we have accessed the ultimate truth. Instead, we make contingent arguments that privilege a particular interpretation for the purpose of political contestation. We put forward the best analysis we can craft to challenge dominant representations and lay bare their ideological underpinnings. However, while doing so, we also remember that interpretation is always open to challenge and reinterpretation. This does not weaken political resistance, but rather dismantles ideological claims of certainty. In this way, a cultural studies refashioning of the activist slogan "speak truth to power" might be "deconstruct truth-claims to expose power."

But is it only academics, with their sophisticated analytical tools, who are capable of deconstructing and thereby resisting hegemonic representations? Is the average media consumer doomed to be subject to ideological indoctrination? Hall's answer is no. In his essay, "Encoding and Decoding in the Television Discourse," Hall outlines the ways that hegemonic representation can both indoctrinate particular messages and incite consumers of representation to negotiate and resist those messages.[26] Using the example of television programming, Hall breaks down different moments in the production and interpretation of meaning. He argues that while television producers may encode particular messages based on institutional and ideological factors, the audience could decode these messages in a variety of ways.

Hall delineates three reading practices, or interpretive processes, to emphasize the ways that audience members actively participate in making sense of the meaning of the program. When an audience member internalizes the dominant and intended ideological message of the text—that is, the message that has been encoded by the producers of the program—Hall calls this the *preferred reading*. In this reading, the consumer and the creator are in semiotic alliance. When an audience member accepts the broad, abstract, hegemonic message of the program, but updates, adapts, or modifies its implications for his or her own particular context, this is referred to as a *negotiated reading*. This reading entails contradiction and ambivalence toward the text. Finally, when a viewer decodes the hegemonic message as ideology and interprets the implicit truth-claims and identity constructions as reflecting dominant interests rather than reality, this is understood as an *oppositional reading*. Here, the reader goes against the normative grain of the text, for example, by identifying with the villain of a story and disdaining the hero.

Hall's emphasis on diverse interpretative trajectories and the contradictory possibilities of reception thus challenges an overly deterministic understanding of audience reception. Such a semiotic model offers the exciting possibility of resistance and change by recognizing active decodings that range from total agreement with to complete rejection of a text's latent ideological message.

Of course when a scholar is analyzing a text to determine what constitutes the dominant encoding and what is entailed by a preferred, negotiated, or oppositional reading, there are no easy answers. Indeed, some critics have interpreted Hall's schema as overly reductionist in both the decoding and the encoding stages. The suggestion that a program contains a singular discernable dominant code ignores the possibility that the text can contain multiple and even conflicting ideologies.[27] The idea that readers can be roughly broken down into three categories that range from passive acceptors to active resisters further reduces the complexity of reading practices. However, such objections tend to ignore Hall's guiding principle: "without guarantees." As we have discussed above, Hall's theory of media representation is that

---

26 Stuart Hall, "Encoding and Decoding in the Television Discourse," *CCCS Stencilled Paper* 7 (1973).

27 Daniel Chandler, "Semiotics for Beginners," http://www.Aber.Ac.uk/media/Documents/S4B (accessed December 22, 2013).

deconstruction and analysis can never guarantee access to the truth of the text. At its best, the encoding/decoding framework offers analytical tools to open up the complexity of a text and its effects, not to foreclose a plurality of interpretations.

Hall's theory that meaning is made through an interactive process of construction, representation, and variable interpretation advances the notion that signification is not static but dynamic. To convey this multistaged and multilayered process, Hall uses the concept of **signifying practices**, which refers to the meaning-making behaviours that constitute the interconnected relationship between creation and reception. In this way, the consumer of the text plays just as vital a role as the designer of the text in the production of meaning.[28]

Stereotyping

When analyzing a signifying practice from a critical perspective, Hall asks us to interrogate the text—that is, go beyond the surface meaning and consider what underlying elements support the logic of the story. Let's consider some interrogative tools and methodologies that can help us decode, deconstruct, and expose the ideological agenda of a representation, and recognize the oppositional or counterhegemonic elements that may reside within. While not all of the following analytical tools will be relevant to a final analysis of the text you are seeking to decode, it may be useful to try them all at first to see what ideas come forth. The following examples will focus on narrative texts, as opposed to nonverbal or purely visual productions.

When you seek to decode a text, a crucial step is to engage with one of the most insidious signifying practices: **stereotyping**. Whether in fiction or nonfiction, stereotypical representation is a knowledge claim that characterizes a social identity to a fixed and limited set of characteristics. While stereotypes need not be pejorative on their face (e.g., the stereotype that Asian people are good at math), they are reductionist and deny the full range of human diversity and complexity of particular groups. At their worst, stereotypes legitimate the stigmatization of such groups and naturalize the socioeconomic, political, and racial status quo. Stereotyping is accordingly a divisive practice. As Hall states,

> It sets up a symbolic frontier between the "normal" and the
> "deviant," the "normal" and the "pathological," the "acceptable" and

---

28 Hall, *Representation: Cultural Representations and Signifying Practices*, 33.

the "unacceptable," what "belongs" and what does not is "**Other**," between "insiders" and "outsiders," Us and Them. It facilitates the "binding" or bonding together of all of Us who are "normal" into one "imagined community"; and it sends into symbolic exile all of Them—"the Others"—who are in some way different—"beyond the pale."[29]

Hall's description helps to highlight the many guises that stereotyping can take. Stereotypical judgments can be justified by sociological, medical, moral, and political discourse. Hall also draws attention to the social bonding and community building that stereotyping can achieve: Those deemed "normal" connect to one another and reaffirm their normality through the process of exiling Others. Stereotypes are also a key source of governmentality because individuals may seek to distance themselves from stereotyped groups. For example, a person from a community that has been subject to negative stereotyping may choose not to dress in what might be considered "ethnic" garb, in order to dissociate him or herself from this stigmatized identity.[30]

But how can we contest stereotypes? Perhaps the first step is simply to notice them. When you read a narrative text, consider which characteristics seem to cluster around the most negative, the most silent, or the most ridiculed figures. Questions you might want to consider include, What types of people are portrayed as multidimensional characters, and what types are rendered in a one-dimensional way? Do the one-dimensional characters tend to be members of a certain race, class, age, gender, sexuality, or other identifiable group? How is their body marked through dress, hairstyles, accessories, tattoos, piercings, and so on? What personality traits do they possess, and how does this compare to the main characters? Identifying particular figures as stereotypes and interrogating how they are stereotyped contests the implicit truth-claims embedded in the representation. Such deconstructions can work to expose and denaturalize the oversimplification, objectification, animalization, or demonization of otherized groups.

While deconstructing stereotypes in this way is one important counterhegemonic practice, constructing and recognizing alternatives can be equally effective. You may want to seek out and analyze signifying practices that portray a marginalized group in multidimensional, contextualized or positive ways. Often, such counterhegemonic representations are found in alternative (as opposed to popular) mediums. Take the representation of

---

29 Hall, *Representation: Cultural Representations and Signifying Practices*, 258.
30 Erving Goffman, *Stigma: Notes on the Management of Spoiled Identity* (Englewood Cliffs, NJ: Prentice-Hall, 1963).

prisoners, for example. In popular culture, like the hit HBO television show *Oz* (1997–2003), inmates are generally represented as sadistic, monstrous, and unrepentant savages who must be kept behind bars for the safety of good, normal, law-abiding citizens.[31] Black inmates are represented as particularly brutal.[32] But in the alternative publication "Prisoners of the War on Drugs," the systemic factors that keep members of poor communities vulnerable to criminalization and incarceration are explored (see Figure 3.2).[33]

Despite the fact that the text is in comic form, it still manages to represent how social and economic factors perpetuate the criminalization cycle. It further combats stereotyping by humanizing those caught in the criminal justice system while depicting the devastating ripple effects that prisons can have on inmates' families and communities.

Satire is another contesting strategy that undermines the power of stereotypes. But unlike positive, humanizing, and contextual representations, satire does not reject stereotypes—it works with them, or better put, it reworks them. A good starting point to consider the significance of satire is the *Oxford Dictionary of English*, which defines the term as "the use of humour, irony, exaggeration, or ridicule to expose and criticize people's stupidity or vices, particularly in the context of contemporary politics and other topical issues."[34] To recognize satire, one must be able to read a text on multiple levels. Consider the popular satirical film *Team America: World Police* (2004), which, on a surface reading, depicted Arabs as maniacal terrorists and Americans as glorious champions. However, a deeper analysis of the satirical tone of the film suggests that the caricaturing of evil Arabs actually subverts stereotyping and xenophobia. As Jeremy C. Fox states, "The terrorists in the film speak the kind of gibberish Arabic you could imagine coming from the mouths of patriotic adolescents in study halls across the country."[35] Meanwhile, the American "heroes" are portrayed as monomaniacal zealots, unconcerned, for example, that they have demolished Paris or destroyed the pyramids in Egypt in their bid to keep the world "safe." Satire thus takes

---

31 Bill Yousman, "Inside Oz: Hyperviolence, Race and Class Nightmares, and the Engrossing Spectacle of Terror," *Communication and Critical/Cultural Studies* 6, no. 3 (2009): 265–84.

32 Ibid., 276.

33 Sabrina Jones, Ellen Miller-Mack, and Lois Ahrens, "Prisoners of the War on Drugs," The Real Cost of Prisons Project (2005), http://www.realcostofprisons.org/war_on_drugs.pdf (accessed December 22, 2013).

34 *Oxford Dictionary of English*, 3rd ed., s.v. "satire."

35 Jeremy C. Fox, "Marionettes Doing the Dirty: *Team America: World Police*," film review (May 13, 2006), http://www.pajiba.com/film_reviews/team-america-world-police.php (accessed April 5, 2014).

Figure 3.2 Cycles of exile

These ideas are based on the work of Dina R. Rose and Todd R. Clear: "Incarceration, Reentry and Social Capital: Social Networks in the Balance," 12/01
Prisoners of the War on Drugs by Sabrina Jones • © 2005 The Real Cost of Prisons Project • www.realcostofprisons.org

stereotypes to a comical extreme to critique and make visible their ideological underpinnings.

Semiotic Tools

The next two analytical tools to consider are an extension of semiotic theory. We have already discussed how the signified and the signifier work together to make a sign intelligible within a set of cultural codes. Another important aspect of the way signs work to communicate meaning is their relationship to other signs, both similar and different. To understand the sign *criminal*, one must have a sense of the sign *law*. After all, how else can one signify a criminal without first having an understanding that there are laws that can be broken? Signs are further defined by negation and binary opposition. For example, the sign *criminal* is partly signified by its constructed binary opposite: *victim*. One way that critical criminologists might challenge this dichotomy is to argue that most people designated as *criminals* are also victims of poverty, social marginalization, and overpolicing, as you will find in Chapter 9: Crime and Social Classes: Regulating and Representing Public Disorder.

Hall suggests that we must pay attention not just to what is present in a text, but also to what is absent. When scrutinizing a representation, we have already discussed how we should look to background characters as possible conveyers of stereotypes. Sometimes, however, the most pernicious signifying practice doesn't work through explicit stereotyping, but instead through conspicuous absence. As Hall explains, "Every image that we see is being read in part against what isn't there."[36] For example, consider a climactic scene in the blockbuster movie *The Dark Knight Rises* (2012). Toward the end of the film, the city of Gotham has been appropriated by violent anti-capitalist anarchists who have managed to keep the police force at bay for five months. When the police are freed, they clash with the anarchists in a ferocious street fight. Out of narrative context, such a scene might invoke fear of police brutality, or at least excessive force. Yet through the plot structure of the film, the preferred reading is that you cheer for the cops who are "liberating" the streets. In part, this message works through absence. Earlier scenes in the film depict ordinary citizens in full support of the anarchist takeover. But as scholar–blogger Aaron Bady observes, in this scene, "the people we see the cops beating up are not citizens, but a hyper organized criminal conspiracy."[37]

---

36 Hall, *Representation and the Media*, 15.

37 Aaron Bady, "Do Not Go Gentle into that Dark Knight," *The New Inquiry*, July 25, 2012, http://thenewinquiry.com/blogs/zunguzungu/do-not-go-gentle-into-that-dark-knight/ (accessed April 5, 2014).

They are objectified. Absent are the ordinary citizens who previously sympathized with the anti-capitalist cause. Moreover, the movie audience does not witness the aftermath of dead and mutilated bodies—the inevitable result from such a violent confrontation.

Further, it is possible to interpret *The Dark Knight Rises* as invoking current political events without expressly referring to them—another kind of "absence" that speaks volumes. While Gotham is, of course, not a real city, and the exact plot details are fictional, numerous critical thinkers have read the 2012 film in the context of the 2011 Occupy Wall Street movement. Both the demonstrators in New York City and the anarchists in Gotham City are engaging in direct action to protest the staggering gap between the rich and the poor. In addition, one of the most patent cinematic invocations of the Occupy movement is when the fictional anarchists literally take over Gotham's stock exchange. In light of this striking parallel, and regardless of the director's personal intentions, the film's depiction of the anarchists as unjust, homicidal, and fanatical can thus be interpreted as an indictment of the Occupy movement, or at least a warning that anti-capitalist protestors are brainwashed thugs.[38] Absence can thus be a way to hide the ramifications of an adrenaline-pumping action scene as well as a way to intervene in political debates under the guise of entertainment.

Emotions, Identities, and Privilege

The final source of insight to consider is your own subjective experience. When you seek to decode a signifying practice, observe your own emotional interaction with the text. If you know you are going to analyze a particular film, for example, try not to intellectualize your viewing the first time you watch it, but rather allow your feelings to be swayed by the narrative. For many students, such an exercise may feel "biased" or "anti-intellectual"; most likely, teachers and professors have taught you that your personal opinion of a text is irrelevant or misleading. Perhaps you have been instructed that an "objective" analysis of a text looks for evidence within the text or cites recognized scholarly perspectives from secondary material. This is sound advice. But what is being suggested here is not that you base your entire analysis on your emotional reaction, but rather that you simply take notice of it because it may have significance for your final evaluation. For example,

---

38 "Christopher Nolan: *Dark Knight Rises* Isn't Political: Despite Echoes of Occupy Wall Street in Finale of Nolan's Batman Trilogy, Director Argues He Has No Particular Message," *Rolling Stone*, July 20, 2012, http://www.rollingstone.com/movies/news/christopher-nolan-dark -knight-rises-isn-t-political-20120720 (accessed April 5, 2014).

if you believe your identity or your personal experiences have had an impact on your emotional reception of the text, then note this down. Whether the text made you feel angry or affirmed, excited or indifferent, this has value and may prove relevant in your decoding.

One reason that a text may elicit a particular affective experience could be based on your identity. For example, my roots stem from India and Pakistan, and my religious background is Islamic. When I watch depictions of Muslims or South Asians, I feel implicated by the text. This reaction is, of course, heightened by the current post-9/11 geopolitical moment that has brought Islam, and by extension all people racialized as "brown," into the spotlight. But understanding the nexus between identity and analysis is tricky. It should be noted that while I may find a text like the movie *Ironman* (2008) Islamaphobic, another person with a similar background might judge the movie as properly distinguishing between "lawful" and "criminal" Muslims, thereby countering the racist homogenization and demonization of all Muslims.

An absolute claim about how people of certain backgrounds will or should experience a text is a form of **identity politics** grounded in essentialism. Absolutism should be avoided because it ignores the diversity of perspective that exists within all categories of people. Again, as Stuart Hall reminds us, when analyzing a particular representation there are no guarantees that we have accessed the most persuasive or relevant interpretation. Nonetheless, it is still an important exercise to consider how identity may influence the reception and decoding of a text, particularly for those whose identities have been subject to stereotyping.

An inquiry into how identity may inform our assessment of a representation includes taking into account not just the characteristics that make us vulnerable, but also those that bring us privilege. As you analyze a signifying practice, take a moment to consider how elements in the text may naturalize or legitimize your own privileges or sense of self. For example, a white, middle-class person with liberal leanings may rejoice in reading *The Help* (2011) because, while it addresses some aspects of race and class oppression in the 1960s, it features and centralizes the heroic actions of a white protagonist fighting to expose racial injustice. Indeed, the Association of Black Women Historians says of *The Help*, it "distorts, ignores, and trivializes the experiences of black domestic workers" while narrating a "... coming-of-age story of a white protagonist, who uses myths about the lives of black women to make sense of her own."[39] Whether you agree with this critique or not,

---

39 "An Open Statement to the Fans of *The Help*," Association of Black Women Historians, http://www.abwh.org/index.php?option=com_content&view=article&id=2%3Aopen-statement-the-help (accessed April 5, 2014).

the self-reflective exercise is important because it can help you recognize whether you might have personal investments in a narrative's ideology.

Another place to consider privilege is within the text itself. Students who analyze signifying practices often target representations of otherized characters (e.g., racialized or queer characters) to expose pejorative stereotyping. But to challenge privilege, it is just as important to scrutinize representations of those who are not marked as other. This is because one of the ways that privilege sustains itself is by flying under the radar. The characteristics that come with unearned privilege pass as normal, generic, and universal. As Michael Kimmel says, "To be white, or straight, or male, or middle class is to be simultaneously ubiquitous and invisible. You're everywhere you look, you're the standard against which everyone else is measured."[40] It is those who deviate from this "normal" who become particularized, who must be named. Think about how movies associated with feminine interests and targeted toward female audiences are labelled, often in a derogatory fashion, as "chick flicks." Compare that to movies associated with masculine interests and targeted toward male audiences, which are typically referred to in nongendered terms, for example, as "action films." When we seek to execute a full interrogation of a signifying practice, it is thus important to consider not only the ways our own privilege may structure our enjoyment or distaste, but also how privileged characters, characteristics, and perspectives are valorized and maintained.

Conclusion

This chapter has sought to introduce you to the cultural studies approach to analysis and to methodological tools that engage with the politics of representation and criminalization. While we considered the views of many different scholars, of most relevance was Stuart Hall's approach, which challenges the conception of representation as a mimetic practice that simply reflects reality. You were asked to think about representation as a signifying practice, where both the creator and the consumer of a text play roles in producing meaning and constructing reality. Our review of semiotics invited you to consider how language and discourse can perpetuate ideologies and hegemonic constructions of criminality.

But what is the effect of a text, and how do we decode it? We theorized about how a text may be received, what behavioural impact it might have, and what relationships and identifications it might evoke. Stereotyping was

---

40 Michael S. Kimmel and A.L. Ferber, *Privilege: A Reader* (Boulder, CO: Westview Press, 2003), xiv. See also Richard Dyer, *White: Essays on Race and Culture* (London: Routledge, 1997).

Figure 3.3 The power of white privilege

highlighted as a particularly powerful and insidious signifying practice that deserves interrogation. Semiotic interpretive frames further help to open up a text by considering how signs work through similarity, opposition, and absence. We ended by considering how our emotions can be a source of insight and how the identity and privilege of both readers and represented figures might be relevant in understanding the political significance of a text.

Finally, as we have stated throughout the chapter, we must remember that the constructivist approach to cultural studies rejects any guarantees of the "truth" of an interpretation. We must acknowledge that our arguments and our interpretations are influenced by our sociocultural and historical position, and thus are open to reinterpretation and contestation. This acknowledgement should not cause you to throw up your hands and abandon the project of representational analysis. Rather, this is cause to be optimistic. It is the very contestation of meaning—the meaning of a sign, a representation, a thing, an idea—that opens up space for both struggle and social transformation.

Study Questions

Consider Figure 3.3 by political cartoonist Keith Knight. What is of particular relevance to this chapter is that the comic depicts a representation of three audience members responding to a representation, and in this way helps us to analyze the politics of representation at two levels.

1. In what way does the comic itself engage in the politics of representation?
2. How does the comic subvert hegemonic constructions of crime?
3. How are stereotypes, identities, and emotions addressed in the comic?
4. What is your emotional response to this comic?
5. What concepts have we studied in this chapter that would explain why the three audience members are responding to the newscast in different ways?

Exercise

Identify a crime drama television show that is current and popular. Watch a random episode and consider the three types of readings outlined by Stuart Hall: preferred, negotiated, and oppositional. In a paragraph, write down what you believe to be the preferred reading of the show. When doing this, consider the ideological underpinnings of the narrative, the characters who are most likeable and unlikeable, and what you perceive to be the normative conclusion of the story. In a second paragraph, discuss what might be a negotiated reading of the show. When doing this, consider how someone might accept the broader ideological message or moral of the show, while adapting or modifying elements to suit a different set of circumstances. In the final paragraph, imagine what might constitute an oppositional reading of the show. When doing this, consider how the viewer might reject the underlying message of the narrative, sympathize with an "unlikeable" character, or identify the ways broader socioeconomic, political, or racial hierarchies are naturalized.

Remember that viewers may interpret the show in different ways, and that there are no strict rules regarding what constitutes a preferred, negotiated, or oppositional reading. Rather, this exercise is meant to cultivate your own analytical skills in engaging with the politics of criminal representation.

Keywords

politics of representation; cultural studies; Marxist; language; semiotics; signifier; signified; signifying practices; discourse; power; governmentality; ideology; hegemony; cultivation theory; parasocial interaction; identification; stereotyping; Other; identity politics

Bibliography

"An Open Statement to the Fans of *The Help*." Association of Black Women Historians. http://www.abwh.org/index.php?option=com_content&view=article&id=2%3Aopen -statement-the-help (accessed April 5, 2014).

"Christopher Nolan: *Dark Knight Rises* Isn't Political: Despite Echoes of Occupy Wall Street in Finale of Nolan's Batman Trilogy, Director Argues He Has No Particular Message." *Rolling Stone*, July 20, 2012. http://www.rollingstone.com/movies/news/christopher -nolan-dark-knight-rises-isn-t-political-20120720 (accessed April 5, 2014).

Agustín, Laura Maria. *Sex at the Margins: Migration, Labour Markets and the Rescue Industry*. London: Zed Books, 2007.

Anderson, Craig A. "An Update on the Effects of Playing Violent Video Games." *Journal of Adolescence* 27, no. 1 (2004): 113–22. http://dx.doi.org/10.1016/j.adolescence .2003.10.009.

Bady, Aaron. "Do Not Go Gentle into that Dark Knight." *The New Inquiry*. July 25, 2012. http://thenewinquiry.com/blogs/zunguzungu/do-not-go-gentle-into-that-dark -knight/ (accessed April 5, 2014).

Bushman, Brad J., and L. Rowell Huesmann. "Short-Term and Long-Term Effects of Violent Media on Aggression in Children and Adults." *Archives of Pediatrics & Adolescent Medicine* 160, no. 4 (2006): 348–52. http://dx.doi.org/10.1001/archpedi.160.4.348.

Chandler, Daniel. "Semiotics for Beginners." http://www.Aber.Ac.uk/media/Documents/ S4B (accessed December 22, 2013).

Cohen, Jonathan. "Defining Identification: A Theoretical Look at the Identification of Audiences with Media Characters." *Mass Communication & Society* 4, no. 3 (2001): 245–64. http://dx.doi.org/10.1207/S15327825MCS0403_01.

Destutt de Tracy, Antoine, and Henri Gouhier. *Élements D'idéologie*. Paris: J.Vrin, 1970.

Drotner, Kirsten. "Dangerous Media? Panic Discourses and Dilemmas of Modernity." *Paedagogica Historica* 35, no. 3 (1999): 593–619. http://dx.doi.org/10.1080/ 0030923990350303.

Dyer, Richard. *White: Essays on Race and Culture*. London: Routledge, 1997.

Fox, Jeremy C. "Marionettes Doing the Dirty: *Team America: World Police*." Film Review. May 13, 2006. http://www.pajiba.com/film_reviews/team-america-world-police .php (accessed April 5, 2014).

Gentile, Douglas A., Paul J. Lynch, Jennifer Ruh Linder, and David A. Walsh. "The Effects of Violent Video Game Habits on Adolescent Hostility, Aggressive Behaviors, and School Performance." *Journal of Adolescence* 27, no. 1 (2004): 5–22. http://dx.doi.org/ 10.1016/j.adolescence.2003.10.002.

Gerbner, George, and Michael Morgan. *Against the Mainstream*. New York: Peter Lang, 2002.

Goffman, Erving. *Stigma: Notes on the Management of Spoiled Identity*. Englewood Cliffs, NJ: Prentice-Hall, 1963.

Grohol, John M. "The Link between Video Games and Violence." *Psych Central* (2008). http://psychcentral.com/blog/archives/2008/05/17/the-link-between-video -games-and-violence/ (accessed September 6, 2012).

Hall, Stuart. *Representation and the Media (audiovisual)*. Massachusetts: Media Education Foundation, 1997.

Hall, Stuart. *Representation: Cultural Representations and Signifying Practices*. Thousand Oaks: Sage in association with the Open University, 1997.

Hall, Stuart et al. *Policing the Crisis: Mugging, the State, and Law and Order*. London: Macmillan, 1978.

Jaworski, Adam, and Nikolas Coupland, eds. *The Discourse Reader*. London: Routledge, 1999.

Jones, Sabrina, Ellen Miller-Mack, and Lois Ahrens. "Prisoners of the War on Drugs." The Real Cost of Prisons Project (2005). http://www.realcostofprisons.org/war_on_drugs.pdf (accessed December 22, 2013).

Kay, Fiona M., and Joan Brockman. "Barriers to Gender Equality in the Canadian Legal Establishment." *Feminist Legal Studies* 8, no. 2 (2000): 169–98. http://dx.doi.org/10.1023/A:1009205626028.

Kimmel, Michael S., and Abby L. Ferber. *Privilege: A Reader*. Boulder, CO: Westview Press, 2003.

Milburn, Sharon Seidman, Dana R. Carney, and Aaron M. Ramirez. "Even in Modern Media, the Picture Is Still the Same: A Content Analysis of Clip Art Images." *Sex Roles* 44, no. 5 (2001): 277–94. http://dx.doi.org/10.1023/A:1010977515933.

Murray, John P. "Media Violence: The Effects Are Both Real and Strong." *American Behavioral Scientist* 51, no. 8 (2008): 1212–30. http://dx.doi.org/10.1177/0002764207312018.

Oatley, Keith. "Meetings of Minds: Dialogue, Sympathy, and Identification in Reading Fiction." *Poetics* 26, no. 5 (1999): 439–54. http://dx.doi.org/10.1016/S0304-422X(99)00011-X.

Olson, Cheryl K., Lawrence Kutner, and Eugene V. Beresin. "Children and Video Games: How Much Do We Know?" *Psychiatric Times* 24, no. 12 (2007): 41–45.

Oxford Dictionary of English, 3rd ed., s.v. "satire."

de Saussure, Ferdinand, Charles Bally, Albert Sechehaye, et al. *Course in General Linguistics*. New York: McGraw-Hill, 1996.

Schultz, Ulrike, and Gisela Shaw. *Women in the World's Legal Professions*. Oxford: Hart Publishing, 2003.

Surette, Ray. *Media, Crime, and Criminal Justice: Images, Realities, and Policies*. Belmont: Wadsworth, 2010.

Yousman, Bill. "Inside Oz: Hyperviolence, Race and Class Nightmares, and the Engrossing Spectacle of Terror." *Cultural Studies* 6, no. 3 (2009): 265–84.

four
The Politics of Counting Crime

MICHAEL S. MOPAS

Introduction

Numbers and statistics play a vital role in shaping what we know about crime. We rely heavily on quantitative data to tell us everything from how many violent offences occurred in a given year and whether or not these instances are on the rise, to the rate of **recidivism** among offenders given community sentences. So although they lack rich ethnographic detail that may help us better understand why a person would commit a violent act in the first place or why certain rehabilitation programs work for one individual and not another, this type of information can offer a snapshot of broader trends and patterns. And much like a photograph, we assume that these figures accurately capture and depict what is really going on around us.

There are numerous ways in which we can go about studying crime, yet we tend to value quantitative research as a more legitimate way of knowing. We believe that number crunchers are able to get at the "truth" by employing scientific methods to produce findings that are free of personal bias and subjective interpretation. These truth-claims are extremely powerful weapons in public debates over crime control policies. The issue of crime and how best to respond to it is highly emotional and politically charged, and thus any groups who can point to "cold hard facts" are more likely to be trusted and heard. Dismissing any empirical evidence that contradicts these views, many of us still believe that scientific research should trump ideology as the primary basis for creating public policy.

Yet, since few of us know how these studies are carried out or have the basic skills needed to assess the validity of the results, we are forced to believe that what researchers tell us is true. For most individuals, the decision to accept a claim as fact is based not on a thorough evaluation of the research, but on our perceptions about the credibility of the researcher. And even though many of us are taught to be critical consumers of information by carefully evaluating the sources and by acknowledging that unscrupulous people can always fudge the numbers to promote their own agendas, this type of critical thinking is limited and reinforces a false dichotomy between "good" and "bad" research. More specifically, we end up promoting the idea that "bad" quantitative studies use numbers that are made up or falsified, while "good" ones are scientifically rigorous and allow the truth to simply "speak for itself."

In this chapter, I challenge this approach by suggesting that all numbers and statistics—regardless of who generates them and their underlying motivations—are socially produced. Drawing on insights from the field of **science and technology studies** (STS), I contest the notion that by following the rules of scientific inquiry we can produce "objective" facts about the world. Instead, I argue that what we classify as a scientific truth is not the product of a system of knowledge that allows nature to speak, but the outcome of human achievement. To illustrate this point, I "open up the **black box**"[1] of crime statistics to expose the underlying mechanisms that go into their production and highlight the human interests and actions involved. I then show how these supposedly "neutral" numbers have been used to promote and legitimize a positivist approach to dealing with crime that works on the premise that criminality is natural and resides within specific bodies and spaces. Far from being instruments of objective truth-telling, numbers and statistics are inherently political and cannot be disentangled from the broader social contexts in which they are produced and used. I begin this chapter by discussing how it is that we have come to equate quantitative research with truth and objectivity.

Finding Truth through Science

Our current faith in quantitative research to generate facts can be traced back to the Enlightenment period of the late eighteenth century and the shift toward science and reason as the primary mechanisms for advancing human knowledge. Ironically, although many of us tend to blindly accept the validity of "scientific" findings, the very notion that we should look to science as a means to better describe and explain our world emerges out of a critique of earlier forms of unquestioned epistemologies. The Enlightenment, or the "Age of Reason," ushered in a new way of thinking with intellectuals denouncing superstition, prejudice, common sense, and tradition as the proper ways of knowing.

In his famous essay published in 1784 entitled "What Is Enlightenment?" philosopher Immanuel Kant encouraged citizens to "dare to know" and to "have the courage to use your own reason":

---

1 Richard Whitley, "Black Boxism and the Sociology of Science: A Discussion of the Major Developments in the Field," in *The Sociology of Science*, ed. Paul Halmos (Keele: University of Keele, 1972), 61–92.

Don't just do what your priest or what your parents tell you; mistrust tradition; mistrust received opinion; exercise your critical faculties and question everything you were trained to believe. What we have inherited from the past, from tradition, from authority, is unexamined and probably wrong.[2]

Enlightenment philosophers believed that all individuals—not just highly educated men—were rational and had the capacity for critical thought, which they must use to dispassionately interrogate what they consider to be true.[3]

However, to be "enlightened" meant more than just being a skeptic. The Enlightenment period also brought with it a concern for the methods by which we come to know the things we know. Knowledge was no longer something that was passed down from religious leaders or other authority figures. On the contrary, knowledge had to be produced and verified according to a set of rules and procedures that we now commonly refer to as the **scientific method**. Only knowledge produced in this manner could be deemed valid. This belief that one must employ a certain methodology to generate facts about the world is a lasting legacy of the Enlightenment that remains with us today.

A school of thought known as **positivism** would later formalize many of these ideas about how it is we can produce knowledge. Positivism originated out of the work of Enlightenment thinkers like Henri de Saint-Simon, Pierre-Simon Laplace, and Auguste Comte. A key principle of positivism is that all claims to truth must be proven with empirical evidence. Positivist philosophers believe in an external reality that exists outside of human beings—that is, independently of our own subjective experiences of it—that can be objectively studied and observed. This reality operates according to its own set of natural laws that create stability and order. For positivists, the primary goal of research is to uncover these facts about the world and the underlying laws that govern them.[4]

Positivist thinkers assume that the world follows causal laws whereby all phenomena are prompted by some external force. This law of cause and effect applies to both the physical and the social worlds. Thus, like all other things, positivists believe that human behaviour was determined by an outside cause. Émile Durkheim used the term *social facts* to describe these things that exist independently from us, but coercively shape and influence our

---

2 Mariana Valverde, *Law and Order: Images, Meanings, Myths* (New Brunswick: Rutgers University Press, 2006), 2.
3 Ibid.
4 Ted Palys, *Research Decisions: Quantitative and Qualitative Perspectives*, 3rd ed. (Toronto: Nelson, 2003), 5.

actions.[5] As will be discussed later in this chapter, this belief that external forces determine one's behaviour called into question the existence of personal autonomy and human agency.

For positivists, then, the discovery of causal relationships allows us to generate generalized explanations for a wide range of events and occurrences. The aim is not to uncover the underlying factors that account for every single case, but to produce a "big picture" understanding of what "typically" happens or how the majority of people "normally" behave.[6] Through a process of deductive reasoning, scientists can test these general laws of cause and effect against their observations in the hopes of further refining and improving knowledge about the world. Once discovered, these causal laws are thought to be universal, holding true regardless of time, space, or cultural context, and can be used to explain why things are the way they are.

Positivists also assume that uncovering these causal laws will permit us to make reasonable predictions about the likelihood of future events.[7] For positivists, a true understanding of a phenomenon can only be demonstrated through one's ability to predict its occurrence.[8] However, as noted earlier, positivists are more interested in finding general trends and patterns than in developing nuanced explanations of individual cases. Consequently, most positivists do not believe the causal laws they discover could predict the specific behaviour of a particular person in a given situation, nor do they believe in absolute determinism.[9] Many positivist thinkers acknowledge that people are not machines and therefore do not always behave in the exact same way. Instead, most positivists maintain that the causal laws are probabilistic in nature and generally hold for large groups of people or occur in many situations.[10] So, while they cannot predict what might happen in definitive terms, positivists believe they can determine the likelihood that, under certain conditions, most individuals would behave in a particular way.

Prediction and scientific explanation are not the only goals of positivist research. Positivists also believe that if we clearly understand how the world works, we are not only able to predict but also control the future. Knowledge can therefore be used for instrumental purposes. As soon as we discover the laws that govern human nature, we can use them to alter social relations and

---

5　Émile Durkheim, *The Rules of the Sociological Method*, trans. W.D. Halls (New York: The Free Press, 1982 [1895]).

6　Palys, *Research Decisions*, 7.

7　W. Lawrence Neuman, Bruce Wiegand, and John A. Winterdyk, *Criminal Justice Research Methods: Qualitative and Quantitative Approaches*, Canadian ed. (Toronto: Pearson, 2006), 68.

8　Palys, *Research Decisions*, 8.

9　Ibid.

10　Neuman, Wiegand, and Winterdyk, *Criminal Justice Research Methods*, 68.

to improve how things are done.[11] So how do we know that the theories we develop accurately describe reality?

According to positivist philosophers, theories must be "positively" verified through observation before they can be accepted as truth.[12] Through empirical research, positivists attempt to "see" the realities of the natural world that exist outside of our socially produced world of ideas, values, and beliefs.[13] For positivists, knowledge that can be substantiated and consistent with observable evidence is superior to intuition, emotion, common sense, and other ways of knowing.[14] As such, only the external causes and effects that are most amenable to observation and measurement are legitimate objects of research—all other forces that cannot be witnessed are deemed unworthy of study (e.g., a person's underlying thoughts or motives).[15]

For positivists, only the unbiased observer can find truth, and it is only through science that one can systematically observe the world in an objective, disinterested, and detached manner.[16] The term *science* refers to the set of norms, procedures, techniques, and instruments used by those in the scientific community to generate facts that transcend personal prejudices and biases. It is also a social institution made up of scientists and researchers and the various values, beliefs, and practices they must adhere to. As new scientists enter the community, they are socialized into accepting these ideals and principles as part of their membership. The institutional norms of this community help to keep members in check and allow them to produce facts. Claims that can be confirmed through observation are viewed as scientific and meaningful, while those that cannot be verified are labelled as "pseudo-scientific" or "junk science." In this way, science refers to not only the system for producing knowledge, but also the knowledge that is produced from this system. For many positivists, this knowledge comes in the form of numbers.

The Objectivity of Numbers

The practices of measurement and quantification have long been, and still remain, central to the positivist tradition.[17] For many people, positivism is

---

11 Ibid., 67.
12 Stewart Richards, *Philosophy and Sociology of Science: An Introduction* (Oxford: Basil Blackwell, 1987), 198; David Hess, *Science Studies: An Advanced Introduction* (New York: New York University Press, 1997), 8.
13 Neuman, Wiegand, and Winterdyk, *Criminal Justice Research Methods*, 70.
14 Ibid.
15 Palys, *Research Decisions*, 6.
16 Richards, *Philosophy and Sociology of Science*, 201.
17 Ian Hacking, *The Taming of Chance* (Cambridge: Cambridge University Press, 1990), 5.

synonymous with quantitative methodologies. Although being a quantitative researcher does not necessarily mean that one is a positivist, being a positivist does imply the use of a quantitative approach.[18] This affinity toward numbers is in keeping with many of the key assumptions of positivism regarding the state of nature and how we can properly study it. First, measuring and counting is one of the most direct ways that positivists can go about observing broad social trends and patterns. Through the use of large-scale surveys, positivist researchers can gather a large number of observations that can tell us something about how the world "typically" works. Moreover, since positivists only count things that can be observed, it is assumed that these numbers are empirical in nature and can therefore be trusted.

Second, the practice of quantification allows positivists to translate research into a language that is standardized and can be shared. Turning research findings into numbers, graphs, and formulas enables a wider distribution and consumption by an audience separated by time and space. As Theodore Porter argues, quantification is a "technology of distance."[19] He writes:

> The language of mathematics is highly structured and rule-bound. It exacts a severe discipline from its users, a discipline that is very nearly uniform over most of the globe ... Since the rules for collecting and manipulating numbers are widely shared, they can easily be transported across oceans and continents and used to coordinate activities or settle disputes ... Quantification is well suited for communication that goes beyond the boundaries of locality and community.[20]

However, the standardization of counting practices provides members of the scientific community with more than just a shared language. The use of quantitative methodologies also gives researchers a way to "objectively" study the world.

As discussed earlier, positivists assert that scientific research must be conducted in a dispassionate and depersonalized manner in order for findings to be deemed legitimate and meaningful. One way this can be achieved is by limiting the contact between the researcher and the objects under investigation. For positivists, one of the biggest concerns is that researchers will somehow overidentify with those they study and become "so attuned and sensitive to the culture or group they're investigating that they take on the perspective

18 Palys, *Research Decisions*, 5.
19 Theodore Porter, *Trust in Numbers: The Pursuit of Objectivity in Science and Public Life* (Princeton: Princeton University Press, 1995), ix.
20 Ibid.

of that group's members, leaving their supposedly more appropriate detached, analytical perspective behind."[21] As Ted Palys explains, the assumption is that "the closer one comes to dealing with people on a one-to-one basis, the more dangerous the situation becomes, since one might be tempted to resort to metaphysical concepts such as thoughts, perceptions, attitudes and values."[22] Quantitative methodologies prevent the researcher from overidentifying with his or her subjects by keeping the data far removed from the source.

By limiting research to the counting of observable events and employing standardized practices that are open to public scrutiny, it is assumed that researchers can remain neutral while minimizing the "need for intimate knowledge and personal trust" with those they study. For positivists, then, the practice of quantification allows us to "produce knowledge that is independent of the particular people who make it" by keeping the researcher's judgments and subjectivities out of the equation.[23] As Kevin Haggerty suggests, "numbers are a powerful technology of objectification."[24] Once they are produced and circulated for consumption, the numbers generated by researchers become objects that are believed to speak for themselves as the circumstances of their production disappear from view.

Thus, for positivist thinkers, quantitative methodologies provide a system of "mechanical objectivity" that generates knowledge based on the application of explicit rules.[25] According to Theodore Porter, "[o]bjectivity derives not mainly from the wisdom acquired through a long career, but from the application of sanctioned methods, or perhaps the mythical, unitary 'scientific method,' to presumably neutral facts."[26] Furthermore, "[t]here should be no room for biases of the researcher to corrupt the results."[27] This approach to objectivity is often taken up in practice as a way to promote political democracy. The current push for evidence-based policy is rooted in this belief: For policy to be seen as just and reasonable, government initiatives must be based on scientific research and not on political ideology:

> The appeal of numbers is especially compelling to bureaucratic
> officials who lack the mandate of a popular election, or divine
> right. Arbitrariness and bias are the most usual grounds upon which

---

21 Palys, *Research Decisions*, 7.
22 Ibid.
23 Porter, *Trust in Numbers*, ix.
24 Kevin Haggerty, *Making Crime Count* (Toronto: University of Toronto Press, 2001), 6.
25 Porter, *Trust in Numbers*, 7; Lorraine Daston and Peter Galison, "The Image of Objectivity," *Representations* 40 (1992): 81–128.
26 Porter, *Trust in Numbers*, 7.
27 Ibid.

such officials are criticized. A decision made by the numbers (or by explicit rules of some other sort) has at least the appearance of being fair and impersonal. Scientific objectivity thus provides an answer to a moral demand for impartiality and fairness. Quantification is a way of making decisions without seeming to decide. Objectivity lends authority to officials who have very little of their own.[28]

By removing the fallibility and potential bias associated with human subjectivity, it is assumed that the use of "mechanically" produced numbers allows us to establish an objective understanding of the world and create public policies that are fair and just.

From Theory to Practice: Collecting Statistics on Deviant Populations

The idea that we can use quantitative research techniques to make sense of the world and to discover the underlying patterns that exist within it was adopted early on by emerging nation-states across Europe.[29] As a result of the growing industrialization and urbanization of the 1800s, government institutions evolved into bureaucracies that began seeing it as their mission to generate, compile, and archive detailed information about citizens. Many kinds of human behaviours, especially forms of deviance such as crime, suicide, vagrancy, and disease, came to be counted.[30] These statistics appeared consistent over time, lending support to the positivist belief that our world operated according to certain laws of probability. Moreover, the numbers generated by state bureaucracies allowed individuals to be classified as either normal or deviant. People could be deemed "normal" if they conformed to the central tendency of these laws of probability, while those at the extremes were considered pathological or deviant.[31]

The adoption of this probabilistic view of the world directly challenged the determinism that was dominant throughout the nineteenth century. It was now possible to see that the world might be regular and predictable,

---

28 Ibid, 8.
29 Hacking, *The Taming of Chance*; Piers Beirne, *Inventing Criminology: Essays in the Rise of Homo Criminalis* (Albany: State University of New York Press, 1993); Simon Cole, *Suspect Identities: A History of Fingerprinting and Criminal Identification* (Cambridge, MA: Harvard University Press, 2001); Haggerty, *Making Crime Count*; Mike Maguire, "Criminal Statistics and the Construction of Crime" in *The Oxford Handbook of Criminology*, 5th ed., ed. Mike Maguire, Rod Morgan, and Robert Reiner (Oxford: Oxford University Press, 2007).
30 Hacking, *The Taming of Chance*.
31 Ibid.

but still not subject to universal laws that determine what will happen in the future. This was made possible by the growing practice of enumerating people and their habits. The enthusiasm toward counting and the growing use of statistics have had a profound impact on how we see the world and those within it. As Ian Hacking observes, "[t]he systematic collection of data about people has affected not only the ways in which we conceive of a society, but also the ways in which we describe our neighbour."[32] This practice has also "profoundly transformed what we choose to do, who we try to be, and what we think of ourselves."[33]

Our preoccupation with numbers and probabilities remains with us today. We are not only trained in numeracy, but we are also encouraged to view the world through an actuarial lens. This is evident in the way we are made to think about the various risks that surround us in terms of probabilities. Whether we are talking about natural disasters or diseases and illnesses, we have become obsessed with knowing the likelihood of these things occurring in the hopes that we can take action to change the odds. Thus, individuals who are more than 20 pounds over their "ideal" weight may be persuaded to change their diets and get more exercise when faced with the "statistical reality" that, on average, people in this category are more likely to die of heart disease or develop diabetes. Thus, the collection of statistical data not only allows certain regularities to become visible, but potentially actionable. In fact, one of the major reasons that governments began gathering aggregate data about its citizens was to identify those individuals who fell outside the social norm so that these supposedly "deviant" subgroups could be controlled and possibly improved.[34] The data collected helped establish the idea of "average" or "normal" behaviour and has led to new kinds of social engineering aimed at modifying and "normalizing" abnormal classes of people. Gathering data about populations was therefore an important step in the broader project of state regulation.

As Michel Foucault has argued, the collection of aggregate statistics about a population has played a crucial role in the practice of liberal governance.[35] For Foucault, a certain mentality—what he called *governmentality*—has

---

32 Ibid., 3.
33 Ibid.
34 Ibid.
35 Michel Foucault, *Discipline and Punish: The Birth of the Prison* (New York: Vintage, 1977); Michel Foucault, *The History of Sexuality*, vol. 1, *An Introduction*, trans. Robert Hurley (New York: Vintage, 1978); Michel Foucault, "Governmentality," in *The Foucault Effect: Studies in Governmentality*, ed. Graham Burchell, Colin Gordon, and Peter Miller (Chicago: University of Chicago Press, 1991), 87–104.

become the basis of all modern forms of political thought and action.[36] Central to this project of biopolitics is the need for authorities to know a population: If a certain population (criminals, the mentally ill, etc.) can be studied, measured, and classified as "deviant" or outside of the norm, they can be acted upon and possibly changed. Thus, by producing a particular category of knowable people, a range of strategies and programs can be created in which some individuals (e.g., experts, health practitioners) are able to exercise their authority and work on others (e.g., patients, offenders) to make them different in some way.[37] Using the statistical knowledge collected from surveys, censuses, and reports, these subjects can be classified, rendered knowable, and made amenable to certain forms of intervention.[38]

In the section that follows, I discuss the role that quantification and statistics played in creating an entirely new category of people known as *repeat offenders* and how this led to a dramatic change in the way we understand and respond to the issue of crime.

Putting Numbers to Work: Creating the Repeat Offender

The advent of crime statistics provides a clear illustration of how the collection of data about a particular population has influenced the way in which they are governed. The first attempts to measure crime in a systematic way occurred in France in the late 1820s when moral statisticians promoted the practice as a means to discover the underlying laws and regularities of the social world akin to those found in the natural world.[39] The adoption of this positivist worldview, coupled with the expansion of state bureaucracies that increasingly saw their mission as generating and archiving information about citizens (especially stigmatized individuals like criminals), allowed the French government to start counting the number of crimes being committed and documenting where and when these offences were taking place.[40] In 1829, France was able to compile these data to publish its first annual report on national crime statistics.

Although governments have always been in the business of knowing about their citizens, it was not until the Industrial Revolution and the birth of the modern era in the early nineteenth century that state institutions

---

36 Nikolas Rose, Pat O'Malley, and Mariana Valverde, "Governmentality," *Annual Review of Law and Social Science* 2, no. 1 (2006): 86.

37 Dawn Moore, *Criminal Artefacts: Governing Drugs and Users* (Vancouver: UBC Press, 2007).

38 Haggerty, *Making Crime Count*.

39 Maguire, "Criminal Statistics and the Construction of Crime," 207.

40 Cole, *Suspect Identities*, 9.

began collecting detailed records of individuals and developing the tools and systems to do so. With these structures in place, governments now had the capacity to create identities for people that "existed outside the physical body, in the files and paper records of some government bureaucracy."[41] Those who were caught and convicted of committing a crime would now have a criminal record of their actions that could be archived by the state. So, for public officials, it was not just about measuring how much crime was out there, but keeping track of who was committing these offences.

The ability to keep count of criminal activity has had a profound impact on how we understand crime. The crime statistics that began to appear in continental Europe in the 1820s showed that a small number of repeat offenders were responsible for a large proportion of crimes committed. These findings directly challenged many of the dominant assumptions during this period regarding crime and how best to respond to it. In the late eighteenth century, jurists like Cesare Beccaria advanced what they believed to be a more rational approach to crime by suggesting that criminal sentences be based on the specific offence committed. The idea that "the punishment must fit the crime" is a key principle of what is now commonly referred to as the classical school of criminology. Classical thinkers believed that setting the punishment proportionate to the crime would create a more fair and effective system of justice by limiting judicial discretion. When deciding on a sentence, judges were required to look at the offence and not take into account the criminal history or personal circumstances of the offender. Offenders would be given sentences that fit the crime irrespective of who they were or what they might have done in the past. The classical school of thought provided the philosophical foundation upon which many criminal justice systems were built. As a result, by the late nineteenth century, offenders across Europe and elsewhere were being punished proportionately to their offences.[42]

This practice drastically changed as soon as national crime statistics became available. Although the accuracy of these numbers could not have been very great, they provided positivist reformers with the evidence they needed to challenge many of the key assumptions of classical jurisprudence. Rather than seeing crime as a rational act that all individuals have an equal chance of committing, positivists could now point to the statistics to demonstrate that a disproportionate amount of crime was being committed by a certain segment of the population. This new way of thinking about crime,

---

41 Ibid., 10.
42 Ibid., 14.

coupled with new technologies of identification and record keeping, would have direct consequences for the criminal justice system and approaches to recidivism.

More specifically, the habitual offender was now conceived as an object of scientific inquiry. Scientists began looking for the underlying physical causes that drove certain individuals to reoffend. An entire field of **criminal anthropology** emerged—spearheaded by Cesare Lombroso and his many followers—aimed at examining the so-called born criminal. This group of Italian School criminologists, as they later became known, drew heavily on Charles Darwin's theory of evolution and believed that criminals and other deviants were biologically different from normal, law-abiding citizens.

Although they still accepted the idea that criminality could be caused by poor social conditions, members of the Italian School focused their attention on heredity to explain crime. These criminologists believed that criminals were the products of "bad stock" who were less evolved than the rest of the population, and that one could look toward the criminal's body for visible signs of these innate differences.[43] Using various tools from anthropology, Lombroso and others began measuring the bodies of prisoners and created an extensive list of common physical features or "stigmata" that were thought to be indicators of an inherited propensity to commit crime, ranging from sloping foreheads and heavy jaws to excessively long arms and receding brows. Some researchers, like Francis Galton (cousin of Charles Darwin), assumed that visible markers on one's body could be read to identify specific criminal types who were predisposed to committing a particular set of offences.

This new approach to thinking about crime and criminality would have a profound impact on the administration of criminal justice in places like Britain and the United States. If a disproportionate amount of crime was being committed by a group of habitual offenders who could now be identified by the presence of certain physical features, then they could be separated from the "first timer" and treated accordingly. Repeat offenders were given much harsher sentences and, in some instances, sent to serve time in separate prisons. This was done to keep the redeemable, first-time offenders from the potentially corrupting influence of the irredeemable "born criminal" and the prison environment more generally.

A much more ambitious project was to use these data on the physical features of the criminal to proactively prevent crimes from occurring. For example, some police departments in the United States began putting theories of criminal physiognomy into practice by training detectives to identify

---

43 Ibid., 23.

specific criminal types by their facial characteristics.[44] In many cases, this type of physiognomic profiling (a practice very similar to the racial profiling that goes on today) would result in individuals being arrested for simply looking like a criminal.[45] The eugenics movement, which began in the late 1800s in the United States and gained popularity in a host of other countries until about the 1930s, took many of these ideas about heredity and prevention to even greater—and more devastating—heights.

Still Looking for Signs of Criminality

Many of the theories about criminality put forward by Lombroso and others proved to be false. Rather than predicting who was more likely to commit a crime, the programs put in place simply justified and legitimized the racism (as well as the sexism, classism, ableism, etc.) that permeated the criminal justice system. The stereotypes about certain racialized groups and their supposed criminal tendencies now had science to support an already erroneous and spurious claim. Although critics were successful at pointing out the methodological problems and the direct violations of civil liberties and human rights that take place when we punish people before a crime has been committed, the legacy of positivist criminology lives on.

Like in the past, new methods of criminal record keeping and data collection continue to propel renewed hope in our ability to accurately predict future criminality. For example, law enforcement officials initially created DNA databanks as a way to store genetic information about convicted sex offenders and other types of serious criminals. From very early on, these databanks proved to be invaluable in helping police find suspects in both current and cold cases. Any DNA evidence left at a crime scene could now be checked against the genetic profiles found in the databank, possibly leading police to the culprit(s). In addition to its use in criminal investigations, the DNA databank—alongside the various advancements in forensic crime scene analysis—serves as a powerful deterrent to offenders with genetic information on file. Convicted offenders released back into the community must now think twice before reoffending, knowing that any traces of their DNA can be linked back to them.

However, the idea that we can prevent crimes from occurring goes beyond the possible deterrent effect on already-convicted offenders. Since the discovery of DNA, we have entered the so-called genetic age that has brought with it the belief that who we are—and who we are to become—is

---

44 Ibid., 24.
45 Ibid.

rooted in our genes. Though scientists have been careful not to suggest the existence of a "crime gene" that will place their owners on an unavoidable path toward a life of crime, many scholars have argued that certain individuals are genetically predisposed to "anti-social behaviour" when faced with adverse social conditions (e.g., poverty, maltreatment, chaotic home environment).[46] Although they acknowledge the importance of one's environment in shaping behaviour, these researchers place much of their attention on genetics and often promote treatments and therapies that target these biological factors.

Alongside these projects that aim to "cure" the underlying causes of criminality, we have also witnessed the emergence of a more future-oriented approach to governance that seeks to prevent crime rather than treat its root origins. Under this regime, aggregate data regarding the common traits, experiences, and patterns of behaviour among offenders are collected to create risk assessment tools that can be used to determine future crime and criminality.[47] This statistical knowledge is then used to identify the specific factors that put certain people, places, and things "at risk" in the hopes that these conditions can be effectively managed or eliminated.[48] One way this is done is by focusing on the **criminogenic** people and places that are statistically more likely to be linked to crime. Intelligence-led policing is one approach to crime control that builds on these ideas of risk assessment and risk management using a "strategic, future-oriented and targeted approach to crime control, [and] focusing upon the identification, analysis and management of persisting and developing problems or risks."[49] Rather than simply reacting to crimes as they occur, police departments may choose to rely on crime data to target particular populations or to allocate greater policing resources to city "hot spots" that they can place under greater surveillance. Because of shrinking budgets, police departments in both Canada and the United States are increasingly having to rely on highly sophisticated mathematical algorithms—often developed by criminologists in collaboration

---

46 Terrie Moffitt, "Adolescence-Limited and Life-Course Persistent Antisocial Behavior: A Developmental Taxonomy," *Psychological Review* 100 (1993): 674–701; Adrian Raine, "Biosocial Studies of Antisocial and Violent Behavior in Children and Adults: A Review," *Journal of Abnormal Child Psychology* 30, no. 4 (2002): 311–26.

47 David Garland, "'Governmentality' and the Problem of Crime: Foucault, Criminology, Sociology," *Theoretical Criminology* 1 (1997): 171–214; Robert Castel, "From Dangerousness to Risk" in *The Foucault Effect: Studies in Governmentality*, ed. Graham Burchell, Colin Gordon, and Peter Miller, 281–98 (Chicago: University of Chicago Press, 1991).

48 Mathieu Deflem, "Surveillance and Criminal Statistics: Historical Foundations of Governmentality," *Studies in Law, Politics and Society* 17 (1997): 149–84.

49 Willem de Lint, "Intelligence in Policing Security: Reflections on Scholarship," *Policing and Society* 16, no. 1 (2006): 1–6.

with statisticians and mathematicians—to determine where criminal activity is likely to occur and to inform future crime prevention campaigns.

In addition to identifying the various risk factors that lead to crime, statistical knowledge is also employed to locate the people, places, and things that are most likely to be victimized so that precautionary measures can be taken to prevent their future victimization.[50] Through various crime prevention programs initiated by both state and nonstate agencies (e.g., insurance companies), citizens are made aware of their chances of becoming a victim of crime and are made responsible for taking the appropriate steps to reduce their risk.[51] From purchasing a home alarm system to ensuring that valuables are never left in plain view in one's car, citizens are encouraged and increasingly expected to play a much more active role in ensuring their own personal safety and security. In a similar fashion, physical spaces have also become targets of intervention. Using principles from an increasingly popular approach known as Crime Prevention through Environmental Design (CPTED), architects and urban developers are trying to "design out" crime and disorder by altering the built environment in ways that make it more difficult for individuals to engage in certain activities. From changing the layout of a space to improve natural surveillance to installing "bum-proof" benches that prevent people from lying down or staying in one space for too long, an assortment of target-hardening techniques are employed to make locations less susceptible to crime and disorder.[52]

These crime prevention strategies are often animated and legitimized through crime statistics. The data collected are not only used to establish predictable patterns of offending that can then be acted upon, but serve as "hard" evidence for one's likelihood of victimization and statistical proof for why precautions need to be taken. Underlying this future-oriented and preventative approach to crime is a much broader shift in how we come to think about offenders. Although many researchers and practitioners still pathologize deviance and engage in the long-standing tradition of trying to identify criminals from noncriminals, this perspective has given way to a greater appreciation of crime as "normal."[53] From this perspective, criminals

50 Deflem, "Surveillance and Criminal Statistics."
51 Pat O'Malley, "Risk and Responsibility," in *Foucault and Political Reason: Liberalism, Neoliberalism, and Rationalities of Government*, ed. Andrew Barry, Thomas Osborne, and Nikolas Rose, 189–208 (Chicago: University of Chicago Press, 1996); David Garland, "The Limits of the Sovereign State: Strategies of Crime Control in Contemporary Society," *British Journal of Criminology* 36, no. 4 (1996): 445–71; David Garland, *The Culture of Control: Crime and Social Order in Contemporary Society* (Chicago: University of Chicago Press, 2001).
52 Mike Davis, *City of Quartz: Excavating the Future in Los Angeles* (New York: Verso, 1990).
53 Haggerty, *Making Crime Count*, 50; Garland, "'Governmentality' and the Problem of Crime."

are no longer assumed to be inherently different from the general population but are seen instead as rational actors who weigh the costs and benefits of their actions. Criminals are thus viewed as "statistical beings" that operate with certain regularities.[54] Indeed, all of these crime prevention strategies are based on the assumption that offenders behave in rational and predictable ways—a belief that is constituted and reinforced through numbers and statistics.

Seeing Crime Statistics as Socially Constructed

From the discussion above, we can see how statistics are mobilized to help construct our conception of the "criminal." On the one hand, positivist criminologists interested in identifying the underlying pathologies that produce criminality and distinguish criminals from the rest of the population can make use of a variety of statistical instruments to measure and quantify these differences. At the same time, we have witnessed the normalization of crime that treats such behaviours as rational and highly predictable. In both instances, we depend on statistics to support our claims and to inform our approach to dealing with crime. Whether they are used to demonstrate inherent differences between criminals and noncriminals or as a means to identify stable patterns of crime, numbers are crucial. However, the fact that they can be used to support diametrically opposite views about the nature of crime and criminality (e.g., crime is abnormal versus crime is normal) illustrates the malleability and interpretive flexibility of quantitative data.[55]

Thus, far from being instruments of objective truth-telling, numbers and statistics are highly political and cannot easily be disentangled from the broader social settings in which they are produced and used. By no means is this a new argument. Over the past few decades, various scholars have placed the reliability and validity of crime statistics, and the science upon which they are based, under tremendous scrutiny. In particular, many have argued that crime statistics (like all other statistics) are socially constructed. But what exactly do we mean when we say that crime statistics are *social constructions*?

To many people, there is a tendency to confuse social constructivism with the idea that numbers and statistics are "made up" and intentionally designed to deceive. The main concern here is that unscrupulous individuals can manipulate numbers and statistics to fabricate a partial image of the

---

54 Garland, "'Governmentality' and the Problem of Crime," 187.
55 Trevor Pinch and Wiebe Bijker, "The Social Construction of Facts and Artefacts: Or How the Sociology of Science and the Sociology of Technology Might Benefit Each Other," *Social Studies of Science* 14, no. 3 (1984): 399–441.

"truth" that serves their own interests. Put simply, numbers and statistics can be used to tell lies. That we equate quantitative data with lying seems somewhat in keeping with the plethora of popular books that have recently surfaced on this subject. Books like *How to Lie with Statistics*, *How Numbers Lie*, and *Damned Lies and Statistics* make this association quite explicit in their very titles.

Readers of these books are left with the general impression that numbers and statistics cannot be trusted and that we, the public, need to become "numerate" and more critical consumers of these data. However, thinking critically often means watching out for potential bias and questioning the motivations of the authors. As a result, we are encouraged to focus not on the statistics, but on the people who might purposely misuse them. As Joel Best puts it, "[o]ne might conclude that statistics are pure, unless they unfortunately become contaminated by the bad motives of dishonest people."[56] Thus, if we want to protect ourselves from being duped, we need to be able to spot unscrupulous researchers who purposely fudge their statistics.

Of course, we can never really get into peoples' heads to find out if they are being honest with their numbers. The only way we can truly guard ourselves against being misled is by carefully interrogating the methods used to generate the numbers and asking whether or not the study was "scientific." So, although we might not ever know the true intentions of the researcher, we can look to see if the numbers were "honestly" produced by examining how a study was carried out. Here, what separates real science from junk science is the adherence to the rules of science. By following proper procedures and protocols and having their work open to public scrutiny, we believe that the subjectivity and personal interests of the researcher can be kept at bay to allow the study results to speak for themselves.

However, by accepting the notion that "bad" numbers only come from "bad" studies, we lose sight of some of the broader critiques concerning statistics and quantitative research more generally. In particular, we are left with the impression that "bad" numbers are socially constructed and a mere reflection of the personal biases of the researcher, while "good" numbers come out of scientific research that permit the data to "speak the truth." I want to challenge this assumption by suggesting that all statistics—irrespective of who generates them and their underlying motivations—are humanly produced. This position draws heavily from the seminal work that has emerged out of STS, which is the interdisciplinary field of research that looks closely at the ways in which scientific facts and technological artifacts come to be

---

56 Joel Best, *More Damned Lies and Statistics: How Numbers Confuse Public Issues* (Berkeley: University of California Press, 2004), xiv.

produced. Many STS scholars, particularly those who work out of a constructivist tradition, examine how various social factors influence and shape the content of science and technology.[57]

The argument that all statistics are humanly produced is based on the assumption that all scientific knowledge is theory laden and always "underdetermined" by the evidence. Unlike positivist thinkers, STS scholars challenge the notion that we can get at the truth through scientific observations. On the contrary, these scholars argue that regardless of the methods we employ, it is impossible for us to be completely objective and see the world from a position of nowhere. The natural world cannot be viewed outside of human subjectivity and experience. From what we choose to accept as "valid" or "reliable" evidence to the way in which we interpret the data, our observations are informed by the theories, paradigms, and worldviews we adopt and are highly contingent upon the decisions we make about how and what we choose to study.[58] Even if we did accept that science allows us to see the world objectively, STS scholars counter that there is never enough evidence for us to say with any certainty that our theories are true since there is always a possibility that a future observation will prove our claims wrong.

Thus, whether we choose to accept something as a scientific fact is not determined by the evidence, but by human beings and the social processes that we develop to make this decision. Science always contains a sizable element that is socially determined or contingent upon the social context in which it is generated.[59] This becomes quite obvious when we consider how crime statistics are produced.

So What Do Crime Statistics Tell Us?

In Canada and in other parts of the world, official crime data are based on crimes that are reported by the police. Although it might seem quite intuitive to use police reports as a way to measure the amount of crime, the practice is not without its problems. In particular, many have questioned the referentiality of these data.[60] In other words, do these official statistics tell us about crime per se? Or are they more a reflection of the practices and policies of the police and the public's confidence (or lack thereof) in this organization? Indeed, there are a variety of factors outside of actual crimes committed that may greatly influence these data. Criminologists have used the metaphor of

---

57 Hess, *Science Studies*, 82.
58 Ibid., 52.
59 Richards, *Philosophy and Sociology of Science*, 205.
60 Haggerty, *Making Crime Count*, 25.

a "crime filter" to describe how certain criminal acts are screened out from inclusion in official records.[61]

One of the biggest factors influencing crime statistics is public reporting. For a variety of reasons, not all crimes are reported to the police. Some individuals might not know a crime has occurred, or they may perceive an incident to be not serious enough to warrant a call. Others might fear authorities or have little faith in their ability to deal with a situation, thereby making them reluctant to report their victimization. These unreported cases are commonly referred to as the **dark figure of crime**.[62] Sexual assault is one type of crime that is often underreported. Not being believed, fear of reprisals, and feelings of shame and humiliation are just a few reasons why a victim of sexual assault may choose not to report the incident to police. However, alongside these filters that contribute to an underreporting of criminal activity, there are a variety of other factors that may have the complete opposite effect. For example, media campaigns that encourage citizens to take cyberbullying seriously might result in more calls to the police for assistance in these matters. Thus, whether they have a positive or negative impact on reporting, these factors will invariably affect the overall crime rate.

Even when crime is reported to the police, there is no guarantee that the incident will make it into the official records. There are a number of institutional factors that may influence how the police respond to a call. Police dispatchers may not view an incident as a serious matter or divert the call to a more appropriate organization. In fact, a vast majority of calls to the police are never forwarded to officers.[63] Police officers also have a tremendous amount of discretion and may choose not to lay a charge or write a report, especially if this means avoiding tedious paperwork. Yet without this paperwork, the incident is not officially recorded. On a much broader level, departmental policies can also influence crime data. Public pressure to crack down on certain types of offences or internal demands to "pad the stats," for instance, may lead to changes in policy priorities resulting in greater arrests and reports.

The examples presented above serve to illustrate how crime rates can drastically fluctuate irrespective of any actual changes in criminal behaviour. Rather than being an indicator of the amount of crime that is out there, official statistics may be more of a reflection of public reporting patterns and police activity. However, even when an incident passes through the filter to be recorded as an official crime statistic, a number of decisions have to be

---

61 Palys, *Research Decisions*, 234; Haggerty, *Making Crime Count*, 29–30.
62 Palys, *Research Decisions*, 234.
63 Peter Manning, "Information Technologies and the Police," in *Modern Policing*, ed. Michael Tonry and Norval Morris, 349–98 (Chicago: University of Chicago Press, 1992).

made about how this is counted. For example, how exactly do we record a crime spree that saw the commission of six different crimes with four victims perpetrated by two individuals? More specifically, how many crimes should be counted here?

To deal with these sorts of issues and to allow for standardized reporting across jurisdictions and police forces, Canada has joined the United States and other countries in adopting the **Uniform Crime Reporting (UCR) Survey**.[64] The UCR provides basic counting rules (e.g., for crimes of violence, one counts the number of victims; for property crimes, one counts the number of events; and for multiple offences, only the most serious offence is counted).[65] So, although UCR rules greatly simplify how we count crime and permit us to compare data across jurisdictions, they also greatly diminish the accuracy of the statistics. For instance, these rules produce a drastic underestimation of the number of offences reported by police.[66]

Despite their appearance as objective indicators of criminal behaviour, official crime statistics—like all other statistics—are socially constructed and the outcome of a human process: "Every statistic ... is shaped by the process which operationally defines it, the procedures which capture it, and the organization which interprets it."[67] Yet, because of their presumed objectivity and connections to science, these supposedly unbiased and dispassionate statistics are subject to far less scrutiny than other forms of research. Quite the opposite, there is a tendency to think that numbers simply appear through quantitative research to tell us the truth about the world.

However, as I have shown here, numbers can never truly speak for themselves. On their own, numbers are hollow and void of any real significance. Beyond informing us about how much there is of whatever has been measured, there is nothing inherent in these numbers that tells us anything about the phenomenon they are believed to represent—it is only when these numbers are imbued with meaning and given voice by others that they become relevant.

For example, the fact that there were a total of 10 homicides reported in Ottawa in 2011, while interesting, tells us very little (aside from the fact that there were 10 homicides reported in Ottawa in 2011). This number derives much more meaning from how others interpret it and the ways in which it is mobilized to communicate certain claims. Thus, if we take this same number and compare it to those of other Canadian cities, we can now state

---

64 Palys, *Research Decisions*, 237.

65 Ibid.

66 Ibid.

67 Wesley Skogan, "Measurement Problems in Official and Survey Crime Rates," *Journal of Criminal Justice* 3 (1975): 17.

that Ottawa is near the bottom when it comes to homicides and was ranked eighth out of 10 cities with populations of 500,000 or more.[68] We might also use this number, as former Ottawa Police Chief Vern White did, to proclaim that Ottawa is a safe city and that "compared to some of the other major cities in Canada, we're in good shape."[69]

Although 10 homicides in one year may seem like a low figure, there is nothing intrinsic about this number that tells us that Ottawa is a safe city. It is only when we compare this number to other cities and mobilize it as evidence of safety that the number takes on this meaning. One could just as easily make a counterclaim that a city's goal should be zero homicides and that this number is unacceptable. We might then use the 10 homicides to justify changes in policing practices or the introduction of tougher crime laws. The main point here is that it is not the raw numbers that count (so to speak), but what others say these numbers tell us and what we, in turn, do with these numbers that matters. Viewed in this light, we can think of crime statistics as rhetorical devices that can be mobilized by various actors to legitimize their claims and to promote certain initiatives.

In this way, numbers can be made to speak. And quite often these numbers are taken up as the voice of authority. As opposed to words and language that can be inflammatory and sensational and are always linked to the speaker or author, numbers allow us to communicate certain ideas in a format that appears highly unemotional and completely detached from human beings. Consequently, we end up believing that these numbers are objective, reliable, and valid measures that give us an unbiased and impartial picture of the truth. This blind faith in statistical data is disconcerting when we consider how these data are taken up to legitimize causal connections between crime and particular categories of people. Even more troubling is how this type of scientific research on who commits crime may be used as a basis for making predictions about future criminality, often leading to extremely questionable crime control policies and practices.

Fixing Criminal Bodies and Predicting Future Criminality

In the previous section, I challenged the reader to think critically about the supposed objectivity of official crime statistics by pointing out the subjectivity that goes into their production. More specifically, I argued that it is impossible

---

68 Scott Taylor, "Ottawa Low on Murder Count," *Ottawa Sun*, January 2, 2011, http://www .ottawasun.com/news/ottawa/2011/01/02/16735311.html (accessed August 15, 2012).

69 Danielle Bell, "Bloody Year in Bytown," *Ottawa Sun*, November 12, 2011, http://www .ottawasun.com/2011/11/19/bloody-year-in-bytown (accessed August 15, 2012).

for us to know whether these statistics are telling us about criminal behaviour or the work of the criminal justice system. To this day, there is no single theory that adequately explains why people commit crime and no method of prediction that has ever been proven successful. Still, many researchers continue to believe that we can identify and target the biological factors that predispose an individual to engage in criminal activity. Underlying all of these attempts at diagnosis and forecasting is the positivist belief that if we develop the proper tools for scientific observation, we can see the "truth" about crime. As discussed earlier, scholars from the Italian School, for example, relied heavily on the science of anthropology to measure and analyze criminal bodies. In their search for the "born criminal," Lombroso and others turned their forensic gaze toward the most obvious of places: prisons.

Although it might seem reasonable to look for criminals in prison, this selection strategy rests on a number of important assumptions. First, it assumes that there is a segment of the population known as *criminals* who are inherently different from normal citizens and that only these individuals would commit offences so serious that they would land in prison. Yet, even if we accept that "born criminals" do exist, that they are the ones responsible for committing the majority of crimes, and that they can be found in our prisons, we must also assume that the criminal justice system is perfectly capable of detecting these individuals. More specifically, we have to assume that the criminal justice system is fair and that only individuals who fall into Lombroso's category of "criminal" are incarcerated.

However, as we know, the criminal justice system is far from perfect. There are individuals in our prisons who have been wrongfully convicted, while many others who have committed serious criminal acts will never set foot in a jail cell. By using prison populations as a site to examine the criminal body, Lombroso and others failed to account for the extraneous variables outside of one's own criminality that may determine the likelihood of incarceration. Indeed, not all individuals have an equal chance of being arrested and sent to prison—the prisons studied by Lombroso in the 1800s were as disproportionately represented by visible minorities and the poor as they are today.

Although some might see this as a clear indication that certain racialized or economically disadvantaged groups are more "criminal" than others, one cannot ignore the existing social inequalities that help to explain the differences in numbers. Poor and racialized people may be more likely to end up in prison not because of some kind of inherited biological or genetic trait that makes them more prone to commit crime than the rest of the population, but as a result of poverty and poor social conditions that may force some individuals into crime. These individuals may also have their activities more closely watched by law enforcement and thus have a far greater chance of being arrested. In stark contrast, the wealthy and powerful in our society are not only less likely to be under police scrutiny, but they also have the resources to keep them out of prison should they find themselves in trouble with the law.

A second major assumption we must accept is that our laws reflect universal and fixed norms of society. If we are to believe that there are born offenders, then we must also accept that the crimes they commit are naturally or inherently criminal. In other words, we must hold on to a positivist worldview that criminals and the crimes they commit are "real" and exist independently from how we choose to define them. Although one could argue that there are certain types of actions that we could all agree are wrong and should be criminalized, the laws we have that make these acts illegal are socially constructed. A society determines what is a crime and who is a criminal by the laws it creates and the ways in which these laws are enforced. As a result, there are various acts that are illegal in some places and at certain moments in history and not others.

This, in turn, brings into question whether or not it is appropriate to classify people who have broken socially defined laws as natural born criminals. How do we claim that certain individuals are inherently criminal when the criteria used to determine criminality are socially constructed and liable to change? Indeed, many of the prisoners that Lombroso and other researchers studied and labelled as born criminals would not be criminalized or incarcerated in North America today. The main point here is that every scientific study on crime and criminality is based on highly subjective decisions about what we define as a crime, who we identify as a criminal, and how we choose to explain their criminality. The subjectivity inherent in this research, however, is often hidden from view by the appearance of objectivity that is commonly associated with science and numbers. Thus, as critical criminologists, we need to deconstruct these claims to truth and work toward making the subjective nature of this type of criminological research much more visible.

Conclusion: Questioning Numbers

In this chapter, I have been quite critical of the ways in which positivist criminologists have equated numbers and statistics with truth. However, it is important to note that critical scholars are just as guilty of using quantitative data to make statements of fact about crime and criminality. Most recently, we have seen a number of critical criminologists pointing to the "cold hard facts" of official data as evidence that crime in Canada is on the decline to challenge the "tough on crime" policies introduced by the Conservative federal government. Ironically, these are often the same scholars who engage in research aimed at deconstructing and destabilizing the truth-claims made by experts. Thus in one instance critical scholars can be constructivists who assert that the very notion of crime is socially constructed. Yet at other times these same scholars adopt a positivist stance and turn to science to "prove" that their claims are based on unbiased evidence. However, by doing so we leave ourselves open to criticism for only accepting scientific "truths" as valid when they support our own political viewpoints. We can also be challenged for being elitists who know when facts are true and when they are not.

However, I suggest that if we want to be taken seriously we cannot oscillate between two diametrically opposite perspectives and be constructivists in one moment and positivists in the next. Instead, we need to be consistent in how we view the world by assuming that all forms of knowledge are socially produced. So, rather than reifying science as the way to truth and equating quantitative data with fact and objectivity, we have to acknowledge that scientific evidence is just as partial and theory laden as other ways of knowing. We need to recognize that, regardless of methodology, all studies of crime (including our own) are inherently political since they cannot be disentangled from the broader social and cultural contexts in which they are produced and the personal beliefs and values that inform them.

In addition to being critical about how scientific facts about crime and criminals are constructed, it is important that we also pay close attention to the ways in which this knowledge gets mobilized and communicated. As I have shown in this chapter, the data we collect and the ways they are interpreted can have a profound impact on how we approach the issue of crime and its control. Moreover, our decision to accept certain statements as true can turn them into black boxes in which they "become stable entities, processes, or laws, dissociated from the circumstances of their production."[70] Once this is achieved, a claim can readily be circulated and accepted as truth, while all of the work that went into transforming the assertion into fact disappears from view.

The status of a truth-claim is therefore always dependent on what happens to it when placed in the hands of others.[71] The making and black-boxing of facts is thus a collective process. When confronted with a black box, we make a number of decisions as to whether or not we take it up, reject it, reopen it, or drop it through lack of interest.[72] These decisions have

---

70 Michael Lynch, "The Discursive Production of Uncertainty: The OJ Simpson 'Dream Team' and the Sociology of Knowledge Machine," *Social Studies of Science*, 28, no. 5–6 (1998): 829–68.

71 Bruno Latour, *Science in Action: How to Follow Scientists and Engineers through Society* (Cambridge, MA: Harvard University Press, 1987), 29.

72 Ibid.

direct consequences: If we believe a fact without question, then we make the black box more solid; but if we reject the fact, it is weakened and its spread is interrupted. As critical scholars, it is incumbent upon us to remain skeptical and to always open up these black boxes of criminological knowledge to highlight the human subjectivities and political interests that are inherent in this type of research.

Study Questions

1. What do we mean when we say that crime statistics are socially constructed? Do official crime statistics accurately reflect the actual amount of crime happening within our communities? Why or why not?

2. How are crime statistics political? What role do crime statistics play in shaping our understanding of crime and how we deal with offenders?

3. Is it possible to study crime objectively? Why or why not?

4. Why is it important to be critical of official crime statistics? What do we mean when we say that crime statistics are "black boxed"? What are some of the dangers and possible implications of treating crime statistics as black boxes?

Exercise

1. Find a news article that presents recent crime statistics or the results of a quantitative criminological study (the lengthier and more detailed, the better). Critically analyze the article by considering the following questions:

    a. How are these crime statistics or research findings represented in the article? Pay particular attention to the language used. Are there graphs or tables? If so, how are they presented? What effect does this have on how we view the statistics or research findings?

    b. Are the statistics or research findings presented as "fact"? If so, how?

    c. Who are called upon as experts to interpret the statistics or research findings? How are the statistics or research findings interpreted? Are the statistics or research findings used to promote changes to law or public policy?

    d. Are the statistics or research findings ever called into question? If so, how and by whom?

    e. Are there any important details about the statistics or research study that have been left out of the article? How might the inclusion of these details affect our interpretation of the statistics or research findings? Are there other ways in which the statistics or research findings could have been interpreted?

Keywords

recidivism; science and technology studies; black box; scientific method; positivism; criminal anthropology; dark figure of crime; Uniform Crime Reporting Survey

Bibliography

Beirne, Piers. *Inventing Criminology: Essays in the Rise of Homo Criminalis.* Albany: State University of New York Press, 1993.

Bell, Danielle. "Bloody Year in Bytown." *Ottawa Sun,* November 19, 2011. http://www.ottawasun.com/2011/11/19/bloody-year-in-bytown.

Best, Joel. *More Damned Lies and Statistics: How Numbers Confuse Public Issues.* Berkeley: University of California Press, 2004.

Castel, Robert. "From Dangerousness to Risk." In *The Foucault Effect: Studies in Governmentality,* edited by Graham Burchell, Colin Gordon, and Peter Miller, 281–98. Chicago: University of Chicago Press, 1991.

Cole, Simon. *Suspect Identities: A History of Fingerprinting and Criminal Identification.* Cambridge, MA: Harvard University Press, 2001.

Daston, Lorraine, and Paul Galison. "The Image of Objectivity." *Representations* 40, no. 1 (1992): 81–128. http://www.jstor.org/stable/2928741.

Davis, Mike. *City of Quartz: Excavating the Future in Los Angeles.* New York: Verso, 1990.

Deflem, Mathieu. "Surveillance and Criminal Statistics: Historical Foundations of Governmentality." *Studies in Law, Politics, and Society* 17 (1997): 149–84.

Durkheim, Émile. *The Rules of the Sociological Method.* Translated by W.D. Halls. New York: The Free Press [1895], 1982.

Foucault, Michel. *Discipline and Punish: The Birth of the Prison.* New York: Vintage, 1977.

Foucault, Michel. *The History of Sexuality.* Vol. 1, *An Introduction.* Translated by Robert Hurley. New York: Vintage, 1978.

Foucault, Michel. "Governmentality." In *The Foucault Effect: Studies in Governmentality,* edited by Graham Burchell, Colin Gordon, and Peter Miller, 87–104. Chicago: University of Chicago Press, 1991.

Garland, David. "'Governmentality' and the Problem of Crime: Foucault, Criminology, Sociology." *Theoretical Criminology* 1, no. 2 (1997): 173–214. http://dx.doi.org/10.1177/1362480697001002002.

Garland, David. *The Culture of Control: Crime and Social Order in Contemporary Society.* Chicago: University of Chicago Press, 2001.

Garland, David. "The Limits of the Sovereign State: Strategies of Crime Control in Contemporary Society." *British Journal of Criminology* 36, no. 4 (1996): 445–71. http://dx.doi.org/10.1093/oxfordjournals.bjc.a014105.

Hacking, Ian. *The Taming of Chance.* Cambridge: Cambridge University Press, 1990.

Haggerty, Kevin. *Making Crime Count.* Toronto: University of Toronto Press, 2001.

Hess, David. *Science Studies: An Advanced Introduction.* New York: New York University Press, 1997.

Latour, Bruno. *Science in Action: How to Follow Scientists and Engineers through Society.* Cambridge, MA: Harvard University Press, 1987.

de Lint, Willem. "Intelligence in Policing Security: Reflections on Scholarship." *Policing and Society* 16, no. 1 (2006): 1–6.

Lynch, Michael. "The Discursive Production of Uncertainty: The OJ Simpson 'Dream Team' and the Sociology of Knowledge Machine." *Social Studies of Science* 28, no. 5–6 (1998): 829–68. http://dx.doi.org/10.1177/030631298028005007.

Maguire, Mike. "Criminal Statistics and the Construction of Crime." In *The Oxford Handbook of Criminology*, 5th ed., edited by Mike Maguire, Rod Morgan, and Robert Reiner, 206–44. Oxford: Oxford University Press, 2007.

Manning, Peter. "Information Technologies and the Police." In *Modern Policing*, edited by M. Tonry and N. Morris, 349–98. Chicago: University of Chicago Press, 1992.

Moffitt, Terrie. "Adolescence-Limited and Life-Course Persistent Antisocial Behavior: A Developmental Taxonomy." *Psychological Review* 100, no. 4 (1993): 674–701. http://dx.doi.org/10.1037/0033-295X.100.4.674.

Moore, Dawn. *Criminal Artefacts: Governing Drugs and Users.* Vancouver: UBC Press, 2007.

Neuman, W. Lawrence, Bruce Wiegand, and John A. Winterdyk. *Criminal Justice Research Methods: Qualitative and Quantitative Approaches.* Canadian edition. Toronto: Pearson, 2006.

O'Malley, Pat. "Risk and Responsibility." In *Foucault and Political Reason: Liberalism, Neo-Liberalism and Rationalities of Government*, edited by Andrew Barry, Thomas Osborne, and Nikolas Rose, 189–208. Chicago: University of Chicago Press, 1996.

Palys, Ted. *Research Decisions: Quantitative and Qualitative Perspectives.* 3rd ed. Toronto: Nelson, 2003.

Pinch, Trevor, and Wiebe Bijker. "The Social Construction of Facts and Artefacts: Or How the Sociology of Science and the Sociology of Technology Might Benefit Each Other." *Social Studies of Science* 14, no. 3 (1984): 399–441. http://dx.doi.org/10.1177/030631284014003004.

Porter, Theodore M. *Trust in Numbers: The Pursuit of Objectivity in Science and Public Life.* Princeton: Princeton University Press, 1995.

Raine, Adrian. "Biosocial Studies of Antisocial and Violent Behavior in Children and Adults: A Review." *Journal of Abnormal Child Psychology* 30, no. 4 (2002): 311–26. http://dx.doi.org/10.1023/A:1015754122318.

Richards, Stewart. *Philosophy and Sociology of Science: An Introduction.* Oxford: Basil Blackwell, 1987.

Rose, Nikolas, Pat O'Malley, and Mariana Valverde. "Governmentality." *Annual Review of Law and Social Science* 2, no. 1 (2006): 83–104. http://dx.doi.org/10.1146/annurev.lawsocsci.2.081805.105900.

Skogan, Wesley G. "Measurement Problems in Official and Survey Crime Rates." *Journal of Criminal Justice* 3, no. 1 (1975): 17–31. http://dx.doi.org/10.1016/0047-2352(75)90096-3.

Taylor, Scott. "Ottawa Low on Murder Count." *Ottawa Sun*, January 2, 2011. http://www.ottawasun.com/news/ottawa/2011/01/02/16735311.html.

Valverde, Mariana. *Law and Order: Images, Meanings, Myths.* New Brunswick: Rutgers University Press, 2006.

Whitley, Richard. "Black Boxism and the Sociology of Science: A Discussion of the Major Developments in the Field." In *The Sociology of Science*, edited by Paul Halmos, 61–92. Keele: University of Keele, 1972.

PART II

Intersections

In this part of the book, we examine the broad social intersections through which criminalization processes, as well as the dynamics of representations of crime, can be concretely examined. The bodies of subjects entangled with the law, whether as victims, accused, or agents of the law, matter for how legal processes unfold and for the ways that crime is understood as a social fact. The ways in which race, gender, sexuality, and class intersect with one another and with processes of criminalization are the focus of this section.

Each of the chapters in this section emphasizes the relational nature of social positions: One cannot have "the West" without the (racialized) "rest" (Chapter Five), masculinity without femininity (Chapters Six and Seven), "normal" without "abnormal" sexual subjects (Chapter Eight), or wealth without poverty (Chapter Nine). But more than simple dichotomies, each of these chapters focuses on the complex processes that produce shifting, dynamic, and particularized social relations as they become visible through an examination of criminalization, representation, and regulation. The authors in this section sometimes use different terminologies to get at these complex processes: *intersectionality, conjunctural analysis, mutual constitution,* and *interdependency.* The overall theme, however, is the same: When considering the relationships between race, gender, sexuality, and class, we must focus on them as interrelated and interdependent forces. Race is always gendered, sexuality is always racialized, and class permeates gendered subjectivities. Thus, while each chapter takes a distinct starting point, you will find that no chapter in Part Two offers a neat or simple formulation of a single social identity or relation. To the contrary, each of the authors raises important and complex questions about the intersections among these social relations and the processes of criminalization and regulation.

In "Racialization, Criminalization, Representation" (Chapter Five), Carmela Murdocca offers a historical and theoretical account of the production of race and the processes of racialization in Western history, demonstrating how these are socially constructed ideas that are key to modernity. Her analysis demonstrates the ways that colonial forms of knowledge are intertwined with issues of racialization, representation, and criminalization. The simultaneous production of racialized understandings and definitions of criminal behaviour has had profound effects on the ways that racialized individuals are linked to crime, and to the enormously disproportionate burden people of colour have borne as both objects of the criminal justice system and as victims of crime.

In Chapter Six, "Gendering Crime: Men and Masculinities," Ruthann Lee turns our attention to the particular ways in which masculinity, race, and criminalization play out on the representational field. After charting the "discovery" of masculinity as an important issue within criminology and the contemporary "crisis of masculinity" that has taken hold in the wake of the shifting significances of masculinity in the contemporary world, Lee offers a unique perspective on two mainstream Hollywood films—*Better Luck Tomorrow* (2002) and *Harold & Kumar Escape from Guantanamo Bay* (2008)—and demonstrates the ways in which such films both reproduce but also play with dominant cultural messages about race, masculinity, and crime. The choice of films is important, as both of these movies star South or East Asian men, thus shifting the analysis away from the typical Black–white racial relations that dominate a great deal of crime and representation discussions. As Lee shows in this chapter, the concept of masculinity is a useful entry point for examining intersections of gender and race with processes of criminalization and the shifting, complex, and uneven ways that race, masculinity, crime, and criminality are represented in popular culture.

In a similar vein, but with a focus on women and femininities, in "Women Gone Bad? Women, Criminalization, and Representation" (Chapter Seven) Amanda Glasbeek examines the links between the production of knowledge about female crime and the regulation of a normative femininity. Her chapter aims to decode how and what we know about women and crime by demonstrating the links between popular representations of female criminals, the production of criminological knowledge about female crime, and the experiences of women in the criminal justice system. As she shows, the policing of a white, heterosexual, and middle-class normative femininity is often the object of criminological knowledge, both popular and academic, and such representations of women and crime tend to tell us more about gender than they do about crime.

Chapter Eight, "Sexual Regulation: Sexing Governmentality; Governing Sex," by Deborah Brock, asks us to think critically about the governance of sexuality. Brock asks "How do you 'know' what you 'know' about sex, and particularly the connection between sex and crime? Where do those images and ideas come from?" Drawing on Foucault's ground-breaking work on the discursive explosion since the nineteenth century in the West that has produced contemporary sexual subjectivities, Brock demonstrates that how and what we know about sex is inseparable from the medical, legal, psychological, and personal power–knowledge relations that constitute sex as a discrete area of inquiry. Thus, while we have an enormous number of laws and regulations about sex (many of them prohibitive—who can have sex with whom, for example), sex and sexuality occupy a governmental field that extends far beyond the juridical domain. Drawing also on the central theme of Part Two, Brock demonstrates the ways that sexuality is mutually constitutive with race, gender, and class and exists within a complex set of regulations, including self-regulation, which illustrate that sex is indeed complicated.

While the significance of class to processes of criminalization has long been recognized in sociological explanations of crime, in "Crime and Social Classes: Regulating and Representing Public Disorder" (Chapter Nine), Marie-Eve Sylvestre complicates such analyses by historicizing these class differences and following them into the present. Drawing on historical continuities and changes, this chapter focuses on the ways that criminalization and the representation of crime not only reflect but are also constitutive of class differences. Taking into account the work of Marx, Foucault, Bourdieu, and others, and using the examples of vagrancy, homelessness, and street gangs to illustrate her arguments, Sylvestre demonstrates the multiple forms and sites of power that shape our understanding of crime and the reality of punishment in everyday life.

Readers can expect that each individual chapter will help them understand the social bases for criminalization processes. In addition, when these chapters are read together they demonstrate the importance of understanding the connections between social bases of inequality and the regulation and representation of crime.

five
Racialization, Criminalization, Representation

CARMELA MURDOCCA

Introduction

Few news stories or representations of crime are without reference to the cultural identity or race of those involved. The ways in which people are understood as racialized matters a great deal for the ways in which people are subject to processes of criminalization. Few narrations, stories, or representations of crime, whether operating as "truths" (e.g., news stories) or as fictions (e.g., television shows or mainstream films), fail to tell a story about *race*. At the same time, few representations of crime consider the ways that criminalization might also be important to examining racialized identities for individuals and for entire nations.

This chapter examines the relationship between criminalization, representation, and **racialization** by addressing the following questions: What is race and racialization? How is the process of criminalization also racialized? What are the politics of racialization, criminalization, and representation? This chapter draws from the fields of critical race theory, colonial legal studies, postcolonial theory, and cultural studies to provide insights into the processes of racialization, representation, and state practices of regulation and criminalization.

Historicizing and Globalizing Race: Some Definitions

Race is not only one of the most important subjects in the fields of sociology and criminology, it is one of the defining ideas in modern Western societies. As a result, it is important to consider a historical and geographical genealogy of contemporary Western and North American ideas about race and racism. Postcolonial and critical race scholars suggest that race is a European invention and that the concept of *race* is a distinctly modern idea.[1] Spanning from the fifteenth century onward, a series of philosophical, cultural, economic, and political events were key ingredients to the development of the modern

---

1 Howard Winant, "Race and Race Theory," *Annual Review of Sociology* 26 (2000): 169–85; David Goldberg, *Racist Culture: Philosophy and the Politics of Meaning* (Cambridge, MA: Blackwell, 1993).

concept of race. In other words, race is an idea that emerged from and was produced out of specific historical and geographical circumstances.

The Enlightenment, for example, spawned a set of philosophical ideas that have defined the modern era and are key to understanding our current ideas about race.[2] As noted in Chapter One, Enlightenment thinking is the cornerstone of much of our contemporary views on crime. Some of the hallmarks of Enlightenment thought include the centrality of reason, the rise of empiricism and science, universalism and the search for general laws, the notion that the human condition can be improved, the rise of secularism, the idea of progress, and the fundamental belief in freedom. But the Enlightenment was not only a set of intellectual ideas. From the fifteenth century to the present day, colonial projects around the world provided the political and geographical context within which many Enlightenment ideas about human beings, gender, race, and racialization flourished. The emergence of processes of colonization, especially the development and expansion of the transatlantic slave trade, led to the globalization of markets and economies. The impact of these historical, political, and economic processes continues to carry implications for our current understandings of race.

Race, then, is an *idea*, which suggests that it is a created concept—a constructed concept with a history and a past. Most critical race scholars maintain that race is a social, political, and cultural construction; it is a concept that a culture ascribes to a group of people that is believed to have real or imagined bodily differences. Race "signifies and symbolizes sociopolitical conflicts and interests in reference to different types of human bodies."[3] Race is not biologically determined, nor is race an objective social or political fact.

As a created concept, race is a **social construction**. To speak about race as a social construction means that social, historical, political, and economic processes shape the meaning that is given to race over time (through different decades and centuries) and across geographical areas (in different nations and territories) and as a result of changing cultural and social formations. The idea of race as a social construction helps us to understand that the construction of race (much like the construction of crime and criminalization) is the result of social, cultural, and historical processes. Racialization, therefore, is a

---

2 Although the eighteenth century is often referred to as the Age of Enlightenment, philosophical writings related to what is described as the Age of Reason dating back to the fifteenth century set in motion many hallmarks of the Age of Enlightenment. Some of the philosophers and scholars associated with the Age of Reason include René Descartes (1596–1650), Benedict de Spinoza (1632–77), Thomas Hobbes (1588–1679), John Locke (1632–1704), David Hume (1711–76), Jean-Jacques Rousseau (1712–78), and Immanuel Kant (1724–1804).

3 Winant, "Race and Race Theory."

process that is produced through sociopolitical, legal, economic, and cultural formations and meanings. Racialization, then, signifies and emphasizes the *processes* through which ideas about race are constructed. As Steve Garner observes, "The concept of racialisation is based on the idea that the object of study should not be 'race' itself, but the process by which it becomes meaningful in a particular context. In fact, racialisation has now become one of the key ways that academics make sense of the 'meanings of race.'"[4]

These terms—*race, racialization,* and *racism*—have developed through significant historical transformations including colonialism, the rise of capitalism, Enlightenment thinking, transatlantic slavery, and indentured servitude. These significant historical, political, economic, and cultural processes produced the ideas concerning race that we are familiar with today.

Colonialism and Imperialism

There are different forms of colonialism, and colonial projects emerged in distinct ways in different historical periods and in different geographical locations. **Colonialism** is a political "project that extends a nation's sovereignty over territory beyond its borders by the establishment of either settler colonies or administrative dependencies in which **indigenous populations** are directly ruled, displaced" and murdered.[5] Colonizers generally dominate resources, labour, and markets and also impose legal, sociocultural, and linguistic structures on subject populations.[6]

Colonialism is often linked to imperialism, and the terms are often used interchangeably. It is useful, however, to distinguish between the terms both spatially and geographically. **Imperialism** refers to the economic and political processes of extending the dominance of an empire, nation, or metropolitan centre over foreign entities, or of acquiring and holding colonies and dependences.[7] As Ania Loomba explains, "[t]hus the imperial country is the 'metropole' from which power flows, and the colony or neo-colony is the place which it penetrates and controls. Imperialism can function without formal colonies (as in the United States today) but colonialism cannot."[8]

European colonialism and imperialism can be characterized through different historical phases spanning from the fifteenth century to the

---

4 Steve Garner, *Racisms: An Introduction* (London: Sage, 2010), 19.
5 *New World Encyclopedia*, s.v. "Colonialism."
6 Ibid.
7 Ania Loomba, *Colonialism/Postcolonialism* (London: Routledge, 1998), 4–8.
8 Ibid., 7.

present day. In Canada, **settler colonialism** was the type of colonial project that proliferated. Settler colonialism is a racial project that is dependent on the usurpation of land and the legal, administrative, cultural, and bureaucratic governance of indigenous populations. As Sherene H. Razack explains:

> A white settler society is one established by Europeans on non-European soil. Its origins lie in the dispossession and near extermination of Indigenous populations by the conquering Europeans. As it evolves, a white settler society continues to be structured by a racial hierarchy. In the national mythologies of such societies, it is believed that white people came first and it is they who principally settled the land; Aboriginal people are presumed to be mostly dead or assimilated. European settlers thus *become* the original inhabitants and the group most entitled to the fruits of citizenship. A quintessential feature of white settler mythologies is, therefore, the disavowal of conquest, genocide, slavery, and the exploitation of the labour of **peoples of colour**. In North America, it is still the case that European conquest and colonization are often denied, largely through the fantasy that North America was peacefully settled and not colonized.[9]

Despite their common status "as colonies and subsequently as 'Dominions' in the early twentieth century," Canada, Australia, and New Zealand emerged as liberal states in relation to encounters with and governance of indigenous peoples.[10] Dominions refer to the self-governing nations within the British Commonwealth. Often understood to be an exception among settler states because it was "the first settler society to gain independence,"[11] the United States similarly "anchored its subsequent legitimacy on acknowledgement and annulment in its relations with Native Americans."[12]

In addition to colonization, the transatlantic slave trade, indentured servitude, and the rise of industrialization and capitalism together had a profound effect on the emergence of particular forms of racialization in

---

9 Sherene H. Razack, "Introduction: When Place Becomes Race," in *Race, Space and the Law: Unmapping a White Settler Society*, ed. Sherene H. Razack, 1–20 (Toronto: Between the Lines, 2002). Emphasis in original.

10 A.E. Coombes, *Rethinking Settler Colonialism: History and Memory in Australia, Canada, Aotearoa New Zealand and South Africa* (Manchester: Manchester University Press, 2006), 1.

11 D. Stasiulus and N. Yuval-Davis, *Unsettling Settler Societies: Articulations of Race, Ethnicity and Class* (London: Sage Publications, 1995), 6.

12 Elizabeth A. Povinelli, *The Cunning of Recognition: Indigenous Alterities and the Making of Australian Multiculturalism* (Durham: Duke University Press, 2002).

Western nations—indeed, these were the tools of colonial projects. The transatlantic slave trade occurred simultaneously with European colonialism from the mid-fifteenth century to the end of the nineteenth century. Historians suggest that the slave trade was responsible for the forced migration, trafficking, indentured servitude, and enslavement of 12 to 15 million people from Africa to the Western hemisphere. The interactions and connections between colonialism, slavery, and the rise of capitalism spawned what critical race theorist Howard Winant describes as the *modern world system*:

> The idea of "race" began to take shape with the rise of world
> political economy. The onset of global economic integration,
> the dawn of the seaborne empire, the conquest of the Americas,
> and the rise of the Atlantic slave trade, were all key elements in
> the genealogy of race. The concept emerged over time as a kind
> of world-historical *bricolage*, an accretive process that was part
> theoretical, but much more centrally practical. Though intimated
> throughout the world in innumerable ways, racial categorization of
> human beings was a European invention. It was an outcome of the
> same world-historical processes that created European nation-states
> and empires, built the "dark satanic mills" of Britain (and the even
> more dark and satanic sugar mills of the Brazillian Reconcavo and
> the Caribbean), and explained it all by means of Enlightenment
> rationality.[13]

The implication of these world historical processes suggests a profound and complicated genealogy for the concept of race. These processes were and are cumulative, requiring philosophical ideas (the central tenets of Enlightenment thinking) and human action and reaction. In this sense, it is inaccurate to suggest that colonization and the transatlantic slave trade were top-down processes. Indeed, colonization required extreme forms of violence and was accomplished through economic exploitation and the genocide of indigenous peoples. The colonized, the enslaved, and the exploited, however, were not merely passive victims of the globalizing economic process of colonialism, slavery, and other forms of economic and political exploitation. It is important to think about these historical processes as dynamic in form and consequence, rather than simply as exploitative.

---

13 Winant, "Race and Race Theory."

Edward Said and Colonial Discourse

Edward W. Said (1935–2003) is a central thinker in the development of the field of **postcolonial studies**,[14] which is an interdisciplinary field of study that focuses on the historical, political, economic, cultural, legal, and social effects of colonialism. Although the "post" in postcolonialism carries the connotation of *after* colonialism, "it has been suggested that is more helpful to think of post-colonialism not just as coming literally after colonialism and signifying its demise, but more flexibly as the contestation of

Figure 5.1 Edward Said

---

14 Other notable writers in the field of postcolonial studies are Frantz Fanon and Gayatri Spivak.

colonial domination and the legacies of colonialism."[15] Said's influential book *Orientalism* (1978) is said to have generated the field of postcolonial studies. In *Orientalism*, Said uses Michel Foucault's notion of discourse to argue that the *idea* of the Orient was produced "politically, sociologically, militarily, ideologically, scientifically, and imaginatively" through European colonial projects, and conversely that "European culture gained in strength and identity by setting itself off against the Orient as a sort of surrogate and even underground self."[16] As noted in Chapter One, for Michel Foucault, knowledge and discourse are produced through sets of *discursive formations* that determine, define, and construct the objects, concepts, paradigms, theoretical formulations, and methodological resources that are available in a given culture.

In *Orientalism*, Edward Said applies Michel Foucault's concepts of discourse and discursive formation to European or Western representations of the "Eastern" world. Said argues that a complex set of representations and fabrications produced the discursive formation of the "Orient." He argues that Orientalism is "a system of knowledge about the Orient, an accepted grid for filtering the Orient into Western consciousness."[17] For Said, the historical and contemporary record reveals that distorted representations of the East are so powerful that we can discern the lasting effects in anthropological, sociological, biological, linguistic, racial, economic, artistic, political, and cultural processes.

The significance of Said's work for the social sciences rests on the connection that he established between the economic, political, *as well as* cultural process of colonial projects. In short, Said's path-breaking work reveals how colonialism is structural (political and economic) as well as cultural. As Said argues, colonialism and imperialism not only require military and governmental power, but also require an *idea of empire*. In his later work, *Culture and Imperialism* (1993), Said maintains that colonial contests over land and geography are "complex and interesting because it is not only about soldiers and cannons but also about ideas, about forms, about images and imaginings." Said continues:

> Neither imperialism nor colonialism is a simple act of accumulation and acquisition. Both are supported and perhaps even impelled by impressive ideological formations that include notions that certain territories and people *require* and beseech domination, as well as forms of knowledge

---

15 Loomba, *Colonialism/Postcolonialism*, 16.
16 Edward W. Said, *Orientalism* (New York: Random House, 1978).
17 Ibid., 6.

affiliated with domination: the vocabulary of classic nineteenth century imperial culture is plentiful with words and concepts like "inferior" or "subject races," "subordinate peoples," "dependency," "expansion," and "authority." Out of the imperial experiences, notions about culture were clarified, reinforced, criticized, or rejected.[18]

In other words, colonialism, imperialism, and empire-building need to be understood not only for the accumulation of capital but also as cultural manifestations concerning the production of *ideas and representations* about race.

Natural law—the idea that there is a set of universal laws that govern all human behaviour—is a key Enlightenment idea. Natural law dictates that if you believe that there are universal laws that govern human behaviour, correspondingly you believe that all human beings are bound by a common humanity. Many Enlightenment thinkers were invested in the idea of the "human"—the category of "human" came to be an important signifier of ideas related to race and racialization. At the same time, however, many of these philosophers advanced the idea that there were inherent differences between human beings. Critical race scholar David Theo Goldberg argues that the more universal and abstract the idea of the human became during this period, the more the historical record reveals that a notion of difference, categorization, classification, value, and hierarchy came to be associated with distinctions between human beings.[19] For example, in the eighteenth century and onward, indigenous peoples were often perceived and represented by colonizers as "savage," "barbaric," and subhuman. These representations were also applied to peoples of African origin. Ideas about race, gender, and culture were key ingredients in colonial projects in the marking of "otherness." These discourses and representations related to racial otherness can be referred to as *colonial racism*. Figure 5.2 shows some of the powerful "either/or" notions of Indian authenticity that were fashioned during the late nineteenth and early twentieth centuries by colonial society that relied on a wide variety of associated binaries.

Legal systems, and the criminal justice system in particular, played a central institutional and practical role in legitimizing the ideas and representations of colonial and imperial projects. The discourse of race and racism at this time—from ideas about inferior races, savages, and barbaric peoples—were racial narratives and stories that highlighted ideas about lawlessness. And these discourses were produced through law. As Geeta Chowdhry and Mark

---

18 Edward W. Said, *Culture and Imperialism* (New York: Random House, 1994), 9. Emphasis in original.
19 Goldberg, *Racist Culture.*

Figure 5.2 Binaries of authenticity

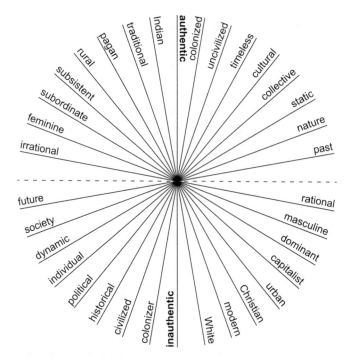

In the late nineteenth century and the early twentieth, colonial society fashioned a powerful "either-or" notion of Indian authenticity that relied on a wide variety of associated binaries, a sampling of which are shown here.

Beeman explain, "the development of a coercive and extra-legal apparatus was central to the creation of fear and maintenance of order in colonized territories ... Whether the Europeans saw themselves as part of a *mission civilisatrice* or as safeguarding their possessions in a 'wild' landscape among 'savage' inhabitants, power was intrinsic to the colonizing structure. In turn, such power was ensured through colonial edicts and policies that protected colonial interests against those of the colonized, through the criminalization of cultural practices and through brute force."[20]

Modern racism has its origins in the colonial encounter. At the centre of colonial projects is the figure of the racialized, colonial subject that was made through anthropological and scientific discourse (scientific racism) of

20 Geeta Chowdhry and Mark Beeman, "Situating Colonialism, Race, and Punishment," in *Race, Gender and Punishment: From Colonialism to the War on Terror*, ed. Mary Bosworth and Jeanne Flavin, 13–31 (New Brunswick: Rutgers University Press, 2007), 18.

the eighteenth and nineteenth centuries, which constructed race as a hierarchical and biological category. Many scholars caution, however, that we should not draw a direct line between eighteenth-century representations of indigenous or racialized people to the present day because ideas about what it means to be human, "authentically Indian," and white shift through time and through geographical space. For example, in her study of the social and political implications of ideas about "real Indians" in the Pacific Northwest, Paige Raibmon shows how government officials, anthropologists, social reformers, settlers, missionaries, and tourists developed shifting definitions of "Indianness" and "Indian authenticity" in ways that secured settler claims to sovereignty, land, and resources and curtailed indigenous claims to land and resources (see Figure 5.2). Interestingly, Raibmon demonstrates that indigenous people often used similar definitions of "Indianness" to secure the legal, social, and political possibilities for survival in the context of colonialism. A striking example of these representations of "Indianness" is the performance of the Kwakwaka'wakw from Vancouver Island at the Chicago World's Fair in 1893. I quote Raibmon's description and analysis of the performance at length because it addresses distinct links between race, representation, criminalization, and resistance in a colonial context:

> That night the troupe performed a dance adapted from their sacred winter ceremonial, the root of the spiritual and material order. When the two main performers stepped to the side of the stage and pulled off their shirts, the audience assumed the performance had ended. At that moment, however, the rest of the troupe surrounded the two young men and began singing and chanting to the beat of a drum. Horror struck spectators as the troupe's leader, George Hunt, used a razor to slash four deep gashes across the back of each initiate. Neither man flinched. The performance and music continued with George Hunt offering his arm to one of the young Kwakwaka'wakw men who "sank his teeth into Hunt's arm until he was dragged away, apparently having bit off a piece of flesh the size of a silver dollar" ... The spectators in Chicago watched with a mixture of fascination and revulsion as their most lurid imaginings of wild and savage Indians played out before their eyes. Like colonial officials in British Columbia, they misinterpreted Kwakwaka'wakw as attached to superstition, in opposition to modernity and change ... the Kwakwaka'wakw asserted their right to simultaneously engage modernity and tradition in distinctly indigenous—distinctly Kwakwaka'wakw—ways. The Kwakwaka'wakw found themselves at the centre of an ideological dispute within colonial society. On

the one hand, anthropologists and tourists encouraged them to enact the most "traditional" elements of their culture, while on the other, missionaries and government officials pressured them to abandon "tradition" in favour of "civilization" ... When they returned home, they used wages from the trip to further frustrate church and state officials, and in so doing continued a long pattern of using wage labour for their own devices. The Kwakw*aka*'wakw performers in Chicago played colonial viewpoints off one another in a manner that furthered their attempts to retain control of their lives. They rejected dichotomies that animated colonial ideas at the same time as they used them.[21]

This story about the Kwakw*aka*'wakw highlights the contestations and struggle of living in a colonial society. The interwoven relationships among the cultural, legal, representational, and political processes within which indigenous peoples, colonial officials and administrators, merchants, settlers, travellers, missionaries, teachers, scientists, domestic servants, and labourers interacted highlights the complex social systems in colonial societies. These representational practices provided the content and form of criminalization and regulation in colonial societies. In the Canadian context, for example, Constance Backhouse has shown how the *Wanduta* case criminalized Aboriginal dance in Manitoba in 1903. Backhouse reveals how, although settlers viewed Aboriginal dance with fascination, the Canadian government passed laws prohibiting ceremonial dance in 1884. As Backhouse explains, there were gendered and racialized rationales for criminalizing Aboriginal dance:

> The non-religious reasons that whites tendered for opposing Aboriginal dance were many and varied. Some of the more spurious claims by the superintendent general of Indian Affairs was that "Indians raised dust with their dancing and the women's failure to clean it up spread such diseases as tuberculosis." Deputy Superintendent of Indian Affairs Frank Pedley advanced the theory that dancing caused "physical deterioration" and "mental instability."[22]

---

21 Paige Raibmon, *Authentic Indians: Episodes of Encounter from the Late-Nineteenth-Century Northwest Coast* (Durham: Duke University Press, 2005), 15–17.

22 Constance Backhouse, *Colour-Coded: A Legal History of Racism in Canada, 1900–1950* (Toronto: University of Toronto Press, 2001), 35.

Borrowing from Mary Louise Pratt's influential book *Imperial Eyes* (1992), historians of colonialism describe the complex social, political, legal, and cultural worlds of colonial societies as "contact zones," which refers to "the space of colonial encounters ... in which peoples geographically and historically separated come into contact, usually involving conditions of coercion, radical inequality and intractable conflict."[23] Colonial discourse and representations, then, are one place where we can begin to ask questions about and think through the complexities of lasting and ongoing effects within colonial societies. Prioritizing questions of discourse and representation "indicates a new way of thinking in which cultural, intellectual, and political processes are seen to work together in the formation, perpetuation and dismantling of colonialism."[24]

Frantz Fanon and "Racialization"

There is yet another important genealogy related to the concept of racialization. This genealogy emerges from the anti-colonial revolutionary writings of Frantz Fanon. Frantz Fanon (1925–1961), born in Martinique, was an Algerian–French psychiatrist, philosopher, humanist, and revolutionary anti-colonial writer. Fanon supported the Algerian anti-colonial struggle for independence from colonial France. His writings have been influential in the fields of critical race studies, postcolonial studies, and social movement studies.

Fanon's most influential writing appears in two of his books: *Black Skin, White Masks* (1952) and *The Wretched of the Earth* (1961). In *Black Skin, White Masks*, Fanon explores the psychological and social effects of living as a Black man in a colonial world. He developed and advanced a theory that argued that European colonialism created a binary world—a **Manichean** world—whereby sharp and distinct categories of domination and subjection structure social, political, and economic relations. The colonizer/the colonized, Black/white, civilized/barbaric, respectable/degenerate became profound psychic and social orders of domination for colonized people in a colonized world.[25] These sharp distinctions have the effect, Fanon argues, of splitting humanity into two categories: human and subhuman. It is in the context of this distinction that Fanon first uses the phrase *to racialize* when contrasting it

---

23 Mary Louise Pratt, *Imperial Eyes: Travel Writing and Transculturation* (New York: Routledge, 1992), 6.
24 Loomba, *Colonialism/Postcolonialism*, 54.
25 Frantz Fanon, *Black Skin, White Masks* (New York: Grove Press, 1967); Frantz Fanon, *The Wretched of the Earth* (New York: Grove Press, 1963).

Figure 5.3 Frantz Fanon

from the phrase *to humanize*, thereby signalling the ways in which processes of racialization eject certain people from the very category of human. In this sense, racialization can be viewed as assisting processes of domination, oppression, subjugation, violence, and marginalization. Racialization, therefore, is about **relations of power**: "Racialisation represents an essential sociological tool because it draws attention to the *process* of making 'race' relevant to a particular situation and context and thus requires an examination of the precise circumstances in which this occurs: who the 'agents' are; who the actors are."[26]

What, then, is "**racism**"? As Ali Rattsani argues, "Racialization tells us that racism is never simply racism, but always exists in complex imbrication

---

26 Garner, *Racisms*, 21. Emphasis in original.

with nation, ethnicity, class, gender and sexuality, and therefore a dismantling of racism also requires, simultaneously as well as in the long run, a strategy to reduce relevant class inequalities, forms of masculinity, nationalism and other social features, whereby racisms are reproduced in particular sites."[27] Racialization is central to and interwoven into state governance, law and administration, and systems of representation. As I have noted, race is an idea—a multidimensional concept that changes over time and through different geographical places. In our contemporary world, we view racial difference as fixed and set in stone. The fixity of race results from the idea that race largely and exclusively refers to phenotype (observable characteristics and traits, like skin colour). Critical race and postcolonial scholars encourage us to challenge this view based on its historical inaccuracy and the legacy of scientific or biological racism that supports it. What we know about the concept of "race" comes from the stories that we tell about race and the forms of governance that assist in the organization of knowledge about race. Whether these stories are derived from popular media, such as television shows, movies, newsfeeds, Twitter, or Facebook, or through formal governmental and legal processes, they rely on ideas about race that have a long history in Western culture. A comparative approach, one that globalizes our analyses of race, has been lacking in the research.[28]

Racialization, Representation, Criminalization

Despite the strengths of postcolonial and critical race scholarship, with a few exceptions the field of criminology has paid little attention to addressing the practices, ideas, and representations associated with colonialism.[29] One of the first scholars to examine the significant relationship between racialization, criminalization, and representation was Stuart Hall in his 1978 book *Policing the Crisis: Mugging, the State, and Law and Order.*

Policing the Crisis examines the racialized moral panic over the perceived rise of mugging in Britain. Hall argues that *mugging* was a term invented by the British press with a series of news stories; the phrase **moral panic** was made famous by the sociologist Stanley Cohen. Cohen suggests that at times

---

27 Ali Rattansi, "Racialization," in *Racializtaion: Studies in Theory and Practice*, ed. Karim Murji and John Solomos (London: Oxford University Press, 2005), 296.

28 Ann Laura Stoler, "Between Metropole and Colony: Rethinking a Research Agenda," in *Tensions of Empire: Colonial Cultures in a Bourgeois World*, ed. Frederick Cooper and Ann Laura Stoler, 1–58 (Berkeley: University of California Press, 1997); Yasmin Jiwani, "Race and the Media: A Retrospective and Prospective Gaze," *Canadian Journal of Communications* 34, no. 4 (2009): 735–40.

29 Stuart Hall et al., *Policing the Crisis: Mugging, the State, and Law and Order* (London: Macmillan, 1978).

of social unrest, folk devils and moral panics serve to offer a sense of control over these events, groups, and individuals who appear to threaten societal norms. Cohen argues that "a moral panic is a reaction by a group of people based on the false or exaggerated perception that some cultural behavior or group, frequently a minority group or a subculture, is dangerously deviant and poses a menace to society."[30]

Some more recent sociologists who explore the concept of the "risk society" (as Browne and French examine in Chapter Ten) suggest that the notion of moral panic is one that has little value at present because of the almost constant and routine reporting of moral panics, social crises, or social fears and anxieties (whether they are related to crime, health, or environmental issues) by the media, which undermines the very notion of a moral panic.[31] In addition, scholars relying on Foucauldian ideas concerning social and moral regulation and governance suggest that the framework of a moral panic constructs a dichotomy between irrational fears (a panic) and "real truth" and empirical reality.[32] In short, moral panics become a variant of social anxiety about crime rather than a dimension of broader governmental forms of moral and social regulation.

In other words, moral panics are not exceptional—they have become the routine. Nevertheless, at the time of Hall's study, the moral panic around mugging was significant. Hall suggests that news stories constructed mugging as a symbol for a range of social problems involving national anxieties about poverty, drugs, Black people, urban crime, and homelessness.[33] The news campaign against mugging had a distinct form of racial representation: Mugging became synonymous with crimes committed by young Black men.

Hall shows that much of the media attention directed at mugging also focused on court and other criminal justice responses. Courts, lawyers, and police officials were celebrated for issuing lengthy and exemplary sentences in the interest of public safety. Hall's study demonstrated the important links between racialization, media representation, and changes in law, order, and governance. Hall drew heavily on Antonio Gramsci's concept of hegemony to demonstrate the connections between representation, racialization, and state governance. **Hegemony** is the process through which ruling states or groups maintain their dominance by convincing those whom they

---

30 Stanley Cohen, *Folk Devils and Moral Panics* (London: MacGibbon and Kee, 1972).

31 Dawn Moore and Mariana Valverde, "Maidens at Risk: 'Date Rape Drugs' and the Formation of Hybrid Risk Knowledges," *Economy and Society* 29, no. 4 (2000): 514–31.

32 Ibid.

33 Ibid., 522. Today, perhaps a similar argument can be made about the media concern with panhandling.

Figure 5.4 Young racialized man mugging woman on street

dominate (citizens, the underclass) that they share the same values and interests as the ruling group. This is accomplished through coercion and consent.
In the case of the so-called mugging crisis in Britain, Hall demonstrated the
ways in which the media acted as the "legitimators" of state moral and social
regulation.[34]

Importantly, Hall historicized the crime of mugging by showing its
similarities to nineteenth-century footpads and garrotters (petty or street
thieves).[35] Reviewing statistics concerning street crime, Hall also found no
evidence to indicate that street crime was increasing at a rate that would
cause a moral panic. In labelling certain Black youths as "muggers," Hall
found that the invented category of *mugger* produced the statistical evidence
used to indicate a rising level of street crime that was reported in the news.
This "new" category of crime and the "new" rising statistics were used to
legitimize the "get tough on crime" measures adopted by the government
and the police. Grounding their coverage of the "mugging crisis" in statements such as "everybody thinks" that mugging is a problem or "the public
has to be protected," public opinion was quickly mobilized in support of a

---

34 Hall et al., *Policing the Crisis*, 76.
35 Ibid.

Figure 5.5 Toronto Police Chief Bill Blair stands next to a poster of victims of gang violence as he announces a string of arrests and charges against gang activity in Scarborough in what was dubbed Project Pathfinder in 2007

law-and-order approach to this crime problem.[36] This feedback loop between public opinion, media representation, state and police practice, and processes of racialization demonstrates the idea of hegemony quite acutely: "modes of consent" (i.e., the transformation of public opinion through media representation) working with and through "modes of coercion" (i.e., the state, law, and police response to the *new* crime problem).[37]

Stuart Hall's significant study allows for an examination of a range of contemporary media representations concerning racialization and criminalization. Today, the analysis of mugging advanced by Hall can be applied to the context of gun and gang violence in urban centres in Canada. Distinct regional variations demonstrate the connections between public opinion, media representation, police practice, and the process of racialization. In Toronto, representations of gun violence often link young Black men, gang violence, and new approaches to policing to combat the "escalating" problem.

---

36 Ibid.
37 Ibid.

Figure 5.6 Indian Posse tattoo

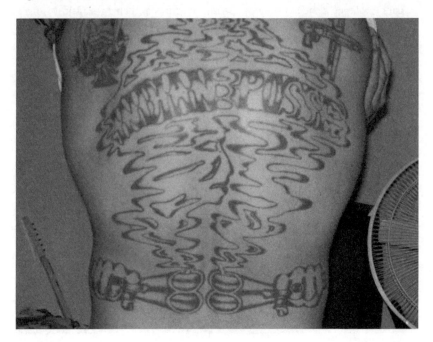

Project Pathfinder, for example, is a Toronto Police Service initiative targeting specific low-income and racialized neighbourhoods for gang activity.[38]

In the province of Saskatchewan (and in Manitoba and Alberta), gang violence is focused on young indigenous men who are involved in organized crime.[39] The report of the Saskatchewan Criminal Intelligence Service Organization, for example, identifies connections between "poverty, violence, absent parenting, and urban migration, combined with blocked opportunities and substance abuse"[40] as combined factors that lead to gang activity. The report uses visual representations of graffiti, leather jackets, and tattooing as visual signs, signifiers, and forms of representation that provide evidence of gang activity. News reporting in Canada also repeatedly shows mug shots of

---

38 See Toronto Police Service, "Project Pathfinder Nets More Arrests," http://www.torontopolice .on.ca/modules.php?op=modload&name=news&file=article&sid=1626 (accessed February 21, 2013).

39 Criminal Intelligence Service Organization, "2005: Intelligence Trends—Aboriginal Based Gangs in Saskatchewan," 1, no. 1 (Winter 2005). See also Joe Friesen, "The Ballad of David Wolf," *Globe and Mail*, June 18, 2011, http://www.theglobeandmail.com/news/national/the -ballad-of-daniel-wolfe/article1357474/?page=all (accessed February 21, 2013).

40 Ibid.

Figure 5.7 Racialized youth being investigated by police

unnamed young indigenous men, declaring "Native gangs spreading across Canada."[41] These images function as representational placeholders for crime, youth violence, urban centres, and the problem of "race."

In Vancouver and Surrey, media representation, police practice, and state regulation has focused on young Punjabi and Sikh men involved in crime. The documentary film *Warrior Boyz* (2008) chronicles some of the obstacles that second-generation Sikh and Punjabi youth face in British Columbia as they navigate racism in schools, lack of employment opportunities, and social disenfranchisement.

Whether gang or gun violence occurs in Toronto, Vancouver, or Regina, the figures of young, racialized men (whether Black, indigenous, or Sikh) function as representational signs of social, economic, and community-based needs for new forms of regulation. The report from the Saskatchewan Criminal Intelligence Service Organization concludes that gang violence "costs the community" through the combined factors of "increased crime or fear of crime," "increased (property) insurance," and "decline of property values."[42] These types of discourses concerning gun and gang violence are produced through the circulation of understandings of representation, regulation,

---

41 Canadian Press, "Native Gangs Spreading across Canada," *CBC News*, March 16, 2010, http://www.cbc.ca/news/canada/manitoba/native-gangs-spreading-across-canada-1.873168 (accessed November, 19, 2013).

42 Criminal Intelligence Service Organization, "2005: Intelligence Trends."

and racialization. Yasmin Jiwani has described connections between racialization and criminalization as "the criminalization of 'race' (and) the racialization of crime," whereby ideas about race and racialization are not only inseparable from forms of regulation and criminalization, but also offer content to forms of regulation and criminalization.[43]

The relationship between criminalization, representation, and regulation can have deadly consequences for certain marginalized people. Sherene Razack's analysis of the murder of Pamela George, an indigenous woman, is a sobering reminder that racialization, representation, and forms of state and nonstate regulation can have dire consequences. George was murdered by two young white university students who "following oral sex, took turns brutally beating her and left her lying with her face in the mud."[44] Razack argues that George's murder should be understood as gendered racial violence where "the racial or colonial aspects of this encounter are more prominently brought into view by tracing two inextricably linked collective histories: the histories of the murderers, two middle-class white men, and of Pamela George, a Saulteaux woman."[45] By reviewing the transcripts from the murder case, Razack asks the following questions: How does the history of colonialism and racism in Canada directed at indigenous peoples help us shed light on Pamela George's murder? What is it about the biographies of George and her murderers that brought them into a violent encounter with each other? What about the histories of the white men made it possible for them to brutally murder George? What was it about Pamela George that not only made her especially vulnerable but also made her a target? Through analyzing the court transcripts, Razack's analysis concludes that forms of racialization, representation, and regulation resulted in George's "absence" from her own murder trial: "If this exploration of Pamela George's murder trial does anything at all, my hope is that it raises consciousness about how little she mattered to her murderers, their friends and families, and how small a chance she had of entering the court's and Canadian society's consciousness as a person."[46]

There has been much attention drawn to the fact that the murder of Pamela George is but one episode in a longer history of violence in the lives of indigenous women. According to the Native Women's Association of

---

43 Yasmin Jiwani, "The Criminalization of 'Race,' the Racialization of Crime," in *Crimes of Colour: Racialization and the Criminal Justice System in Canada*, ed. Wendy Chan and Kiran Mirchandani, 67–86 (Toronto: University of Toronto Press, 2002).

44 Sherene H. Razack, "Gendered Racial Violence and Spatialized Justice: The Case of Pamela George," in *Race, Space and the Law: Unmapping a White Settler Society*, ed. Sherene H. Razack (Toronto: Between the Lines, 2002), 124.

45 Ibid., 126.

46 Ibid., 156.

Figure 5.8 Advocacy in support of indigenous women

Canada (NWAC), "approximately 60% of 3000 women that have gone missing or been murdered in Canada since 1980 are Native, with approximately
500 cases outstanding in BC alone."[47] The official number of cases according
to NWAC is 583. The discrepancy between these numbers can be attributed to a lack of funding for widespread research, most recently manifest in
the government's cutting of funds to NWAC's Sisters in Spirit campaign.[48]
Many indigenous and non-indigenous advocacy groups, including Amnesty
International, are calling on the local, provincial, and federal governments to
address this historical and systemic issue. The "Stolen Sisters" report produced
by Amnesty International calls upon the state to address the following root
causes of violence in the lives of indigenous women in Canada:

1. The role of racism and misogyny in perpetuating violence
   against indigenous women.
2. The sharp disparities in the fulfillment of indigenous women's
   economic, social, political, and cultural rights.

---

47 Ibid.

48 Native Women's Association of Canada, "Missing and Murdered Aboriginal Women and Girls,"
http://www.nwac.ca/research/nwac-reports (accessed February 22, 2013).

3. The continued disruption of indigenous societies caused by the historic and ongoing mass removal of children from indigenous families and communities.

4. The disproportionately high number of indigenous women in Canadian prisons, many of whom are themselves the victims of violence and abuse.

5. Inadequate police response to violence against indigenous women as illustrated by the handling of missing persons cases.[49]

Critical Race Theory

Many of the insights advanced in this chapter are consistent with a theoretical approach known as critical race theory. **Critical race theory** is an interdisciplinary theoretical approach that examines race and processes of racialization in social, legal, political, cultural, and economic processes. Critical race theory emerged out of sociolegal scholarship and focuses on the role of race and racism in the law and legal processes.

Even though many disciplines (from sociology, political science, criminology, cultural and film studies, queer theory, and Chicano/a and Latino/a studies) continue to develop and advance critical race theory, there are some basic ideas that guide the approach. Critical race theory starts from the premise that racism is a central feature of advanced liberal and capitalist societies. Racism, therefore, is not exceptional to an otherwise liberal, equal, and democratic society; rather, racism is interwoven into the very fabric of these societies. Given this view, critical race theorists do not adhere to the idea that the law is impartial or neutral and applies equally to everyone. Instead, critical race theorists suggest that the law (and legal processes) is a product of societies that are profoundly organized by and through ideas about race.

To understand how processes of racialization work in advanced liberal and capitalist societies, critical race theorists generally rely on a methodological approach that foregrounds intersectionality and the use of personal narratives and storytelling. The notion of **intersectionality** advances the idea that to examine structures of knowledge, power relations, and social and legal phenomena, we must address the wider historical, political, and social context while recognizing the ways in which the interlocking systems of

---

49 Amnesty International, "Stolen Sisters: A Human Rights Response to Discrimination against Indigenous Women in Canada," October 4, 2004, http://www.amnesty.ca/research/reports/ stolen-sisters-a-human-rights-response-to-discrimination-and-violence-against-indig (accessed April 8, 2014).

race, gender, sexuality, and class simultaneously structure social and political relations. Critical race legal theorist Kimberlé Williams Crenshaw coined the word *intersectionality* to explain the multiple ways in which race and gender interact in Black women's lives. She explains intersectionality in the following manner:

> Consider an analogy to traffic in an intersection, coming and going in all four directions. Discrimination, like traffic through an intersection, may flow in one direction, and it may flow in another. If an accident happens in an intersection, it can be caused by cars traveling from any number of directions and, sometimes, from all of them. Similarly, if a Black woman is harmed because she is in an intersection, her injury could result from sex discrimination or race discrimination ... But it is not always easy to reconstruct an accident: Sometimes the skid marks and the injuries simply indicate that they occurred simultaneously, frustrating efforts to determine which driver caused the harm.[50]

In addressing questions *simultaneously*, critical race theorists and researchers often rely on the use of experiential knowledge, or personal experiences and narratives. As Daniel Solorzano explains, "Critical race theory recognizes that the experiential knowledge of women and men of color is legitimate, appropriate, and critical to understanding, analyzing, and teaching about racial subordination ... Indeed, critical race theory views this knowledge as a strength and draws explicitly on the person of color's lived experiences by including such methods as storytelling, family history, biographies, scenarios, parables, cuentos, chronicles, and narratives."[51] Finally, critical race theories offer a distinct commitment to social justice that draws our attention to the limits of the law in pursuing, seeking, and eradicating injustice. Critical race approaches invite us to ask the following question: What political, cultural, social, interpersonal, and economic engagements (other than the law) may be necessary in the pursuit of social justice?

---

50 Kimberlé Williams Crenshaw, "Demarginalizing the Intersection of Race and Sex: A Black Feminist Critique of Antidiscrimination Doctrine, Feminist Theory and Antiracist Politics," *University of Chicago Legal Forum* (1989): 139–67.
51 Daniel G. Solorzano, "Critical Race Theory, Race and Gender Microaggressions, and the Experience of Chicana and Chicano Scholars," *International Journal of Qualitative Studies in Education* 11, no. 1 (1998): 121–36.

Conclusion

This chapter has addressed some of the ways in which "race" and racialization are defined through a historical framework that considers the emergence of the concept of race through the process of colonization and slavery in the Western world. In addition, we have explored how colonial forms of knowledge are intertwined with issues of racialization, representation, and criminalization. Recently, there has been talk that we live in a post-racial world. This chapter suggests that historical, economic, and political ideas pertaining to race are interwoven into the very fabric of our society, rendering the notion of "post-racial" inaccurate. Howard Winant captures the implications of identifying these historical processes, suggesting that it "is not to say that the European attainment and world-encompassing power 'gave rise' to race. Indeed it is just as easy to argue the opposite: that the modern concept of race 'gave rise to,' or at least facilitated the creation of, an integrated sociopolitical world, a modern authoritarian state, the structures of an international economy, and the emergence over time of a global culture. We must recognize all these issues as deeply racialized matters."[52]

Study Questions

1. What are race, racialization, and racism? What is the relationship between colonization and racialization?
2. What are the connections between the politics of representation, criminalization, and racialization?
3. What are some of the central tenets of critical race theory?

Exercise

Look for images in the dominant culture that depict particular ideas about race and racialization. How might some of the ideas advanced in this chapter assist in analyzing these images? How would a critical race theorist analyze these images?

Keywords

racialization; race; colonialism; indigenous populations; imperialism; settler colonialism; people of colour; postcolonial studies; social construction; Manichean; relations of power; racism; moral panic; hegemony; critical race theory; intersectionality

---

52 Winant, "Race and Race Theory."

References

Amnesty International. "Stolen Sisters: A Human Rights Response to Discrimination against Indigenous Women in Canada." October 4, 2004. http://www.amnesty.ca/research/reports/stolen-sisters-a-human-rights-response-to-discrimination-and-violence-against-indig (accessed April 8, 2014).

Backhouse, Constance. *Colour-Coded: A Legal History of Racism in Canada, 1900–1950.* Toronto: University of Toronto Press, 2001.

Canadian Press. "Native Gangs Spreading across Canada." *CBC News*, March 16, 2010. http://www.cbc.ca/news/canada/manitoba/native-gangs-spreading-across-canada-1.873168 (accessed November 19, 2013).

Chowdhry, Geeta, and Mark Beeman. "Situating Colonialism, Race, and Punishment." In *Race, Gender and Punishment: From Colonialism to the War on Terror*, edited by Mary Bosworth and Jeanne Flavin. New Brunswick: Rutgers University Press, 2007.

Cohen, Stanley. *Folk Devils and Moral Panics.* London: MacGibbon and Kee, 1972.

Coombes, A.E. *Rethinking Settler Colonialism: History and Memory in Australia, Canada, Aotearoa New Zealand and South Africa.* Manchester: Manchester University Press, 2006.

Crenshaw, Kimberlé Williams. "Demarginalizing the Intersection of Race and Sex: A Black Feminist Critique of Antidiscrimination Doctrine, Feminist Theory and Antiracist Politics." *University of Chicago Legal Forum* (1989): 139–67.

Criminal Intelligence Service Organization. "2005: Intelligence Trends—Aboriginal Based Gangs in Saskatchewan." 1, no. 1 (Winter 2005).

Fanon, Frantz. *The Wretched of the Earth.* New York: Grove Press, 1963.

Fanon, Frantz. *Black Skin, White Masks.* New York: Grove Press, 1967.

Friesen, Joe. "The Ballad of David Wolf." *Globe and Mail*, June 18, 2011. http://www.theglobeandmail.com/news/national/the-ballad-of-daniel-wolfe/article1357474/?page=all (accessed February 21, 2013).

Garner, Steve. *Racisms: An Introduction.* London: Sage, 2010.

Goldberg, David Theo. *Racist Culture: Philosophy and the Politics of Meaning.* London: Blackwell, 1993.

Hall, Stuart, et al. *Policing the Crisis: Mugging, the State, and Law and Order.* London: Macmillan, 1978.

Jiwani, Yasmin. "Race and the Media: A Retrospective and Prospective Gaze." *Canadian Journal of Communication* 34, no. 4 (2009): 735–40.

Jiwani, Yasmin. "The Criminalization of 'Race,' the Racialization of Crime." In *Crimes of Colour: Racialization and the Criminal Justice System in Canada*, edited by Wendy Chan and Kiran Mirchandani, 67–86. Toronto: University of Toronto Press, 2002.

Loomba, Ania. *Colonialism/Postcolonialism.* London: Routledge, 1998.

Moore, Dawn, and Mariana Valverde. "Maidens at Risk: 'Date Rape Drugs' and the Formation of Hybrid Risk Knowledges." *Economy and Society* 29, no. 4 (2000): 514–31. http://dx.doi.org/10.1080/03085140050174769.

Native Women's Association of Canada. "Missing and Murdered Aboriginal Women and Girls." http://www.nwac.ca/research/nwac-reports (accessed February 22, 2013).

New World Encyclopedia, s.v. "Colonialism."

Povinelli, E.A. *The Cunning of Recognition: Indigenous Alterities and the Making of Australian Multiculturalism.* Durham: Duke University Press, 2002. http://dx.doi.org/10.1215/9780822383673.

Pratt, Mary Louise. *Imperial Eyes: Travel Writing and Transculturation.* New York: Routledge, 1992.

Raibmon, Paige. *Authentic Indians: Episodes of Encounter From the Late-Nineteenth-Century Northwest Coast.* Durham, NC: Duke University Press, 2005. http://dx.doi.org/ 10.1215/9780822386773.

Rattansi, Ali. "Racialization." In *Racialization: Studies in Theory and Practice*, edited by Karim Murji and John Solomos. London: Oxford University Press, 2005.

Razack, Sherene H., ed. *Race, Space and the Law: Unmapping a White Settler Society.* Toronto: Between the Lines, 2002.

Said, Edward W. *Orientalism.* New York: Random House, 1978.

Said, Edward W. *Culture and Imperialism.* New York: Random House, 1994.

Solorzano, Daniel G. "Critical Race Theory, Race and Gender Microaggressions, and the Experience of Chicana and Chicano Scholars." *International Journal of Qualitative Studies in Education* 11, no. 1 (1998): 121–36. http://dx.doi.org/10.1080/ 095183998236926.

Stasiulus, D., and N. Yuval-Davis. *Unsettling Settler Societies: Articulations of Race, Ethnicity and Class.* London: Sage Publications, 1995.

Stoler, Ann Laura. "Between Metropole and Colony: Rethinking a Research Agenda." In *Tensions of Empire: Colonial Cultures in a Bourgeois World*, edited by Frederick Cooper and Ann Laura Stoler, 1–58 Berkeley: University of California Press, 1997. http:// dx.doi.org/10.1525/california/9780520205406.003.0001.

Toronto Police Service. "Project Pathfinder Nets More Arrests." http://www.torontopolice .on.ca/modules.php?op=modload&name=news&file=article&sid=1626 (accessed February 21, 2013).

Winant, Howard. "Race and Race Theory." *Annual Review of Sociology* 26, no. 1 (2000): 169–85. http://dx.doi.org/10.1146/annurev.soc.26.1.169.

six
Gendering Crime:
Men and Masculinities

RUTHANN LEE

Introduction

Let's begin our discussion of masculinities and criminalization with a quick exercise. Picture in your mind someone committing a criminal act. What was the gender of the person you imagined? Was the person racialized? When you engage in this kind of imagining, you are already implicated in representational practices; exploring how this happens is a central objective of this chapter. How are representations of masculinity and crime in popular media like Hollywood films socially constructed and historically produced through systems of power? What knowledge claims are made in Hollywood films when different men break the law and commit crime?

This chapter historicizes the meanings and representations of **masculinities** and their relationships to the criminalization process. It explores shifting representations of masculinities in Hollywood films to challenge the myths and stereotypes that surround crime and to demonstrate how popular media function as practices of governing. As we undertake our analysis, we will foreground processes of racialization because they occupy a "privileged" place in processes of representation and criminalization, and because in popular culture masculinities are always already racialized, even where the process of racialization is "unmarked" as white. We will use an intersectional and relational analysis for reading representations of masculinity and crime, because masculinities are always temporal, contingent, and contested. The concept of masculinity itself requires investigation, and we will do this by comparing two ways of understanding masculinity and crime: a **conservative analysis** versus a **feminist analysis**.

The Politics of Representation

Let's review what we mean by the politics of representation. By now you should be aware that doing an analysis of the politics of representation is more complicated than performing a simple media analysis. To analyze the politics of representation, we need to ask ourselves the following questions: Where do images come from? Who produces these images? How is meaning closed down in representation? Who is silenced in the production of images? Based on our discussion of cultural studies scholar Stuart Hall's work in Chapter Three, we can conclude that (1) all representations are produced through relations of power, (2) the purpose of power and the ambition of ideology are to fix a particular meaning to a specific set of images, and (3) representation is a site of contestation and struggle.[1]

Hall's idea that the goal of power and ideology is to fix meaning to an image suggests that media images in popular culture significantly influence how we understand and interpret our social world. To conduct a highly sophisticated analysis of these media images we need to place them within a historical, political, economic, and cultural conjuncture. An analysis of the politics of representation is crucial to challenging our assumptions about crime and criminality. Recall from Chapter Three that much of people's knowledge about crime and criminality does not come from personal experience but from mediated sources of data, including forms of popular culture like Hollywood film. As a result, our own understandings about criminality are usually filtered through external sources that provide a context and language for how we interpret our perceptions. Hollywood films thus provide a rich site for considering issues of criminalization and regulation. They are important cultural texts for examining our everyday assumptions about criminalization because they recycle and create old and new ideas about the social organization of race, class, gender, sexuality, bodies, and nations.

As noted in Chapter Five, *racialization* refers to the construction of race as a social and historical process whereby "race" is given meaning associated with the physiological or cultural characteristics of a group of people. Even though "race" as a category of identity is one that is socially constructed, the material effects of this social construction are very real. Racism systematically confers privilege to white bodies and places non-white bodies in disadvantaged positions. Thus, the everyday impacts of racism can be harmful, often violent, and painful for people of colour. However, it is important to recognize that not all racialized bodies are impacted in the same way. Racism works differently for differently racialized people.[2]

---

1 Stuart Hall, "The Work of Representation," in *Representation: Cultural Representations and Signifying Practices*, ed. Stuart Hall, 13–74 (Thousand Oaks: Sage, 1997).

2 For example, Aboriginal groups encounter unique and systematic forms of racism involving the appropriation of land and cultural genocide that are distinct from the denial of rights and privileges to other racialized groups in Canada (Bonita Lawrence and Ena Dua, "Decolonizing Anti-Racism," *Social Justice* 32, no. 4 [2005]: 120–43).

Our knowledge of who commits crime and the kinds of crime they commit is typically informed by stereotypical constructions of race found in many classic Hollywood movies. For example, think of the stereotype of the male Italian mafia boss portrayed in the 1972 film *The Godfather*, or the stereotype of violent Black male street criminals shown in "hood" films from the 1990s such as *Menace II Society* or *Boyz N the Hood*. These one-dimensional and demonizing portrayals evacuate the social and historical context in which criminalized forms of racialized masculinities are performed and produced. Exploring how this happens can be enriched by a **conjunctural analysis**, which asks nuanced questions about the nature of representations and media images. For instance, what are the economic, political, and cultural forces of a given time and place? How are representations of modern masculinity in Hollywood films tied to specific forms of national identity and ideas about citizenship?[3] What are the implications for the social organization of race, class, gender, sexualities, age, religion, nation, citizenship, and dis/ability? A conjunctural analysis helps us locate the production conditions of a film—that is, when, why, and how it was made. This, in turn, can help us figure out why and how certain representations exist. Let's now think about the representational practices of late twentieth and early twenty-first century Hollywood movies within the context of "the crisis of masculinity."

The "Problem" of Masculinity

During the late 1990s, debates about a **crisis of masculinity** emerged in popular discourses of Europe and North America. The so-called crisis of masculinity refers to the sentiment of men who felt emasculated by **second-wave feminism**, which gained momentum in the late 1960s. Rather than pinpointing changes to the global economy and the industrial manufacturing sector that occurred after World War II, many men blamed women for taking away their social and economic status. At this time, the labour market fluctuated drastically with a decline in male-occupied factory jobs and a sharp rise in service work that required the domestic skills of female workers. More than ever before, women were receiving jobs, making money, and becoming financially independent. The rising sense of emasculinization was best articulated in a now-infamous book published in 1990 by American author

---

3 The films I discuss deal with themes of race, crime, and masculinity in a US context, which is a major limitation of using Hollywood films as a site of analysis because the United States and Canada have distinct and important historical, political, economic, and cultural differences.

Robert Bly called *Iron John: A Book about Men*.[4] Using subtly misogynist and anti-feminist claims, *Iron John* characterizes an extreme social response of men under conditions of economic uncertainty, which sees women's economic advancement as a threat to traditional forms of male power and authority.

For many criminologists, the "crisis of masculinity" is highly loaded. In modern Western societies men—as opposed to women—are far more likely to commit crime. As Richard Collier points out, "the criminal justice system is quite simply dominated by men."[5] In Canada, nearly 80 per cent of accused criminals are men, and 94 per cent of the federal prison population is male.[6] Yet until recently, most contemporary scholars have rarely discussed this fact.

When critical scholars examine gender relations, the focus tends to centre on a discussion of women and the construction of femininity so that gender is equated with the categories of women and the feminine. In this way, the categories of men and the masculine seem invisible. In other words, it is easy to forget that men are gendered. This omission is a symptom of **patriarchy**, or the historically unearned privilege that systematically accrues to men and forms of masculinity. Thus, it is crucial to remember that masculinity, like femininity, is a social construction and therefore an important category of analysis for critical criminologists.[7] Moreover, since men more frequently commit crime, it seems rather obvious that criminologists should take a closer look at the concept of masculinity.

What do we mean, exactly, when we talk about *masculinity*? It can be a rather vague or imprecise term. For the past 30 years or so, critical and feminist scholars in the West have studied and tried to define the concept of masculinity in a precise way. First of all, most contemporary scholars agree that like other aspects of identity masculinities are socially constructed. For instance, critical legal scholar Richard Collier argues that "the social meaning(s) of masculinity/ies are not 'given' or 'determined' (be it by biology

---

4 Robert Bly, *Iron John: A Book about Men* (Malden: Addison-Wesley, 1990). In retaliation to the women's liberation movement, *Iron John* calls for a **mythopoetic men's movement** to liberate men from the constraints of the modern world, which keep them from being in touch with their true masculine nature, and is best known for the rituals that take place during their gatherings. Leaders of the movement believe that modernization results in the feminization of men and the loss of the "deep masculine." The movement emphasizes homosocial rites of passage that secure and sustain the indestructible hardness of manhood.

5 Richard Collier, *Masculinities, Crime and Criminology* (London: Sage Publications, 1998), 2.

6 Tina Hotton Mahoney, "Women and the Criminal Justice System," Statistics Canada, April 2011, Table 11.

7 It is important to recognize that specifically examining men and masculinity in relation to crime is not to claim that women and children do not commit crime. Nor does it indicate that female offenders are treated differently than male offenders in the criminal justice system. It also does not intend to minimize how women are usually the victims or survivors of men's crimes.

or psyche)."[8] In this way, a social constructionist view of masculinities recognizes that the meanings of masculinity shift over time and place. Put differently, critical and feminist scholars want to avoid essentialist understandings of masculinity. Essentialism refers to the belief that people or things have an underlying and unchanging "essence." It describes any statement that attempts to close off the possibility of changing human characteristics. The term *essentialism* is often used when human behaviour is explained through biological or scientific explanations and social or cultural forces are ignored. For example, the stereotypical notion that all men are aggressive and violent by nature or that all men are ruled by testosterone are essentialist ideas. Keep in mind that even though masculinities are—like the concept of race—socially constructed, there are direct, everyday, material effects associated with the lived experience of masculinity; when I refer to *the material*, I am referring to the everyday, concrete, tangible experiences of real people.

A second important point about masculinities that critical and feminist scholars agree upon is that the concept of masculinity needs to be pluralized. In other words, there is not just one form of masculinity—there are multiple definitions and ways of embodying masculinity. Further, masculinities are relational, a claim that enables critical and feminist scholars to emphasize an analysis of power relations that illuminates how different masculine subjects are unevenly and contradictorily positioned through specific historical, economic, cultural, and political processes. R.W. Connell, a well-known gender theorist who specializes in masculinity studies, helps us better understand how masculinities are relational. He argues that not all masculinities are constituted equally, and he is credited for coining the now widely used concepts of **hegemonic masculinity** and **subordinate masculinity** to explain this idea.[9] Some scholars also refer to these as *dominant masculinities* and *outlaw masculinities*, respectively.

The application of an intersectional and relational analysis reveals that masculinities are formed by and through other social relations. Recall that an intersectional analysis recognizes how individuals occupy and embody multiple social locations, subject positions, and identities.[10] It makes central

---

8 Collier, *Masculinities, Crime and Criminology*, 3.

9 Robert W. Connell and James W. Messerschmidt, "Hegemonic Masculinity: Rethinking the Concept," *Gender & Society* 19, no. 6 (2005): 829–59. Hegemony refers to a process by which ruling groups maintain dominance, convincing those they subordinate that they share the same values and interests as the ruling groups. This is accomplished through the organization of consent rather than direct forms of violence or coercion.

10 Kimberlé Crenshaw, "Mapping the Margins: Intersectionality, Identity Politics, and Violence against Women of Color," *Stanford Law Review* (1991): 1241–99; Combahee River Collective, "A Black Feminist Statement," in *This Bridge Called My Back: Radical Writings by Women of Color*, 210–18 (New York: Kitchen Table Women of Color Press, 1982).

how individuals embody and live a range of social locations and subject positions, including race, class, gender, sexualities, age, religion, citizenship, dis/ability, and so on. In this way, an intersectional analysis helps us recognize the multiplicity of our identities. It also helps explain why not all people react in exactly the same way to the same media or representation. Recall from Chapter Three that our subjective experiences and identities inform how we decode or interpret a signifying practice. Since we are all differently located within relations of power and privilege, we each have different ways of responding to images and ideas, including stereotypes of race and masculinity.

Some of the characteristics associated with hegemonic masculinity include being middle or upper class, able-bodied, white, and straight/**heterosexual**. Other dominant identity categories could be added here, such as being English speaking, university educated, and Anglo-Saxon—and you can probably think of even more categories. The characteristics of subordinate or outlaw masculinities tend to be the inverse of hegemonic masculinities—for instance, gay, **queer**, nonheterosexual, non-white, immigrant, and working class. We could also include non-English speaking, non-Protestant, and disabled.

When we recognize that masculinities are shaped by different social locations, we can develop a more complex analysis of patriarchy. We can acknowledge that even though all men benefit from a system of patriarchy in which social institutions and processes confer authority to men over women and children, not all men are positioned equally in relation to each other. Likewise, we can see that men and women can be differently positioned relative to each other, which signals the contradictory power relations between, for example, a white upper-class woman and a Black working-class man.

Finally, we can recognize that what individual men do with their power—how they enact agency—as well as how they negotiate their relative privilege is undetermined. Even though a group of men might share the same social locations, access similar opportunities, and suffer the same structural disadvantages, it is impossible to predict whether they will make the same life decisions or behave in the same way.

What Does It Mean to Be a "Real Man"?

Hegemonic or dominant forms of masculinity define what it means to be a "real man," which include the destructive characteristics described by critical criminologists Tim Newburn and Elizabeth Stanko: "In modern western patriarchal culture the dominant or hegemonic masculine form is aggressive and misogynist."[11] In the documentary *Tough Guise*, Jackson Katz, a US anti-violence educator and author, points to how aggression and misogyny permeate images of men in action films to endorse and glorify violent forms of masculinity. Katz explains that in popular films, as well as in many advertisements and television shows, the seemingly benign father of a middle-class, white, North American nuclear family embodies this idealized and normative form of masculinity.[12] Typically, this patriarchal figure is a strong and dependable breadwinner who protects his wife and children at all costs, often through violent acts. This is where misogyny is revealed: As a patriarch, the "real man" also uses violence to punish women if they betray, overstep, or disobey him. Katz documents how the idealized father figure in Western popular culture circulates within a traditional gender order. As a result, patriarchy remains naturalized and unquestioned.

The patriarchal archetype indicates that there are limited and disconcerting ways to be a "real man." This idealized form of manhood is a measuring stick against which all men are judged, and problem and criminal masculinities are evaluated against the masculine ideal. Outside this ideal of manliness and fatherhood lie suspect masculinities. These are the non-normative, subordinate, or outlaw masculinities that are inversely related to hegemonic or dominant masculinities. Suspect, subordinate, or outlaw masculinities refer to gay, nonwhite or racialized, poor, immature, immigrant, uneducated, and unmarried men, or they are a combination of these categories. These forms of masculinities are frequently discredited and oppressed. Thus, certain masculinities are privileged while others are considered deviant and troublesome.

Yet scholars of masculinity importantly point out that "racial and class disadvantages combine not only to reduce opportunities but also to heighten the salience of certain forms of manliness."[13] In this way, the idealized masculine identity is something that is always only *temporarily* accomplished. It takes a concerted amount of work and effort to produce and perform a normative or hegemonic masculine identity—in other words, hegemonic masculinities are always unstable and incomplete.

---

11 Tim Newburn and Elizabeth Anne Stanko, *Just Boys Doing Business? Men, Masculinities and Crime* (New York: Routledge, 1994), 4.

12 *Tough Guise: Violence, Media, and the Crisis in Masculinity*. DVD, dir. Sut Jhally, narr. Jackson Katz (North Hampton: Media Education Foundation, 1999). Katz's more recent work examines how an epidemic of gendered gun violence in America is linked to hegemonic masculinity and US nationalism. See Jackson Katz, "Memo to Media: Manhood, Not Guns or Mental Illness, Should Be Central in Newtown Shooting," *Huffington Post*, http://www.huffingtonpost.com/jackson-katz/men-gender-gun-violence_b_2308522.html (accessed April 29, 2013).

13 Newburn and Stanko, *Just Boys Doing Business?* 3.

Unpacking "the Crisis": Conservative and Feminist Approaches

Criminologists engage in controversial debates about the problems of masculinity and crime. Contemporary conservative scholars believe that the "crisis of masculinity" leads to the rise of broken homes, single-parent families with wayward children—and ultimately an escalation of crime. The solution, according to a conservative analysis, is to re-establish traditional gender roles and a patriarchal family system through the assertion of strong "family values." All men should aspire to be "real men," or hardworking providers and breadwinners. Consequently, men, fathers, and husbands must remain in the public sphere whereas women, mothers, and wives are relegated to the private sphere—in other words, women should stay at home and take care of children and the elderly. Most significantly, the heterosexual, nuclear family and traditional home must be protected at all costs.

In the context of the United States and Canada, "protecting the home" is a common euphemism for protecting the nation against the "Other." The "Other" might refer to terrorists, noncitizens, immigrants, refugees, or other xenophobic categories of identity. After the events of 9/11, the rise of the national security state under the Bush administration (not coincidentally coordinated under the Department of *Home*land Security) led to the growth of a more insular and isolated national culture in both the United States and Canada. This concern for national security is reflected in the numerous Hollywood war movies produced and released each year that celebrate the individual heroism of men in war. Xenophobic anxiety and preoccupations with national security are noticeable in the two Hollywood films analyzed in this chapter.

We can now contrast the conservative perspective with a feminist one. As discussed earlier, most feminist scholars view masculinity as more complicated than a singular or unitary form would suggest. Through the concept of intersectionality,[14] feminist scholars recognize that social subjects are complex

---

14 More recently, feminist and other critical scholars have used the concept of **assemblage** to counter how intersectionality theory relies on modern Western identity categories that are not necessarily applicable in all historical and geographical contexts. The concept of assemblage accounts for the ways in which categories of identity and subjectivity are constantly shifting and produced relationally. As you learned in Chapter Three, meanings are not fixed—they are unstable and fluid. Meanings are often contested, and the revisioning of representations by social movements is one of the primary means through which meanings are challenged. The concept of an assemblage recognizes that activism and solidarity movements do not need to be established through a shared identity or identity politics, and they can be temporary, ongoing, and unpredictable. In other words, assemblages are not based on concrete or stable identity formations. This enables us to consider wider possibilities for the politics of resistance in relation to the representation and regulation of crime and criminality.

and multilayered. Although feminists, like conservatives, also believe that there is a "crisis of masculinity," feminists contest the idealized construction of what it means to be a "real man" and at the same time expose and problematize how this idealized form of masculinity factors into crime. Put another way, feminists want to challenge criminology's historic failure to adequately address men's overwhelming involvement in crime—as well as the issue of men's violence against women.

It is easy to forget that the categories of masculinity and femininity are relatively recent concepts in modern Western history. Like race, the concepts of masculinity and femininity are tied to Enlightenment notions of civilization, progress, and the development of modern Western nations (see Chapter Five). Subsequently, Newburn and Stanko draw attention to the importance of keeping a historical context in mind when analyzing the relationship between masculinities and crime:

> It is crucial ... to think about the power and variety of masculine values, the processes by which they become internalized, the processes of identification, the ways in which certain core values become associated with specific social groups, together as an historical analysis of masculinities and masculine practices.[15]

Accordingly, when feminists study how meanings of masculinity and femininity shift over time, they reveal that men's and women's roles and behaviours also change significantly throughout history. In this way, feminist criminology enables us to recognize that men's disproportionate involvement in crime and violence is never absolute.

The Limits of Theorizing Masculinities

Even though an analysis of masculinities can be useful for thinking about processes of criminalization, there are some important limitations. First, the concept of masculinities is politically ambiguous. For instance, if we compare conservative and feminist approaches to analyzing crime, we observe that the concept of *masculinity* can be used to reinforce both progressive and regressive (or both left- and right-wing) political agendas.

Second, the singular concept of masculinity carries an underlying essentialism whereby men are automatically and exclusively equated with masculinity. Yet with the emergence of queer and **transgender** theory

---

15 Newburn and Stanko, *Just Boys Doing Business?* 2.

and practices, we know that masculinity can apply to men, women, and **genderqueer** people. Third, the analysis of masculinities can be conceptually inaccurate, particularly when the category of masculinities is used in a transcultural or transhistorical way. In other words, the idea that masculinities are pluralized does not address the problem of universalism, which is a process or idea that fails to consider cross-cultural differences or previous historical variation. Since the category of masculinity is a modern Western construction, as a theoretical concept masculinity is largely **ethnocentric** and **Eurocentric** with limited applications in non-Western contexts.

Exploring Race, Masculinities, and Crime in Hollywood Films

Men of colour, especially young Black men, are overrepresented in the criminal justice system.[16] This is directly related to the practices of settler colonialism, slavery, and racial segregation in both the United States and Canada. The complicated history of US anti-Black racism is thematically reflected in many Hollywood movies that both reinforce and subvert or destabilize stereotypes of Black male youth as criminals, including a now-classic genre of African American films such as *Boyz N the Hood* (1991), *Menace II Society* (1993), and *Do The Right Thing* (1989).

But how are other racialized groups of men represented in relation to crime? The films I discuss in this chapter do not feature young Black men. Instead, they focus on other young men of colour—more specifically, East Asian and South Asian men. Scholarship on race and criminalization often focuses on Blackness, which can unintentionally reinforce stereotypes about Black male criminals by neglecting a relational and intersectional understanding of racialized masculinities.[17] By critically examining the depiction of criminalized Asian men in popular culture, we can deepen our critical analysis of race, racism, and processes of racialization, which is often reduced to a Black–white **binary**, especially in a US context.[18]

Let's look more carefully at how racialized masculinities are relationally produced through the **tropes** of crime and criminality by examining

16 Kelly Welch, "Black Criminal Stereotypes and Racial Profiling," *Journal of Contemporary Criminal Justice* 23, no. 3 (2007): 276–88.

17 Scot Wortley, "Hidden Intersections: Research on Race, Crime, and Criminal Justice in Canada," *Canadian Ethnic Studies* 35, no. 3 (2003): 99–117.

18 Juan F. Perea, "The Black/White Binary Paradigm of Race: The Normal Science of American Racial Thought," *California Law Review* 85, no. 5 (1997).

two contemporary films: *Better Luck Tomorrow* and *Harold & Kumar Escape from Guantanamo Bay*. What messages do these films convey about race, masculinities, and crime? How are certain stereotypes about race, age, sexuality, and class both reinforced and subverted in various scenarios? How do power relations operate between different Asian and non-Asian characters? Although certain racial and gender stereotypes about crime might seem obvious in these films, at other moments representations of criminality are more complex, ambiguous, or contradictory. The following analysis focuses on scenes that demonstrate this complexity, contradiction, and ambiguity.

Unearned Innocence and Ambivalent Masculinities: Better Luck Tomorrow

Better Luck Tomorrow (*BLT*) is a feature-length film directed by **Asian American** director Justin Lin that premiered at the Sundance Film Festival in 2002. It is categorized as a crime/drama that highlights an almost exclusively Asian American male cast. *BLT* was initially produced as an independent film. However, after receiving rave reviews the film was picked up for mass distribution by MTV Films, a subsidiary of Paramount Pictures that is primarily aimed at a youth audience. Even though *BLT* carries a restricted rating it was successfully marketed as a "teen movie," and it was the first-ever Asian American film to be distributed by MTV Films. Within a year, the movie grossed about $3.8 million, while its production budget was estimated at only $250,000.[19] By acquiring *BLT* for Hollywood, MTV recognized a viable commercial market that targets Asian American teenagers but also appeals to a larger group of youth consumers.

Film scholar Margaret Hillenbrand suggests that *BLT* subversively and uniquely melds two popular film genres:

> *BLT*'s most obvious parodic move is to co-opt ... the teen flick and the gangster movie—and to rescript, recast and reedit them for Asian America ... By slotting Asian American men into these well-worn cinematic models of masculinity, the film gestures powerfully to the absence of any established paradigms that they can call their own.[20]

---

19 "Better Luck Tomorrow," *Box Office Mojo*, http://www.boxofficemojo.com/movies/?id =betterlucktomorrow.htm (accessed April 29, 2013).

20 Margaret Hillenbrand, "Of Myths and Men: *Better Luck Tomorrow* and the Mainstreaming of Asian American Cinema," *Cinema Journal* 47 no. 4 (2008): 64.

To illustrate, *BLT*'s promotional posters label each central character as a teenage caricature such as "the boyfriend," "the beauty," "the clown," "the muscle," "the mastermind," and "the overachiever."[21] These social archetypes make reference to conventional white American teenage stereotypes and transfer them into an Asian American context. The list signals a purposeful attempt to shift and expand mainstream imaginings of Asian American identity in popular culture. Such insertions reconfigure and complicate (albeit in limited ways) dominant understandings of Asian American teenagers by supplementing existing racial stereotypes with new ones. Recall from Chapter Three that racial stereotypes operate as knowledge claims that naturalize the white status quo and reduce people of colour to a set of narrow characteristics. *BLT* reworks the Asian American "**model minority**" stereotype—or the construction of Asians as a hardworking, law-abiding, thrifty, family-oriented, upwardly mobile, and most successfully assimilated minority group in the United States—in prominent and largely unexpected ways.

BLT's conditions of production and reception are shaped by its connections to an Asian American social movement, or a form of identity politics that is linked to the 1960's civil rights movement and the Vietnam War. Film scholar Renee Tajima explains that Asian American films have functioned historically as a cinema of opposition and criticism.[22] Since the late 1960s, a major concern of Asian American filmmakers has been to reclaim subjugated historical narratives and to present more accurate representations of Asian American identities.

Cultural theorist Richard Fung asserts that in popular culture, Asian American men are usually stereotyped as martial artists, warriors, or villains (see Figure 6.1) and have limited visibility in Hollywood films overall.[23] *BLT* responds to this historical invisibility and lack of diversity of Asian male representation in film.[24] Nonetheless, the film has generated controversy among a number of critics, mostly Asian American scholars, for its representation of

---

21 See the film poster image, available at http://www.impawards.com/2003/better_luck _tomorrow.html.

22 Renee Tajima, "Moving the Image: Asian American Independent Filmmaking 1970–1990," in *Moving the Image: Independent Asian Pacific American Media Arts*, 10–33 (1991).

23 Richard Fung, "Looking for My Penis: The Eroticized Asian in Gay Video Porn," in *How Do I Look? Queer Film and Video*, ed. Bad Object-Choices, 145–68 (Seattle: Bay Press, 1991).

24 Director Justin Lin has explicitly stated that "as an Asian American filmmaker, I wanted to make a movie that was real and non-apologetic, one that resisted the standard stories and stereotypes of recent Asian American cinema ... While the film heavily deals with identity politics, I tried to steer clear of being didactic or polemic." See "Director's Notes," *Better Luck Tomorrow*, http://www.betterlucktomorrow.com/html/index.php?id=about&ImgId=05&banid =notes (accessed July 18, 2009).

Figure 6.1 Asian male stereotype: The ninja-warrior-villain

Asian American youth. Some critics say that the movie is "irresponsible" for the way it portrays young Asian Americans. Others say it is "ground-breaking" for providing more complex representations of Asian American characters.[25] These conflicting interpretations signal the contradictory messages conveyed throughout the film concerning the politics of race, crime, and masculinity.

In brief, *BLT* features a group of Asian American high school students who live in an upper-middle-class suburb of Los Angeles. The film is voiced through the character of Ben Manibag (Parry Shen), an extremely intelligent

---

25 See Konrad Ng, "Justin Lin, Asian American Cinema and Social Media," *flowtv.org*, http://flowtv.org/2010/02/"you-offend-me-you-offend-my-family"-justin-lin-asian-american-cinema-and-social-media-konrad-ng-university-of-hawaii-at-manoa/

17 year old who is determined to graduate at the top of his class and get into the best Ivy League university. In order to diminish the pressures of academic perfection, Ben leads a double life as a perpetrator of mischief and petty crime along with his two friends, Virgil (Jason Tobin), a brilliant yet socially inept character, and Virgil's cousin Han (Sung Kang), a brawny silent type who expresses his frustrations through violence directed at Virgil. Ben, Virgil, and Han befriend another student named Daric (Roger Fan), the senior valedictorian and another archetypal overachiever and perfectionist. Daric leads the rest of the group into an increasingly dangerous set of scams that escalate from selling cheat sheets to stealing computer equipment to eventually dealing drugs and guns. The group gains notoriety as a suburban gang at their high school.

The boys' nemesis is Steve (John Cho), the boyfriend of Stephanie (Karin Anna Cheung). Stephanie is also Ben's romantic interest. Steve attends a nearby private school and embodies the ideal Asian American man: He is wealthy, academically accomplished (having been accepted to numerous Ivy League schools), conventionally attractive, and his (hetero)masculinity is affirmed by his suggested relationship with a white female classmate. When Steve asks the boys to rob his parents' house to "give them a wake-up call," the boys collectively decide to teach him a lesson. They deem Steve to be an arrogant, ungrateful, and spoiled son. However, the night of the planned confrontation with Steve spins out of control and ends with his symbolic and horrifically violent murder by the four other boys. The film's ending remains intentionally open ended and "morally ambiguous."[26] What is significant is that even though the other students are well aware of their criminal activities, the boys are never accused of or arrested for their crimes. Why might this be?

Deconstructing the Asian American "Model Minority" Stereotype

In Chapter Three we learned that an analysis of the politics of representation includes a deconstruction of stereotypes that are produced in media texts like films.[27] What stereotypes about masculinity, race, class, age, citizenship,

---

26 Lin has commented: "It was never my interest to show cause and effect, right and wrong. Instead, I wanted to be true to the characters. The morally ambiguous denouement is directly related to the moral confusion of the characters. More than that, however, it was extremely important for me to create a dialogue after the film's closing credits rather than give the viewer a traditional narrative closure. I'd much prefer the film to raise questions rather than present some sort of 'answer.'" See "Director's Notes," *Better Luck Tomorrow*, http://www.betterlucktomorrow.com/html/index.php?id=about&ImgId=05&banid=notes (accessed July 18, 2009).

27 Hall, "The Work of Representation."

and nation are at work in *BLT*? Does the double-edged "model minority" stereotype work to grant the boys an unearned innocence?

Cultural theorists such as Lisa Lowe and Aihwa Ong link the seemingly positive model minority stereotype to the historical emergence of successful capitalist states in Asia. This emergence necessitated global economic restructuring for US capital, exacerbating American anxiety about Asia. Throughout the twentieth century, the Asian immigrant was configured as an internal threat to the national body—the "**yellow peril**"—blatantly illustrated by the classification of Asian-origin immigrants as "aliens ineligible to citizenship," which was written into late nineteenth- and early twentieth-century US immigration laws.[28] However, this image more recently shifted to pose Asians as a domesticated model minority. While on the one hand Asian states are conceived of as external competitors in overseas imperial wars and in the global economy, on the other hand Asian immigrants remain an essential racialized labour force within the domestic national economy. In this way, the model minority myth establishes Asian Americans as hardworking, law-abiding, thrifty, family-oriented, education-revering people who have made it in American society and should serve as a "model" for other, less virtuous minorities, especially Blacks.[29]

BLT explicitly plays with the model minority stereotype that portrays Asian Americans as the least rebellious and most successfully assimilated racial group in the United States. For instance, the boys' parents (who are presumably first-generation Asian American immigrants) are conspicuously absent from the film, yet their influence and authority over their sons' behaviour is indicated most obviously in the boys' understanding that social mobility must be achieved through higher education and conformity. As Ben states in an early voice-over, "Our straight A's were our alibis, our passports to freedom. Going to a study group could get us out of the house until four in the morning. As long as our grades were there, we were trusted." Virgil's and Han's characters further indicate the boys' loyalty and obedience toward their parents. For example, Virgil articulates enormous fear of his father's reaction if he were to be arrested for participating in beating up another student, and Han's brusque response to Steve's plan to betray his parents through house robbery is "That dude's fucked!"

---

28 Lisa Lowe, *Immigrant Acts: On Asian American Cultural Politics* (Durham: Duke University Press, 1996); Aihwa Ong, *Flexible Citizenship: The Cultural Logics of Transnationality* (Durham: Duke University Press, 1999).

29 Claire Jean Kim and Taeku Lee, "Interracial Politics: Asian Americans and Other Communities of Color," *PS: Political Science and Politics* 24 no. 3 (2001): 631–37.

Interestingly, in the film, Daric recognizes that the model minority stereotype can work to his advantage. He crushes Ben's sense of pride at making the high school basketball team by writing a school newspaper article about affirmative action and school sports, for which he wins a journalism award. Daric tells Ben that he is the obvious "token Asian" on the team, destroying Ben's innocent belief in American meritocracy. Daric also teases Ben for working at a local fast-food restaurant and asks him to participate in a money-making scheme of selling and distributing cheat sheets to other students, drawing on their status as academic overachievers to conceal their illicit activities. In this example, the model minority stereotype inadvertently thwarts a racialized process of criminalization.

Virgil informs us that Daric lives alone in a large house. Daric's parents reside in Vancouver, reflecting what Aihwa Ong describes as an increasingly common family arrangement of flexible citizenship among affluent classes of Hong Kong professional migrants.[30] All of the main characters in *BLT* reside in an upper-middle-class suburb of Los Angeles, demonstrating the establishment of Asian communities in formerly white neighbourhoods:

> By locating themselves in white suburbs rather than in Chinatown, and by making a living not as restaurant workers but as Pacific Rim executives, well-to-do Asian newcomers breach the spatial and symbolic borders that have disciplined Asian Americans and kept them on the margins of the American nation. This "out-of-placeness" of new Asian immigrants reinforces the public anxiety over the so-called thirdworldization of the American city, a term that suggests both economic and ethno-racial heterogeneity, over which white Americans are losing control.[31]

In *BLT*, this white American suburban anxiety is reflected in a scene where the four boys arrive uninvited to a neighbourhood party. Although the boys are mocked by a racially mixed group of young men from their school (interestingly, there is another male Asian student in the group), the group is clearly led by a white student who taunts Ben's group by inquiring why they're not "at Bible study." When the white student directly targets Daric with the racist insult "Who are you trying to be? A Chinese Jordan?" making reference to professional basketball player Michael Jordan, an enraged Daric draws out a gun, which he points at the white student and the crowd

30 Ong, *Flexible Citizenship*.
31 Ong, *Flexible Citizenship*, 100.

Figure 6.2 Upper-class American suburbia

of observers. A fight ensues and the white student is left unconscious; all four of the boys participate in his beating.

It could be argued that the boys' possession of a gun functions as a phallic symbol—a compensatory device that stands in for the absence of masculine power held by Asian American men and an indication of the social capital that the boys lack. As Ong states,

> Long viewed as coolies, houseboys, and garment workers, but now upgraded to members of a law-abiding and productive model minority, each new wave of Asian immigrants has to contend with the historical construction of Asian others as politically and culturally subordinate subjects.[32]

Ong further contends that many Asian Americans seek to convert symbolic capital into cultural capital to attain higher social standing in white American society. This includes acquiring class markers, such as name-brand clothing, automobiles, real estate, art, and other kinds of property. The arrival of wealthy Asian immigrants poses challenges to white Americans'

---

32 Ibid., 101.

understanding of themselves as privileged US citizens who should take no back seat to foreigners, especially not to Asians. But as Ong asks, "will the accumulation of cultural, and not just economic, capital by these well-heeled immigrants change such nativist perceptions"?[33]

Correspondingly, in a liberal American framework the popularity of *BLT* with many American film critics and non-Asian audiences could be attributed to an easily digestible oppositional politics. Or the film's commercial success might also reflect cultural studies scholar Gina Marchetti's view on the historical function of Asian representation in Hollywood cinema:

> Hollywood used Asians, Asian Americans, and Pacific Islanders as signifiers of racial otherness to avoid the far more immediate racial tensions between Blacks and whites or the ambivalent mixture of guilt and enduring hatred toward Native Americans and Hispanics.[34]

BLT's reconfiguration of Asian American masculinity functions within a US racial hierarchy, which points to the insidious workings of the model minority myth, which

> functions ideologically to reproduce racial hierarchy in America by essentializing and homogenizing Asian American experiences, exaggerating Asian American prosperity and downplaying Asian American needs, delegitimizing black demands for social programs, and legitimating racially discriminatory arrangements ... Indeed, institutional power holders sometimes cite the model minority myth as justification for giving preferential treatment to Asian Americans over blacks. To the extent that Asian Americans themselves buy into this myth and evince feelings of superiority towards blacks, the racial hierarchy becomes that much more entrenched.[35]

BLT presents a timely opportunity to explore the political tensions among Black and Asian communities by comparing it to the related genre of African American hood films that flourished during the 1990s, which similarly

---

33 Ibid., 101.
34 Gina Marchetti, *Romance and the "Yellow Peril": Race, Sex, and Discursive Strategies in Hollywood Fiction* (Berkeley: University of California Press, 1993), 6.
35 Kim and Lee, "Interracial Politics," 634.

targeted a growing market of racialized consumer youth.[36] For instance, how might we examine *BLT* to problematize the ways in which Asian Americans are implicated in reproducing racial prejudices against other nonwhite—and specifically Black—people?[37] Given that "black–Korean conflict has been memorialized in popular films and television programs,"[38] *BLT*'s lack of Asian and Black interaction is somewhat curious. Instead, *BLT* provides a tentative exploration of some volatile and complicated issues of relationality among differently racialized diasporic groups in the United States. For example, after the fight scene the boys quickly escape from the party in Han's car. In this getaway scene, another vehicle with two racialized (possibly Latino or Filipino) young men pull up beside Han's car. Virgil (who remains oblivious to the interaction occurring with the young men in the other vehicle) maintains a run-on dialogue that presents the Asian boys' initial feelings of exhilaration and empowerment. However, when the Latino/Filipino boys make threatening gestures and flash their much larger gun at Han, Daric, and Ben, the East Asian boys are made aware of their comparatively inferior level of masculinity. Although this scene reveals the relational aspect of racialized masculinities and the constructed and performed nature of such identities, it arguably reinforces the "hyper-machismo" stereotype of Latino men. Moreover, apart from this scene, interracial or cross-racial interactions are limited to white–Asian relationships.[39]

In *BLT*, the uneasy paradox of the model minority myth is revealed in that the boys are never charged for their violent assault on the white male student at the party. At first, Ben is convinced that all four of them will be

---

36 Ella Shohat and Robert Stam remark that "any binary grid which pits Anglo Whiteness against Black/Red/Yellow others inevitably misses the complex contradictory gradations of syncretized culture." *Unthinking Eurocentrism* (London: Routledge, 1994), 237. See also Spike Lee's *Do The Right Thing* (1989), a film that "foregrounds not only the tensions but also the begrudging affinities between Italian-Americans and African-Americans. The film implicitly calls attention to how some members of recent immigrant communities have used Blacks as a kind of 'welcome mat,' as a way of affirming, through anti-Black hostility, their own insecure sense of American identity." Ibid.

37 See Jared Sexton, "Proprieties of Coalition: Blacks, Asians, and the Politics of Policing," *Critical Sociology* 36, no. 1 (2010): 87–108; Jared Sexton, "People-of-Color-Blindness: Notes on the Afterlife of Slavery," *Social Text* 28, no. 2 (2010): 31–56; Tamara K. Nopper, "Colorblind Racism and Institutional Actors' Explanations of Korean Immigrant Entrepreneurship," *Critical Sociology* 36, no. 1 (2010): 65–85.

38 Kim and Lee, "Interracial Politics," 64.

39 Indeed, as Hillenbrand declares, "crude ethnic stereotypes recur across the film. The jocks and gangbangers familiar to us from the sequence just described are White and non-White in an axiomatic, *a priori* way, with the White jock as dumb as the non-White gangbangers are thuggish. And the blonde girl with whom Steve two-times Stephanie is referred to unblinkingly in the credits as 'Steve's Barbie.'" "Of Myths and Men," 69.

caught since most of their schoolmates are aware of the incident. However, the boys are never accused of the crime. In this sense, the model minority stereotype has worked in their favour by granting them unearned innocence.

In the same way, all four boys remain quiet about Steve's murder. Ben's closing voice-over indicates his complacency about not knowing what will happen next and hopes for "better luck" in the future. His momentary sense of security, however, seems to rely on the knowledge that keeping silent will work in his favour—the boys will most likely not be suspected of murder or violence, as verified by the house party incident. Ben's moral ambivalence signals his position of privilege in relation to other racialized masculine subjects and signals an uneven process of criminalization that applies to certain Asian American men. Here we can heed Asian American scholar Oscar V. Campomanes's important claim that American race relations must be analyzed within a global and historical context of US imperialism. Campomanes reminds us that Asian American studies emerged from the anti-imperialist movements of the 1960s—specifically in opposition to the Vietnam War. As a result, critical scholars must revoke popular immigrant assimilation narratives and the Asian American model minority myth:

> We need to chart the powerful effects of these rhetorical conventions in condoning the self-erasure of U.S. imperialism and their consequences for those who were absorbed through neocolonial and postcolonial annexation: Filipinos, Hawaiians and Pacific Islanders from 1898 onward, Southeast Asian refugees in the 1970s ... This is a task that requires initiative and collaborative work among us, given the politically forbidding and logistically overwhelming aspects of the subject.[40]

On the one hand, *BLT* subverts the model minority myth by presenting its (East) Asian American male characters as reckless, flawed, and lacking in remorse for their misdeeds and brutality. On the other hand, none of the characters is suspected, accused, or arrested for their involvement in serious crimes, which include a gang beating, weapon possession, drug dealing, and murder, signalling how the model minority myth operates in perplexing ways. The newly established and noncriminalized Asian American masculinities in *BLT* depict how only certain privileged classes of Asian American groups have acquired cultural mobility and modes of visibility that are

---

40 Oscar V. Campomanes, "New Formations of Asian American Studies and the Question of US Imperialism," *Positions* 5, no. 2 (1997): 538.

Figure 6.3 Guantanamo Bay airplane

increasingly transnational in scope. But if the objectives of Asian American cultural politics remain critical and oppositional, how have newer representations of Asian American masculinities and crime shifted in the post-9/11 moment, if at all?

(Un)worthy Citizens: Post-9/11 Masculinities in Harold & Kumar Escape from Guantanamo Bay

Much like *BLT*, the Hollywood-produced comedy *Harold & Kumar Escape from Guantanamo Bay* (*H&K*) features the narrative of two young, upwardly mobile Asian American men from New Jersey.[41] The film satirically exposes the prevalence of US racism and, in so doing, challenges viewers to reconsider racial stereotypes. The main characters, Harold Lee (John Cho) and Kumar Patel (Kal Penn), are ostensibly based on the co-writers' real-life

---

41 The film was co-written and directed by white Jewish American directors John Hurwitz and Hayden Schlossberg. The distributor, New Line Cinema, is a New-York based company that started by targeting an expanding market for foreign and art films on US college campuses from the late 1960s. New Line distributed *H&K* internationally in over 14 countries. See "Harold & Kumar Escape from Guantanamo Bay," *IMDb*, http://www.imdb.com/title/tt0481536 (accessed April 29, 2013).

friends from high school and university. Harold and Kumar are best friends in their early twenties who are identified as Korean American and Indian American (in Canada, they would be identified as East Asian and South Asian, respectively). The pair attended reputable US universities and are expected by their families to enter professions—Kumar to become a medical doctor like his brother and father, and Harold to use his business degree to work his way up the corporate ladder.[42]

However, Harold and Kumar are also potheads, and the film narrative relies on drug-related humour[43] as well as controversial racial jokes and the ironic play of Asian American stereotypes. *H&K* carries an R rating for "strong crude and sexual content, graphic nudity, pervasive language and drug use," yet, like *BLT*, it targets a US—and increasingly global—market of youth consumers.

The film also deals explicitly with the politically loaded topic of Guantanamo Bay, the US detention centre located in Cuba that has held over 700 detainees on terrorist-related charges since it opened in 2002 under the Bush administration. Many of the ex-prisoners were falsely accused and tortured under major human rights violations despite international protests.[44]

In her compelling study of middle-class Asian Indian and American community groups, cultural theorist Inderpal Grewal suggests that purportedly "new" dangers and the post-9/11 War on Terror are in fact a fulfillment of neoliberal American agendas since the 1990s. Like many other scholars, Grewal draws attention to the troubling aftermath of 9/11 under the Bush administration, which dramatically increased state surveillance and racial profiling of "Muslim males, male converts to Islam, and those who 'look Muslim' or Middle Eastern at airports within the US."[45]

The terrorist stereotype is not at all new—it is related to a long history of imperialism and eighteenth- and nineteenth-century representations of Muslims as a threat to Western society. As you learned in Chapter Five, it is a form of racism referred to as **Orientalism**, a term coined by

---

42 *Escape from Guantanamo Bay* is a sequel to Hurwitz and Schlossberg's previous film *Harold & Kumar Go to White Castle* (2004, dir. Danny Leiner), which establishes Harold and Kumar as recognizable Asian American stereotypes.

43 The film is modelled after the "stoner road comedies" of the 1970s, like *Cheech and Chong*.

44 Even after prisoners were released, their home countries often refused to take them back. Former prisoners are left homeless without any formal rights to citizenship. Despite Democratic President Barack Obama's initial efforts to close the Guantanamo Bay camps and transfer the detainees in 2009, there have been continuous delays in its closure because of legal processing issues and opposition from Congress members. As of September 2012, 167 detainees remain in the Guantanamo Bay camps.

45 Inderpal Grewal, *Transnational America: Feminisms, Diasporas, Neoliberalisms* (Durham: Duke University Press, 2005), 15.

postcolonial scholar Edward Said to refer to the discursive invention of the Orient, whereby the so-called East (i.e., Middle-Eastern countries and Islamic or Arab societies) is viewed as backwards and inferior to Western European and North American societies. Eastern men are typically viewed as barbaric, savage, and inherently prone to violence. Eastern women are typically viewed as passive, silent, and in need of saving.[46] The terrorist stereotype comes from a legacy of Orientalist discourses that serve to justify ongoing US and European invasion and expansion within the Middle East. As explained in the previous chapter, colonialism, imperialism, and empire-building need to be understood not only for their accumulation of capital, but also as cultural manifestations concerning the production of Orientalist ideas and representations.

However, Grewal points out that in the current post-9/11 and neoliberal era, Asian American subjects are *contradictorily* produced in the United States through new forms of consumer citizenship. In other words, Asian Americans are a class-stratified group with unequal levels of access to cultural, political, and economic resources. Overall, Grewal's research helps contextualize the unexpected commercial success and popularity of *Harold & Kumar Escape from Guantanamo Bay*, in which the Asian American male protagonists are mistakenly identified as terrorists and noncitizens.

H&K begins with a fateful trip to Amsterdam, where Kumar tries out a "smokeless bong" in the airplane toilet. Kumar is discovered, the bong is mistaken for a bomb, and Kumar for an Arab terrorist. After attempting to explain the misunderstanding, Harold is arrested as an accomplice and the pair is placed in the custody of the Department of Homeland Security. The lead investigator is portrayed as a paranoid racist and xenophobic white male who longs to eliminate all foreign evildoers. For example, he insists on using a Korean language interpreter to interrogate Harold's parents even though they speak flawless English and declare their 40-year American citizenship. Kumar's father, depicted as an articulate medical doctor, is similarly dismissed. Unlike *BLT*, *H&K*'s audiences meet Harold and Kumar's parents, who assert their sons' innocence as "good boys" and model citizens who are incapable of crime. Despite their parental pleas, Harold and Kumar are promptly flown off to Guantanamo Bay without hope of appeal or release.

Competing stereotypes of racialized masculinities are at work in this movie. Kumar's character actively and repeatedly challenges the stereotype of the

---

46 Edward Said, *Orientalism* (New York: Vintage, 1979). This gendered stereotype of Eastern women appears to be at work in the portrayal of Kumar's mother, who never speaks in the movie.

brown man as terrorist, accusing an airport security officer of racial profiling, for example. In contrast, Harold appears to embody the model minority stereotype, pleading for innocence by claiming to be a good American
citizen. Harold is terrified of breaking the law, getting into trouble, and losing
respect among his family and peers. Throughout the film, his tentative belief
in US meritocracy is juxtaposed with Kumar's insistent skepticism and outrage
at a racially unjust government. Nonetheless, unlike the boys in *BLT*, this
Asian American duo is far less ambivalent about their status as US citizens
who are entitled to the individual protections and democratic freedoms of
America. Bolstered by their middle-class and educational privilege, Harold
and Kumar are savvy about their formal and cultural rights to US citizenship.
As such, they struggle far less with conflicts over cultural identity and issues of
belonging. By further example, Harold (who is bullied by his racist white male
co-workers) gets ultimate revenge not only by "getting the girl" at the end
of the movie, but also through his class privilege. As we learned in Chapter
Three, when we seek to execute a full interrogation of a signifying practice,
it is important to consider how privileged characters, characteristics, and perspectives are valorized and maintained. Harold and Kumar's "escape" from
Guantanamo Bay and criminality thus reflect their triumphant navigation
and reconfiguration of a mainstream American—and transnational—cultural
landscape, exemplified by their privileged access to global mobility and capital.

Heteronormative Patriots

Harold and Kumar spend much of the film establishing themselves as innocent, loyal, and worthy American citizens—patriotically defending their
rights to pleasure, freedom, and in Kumar's case excessive consumption.[47] For
instance, during their very brief stint at Guantanamo Bay, the duo encounters
a neighbouring pair of vengeful and unapologetic inmates who claim to
be genuine terrorists (albeit from an unidentified nation or organization).
When the neighbouring inmates draw attention to the global harms caused
by American imperialism, Harold and Kumar vehemently defend their
unfettered rights to US capitalist consumption (epitomized by the American

---

47 Rahul Hamid argues that "Kumar best represents this connection between pleasure and
America's freedom … For immigrants who come to this country for freedom, economic
opportunity, and a better life, Kumar's exuberance is more than just empty hedonism—it
is essential to becoming an American and realizing the country's promise. For second-
generation children like Harold and Kumar, that does not necessarily mean reaching for the
highest professional attainment, as their parents might have done, but rather it means finding
acceptance in the glorious, mediocre middle." Rahul Hamid, "Film Review: *Harold and Kumar
Escape from Guantanamo Bay*," *Cineaste* 33, no. 4 (Fall 2008): 58.

doughnut) and express their indignation and disgust at the terrorists' anti-American sentiments and lack of remorse for the 9/11 attacks.

Without a doubt, the film's farcical and deranged depiction of the Guantanamo Bay inmates, as well as its ridiculously over-the-top portrayal of a corrupt and bigoted investigator, is meant to garner sympathy for the innocent protagonists. But at a deeper level, *H&K's* apparently absurd representation of "real terrorists" dangerously resonates with homophobic, misogynist, and racist constructions of terrorist masculinities promoted through transnational media outlets:

> The depictions of masculinity most rapidly disseminated and globalized at this historical juncture are terrorist masculinities: failed and perverse, these emasculated bodies always have femininity as their reference point of malfunction, and are metonymically tied to all sorts of pathologies of the mind and body—homosexuality, incest, pedophilia, madness, and disease … the terrorist is concurrently an unfathomable, unknowable, and hysterical monstrosity, and yet one that only the exceptional capacities of the U.S. intelligence and security systems can quell.[48]

Moreover, the film's representation of "real terrorists" implies that there are actual threats to American national security that must be contained, if not exterminated. As such, the existence of Guantanamo Bay and the surveillance practices of the national security state are duly warranted. To distinguish themselves from "real terrorists," Harold and Kumar deploy what Jasbir K. Puar and Amit S. Rai describe as **heteronormative patriotism**, or a particular performance of racialized heteromasculinity that displaces queerness and deviance onto the bodies and subjectivities of pathologized, inhuman terrorist "others" while simultaneously producing docile, respectable, normative, white, and sometimes **homosexual** Western citizen subjects (see also Chapter Eight).[49] As Puar and Rai point out, the primary rationale for the War on Terror has not been to retaliate and prevent further terrorist attacks; rather, justifications have largely been based on gendered and racialized discourses that demonize the Taliban's allegedly brutal treatment of women. In this bizarre appropriation of US **liberal feminism**, this process reinscribes

48 Jasbir K. Puar, *Terrorist Assemblages: Homonationalism in Queer Times* (Durham: Duke University Press, 2007), xxiii.

49 Jasbir K. Puar and Amit S. Rai, "Monster, Terrorist, Fag: The War on Terrorism and the Production of Docile Patriots," *Social Text* 20, no. 3 (2002): 117–48.

a global imperialist and neoliberal agenda under the humanitarian guise of saving Afghan women:

> [O]n the one hand, the United States is being depicted as feminist and gay-safe by this comparison with Afghanistan, and on the other hand, the U.S. state, having experienced a castration and penetration of its capitalist masculinity, offers up narratives of emasculation as appropriate punishment for bin Laden, brown-skinned folks, and men in turbans.[50]

Puar and Rai further argue that the production of heteronormative patriots works more insidiously to "[incite] violence against queers and specifically queers of color."[51] Accordingly, there are no American homosexual people of colour to be found in *H&K*, and Harold and Kumar's heteromasculinities are resolutely affirmed through their constant (hetero)sexist banter, subtle disparagement of gays and queers, and battles for female affection.

The success of the film can in many ways be attributed to the representation of the Bush administration. Then-President George W. Bush is portrayed as a harmless, ordinary man from Texas who, like Kumar, struggles to please his father, George Bush, Sr.[52] After an accidental encounter with President Bush, during which Harold and Kumar secure a homosocial and infantilizing bond with him, the young men receive a presidential pardon. The two young men effectively establish themselves as middle-class, heterosexual citizens of the United States (with their only deviance being that they smoke pot). Harold and Kumar are politically moderate, loyal Asian Americans who merit citizenship—in contrast to anti-US, morally suspect, fundamentalist Muslim terrorists who deserve to be criminalized and punished.

Conclusion

The concept of masculinities is a complex but useful entry point for examining intersections of gender and race with processes of criminalization and the shifting and uneven ways that race, masculinity, crime, and criminality are represented in popular culture. We began this chapter by reviewing how a conjunctural analysis of the politics of representation asks us to interrogate

---

50 Ibid., 126.
51 Ibid.
52 By the end of this scene, Kumar—the suspected terrorist—actually identifies and empathizes with George W. Bush. Unsurprisingly, the US government under the Bush administration did not ban the film.

the nature of media representations by considering the economic, political, and cultural forces of a given time and place. We applied this conjunctural approach to investigate the "crisis of masculinity" that is portrayed in media and popular culture, which is of key concern to both conservative and feminist scholars of criminology.

We identified the historical conditions of production and reception for Asian American films, and we applied a feminist intersectional and relational analysis of Asian American masculinities to examine how the contemporary portrayal of criminalized Asian American masculinities in Hollywood cinema is distinct from other representations of young men, particularly Black male youth. These cinematic representations of young Asian American men simultaneously invoke and challenge Orientalist myths, yellow peril ideologies, and model minority stereotypes. They are tied to specific colonial histories, national identities, and forms of consumer citizenship. As critical viewers and consumers of popular culture, this discussion enabled us to consider how shifting ideas about race, masculinity, crime, and criminality are intimately connected to projects of nation-building, practices of governance, and global consumer capitalism. Overall, we can use this analytical opportunity to reflect on and inform our activist struggles and engagements in projects of resistance and social transformation.

Study Questions

1. What is the difference between a conservative and a feminist approach to understanding crime and criminality? How do these approaches understand the "crisis of masculinity" as it relates to crime?
2. What are "model minority" and "yellow peril" stereotypes? Historically, why and how do these stereotypes construct Asian Americans as both normative and deviant citizens? How do these stereotypes operate to criminalize certain racial groups in popular films like *Harold & Kumar Escape from Guantanamo Bay*?

Exercise

A related issue concerning Asian stereotypes and anti-Asian racism in Canada is the *Maclean's* "Too Asian?" controversy.[53] Read the original article published in 2010. What is the main debate or problem raised by the article?

---

53 See the original article at http://www.macleans.ca/news/canada/too-asian/

Discuss and compare how Asian students are represented in relation to white students and other racialized groups. Can you identify "yellow peril" and "model minority" discourses at work? How is the article also gendered? What representations of Asian masculinities are portrayed, and what purpose do they serve?

Keywords

masculinities; conservative analysis of crime; feminist analysis of crime; conjunctural analysis; second-wave feminism; crisis of masculinity; patriarchy; hegemonic masculinity; subordinate masculinity; heterosexual; queer; transgender; genderqueer; binary; Asian American; model minority; yellow peril; Orientalism; heteronormative patriotism; homosexual; liberal feminism

References

Bly, Robert. *Iron John: A Book about Men.* Malden: Addison-Wesley, 1990.

Campomanes, Oscar V. "New Formations of Asian American Studies and the Question of US Imperialism." *Positions* 5, no. 2 (1997): 523–50. http://dx.doi.org/10.1215/10679847-5-2-523.

Collier, Richard. *Masculinities, Crime and Criminology.* London: Sage Publications, 1998.

Combahee River Collective. "A Black Feminist Statement." In *This Bridge Called My Back: Radical Writings by Women of Color,* edited by Cherrie Moraga and Gloria Anzaldua, 210–18. New York: Kitchen Table Women of Color Press, 1982.

Connell, Robert W., and James W. Messerschmidt. "Hegemonic Masculinity: Rethinking the Concept." *Gender & Society* 19, no. 6 (2005): 829–59. http://dx.doi.org/10.1177/0891243205278639.

Crenshaw, Kimberlé. "Mapping the Margins: Intersectionality, Identity Politics, and Violence against Women of Color." *Stanford Law Review* 43, no. 6 (July 1991): 1241–99. http://dx.doi.org/10.2307/1229039.

Fung, Richard. "Looking for My Penis: The Eroticized Asian in Gay Video Porn." In *How Do I Look? Queer Film and Video,* edited by Bad Object-Choices, 145–68. Seattle: Bay Press, 1991.

Grewal, Inderpal. *Transnational America: Feminisms, Diasporas, Neoliberalisms.* Durham: Duke University Press, 2005. http://dx.doi.org/10.1215/9780822386544.

Hall, Stuart. "The Work of Representation." In *Representation: Cultural Representations and Signifying Practices,* edited by Stuart Hall, 13–74. Thousand Oaks: Sage, 1997.

Hamid, Rahul. "Film Review: *Harold and Kumar Escape from Guantanamo Bay.*" *Cineaste* 33, no. 4 (Fall 2008): 57–58.

Hillenbrand, Margaret. "Of Myths and Men: *Better Luck Tomorrow* and the Mainstreaming of Asian America Cinema." *Cinema Journal* 47, no. 4 (2008): 50–75. http://dx.doi.org/10.1353/cj.0.0024.

Katz, Jackson. "Memo to Media: Manhood, Not Guns or Mental Illness, Should Be Central in Newtown Shooting." *Huffington Post.* http://www.huffingtonpost.com/jackson-katz/men-gender-gun-violence_b_2308522.html (accessed April 29, 2013).

Kim, Claire Jean, and Taeku Lee. "Interracial Politics: Asian Americans and Other Communities of Color." *PS: Political Science and Politics* 24, no. 3 (2001): 631–37.

Lawrence, Bonita, and Enakshi Dua. "Decolonizing Antiracism." *Social Justice* 32, no. 4 (2005): 120–43.

Lowe, Lisa. *Immigrant Acts: On Asian American Cultural Politics.* Durham: Duke University Press, 1996.

Mahoney, Tina Hotton. "Women and the Criminal Justice System." Statistics Canada, April 2011, Table 11.

Marchetti, Gina. *Romance and the "Yellow Peril": Race, Sex, and Discursive Strategies in Hollywood Fiction.* Berkeley: University of California Press, 1993.

Newburn, Tim, and Elizabeth Anne Stanko. *Just Boys Doing Business? Men, Masculinities and Crime.* New York: Routledge, 1994.

Ng, Konrad. "Justin Lin, Asian American Cinema and Social Media." *Flowtv.org.* http://flowtv.org/2010/02/"you-offend-me-you-offend-my-family"-justin-lin-asian-american-cinema-and-social-media-konrad-ng-university-of-hawaii-at-manoa/ (accessed February 21, 2010).

Nopper, Tamara K. "Colorblind Racism and Institutional Actors' Explanations of Korean Immigrant Entrepreneurship." *Critical Sociology* 36, no. 1 (2010): 65–85. http://dx.doi.org/10.1177/0896920509347141.

Ong, Aihwa. *Flexible Citizenship: The Cultural Logics of Transnationality.* Durham: Duke University Press, 1999.

Perea, Juan F. "The Black/White Binary Paradigm of Race: The Normal Science of American Racial Thought." *California Law Review* 85, no. 5 (1997): 1213–58. http://dx.doi.org/10.2307/3481059.

Puar, Jasbir K. *Terrorist Assemblages: Homonationalism in Queer Times.* Durham: Duke University Press, 2007. http://dx.doi.org/10.1215/9780822390442.

Puar, Jasbir K., and Amit S. Rai "Monster, Terrorist, Fag: The War on Terrorism and the Production of Docile Patriots." *Social Text* 20, no. 3 (2002): 117–48.

Said, Edward. *Orientalism.* New York: Vintage, 1979.

Sexton, Jared. "Proprieties of Coalition: Blacks, Asians, and the Politics of Policing." *Critical Sociology* 36, no. 1 (2010): 87–108. http://dx.doi.org/10.1177/0896920509347142.

Sexton, Jared. "People-of-Color-Blindness: Notes on the Afterlife of Slavery." *Social Text* 28, no. 2 (2010): 31–56. http://dx.doi.org/10.1215/01642472-2009-066.

Shohat, Ella, and Robert Stam. *Unthinking Eurocentrism.* London: Routledge, 1994.

Tajima, Renee. "Moving the Image: Asian American Independent Filmmaking 1970–1990." In *Moving the Image: Independent Asian Pacific American Media Arts*, edited by Russell Leong, 10–33. Los Angeles: Asian Pacific American Media Arts, 1991.

Tough Guise: Violence, Media, and the Crisis in Masculinity. DVD. Dir. Sut Jhally, narrated by Jackson Katz. North Hampton: Media Education Foundation, 1999.

Welch, Kelly. "Black Criminal Stereotypes and Racial Profiling." *Journal of Contemporary Criminal Justice* 23, no. 3 (2007): 276–88. http://dx.doi.org/10.1177/1043986207306870.

Wortley, Scot. "Hidden Intersections: Research on Race, Crime, and Criminal Justice in Canada." *Canadian Ethnic Studies* 35, no. 3 (2003): 99–117.

seven

Women Gone Bad? Women, Criminalization, and Representation

AMANDA GLASBEEK

Introduction

As I was writing this chapter, I received an "urgent" email from my university's media department asking me to participate in a news segment for a national broadcaster on a breaking news story. The item in question was about a woman who had been charged by Toronto police with first-degree murder in a "ferocious" killing of a young man in 2012.[1] I was specifically asked to comment on the element that made this story newsworthy—namely, that the accused killer was a woman. As it turned out, I was out of the country when this request came in and was unable to comply. But the very request raises key issues about the relationship between women, crime, and representation. Had I responded, I might well have found a short way to say what this chapter seeks to explain at more length: Despite significant feminist changes over the past 40 years, it remains the case that our Western ideas of **normative femininity** are incompatible with our ideas about crime, and especially violent crime. In short, (white, middle-class, heterosexual) femininity and violence are seen as opposite ideals, so when women commit crimes of aggression, they not only violate the law but also appear to betray their gender.[2] The core argument this chapter makes is that representations of women and crime—in the media, in law, and in criminology—often teach us more about gender than they do about crime.

To understand this argument, it is important to attend to the constructions of normative femininity and to think critically about the ways in which (some) women's breach of these social codes produces public anxiety about shifting gender norms. In other words, this chapter aims to highlight and decode how and what we know about women and crime. This is done in four parts. I begin with some brief definitional issues aimed at situating

---

1 G. Slaughter, "Woman Charged with First-Degree Murder in 'Ferocious' Killing of George Fawell," *Toronto Star*, April 4, 2013.
2 Elizabeth Comack and Gillian Balfour, *The Power to Criminalize: Violence, Inequality and the Law* (Halifax: Fernwood Publishing), 61.

gender as a concept in this chapter. I then look at the long-term legacy of Lombrosian ideas on representations of women's criminalization. While much of Lombroso's criminal anthropology has been systematically debunked (see Chapter Four, for example), many of his ideas can be seen in the contemporary story that gets told about female criminalization. The third section of this chapter will look at the contemporary story, with a specific focus on the ways in which young women's violent crimes have produced a degree of social anxiety that is out of proportion to the significance of the crimes themselves. Finally, I will look at some new lines of resistance that feminists, and especially young feminists, are posing to these traditional representations of female criminalization.

Understanding Gender

As other chapters in this textbook also demonstrate with respect to other social relations such as race and sexuality, **gender** is socially constructed, historically contingent, and open to contestation. It has long been a staple observation of **feminism** that *sex* refers to our physical differences while *gender* refers to the social meanings that are attributed to those physical differences. This approach has allowed feminist scholars to trace the different meanings and differential power relations associated with being male or being female (i.e., masculinities and femininities) both across and within time and place. While there is often a tendency to conflate "gender" with "women," as if men do not have a gender, recent scholarship has begun to pay much more attention to the significance of masculinities and to the ways that men are gendered. This has been a significant development for criminology, given that men commit the overwhelming majority of crime. Chapter Six explored the relationship between masculinity, criminalization, and representation, so this chapter will focus on women and femininity.

Nonetheless, it is important to recognize that masculinities and femininities are relational—that is, they can only exist together and they define each other. Take a moment to think about how you might describe ideal portrayals of masculinity and femininity. Even if you don't live up to or even aspire to live up to these descriptions, you probably listed qualities like "strong," "powerful," and "assertive," for masculinity and "delicate," "vulnerable," and "passive" or "emotional" for femininity. Although the content of these categories may change over time, and although these qualities define no one in particular, we are all familiar with them as normative expectations that we may try to achieve, resist, or actively subvert. Scholars also describe these as "situational," meaning that we perform different aspects of our gender in front of different audiences and in different situations.[3] As Chapter Six describes in more detail, these idealized forms of gender performance are referred to as *hegemonic masculinity* and *emphasized femininity* (or what we call here *normative femininity*).[4] We may express these socially constituted gendered identities regardless of our biological qualities. Someone born with a penis may express himself as a highly emotional, vulnerable person, for example. What is important is that these gender expressions are arrayed in hierarchical and oppositional relationships to one another. Thus, not only is being strong and assertive associated with masculinity, but these are defined through their opposition to, and as more socially valuable than, the feminine qualities of vulnerability and passivity.

Increasingly, feminist scholars argue that gender is not something that we *are* so much as it is something that we *do*.[5] Scholars refer to this as embodied structured action: "The key to understanding the maintenance of existing gendered social structures is the accomplishment of gender through embodied social interaction—the doing or practicing of gender."[6] This approach further challenges any assumed relationship between our bodies and our gendered identities. As feminist anthropologist Emily Martin discovered in her famous study of biology textbooks used in medical schools, even what we think we know about our bodies may tell us more about the social constructions of ideal masculine and feminine roles than about our biology. Martin's analysis of the ways in which these textbooks described reproductive biology found that eggs were described as passive, either drifting or being transported along the fallopian tubes, while sperm were presented as active, determined, and strong in their mission to find the egg which, like Sleeping Beauty, was waiting to be rescued and kissed (or penetrated) by the heroic sperm.[7] This kind of study shows that our cultural knowledge of gender may come before our "scientific" understandings of our physiology.

Similar arguments can be made about the representations of women in criminology. Until the advent of academic feminism in the 1970s and 1980s, theories about women and crime reflected accepted ideas about and expectations of women more than they have offered empirically grounded theory

---

3 James W. Messerschmidt, *Gender, Heterosexuality and Youth Violence: The Struggle for Recognition* (Lanham, MD: Rowman and Littlefield, 2012).

4 R.W. Connell, *Masculinities* (Berkeley: University of California Press, 1995).

5 C. West and D.H. Zimmerman, "Doing Gender," *Gender and Society* 1, no. 2 (1987): 125–51.

6 James W. Messerschmidt, *Crime as Structured Action: Gender, Race, Class, and Crime in the Making* (Thousand Oaks: Sage, 1997), 40.

7 Emily Martin, "The Egg and the Sperm: How Science Has Constructed a Romance Based on Stereotypical Male-Female Roles," *Signs: Journal of Women in Culture and Society* 16, no. 3 (1991): 485–501.

and—even more important to feminist theorizing—theory grounded in the experiences of women themselves.[8] In particular, the legacy of Lombroso's ideas about "criminal women" has been profound, and these ideas have had much longer-lasting effects on criminological theory than his other contributions to criminology. As Nicole Hahn Rafter and Mary Gibson point out, this enduring influence is attributable to the fact that his theorizing was in keeping with prevailing gender ideologies:

> [T]he fundamental reason behind the continuing influence of
> Lombroso's work lay with the way it built on age-old myths about
> women's nature. ... [T]hese myths were so ubiquitous and their truths
> so seemingly obvious that criminologists, while questioning many
> other aspects of Lombroso's work, left them intact. They did not
> undergo serious questioning until the renaissance of the women's
> movement in the 1970s.[9]

Even as feminist scholars have managed to unsettle the apparent "truths" about women that had become embedded in criminology, it continues to be the case that popularly held ideas about the ostensible natures of women are important determinants in the relationship between women, criminalization, and regulation. In other words, popular, legal and criminological representations of women often intertwine.

Following Foucault's advice to attend seriously to the ways that truth-claims are productive (see Chapter One), this chapter doesn't seek to disentangle these threads to determine the "real" story about women and crime. Rather, the point here is to try to learn what this entanglement can teach us about the interaction between the representation, criminalization, and regulation of women. Drawing on a governmentality framework, it is also the argument of this chapter that the representation of female criminalization is an important technology through which the boundaries of normative femininity are made intelligible and governable. In other words, women as a group are produced and regulated by the production of knowledge about female crime. This is not the same as saying that all women are regulated in the same way or with the same consequences; as will become apparent as you read this chapter, race, class, and sexuality matter for the ways that women encounter

---

8 See Kathleen Daly and Meda Chesney-Lind, "Feminism and Criminology," in *Gendered (In)Justice: Theory and Practice in Feminist Criminology*, ed. P. Scram and B. Koons-Witt, 9–48 (Waveland Press, 2004) for a discussion of the distinction between criminologies about women and specifically *feminist* criminologies.

9 Nicole Hahn Rafter and Mary Gibson, eds., "Editors' Introduction," in *Criminal Woman, the Prostitute, and the Normal Woman*, C. Lombroso and G. Ferrero (Durham: Duke University Press, 2004), 27.

or are treated by the criminal justice system. Moreover, these differences are significant, and we need to be attentive to the intersections between axes of inequality and criminalization. Nonetheless, it is also the case that—in part through a denial of these important differences—the links between representation and criminalization are, for women, a form of regulation itself. This has implications both within but also beyond the terrain of women and crime.

Lombroso and the Construction of the "Female Offender"

Most feminist accounts begin the story of women's representation within crime and criminology with Cesare Lombroso, who is generally considered to be the key founder of modern criminology. While much can be (and has been) said about Lombroso's criminology (see, for example, Chapter Four), for feminist criminologists two things are of particular importance. First, as noted earlier, the legacy of Lombroso's theories for criminologies of women has been profound, even as his theories relating to "criminal man" were unsettled relatively quickly. Second, the place of the body in Lombroso's criminology is significant. Key to the development of modern positivist criminology was a *double entendre* centred on the body: There was, in nineteenth-century scientific thought, a focus on what we now call the social body (i.e., society) as well as a growing concern with the bodies of individuals within society. These twinned ideas were captured in the term *degeneracy*. Lombroso, a physician by training, was among those of the educated and reforming elite of the nineteenth century who saw society as a body threatened by the degenerative disease of crime; at the same time, he was part of a community who increasingly saw the body of the criminal as a sign of social dangerousness or an embodiment of degeneracy.[10] In Lombroso's words, the key to this new approach to criminology was to determine "in what manner and to what degree it is necessary for the health of society to limit the rights of delinquents."[11]

This scientific or medical model of criminality—the criminal body as diseased while crime infected the body politic—is a key defining idea of the Lombrosian project. The body became the site on which criminology operated; it became a "social text" that required scientific experts (criminologists) who would know how to read it.[12] Through these readings of

---

10 David Horn, "This Norm Which Is Not One: Reading the Female Body in Lombroso's Anthropology," in *Deviant Bodies: Critical Perspectives on Difference in Science and Popular Culture*, ed. Jennifer Terry and Jacqueline Urla, 109–28 (Bloomington: Indiana University Press, 1995).
11 As cited in Horn, "This Norm Which Is Not One," 111.
12 Ibid., 109.

bodies, Lombroso also famously declared that there was such a thing as a "born criminal." This criminal man was also atavistic—that is, an evolutionary throwback whose degeneracy threatened the social body and on whose body such signs of degeneracy would be readable. A science of bodies would thus make intelligible, or render both visible and therefore governable, the "dangerousness" that was itself the object of the new criminological project.

La donna delinquente was the first modern criminology text that aimed to apply this new science of crime to women. Co-authored by Lombroso and his son-in-law, Guglielmo Ferrero, it appeared in English as *The Female Offender* in 1895, two years after its original publication in Italian (and 16 years before an English translation of *Criminal Man*, originally published in 1876).[13] Translating the concept of the born, atavistic criminal into a theory about women, however, proved difficult. Indeed, the two men would have to engage in a remarkably "tortured logic"[14] to apply the theory of atavism, degeneracy, and embodied criminality to women. Nonetheless, it is the criminal woman who outlasted Lombroso, long after the idea of the criminal man fell under intellectual challenge.

The first problem that Lombroso and Ferrero encountered when trying to articulate a theory of criminal woman was that the theory of atavism already proposed that women, as a group, were on the less evolved stage of human development. Criminal man, Lombroso had argued, was linked by abnormal anatomy and physiology to insane persons, epileptics, and evolutionary throwbacks that included the ape, the child, the woman, prehistoric man, and the contemporary savage.[15] But, if women were already atavistic, and if criminals were atavistic, then it should follow that women were *more* criminal than men. However, women had (and still have) dramatically lower crime rates than men do. Rather than concluding that this might suggest that women were more evolved than men, Lombroso and Ferrero employed two manoeuvres to arrive at a different set of conclusions. First, they argued that women's lack of involvement in crime was proof of their inferiority because it indicated a lesser degree of variety and initiative among women, which itself was taken to be proof of a lack of evolution. Women's normality thus became a pathology.[16] Second, Lombroso and Ferrero changed the definition of crime to include a much-expanded definition of prostitution that included all forms of marriage

---

13 Rafter and Gibson, "Editors' Introduction," 4.
14 Ibid., 10.
15 See Chapter Five for an elaboration of the influence of racist colonial ideas on criminological thought and, by the same token, the influence of perceptions of crime on the development of a particular kind of colonial, "scientific" racism.
16 Horn, "This Norm Which Is Not One," 121.

in "savage" societies (reinforcing racialized colonial hierarchies) as well as any form of sexual activity outside marriage. Among women, Lombroso and Ferrero argued, criminality had almost always taken the form of prostitution: "The primitive woman was rarely a murderer, but she was always a prostitute."[17] Suddenly, the social body was full of degenerate women.

Having recategorized female criminality in these ways, Lombroso and Ferrero were then able to return to the original theories of atavism and criminal anthropology and conclude that, if most women, including female criminals, did not show obvious signs of degeneracy, prostitutes, as the quintessential female criminal, tended to show many of them (see Figure 7.1).

It still required considerable expertise to read the female body as criminal, especially in the case of prostitution, in part because the nature of the trade meant that women engaged in sex work tended to profit from a presentation of themselves as appealing. Women, therefore, masked their signs of degeneracy through clothing and makeup, which could only be revealed through scientific study and long-term signs of degeneracy. The physical signs of decay that Lombroso attributed to female offenders, such as sunken cheekbones and slack jaws, wrinkles and scars, and general lost beauty, were not considered attributable to poverty, lack of nutrition, sexually transmitted diseases, experiences of violence, or other possible occupational hazards of sex work. Rather, these were read as proof of the women's "real" nature as morally weak degenerates who were socially dangerous.

Importantly, this recasting of female criminality created a triangular scheme through which the normal woman, the female offender, and the prostitute were linked together.[18] In one corner stood the prostitute, the true or exemplary expression of female degeneration. In another corner was the born criminal, the theory that was developed for men but which, according to Lombroso and Ferrero, was exceptional in women both because of its rarity and because of women's general inferiority: "The born female criminal is, so to speak, doubly exceptional as a woman and as a criminal. For criminals are an exception among civilized people, and women are an exception among criminals. ... As a double exception, the criminal woman is consequently a monster."[19] In this formulation, to be feminine and a criminal were constructed as polar opposites. In the third corner of the triangle was the normal woman, who herself was constructed as inherently unstable: She was weak, inferior, undifferentiated, latently immoral, and always possibly a

---

17 Cesare Lombroso and Guglielmo Ferrero, *Criminal Woman, the Prostitute, and the Normal Woman,* trans. Nicole Hahn Rafter and Mary Gibson (Durham: Duke University Press, 2004), 48.

18 Horn, "This Norm Which Is Not One," 120.

19 Lombroso and Ferrero, *Criminal Woman, the Prostitute, and the Normal Woman,* 183.

Figure 7.1 Physiognomy of Russian female offenders

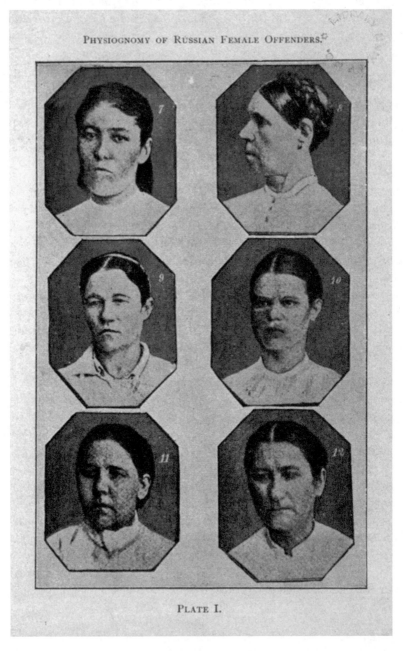

Source: Lombroso and Ferrero, *Criminal Woman, the Prostitute, and the Normal Woman.*

prostitute. The short and slippery slope from normality to criminality for women, according to Lombroso and Ferrero, could typically be held in check by maternity and sexual restraint: "[The criminal woman's] normal sister is kept in the paths of virtue by many causes, such as maternity, piety, weakness, and when these counter influences fail, and a woman commits a crime, we may conclude that her wickedness must have been so enormous before it could triumph over so many obstacles."[20]

As you can see, this theory placed all women under suspicion and as requiring constant surveillance. As David Horn has argued, "what emerged from Lombroso's studies was less the (hoped for) transparent pathology of the female offender than the barely legible *potential* dangerousness of the normal woman."[21] Arguably, this is the reason for the enduring legacy of Lombrosian theories. As the rest of this chapter will show, although Lombroso's methodological approach has been well and truly debunked, many of his core ideas about the female offender remain alive and well. Women's appearance; their race, class, and sexuality; processes of **monsterization**; and, most of all, an idealized (if never really achieved) notion of "normality" all continue to affect women's criminalization and regulation.

Contemporary Representations of Women and Crime

One need not look very far to see many of Lombroso's ideas about women in contemporary popular representations of female offenders. For example, in her study of the representation of female offenders on the reality television show *America's Most Wanted*, Lisa Bond-Maupin found that women's crimes were represented as embodied deviance, typically signalled through their sexual identities.[22] Indeed, the sexuality of women offenders was often presented as both central to their crimes and as inherently dangerous. A common representation of female offenders on *America's Most Wanted* was that they were seductive, preoccupied with sex, and sexually manipulative, and their often-male victims were unable or unwilling to resist their sexual advances. These hyper-sexualized images were also linked back to the women's (failed) performance of "normal" femininity; that is, sexual promiscuity or aggression was taken as one major sign, among others, of the women's failure to be "good" women and was linked to the urgency of their capture or to the particular heinousness of their crimes.

---

20 Ibid.
21 Horn, "This Norm Which Is Not One," 109.
22 Lisa Bond-Maupin, "'That Wasn't Even Me They Showed': Women as Criminals on *America's Most Wanted*," *Violence Against Women* 4, no. 1 (1998): 30–44.

At the same time, studies of popular representations of women and crime show that motherhood can act as a redeeming quality. Women who are mothers tend to be seen as less dangerous than those who forsake a maternal role. But motherhood is a tricky subject. Women who violate this role through the killing of family members are typically represented as monstrous. A media analysis of representations of female offenders on *Law and Order: Special Victims Unit* found that "the worst female criminals are nearly always mothers of some kind."[23] This fictional depiction of the "monstrous maternal," which "emphasizes the threat posed to men by women, particularly mothers, and [which] suggests that it is women who pose the real threat to the social order,"[24] alongside the general sexualized embodiment of deviance in other popular representations of female offenders would not have surprised Lombroso, even though they appeared roughly 100 years after the original publication of *The Female Offender*.

Similar representational themes take shape in everyday life as well. For example, in 1995 a Quebec Superior Court judge, when sentencing a woman for the second-degree murder of her husband, declared "People say, and I believe it, that when they fall, women reach a level of baseness that the most vile man couldn't reach."[25] Sylvie Frigon's historical analysis of the 28 Canadian women found guilty of killing their husbands (and condemned to death) between 1866 and 1954 illuminates the ways in which the trials relied more on constructions of femininity and the women's moral character than they did on "scientific" evidence. Women's physical appearances, their performances as mothers, and their comportment within their marriages were all taken into account in the courtroom as well as in the press: "the outcome of the trials ... and the dramatic quality of those trials are due in large part to the construction of the moral character and the history of the women concerned. The evidence ... becomes secondary."[26] In these ways, representations of femininity and the criminalization of women intertwine, often to the point of becoming indistinguishable.

In trying to understand the persistence of such themes, it is useful to begin by acknowledging that a part of the reason that women appear as anomalies in many of our understandings of crime, both popular and

23 Lisa M. Cuklanz and Sujata Moorti, "Television's 'New' Feminism: Prime-Time Representations of Women and Victimization," *Critical Studies in Media Communication* 23, no. 4 (2006): 315.

24 Ibid.

25 "Comments on Jews, Women Shock the Court," *Edmonton Journal*, December 8, 1995, A8.

26 Sylvie Frigon, "Mapping Scripts and Narratives of Women Who Kill Their Husbands in Canada, 1866–1954: Inscribing the Everyday," in *Killing Women: The Visual Culture of Gender and Violence*, ed. A. Burfoot and S. Lord (Kitchener-Waterloo: Wilfrid Laurier Press, 2006), 16.

criminological, is because female criminals have been "too few to count,"[27] both historically and into the present. That is, while women have always found themselves charged with a wide variety of criminal offences, they have rarely been proportionately represented in crime statistics. To the contrary, crime has been a decidedly masculine affair: Adult women comprise only 22 per cent of those charged with a criminal offence in Canada, and the majority of those criminal offences (65 per cent) are for nonviolent offences such as theft (32 per cent of adult women's cases), administration of justice charges (20.3 per cent), traffic violations (11.9 per cent), and other federal statute offences, such as violations of the Narcotics Control Act (10.6 per cent).[28] Women whose cases proceed to the courtroom are more likely than men to be found not guilty: in 2008–09, 59 per cent of all cases involving women ended in a guilty verdict, compared to 68 per cent of men's cases.[29] And even when found guilty, women are less likely to get a custodial sentence than men. Women constitute only 11 per cent of provincial/territorial prisoners in Canada and 6.4 per cent of the federal prison population.[30] Women, then, are a significant minority of offenders, and as a result when we think of crime or of criminals we often tend to think of men.

Women's lower rates of prosecution, conviction, and incarceration have led some to argue that women get more lenient treatment in the criminal justice system than do men simply because they are women. This is known as the **chivalry thesis**, which assumes that criminal justice officials are men who express their masculinity in part through a gentle approach to women who are in need of protection because of their inherent weakness or vulnerability. A closer look at women's patterns of criminalization, however, shows that this is not a very accurate way of explaining gender-specific crime patterns. Women's lower rates of conviction and incarceration can be explained, in large measure, by the fact that women tend to commit less serious crimes than men do and are less likely than men to appear before the courts on multiple charges.[31]

However, it is also important to disaggregate the category of "woman" to get a fuller sense of both women's contemporary criminalization patterns

---

27 Ellen Adelberg and Claudia Currie, eds., *Too Few to Count: Canadian Women in Conflict with the Law* (Vancouver: Press Gang Publishers, 1987).

28 By way of comparison, the breakdown of the top 66 per cent of men's charges is crimes against the person (24.4 per cent), crimes against property (22 per cent), and administration of justice charges (20 per cent). Tina Hotton Mahony, "Women and the Criminal Justice System," Statistics Canada, April 2011, Table 10, 26.

29 Ibid., 27.

30 Ibid., Table 11, 31.

31 Ibid.

as well as why the chivalry thesis cannot explain the outcome of women's cases. Particularly noteworthy is the high rate of imprisonment for Aboriginal women, who are even more overrepresented in prison populations than Aboriginal men. Aboriginal women constitute nearly 20 per cent of all provincial and territorial prison populations and 30 per cent of all women federal inmates, even though Aboriginal people constitute only 3.9 per cent of the Canadian population.[32] This alone suggests that not all women benefit from the "protection" of their femininity. As Elizabeth Comack and Gillian Balfour found in their research on cases involving violence before the Manitoba Court of Queen's Bench, Aboriginal women were treated much more harshly than their white counterparts, and their violence was taken to be both more serious but also less shocking than violence committed by white women.[33] More generally, both historically and into the present day there has been a consistently harsh treatment of women "who deviate from accepted standards of feminine behavior."[34] Thus, rather than chivalrous courts a complex range of **extralegal factors**, including the intersections of race, class, gender, and sexuality and the interplay between these and normative femininity, influence both criminalization and criminal court outcomes.

Troubling Contemporary Representations of Women

Clearly, there is more to the story of the gender-specific representations of women's criminalization than simply numbers. Much more interesting is the ways in which women's criminalization takes on specific sets of meanings and becomes a terrain on which a series of public conversations about proper femininity gets staged. This is especially true for young women, whose rates of crime (especially violent crime) have increased over the past two decades.[35] Indeed, the increases in young women's offending has captured an

---

32 Ibid.

33 Gillian Balfour and Elizabeth Comack, *Criminalizing Women* (Halifax: Fernwood Publishing, 2004).

34 Helen Boritch, "Gender and Criminal Court Outcomes: An Historical Analysis," in *Crime and Deviance in Canada: Historical Perspectives*, ed. C. McCormick and L. Green, 124–47 (Toronto: Canadian Scholars' Press, 2005).

35 All women's crime rates have increased over the past few decades. In 1979, women constituted 15 per cent of all criminally charged persons, compared to 22 per cent in 2009. However, young women's crime rates are three times higher than adult women's crime rates. Some of the reasons for these increases are discussed in the body of this chapter. For an excellent overview of women's criminalization rates and patterns, see Gillian Balfour, "Prostituted, Policed, and Punished: Exploring the Victimization, Criminalization, and Incarceration of Women in Canada," in *Diversity, Crime, and Justice in Canada*, ed. B. Perry, 210–29 (Toronto: Oxford University Press, 2011).

enormous amount of public attention. Movies such as *Mean Girls* (2004) as well as books with titles such as *Odd Girl Out: The Hidden Culture of Aggression in Girls*[36] (which was the basis of an Oprah Winfrey special entitled "The Hidden Culture of Aggression in Girls") and a litany of newspaper features with titles like "Girls Get Violent,"[37] "Bad Girls Go Wild,"[38] and "Violent Young Women Are Spiking the Punch"[39] are indicative of a surfeit of public conversations about "girl violence."[40]

These kinds of popular news sources tend to share some features in common. For example, most begin by citing seemingly alarming official statistics. Thus, Rebecca Fowler (reporting on British crime rates) notes that "In the past five years female violent crime has risen by 12 per cent, four times the rate among men, and offences involving women carrying out assault, robbery, murder and drug-related crimes has increased by 250 per cent since 1973."[41] Similarly, a 2005 *Newsweek* article reported that the number of American young girls arrested for aggravated assault had doubled over the past two decades, while the number of girls arrested for possession of a weapon had increased "by a whopping 125 percent."[42] A *Vancouver Sun* article noted "the number of females charged with violent crime has been increasing twice as fast over the last decade as the number of males."[43] And a newspaper from Australia reports that "according to new national crime figures women are now outpacing men in the violence stakes, with the rate of women committing assaults jumping 49 percent since the mid 1990s."[44]

Certainly, without contextualization these numbers may appear upsetting. But upon closer examination these apparently factual and statistical documentations of "a burgeoning national crisis"[45] of rising female violence are misleading. Notice, for example, that the increases are all discussed as percentage increases. This does not give us a sense of the actual number of women under discussion. For example, if no young woman was charged with a violent

---

36 Rachel Simmonds, *Odd Girl Out: The Hidden Culture of Aggression in Girls* (New York: Random Books, 2002).

37 Rebecca Fowler, "Girls Get Violent," *The Independent*, May 2, 1996.

38 Julie Scelfo, "Bad Girls Go Wild," *Newsweek* 145, no. 24 (June 13, 2005): 66–67.

39 Richard Noone and Leigh Van Den Broeke, "Violent Young Women Are Spiking the Punch," *The Daily Telegraph*, August 9, 2012.

40 For an elaborated discussion, see Jessica Ringrose, "A New Universal Mean Girl: Examining the Discursive Construction and Social Regulation of a New Feminine Pathology," *Feminism and Psychology* 16, no. 4 (2006): 405–24.

41 Fowler, "Girls Get Violent."

42 Scelfo, "Bad Girls Go Wild."

43 Cited in Amber Richelle Dean, "Locking Them Up to Keep Them 'Safe': Criminalized Girls in British Columbia" (Vancouver: Justice for Girls, 2005), 1.

44 Noone and Van Den Broeke, "Violent Young Women Are Spiking the Punch."

45 Scelfo, "Bad Girls Go Wild."

offence in one year, and two young women were so charged the following year, one could correctly assert that there had been a 200 per cent increase in female violent offending.[46] Two violent women, however, are unlikely to be understood as a "burgeoning national crisis." And indeed the numbers are small: In Canada in 2008–09, the number of cases involving a young woman charged with a violent offence was 3,528 (compared to 10,921 male youth).[47]

The overall crime statistics also need to be contextualized within larger patterns of the policing of young people more generally. Even at their highest point in the 1990s, when arrests of young people spiked in Canada before going down again after 2002, young women's and men's violent offences combined only accounted for 24 per cent of all crimes committed by youth.[48] Most of these are for common assault, the least severe violent offence and, for young women, many of these offences are committed in the context of self-defence.[49] Some critics of the "girls gone bad' thesis also point out that there has been a phenomenon known as *up-criming* over the course of the last decade, meaning that offences that previously would not have come to the attention of the police are now being reported and prosecuted. This is particularly the case for young people, for whom zero-tolerance policies on bullying has led to an increase in the number of youths charged with assault.[50]

What is interesting about the "girls gone bad" thesis, however, is not that the numbers are wrong or misleading—although they obviously are—but that the idea of "bad girls" is considered interesting and newsworthy to begin with. Another feature these types of representations have in common is that they typically open with anecdotes of a shocking event. Thus, the *Newsweek* article "Bad Girls Go Wild" opened with the following:

> When police arrived on the scene of a fatal stabbing last week ...
> they were stunned by what they saw. The victim, an 11-year-old
> girl, lay crumpled on the floor, the front of her "Dora the Explorer"
> T-shirt bloodied. The weapon, a steak knife, was in the kitchen sink.

---

46 Kim Pate, "Young Women and Violent Offences: Myths and Realities," *Canadian Woman Studies* 19, no. 1 & 2 (Spring/Summer 1998): 39–43.

47 Mahony, "Women and the Criminal Justice System," Table 10, 26. Note that this is a count of cases, not persons.

48 Dean, "Locking Them Up to Keep Them 'Safe,'" 1.

49 Ibid. The use of violence in self-defence also explains much about the increases in violent offence charges against adult women. See Elizabeth Comack, Vanessa Chopyk, and Linda Wood, "Aren't Women Violent, Too? The Gendered Nature of Violence," in *Marginality and Condemnation: An Introduction to Criminology*, 2nd ed., ed. C. Brooks and B. Schissel, 330–50 (Halifax: Fermwood Publishing, 2008).

50 Meda Chesney-Lind and Lisa Pasko, *The Female Offender: Girls, Women and Crime*, 2nd ed. (Thousand Oaks: Sage, 2004), 38.

And the perpetrator, visibly upset and clinging to her mother ... was a little girl in a ponytail, only 9 years old. A few days later, she stood in white socks and shiny black dress shoes before a judge, listening as her lawyer entered a plea of not guilty.[51]

Notice the series of juxtapositions here. On the one hand are images of "good" femininity, which is equated with innocence: the Dora T-shirt, a little girl "clinging to her mother" with a ponytail, white socks and dress shoes, and the domestic setting of the kitchen. On the other hand is the "stunning" news that these images of femininity are structured by violence: a "crumpled" victim, a steak knife, a bloodied T-shirt, and a court of law. As the empirical evidence noted above teaches us, this case is hardly representative of female youth crime in general, or even the reasons for the (temporary) spike in female violent crimes in particular. But this sensational reporting, which so clearly juxtaposes femininity and violence, does tell us a great deal about a set of concerns that traditional "girlhood" is in danger.

In case this argument about crime as a sign of endangered femininity was in doubt, the explanatory framework for this apparent upsurge in female violence offered by the same *Newsweek* article makes it clear:

> Part of this spike in violence is related to evolving sex roles. Historically, boys have received messages from the culture that connect masculinity with physical aggression, while girls received opposite messages, encouraging passivity and restraint. Now girls are barraged with images of "sheroes" ... giving them a wider range of role models and tacit permission to alter their behavior. ...The women's movement, which explicitly encourages women to assert themselves like men, has unintentionally opened the door to girls' violent behavior.[52]

A similar argument is made in the British newspaper *The Independent*: "Women's lives have been transformed by a growing sense of equality with men, yet it is as if the next generation of women are taking up some of the darkest aspects of male behaviour and making it part of their own response to their frustrations and fears."[53] In other words, the crisis of femininity that these articles bemoan is, in large measure, the fault of the women's movement.

This idea that the women's movement is responsible for female crime is not a new one. In 1975, in one of the earlier attempts to include women in

---

51 Scelfo, "Bad Girls Go Wild."
52 Ibid.
53 Fowler, "Girls Get Violent."

Figure 7.2 Woman throwing a punch (Sydney, Australia)

criminological theorizing, Freda Adler had written that "the movement for full equality has a darker side. ... In the same way that women are demanding full opportunity in the fields of legitimate endeavor, a similar number of determined women are forcing their way into the world of major crimes."[54] This is known as the **masculinization thesis**, the general assumption of which is that because of changes to gender roles women are acting more and more like men, including through participation in crime. By the same token, this theory suggests that women who do commit crimes are masculine, or masculinized. While the causal logic here is not always clear (are women who commit crimes masculinized by doing so, or are women who are more masculine more likely to commit crimes?), what is certain is that committing crime and being feminine are two different things. Interestingly, this kind of theorizing appears in different historical eras, consistent with periods during which an active women's movement has made gains in the public sphere.[55]

---

54 Freda Adler, *Sisters in Crime* (New York: Random Books, 1975), 3.

55 See Meda Chesney-Lind and Michele Eliason, "From Invisible to Incorrigible: The Demonization of Marginalized Women and Girls," *Crime, Media, Culture* 2, no. 1 (2006): 29–47. They trace this theory past the contemporary women's movement and show how it rears itself each time women have made any gains in the public sphere. Indeed, Lombroso and Ferrero wrote *La donna delinquente* in a period in which a strong women's movement existed in Italy, at least one prominent member of which was a regular visitor to the Lombroso home. Thus, Rafter and Gibson speculate that "Lombroso's home life, together with the [existence of] the women's movement, may from time to time have led [Lombroso] to view women with annoyance and even trepidation" (Rafter and Gibson, "Editors' Introduction," 13).

The idea that increases in female crime are attributable to changing gender roles is not particularly helpful in advancing our understanding of the criminalization of women. While the masculinization thesis does try to account for female crime, it does little to change the association between criminality and masculinity. To the contrary, it assumes that you can simply "add women and stir" to existing explanations of crime, as if "the same forces that propel men into violence will increasingly produce violence in girls and women once they are freed from the constraints of their gender."[56] Just as troubling, this theorization seems to suggest that constraints on women's liberation might be beneficial. After all, if female crime is blamed on the blurring of sex roles, then presumably returning to more clear gender boundaries and traditional roles would help to solve a "burgeoning" social problem.

You should be able to see that the masculinization thesis is less a verifiable theory about crime than it is a cultural message about femininity and masculinity. And it is as a cultural message that it retains its force and continues to shape popular discourses about female criminality. This has real repercussions for criminalized women: The more women deviate from ideal notions of femininity, the more likely they are to be viewed as dangerous and in need of control and restraint.

Perhaps the most explicit example of this kind of representation is the movie *Monster* (2003), which depicted the events leading to the capture, prosecution, and execution of real-life female criminal Aileen Wuornos, who was known as the first female serial killer. She was a working prostitute who killed seven men in Florida between 1989 and 1990. At the time that she committed the murders, she was also living in a romantic relationship with another woman. In other words, she was poor, a prostitute, a lesbian, and a violent offender. In the Hollywood representation of her crimes, the director, Patty Jenkins, wanted to portray Wuornos in as sympathetic a light as possible. Indeed, Jenkins's explicitly feminist approach to the subject is evident throughout the film as we, the audience, are called upon to identify and sympathize with the apparent villain of the story.

Nonetheless, there are some elements of the film that are noteworthy for a study of the links between discursive representations of femininity and our understandings of criminalization, and especially of women engaged in violent crime.[57] In particular, the film situated Wuornos's "killing spree" as having begun when she began her lesbian relationship and, in fact, plays on a flattened stereotype of the "butch" lesbian: Wuornos is portrayed as highly masculinized through her dress, movement, and speech; her physical contrast to her

---

56 Chesney-Lind and Eliason, "From Invisible to Incorrigible," 31.
57 Ibid., 37–38.

petite romantic partner; and her breadwinning role in the relationship. Thus, the killings appear as a misguided attempt to act in a traditionally masculine role of provider and protector in a same-sex relationship. The very title of the film is itself revealing: Not only does it dehumanize Wuornos, but it conforms to Lombrosian ideas about the "doubly exceptional" nature of female crime: "For a movie that is supposedly sympathetic to the horribly abused Wuornos, to name the film *Monster* is to perpetuate myths about women."[58]

Women of colour are also poorly served by the representational links between normative femininity and criminalization, especially by the discursive construction of femininity as nonviolent. Young women of colour, for example, are often portrayed as both violent and as gang members and therefore as nonfeminine.[59] And just as it seems difficult to imagine young white women as violent, so too it seems hard to situate young women of colour as victims. This is nowhere more apparent than in the tragic 1997 killing of Reena Virk, a South Asian teenager killed by other teenagers who were mostly young women and mostly white. Despite the racial differences between the victim and her perpetrators, this murder was immediately taken up by the media as an incident of "girl-on-girl" violence. To the extent that race was visible, as a South Asian person Virk was racialized, and the fact that she was not white along with other markers of her physical appearance—she was overweight, very tall for her age, and considered "plain"—were taken up as self-evident indicators of Virk's lack of fit within a community of teenagers. In other words, Virk's physical characteristics were *her* problem and offered as a part of the explanation for why she might be tormented by other female teenagers. The "girl violence" thesis was further cemented by the suggestion that the catalyst for the murderous attack on Virk had been Virk's attempts to contact the boyfriends of the other girls.[60]

What did not receive comment and thus remained invisible was the racial identity of her killers. That is, whiteness did not "mark" them as privileged in the same way that being brown marked Virk as disadvantaged. "Erasing race"[61] in this way is precisely what allowed Virk's murder to be characterized as an instance of girl violence. As Sheila Battacharya argues, this explanation "assumes all girls are horizontally positioned to each other despite differences

58 Ibid.

59 Chesney-Lind and Pasko, *The Female Offender*.

60 For a full recounting of the complex facets of this case, see Mythilli Rajiva and Sheila Batacharya, eds., *Reena Virk: Critical Perspectives on a Canadian Murder* (Toronto: Canadian Scholars' Press, 2010).

61 Yasmin Jiwani, "Erasing Race: The Story of Reena Virk," in *Violence against Women: New Canadian Perspectives*, ed. K. McKenna and J. Larkin, 441–52 (Toronto: Inanna Publications, 2002).

in power between them."[62] This construction of a "universal mean girl"[63] renders racialized acts of violence invisible and creates a self-fulfilling fantasy about a normative femininity that is endangered by "girls gone bad." Not only does this approach fail to adequately explain tragedies like the murder of Reena Virk, but it also means that women who do not meet these normative standards—lesbians (especially "butch" lesbians), women of colour, women who are overweight or "plain," and so on—are already seen as potentially suspect. The policing of female crime can often look a lot like the policing of racialized and sexualized gender roles more generally.

The refusal to acknowledge that normative femininity is violent not only ignores histories of violences committed by white women (think, for example, of slavery in the American South),[64] but it also means that when white women use violence, including lethal violence, the general reaction is one of shock that begins a desperate search for explanations that will allow us to maintain the vision of femininity as it is and to understand why some women are failing or refusing to live by its normative standards. Explanations such as the chivalry thesis, the masculinization thesis, and the "girls gone bad" thesis all reinforce a narrow definition of femininity while demonizing those women and girls who cannot or will not conform to this narrow definition. Rather than questioning normative femininity and the power structures it is situated within, women and girls themselves become the problem and their behaviours and actions are read as evidence of dangerous changes to a social order. Such representations, however, have not gone unchallenged. The final section of this chapter looks at one site where feminists have begun to change the way that crime and women's bodies are represented.

Victimization, Femininity, and Feminist Resistance

Our representational fields may not provide much discursive space for women who commit crimes, especially violent crimes, but women as victims of crime are overwhelmingly represented in both criminology and popular renderings of crime.[65] This makes sense if we understand the significance of normative femininity, with its emphases on vulnerability, passivity, and dependence. It also makes sense in terms of the changes to criminology brought

---

62 Sheila Batacharya, "Racism, 'Girl Violence,' and the Murder of Reena Virk," in *Girls' Violence: Myths and Realities*, ed. C. Adler and A. Worrall (New York: State University of New York Press, 2004), 68.

63 Ringrose, "A New Universal Mean Girl."

64 Batacharya, "Racism, 'Girl Violence,' and the Murder of Reena Virk."

65 As noted earlier in the chapter, this is especially true for white women or women who meet the criteria for normative femininity.

about through feminist interventions, which have focused largely (although by no means exclusively) on violence against women as an important area for criminological research. A focus on women's victimization also makes sense in terms of statistics: Although women and men tend to be victims of violent crime at roughly equal rates, women are the overwhelming majority (87 per cent) of victims of sexual assault, and women are much more likely than men to be victimized by someone they know. Almost half of all violent incidents involving female victims are committed by spouses or intimate partners, while another 42 per cent of violent incidents involving female victims are committed by other family members and acquaintances.[66]

Despite this clearly gendered spatialization of violence, most representations of violence against women focus on **stranger danger** in public spaces. This includes a great deal of police advice to women on how to keep safe. As Elizabeth Stanko's analysis of police advice pamphlets aimed at helping women stay safe when going out in public illustrates, such official advice includes tips telling women to walk confidently, avoid lingering at darkly lit bus stops, keep to well-lit roads, tell family and friends where you are going, keep your hands free in case you need to engage in self-defence, not drink too much alcohol or consume too many drugs that your judgment might be undermined, park in well-lit areas, and be constantly alert to your surroundings.[67] This kind of advice makes women responsible for the risk of violence against them by targeting women's behaviours and movements as potential victims, a process known as **responsibilization**. Stanko argues that these forms of advice literature and techniques of responsibilization are productive of good femininity: Good women are those who do not, for example, drink to excess, wander around the city without telling anyone where they are, or dress or carry themselves in ways that accentuate their sexuality.[68] Such forms of crime prevention are also productive of particular ideas about women's bodies, specifically that women *are* vulnerable and weak and therefore in need of protection. The awful irony of this production of femininity is that it is these very qualities that make women appear rape-able.[69]

Recently, feminists have turned these messages of responsibilization on their heads. Thus, on January 24, 2011, when a Toronto police officer told

---

66 Mahony, "Women and the Criminal Justice System," Table 1, 7.

67 Elizabeth Stanko, "Warnings to Women: Police Advice and Women's Safety in Britain," in *Crime Control and Women: Feminist Implications of Criminal Justice Policy*, ed. S. Miller, 52–71 (Thousand Oaks: Sage Publications, 1998).

68 Elizabeth Stanko, "Safety Talk: Conceptualizing Women's Risk Assessment as a Technology of the Soul," *Theoretical Criminology* 1, no. 4 (1997): 479–99.

69 Alex Campbell, "Keeping the 'Lady' Safe: The Regulation of Femininity through Crime Prevention Literature," *Critical Criminology* 13 (2005): 119–40.

Figure 7.3 SlutWalk Toronto

a group of university students who had gathered to discuss safety on their campus that "women should avoid dressing like sluts in order not to be victimized," those same women students responded by forming the organization SlutWalk. SlutWalk "began because a few people had had *enough* of victim-blaming, of slut-shaming and sexual profiling and policing."[70] SlutWalk began as a march in February 2011 and has since grown to an annual event in cities around the world, organized by women who are seeking to change the ways that violence against women is represented (see Figure 7.3).

Similar grassroots groups have emerged elsewhere with the same message. For example, in 2008 there were a series of sexual assaults in a residential neighbourhood in Edmonton that involved the rapist breaking into the homes of his victims:

> The police response to the situation was to warn women to "lock their doors and windows," while no specific information about the perpetrator was given out. The vague warnings and media sensationalism contributed to a community of fear. Women were afraid to go out at night, afraid to walk home alone, and afraid to be by themselves.[71]

---

70 SlutWalk Toronto, http://www.slutwalktoronto.com (accessed April 12, 2014). Emphasis in original.

71 Garneau Sisterhood, http://garneausisterhood.weebly.com/garneau-rapist.html (accessed February 1, 2013).

Figure 7.4 Garneau Sisterhood poster campaign

In response, a group calling itself the Garneau Sisterhood emerged and conducted a poster campaign that aimed at directly intervening in these dominant messages of female victimization and vulnerability (see Figure 7.4). Posters were crudely constructed, often hand printed, and contained messages such as "There is no such thing as an isolated attack on an individual woman. When a sister is raped, it is a rape of the sisterhood. The sisterhood is watching." Some posters invited community members to question police tactics while others challenged rape myths: "Start questioning offenders instead of survivors" and "Rape happens because of rapists." Other grassroots groups of feminists have adopted similar tactics. At York University, a group of women concerned about the number of reported sexual assaults on campus and disappointed that the responses from the police and campus security were the usual encouragements to be vigilant and aware of their surroundings decided to invert the message and to responsibilize men. One example of this was through a sticker campaign with messages like "YOU be vigilant! Don't rape!"[72]

---

72 Naoko Ikeda and Emily Rosser, "*You* Be Vigilant! Don't Rape! Reclaiming Space and Security at York University," *Canadian Woman Studies* 28, no. 1 (Fall 2009/Winter 2010): 37–43.

These feminist initiatives, many of which are being organized and sustained through the activism of young women, are direct interventions into a **rape culture** that suggests that women are responsible for the violence that occurs against them. It is significant that these new forms of resistance often come in the way of simple inversions of representations of sexual assault itself. Turning the focus away from the victims and onto the perpetrators of sexual violence brings into question the relationship between masculinity and crime rather than continuing to police femininity. This is not a direction that Lombroso would have foreseen—or likely welcomed.

Conclusion

When thinking about women, criminalization, and representation, one striking theme is the blurring of fact and fiction. Our ideas about normative femininity, the representations of female offenders and victims in fictional settings such as movies and television, and the ways in which women's crime is dealt with by the law as well as in criminological theorizing, are interwoven and indeed often inseparable. As Sylvie Frigon has noted, "representations [of offending women involved in actual crime] become cultural artefact and social norm. In fact, films, plays, documentaries, and TV shows can be charted through the blurred boundaries of fact and fiction as participating in the evolution of the characterization of women as fallen."[73] Moreover, these are age-old themes that can be linked to Lombrosian criminology, in which women were represented as monsters, as always suspect, and as in need of constant policing. One is tempted, in fact, to read Lombroso and Ferrero's text on the female offender as fiction, so rife is it with fantasies about what they seem to *hope* "normal" women are like.[74] But, as with the interpretations of the egg and the sperm, knowledge production is never objective, and perhaps the line between fact and fiction is not so clear after all.

What studying the relationship between women, criminalization, and representation can teach us, then, is less any "truths" about the particular characteristics of the female offender than it can tell us something—indeed, perhaps a lot—about dominant narratives of gender in our society. As the example of the media panic about the violent girl demonstrates, representations of women behaving in seemingly "unwomanly" ways should be treated less as observations about statistical "facts" or worrisome crime waves and more as reflections on the anxiety about shifting power relations and a nostalgic

---

73 Frigon, "Mapping Scripts and Narratives of Women Who Kill Their Husbands," 17.

74 Lombroso and Ferrero used the existence of folk tales about women's nature as part of their "evidence" for their construction of the female offender.

longing for clearer boundaries and perhaps less power for women. We must also be attentive to what these narratives tell us about race and sexuality, among other social relations, and remember that power is not evenly distributed, even among girls who may well have relatively less power than boys.

What may be most startling about these narratives of femininity and crime is their remarkable consistency over time. Indeed, we can see a contemporary version of the "girls gone bad" thesis emerging in the social anxieties that are being expressed over the relatively new phenomenon of sexting. Once again, young women (as an undifferentiated group) are being held responsible for the dangers that may result from exercising their own sexual autonomy, while simultaneously such expressions of sexual autonomy are seen as dangerous breaches of feminine codes.[75] But perhaps this example offers hope for a different ending as well. To the backlash that has accompanied the shifting gender relations that are encoded into the social meanings around sexting, feminists, especially young feminists, are responding by turning the attention away from young women and onto the rape culture that tries to appropriate women's bodies and to define them through narrow standards. Shifting the attention away from the policing of women's gendered bodies and roles and onto a critique of the dominant narratives is one significant move that can break the historical links between representations of women's criminalization and normative expectations. Perhaps even more significantly, such a move has the potential to develop a new vocabulary that is capable of enriching rather than limiting how and what we know about women and crime.

Study Questions

1. What is *normative femininity* and what is its relationship to crime?
2. What are the masculinization thesis, the chivalry thesis, and the "girls gone bad" thesis? Why are these not useful explanations for female crime?
3. How do fictional and the nonfictional stories about female crime overlap?

Exercise

Look for media representations of women accused of violent crimes. These may be factual or fictional representations. What kinds of explanations are

---

75 Lara Karaian, "Lolita Speaks: 'Sexting,' Teenage Girls and the Law," *Crime Media Culture* 8, no. 1 (April 2012): 57–73.

offered for these crimes? Are the women "monsterized"? How do other social relations such as sexuality and race figure in the representation? In what ways might these representations be said to be reflections on normative femininity? Are the interventions of groups like SlutWalk and the Garneau Sisterhood effective in changing the "story" about women and girls' criminalization?

Keywords

normative femininity; gender; feminism; monsterization; chivalry thesis; extralegal factors; masculinization thesis; stranger danger; responsibilization; rape culture

References

Adelberg, Ellen, and Claudia Currie, eds. *Too Few to Count: Canadian Women in Conflict with the Law.* Vancouver: Press Gang Publishers, 1987.

Adler, Freda. *Sisters in Crime.* New York: Random Books, 1975.

Balfour, Gillian. "Prostituted, Policed, and Punished: Exploring the Victimization, Criminalization, and Incarceration of Women in Canada." In *Diversity, Crime, and Justice in Canada,* edited by B. Perry, 210–29. Toronto: Oxford University Press, 2011.

Balfour, Gillian, and Elizabeth Comack. *Criminalizing Women.* Halifax: Fernwood Publishing, 2004.

Battacharya, Sheila. "Racism, 'Girl Violence,' and the Murder of Reena Virk." In *Girls' Violence: Myths and Realities,* edited by C. Adler and A. Worrall, 61–80. New York: State University of New York Press, 2004.

Bond-Maupin, Lisa. "'That Wasn't Even Me They Showed': Women as Criminals on *America's Most Wanted.*" *Violence Against Women* 4, no. 1 (1998): 30–44. http://dx.doi.org/10.1177/1077801298004001003.

Boritch, Helen. "Gender and Criminal Court Outcomes: An Historical Analysis." In *Crime and Deviance in Canada: Historical Perspectives,* edited by C. McCormick and L. Green, 124–47. Toronto: Canadian Scholars' Press, 2005.

Campbell, Alex. "Keeping the 'Lady' Safe: The Regulation of Femininity through Crime Prevention Literature." *Critical Criminology* 13, no. 2 (2005): 119–40. http://dx.doi.org/10.1007/s10612-005-2390-z.

Chesney-Lind, Meda, and Michele Eliason. "From Invisible to Incorrigible: The Demonization of Marginalized Women and Girls." *Crime, Media, Culture* 2, no. 1 (2006): 29–47. http://dx.doi.org/10.1177/1741659006061709.

Chesney-Lind, Meda, and Lisa Pasko. *The Female Offender: Girls, Women and Crime.* 2nd ed. Thousand Oaks: Sage, 2004. http://dx.doi.org/10.4135/9781452232157

Comack, Elizabeth, and Gillian Balfour. *The Power to Criminalize: Violence, Inequality and the Law.* Halifax: Fernwood Publishing, 2004.

Comack, Elizabeth, Vanessa Chopyk, and Linda Wood. "Aren't Women Violent, Too? The Gendered Nature of Violence." In *Marginality and Condemnation: An Introduction to Criminology,* 2nd ed., edited by C. Brooks and B. Schissel, 330–50. Halifax: Fernwood Publishing, 2008.

Connell, R.W. *Masculinities.* Berkeley: University of California Press, 1995.

Cuklanz, Lisa M., and Sujata Moorti. "Television's 'New' Feminism: Prime-Time Representations of Women and Victimization." *Critical Studies in Media Communication* 23, no. 4 (2006): 302–21. http://dx.doi.org/10.1080/07393180600933121.

Daly, Kathleen, and Meda Chesney-Lind. "Feminism and Criminology." In *Gendered (In)Justice: Theory and Practice in Feminist Criminology*, edited by P. Scram and B. Koons-Witt, 9–48. Long Grove, IL: Waveland Press, 2004.

Dean, Amber Richelle. *Locking Them Up to Keep Them 'Safe': Criminalized Girls in British Columbia*. Vancouver: Justice for Girls, 2005.

Fowler, Rebecca. "Girls Get Violent." *The Independent*, May 2, 1996.

Frigon, Sylvie. "Mapping Scripts and Narratives of Women Who Kill Their Husbands in Canada, 1866–1954: Inscribing the Everyday." In *Killing Women: The Visual Culture of Gender and Violence*, edited by A. Burfoot and S. Lord, 3–20. Kitchener-Waterloo: Wilfrid Laurier Press, 2006.

Garneau Sisterhood. http://garneausisterhood.weebly.com/garneau-rapist.html (accessed February 1, 2013).

Horn, David. "This Norm Which Is Not One: Reading the Female Body in Lombroso's Anthropology." In *Deviant Bodies: Critical Perspectives on Difference in Science and Popular Culture*, edited by Jennifer Terry and Jacqueline Urla, 109–28. Bloomington: Indiana University Press, 1995.

Ikeda, Naoko, and Emily Rosser, "*You* Be Vigilant! Don't Rape! Reclaiming Space and Security at York University." *Canadian Woman Studies* 28, no. 1 (Fall 2009/Winter 2010): 37–43.

Jiwani, Yasmin. "Erasing Race: The Story of Reena Virk." In *Violence against Women: New Canadian Perspectives*, edited by K. McKenna and J. Larkin, 441–52. Toronto: Inanna Publications, 2002.

Karaian, Lara. "Lolita Speaks: 'Sexting,' Teenage Girls and the Law." *Crime, Media, Culture* 8, no. 1 (April 2012): 57–73. http://dx.doi.org/10.1177/1741659011429868.

Lombroso, Cesare, and Ferrero Guglielmo. *Criminal Woman, the Prostitute, and the Normal Woman*, translated and introduced by N.H. Rafter and M. Gibson. Durham: Duke University Press, 2004.

Mahony, Tina Hotton, "Women and the Criminal Justice System." Statistics Canada. April 2011.

Martin, Emily. "The Egg and the Sperm: How Science Has Constructed a Romance Based on Stereotypical Male-Female Roles." *Signs* 16, no. 3 (1991): 485–501. http://dx.doi.org/10.1086/494680.

Messerschimdt, James W. *Gender, Heterosexuality and Youth Violence: The Struggle for Recognition*. Lanham, MD: Rowman and Littlefield, 2012.

Messerschmidt, James W. *Crime as Structured Action: Gender, Race, Class, and Crime in the Making*. Thousand Oaks: Sage, 1997.

Noone, Richard, and Leigh Van Den Broeke. "Violent Young Women Are Spiking the Punch." *The Daily Telegraph*, August 9, 2012.

Pate, Kim. "Young Women and Violent Offences: Myths and Realities," *Canadian Woman Studies* 19, no. 1 & 2 (Spring/Summer 1998): 39–43.

Rafter, Nicole Hahn, and Mary Gibson. "Editors' Introduction." In *Criminal Woman, the Prostitute, and the Normal Woman*, C. Lombroso and G. Ferrero, 4–31. Durham: Duke University Press, 2004.

Rajiva, Mythilli, and Sheila Batacharya, eds. *Reena Virk: Critical Perspectives on a Canadian Murder*. Toronto: Canadian Scholars' Press, 2010.

Ringrose, Jessica. "A New Universal Mean Girl: Examining the Discursive Construction and Social Regulation of a New Feminine Pathology." *Feminism & Psychology* 16, no. 4 (2006): 405–24. http://dx.doi.org/10.1177/0959353506068747.

Scelfo, Julie. "Bad Girls Go Wild." *Newsweek* 145, no. 24 (June 13, 2005): 66–67.

Simmonds, Rachel. *Odd Girl Out: The Hidden Culture of Aggression in Girls*. New York: Random Books, 2002.

Slaughter, G. "Woman Charged with First-Degree Murder in 'Ferocious' Killing of George Fawell." *Toronto Star*, April 4, 2013.

SlutWalk Toronto. http://www.slutwalktoronto.com/ (accessed April 12, 2014).

Stanko, Elizabeth. "Warnings to Women: Police Advice and Women's Safety in Britain." In *Crime Control and Women: Feminist Implications of Criminal Justice Policy*, edited by S. Miller, 52–71. Thousand Oaks: Sage Publications, 1998. http://dx.doi.org/10.4135/9781452243207.n4.

Stanko, Elizabeth. "Safety Talk: Conceptualizing Women's Risk Assessment as Technology of the Soul." *Theoretical Criminology* 1, no. 4 (1997): 479–99. http://dx.doi.org/10.1177/1362480697001004004.

West, C., and D.H. Zimmerman. "Doing Gender." *Gender & Society* 1, no. 2 (1987): 125–51. http://dx.doi.org/10.1177/0891243287001002002.

eight
Sexual Regulation: Sexing Governmentality; Governing Sex

DEBORAH BROCK

Introduction

What do you think about when you think about sex? For the purposes of this chapter, we want to shift your thinking away from your immediate bodily desires, pleasures, and fears to the somewhat abstract realm of social thought, although we will periodically ask you to "check in" with your own imagination and corporeal existence. As we undertake this process, you will find that in studies of sexuality, thinking about sex is typically not very sexy, although it does provide a particularly fascinating lens for explorations of social life. The approach that we will take to the study of sexual regulation is the governmentality approach first developed by Michel Foucault (see Chapter One). Many sexuality scholars have been drawn to a Foucauldian and governmentality approach for its ability to explore how the dynamic relation between power and knowledge shapes our beliefs, feelings, identities, and actions as well as the broader social context in which we live. You will find that the most common form of sexual regulation in the West today is **self-governance**, through the impetus to be healthy, responsible, self-managing, skilled, open-minded, empowered, self-actualizing, ethical, legal, patriotic, and ... fulfilled. Like it or not, sex is indeed complicated.

This chapter will begin by introducing the conceptual and analytic framework for our inquiry, then discuss the significance of juridical power, legal and philosophical discourses, material conditions, and social movements for studies of sexual regulation. Next, you will be asked to think about how certain claims about normality and abnormality figure into the regulation of sex. We can then explore in more detail how Foucault's work on the history of sexuality has transformed the way in which sexual regulation is understood, and how it has introduced a relatively new approach that explores the government of sex. Finally, you will become acquainted with several significant examples of contemporary sexual governance: sexualization and racialization, homonormativity and homonationalism, and the regendering of commercial sex.

First, let's establish what is meant by *sex*. **Sex** is commonly used in two ways. The first refers to the labels of female or male that are assigned to bodies on the basis of their anatomical characteristics. Sex, in this respect, corresponds to **gender**, expressed in the labels of "woman" and "man," and the social meanings assigned to those labels. As Chapter Seven also pointed out, critical gender theorists believe that the social meanings given to gender shape our understanding of anatomical sex differences, rather than the reverse relation that is assumed in more conventional analyses.

The second common use of sex refers to erotic practices. Since the late nineteenth century, sexual practices have come to be regarded as establishing the basis of **sexual identity** and how people are to be treated on the basis of that identity. **Sexuality** refers to the representation and social meaning that is accorded to sexual practices and identities. Sexuality is commonly regarded as a core element of identity (how people should be known and understood) and as rooted in biologically based determinants. Our task here is to move beyond this **essentialism** and unpack the social meanings assigned to sex, sexuality, and sexual identity.[1] In the process, we will find that the concept of *sex* groups together as an "artificial unity," according to Michel Foucault, "anatomical elements, biological functions, conducts, sensations, and pleasures" and attributes to them a shared meaning and a shared causality. This unitary view assumes that the physical and psychological experiences of sex together drive much of human behaviour, and that sex is something requiring detailed investigation to expose its secrets.[2]

What should be particularly clear is that sexual meaning is enmeshed in a complex nexus of power and that sexual expression is often the target of specific regulatory practices. For example, sex is an area of social, religious, ethical, medical, and political concern and a preoccupation of numerous social movements. Sex has been surrounded by taboo and secrecy, yet discussed endlessly. Digging deeply into the character of a person's sexuality has become a means of uncovering the "truth" about the person. The heterosexual, homosexual, pervert, delinquent, slut, sex addict, nymphomaniac, frigid woman, swinger, exhibitionist—these are all taken to describe what already exists in the character of a person. Following from Foucault, sexuality theorists now contend that naming people in this way is mutually constitutive of the person and the sexual meaning being ascribed to the person. It is suggestive of how that person and those actions should be known and treated.

---

1 More fulsome explanations of these concepts are provided in the glossary. In this chapter, *sex* serves as a short form for erotic practices, and the precise meaning will be determined by the context in which the concept is used.

2 Michel Foucault, *The History of Sexuality*, vol. 1, *An Introduction*, trans. Robert Hurley (New York: Vintage, 1978), 154.

The construction of social categories such as gender and race works in the same way. For example, claiming certain "truths" about sex is often akin to attributing appropriate forms of conduct to women and men. In other words, **truth-claims** can construct gender through ascribing what it means to be a woman or a man. Or truth-claims can construct the meanings of race by ascribing certain social, intellectual, sexual, and other attributes to "raced" bodies.

This suggests that when we are talking about sex, we are often really talking about something else. For example, for feminists sexual assault is a practice of patriarchal violence rather than erotic gratification. Patriarchal actions may simultaneously be informed by racist assumptions about racialized women or by a denigration of women because of their perceived economic class. For anti-racist scholarship, the sexualization of nonwhite bodies is simultaneously, if not primarily, a practice of racialization. These are good examples of what is meant by "mutually constitutive," as here we see how the meaning of sexuality is created interdependent with the meaning of race or class. We can also see how these processes work together to create **stereotypes** that justify social inequality.

Even when we conceive of sex narrowly as something related to erotic desire, sex gets complicated. It can be associated with the fear of an unwanted pregnancy or of a sexually transmitted infection. It can be experienced as a threat or a violation if it is unwanted. Sex can be synonymous with the excitement of desire and with delight in the pleasures of the body of another. Or it can invoke shame for our unruly and persistent desires. Sex, then, is a locus of both pleasure and danger.[3] It is personal, political, and inextricable from power. We will highlight just some of these dimensions in the coming pages as we unpack the complex and multifaceted character of the government of sex.

By this point in the book you will be well aware that not all regulation is juridical and legal and that it does not only involve prohibitions, constraints, and controls. This is why many scholars explore sexual regulation using a governmentality approach. Let's begin with an engagement with sociolegal relations, then move on to thinking about how these are implicated in the shifting meanings of the normal and the abnormal as we build our case for a governmental approach.

---

3 Several important early texts that engage with these dynamics are Carol Vance, ed., *Pleasure and Danger: Exploring Female Sexuality* (London: Routledge and Kegan Paul, 1984); Rosalind Coward, *Powers of Desire* (London: Paladin Books, 1984); Mariana Valverde, *Sex, Power and Pleasure* (Toronto: Women's Press, 1985).

What Does Law Have to Do with It?

Before you began this chapter, you may have anticipated reading a lot about the character, incidence, and prevalence of sex-related crime, given the pervasiveness of accounts of sex crimes in North American popular culture and in the news. It should be clear by now that we are taking quite a different approach to sexual regulation. However, this is a good point to think again about the politics of representation, because the images and ideas about sex and sexuality, criminogenic contexts, and victims and perpetrators that are already in your mind will have established an a priori framework for your reading. How do you "know" what you "know" about sex, and particularly the connection between sex and crime? Where do those images and ideas come from? Other chapters in this book have engaged directly with popular cultural forms like Hollywood movies. Try now applying that kind of analysis to the subject of sex and crime.[4]

Relatedly, you may have anticipated reading more than you will about specific laws that regulate sexuality. Indeed, there may be no other area of human activity as highly regulated as sexual expression, including bodily erotic practices (sex acts), textual practices such as producing images and writing about sex, communicating through the mail or on the Internet, or shipping sexually explicit texts across borders. The statutes of the Criminal Code of Canada provides a rather lengthy **taxonomy** of prohibitions addressing what can and cannot be done sexually by whom and with whom. Some of the most well known are provisions regulating sexual assault, sexual offences against children, prostitution, pornography, and sex in public places, although there is a plethora of less well-known statutes. The history of these statutes is grounded in morals-based claims about appropriate and inappropriate forms of conduct and suggests that legal expectations were organized to uphold certain gender, age, race, and class relations of their time.[5]

We could assume from these statutes that sexual regulation is largely negative and prohibitive in character. Indeed, the history of sexual regulation in the West is strongly linked to the dominance of a conservative perspective on sexuality, through which sexuality is regarded as largely a negative disruptive force that needs to be repressed and regulated lest people fall into

---

4 You can also explore the scholarly work of Ummni Khan, who wrote Chapter Three: The Politics of Representation. Her publications include "Putting a Dominatrix in Her Place," *Canadian Journal of Women and the Law* 21, no. 1 (2009): 143–76; "A Woman's Right to Be Spanked: Testing the Limits of Tolerance of S/M in the Socio-Legal Imaginary," *Law & Sexuality: A Review of Lesbian, Gay, Bisexual and Transgender Legal Issues* 18, no. 1 (2009): 79–120.

5 Part Five of the Code still refers to "Sexual Offences, Public Morals, and Disorderly Conduct."

moral danger. For religious conservatives, the primary purpose of sexuality is reproduction, and the proper context for sexuality is between differently sexed (female and male) married partners in the heterosexual, monogamous family. In contrast, the liberal perspective suggests that sex between consenting adults that does not cause harm is essentially a private matter, although some limited forms of public sexual expression will also be tolerated. What goes on between consenting adults in private is not the law's business.[6] Keep in mind, though, that neither perspective is "pure" in that each will contain elements of the other. More particularly, people's often-idiosyncratic belief systems do not rigidly correspond to a particular theory or philosophy.

The rising influence of liberalism over the course of the twentieth century occurred in a context of significant social and economic changes. These included the shift from rural to urban industrial economies and the increased size, complexity, and anonymity of urban centres. The implications for social life were vast. Notably for our analysis, this made possible the formation of distinct sexual and other subcultures based on shared collective identities and the formation of social movements demanding greater sexual freedoms. It is not surprising that the social movements of the 1960s and early 1970s, even where they were premised on radical political agendas for social transformation, owe part of their success to the rise of liberalism, which created some (however limited) political space for people to challenge the prevailing conservative moral order.[7]

Most recognizably, social movements have sought greater freedoms through law reform. On some sex-related issues, social movements demanded more regulation (including rape, sexual assault and abuse, and other gender-based violence) and on other issues less regulation (including successful political struggles to decriminalize homosexuality and abortion) while still others (most notably, pornography and prostitution) remained highly contested within and between social movements. The scale of legal change in Canada provides a worthy example of the impact of these political struggles because they have shifted public and political discourse about the appropriate role of law in the regulation of sex. For example, legal scholar Elaine Craig's study of public law has identified some important changes in the Supreme Court of Canada's approach to sexuality-related issues.[8]

---

6 The conservative perspective contrasts even more sharply with libertarianism, which claims that there should be as few social and legal constraints on an individual's right to sexual expression as possible.

7 It can also be argued that the rise of liberalism owes much to the articulation of more radical demands of the left and the labour movement, in the context of which liberal social reform provided a hegemonic alternative.

8 Elaine Craig, *Troubling Sex: Towards a Legal Theory of Sexual Integrity* (Vancouver: UBC Press, 2012).

These changes indicate how court decisions are influenced by the prevailing social ethos of their times.

The first change entails a reordering of legal interpretations of what constitutes nonconsensual sex and a corresponding shift in regulatory approaches. This includes significant changes to the Criminal Code, such as the replacement of rape with sexual assault provisions in 1983, somewhat more recognition of sexual assault victims' right to privacy, changes to evidence law affecting victims of sexual assault, changes to the age of consent, and an expansion of legislation covering the sexual abuse of children.

The second change involves the relationship between law reform and **homonormativity** (the adoption of mainstream values and beliefs by LGBTQ individuals to assimilate and achieve acceptance), including an expansion of anti-discrimination law concerning sexual orientation, legal rights and recognitions for same-gender couples, and accompanying changes to family law.

The third change is the replacement of morality-based reasoning with harm-based reasoning in the regulation of sexual expression. This includes changes to the regulation of indecency and pornography. Mariana Valverde's research finds that this shift has also occurred in legal decisions about prostitution. While the moralization of sex work has not disappeared, courts must now focus on harm-based claims—for example, that street solicitation by sex workers is a public nuisance.[9]

Social movements have been instrumental in shifting public opinion and culture, thereby making law reform imaginable, and in providing the conditions of possibility for legal judgments. Sexuality is, as Elaine Craig finds, "constituted through the norms, social practices, relationships, and discursive regimes that describe and regulate it,"[10] yet law must simultaneously use these same social conditions to judge that which is constituted. This tension is inescapable because law itself has become a governmental technology. This can be attributed, above all, to processes of **normalization**, something that Foucault considered to be among the most effective means of regulation in contemporary Western societies. This does not mean that the juridical system of law has become less important (indeed we have seen a proliferation of legal specifications, strategies, and techniques), but rather that

> the law operates more and more as a norm, and ... the judicial
> system is increasingly incorporated into a continuum of apparatuses

---

9 Mariana Valverde, "The Harms of Sex and the Risks of Breasts: Obscenity and Indecency in Canadian Law," *Social and Legal Studies* 8, no. 2 (June 1999): 181–97.
10 Craig, *Troubling Sex*, 9.

(medical, administrative, and so on) whose functions are for the most part regulatory. A normalizing society is the historical outcome of a technology of power centred on life.[11]

Law is now interdependent with an array of disciplines, such as medicine, the psy disciplines (including psychology, psychiatry, and related approaches aimed at understanding and treating the mind), and criminology. These comprise the governmental technologies that together organize social life[12] through the exercise of what Foucault referred to as **biopower**, a concept that you first read about in Chapter One. In *The History of Sexuality, Volume 1*, Foucault introduced a particular notion of biopower[13] as a set of social processes that take two main forms. First, the disciplining of the body through penetrating and shaping our very sense of ourselves, and second, intervention into the life of the population as an entirety (e.g., the statistical measurement of births, deaths, and illnesses) through the development of knowledge and techniques to administer populations for "the calculated management of life."[14] These two forms of biopower meet in sexuality, which Foucault referred to as an "an especially dense transfer point for relations of power."[15] By the conclusion of this chapter, you should be able to summarize why Foucault could make such a statement. However, you should not lose sight of the privileged place that the making of law, its administration, and enforcement hold as techniques of biopower in the regulation of sex.

The Normal and the Abnormal

What does it mean to be normal? Stop and think about this for a minute before reading on. In the course of answering this question, did you also think about what it means to be *not* normal? Likely you did, because it is difficult to understand the meaning of one without the other. This is because

---

11 Foucault, *The History of Sexuality*, 144.

12 Nikolas Rose and Mariana Valverde have argued that we must similarly examine the "legal complex": "As an example, it is now commonplace to ask how 'the law' regulates 'sexuality.' But we would prefer to ask how does a particular problem—say that of homosexual relations or prostitution—come to emerge as a target for government, and what role is played by legal institutions, functionaries and calculations in this? Hence, to investigate the legal complex from the perspective of government is to analyse the role of legal mechanisms, legal arenas, legal functionaries, legal forms of reasoning and so on in strategies of regulation." Nikolas Rose and Mariana Valverde, "Governed by Law?" *Social and Legal Studies* 7, no. 4 (1998): 541–51.

13 Foucault employed the concept of biopower in different ways throughout his scholarly career. For example, in *The Birth of Biopolitics* he treated it as synonymous with biopolitical power and closely tied to the activities of the nation-state. See Michel Foucault, *The Birth of Biopolitics: Lectures at the Collège de France, 1978–1979* (New York: Palgrave MacMillan, 2008).

14 Foucault, *The History of Sexuality*, vol. 1, 140.

15 Ibid., 103.

the ideas of normality and its opposites are co-constituted—each can only occur and only make sense in the context of the other. They were, quite literally, made for one another.

When you think about sexual regulation in this way, the first idea that might come to mind is the control of **deviance** and only then what it means to be *normal*. Deviance is not simply a matter of people acting badly. Rather, deviance is constituted through the definition and regulation of difference through identifying, naming, and judging behaviours, identities, ideas, appearances, and so on as violations of social norms, rules, or laws. Certainly studies of sexual regulation convey a fascination with the rule breakers: the pervert, the prostitute, the criminal sexual psychopath, the pornographer, or the pedophile. Some of these studies reaffirm (whether intentionally or unintentionally) the marginality of deviant identities and practices, while others (such as the perspective that prostitution is a form of work that bears marked similarities to other forms of labour) challenge rather than reinscribe the notion of deviance. Notions of the *abnormal* overlap with the deviant and function in similar ways. Foucault suggested that we think about the constitution of the abnormal as regulatory practice so that we can account for how the notion of abnormality comes about in particular instances and chart, through his **genealogical method**, how the state of abnormality was written onto particular bodies, forming the deviant, abject, monstrous, pathologized, and other marginalized identities.[16]

A growing number of studies of sexuality focus on normativity rather than the deviant or abnormal as a means of demonstrating their interdependence and their co-constitution. For example, the degradation of the "whore" cannot properly be understood without knowing the value of the virgin. The label "slut" functions as much to compel girls and women to be good as to punish the transgressors. That said, this kind of simplistic binary thinking has obscured the complexities of people's actual fantasies and practices. Now, perhaps more than ever, the distinction between the normal and the deviant or abnormal cannot be so clearly demarcated when it comes to sex. The proliferation of erotic images and services targeted toward women is a case in point, as growing numbers of North American women have become consumers of increasingly sexually explicit books, videos, and Internet sites. Women whose sexual interests would have been considered prurient or pathological until fairly recently are now pursuing the new normal, reading explicit and kinky erotic fiction, shopping for sex toys together,

16 Michel Foucault, *Abnormal: Lectures at the Collège de France, 1974–1975* (New York: Picador, 2003).

and sharing detailed information about their sexual experiences. Norms change. As Judith Butler comments, a "norm only persists as a norm to the extent that it is acted out in social practice and re-idealized and reinstituted in and through the daily social rituals of bodily life."[17] Perhaps more than any other area, sexuality is a place where the normal is challenged and transgressed—punched full of holes. One of the "truths" about sexuality in the contemporary West is that it is a site of transgression; indeed, the best sex, and our true sexual selves, can only be found that way. Paradoxically, challenging the normal is the new normal.

Yet it is too simple to conclude that normalization is displacing deviance as adventurous sex and more and better sex becomes not only permissible but compulsory for the healthy, well-adjusted woman. At the same time, the naming of an expanding array of human sexual desires and activities as pathologies means that increasing numbers of us are implicated, however suggestively. The *Diagnostic and Statistical Manual*[18] now surpasses law in its detailed taxonomy of "abnormal" sex. Michel Foucault's genealogies of madness and the birth of the clinic explored how the psy disciplines have come to be among the most influential discourses of our time. His first volume of the *History of Sexuality* illustrates how medical and psy disciplines are primarily responsible for creating sexuality as we now know it.

Michel Foucault and *The History of Sexuality*

There may be no other realm of activity in the contemporary Western world as sex for which so many demands for freedom from regulation have been made, as individuals and groups attempt to wrest themselves from the grip of power. And perhaps no single scholar has been as influential on the development of sexuality studies, and has so transformed our views of the regulation of sexuality, as Michel Foucault. Fortuitously for sexuality studies, Foucault introduced his new approach to power in *The History of Sexuality, Volume 1*.[19]

Foucault employed his analysis of power and his genealogical method, which you explored in Part One of this book, not to establish the truth or falsity about sex but to explore how truth-claims come to be made and take hold. This required a mapping of interconnections between the organization of knowledge, the deployment of discourse, and the flow of power. He began

---

17 Judith Butler, *Precarious Life: The Powers of Mourning and Violence* (New York: Verso, 2004), 48.

18 American Psychiatric Association, *DSM-5: Diagnostic and Statistical Manual of Mental Disorders*, 5th ed. (Arlington: American Psychiatric Publishing, 2013).

19 Volume 2 was published just before Foucault's death in 1984. Volume 3 was published posthumously in 1986.

his studies of sexuality by examining events in Western Europe during the late nineteenth to early twentieth centuries, a period that has commonly been understood as a time of increasing sexual repression. Foucault found that, while sexual repression did indeed occur at this time, it was situated within a proliferation of discourses about sexuality. Rather than silences, repressions, and prohibitions, sex became something to talk about. Sexual fantasies and practices were identified, classified, and managed through "techniques" of diagnosis, training, and treatment, particularly in the newly developing psy disciplines and in medicine. New identities were created based on the perceived truths about an individual's sexuality. Nothing was to be hidden from view or escape the judgment of emerging **expert knowledge** in the medical and social sciences, which together produced a new **truth regime** about sex. It is not possible, therefore, to talk about sexuality as something that exists separate from power. But does that mean that we can ultimately free ourselves from power through the liberation of our sexuality? As you learned in Chapter One, Foucault said *no*.

Power, Knowledge, Discourse

Foucault identified four operations of power in sexuality that indicate how people in the West have been, in effect, "made up" as sexual beings since the late nineteenth century.[20] These take us beyond the simple equation that power = prohibition and repression, and power can therefore be resisted and overcome. First, he found that while "peripheral sexualities" came under increasing surveillance and persecution this was not to make them disappear. Rather, the aim was to develop knowledge about them. A medico-sexual regime was produced with the aim of exploring the family, children's sexuality, and so on. Second, a "new specification of individuals" was created that entailed the "incorporation of perversions" into individual bodies. Most notably, the homosexual was constituted as a particular kind of perverse individual through the combined forces of psychology, psychiatry, and medicine:[21]

> As defined by the ancient civil or canonical codes, sodomy was a category of forbidden acts; their perpetrator was nothing more than the juridical subject of them. The nineteenth-century homosexual became a personage, a past, a case history, and a childhood, in addition

---

20 On "making up" people, see Ian Hacking, "Making up People," in *Reconstructing Individualism*, ed. T. Heller, M. Sosna, and D. Wellbery (Stanford: Stanford University Press, 1986), 222–36.

21 Foucault assigns a precise date to this constitution: the 1870 publication of "Contrary Sexual Feelings" by Carl Westphal.

to being a type of life, a life form, and a morphology, with an indiscreet anatomy and possibly a mysterious physiology. Nothing that went into his total composition was unaffected by his sexuality. It was everywhere present in him: at the root of all his actions because it was their insidious and indefinitely active principle; written immodestly on his face and body because it was a secret that always gave itself away. It was consubstantial with him, less as a habitual sin than as a singular nature. ...The sodomite had been a temporary aberration; the homosexual was now a species.[22]

This does not mean that same-gender acts did not occur before the homosexual came into being; it does mean that the person identified with particular erotic practices, who we now identify as homosexual, was not understood in the same way.

Third, the operation of power involved intensive study, analysis, and discussion of sexuality within a framework of health and pathology. Conversely, this scrutiny had the effect on the body of "intensifying areas, electrifying surfaces, dramatizing troubled moments. It wrapped the sexual body in its embrace."[23] So the operation of power had a twofold effect: While power was reconfirmed as powerful, pleasure's scrutiny brought sex to the foreground and animated it in "a sensualization of power and a gain of pleasure."[24] Pleasure gripped the imagination and held the body in its sway.

Fourth, rather than simply reducing appropriate sexuality to the heterosexual conjugal couple, an apparatus of power–knowledge was created whose influence went well beyond law and taboo. It was less a means of inhibition of sexualities than a mechanism for inciting and multiplying sexualities through "a mode of specification of individuals." This new science of sex, however, did contain a morality disguised as medical expertise, and "claiming to speak the truth, it stirred up people's fears."[25] For example, the medical declaration that onanism (masturbation) was dangerous to the individual, the whole society, and the species was no doubt ineffective in curtailing solitary pleasures all together. It did, however, provide a scientific rationale that buttressed shame-inducing religious edict and weighed heavily upon the furtive young person the responsibility for maintaining a healthy nation and a larger moral order.

---

22 Foucault, *The History of Sexuality*, vol. 1, 43.
23 Ibid., 44.
24 Ibid., 44–45.
25 Ibid., 53.

We can see from these four developments that a new technology of sex emerged that was a shared concern of secular disciplines, including pedagogy (with a focus on the sexuality of children), medicine (notably concerned with the sexual physiology of women), and economics (through an interest in the regulation of births), making sex a social concern that went well beyond an impetus toward control and punishment. These were not new concerns, but they were taken up in a new way. Sustaining the normal life, and life itself, rather than a focus on punishment and death were key objectives in the exercise of biopower shared by emerging disciplines in the social sciences and medicine and by the expanding apparatus of the state.

Foucault's concern was not to dismiss older ideas about sex as ideological—he did not attempt to replace an old truth with a new truth. Rather, he showed how historically specific power–knowledge[26] dynamics produced and deployed particular discourses about sexuality. These discourses proliferated through the establishment of new orders of knowledge, including pedagogy, medicine, sexology, psychiatry, and criminal justice. Their targets included families (children, parents, couples, adolescents), schools, workplaces, prisons, and asylums. Potential perils existed everywhere. The solution was to diagnose, report, prescribe, and treat using the emerging techniques of demography, biology, medicine, psychiatry, psychology, and pedagogy. This meant that there was less a singular discourse about sex than "a multiplicity of discourses produced by a whole series of mechanisms operating in different institutions."[27] Sex "became something to say, and to say exhaustively."[28]

How does this shift our views of the regulation of sex? First, Foucault compelled us to rethink power and to provide more nuanced accounts of power flows. As you learned in Chapter One, power is everywhere and it comes from everywhere—it is **relational**. Second, Foucault's approach was instrumental in decentring the state and law from analyses of regulation. Law and the state are effects of power, not the sources of it, so "the state is nothing else but the mobile effect of a regime of multiple governmentalities."[29] Third, even where power works to secure domination, we can see that it has a productive and creative character, producing new identities, new discourses, new desires. Fourth, Foucault challenged the idea that we can free ourselves from power because "where there is desire, the power relation is already

---

26 It is not that institutions like the nation-state, families, media, and the education system cease to matter; rather, they are privileged sites for the enactment of power, sites through which particular discourses are enabled and lived. Social institutions are not the source of power.

27 Foucault, *The History of Sexuality*, vol. 1, 33.

28 Ibid., 32.

29 Foucault, *Abnormal*, 77.

present."[30] For Foucault, pleasure is inextricable from power, not antithetical to it. Pleasure is not circumscribed by power, but rather proliferates through it— power is diffuse, intricate, and omnipresent. Finally, we can see that the organization of power–knowledge about sexuality through biopower targets the capacities, energies, and pleasures of *bodies*. It was the potential of human bodies that made sexuality such an important focus for investigation and imagination.

The Sexual Politics of Normalization and the Government of Sex

We are now in a position to say that sex, in the multiple ways that we understand it, was brought into being or constituted simultaneously with its identification as a target for a plethora of regulatory strategies. We know it is inseparable from the discourses about it and from power–knowledge relations in which it is constituted as a problem or as an issue of health and well-being. We have established how we have come to regard sexuality as so important to our sense of self and so crucial to our health and happiness. This too is sexual regulation. Foucault's approach has been enormously helpful in demonstrating how the normal, the natural, the abnormal, the deviant, the perverse, and so on come to be designated as such and provides insights into the making of the normal and the natural as privileged and crucial social accomplishments. We can now briefly focus on three significant examples (there are many more) of how sex and sexuality are governed in the current conjuncture to significant social, political, and economic effect. These examples are racialization and sexualization, homonormativity and homonationalism, and the proliferation of commercial sex.

Racialization and Sexualization

Early in this chapter, it was suggested that when we talk about sex and sexuality we are often really talking about something else. This provides an entry point for considering the following: How has racialization occurred contingent upon sexualization? How has the simultaneous sexualization and racialization of particular bodies constituted those bodies as sites of governance?

Anne McClintock and Laura Ann Stoler have been particularly helpful in explaining how these associations were produced through an apparatus of sexual knowledge created during colonial expansion and early modernity.[31] In *The*

---

30 Foucault, *The History of Sexuality*, vol. 1, 81.

31 Ann McClintock, *Imperial Leather: Race, Gender, and Sexuality in the Colonial Contest* (New York: Routledge, 1995); Laura Anne Stoler, *Race and the Education of Desire: Foucault's History of Sexuality and the Colonial Order of Things* (Durham: Duke University Press, 1995).

History of Sexuality, Volume 1, Foucault considered how a science of sexuality was used to justify racism and to ground this racism in the "rational" pursuit of scientific "truth," the biological advancement of the human species, and the advancement of "civilization" itself.[32] Stoler's work found a critical absence in Foucault's *History of Sexuality, Volume 1*, because it focuses exclusively on Western Europe and the formation of the bourgeois self, and does not consider the impact of Western European colonialism on the formation of its truth regimes—"truths" that justified imperial projects. In effect, Stoler re-read *The History of Sexuality* to explore the implications of taking race into account in Foucault's classic text. In her own research into Dutch and French colonial projects, Stoler determined that the colonies functioned as "laboratories of modernity" during the scientific revolution that began in the sixteenth century.[33]

Race, like sexuality, has a genealogy.[34] Our contemporary understanding of race began within the context of emerging sciences that advanced the notion of European civilization in contradistinction to the "savages" of Africa and North America and placed these social contexts on an evolutionary scale represented most directly through a system of classification of peoples into distinct racial categories.[35] The taxonomic ordering of people into races was based on shared physical markers like skin colour, bone structure, and hair. Perceived physiological potential, intellectual aptitudes, and moral qualities were assigned to people as traits on the basis of these shared markers, as well as common cultural and geographical origins. These traits were correlated with evolution: The less evolved the race, the greater the predisposition to carnality and the larger the danger to the civilizing process. In other words, a hierarchy of value was assigned based on the **Eurocentric** values and assumptions that informed scientific method, providing a rationale for European imperial projects and a justification for practices such as slavery

---

32 This was pursued somewhat more fully in his lectures at the Collège de France, reproduced in *"Society Must Be Defended": Lectures at the Collège de France, 1975–1976* (New York: Picador, 2003). Here Foucault explored racialization as the historically first exercise of biopower.

33 Stoler, *Race and the Education of Desire.*

34 As you read in Chapter Five, "race" only exists through its constitution. As W.E.B Du Bois noted in *The Souls of Black Folk*, commonly used markers of race such as hair, bone structure, and skin colour cannot be correlated with genetic differences, cultural patterns, or intellectual traits. See W.E.B. Du Bois, *The Souls of Black Folk* (Chicago: A.C. McClurg & Co., 1903). Stuart Hall finds that "Human genetic variability *between* different populations normally assigned to a racial category is not significantly greater than it is *within* those populations." Despite this, race has become one of the "great classificatory systems of difference between people" (see Stuart Hall, *Race: The Floating Signifier* [transcript] [Northhampton: Media Education Foundation, 1997]).

35 Ladelle McWhorter provides a genealogy of the concept of race that places its use in its current understanding at approximately 1800, about the same time as the discipline of biology appeared. Ladelle McWhorter, "Sex, Race, and Biopower: A Foucauldian Genealogy," *Hypatia* 19, no. 3 (Summer 2004): 38–62.

and racial segregation.[36] Colonial projects, abetted by the newly emerging sciences, were early instances of biopower, penetrating and disciplining bodies and managing populations and making possible contemporary forms of racism.[37]

The constitution of people as sexual and raced beings has similar historical trajectories and contemporary articulations. For example, whiteness and heterosexuality are normalized, natural, and nonproblematic; heterosexuality is never a problem for heterosexuals and, as Richard Dyer comments, white people simply regard themselves as nonraced.[38] What is more, we can find plentiful examples of how racialization and sexualization are mutually constitutive; they depend on one another to be what they are. For example, in North American popular culture, representational practices suggest that Asian men are not particularly erotic beings,[39] while Asian women are typically exoticized and portrayed as sexually available. Both Black women and men are represented as hyper-sexualized, suggesting dangerousness for Black men and reproductive irresponsibility for Black women.[40]

Stoler's research is also suggestive of the ways in which sexuality, racialization, and nationalism were conjoined in colonial projects, "confirming" European bourgeois superiority, building empires, and contributing to the hegemony of the nation-state. Our next discussion provides a contemporary example of the meeting of sexuality and nationalism through a reconfiguration of governmental power: the development of homonormativity as a privileged form of **sexual citizenship**.

---

36 Stoler's research also demonstrated how the constitution of race was key to the constitution of the bourgeois self. It was racialized and working-class bodies that laboured, making it possible for the bourgeoisie to affirm itself, in the process inventing and then focusing on "the self."

37 Stoler, *Race and the Education of Desire*, 15.

38 Richard Dyer, *White* (London: Routledge, 1997).

39 For example, see Richard Fung, "Looking for My Penis: The Eroticized Asian in Gay Video Porn," in *How Do I Look? Queer Film and Video*, ed. Bad Object-Choices, 145–68 (Seattle: Bay Press, 1991).

40 This is not accidental, as historical research amply demonstrates. Since the beginning of the slave trade and throughout the history of colonial projects, representations of the sexually dangerous Black man are pervasive. The most common were rape narratives that posed Black men as a menace to white women, a mythology that served as a justification for the practice of lynching in the southern United States. For example, see Stoler, *Race and the Education of Desire*; Ann Laura Stoler, "Carnal Knowledge and Imperial Power: Gender, Race, and Morality in Colonial Asia," in *The Gender Sexuality Reader*, ed. Roger Lancaster and Micaela di Leonardom, 13–36 (New York: Routledge, 1997); Siobhan Somerville, "Scientific Racism and the Emergence of the Homosexual Body," *Journal of the History of Sexuality* 5, no. 2 (October 1994): 243–66; Ladelle McWhorter, *Racism and Sexual Oppression in Anglo-America: A Genealogy* (Bloomington: Indiana University Press, 2009).

Homonormativity and Homonationalism

For those people born in Canada after 2000, gay marriage has always been around.[41] It is now entrenched as part of the normative order of things. For most, it is simply a nonissue. Indeed, for many the legal recognition of gay marriage is even a source of national pride—a symbol of Canada's progressivism, equality, and respect for the rights and dignity of all people. The winning of lesbian and gay[42] legal rights now occupies the **liminal** space of being simultaneously a radical and extraordinary social change and an embracement of conventionality through the adoption of a normative model of family life. Lesbians and gays have, it seems, won the right to be "boring." Others can provide a detailed account of how this legal transformation came about[43] or debate the merits of the pro- and anti-gay marriage positions. Our more modest purpose here is to think about how these changes express a reconfiguration of governmental power.

As noted earlier in this chapter, Elaine Craig identified several recent significant shifts in the regulation of sexuality. The second was the phenomenon identified by Lisa Duggan as "the new homonormativity" embodied in the white middle-class gay who is family oriented, consumption motivated, and a patriotic citizen and thus deserving of social recognition and legal rights.[44] The homosexual, in other words, has accomplished some limited legitimacy through living as a "minority group" within the regime of the "normal" life, daily making the "normal" gay. This entails the adoption of **heteronormative**[45] values and beliefs by lesbians and gays to assimilate and to achieve

---

41 Canada's Civil Marriage Act was passed on July 20, 2005, providing a definition of marriage in gender-neutral terms.

42 I prefer to use this mainstream term in this context, rather than the more ambiguous, fractured, and potentially politically challenging concept of "queer" or the more inclusive alphabet approach to naming sexual identities (i.e., LGBTQ) precisely because I am discussing the mainstreaming of lesbian and gay rights, a shift of less personal and political significance for those who identify as transgendered or queer. That said, the concept of queer is the preferable term where the objective is to break down a binary model of gay and straight and to capture some of the ambiguity and fluidity of sexual identities and conduct.

43 For example, see Craig, *Troubling Sex*; Miriam Smith, *Lesbian and Gay Rights in Canada: Social Movements and Equality Seeking, 1971–1995* (Toronto: University of Toronto Press, 1999).

44 Lisa Duggan "The New Homonormativity: The Sexual Politics of Neoliberalism," in *Materializing Democracy: Toward a Revitalized Cultural Politics*, ed. Russ Castronovo and Dana D. Nelson, 175–94 (Durham: Duke University Press, 2002).

45 This concept describes the positioning of heterosexuality as the normal and natural expression of human sexuality. While other identities and expressions *may* (or may not) be tolerated, it is heterosexuality that is represented as personally fulfilling, socially valued, and rewarded. The heteronormative couple in turn commits to cohabitation, sexual exclusivity, the creation of a family, the formation of an interdependent economic unit, labour force participation, and responsible citizenship.

some degree of acceptance. Homonormativity, in other words, is consistent with what Andrea Smith refers to as a "minoritizing logic of toleration."[46]

Neoliberal logics have been deployed in the making of homonormativity through three main strategies. First, the expansion of liberal legal–political rights, including the decriminalization of some sex acts, and the acquisition of cohabitation and marriage rights, adoption rights, spousal benefits (consequently leading to divorce rights, alimony, and child support rights), and so on.[47] Second, **familialization** entails the pursuit of the heteronormative model of family life associated with white middle-class life in Western capitalist countries.[48] Third, homonormativity embraces status accomplishment through **consumption**. Unlike the other major philosophy of the welfare state and the free flow of capital, it does not rely on conservative moral claims. Rather, it benefits from corporate recognition of a new target consumer market: middle-class, relatively affluent gays and lesbians. Simple representations of lesbian or gay couples (think IKEA ads) has been demonstrated to be remarkably successful in promoting corporate loyalty.[49]

Homonormativity, then, is not simply a matter of gaining increasing freedom *from* regulation. We can also conceptualize homonormativity as a new mode of governance—few other pressures are so pervasive as the impetus to be "normal" (even if we are not "good")—to embrace domesticity and familialization, neoliberal capitalism, patriotism, and nationalism. It is patriotism and nationalism that I want to turn to next because of the crucial role that they have played in promoting homonormativity in post-9/11 North America and Western Europe.

The phenomenon of **homonationalism** has been widely discussed, particularly in the US context where its effects were most pronounced in the

---

46 Andrea Smith, "Queer Theory and Native Studies: The Heteronormativity of Settler Colonialism," *GLQ* 16, no. 1–2 (2010): 42–68.

47 Less remarked upon is that presumed economic autonomy between cohabiting couples—which was crucial to securing state benefits, including financial support and medical care for low-income partners—has been largely lost.

48 Albeit well after the securing of numerous legal rights in Canada and much of Western Europe, the ruling political ethos is shifting in the United States. The campaign for gay marriage validated the otherwise "traditional" family so markedly that by early 2013 an American organization calling itself the Institute for American Values felt compelled to reverse its position against gay marriage and launch its own campaign for the recognition of gay marriage as a means of saving the institution of marriage itself in face of the institution's declining popularity among middle-class heterosexual Americans.

Editorial, "Gay Marriage Becomes an American Value," *Globe and Mail*, January 30, 2013, http://www.theglobeandmail.com/globe-debate/editorials/gay-marriage-becomes-an -american-value/article8016520/Q6 (accessed January 30, 2013).

49 Although gay positive advertisements appear to overwhelmingly represent and appeal to white, middle class gay male consumers; the target market most likely to have a high disposable income.

Figure 8.1 An IKEA family, Italy 2011

context of "the War on Terror."[50] Homonationalism entails the incorporation of lesbian and gay individuals into nationalist and patriotic projects in defence of the nation. In contrast to the Cold War period,[51] to be lesbian or gay is no longer considered a threat to the nation, provided that one stands united with the nation against external threats. In turn, nation-states claim a **sexual exceptionalism**, according to Jasbir Puar. The support of sexual freedoms for women and gays has become a hallmark of a nation's superiority. Sexual exceptionalism has been mobilized to advance the interests of Western nations through acts of diplomacy, policy decisions, and the exercise of military power. Thus, patriotic lesbians and gays have embraced a sexual citizenship that aligns them with biopolitical strategies whose aim is to re-secure international alignments first established through colonial projects.

The "good" gay, then, is a patriotic and loyal citizen. Such a claim would have seemed an anathema to the sexual liberation movements of the recent past. It indicates an abandonment of the more radical social visions and projects that informed sexual liberation politics, which were typically linked to broader left critiques of capitalism and imperialism. Not surprisingly, then, homonormativity has had considerable appeal for those who may be lesbian or gay but are politically and economically liberal or conservative. However, not everyone wants to fit this model, and not everyone can.[52]

To summarize, the rise of homonormativity and homonationalism provides excellent examples of how governmental power works. Discourses and practices for sexual liberation have shifted the juridical field away from regulation through criminal law to an embracement of same-sex rights in the context of a neoliberal political and economic ethos. Lesbians and gays who willingly embrace the mainstream (and whose economic, ethno-racial, and citizenship status make that possible) govern themselves accordingly in a couple of ways. First, they fashion

---

50 For example, see Jasbir K. Puar, *Terrorist Assemblages: Homonationalism in Queer Times* (Durham: Duke University Press, 2007); Jasbir K. Puar, "Mapping US Homonormativities," *Gender, Place and Culture* 13, no. 1 (February 2006): 67–88.

51 During the Cold War, being lesbian or gay in public service was a potential threat to "national security" because of the alleged risk of blackmail by the enemy. See Gary Kinsman and Patrizia Gentile, *The Canadian War on Queers: National Security as Sexual Regulation* (Vancouver: UBC Press, 2010).

52 For example, those who wish to live nonmonogamous lives, to be a gender nonconformist, or who prefer to work toward more radical social transformation do not fit this new model. Others occupy a liminal position (e.g., the gay Muslim immigrant) in relation to this model. Anna Agathangelou, Daniel Bassicus, and Tamara Spira provide helpful accounts of the prevalence of racialized discourses of inclusion and exclusion, notably the Orientalism of anti-Muslim politics; Anna M. Agathangelou, M. Daniel Bassichis, and Tamara L. Spira, "Intimate Investments: Homonormativity, Global Lockdown, and the Seductions of Empire," *Radical History Review* 100 (2008): 120–43.

Figure 8.2 Avid consumer of the *Fifty Shades* phenomenon

themselves as worthy political subjects. Second, they fashion themselves in the more conventional sense of the term, specifically through the consumption practices that signify a mainstream "lifestyle." In other words, they have stopped marching and gone shopping. This is a fitting place to move on to our third example of contemporary governance, the culture of (sexual) consumption.

Commercial Sex: "Pussy" Goes Public

Who knew that when she was reading *Fifty Shades of Grey* following its publication in early 2012 she was implicated in new techniques of governance? How many Canadian readers of this surprisingly commercially successful erotic trilogy drew a connection between their private reading pleasures and contemporaneous legal challenges to the regulation of swingers clubs and sex work? Or the international political protests organized as SlutWalks, or in defence of the Russian feminist band Pussy Riot?

Early in this chapter I noted that standards of sexual conduct for women are embracing a "new normal": the self-actualizing woman seeking sexual pleasure and new means of sexual expression (albeit commonly through old scripts about what it means to be "sexy"). The intimacies of sex may involve little more than skin and imagination. However, sexuality is enacted within an expanding array of choice and consumption that piques imagination and reorganizes the possible. The mass availability of erotic film and literature, sexually suggestive advertising, lingerie shops, risqué clothing, sex shops, "sex-ercise" classes such as pole dancing and Buti workouts, online encounters, "pick up" bars and clubs, and drink choices (think "sex on the beach") are just some of the more obvious examples that make up a sexually oriented culture from which it is impossible to separate one's individual desires and practices. Negotiating this sexual culture and making decisions about when to say no (or yes) to sex (including how we will dress, dance, or otherwise present ourselves to others, whose gaze we will return, what images we will seek out, and what erotic practices we will engage in) are integral to self-fashioning, or what we can call **projects of the self**. These projects might include taking a pole-dancing class or a course on how to "give great head," have multiple orgasms, or explore BDSM (bondage, discipline, and sadomasochism). It might also include therapeutic efforts to rid oneself of persistent unruly desires that are a source of shame or discomfort. These actions can result from deliberate conscious decisions, but to understand self-fashioning as simply expressing individual freedom of choice is to miss the significance of how techniques of governance shape our values, choices, and conduct.

For those who aspire to be modern, healthy, self-actualizing women, sexuality is no longer limited to "vanilla sex" but is also found in the will to be naughty.[53] The decoupling of sex from reproduction and potentially from emotional commitment; the opening of sexuality to ever-expanding commercial possibilities; and popular cultural representations of women as "cougars," "desperate housewives," seeking "sex in the city," or simply as "girls" produce forms of "empowerment" that place sexuality at the centre of women's identity and accomplishment. They suggest also that commercial sex has been regendered so that women are as important a target market as men.

---

53 To borrow from Foucault's reference to "the will to knowledge" (the subtitle of the UK version of *The History of Sexuality, Volume 1*), a phrase that he adapted from Friedrich Nietzsche.

What does this mean for sexual pleasure? Has it become more varied, more accessible, more democratic? Have inequalities shifted their guise? Is it becoming more difficult to "measure up"? When we fail to be sexy do we also fail to be desirable partners? Do we fail to be women? These are important questions, but they are not the objective of this chapter. The preoccupation here is instead with how the government of sex happens; thinking about the implications for our personal lives is a different but no less important line of inquiry, as are ongoing debates about the sexual commodification, objectification, and exploitation of women.

Sexed subjects, then, are largely responsibilized subjects who take it upon themselves to engage in disciplinary practices of self-examination and self-improvement. Feona Attwood believes that raising these kinds of questions about sexual pleasure suggests that "an endless seduction by sex—whatever that is—and constant self-scrutiny, becomes the newest and most uncertain form of regulation."[54]

It is too easy to simply blame the expansion of consumer culture for these significant historical shifts. Instead, we need to be aware of how consumer culture is produced through the harnessing and combining of discourses of rights, health, materialism, competitive individualism, and progress within neoliberal governance. As with the incorporation of homonormativity, neoliberalism does not discourage "rights" as long as collective rights are used to enable, rather than trump, individual rights. So, for example, women consumers of sexual entertainment are an important target market rather than a moral problem. This indicates why neoliberalism continues to be so successful as an ideological and political project despite its obvious disastrous consequences as an economic project. It has penetrated and reshaped our very subjectivity, emphasizing our freedom and our ability to make choices as empowered sexed subjects.

Conclusion: Power, Knowledge, Pleasure

Governmental techniques are intrinsic to what Jennifer Terry refers to as "the constitution of the subjects and objects of knowledge."[55] How do we come to know ourselves and others as sexually desiring and desirable beings? Who do we desire or not desire? When do we go too far or not far enough? "Sexing people" may sound like an odd formulation, given the common

---

54 Feona Attwood, "Sexed Up: Theorizing the Sexualization of Culture," *Sexualities* 9, no. 1 (2006): 77–94.

55 Jennifer Terry, *An American Obsession: Science, Medicine and Homosexuality in Modern Society* (Chicago: University of Chicago Press, 1999), 14.

assumption that sex simply is and people simply are sexual, but this is precisely what governmental techniques do. Sexed people are or strive to be "fit" subjects in mind and body for whom a healthy sexuality is integral to the person.

Governmental power is not only tightly bound with knowledge (in Foucault's mutually constitutive power–knowledge formulation); we can claim for governmentality a materiality as well—for instance, in the making of the material body, saturated with its sensations and desires. It is a way of theorizing that is enormously useful for making sense of our everyday lives. The ideas presented in this chapter indicate how what appears to be abstract social theory is actually something that is lived daily and bodily and found in our self-knowledge. Do you "know" yourself any differently now?

Sexing people also implicates them as juridical subjects whose actions are judged by law and who make sense of their own sexuality in relation to law, but who simultaneously make and transform law through their ideas and actions. However, rather than "free" ourselves from power, we participate in the proliferation of discourse–power–knowledge about sex as we discover "truths," assert new rights, and identify more boundaries to be crossed. To employ one final quotation from Foucault, "never have there existed more centers of power; never more attention manifested and verbalized; never more circular contacts and linkages; never more sites where the intensity of pleasures and the persistency of power catch hold, only to spread elsewhere."[56]

No matter what the circumstances of intimacy in our everyday or everynight lives,[57] sexuality is always already political. We must not only investigate and question juridical claims, but we must challenge the conditions of normativity for the making of what Judith Butler has referred to as "the livable life."[58] Through this process, we will come to know better the government of sex.

Study Questions

1. How do governmental techniques produce individuals and populations as sites of sexual regulation?

2. What is the role of law in the government of sex? Think about some of the ways that legal regulation is and is not present in governing specific sexed identities, such as the homosexual, the sex worker, and the straight identified woman.

---

56 Foucault, *The History of Sexuality*, vol. 1, 49.
57 Thanks to Becki Ross for this formulation.
58 Butler, *Precarious Life*.

Exercise

Investigate changes to the Criminal Code over the past 50 years. How has the regulation of sex-related conduct shifted during this time? Following the logic outlined in this chapter, in what ways has the government of sex been reconfigured?

Keywords

self-regulation; homonormativity; normalization; sexual citizenship; heteronormative; homonationalism; sexual exceptionalism; projects of the self

References

Agathangelou, Anna, M. Daniel Bassichis, and Tamara Spira. "Intimate Investments: Homonormativity, Global Lockdown, and the Seductions of Empire." *Radical History Review* 100 (Winter 2008): 120–43. http://dx.doi.org/10.1215/01636545 -2007-025.

American Psychiatric Association. *DSM-5: Diagnostic and Statistical Manual of Mental Disorders.* 5th ed. Arlington: American Psychiatric Publishing, 2013.

Attwood, Feona. "Sexed Up: Theorizing the Sexualization of Culture." *Sexualities* 9, no. 1 (2006): 77–94. http://dx.doi.org/10.1177/1363460706053336.

Butler, Judith. *Precarious Life: The Powers of Mourning and Violence.* New York: Verso, 2004.

Coward, Rosalind. *Powers of Desire.* London: Paladin Books, 1984.

Craig, Elaine. *Troubling Sex: Towards a Legal Theory of Sexual Integrity.* Vancouver: UBC Press, 2012.

Du Bois, W.E.B. *The Souls of Black Folk.* Chicago: A.C. McClurg & Co, 1903.

Duggan, Lisa. "The New Homonormativity: The Sexual Politics of Neoliberalism." In *Materializing Democracy: Toward a Revitalized Cultural Politics,* edited by Russ Castronovo and Dana D. Nelson, 175–94 (Durham: Duke University Press, 2002). http://dx.doi.org/10.1215/9780822383901-007.

Dyer, Richard. *White.* London: Routledge, 1997.

Editorial. "Gay Marriage Becomes an American Value." *Globe and Mail,* January 30, 2013. http://www.theglobeandmail.com/globe-debate/editorials/gay-marriage-becomes -an-american-value/article8016520/ (accessed January 30, 2013).

Foucault, Michel. *The Birth of Biopolitics: Lectures at the Collège de France, 1978–1979.* New York: Palgrave MacMillan, 2008. http://dx.doi.org/10.1057/9780230594180.

Foucault, Michel. *Abnormal: Lectures at the Collège de France, 1974–1975.* New York: Picador, 2003.

Foucault, Michel. *Society Must Be Defended: Lectures at the Collège de France, 1975–1976.* New York: Picador, 2003.

Foucault, Michel. *The History of Sexuality.* Vol. 1, *An Introduction.* Translated by Robert Hurley. New York: Vintage, 1978.

Fung, Richard. "Looking for My Penis: The Eroticized Asian in Gay Video Porn." In *How Do I Look? Queer Film and Video,* edited by Bad Object-Choices, 145–68. Seattle: Bay Press, 1991.

Hacking, Ian. "Making up People." In *Reconstructing Individualism*, edited by T. Heller, M. Sosna, and D. Wellbery, 222–36. Stanford: Stanford University Press, 1986.

Hall, Stuart. *Race: The Floating Signifier* (transcript). Northhampton: Media Education Foundation, 1997.

Khan, Ummni. "Putting a Dominatrix in Her Place." *Canadian Journal of Women and the Law* 21, no. 1 (2009): 143–76.

Khan, Ummni. "A Woman's Right to Be Spanked: Testing the Limits of Tolerance of S/M in the Socio-Legal Imaginary." *Law & Sexuality: A Review of Lesbian, Gay, Bisexual and Transgender Legal Issues* 18, no. 1 (2009): 79–120.

Kinsman, Gary, and Patrizia Gentile. *The Canadian War on Queers: National Security as Sexual Regulation.* Vancouver: UBC Press, 2010.

McClintock, Ann. *Imperial Leather: Race, Gender, and Sexuality in the Colonial Contest.* New York: Routledge, 1995.

McWhorter, Ladelle. *Racism and Sexual Oppression in Anglo-America: A Genealogy.* Bloomington: Indiana University Press, 2009.

McWhorter, Ladelle. "Sex, Race, and Biopower: A Foucauldian Genealogy." *Hypatia* 19, no. 3 (Summer 2004): 38–62. http://dx.doi.org/10.1111/j.1527-2001.2004 .tb01301.x.

Puar, Jasbir K. *Terrorist Assemblages: Homonationalism in Queer Times.* Durham: Duke University Press, 2007. http://dx.doi.org/10.1215/9780822390442.

Puar, Jasbir K. "Mapping US Homonormativities." *Gender, Place and Culture* 13, no. 1 (February 2006): 67–88. http://dx.doi.org/10.1080/09663690500531014.

Rose, Nikolas, and Mariana Valverde. "Governed by Law?" *Social & Legal Studies* 7, no. 4 (1998): 541–51. http://dx.doi.org/10.1177/096466399800700405.

Smith, Andrea. "Queer Theory and Native Studies: The Heteronormativity of Settler Colonialism." *GLQ* 16, no. 1–2 (2010): 42–68.

Smith, Miriam. *Lesbian and Gay Rights in Canada: Social Movements and Equality Seeking, 1971–1995.* Toronto: University of Toronto Press, 1999.

Somerville, Siobhan. "Scientific Racism and the Emergence of the Homosexual Body." *Journal of the History of Sexuality* 5, no. 2 (October 1994): 243–66.

Stoler, Ann Laura. "Carnal Knowledge and Imperial Power: Gender, Race, and Morality in Colonial Asia." In *The Gender Sexuality Reader*, edited by Roger Lancaster and Micaela di Leonardom, 13–36 (New York: Routledge, 1997).

Stoler, Laura Anne. *Race and the Education of Desire: Foucault's History of Sexuality and the Colonial Order of Things.* Durham: Duke University Press, 1995.

Terry, Jennifer. *An American Obsession: Science, Medicine and Homosexuality in Modern Society.* Chicago: University of Chicago Press, 1999. http://dx.doi.org/10.7208/chicago/9780226793689.001.0001.

Valverde, Mariana. "The Harms of Sex and the Risks of Breasts: Obscenity and Indecency in Canadian Law." *Social & Legal Studies* 8, no. 2 (June 1999): 181–97. http://dx.doi .org/10.1177/096466399900800202.

Valverde, Mariana. *Sex, Power and Pleasure.* Toronto: Women's Press, 1985.

Vance, Carol, ed. *Pleasure and Danger: Exploring Female Sexuality.* London: Routledge and Kegan Paul, 1984.

nine

Crime and Social Classes: Regulating and Representing Public Disorder

MARIE-EVE SYLVESTRE

Introduction

In Western countries, poor, racialized, uneducated, and unemployed young men and women are disproportionately represented in the criminal justice system. In the United States, young Black males growing up in America's poorest neighbourhoods are five to nine times more likely to be incarcerated or under judicial supervision than white males, and one out of four Black children have had a parent locked up in the last two decades.[1] Immigrants, refugee seekers, and foreigners are substantially overrepresented in European prisons, accounting for up to 60 per cent of the total prison population in some countries.[2]

Similarly, First Nations, Inuit, and Métis people of Canada, who are significantly more likely to live in low-income households and experience food insecurity than the rest of Canadians,[3] while experiencing higher levels of unemployment and lower levels of educational attainment at the time of arrest,[4] are also disproportionately represented in the criminal justice system. In 2010–11, they accounted for 20 per cent of federal admissions in custody whereas they represented approximately 3 per cent of the adult population as a whole.[5] At the provincial level, Aboriginal people are being incarcerated

1 E. Ann Carson and William J. Sabol, *Prisoners in 2011*, Bureau of Justice Statistics, http://www .bjs.gov/index.cfm?ty=pbdetail&iid=4559 (accessed April 13, 2014); Bruce Western, *Punishment and Inequality in the United States* (New York: Russell Sage Foundation, 2006); Loïc Wacquant, "Deadly Symbiosis: When Ghetto and Prison Meet and Mesh," in *Mass Imprisonment—Social Causes and Consequences*, ed. David Garland, 82–120 (London: Sage Publications, 2001).

2 Loïc Wacquant, "Suitable Enemies: Foreigners and Immigrants in the Prisons of Europe," *Punishment and Society* 1 (1999): 215; Eoin O'Sullivan, "Varieties of Punitiveness in Europe: Homelessness and Urban Marginality," *European Journal of Homelessness* 6 (2012): 82; Alessandro De Giorgi, *Rethinking the Political Economy of Punishment* (Aldershot: Ashgate Publishing, 2006).

3 Chantal Collin and Hilary Jensen, *A Statistical Profile of Poverty in Canada* (Ottawa: Library of Parliament, 2009), 16–20.

4 John Patrick Moore, *First Nations, Inuit and Non-Aboriginal Federal Offenders: A Comparative Profile* (Ottawa: Correctional Service of Canada, 2003), http://www.csc-scc.gc.ca/research/ index-eng.shtml.

5 Mia Dauvergne, *Adult Correctional Services 2010–2011*, Statistics Canada (Ottawa: Canadian Centre for Justice Statistics, 2012), http://www.statcan.gc.ca/pub/85-002-x/2012001/article/11715-eng .htm, 11.

up to 10 times more than their proportion in the population, accounting for 77.6 per cent and 11.4 per cent of provincial admissions in custody in Saskatchewan and Ontario, respectively, whereas they represented 11.9 per cent and 1.8 per cent of the population.[6] The disproportion is even higher among female Aboriginal offenders, who represented 41 per cent of all federally incarcerated women.[7]

Finally, and irrespective of race or ethnicity, the most recent studies have shown that only one-third of inmates (36 per cent) kept in Quebec provincial jails had a job (not necessarily a legal one) prior to incarceration, while 52 per cent of them received social assistance.[8] In a 2009–10 study conducted by the John Howard Society of Toronto with 363 inmates in four provincial correctional facilities in the Toronto area, 69 per cent of the respondents experienced residential instability in the two years prior to their incarceration, 24 per cent had used a shelter during that period, and 23 per cent were homeless (living on the street, in places unfit for habitation, in a shelter, or **couch-surfing**). The researchers also found that the rate of homelessness among respondents on being discharged from prison was 22.9 per cent, while that rate had increased to 32.3 per cent within days of discharge.[9]

These alarming numbers raise important issues with respect to crime and social class. Are poor and working-class people more likely to commit crimes than people from more privileged backgrounds and social classes? If so, are class inequalities, socioeconomic disadvantage, and community disorganization linked to higher crime rates? Are poor people more policed, charged, and prosecuted because of their position in society? Or is crime defined, regulated, and represented by certain interest groups so as to shed light on the activities of the poor and the socially excluded while the wealthy elites get away with murder?

In this chapter, I argue that crime and the historical development of punitive practices are related to the management of class relations in society[10] and that the regulation and representation of crime reflect and are constitutive of class differences. The chapter begins by defining social class as an

---

6 Ibid., chart 7, http://www.statcan.gc.ca/pub/85-002-x/2012001/article/11715/c-g/desc/desc07-eng.htm.

7 Ibid., 11.

8 Lise Giroux, *Profil correctionnel 2007–2008: La population correctionnelle du Quebec* (Quebec: Ministère de la sécurité publique, 2011), 19.

9 Amber Kellen, Julie Freedman, Sylvia Novac, and Linda Lapointe, *Homeless and Jailed: Jailed and Homeless* (Toronto: John Howard Society of Toronto, 2010), 20.

10 George Rusche and Otto Kirchheimer, *Punishment and Social Structure* (New Brunswick: Transaction Publishers, 2005); Michel Foucault, *Discipline and Punish* (New York: Vintage Books, 1977).

important principle of differentiation among individuals and groups and discusses its potential impact on the regulation and representation of crime through a brief introduction to different criminological theories that address the dilemma of crime and social classes. The chapter then turns to an examination of the policing and regulation of vagrancy, homelessness, and street gangs. Hidden under the amorphous concept of public disorder, these class-based offences illustrate, both historically and in the present, the impact of differentiated patterns of regulation, representation, and punishment of crime.

Thinking about Class and Crime

The concept of class is used in different contexts and from different theoretical perspectives. In the Marxist tradition, **social classes** are shaped by their relation to the means of production in a specific form of economic organization, which can include slavery, feudalism, or capitalism. Karl Marx defines social classes in industrial societies by the economic relationship between those who own the means of production (capitalists/bourgeoisie) and those who own their own labour power (workers/proletariat). Capitalists are able to accumulate and concentrate wealth because they exploit workers by extracting the **surplus value** from their labour: surplus value is the value produced by workers in excess of the costs related to their labour, including their salaries, and which is then left to be appropriated by the capitalists.[11] Marx also argues that social classes are intrinsically linked to social change. The exploitation of workers leads to class struggles, in which those who own capital (the capitalists) want to protect their exploitative position and workers want to put an end to it. In the Marxist tradition, social classes are therefore collective entities with specific shared economic interests and a consciousness of such interests (class consciousness).[12]

Marx's definition of class has been criticized for conflating theory and practice or for assimilating class on paper to real classes, as well as for its focus on only the relationship to the means of production and its failure to consider the multiple internal divisions in the two proposed classes of his model (bourgeoisie and proletariat) and the inattention to those who do not necessarily fit into these two classes (e.g., the self-employed or peasants).[13]

---

11 Erik Olin Wright, "Foundations of Class Analysis in the Marxist Tradition," in *Alternative Foundations of Class Analysis*, ed. Erik Olin Wright, 6–40, http://www.ssc.wisc.edu/~wright/Found-all.pdf, 14; David F. Greenberg, *Crime and Capitalism—Readings in Marxist Criminology* (Philadelphia: Temple University Press, 1993), 16.

12 George Lukács, *History and Class Consciousness* (London: Merlin Press, 1967).

13 Elliot B. Weininger, "Foundations of Class Analysis in the Work of Bourdieu," in *Alternative Foundations of Class Analysis*, ed. E.O. Wright, http://www.ssc.wisc.edu/~wright/Found-all.pdf, 125.

More contemporary scholars continue to build on Marx's analysis to develop more nuanced explanations of class difference. Sociologist Pierre Bourdieu has made key contributions to our understandings of class in modern society. Like Marx, Bourdieu suggests that class is the dominant principle of social division and is directly related to power and privilege in society.[14] But, according to Bourdieu, social classes are not only constituted by one's position within the relations of production (which is revealed by indicators such as income, occupation, and educational level),[15] but also by cultural practices, symbolic power, and personal characteristics such as gender, age, religion, and ethnicity. Moreover, social classes, such as the peasantry, the working poor, the middle classes, or the bourgeoisie are theoretical constructions that do not exist objectively in reality and are, instead, subjected to the politics of group-making.[16] In other words, the definition and representation of classes themselves are part of a struggle over economic, cultural, and social power and domination in society.[17]

According to Bourdieu, there are at least four forms of **capital** in any given social space: economic, cultural, social (connections, networks), and symbolic capitals.[18] Capitals are "like aces in a game of cards"[19] and refer to the "set of actually usable resources and powers"[20] possessed by each individual. For instance, a university professor arguably possesses a lot of cultural capital and some economic capital, whereas an investment banker possesses a lot of economic capital and social capital and less cultural capital. *Symbolic capital* refers to the actual recognition of the other forms of capitals in any given society. For instance, in North America in the twenty-first century, economic capital is given primary importance. However, in Soviet societies of the twentieth century, another form of capital, political capital (which refers to one's position in the hierarchy of the Communist Party), is necessary to account for the different positions in the social space. As these examples demonstrate, one's position in the social space depends on the global volume and the composition of capital one can mobilize as well as the trajectory of

---

14 Pierre Bourdieu, *Distinction: A Social Critique of the Judgement of Taste*, trans. Richard Nice (Cambridge, MA: Harvard University Press, 1984), 114. Bourdieu writes that class is "a universal principle of explanation."

15 Bourdieu, *Distinction*, 102.

16 Pierre Bourdieu, "What Makes a Social Class? On the Theoretical and Practical Existence of Groups," *Berkeley Journal of Sociology* 32 (1987): 1.

17 For Bourdieu, the paradigm of real groups construction is Marxist theory that succeeds in creating the category of "proletariat"; Pierre Bourdieu, *Practical Reason* (Palo Alto: Stanford University Press, 1998), 31.

18 Ibid., 4.

19 Bourdieu, "What Makes a Social Class?" 4.

20 Bourdieu, *Distinction*, 114.

such capital over time.[21] Such a position, however, is neither static nor real but relational, because it is mediated through the structure of different fields. Social classes are composed of individuals occupying neighbouring positions in a social space—that is, sharing similar conditions of existence—who are more likely to have similar interests, affinities, tastes, and dispositions to produce similar practices (which Bourdieu calls **habitus**).[22]

As a result, classes are not mobilized entities, conscious of their commonalities and interests and fighting against each other in the hopes of attaining some ultimate goal (ending exploitation, for instance, in Marx's theory). Instead, there is a series of individuals predisposed to exist as a class if so mobilized because of their affinities and interests, but also because of their aversion, misrepresentations, and misunderstanding of people from other classes.[23] Moreover, Bourdieu also believed that social classes are the product of a struggle, but in a different sense than Marx. In Bourdieu's opinion, social classes are constituted by the politics of class-making, by which he means that through "endless work of representation" social agents are constantly competing for the existence or nonexistence of social classes.[24] In doing so, they "try to impose their vision of the social world or the vision of their own position in that world and to define their social identity."[25] In his analysis of the space of social positions and the space of lifestyles, in *Distinction*,[26] Bourdieu found that the cultural preferences, aesthetic choices, and personal tastes of a person contributed to constitute social classes. For example, 1960s French professionals and private sector executives tended to prefer golf, whisky, and tennis to, say, fishing and beer, which were more likely to be preferred by foremen and commercial employees. Bourdieu warned us that these preferences or activities were not specific to certain individuals or groups in any substantial or intrinsic sense, but that they were rather relational and always likely to be reconfigured. For instance, it is not unusual that a certain practice associated with the aristocracy at a certain time is given up by this social class as it is adopted by the petit bourgeoisie or the working classes.[27]

To conclude, the concept of social classes as it is used in this chapter refers to social relations constituted by social agents' positions in a social space and which is the object of constant struggles of representation among social agents.

---

21 Ibid.

22 In his translator's introduction to Bourdieu's article, Richard Terdiman defines the habitus as "the habitual, patterned ways of understanding, judging, and acting which arise from our particular position as members of one or several social 'fields' and from our particular trajectory in the social structure." Pierre Bourdieu, "The Force of Law: Toward a Sociology of the Juridical Field," *Hastings Law Journal* 38 (1987): 811.

23 Bourdieu, *Practical Reason*, 10–11.

24 Bourdieu, "What Makes a Social Class?" 11.

25 Ibid.

26 Bourdieu, *Distinction*.

27 Bourdieu, *Practical Reason*, 4. In this text, Bourdieu gives the example of boxing in France.

The Dilemma of Crime and Social Class

The dilemma of crime and social class can be expressed as follows: If social disadvantage and class inequality necessarily lead to crime, how can one explain that not all poor people are criminals? On the other hand, if crime and social classes are not at all connected, why are working and precariat classes (a new form of social class composed of people living in uncertain, insecure conditions) overrepresented in criminalization patterns? Most sociological theories of crime have attempted to address the dilemma of crime and social classes to some extent, from those who emphasize individual or social pathologies (from strain theorists to social disorganization theorists) to social reaction criminologists, including conflict theorists, to Marxist and Foucauldian approaches to deviance and social control.

Some criminologists offered an individualistically oriented response. For instance, in the 1930s strain theorists argued that crime was the result of *anomie*: while dominant groups in society build up the expectation that everybody can achieve economic success, the current economic structure only allows for some to succeed, thus leaving lower classes in a position of frustration and aggression or strain,[28] which is often compounded by racial and sexual discrimination.[29] Other sociologists suggest that crime is not a property of persons, but of groups or communities to which they belong.[30] According to them, poor communities are unable to maintain social control and to realize common law-abiding values because of their level of disorganization deriving from poverty, residential segregation, family disruption, welfare, and high rates of unemployment and economic dislocations.[31]

These approaches tend to pathologize not only individuals but families and communities, and as such they have generated a lot of criticism. Some scholars

---

28 Robert K. Merton, "Social Structure and Anomie," *American Sociological Review* 3 (1938): 672; see also Albert Cohen, *Delinquent Boys* (New York: Free Press, 1955); Cohen suggested that working-class children, who are first socialized to adopt middle-class goals and values but who lack the means to achieve them, resolve the tension by identifying with a delinquent subculture in which they gain status and self-esteem.

29 Richard Delgado, "'Rotten Social Background': Should the Criminal Law Recognize a Defense of Severe Environmental Deprivation?" *Law & Inequality* 3 (1985): 9.

30 Clifford Shaw and Henry McKay, *Juvenile Delinquency and Urban Areas* (Chicago: University of Chicago Press, 1942).

31 Robert J. Sampson and William Julius Wilson, "Toward a Theory of Race, Crime and Urban Inequality," in *Crime and Inequality,* ed. John Hagan and Ruth D. Peterson (Palo Alto: Stanford University Press, 1995), 37; Martin Sanchez Jankowski, *Cracks in the Pavement: Social Change and Resilience in Poor Neighborhoods* (Berkeley: University of California Press, 2008); Elijah Anderson, *Streetwise: Race, Class and Change in an Urban Community* (Chicago: Chicago University Press, 1990).

have contested the misleading association that these authors make between racialization and criminality (see Chapter Five) or between crime and poverty.[32] Edwin Sutherland, who developed the concept of white-collar criminality, was among the first to question the fact that poverty was a cause of crime; after all, poor people do not all commit crime.[33] Writing from another perspective, Jack Katz suggested that we look into the foreground forces of crimes as opposed to the background forces. The lived experience of committing a crime is highly emotional and has both its seductive and its repulsive aspects, which could speak to people of any social class.[34] Katz believes that the proponents of materialistic theories of crime, emphasizing the relationship between crime and materialistic aspirations, do not want to recognize that crime occurs equally among the middle and upper classes, only in different forms (cold-blooded murder versus state bombing of a foreign country, or street corner theft versus offshore tax evasion) because this would send them an image of themselves (as murderers or thieves) that they are not prepared to face.

In turn, critical criminologists suggest that criminology wrongly focuses on the problem of crime and the criminal as opposed to the problem of social reaction (in other words, criminalization and punishment). Some have criticized the association between lower classes and crime by emphasizing policing and punishment practices.[35] Although they do not deny the impact of poverty and racism on one's living conditions and, thus, potentially on life opportunities and involvement with crime, these authors argue that it diverts attention away from the race and class biases in criminal prosecution, in particular as the police target some people based on stereotypes, prejudices, and discriminatory attitudes that police may hold. For instance, in North America people speak of the offence of "driving while Black" to refer to the racial profiling of Black drivers who are routinely stopped and questioned by the police based on pretextual traffic offences (see Chapter Eleven).[36]

---

32 Jerome G. Miller, *Search and Destroy: African-American Males in the Criminal Justice System* (Cambridge: Cambridge University Press, 1996); Michael Tonry, *Malign Neglect: Race, Crime and Punishment in America* (Oxford: Oxford University Press, 1995). For a conservative voice, see Clarence Thomas, "Personal Responsibility," *Regent University Law Review* 12 (1999–2000): 317.

33 Edwin Sutherland, Donald Cressey, and David Luckenbill, *Principles of Criminology* (Dix Hills, NY: General Hall, 1992).

34 Jack Katz, *Seductions of Crime: Moral and Sensual Attractions in Doing Evil* (New York: Basic Books, 1988).

35 See Bernard Harcourt, *Against Prediction: Profiling, Policing and Punishing in an Actuarial Age* (Chicago: Chicago University Press, 2007).

36 David A. Harris, "The Stories, the Statistics and the Law: Why 'Driving While Black' Matters," *University of Minnesota Law Review* 84 (1999): 265; David A. Harris, "Driving While Black and All Other Traffic Offenses: The Supreme Court and Pretextual Traffic Stops," *Journal of Criminal Law & Criminology* 87 (1997): 543.

Studies conducted in Montreal and Toronto all show that nonwhite, young, poor men and women are significantly more likely to be stopped, searched, arrested, and charged.[37]

Moreover, in self-reported surveys about criminality, surprisingly high numbers of people (from 75 to 90 per cent), regardless of their social class, admit having committed illegal acts without having being charged or prosecuted.[38] In this respect, sociologists and anthropologists have convincingly shown that there is considerable variation in the choice of justice systems used to punish people (criminal law, administrative law, civil law) and in the forms of punishment among social classes, which has the effect of hiding middle-class and higher-class criminality.[39] For instance, corporate embezzlement generally tends to be dealt with as an internal management issue or through administrative regulation, whereas small street corner theft is more systematically prosecuted through criminal courts.[40] Similarly, the Voluntary Disclosures Program at Canada Revenue Agency "allows taxpayers to come forward and correct inaccurate or incomplete information or to disclose information they have not reported" without being penalized or prosecuted, thereby transforming offshore fiscal evasion into a banal administrative issue.[41] Despite a relatively recent shift in public mentalities about the importance of white-collar criminality (money laundering, fraud, environmental crimes, etc.), white-collar criminals still tend to be generally punished through the imposition of fines, whereas street criminals typically end up being ticketed *and* incarcerated (see Chapter Fourteen).

For these reasons, many scholars have focused on the criminalization process or on the reasons why some conflictual situations end up

---

37 Paul Eid, *Profilage racial et discrimination systémique des jeunes racisés* (Montreal: Commission des droits de la personne et des droits de la jeunesse du Québec, 2011); Christine Campbell and Paul Eid, *La judiciarisation des personnes itinérantes à Montréal: Un cas de profilage social* (Montreal: Commission des droits de la personne et des droits de la jeunesse, 2009); Commission on Systemic Racism in the Ontario Criminal Justice System, *Report of the Commission on Systemic Racism in the Ontario Criminal Justice System* (Toronto, 1995); Bill O'Grady, Steve Gaetz, and Kristi Buccieri, *Can I See Your ID? The Policing of Youth Homelessness in Ontario* (Toronto: The Homeless Hub, 2011).

38 Marc LeBlanc, "Évolution de la délinquance cachée et officielle des adolescents québécois de 1930 à 2000," in *Traité de criminology empirique*, 3rd ed., ed. Marc LeBlanc, Marc Ouimet, and Denis Szabo, 39–70 (Montreal: Les Presses de l'Université de Montréal, 2003).

39 Vincenzo Ruggiero, *Crime and Markets: Essays in Anti-Criminology* (Oxford: Oxford University Press, 2000).

40 Law Commission of Canada, *What Is a Crime? Challenges and Alternatives*, Discussion Paper (Ottawa: Law Commission of Canada, 2003), 18. On the idea of selectivity, see Ian Taylor, Paul Walton, and Jock Young, *The New Criminology* (London: Routledge, 1973).

41 Canada Revenue Agency, "Voluntary Disclosures Program," http://www.cra-arc.gc.ca/voluntarydisclosures/ (accessed April 24, 2014).

being criminalized while others are not. In the 1960s, liberal criminologist Howard Becker suggested that "*social groups create deviance by making the rules whose infraction constitute deviance* and by applying those rules to particular people and labelling them as outsiders."[42] More critical criminologists, who drew from Marxism, radicalized this proposition and argued that crime was in fact the result of power conflicts and class struggles.[43] In Marxist theory, crime is useful to the capitalists in at least two ways. First, as a commodity, crime produces wealth by creating and maintaining a criminal justice system, including the whole apparatus of police, criminal lawyers, judges, professors, and prisons.[44] Second, crime acts as a mechanism for creating and regulating the labour force and the reserve army of the unemployed (the unemployed who are able to work) for the benefit of industrial capitalism.[45] Therefore, regardless of concessions made to the poor and underprivileged groups,[46] crime is defined and regulated to reflect the long-term interests and concerns of the ruling class as it tries to protect itself against the working class and the dangerous individuals inevitably left out by capitalist economies (the **lumpemproletariat**).[47]

Marxist theory fleshes out key questions with respect to the definition and representation of crime to reflect class power and the role of punishment in the management of class relations, which were echoed in the work of Foucault and other structuralist and poststructuralist scholars. As Chapter One

---

42 Howard S. Becker, *Outsiders: Studies in the Sociology of Deviance* (New York: Free Press, 1963), 9. Emphasis in original.

43 See, for instance, those who identified as "new criminologists": Taylor, Walton, and Young, *The New Criminology*.

44 Karl Marx, "The Usefulness of Crime," in *Crime and Capitalism: Readings in Marxist Criminology*, ed. David F. Greenberg (Philadelphia: Temple University Press, 1993), 52–53. See also Nils Christie, *Crime Control as Industry: Towards Gulags, Western Style*, 3rd ed. (London: Routledge, 2001).

45 Karl Marx, "The Labelling of Crime," in *Crime and Capitalism: Readings in Marxist Criminology*, ed. David F. Greenberg (Philadelphia: Temple University Press, 1993), 54; Rusche and Kirchheimer, *Punishment and Social Structure*.

46 Douglas Hay, "Crime, Property and Authority," in *Albion's Fatal Tree: Crime and Society in Eighteenth-Century England*, ed. Douglas Hay, Peter Linebaugh, John G. Rule, E.P. Thompson, and Cal Winslow (New York: Pantheon Books, 1975), 17; E.P. Thompson, *Whigs and Hunters: The Origin of the Black Act* (New York: Pantheon Books, 1975), 263.

47 See, for instance, Randall Shelden, *Controlling Dangerous Classes: A Critical Introduction to the History of Criminal Justice* (Boston: Allyn and Bacon, 2001); Jeffrey Reiman and Paul Leighton, *The Rich Get Richer and the Poor Get Prison: Ideology, Class and Criminal Justice*, 9th ed. (Boston: Pearson, 2009); Wacquant, "Deadly Symbiosis," Loïc Wacquant, *Punishing the Poor: The Neoliberal Government of Social Insecurity* (Durham: Duke University Press, 2009); Christian Parenti, *Lockdown America: Police and Prisons in the Age of Crisis* (New York: Verso, 1999).

demonstrates, Foucault's influence in criminology is enormous.[48] In *Discipline and Punish,* Foucault built on Georg Rusche and Otto Kirchheimer's work to explain historically the disappearance of public executions and the emergence of imprisonment as punitive techniques. Through his analysis, Foucault develops a theory about the "microphysics of power," referring to the way in which power is not only exercised at the macro level of the State but is also the result of power relationships at a micro level playing out everywhere through, for instance, daily surveillance, inspection, examination, discipline, routine, and rituals.[49] In prisons, the normalization of disciplining the poor is achieved through the imposition and introjection of schedules, rules, and manoeuvres. As you read in Chapter One, for Foucault punishment is not only about repressive power, but also about its relation to the development of knowledge and to **subject creation** (the process through which human beings are made into subjects). Thus, for Foucault punitive practices are political strategies of control over the body (forcing, shaping, and knowing it): "[I]n our societies, the systems of punishment are to be situated in a certain 'political economy' of the body,"[50] by which he means that bodies (and souls) are produced and constituted to serve capitalism. Prison as an institution created the category of the criminal by exercising power and developing knowledge about criminals (through criminology) and by defining, classifying, and categorizing individuals as criminals.[51] Drawing on these critical traditions, other scholars have emphasized the role of cultural and institutional practices and representations that shape our understanding of crime and the reality of punishment in everyday life.[52]

---

48 Foucault also influenced social sciences by the introduction of governmentality studies. See Graham Burchell, Colin Gordon, and Peter Miller, eds., *The Foucault Effect: Studies in Governmentality* (Chicago: Chicago University Press, 1991); David Garland, "Governmentality and the Problem of Crime: Foucault, Criminology, Sociology," *Theoretical Criminology* 1 (1997): 173; David Garland, *The Culture of Control: Crime and Social Order in Contemporary Society* (Chicago: University of Chicago Press, 2001); Malcolm Feeley and Jonathan Simon, "The New Penology: Notes on the Emerging Strategy of Corrections and its Implications," *Criminology* 30 (1992): 449.

49 Foucault, *Discipline and Punish.*

50 Ibid., 172.

51 Ibid.

52 See Garland, *The Culture of Control;* Nicola Lacey, *The Prisoners' Dilemma: Political Economy and Punishment in Contemporary Societies* (Cambridge: Cambridge University Press, 2008); Lacey discusses the dilemma between political economy and cultural studies of punishment (Chapter 1). See also Philippe Bourgois and Jeff Schonberg, *Righteous Dopefiend* (Berkeley: University of California Press, 2009), who draw from Marx, Foucault, and Bourdieu to develop the concept of "lumpen abuse," which refers to the "way structurally imposed everyday suffering generates violent and destructive subjectivities" (p. 19).

As we approach our case studies in the final part of this chapter, we should keep in mind these important insights from Bourdieu, Marx, and Foucault. Crime and criminality are historical, economic, sociopolitical, and cultural constructs. They reflect and are constitutive of a specific form of economic organization: a capitalist market economy.[53] In this economic system, the regulation of the poor through charity or public welfare policies is sometimes replaced by[54] and sometimes supplemented with[55] penal policies used to control those who contradict the social order in various ways. Criminalization also relies upon a series of cultural norms, moral judgments, and political interests of empowered groups and individuals in a society at a precise time of its history, and they are reflected and legitimized through everyday practices. For instance, as we shall see in the case of vagrancy and anti-disorder policies, criminalization is intrinsically connected to certain groups' conception of morality and public order and reflected through the police bureaucratic structure and practices.

Representing Class and Crime

General adherence to the criminal law and to the values of dominant interest groups is achieved through different means. It is first achieved through **ideology**, which consists of a set of conscious and unconscious ideas about the world that are presented and accepted as neutral, natural, and universal. Agents in the criminal justice system, including judges, lawyers, and politicians, refer to official narratives about, for example, individual responsibility or harm prevention to justify the infliction of punishment. These narratives are part of an ideology. This ideology has the effect of legitimating a social order by presenting a series of facts, conditions, or legal categories as neutral when they actually hide political choices and power struggles.[56] Apparent legal neutrality hides the fact that laws are applied mostly to the disadvantaged:

---

53 See Lacey, *The Prisoners' Dilemma*, 60, for a mapping of the varieties of capitalism.

54 Loïc Wacquant, "The Penalisation of Poverty and the Rise of Neo-Liberalism," *European Journal on Criminal Policy and Research* 9 (2001): 401, Loïc Wacquant, "Crafting the Neoliberal State: Workfare, Prisonfare, and Social Insecurity," *Sociological Forum* 25 (2010): 197.

55 Katherine Beckett and Bruce Western, "Governing Social Marginality: Welfare, Incarceration and the Transformation of State Policy," *Punishment and Society* 3 (2001): 43.

56 David Garland, "A Sociological Approach to Punishment," in *Crime and Justice: A Review of Research*, vol. 14, ed. Michael Tonry (Chicago: University of Chicago Press, 1991), 115, 128–29. Legitimation studies in Marxist theory go back to Louis Althusser, "Ideology and Ideological State Apparatuses (Notes toward an Investigation)," in *Lenin, Philosophy & Other Essays*, trans. Ben Brewster (New York: Monthly Review Press, 1971). See Chapter Three for a detailed discussion of ideology.

"In the courts, society as a whole does not judge one of its members, but ... a social category with an interest in order judges another that is dedicated to disorder."[57] Second, adherence is achieved through **hegemony**, a Gramscian concept referring to people's internalization of ruling-class ideas and interests as their own ideas and interests, thus making challenges to the existing social order unthinkable.[58] For example, the crime of theft certainly protects all those who own property, from those who own only a few personal items to the largest landowners of this planet, yet some have more to protect than others.

General adherence to the criminal law is also achieved through social and legal representations of the poor and the criminal. We should not underestimate the effect on our thinking of century-old statutes that hold that the economic and social activities of the poor are suspicious and potentially criminal, while the activities engaged in by aristocrats and landowners to enhance their wealth and capital are seen as an extension of their right to control their property. Yet, as you read in Chapter Three, the control of representations is even more sophisticated. While criminal law first bears upon the poor and the marginal, criminals cannot be merely associated with the precariat classes in people's minds; they have to appear unfamiliar, foreign, even monstrous, and they must be feared and become the poor's enemies.[59] Commenting on crime novels and the use of criminal *fait divers* (news stories), Foucault wrote that "The combination of the *fait divers* and the detective novel has produced for the last hundred years or more an enormous mass of crime stories in which delinquency appears both as very close and quite alien, a perpetual threat to everyday life, but extremely distant in its origin and motives, both everyday and exotic in the milieu in which it takes place."[60]

As a result, the reality of crime also depends on individual agency and cultural practices. The fact that crime reflects empowered groups' interests and the fact that there are several ways in which the general population adheres to this social order does not mean that there is a grand conspiracy on the part of the ruling class to incarcerate and discipline the poor. Remember, social classes are not ready-made categories constituted of self-conscious individuals; they are a series of individuals predisposed to exist as a class

---

57 Foucault, *Discipline and Punish*, 276.

58 Antonio Gramsci, *Selections from the Prison Notebooks* (New York: International Publishers, 1971). See Chapter Three for a detailed discussion of hegemony.

59 Michel Foucault, *Power/Knowledge: Selected Interviews & Other Writings 1972–1977*, ed. Colin Gordon (New York: Pantheon Books, 1980), 46–47.

60 Foucault, *Discipline and Punish*, 296.

because of their commonalities, but also because of their distinctions from people of other classes. Moreover, police, prosecutors and judges, and criminals themselves have a role to play through their everyday practices and acts of resistance, and they shape the definition and regulation of crime in this country.[61] We will now illustrate the complexity of the intersections between crime and social class through our case studies.

The Regulation of "Public Disorder": Vagrancy and Homelessness

The regulation and the criminalization of homeless people show remarkable historical continuity. Vagrancy arguably started to be considered a social problem after the Black Death plague in England in 1348.[62] The first anti-vagrancy statute was passed in 1349, making it a crime to give alms to "many sound beggars [who] refuse to labour," while "giving themselves to idleness and sins, and at times to robbery and other crimes."[63] The wording of that statute set the tone for centuries of misrepresentations of poor and homeless people in Anglo-Saxon countries. In 1824, for example, the United Kingdom adopted An Act for the Punishment of Idle and Disorderly Persons, and Rogues and Vagabonds, providing for the commitment of any person wandering in any public place who begged while "being able wholly or in part to maintain himself or herself, or his or her Family, by Work or by other Means, and wilfully refusing or neglecting to do so."[64] The consistent themes in such statutes is that homeless people (i.e., vagrants) are portrayed as morally inferior, lazy, and dishonest individuals who are to be blamed for their own misfortunes and treated as criminals or potentially serious offenders.

It is clear that there is a strong connection between the adoption of vagrancy statutes and the form of economic organization and class structure that prevailed at the time of its adoption. For William Chambliss, there is little doubt that the first statute was enacted for the purpose of replacing serfdom by "[forcing] laborers to accept employment at a low wage in order

---

61 Garland, *The Culture of Control*, 23–26. Garland was referring to Pierre Bourdieu, "Social Space and Symbolic Power," *Sociological Theory* (1989): 7; and Anthony Giddens, *The Constitution of Society* (Oxford: Polity Press, 1984).

62 John L. Gillin, "Vagrancy and Begging," *American Journal of Sociology* 35 (1929): 424, 427.

63 *Statute of Labourers*, Ed. III, available at http://avalon.law.yale.edu/medieval/statlab.asp (accessed April 13, 2014).

64 *An Act for the Punishment of Idle and Disorderly Persons, and Rogues and Vagabonds*, 1824 (UK), 5 Geo IV, c 83, s 3, available at http://www.legislation.gov.uk/ukpga/1824/83/pdfs/ukpga_18240083_en.pdf (accessed April 13, 2014).

to insure [sic] the landowner an adequate supply of labor at a price he could afford to pay."[65] In sixteenth-century England, vagrancy statutes shifted their focus from labourers to criminals who, "to the great terror of her majesty's true subjects," were attacking merchants transporting goods on the roads.[66] In the United States, Chambliss found that vagrancy statutes were explicitly concerned with the control of undesirable people such as free "Negroes," although there is some evidence that these laws were also used at times to control workers' mobility, particularly during the depression years and in California in an attempt to stop the flight of migrant workers.[67]

Chambliss's class-based analysis was subsequently challenged by some historians and sociologists who argued that vagrancy statutes evolved throughout history as a response to different concerns: from paupers coming by the thousands from the countryside to the cities, challenging the social order through riots, carrying diseases, and overburdening poverty-relief aid mechanisms in the city in the sixteenth century; to prostitutes, pimps, and other wanderers who threatened small town morality in the nineteenth century; and to a catchall category for any undesirable people in twentieth-century North America.[68] Yet this historical research does not refute Chambliss's work but complements it. In fact, if we think about class struggle in a Bourdieusian sense as including struggles over economic power but also over social, cultural, and symbolic forms of power, it is easy to see how the criminalization and regulation of vagrants corresponds to certain groups' interests.

The first Vagrancy Act was adopted in Canada in 1869, modelled upon English legislation.[69] It was replaced by the adoption of the Criminal Code of Canada in 1892.[70] Section 207 of the 1892 Criminal Code created a list of 12 enumerated offences falling within the vagrancy section of the Code and aiming to address a multitude of social issues ranging from labour ("not having any visible means of maintaining himself"; "being able to work and

---

65 William Chambliss, "A Sociological Analysis of the Law of Vagrancy," *Social Problems* 12 (1964): 67, 69.

66 Ibid., 74.

67 Ibid.

68 Jeffrey S. Alder, "A Historical Analysis of the Law of Vagrancy," *Criminology* 27 (1989): 209, 213–16; Paul A. Slack, "Vagrants and Vagrancy in England, 1598–1664," *The Economic History Review* 27 (1974): 360; Mary Anne Poutanen, "The Geography of Prostitution in an Early Nineteenth-Century Urban Centre: Montreal, 1810–1842," in *Power, Place and Identity: Historical Studies of Social and Legal Regulation in Quebec* (Montreal: May 1996).

69 Prashan Ranasinghe, "Reconceptualizing Vagrancy and Reconstructing the Vagrant: A Socio-Legal Analysis of Criminal Law Reform in Canada, 1953–1972," *Osgoode Hall Law Journal* 48 (2010): 55, 62.

70 Criminal Code of Canada, S.C. 1892 (55–56 Vict), c. 29, ss. 207–208.

refusing to do so"; "begging" while not being a "deserving object of charity"); morality ("indecent exhibition," "being a common prostitute," keeping or frequenting a "common bawdy-house"; living "by the avails of prostitution"); mischief (breaking windows, roads, walls, or gardens); and other common nuisances ("loitering," causing a disturbance while being drunk, "disturbing the peace" by discharging firearms, or rioting). A person convicted of one of these various offences was labelled a "loose, idle, disorderly person or vagrant."[71] According to Prashan Ranasinghe, the eclecticism of these offences shows that nineteenth-century Canadians perceived the vagrant in at least three different ways: First, vagrants were thought to be "indolent, lazy and worthless" individuals who did not want to work; second, they were perceived to be "professional" or "habitual criminals," as in the case of prostitutes or tramps, likely to engage in more serious criminality if provided the right opportunity; and finally, they were considered "morally depraved" or "outcasts," belonging to a "self-perpetuating class of citizens who lived without fixed abode."[72] Many of the vagrancy offences listed in section 207 were interpreted by the courts as not applying to "persons of good character" or "respectable citizens."[73] Moreover, references to idleness and disorder as well as explicit distinctions drawn between vagrants and her majesty's "true subjects" have the effect of downplaying the importance of social structures and economic changes, suggesting that homeless people were lazy or morally inferior individuals. Interestingly, Foucault arrived at the same conclusions when writing about France: "Behind the offenses of the vagabond, there is laziness; that is what one must fight against."[74]

Finally, historical patterns of criminalization have emphasized the dangerous character of vagrants and homeless people who represented a threat to society. For instance, Foucault refers to a memorandum on vagabondage published in 1764 in which judge Le Trosne presents vagabonds as useless, dangerous, and barbaric outsiders who "live in the midst of society without being members of it, [they are] in that state that one supposes existed before the establishment of civil society." He also recommended that "[they] should

---

71 Section 207 reads as follows: "Everyone is a loose, idle, or disorderly person or vagrant who ..."
72 Ranasinghe, "Reconceptualizing Vagrancy," 60–61. See also David Bright, "Loafers Are Not Going to Subsist upon Public Credulence: Vagrancy and the Law in Calgary, 1900–1914" *Labour* 36 (1995): 37, 41–42. Bright argues that while North American studies have largely emphasized the fact that vagrancy provisions were used by the ruling class to control the lower classes, Canadian studies have rather insisted on promoting respect for values of order and respectability, occluding evident class interests.
73 Ranasinghe, "Reconceptualizing Vagrancy," 74, footnote 87, referring to *R. v. Kneeland* (1903) 6 CCC 81 (Qc KB) and *R. v. Law* (1924) 42 CCC 123 (Winnipeg Police Ct.).
74 Foucault, *Discipline and Punish*, 106.

be acquired by the state and belong to it as slaves to their masters," and that rewards should be offered to capture them. After all, as Le Trosne observed, "a reward of ten pounds is given for anyone who kills a wolf. A vagabond is infinitely more dangerous for society."[75]

Anti-panhandling statutes and anti-disorder bylaws adopted in Canadian cities in the 1990s and 2000s, such as the Safe Streets Acts of Ontario and British Columbia,[76] as well as red zones or no-go orders issued by criminal courts, are in many ways modern substitutes for vagrancy statutes. The adoption of anti-disorder statutes or bylaws relied on the **broken window theory** (BWT). According to this theory, the absence of social and legal responses to minor offences and to the first signs of disorder in a neighbourhood (a broken window, for example) signals to potential offenders that this neighbourhood is not concerned with preserving order in its public spaces and that crime will be tolerated.[77] The proponents of BWT have associated "panhandlers, drunks, addicts, rowdy teenagers, prostitutes, loiterers, [and] the mentally disturbed"[78] with broken windows or signs of disorder. It is fascinating to see how much resemblance the BWT bears with the logic and rationality used to control the vagrant in the nineteenth century, as illustrated by Foucault in his reference to the policy at Mettray, a juvenile prison: "[T]he least act of disobedience is punished and the best way of avoiding serious offence is to punish the most minor offences very severely."[79] This rationality was based on an "almost universal opinion" expressed by the directors of the *maison centrales* in 1836 about the nature of minor offenders like vagrants: "The minor offenders are generally the most vicious ... Among the criminals, one meets many men who have given in to the violence of their passions and to the needs of a large family. The behaviour of criminals is much better than that of minor offenders; the former are more submissive, harder-working than the latter, who, in general, are pickpockets, debauchees and idlers."[80]

The proponents of BWT also portray homeless people who are deemed responsible for disorderly acts as "disreputable or obstreperous or unpredictable people."[81] Underlying their moral inferiority, they suggest that these

75 Ibid., 88, referring to G. Le Trosne, *Mémoire sur les vagabonds*, 1764.
76 Safe Streets Act, 1999, S.O. 1999, c. 8 (Ontario); Safe Streets Act, S.B.C. 2004, c. 75 (British Columbia).
77 James Q. Wilson and George L. Kelling, "Broken Windows: The Police and Neighborhood Safety," *Atlantic Monthly* 249 (1982): 29.
78 Ibid., 32.
79 Bernard Harcourt, *Illusion of Order: The False Promise of Broken Windows Policing* (Cambridge, MA: Harvard University Press, 2001), 160, referring to Foucault, *Discipline and Punish*, 298.
80 Foucault, *Discipline and Punish*, 245.
81 Wilson and Kelling, "Broken Windows," 30.

people are associated with the threat of having a "stable neighbourhood of families who care for their homes and mind each other's children" transformed into an "inhospitable and frightening jungle" inhabited by "unattached adults."[82] They further compare "respectable people" to "street people," "good citizens" to homeless people, and "good kids" to "criminals or wannabes."[83] The proponents of BWT also insist that homeless people should be held personally responsible and repressed for their choice to live on the streets. They observe that "not all those designated as homeless in these [cases] are in this condition involuntarily. Yet, their choice to live on the streets is disruptive to others."[84] They classify the homeless into groups: the *have-nots*, who are genuinely poor and will eventually move back into mainstream society; the *can-nots*, who are seriously mentally ill or drug addicts; and the *will-nots*, for whom living on the streets is a lifestyle (i.e., a choice).[85] Clearly, we are only one step away from the discourse held about the vagrant who chose not to labour in the late Middle Ages.

Canadian authorities partly relied on the insights and underlying narratives of this theory to build their order-maintenance programs in the 1990s. Adopted in 1999, the Ontario Safe Streets Act aimed "to crack down on aggressive panhandlers and on squeegee people who harass and intimidate motorists."[86] At the time, squeegee kids were described as lazy or dangerous, taking advantage of the public.[87] In British Columbia, Mario Berti writes that a "growing number of panhandlers and 'binners,' as well as people sleeping in doorway alcoves on streets and alleys, in parking lots, and in parks," were interpreted as signs of public disorder[88] and triggered the adoption of their own Safe Streets Act.[89] In Montreal, the police ranked fighting antisocial behaviour among their top priorities in 2003[90] and adopted a policy with respect to disorder that referred to a list of antisocial acts to be closely monitored, which the City of Montreal explicitly endorsed

---

82 Ibid., 31.

83 George L. Kelling and Catherine M. Coles, *Fixing Broken Windows: Restoring Order and Reducing Crime in Our Communities* (New York: Martin Kessler Books, 1996).

84 Ibid., 66.

85 Ibid., 68.

86 *R. v. Banks* (2005), O.J. no. 98 (Ontario Sup. Ct of J.), par. 3, quoting former Ontario Premier Michael Harris.

87 Patrick Parnaby, "Disaster through Dirty Windshields: Law, Order and Toronto's Squeegee Kids," *Canadian Journal of Sociology* 28 (2003): 281.

88 Mario Berti, "Handcuffed Access: Homelessness and the Justice System," *Urban Geography* 31 (2010): 825.

89 Safe Streets Act, S.B.C. 2004, c. 75 (British Columbia).

90 Service de police de la ville de Montréal, Report on the Optimization of the Neighbourhood Police, 2003.

and which included "public consumption of alcohol and drugs," "spitting, urinating, littering," "presence of prostitutes/soliciting," "bothersome presence of
homeless persons or beggars," and "bothersome presence of 'squeegees.'"[91]

The adoption of these bylaws, statutes, and policies against disorder is a
great example of how penal policy is not merely responsive to criminality.
Several scholars have demonstrated the lack of conclusive empirical evidence
to support the connection between physical disorder and serious criminality,
or the fact that broken window policing had produced declines in crime
rates.[92] In fact, many scholars suggest that the policing of disorder is a response
to the social, political, and economic interests of certain empowered groups in
particular neighbourhoods.[93] The definition and policing of disorder reflect,
at least in part, a threat to the economic and political interests as well as to
representations of order and the lifestyles of the upper-middle classes, such as
young professionals and other educated managerial labour and investors in
the late twentieth century.[94] Disorder policing brings to light the tension that
exists between "those who do not have the financial means to provide ... for
a full and meaningful existence and those who are importuned to part with
'any spare change.'"[95] In a previous study in Montreal, I showed that certain
interest groups, including residents' associations, merchants, and business associations, were more likely than other groups to feel threatened by disorder in
the city and were predisposed, given their position in the social space, to be
mobilized to support programs against disorder.[96] It is also easy to see how
certain moral judgments about what a good life should be and how people
should behave in public places transpire from these pieces of legislation.[97]

91 Ibid., Annex 2.
92 Harcourt, *Illusion of Order*; Bernard E. Harcourt and Jens Ludwig, "Broken Windows: New Evidence
from New York City and a Five-City Social Experiment," *University of Chicago Law Review* 73
(2006): 271; Franklin E. Zimring, *The Great American Crime Decline* (Oxford: Oxford University
Press, 2007); John Eck and Edward Maguire, "Have Changes in Policing Reduced Violent Crime?
An Assessment of the Evidence," in *The Crime Drop in America*, ed. Alfred Blumstein and Joel
Wallman (Cambridge: Cambridge University Press, 2000), 207; Jock Young, *The Exclusive Society:
Social Exclusion, Crime and Difference in Late Modernity* (London: Sage Publications, 1999).
93 Steve Herbert, *Citizens, Cops and Power* (Chicago: University of Chicago Press, 2006); William
Lyons, *The Politics of Community Policing* (Ann Arbor: University of Michigan Press, 1997);
Marie-Eve Sylvestre, "Policing the Homeless in Montreal: Is This Really What the Population
Wants?" *Policing & Society* 20 (2010): 432.
94 Parenti, *Lockdown America*; Young, *The Exclusive Society*; Loïc Wacquant, *Prisons of Poverty*
(Minneapolis: Minnesota University Press, 2002).
95 *Federated Anti-Poverty Groups of B.C. v. Vancouver (City)*, 2002, BCSC 105, par. 43.
96 Sylvestre, "Policing the Homeless in Montreal," 449–50.
97 Harcourt, *Illusions of Order*; Marie-Eve Sylvestre, "Disorder and Public Spaces in Montreal:
Repression (and Resistance) through Law, Politics, and Police Discretion," *Urban Geography* 31,
no. 6 (2010): 803–24.

Anti-disorder policies clearly show class biases in law enforcement. In Toronto and Ottawa, there were 16,860 and 4,882 certificates of offences issued against homeless people between 2000 and 2006, respectively, after the Safe Streets Act came into force.[98] In British Columbia, there were 1,370 tickets issued to homeless people between 2005 and 2008.[99] Finally, in Montreal the police issued 64,491 statements of offence for violations of bylaws or the regulations of the Montreal Transportation Society to 8,252 homeless people between April 1994 and December 2010. Almost half of those statements (30,551) were issued in the last five years (2006–10).[100] In all of these cities, including Montreal, these numbers are only the tip of the iceberg.[101] The vast majority of homeless people were rarely able to pay the fines, and because of this they frequently end up being incarcerated. For instance, in Ontario only 0.3 per cent of all certificates of offences issued against homeless people (51 out of 16,860 in Toronto and 14 out of 4,880 in Ottawa) were actually paid between 2000 and 2006.[102] In Montreal, of the 7,650 statements of offence that reached a complete resolution during the period of the first Bellot study (1994–2004), 72.3 per cent were closed after the offender was incarcerated for default of payment.[103] Bellot found that offenders spent, in total, more than 70,000 days in prison for the nonpayment of statements of offence between 1994 and 2004.

Alarmed by the conclusions of these studies, the Quebec Human Rights Commission produced a legal opinion suggesting that the overpenalization of homeless people was a direct consequence of their social profiling by the Montreal police. According to the Commission, *social profiling* refers to "any action taken by one or several persons in a position of authority with respect

---

98 Catherine Chesnay, Céline Bellot, and Marie-Eve Sylvestre, "Taming Disorderly People One Ticket at a Time: The Penalization of Homelessness in Ontario and British Columbia," *Canadian Journal of Criminology and Criminal Justice* 55, no. 22 (2013): 161–85.

99 Ibid.

100 Céline Bellot and Marie-Eve Sylvestre, "La judiciarisation des personnes itinérantes à Montréal: 15 années de recherche, faits et enjeux," The Homeless Hub, www.homelesshub.ca, 2012; Marie-Eve Sylvestre, Céline Bellot, Philippe Antoine Couture-Ménard, and Alexandra Tremblay, "Le droit est aussi une question de visibilité: occupation des espaces publics et parcours judiciaires des personnes itinérantes à Montréal et à Ottawa," *Canadian Journal of Law and Society* 26 (2011): 531.

101 Numbers only include individuals who, at the time of the issuance, provided the address of one of the organizations or shelters working with street youth or the homeless population in the city as their own. Moreover, homeless individuals are also charged with infractions to provincial legislation. For instance, in Ontario tickets are routinely issued in accordance with the Highway Traffic Act, the Liquor Licence Act, the Environmental Protection Act, the Trespass to Property Act, as well as bylaws. These infractions are not included in our numbers.

102 Sylvestre et al., "Le droit est une question de visibilité," 550.

103 Ibid.

to a person or a group of persons, for the purposes of safety, security or public protection, that relies on social condition, whether it is real or presumed, without any reason or reasonable suspicion, with the effect of subjecting that person to differential treatment."[104] In turn, *social condition* refers to a rank, social position, or class attributed to someone principally because of his or her level of income, occupation, and education.[105]

The Commission argued that homeless people were victims of "systemic discrimination" because discrimination ensued from a series of factors, including citywide policies, institutional statements, bylaws, policing practices, and discretion and was not the result of an isolated factor.[106] The Commission estimated that homeless people had received between 30 per cent and 50 per cent of all statements of offences issued in the territory served by the Montreal police in 2004 and 2005. Using the same methodology, Bellot and Sylvestre later found that between 2006 and 2010 homeless people received, on average, approximately 25 per cent of all statements of offences issued by the Montreal police.[107] In contrast, the most recent estimates establish that homeless people represent between 1 to 2 per cent of the population of Montreal.[108]

Anti-disorder campaigns also had a tremendous impact on racial relations in various neighbourhoods. In New York, for instance, complaints of police misconduct increased by 68 per cent in the first three years of implementation of the programs and aggressive stops and searches fell disproportionately on Blacks and Hispanics in the city.[109] In Montreal and Toronto, policies emphasizing the policing of minor offences led to multiple pretextual stops, ID verifications, and arrests among racial minorities.[110] Finally, anti-disorder strategies more recently have also translated into the imposition and enforcement of red zones or no-go orders. Area restrictions, "no-go" orders, and other similar conditions can be issued by police officers in a promise to

---

104 Campbell and Eid, *La judiciarisation des personnes itinérantes à Montréal*, 89–96.

105 André Labonté, *Lignes directrices sur la condition sociale* (Montreal: Commission des droits de la personne et des droits de la jeunesse, 1994).

106 Campbell and Eid, *La judiciarisation des personnes itinérantes à Montréal*.

107 Bellot and Sylvestre, *La judiciarisation des personnes itinérantes à Montréal*.

108 Statistics Canada, *Census 2005*, cited in Campbell and Eid, *La judiciarisation des personnes itinérantes à Montréal*, 43.

109 Eliot Spitzer, *The New York City Police Department's Stop and Frisk Practices: A Report to the People of the State of New York from the Office of the Attorney General* (New York: A.G. Office). Between January 1998 and April 1999 whites, who represent 43.3 per cent of the population in New York City, accounted for 12.9 per cent of all stops, whereas Blacks, who represent 25.6 per cent of the population, and Hispanics, who represent 23.7 per cent, accounted respectively for 50.6 per cent and 33.3 per cent of all stops.

110 Eid, *Profilage racial et discrimination systémique des jeunes racisés*.

appear notice delivered to a person released after arrest to compel his or her attendance in court. They may also be issued by lower court judges as conditions of bail or sentencing to prohibit some individuals from being within the limits of a determined perimeter or from being in a particular place like a park or property that is generally accessible to the public where they were deemed to have committed a criminal offence.[111] While red zones or no-go orders are civil preventive orders by nature, breaches of a court order or of a bail condition constitute a criminal offence.[112] Red zones and other spatial restriction orders have the direct effect of banishing individuals from important parts of town or communities,[113] but perhaps more importantly they provide yet another pretext for law enforcement officers to control poor and marginalized individuals who might not be able to escape the targeted area for different reasons, such as work, family, access to community resources (housing and social services), or social networks.

In this context, disorder, an arguably neutral and general concept, has gained a very specific meaning. As Bernard Harcourt put it, "disorder may contain a lot of order; the disorderly, after all, are not chosen by lot."[114] This definition of disorder was never a given, but the result of social, economic, political, and moral choices. Consider for a moment why urinating in the street when you have no access to public restrooms, consuming alcohol or drugs in public spaces when you do not have the comfort of a home to do so, or begging, soliciting, and **squeegeeing** as street survival strategies are considered more disorderly than other forms of behaviour performed in public spaces, which could include sexual harassment, commercial advertisement and soliciting, and repression of democratic and peaceful protests and public meetings? And this does not even take into account the amount of social disorder that is caused by systemic racism in the workplace, the lack of affordable housing or access to mental health care, governmental cuts in social assistance, and widespread corruption in cities and government contracts.

---

111 Marie-Eve Sylvestre, Dominique Bernier, and Céline Bellot, "Red Zones Orders in Canadian Courts and the Reproduction of Socio-Economic Inequality," *Oñati Socio-Legal Series* (forthcoming).

112 Andrew Ashworth and Lucia Zedner, "Preventive Orders: A Problem of Undercriminalization?" in *The Boundaries of Criminal Law*, ed. R.A. Duff, L. Farmer, S.E. Marshall, M. Renzo, and V. Tadros (Oxford: Oxford University Press, 2010), 64.

113 Katherine Beckett and Steve Hebert, *Banished* (New York: Oxford University Press, 2010).

114 Harcourt, *Illusion of Order*, 19; see also Bernard Harcourt, "Reflecting on the Subject: A Critique of the Social Influence Conception of Deterrence, the Broken Windows Theory, and Order-Maintenance Policing New York Style," *Michigan Law Review* 97 (1998): 291.

Policing Gangs: Putting "Disorder" into Effect

How does the construction of "public disorder" play out through everyday enforcement practices? The demands of powerful interest groups and individuals are reflected in the police bureaucratic reward structure and mission. While there is no conspiracy behind the arrest and policing of the powerless, to act accordingly does make organizational sense. Let's illustrate this idea through an example taken from the policing of gangs.

In his classic 1973 study, William Chambliss discusses the results of a comparative study of police encounters of two gangs of high school boys referred to respectively as "the Saints" and "the Roughnecks," whom he observed during a two-year period spent in the suburb of a large metropolitan area.[115] The Saints were a group of eight white young men from upper-middle-class families, whereas the Roughnecks were a group of six white lower-class young men. Over those two years, he found that the Saints engaged in the following delinquent activities: truancy (missing school); speeding; drunk driving; underage drinking; vandalism; theft of tools, lanterns, and barricades from construction sites; and harassment of women. In comparison, the Roughnecks engaged in underage drinking, fighting, small theft (comic books, books, pens, watches, gasoline, etc.), burglary, loitering in the streets, and public harassment.[116]

Despite the fact that both groups equally engaged in criminal activities, Chambliss discovered that they solicited completely different and opposite reactions from both the school authorities and the police. In fact, school officials did not even seem to notice the Saints's high level of delinquency and, on the rare occasion that they did acknowledge the group's behaviour, they were always ready to forgive them. The Saints were popular in school, with quite a few of them being members of the athletic teams and, even though they missed school on a regular basis and often did not do well on exams or did not hand in their homework, school officials continuously believed them to be "capable of doing better."[117] The police also expressed their belief that the Saints were simply a good bunch of kids who were having some fun; they were rarely arrested, and when they were they were usually able to get away with it by asking for forgiveness.

On the other hand, school officials and the police never forgave the Roughnecks for anything they did and perceived them to be nothing more

---

115 William J. Chambliss, *Power, Politics & Crime* (Boulder: Westview Press, 1999), 100.
116 Ibid., 101–10.
117 Ibid., 105.

than troublemakers. In school, teachers thought that they were uninterested in making something of themselves, and although two of them were excellent football players they were criticized for not playing by the rules and skipping practices. As for the police, they distrusted the Roughnecks. Several members were arrested numerous times while others spent time in reform schools. They were all perceived as "a bad bunch of boys" by both the police and the community as a whole.

Chambliss observed that no one group was more or less delinquent than the other. The Saints missed school every day and vandalized property, whereas the Roughnecks stole items. In terms of economic costs, their respective behaviour led to similar or equal results. In terms of physical harm, the Saints regularly drove while drunk and were often careless on the road in general, whereas the Roughnecks frequently fought. Chambliss did notice, however, that the Saints usually engaged in indoor or "invisible" criminality, while the Roughnecks had a tendency to stay outside and engage in "in your face" street criminality. Finally, the community believed the first group to be "good kids," while the other group was seen as troublemakers.

For Chambliss, there was no conspiracy to arrest members of the lower classes. However, it does make organizational sense to do so. Police officers usually stay out of trouble and face less resistance from offenders upon arrest and less criticism from their superiors if they only deal with the poor while avoiding any encounter with the powerful and "their high-priced lawyers."[118] And perhaps more importantly, a sense of what is deemed to be "criminal" is acquired and internalized by the police through their encounters with the community (i.e., upper-middle-class parents who say that the things their children are doing are merely youthful mistakes, not crimes), as well as from simply being part of the said community.[119] They automatically sort people into those who are likely to do well in life and become respectable individuals and those who will more than likely end up becoming criminals. The forms of sorting and regulation occur through particular forms of representation. As was observed by Chambliss, this categorization is often made in accordance with race and class position. The Saints were well-dressed, well-mannered boys who drove expensive cars, whereas the Roughnecks were "the not-so-well-dressed and the not-so-well-mannered" boys who loitered on street corners. The Saints were apologetic and penitent in their encounters with the police, whereas the Roughnecks were confrontational and hostile. It

---

118 Ibid., 115.

119 Rob White and Chris Cunneen, "Social Class, Youth Crime and Justice," in *Youth Crime and Justice*, ed. Barry Goldson and John Muncie (London: Sage Publications, 2006), 19.

is highly possible that the police may have identified better with one group as opposed to the other; in dealing with these youth, they might have seen in them younger versions of themselves or some of their friends, thinking back nostalgically to a time when they had the right to make mistakes and have fun. As Chambliss's important study makes clear, as a result of the dynamic interaction between institutional incentives and political demands, the police actually retreat to and reinforce a conception of policing as repressive and aimed at protecting corporative interests linked to those of certain groups in the community.[120]

Conclusion

In the last few decades, critical scholars have rightfully referred to the "penalization or criminalization of poverty,"[121] the "governance of social marginality,"[122] the "welfarisation of prisons,"[123] and the "warehousing" of the poor[124] to describe the tragedy of the economic dimensions of criminal justice. Even more tragic is the fact that while such expressions do reflect the reality of crime and punishment in the twenty-first century, they are certainly not recent phenomena. According to Jean-Marie Fecteau, the history of criminalization of poverty has always been about reconciling our understanding of crime as a free and individual act with the collective stigmatization of human misery.[125] This chapter has tried to show that there are historical continuities in criminalization patterns and representations of crime based on class. While certain scholars would be quick to talk about the end of a class-based society, it seems clear that class—understood as an economic but also as a social, cultural and symbolic principle—is still a relevant principle of social division and domination. Empowered classes may not have a class consciousness in the way Marx wanted us to believe, but they certainly do share commonalities and interests and do mobilize their various forms of capital to protect themselves. In turn, these interests are reflected in daily law enforcement practices and representations of crime and disorder.

---

120 Sylvestre, "Policing the Homeless in Montreal."
121 Wacquant, "The Penalisation of Poverty."
122 Beckett and Western, "Governing Social Marginality," 43.
123 Daniel Gilling, "Community Safety and Social Policy," *European Journal on Criminal Policy and Research* 9 (2001): 381, 398; Wacquant, "Crafting the Neoliberal State."
124 Jonathan Simon, "Mass Incarceration: From Social Policy to Social Problem," in *The Oxford Handbook of Sentencing and Corrections*, ed. Joan Petersilia and Kevin R. Reitz (Oxford: Oxford University Press, 2013), 1.
125 Jean-Marie Fecteau, *La liberté du pauvre: Crime et pauvreté au XIXe siècle québécois* (Montreal: VLB Éditeur, 2004), 145.

Study Questions

1. What is the relationship between criminality and economic disadvantage?
2. Think about the concept of harm in society. Is there a class bias in the definition of harm?
3. What are the continuities in the representations of the homeless throughout history and in contemporary times?
4. Does class differ from other identifiable principles of social division, such as religion, race, gender, and ethnicity? Discuss the differences, similarities, and overlaps based on what you have learned about social classes.

Exercise

Consider the following groups of people:

*   Sex workers working at a street corner versus escorts accompanying men on business trips versus waitresses working in a fast-food restaurant off the highway
*   Black bloc protesters smashing bank windows at an anti-globalization demonstration versus unionized strikers defying an injunction to stop obstructing entrance to the premises of a company versus civil rights demonstrators calling for civil disobedience acts against segregation statutes

Compare the different representations of these groups conveyed by the criminal justice system and discuss how the concept of social classes might be relevant in understanding such differences.

Keywords

couch-surfing; social classes; capital; habitus; subject creation; ideology; hegemony; broken window theory; squeegeeing

References

Alder, J.S. "A Historical Analysis of the Law of Vagrancy." *Criminology* 27 (1989): 213–16.
Althusser, L. "Ideology and Ideological State Apparatuses (Notes toward an Investigation)." In *Lenin, Philosophy & Other Essays*. Translated by Ben Brewster. New York: Monthly Review Press, 1971.

Anderson, E. *Streetwise: Race, Class and Change in an Urban Community.* Chicago: Chicago University Press, 1990.

Ashworth, A., and Lucia Zedner. "Preventive Orders: A Problem of Undercriminalization?" In *The Boundaries of Criminal Law,* edited by R.A. Duff, L. Farmer, S.E. Marshall, et al. Oxford: Oxford University Press, 2010. http://dx.doi.org/10.1093/acprof:oso/9780199600557.003.0003.

Becker, H.S. *Outsiders: Studies in the Sociology of Deviance.* New York: Free Press, 1963.

Beckett, K., and Bruce Western. "Governing Social Marginality: Welfare, Incarceration and the Transformation of State Policy." *Punishment and Society* 3, no. 1 (2001): 43–59. http://dx.doi.org/10.1177/14624740122228249.

Beckett, K., and Steve Herbert. *Banished.* New York: Oxford University Press, 2010.

Bellot, C., and Marie-Eve Sylvestre, "La judiciarisation des personnes itinérantes à Montréal: 15 années de recherche, faits et enjeux." The Homeless Hub, www.homelesshub.ca, 2012.

Berti, M. "Handcuffed Access: Homelessness and the Justice System." *Urban Geography* 31, no. 6 (2010): 825–41.

Bourdieu, P. "Social Space and Symbolic Power." *Sociological Theory* 7 (1989): 14–25.

Bourdieu, B. "The Force of Law: Toward a Sociology of the Juridical Field." *Hastings Law Journal* 38 (1987).

Bourdieu, P. "What Makes a Social Class? On the Theoretical and Practical Existence of Groups." *Berkeley Journal of Sociology* 32 (1987): 1–17.

Bourdieu, P. *Distinction: A Social Critique of the Judgement of Taste.* Translated by Richard Nice. Cambridge, MA: Harvard University Press, 1984.

Bourdieu, P. *Practical Reason.* Palo Alto: Stanford University Press, 1998.

Bourgois, P., and J. Schonberg. *Righteous Dopefiend.* Berkeley: University of California Press, 2009.

Bright, D. "Loafers Are Not Going to Subsist upon Public Credulence: Vagrancy and the Law in Calgary, 1900–1914." *Labour* 36 (1995): 37. http://dx.doi.org/10.2307/25143973.

Burchell, G., C. Gordon, and P. Miller, eds. *The Foucault Effect: Studies in Governmentality.* Chicago: Chicago University Press, 1991. http://dx.doi.org/10.7208/chicago/9780226028811.001.0001.

Campbell, Christine, and Paul Eid. *La judiciarisation des personnes itinérantes à Montréal: un cas de profilage social.* Montreal: Commission des droits de la personne et des droits de la jeunesse, 2009.

Canada Revenue Agency. "Voluntary Disclosures Program." http://www.cra-arc.gc.ca/voluntarydisclosures/ (accessed April 24, 2014).

Carson, E. Ann, and William J. Sabol. *Prisoners in 2011.* Bureau of Justice Statistics. http://www.bjs.gov/index.cfm?ty=pbdetail&iid=4559 (accessed April 13, 2014).

Chambliss, W. "A Sociological Analysis of the Law of Vagrancy." *Social Problems* 12, no. 1 (1964): 67–77. http://dx.doi.org/10.2307/798699.

Chambliss, W. *Power, Politics & Crime.* Boulder: Westview Press, 1999.

Chesnay, C., Céline Bellot, and Marie-Eve Sylvestre. "Taming Disorderly People One Ticket at a Time: The Penalization of Homelessness in Ontario and British Columbia." *Canadian Journal of Criminology and Criminal Justice* 55, no. 22 (2013): 161–85. http://dx.doi.org/10.3138/cjccj.2011-E-46.

Christie, Nils. *Crime Control as Industry: Towards Gulags, Western Style,* 3rd ed. London: Routledge, 2001.

Cohen, A. *Delinquent Boys.* New York: Free Press, 1955.

Collin, C., and H. Jensen. *A Statistical Profile of Poverty in Canada.* Ottawa: Library of Parliament, 2009.

Commission on Systemic Racism in the Ontario Criminal Justice System. *Report of the Commission on Systemic Racism in the Ontario Criminal Justice System.* Toronto, 1995.

Dauvergne, Mia. *Adult Correctional Services 2010–2011.* Statistics Canada. Ottawa: Canadian Centre for Justice Statistics, 2012.

De Giorgi, Alessandro. *Rethinking the Political Economy of Punishment.* Aldershot: Ashgate Publishing, 2006.

Delgado, R. "'Rotten Social Background': Should the Criminal Law Recognize a Defense of Severe Environmental Deprivation?" *Law & Inequality* 3 (1985).

Eck, J., and Edward Maguire. "Have Changes in Policing Reduced Violent Crime? An Assessment of the Evidence." In *The Crime Drop in America,* edited by Alfred Blumstein and Joel Wallman. Cambridge: Cambridge University Press, 2000.

Eid, Paul. *Profilage racial et discrimination systémique des jeunes racisés.* Montreal: Commission des droits de la personne et des droits de la jeunesse, 2011.

Fecteau, J.-M. *La liberté du pauvre: Crime et pauvreté au XIXe siècle québécois.* Montreal: VLB Éditeur, 2004.

Feeley, M., and Jonathan Simon. "The New Penology: Notes on the Emerging Strategy of Corrections and Its Implications." *Criminology* 30, no. 4 (1992): 449–74. http://dx.doi.org/10.1111/j.1745-9125.1992.tb01112.x.

Foucault, M. *Discipline and Punish.* New York: Vintage Books, 1977.

Foucault, M. *Power/Knowledge: Selected Interviews & Other Writings 1972–1977.* Edited by Colin Gordon. New York: Pantheon Books, 1980.

Garland, D. "A Sociological Approach to Punishment." In *Crime and Justice: A Review of Research.* Vol. 14. Edited by Michael Tonry. Chicago: University of Chicago Press, 1991.

Garland, D. "Governmentality and the Problem of Crime: Foucault, Criminology, Sociology." *Theoretical Criminology* 1, no. 2 (1997): 173–214. http://dx.doi.org/10.1177/1362480697001002002.

Garland, D. *The Culture of Control: Crime and Social Order in Contemporary Society.* Chicago: University of Chicago Press, 2001.

Giddens, A. *The Constitution of Society.* Oxford: Polity Press, 1984.

Gillin, J.L. "Vagrancy and Begging." *American Journal of Sociology* 35, no. 3 (1929): 424–32. http://dx.doi.org/10.1086/215056.

Gilling, D. "Community Safety and Social Policy." *European Journal on Criminal Policy and Research* 9, no. 4 (2001): 381–400. http://dx.doi.org/10.1023/A:1013195320449.

Giroux, L., *Profil correctionnel 2007–2008: La population correctionnelle du Québec.* Quebec: Ministère de la sécurité publique, 2011.

Gramsci, A. *Selections from the Prison Notebooks.* New York: International Publishers, 1971.

Greenberg, D. *Crime and Capitalism: Readings in Marxist Criminology.* Philadelphia: Temple University Press, 1993.

Harcourt, B. *Against Prediction: Profiling, Policing and Punishing in an Actuarial Age.* Chicago: Chicago University Press, 2007.

Harcourt, B. *Illusion of Order: The False Promise of Broken Windows Policing.* Cambridge, MA: Harvard University Press, 2001.

Harcourt, B. "Reflecting on the Subject: A Critique of the Social Influence Conception of Deterrence, the Broken Windows Theory, and Order-Maintenance Policing New York Style." *Michigan Law Review* 97, no. 2 (1998): 291–389. http://dx.doi.org/10.2307/1290289.

Harcourt, B., and Jens Ludwig, "Broken Windows: New Evidence from New York City and a Five-City Social Experiment." *University of Chicago Law Review* 73 (2006): 271–320.

Harris, D.A. "Driving While Black and All Other Traffic Offenses: The Supreme Court and Pretextual Traffic Stops." *Journal of Criminal Law & Criminology* 87, no. 2 (1997): 544–82. http://dx.doi.org/10.2307/1143954.

Harris, D.A. "The Stories, the Statistics and the Law: Why 'Driving While Black' Matters." *University of Minnesota Law Review* 84 (1999).

Hay, D. "Crime, Property and Authority." In *Albion's Fatal Tree: Crime and Society in Eighteenth-Century England*, edited by Douglas Hay, Peter Linebaugh, John G. Rule, E.P. Thompson, and Cal Winslow. New York: Pantheon Books, 1975.

Herbert, S. *Citizens, Cops and Power*. Chicago: University of Chicago Press, 2006. http://dx.doi.org/10.7208/chicago/9780226327358.001.0001.

Katz, J. *Seductions of Crime: Moral and Sensual Attractions in Doing Evil*. New York: Basic Books, 1988.

Kellen, A., Julie Freedman, Sylvia Novac, and Linda Lapointe. *Homeless and Jailed: Jailed and Homeless*. Toronto: John Howard Society of Toronto, 2010.

Kelling, G.L., and M. Catherine Coles. *Fixing Broken Windows: Restoring Order and Reducing Crime in Our Communities*. New York: Martin Kessler Books, 1996.

Labonté, André. *Lignes directrices sur la condition sociale*. Montreal: Commission des droits de la personne et des droits de la jeunesse, 1994.

Lacey, N. *The Prisoners' Dilemma: Political Economy and Punishment in Contemporary Societies*. Cambridge: Cambridge University Press, 2008. http://dx.doi.org/10.1017/CBO9780511819247.

Law Commission of Canada. *What Is a Crime? Challenges and Alternatives. Discussion Paper*. Ottawa: Law Commission of Canada, 2003.

LeBlanc, Marc. "Évolution de la délinquance cachée et officielle des adolescents québécois de 1930 à 2000." In *Traité de criminology empirique*, 3rd ed., edited by Marc LeBlanc, Marc Ouimet, and Denis Szabo, 39–70. Montreal: Les Presses de l'Université de Montréal, 2003.

Lukács, George. *History and Class Consciousness*. London: Merline Press, 1967.

Lyons, W. *The Politics of Community Policing*. Ann Arbor: University of Michigan Press, 1997.

Marx, K. "The Usefulness of Crime." In *Crime and Capitalism: Readings in Marxist Criminology*, edited by David F. Greenberg. Philadelphia: Temple University Press, 1993.

Marx, K. "The Labelling of Crime." In *Crime and Capitalism: Readings in Marxist Criminology*, edited by David F. Greenberg. Philadelphia: Temple University Press, 1993.

Merton, R.K. "Social Structure and Anomie." *American Sociological Review* 3, no. 5 (1938): 672–82. http://dx.doi.org/10.2307/2084686.

Miller, J.G. *Search and Destroy: African-American Males in the Criminal Justice System*. Cambridge: Cambridge University Press, 1996. http://dx.doi.org/10.1017/CBO9780511621574.

Moore, J.P. *First Nations, Inuit and Non-Aboriginal Federal Offenders: A Comparative Profile*. Ottawa: Correctional Service of Canada, 2003.

O'Grady, W., Steve Gaetz, and Kristi Buccieri. *Can I See Your ID? The Policing of Youth Homelessness in Ontario*. Toronto: The Homeless Hub, 2011.

O'Sullivan, Eoin. "Varieties of Punitiveness in Europe: Homelessness and Urban Marginality." *European Journal of Homelessness* 6 (2012): 69–97.

Parenti, C. *Lockdown America: Police and Prisons in the Age of Crisis*. New York: Verso, 1999.

Parnaby, P. "Disaster through Dirty Windshields: Law, Order and Toronto's Squeegee Kids." *Canadian Journal of Sociology* 28, no. 3 (2003): 281–307. http://dx.doi.org/10.2307/3341925.

Poutanen, M.A. "The Geography of Prostitution in an Early Nineteenth-Century Urban Centre: Montreal, 1810–1842." In *Power, Place and Identity: Historical Studies of Social and Legal Regulation in Quebec.* Montreal: Montreal History Group, May 1996.

Ranasinghe, P. "Reconceptualizing Vagrancy and Reconstructing the Vagrant: A Socio-Legal Analysis of Criminal Law Reform in Canada, 1953–1972." *Osgoode Hall Law Journal* 48 (2010): 55–94.

Reiman, J., and Paul Leighton. *The Rich Get Richer and the Poor Get Prison: Ideology, Class and Criminal Justice.* 9th ed. Boston: Pearson, 2009.

Ruggiero, V. *Crime and Markets: Essays in Anti-Criminology.* Oxford: Oxford University Press, 2000.

Rusche, G., and O. Kirchheimer. *Punishment and Social Structure.* New Brunswick: Transaction Publishers, 2005.

Sampson, R.J., and W.J. Wilson. "Toward a Theory of Race, Crime and Urban Inequality." In *Crime and Inequality*, edited by John Hagan and Ruth D. Peterson, 37–54. Palo Alto: Stanford University Press, 1995.

Sanchez Jankowski, M. *Cracks in the Pavement: Social Change and Resilience in Poor Neighborhoods.* Berkeley: University of California Press, 2008.

Service de police de la ville de Montréal. Report on the Optimization of the Neighbourhood Police, 2003.

Shaw, C., and H. McKay. *Juvenile Delinquency and Urban Areas.* Chicago: University of Chicago Press, 1942.

Shelden, R. *Controlling Dangerous Classes: A Critical Introduction to the History of Criminal Justice.* Boston: Allyn and Bacon, 2001.

Simon, J. "Mass Incarceration: From Social Policy to Social Problem." In *The Oxford Handbook of Sentencing and Corrections*, edited by Joan Petersilia and Kevin R. Reitz. Oxford: Oxford University Press, 2013.

Slack, P.A. "Vagrants and Vagrancy in England, 1598–1664." *Economic History Review* 27 (1974): 360–79.

Spitzer, E. *The New York City Police Department's Stop and Frisk Practices: A Report to the People of the State of New York from the Office of the Attorney General.* New York: A.G. Office.

Sutherland, E., D. Cressey, and D. Luckenbill. *Principles of Criminology.* Dix Hills, NY: General Hall, 1992.

Sylvestre, M.-E. "Disorder and Public Spaces in Montreal: Law, Politics and Discretion." *Urban Geography* 31, no. 6 (2010): 803–24. http://dx.doi.org/10.2747/0272-3638.31.6.803.

Sylvestre, M.-E. "Policing the Homeless in Montreal: Is This Really What the Population Wants?" *Policing and Society* 20, no. 4 (2010): 432–58. http://dx.doi.org/10.1080/10439463.2010.523114.

Sylvestre, M.-E., Céline Bellot, Philippe Antoine Couture-Ménard, and Alexandra Tremblay. "Le droit est aussi une question de visibilité: occupation des espaces publics et parcours judiciaires des personnes itinérantes à Montréal et à Ottawa." *Canadian Journal of Law and Society* 26, no. 3 (2011): 531–61. http://dx.doi.org/10.3138/cjls.26.3.531.

Sylvestre, M.-E., D. Bernier, and C. Bellot. "Red Zones Orders in Canadian Courts and the Reproduction of Socio-Economic Inequality." *Oñati Socio-Legal Series* (forthcoming).

Taylor, I., P. Walton, and J. Young. *The New Criminology.* London: Routledge, 1973. http://dx.doi.org/10.4324/9780203405284.

Thomas, C., "Personal Responsibility." *Regent University Law Review* 12 (1999–2000): 317–27.

Thompson, E.P. *Whigs and Hunters: The Origin of the Black Act*. New York: Pantheon Books, 1975.

Tonry, M. *Malign Neglect: Race, Crime and Punishment in America*. Oxford: Oxford University Press, 1995.

Wacquant, L. "Suitable Enemies: Foreigners and Immigrants in the Prisons of Europe." *Punishment and Society* 1, no. 2 (1999): 215–22. http://dx.doi.org/10.1177/14624749922227784.

Wacquant, L. "Deadly Symbiosis: When Ghetto and Prison Meet and Mesh." In *Mass Imprisonment: Social Causes and Consequences*, edited by David Garland, 95–133. London: Sage Publications, 2001. http://dx.doi.org/10.4135/9781446221228.n8.

Wacquant, L. "The Penalisation of Poverty and the Rise of Neo-Liberalism." *European Journal on Criminal Policy and Research* 9, no. 4 (2001): 401–12. http://dx.doi.org/10.1023/A:1013147404519.

Wacquant, L. *Prisons of Poverty*. Minneapolis: Minnesota University Press, 2002.

Wacquant, L. *Punishing the Poor: The Neoliberal Government of Social Insecurity*. Durham: Duke University Press, 2009. http://dx.doi.org/10.1215/9780822392255.

Wacquant, L. "Crafting the Neoliberal State: Workfare, Prisonfare, and Social Insecurity." *Sociological Forum* 25, no. 2 (2010): 197–220. http://dx.doi.org/10.1111/j.1573-7861.2010.01173.x.

Weininger, E.B. "Pierre Bourdieu on Social Class and Symbolic Violence." In *Alternative Foundations of Class Analysis*, edited by E.O. Wright. http://www.ssc.wisc.edu/~wright/Found-all.pdf.

Western, B. *Punishment and Inequality in the United States*. New York: Russell Sage Foundation, 2006.

White, R., and C. Cunneen. "Social Class, Youth Crime and Justice." In *Youth Crime and Justice*, edited by Barry Goldson and John Muncie, 17–29. London: Sage Publications, 2006.

Wilson, J.Q., and G.L. Kelling. "Broken Windows: The Police and Neighborhood Safety." *Atlantic Monthly* 249 (1982): 29.

Wright, E.O. "Foundations of Class Analysis in the Marxist Tradition." In *Alternative Foundations of Class Analysis*, edited by E.O. Wright, 6–40. http://www.ssc.wisc.edu/~wright/Found-all.pdf.

Young, J. *The Exclusive Society: Social Exclusion, Crime and Difference in Late Modernity*. London: Sage Publications, 1999.

Zimring, F.E. *The Great American Crime Decline*. Oxford: Oxford University Press, 2007.

PART III

Emerging Issues in Canada and Beyond: Connecting the Global to the Local

This book has developed a case for integrating a historical framework that addresses links between representation, governance, and social regulation. This final section examines emerging issues in criminalization to address the interconnections between processes of criminalization in local (Canadian) and global contexts. Each chapter in this section explores timely global contemporary issues, including surveillance, the globalization of human rights regimes, national security and border policing, the nature and extent of corporate crime, and the criminalization of indigenous social movements. Part Three uses the frameworks developed throughout the book to examine these local and global contexts. Each of these chapters reveal the mutual interdependence between local contexts and global formations. In so doing, the authors reveal the ways in which local, national, and global processes are embedded within a single location, event, or case study. Collectively, the authors advance the view that we must begin to unpack the ways in which the global resides in seemingly local forms of representation, regulation, and criminalization. In particular, the authors reveal how (and in what ways) the locus of criminality now extends well beyond the confines of the criminal justice system into dispersed governmental and nongovernmental sites as well as into the lives of ordinary people.

In Chapter Ten, "Profiles and Profiling Technology: Stereotypes, Surveillance, and Governmentality," Martin French and Simone Browne explore the ubiquity of surveillance technologies in every aspect of our lives. French and Browne draw upon a series of examples, including the case of Maher Arar, to reveal links between surveillance technologies, representation, profiling, and criminalization. The analysis in this chapter is animated by a governmentality approach that focuses our analytic attention on the everyday, mundane, and often taken-for-granted exercise of power.

In Chapter Eleven, "Wanted by the Canada Border Services Agency," Anna Pratt explores the Canadian version of the FBI's "Most Wanted Listed." Dubbed the "Wanted by the CBSA List," Pratt provides a sobering analysis of transnational networks and dispersed governmental and nongovernmental agencies, corporations, and individual citizens that are mobilized and inducted into Canada's border security and policing regime. Pratt argues that the CBSA List is only one technology in an expansive, heterogeneous, and well-established "immigration penality" that is enabled in large part by the varied intersections, at the levels of discourse, authorities, and technologies, that effectively blur the boundaries between the domains of criminal justice and immigration.

In the subsequent chapter, Chapter Twelve, "In the Name of Human Rights: Governing and Representing Non-Western Lives in Post 9/11," Marcia Oliver explores a series of prescient questions pertaining to the global and universalizing proliferation of human rights rhetoric and human rights regimes. Oliver asks, "When faced with such continued violence and destruction throughout the world, how are we to make sense and speak of international human rights? How does globalization change the way we think about crime and human rights violations? How are different nations, cultures, and populations represented and positioned within human rights discourse (e.g., superior/inferior, civilized/barbaric, saviour/victim), and how might the circulation of visual images of human suffering contribute to the different and hierarchical ways that the West and non-West are constructed and inform our understandings of the current world order?" Oliver's chapter seeks to challenge the view of liberal rights as inherently "good." In so doing, she lays the groundwork for considering the conceptual paradigms and discourses at stake when discourses of human rights are invoked both locally and globally.

In Chapter Thirteen, "Where Are All the Corporate Criminals? Understanding Struggles to Criminalize Corporate Harm and Wrongdoing," Steven Bittle asks how representations of crime work differently when applied to society's most privileged individuals who own and control large, powerful, and increasingly multinational corporations. Challenging dominant media and government focus on the perils of street crime, Bittle invites us to consider the global, pernicious, and devastating effects of corporate crime. These effects include injuring and killing workers, unsafe working conditions, the impact of dangerous products in the marketplace, toxic waste sites, and illegal accounting and price-fixing practices, among others. Corporate crime is devastating and yet, as Bittle argues, efforts to legislate against corporate crime have rarely resulted in dramatic improvements in corporate responsibility and in most cases have supported rather than threatened corporate capitalism.

In the timely final chapter, "Social Movements and Critical Resistance: Policing Colonial Capitalist Order," Tia Dafnos explores indigenous resistance against histories of colonization in liberal states. Using the case study of the Ontario Provincial Police and the reforms that were adopted after the reclamation at Ipperwash and the shooting death of Dudley George, Dafnos examines the policing of dissent and resistance. Dafnos asks, "How does the conventional definition of 'public order policing' and the concepts of 'order' and 'policing' shape forms of dissent and resistance?" The chapter responds to this question by examining the historical emergence of public order policing in relation to the histories of colonialism, militarization, security, and citizenship.

Collectively, these chapters provide readers with an interdisciplinary and critical framework with which to investigate global and local patterns of criminalization and the politics of contestation and resistance.

ten

Profiles and Profiling Technology: Stereotypes, Surveillance, and Governmentality

MARTIN A. FRENCH AND SIMONE A. BROWNE

Introduction

> At the NSA [United States's National Security Agency], I witnessed with growing alarm the surveillance of whole populations without any suspicion of wrongdoing, and it threatens to become the greatest human rights challenge of our time.
> —Edward Snowden[1]

Surveillance permeates our daily lives in countless ways, though it often operates below the radar. In 2013, however, the secret operation of numerous mass surveillance programs became headline news in mainstream media thanks to the publication of leaked documents made available by Edward Snowden. The secret programs that Snowden brought to light share an affinity with most other types of surveillance: they scoop up, organize, and store data about people, places, and things so that it is close to hand for future analysis and action. As this chapter illustrates, there is nothing necessarily sinister in the organizational impulse to undertake surveillance for the purposes of informing future action. The mundane technologies and practices that make up surveillance become problematic, though, when they interlock with processes of representation, racialization, and criminalization.

As you have learned in previous chapters, the processes of representation, racialization, and criminalization are intimately linked. Through Ummni Khan's discussion of the work of Stuart Hall (Chapter Three), for instance, you learned that representations structure and frame how we think about phenomena. Using the HBO show *Oz* as an example, Khan discussed the mass-mediated projection of racist stereotypes about prison inmates. In this chapter we consider linkages between stereotypical representations, racialization, and

---

1 Edward Snowden, "An Open Letter to the People of Brazil," *Folha de S. Paulo*, December 17, 2013, http://www1.folha.uol.com.br/internacional/en/world/2013/12/1386296-an-open-letter-to-the-people-of-brazil.shtml (accessed December 17, 2013).

criminalization less with an eye to their mass-mediated projections, and more with a view to the way they are enacted in often-hidden processes and signifying practices. By focusing on **profiles** and **profiling technologies**—key mechanisms, or tools, of contemporary surveillance—our goal is to illustrate how surveillance can perpetuate linkages between stereotypical representations, racialization, and criminalization. We accomplish this by once again looking to the concept of governmentality, which focuses our analytic attention on the everyday, mundane, and often taken-for-granted exercise of power.

In what follows, you will learn about how surveillance and governmentality relate to the idea of **social control**. You will learn that studying surveillance provides a way of thinking about governmentality, and also that the concept of governmentality is useful for understanding why surveillance has become so ubiquitous in so many places around the world. We will discuss how profiles and profiling technologies work to enable surveillance, and we will show how profiling is used in the financial, policing, international travel, and medical sectors. By showcasing how profiling and profiling technologies can work in these different sectors, we will illustrate how processes of representation, racialization, and criminalization intersect in surveillance systems. Before jumping into this analysis, however, it will first be worthwhile to begin with an example of just what is at stake when racist and stereotypical representations are embedded into surveillance systems.

Stereotypes, Surveillance, and the Case of Maher Arar

In the weeks and months following September 11, 2001 (hereafter referred to as 9/11), Canadian police and security-intelligence organizations worked feverishly to investigate what was described at the time as an "immanent threat to public safety." Galvanized by the spectacular and tragic attacks that had unfolded in the United States on 9/11, investigators cast a wide net designed to sweep up those suspected to have the capability of facilitating—if not actually executing—an act of terrorism.[2] They sought, especially, those individuals fitting a profile of what was known or suspected about al-Qaeda operatives at that time. Caught up in this investigative net were numerous Canadians of Arab or Middle Eastern descent.

Below we tell the story of one of these Canadians—Maher Arar—because it illustrates how surveillance may be implicated in regulatory or governance

---

2 Arar Inquiry, *Report of the Events Relating to Maher Arar: Factual Background*, vol. 1, *Commission of Inquiry into the Actions of Canadian Officials in Relation to Maher Arar* (Ottawa: Public Works and Government Services Canada, 2006), 14–15.

processes and practices, ranging from overt control to more subtle and covert forms of influence. Arar's story also illustrates the potentially profound consequences that can follow from the misuse of and overreliance on profiles and surveillance. It exemplifies how surveillance can manifest the linkages between social structures like systemic racism, sedimented cultural representations like stereotypes of Muslim identities, and the everyday lived experience of marginalization and oppression.

Before the fall of 2002, Arar was living in Ottawa and going about the affairs of his daily life much as we all do. He was born in Syria, but he immigrated to Canada when he was 17 and became a Canadian citizen in 1991. He completed degrees at McGill University and the Université du Québec and subsequently worked in the communications sector.

In the fall of 2001, Arar came to the attention of authorities because he had met up with Abdullah Almalki at a café in Ottawa. Like Arar, Almalki had also immigrated to Canada from Syria, also becoming a citizen in 1991. Almalki was at that time under investigation by Canadian security forces because he had worked during the early 1990s in Pakistan and Afghanistan. Once Arar was identified as a potential associate of Almalki, he too became the subject of an investigation. He was put under surveillance periodically during the fall of 2001. Although this surveillance yielded nothing unusual about Arar, investigators began collecting more and more information about him. They assembled a substantial dossier on Arar, including, for example, a rental agreement for an Ottawa-area apartment that he had signed, which had named Almalki as an emergency contact. Canadian security forces eventually turned the information they had collected on Arar over to the US Federal Bureau of Investigation without any kind of qualification.[3]

Although there was no evidence of Arar's having done anything wrong, the fact that he had been under surveillance by Canadian security forces cast a pall of suspicion over him. In the political climate of the immediate post-9/11 period, Arar and Almalki—and others who seemed to match a prevailing set of reductive characteristics informing national security investigations—were stereotyped in such a way that their presumption of guilt might as well have been a foregone conclusion.

Even though Arar and Almalki were under investigation in 2001, it is important to note here that their cases would eventually become the subject of public inquiries that would clear them of any suspected wrongdoing. These inquiries also demonstrated that Canadian security forces and

---

3 Ibid., 52–56.

government officials, who were under pressure to preempt another 9/11, bent and broke numerous rules governing the investigation of suspects. Back in 2001, however, before the public knew anything concrete about the fast and loose way authorities were undertaking their investigations, Arar's fateful meeting with Almalki turned him into a "person of interest." Unaware that security forces had begun to assemble a profile on him, Arar travelled to Tunis for a family vacation. Returning to Canada from his vacation in late September 2002, he was detained by the US Immigration and Naturalization Service (INS) while transiting through New York's JFK airport. He was accused of being a terrorist and held in solitary confinement in a New York detention centre for over a week. In spite of strenuously denying this accusation, he was deported to Syria. For the next 374 days—over a year—Arar was kept in a Syrian jail where he was repeatedly interrogated and tortured when not confined in a tiny chamber that he subsequently likened to a grave. In October 2006, Arar was cleared of all charges of terrorism by a Commission of Inquiry held by the Government of Canada. He received a settlement of $10 million. Arar still remains on "no-fly" lists maintained by the US government, however.

Arar would likely never have been deported to Syria had it not been for the fact that Canadian security forces passed unqualified, uncontextualized information about him to American security forces. His story presents us with a worst-case scenario of what can happen when organizations conduct surveillance and use profiles to guide their interactions with individuals, in ways that reduce those individuals' life histories down to a few data points and that operate in the background, unbeknownst to those individuals. It also suggests how surveillance and profiling are implicated in processes of social control and governmentality. Indeed, Arar's case clearly illustrates how surveillance was directly related to the exercise of control over his individual circumstances: The information it generated was used to legitimate his confinement, deportation, illegal interrogation, torture, and incarceration. Beyond the exercise of control over Arar, we can also imagine how a general atmosphere of surveillance might have played a role in the governmentalities circumscribing the everyday life of racialized communities in pre- and post-9/11. To be of Middle Eastern or Arab descent, to be of Muslim faith, to know what happened to Arar and others—and to feel one's self under surveillance—was and remains a potentially terrifying prospect ("If I seem to match a police profile, if I am under surveillance, could the same thing happen to me?"). Under these conditions, the beliefs and practices of racialized communities— indeed, their very capacity for self-determination—may be fundamentally constrained.

Ambiguities and Potentialities of Surveillance

Maher Arar's case presents us with an extreme example of what can happen when surveillance goes wrong. When the everyday practices and processes that underpin surveillance interlock with existing racial stereotypes, for example, it's not just that they reinforce extant forms of systemic racism and criminalization, it's also that they can radically alter an individual's life course in devastating ways. Unlike the projection of racist stereotypes in mass-mediated cultural products like television shows, the projection of racist stereotypes through the practices and processes of surveillance can have immediate and profoundly negative consequences for those under surveillance.

Having said this, we must take care in how we analyze surveillance. It would be overly simplistic to argue that because it can be deeply implicated in systemic racism surveillance is inherently bad. Surveillance by itself did not result in Arar's maltreatment—it was surveillance in the context of aggressive policing, surveillance interlocking with overcooked political rhetoric and widespread systemic racism, surveillance in the service of a vastly unequal global political system, and so on. Besides, there are any number of examples that one could cite where surveillance is regarded as having had positive consequences. Think, for instance, about when public health officials use data from epidemiological surveillance to intervene in influenza outbreaks. Or when satellite images of Earth and aerial photography are put to use for environmental protection by monitoring for cases of illegal dumping. Examples such as these suggest that surveillance can just as easily have positive and desirable outcomes as negative and undesirable outcomes. Accordingly, a good starting point for the analysis of surveillance is to assume that it is neither necessarily good nor necessarily bad, but that it is instead ambiguous with respect to these potentialities. But moving beyond this initial analytic stance requires investigating the conditions under which surveillance might be good or bad and, crucially, investigating who is served—and who is harmed—by surveillance.

Such investigation is important because, as Maher Arar's case so clearly illustrates, the potential for surveillance processes to produce disastrous outcomes is real. Moreover, surveillance-mediated disasters tend to happen to people who are already marginalized in some way, for instance when surveillance and profiling practices interlock with existing stereotypical representations, systemic forms of racism, disadvantage, and processes of criminalization. To help better illustrate the ambiguities and potentialities of surveillance, and how they might interlock with racism and criminalization, we turn now to a discussion of social control and governmentality. This will set up our consideration of surveillance, profiling, and profiling technologies in different sectors of contemporary life.

Surveillance and Governmentality: Moving Beyond Mechanistic Theories of Social Control

Below we will briefly introduce the idea of social control, and then discuss why contemporary scholars have found it necessary to move beyond the mechanistic theories associated with this idea. We next discuss the concept of governmentality, which advances social theory beyond mechanistic understandings of social control. The study of surveillance sheds light on governmentality and, in turn, the concept of governmentality is useful for thinking through some of the dynamics of contemporary surveillance. Using the example of profiles and profiling technologies, we will illustrate the potential of automated and largely hidden forms of governmentality that function through everyday surveillance.

Social Control

Ideas about social control are long-standing in sociology. If we understand social control to describe the processes through which elements of social order are maintained and reproduced, then we may read it into the classic sociological works of Marx, Weber, and Durkheim. In Marx's writings, for example, it is the capitalist mode of production that mediates and controls hierarchic class relations. In Weber's writings, large-scale bureaucratic institutions are a source of control. And in Durkheim's writings, collectively held social facts enable social order. We might think of Marx, Weber, and Durkheim as offering structural explanations for social order. In other words, we might read them as conceptualizing what later came to be called social control in terms of society-wide structures like the capitalist economy, the state bureaucracy, and collectively held social facts.

If we choose not to read the concept of social control into classic sociological works, then we must begin its analysis in the late nineteenth century, when it is thought to have first entered the sociological lexicon.[4] One of the earliest articulations of social control was in an 1896 article entitled "Social Control" by American sociologist Edward Ross. Ross advanced the concept of social control to describe "that ascendancy over the aims and acts of the

---

4 Darin Weinberg, "Social Control," in *Blackwell Encyclopedia of Sociology*, ed. George Ritzer. (Blackwell Publishing: Blackwell Reference Online, 2002), http://www.blackwellreference.com/public (accessed May 2, 2012).

individual which is exercised on behalf of the group."[5] Implicit in this definition is an understanding of society as containing a system of mechanisms that
function—either through reward or punishment—to maintain harmony in
social relations. Also implied is the idea that individual actors, in the absence
of social control mechanisms, would naturally tend toward conflict. In a manner not dissimilar from classic European political theory (as expressed, for
example, by Thomas Hobbes's *Leviathan*), the early theorizations of social
control supposed that self-interested individuals functioned together in
groups largely because of external "social" forces.

Rethinking Social Control, Rethinking Power

The task of analyzing and explaining these social forces—of diagnosing the
precise causes of conflict and the exact means by which social order and harmony is maintained or disrupted—has proven an enduring matter of debate
in sociology. One key issue in this debate concerns the relationship between
coercion and influence. Is social control effected because individual actors are
coerced or forced to take a given course of action, or because they are influenced and persuaded that a given course of action is in their best interests?

Another key issue in this debate concerns the sources of coercion and
influence. To what degree is it possible to speak of autonomous "social" forces
operating in separate spheres from the institutions of sovereign states and
their juridical mechanisms? To what degree, in other words, is it possible
to distinguish influence and coercion as effected through the family or the
community from influence and coercion effected through the government
and other institutions of the state? Early theorizations of social control suggested a stronger distinction between these spheres than many contemporary
scholars are willing to accept. During the 1980s and 1990s, against the backdrop of sustained political challenges to the structures of the welfare state
in several liberal democracies (including Canada, the United States, and the
United Kingdom) scholars took aim at approaches that traced strong distinctions between state and nonstate actors in the analysis of social control.[6]
Arguing that these relied too heavily upon a mechanistic and functionalist
view of social relations, they illustrated, for example, how **neoliberalism** and
neoliberal rationalities created mechanisms for "governing at a distance."[7]

---

5 Edward A. Ross, "Social Control," *American Journal of Sociology* 1, no. 5 (1896): 519.
6 Nikolas Rose, Pat O'Malley, and Mariana Valverde, "Governmentality," *Annual Review of Law and Social Science* 2 (2006): 83–104.
7 Nikolas Rose and Peter Miller, "Political Power beyond the State: Problematics of Government," *British Journal of Sociology* 43, no. 2 (1992): 173.

Coercion and influence, from this perspective, functioned together through a wide array of different forms of authority.[8] Accordingly, mechanistic distinctions between control effected through government and control effected through social forces were viewed as untenable.

Critiques of mechanistic theories of social control were accompanied by a widespread and fundamental rethinking of the nature of power. Power was classically viewed as the exercise of force to make people do (or refrain from doing) something. A king or queen best exemplifies this understanding of power: He or she commands his or her subjects (through law), backed up with the threat of violence (the exercise of power), and thereby secures control over the people in his or her territory. Yet this classic view was challenged, particularly in the latter half of the twentieth century, by a perspective that saw power not only in government, law, and violence, but also diffused throughout the entire social body in the mundane, everyday lived experiences of subjects.

The contrast between these two views of power is evident if we hold together a turn-of-the-twentieth-century definition with a later definition. In Max Weber's monumental *Economy and Society*, power is given the following general definition: "the chance of a man or a number of men [sic] to realize their own will in a communal action even against the resistance of others who are participating in the action."[9] Though Weber expands upon and complicates this initial definition, its general connotation is one of opposing forces locked in struggle; a tug of war or a pitched battle come to mind.

As you read in Chapter One, such definitions of power were criticized and transformed, perhaps most notably by Michel Foucault. In *Surveiller et Punir* published in 1975 (which was translated into English and retitled *Discipline and Punish* in 1977), Foucault proposed to study the "micro-physics" of power, a power "exercised rather than possessed."[10] This approach to studying power was different from the classic approach, especially in its emphasis on effects rather than forces. By emphasizing effects, Foucault was able to distinguish between the well-studied modality of "sovereign power" and the little recognized, distinctively modern modality of "disciplinary power." "Whereas sovereign power is expressed through the symbols of the dazzling force of the individual who holds it," he wrote elsewhere, "disciplinary power is a discrete, distributed power; it is a power which functions

8 Rose, O'Malley, and Valverde, "Governmentality."

9 Cited in Hans Gerth and C. Wright Mills, eds., *From Max Weber: Essays in Sociology* (New York: Oxford University Press, 1958), 180.

10 Michel Foucault, *Discipline and Punish: The Birth of the Prison*, trans. Alan Sheridan (New York: Vintage Books, 1995), 26.

Figure 10.1 Prisoners on public display in a pillory

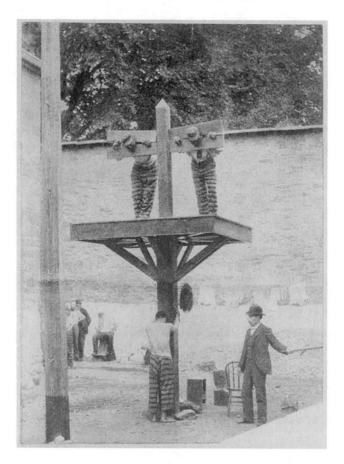

through networks and the visibility of which is only found in the obedience and submission of those on whom it is silently exercised."[11]

We might think of these different modalities of power in terms of their visibility to the social analyst. One is *overt* and easy to recognize in its effects; the other is more *covert* and is more difficult to see in its effects. For example, one is manifest in spectacular punishment (think of prisoners being overtly restrained and put on public display in a pillory; see Figure 10.1), the other in quiet exhortation (think of a parent looking disapprovingly at a rowdy child;

---

11 Michel Foucault, *Psychiatric Power: Lectures at the Collège de France 1973–1974*, trans. François Ewald and Allesandro Fontana, ed. Arnold Davidson (New York: Picador, 2006), 22.

Figure 10.2 A parent and child

see Figure 10.2). The two modalities interlock, but before Foucault much more had been written about overt sovereign power than covert disciplinary power—about power as possessed rather than as exercised at the level of its micro-physics.

From Social Control to Governmentality

This notion of power's micro-physics, its covert exercise and not simply its overt concentration in persons and institutions, prompted a need to supplement classic, structural thinking about social control with a more supple idea. Foucault used the term *governmentality* to describe this idea, which focuses analysis on the broad "ensemble" of institutions, actors, procedures, calculations, and knowledges that make governing possible.[12] According to Nikolas Rose and colleagues, the analysis of governmentalities focuses on

> different styles of thought, their conditions of formation, the
> principles and knowledges that they borrow from and generate,

---

12 Michel Foucault, "Governmentality," in *The Foucault Effect: Studies in Governmentality with Two Lectures by and an Interview with Michel Foucault*, ed. Graham Burchell, Colin Gordon, and Peter Miller (Chicago: University of Chicago Press, 1991), 102.

the practices that they consist of, how they are carried out, their contestations and alliances with other arts of governing. From such a perspective, it becomes apparent that each formulation of an art of governing embodies, explicitly or implicitly, an answer to the following questions: Who or what is to be governed? Why should they be governed? How should they be governed? To what ends should they be governed? ... Further, instead of seeing any single body—such as the state—as responsible for managing the conduct of citizens, this perspective recognizes that a whole variety of authorities govern in different sites, in relation to different objectives. Hence, a second set of questions emerges: Who governs what? According to what logics? With what techniques? Toward what ends?[13]

From this perspective, the concept of governmentality provides analytic cues to guide empirical inquiry. It identifies important questions for research and suggests where researchers might look for answers.

Surveillance and Governmentality

The concept of governmentality can provide important cues for understanding surveillance in everyday life. And in turn, empirical studies of surveillance can offer a means for understanding contemporary governmentalities. Below we provide a brief introduction to surveillance in contemporary life, touching especially on profiles and profiling technologies and suggesting how these are implicated in social control and governmentality.

Thinking explicitly about its relation to human subjects, David Lyon defines surveillance as "any collection and processing of personal data, whether identifiable or not, for the purposes of influencing or managing those whose data have been garnered."[14] "Although it may have protecting, entitling or caring components," he notes, "surveillance expands primarily as a means of power in modern societies, due to military, geo-political and economic dynamics expressed through bureaucratic organizations."[15] Important for Lyon's analysis of surveillance is the ubiquity of information technologies, especially digital technologies, which support all manner of monitoring. These platform technologies provide an infrastructure for linking different kinds of surveillance systems together.

---

13 Rose, O'Malley, and Valverde, "Governmentality," 84–85.

14 David Lyon, *Surveillance Society: Monitoring Everyday Life* (Buckingham: Open University Press, 2001), 2.

15 David Lyon, *Surveillance Studies: An Overview* (London: Polity Press, 2007), 47.

We might think of linked surveillance technologies as creating a giant system that is virtually inescapable. In other words, it is virtually impossible to live untouched by surveillance today except, perhaps, for those on the very margins of social existence. This situation stems from the growing integration of previously discrete surveillance systems. According to Kevin Haggerty and Richard Ericson, such integration "marks the progressive 'disappearance of disappearance'—a process whereby it is increasingly difficult for individuals to maintain their anonymity, or to escape the monitoring of social institutions."[16]

Consider, for example, the following scenario: You might wear a baseball cap to hide your face from the closed-circuit television (CCTV) cameras in your local mall parking lot. But if security guards and police obtain permission to combine CCTV data with, say, cellphone data—and if that data shows that your cellphone was under the camera's gaze at precisely the same time as the running, behatted individual—it could be doubly difficult for you to deny that you were where these surveillance systems say you were. This scenario suggests how seemingly discrete systems—a mall CCTV system and a cellular telephone system—might be linked together to help build up a data set about people. Many other systems could be overlain as well, producing a progressively more detailed profile. Where was your transit pass used on the day in question? Did your bank account balance change in an unusual way in the days following? Did you email anyone or post anything on Facebook that relates you to the incident in question?

What the above scenario underscores is that surveillance is a pervasive feature of contemporary life. We transact with numerous surveillance systems on a daily basis, and these transactions can, under the right circumstances and through data aggregation, be readily connected together. But why should we care if surveillance is becoming more pervasive and interconnected? It's no big deal, you might say, if there are multiple different ways of monitoring your behaviour—no one ever got hurt by being looked at. It is difficult to deny that it is better to be watched than, say, physically assaulted. Yet this does not mean that the experience of being watched is a benign one.

Foucault, whose theorization of the micro-physics of power we discussed above, gave a chilling description of the potential effects of pervasive surveillance. In *Discipline and Punish*, Foucault wrote a now iconic analysis of Jeremy Bentham's ideas about the panopticon (see Chapter One). Foucault's analysis illustrates the idea that, if you feel you are under constant

---

16 Kevin Haggerty and Richard Ericson, "The Surveillant Assemblage," *British Journal of Sociology* 51, no. 4 (2000): 619.

Figure 10.3 Closed-circuit television (CCTV) cameras

surveillance, you will eventually take on the work of your overseer—you will police yourself. Foucault provocatively suggested that although the panopticon was never built as Bentham had envisioned it, the institutions of modern life—the school, the hospital, the factory—had, in decisive respects, taken on an uncanny resemblance to the panoptic prison. The result was a system of discipline that, in theory at least, was diffused throughout the social body and which enrolled subjects into the work of their own discipline. It was a system founded, in other words, upon widespread self-discipline. Based on a reading of Foucault's discussion of the panopticon, it would seem reasonable to conclude that surveillance and imprisonment are but two sides of the same coin.

However, Foucault's broader analysis in *Discipline and Punish* (and other writings) indicates the deeply contested operation of power. It would be overstating things to say that he did not see much of a difference between surveillance and imprisonment. In addition to accounting for the complexities of his analyses, care must be taken when using his ideas to explain contemporary situations. Foucault's arguments were based on a study of transformations that happened during the eighteenth and nineteenth centuries. For this reason, they cannot merely be overlain on the present. Thus, although many scholars have theorized contemporary surveillance in relation to Foucault's ideas—especially his reading of the panopticon—a good deal of adaptation is often viewed as necessary.[17] Some scholars have recently begun to take issue with the use of Foucault's work as a key frame for understanding contemporary surveillance. As they have argued, the panopticon, with its controllingly carceral connotations, does not adequately grasp the dynamics of contemporary surveillance,[18] missing a great deal of activity that, while not necessarily overtly controlling, is nonetheless key in its governing effects.

As we shall now argue, profiles and profiling technologies exemplify how contemporary surveillance, while not functioning in an obviously panoptic way, may nonetheless produce (self)disciplining and normalizing effects in ways that problematically enact stereotypical representations and broader, structural processes like racialization and criminalization. From this perspective, surveillance—including the mundane and often-hidden processes and everyday practices that make it work—may be viewed as a conduit for governmental power in everyday life. If through the conceptual lens of governmentality we understand contemporary governance operating not as "an all-pervasive web of 'social control,'" but rather through "assorted attempts at the calculated administration of diverse aspects of conduct through countless, often competing, local tactics,"[19] then we may glimpse why surveillance has become so central to the smooth functioning of everyday life. The concept of surveillance, in other words, names the processes and practices that help to coordinate and account for the calculated administration of diverse conduct.

Profiles and Profiling Technologies as Surveillance

> Computer profiling ... is understood best not just as a technology of surveillance, but as a kind of surveillance in advance of surveillance, a technology of "observation before the fact." A profile, as the name suggests, is a kind of prior ordering, in this case a model or figure that organizes multiple sources of information to scan for matching or exceptional cases.[20]

Suppose you are looking at an apple sitting on your table. You take out a piece of paper and write down the words "red" and "fruit." You have just

---

17 David Lyon, ed., *Theorizing Surveillance: The Panopticon and Beyond* (Cullompton: Willan, 2006).

18 See, for example, Kevin Haggerty, "Tear Down the Walls: On Demolishing the Panopticon," in *Theorizing Surveillance: The Panopticon and Beyond*, ed. David Lyon, 23–45 (Cullompton: Willan, 2006); Michalis Lianos, "Social Control after Foucault," *Surveillance & Society* 1, no. 3 (2003): 412–30.

19 Rose and Miller, "Political Power beyond the State," 175.

20 William Bogard, *The Simulation of Surveillance: Hypercontrol in Telematic Societies* (Cambridge: Cambridge University Press, 1996), 27.

profiled your apple; that is, you have just represented it according to a couple of its key, identifying characteristics. According to this profile, the object you are looking at is a red fruit. Notice that the two words you have written down are a rather thin representation of your delicious, three-dimensional apple. You would never consider eating the paper instead of the apple. Yet, in spite of its not being very tasty, the profile you have created has a utility. It is smaller, thinner, lighter, more portable, and perhaps also more durable than the thing it is meant to represent. We might think of this profile as more malleable, easier to manipulate and move around, than the apple it stands in for. Depending on your perspective, the profile's attributes may have greater utility than the apple's; if you want to satiate your hunger, you would choose the apple, but if you want to organize your kitchen, if you want to identify, assess, and classify the object you are looking at in relation to the other objects in your kitchen, the profile is what you will reach for. It will tell you to put the apple with other fruit (or maybe with other red items, depending on how you choose to organize your kitchen).

Profiles help us identify, assess, classify, and manage the world around us.[21] But how do profiles and profiling technologies actually work, especially in organizational contexts? And how are they related to surveillance and governmentality? We address these questions below.

Writing about the personal information economy and the consumer profiling industry, Greg Elmer suggests that profiles are like "simulations or pictures of consumer likes, dislikes, and behaviours."[22] They enable, as in the quotation by William Bogard that opened this section, a kind of surveillance in advance of surveillance. In other words, they allow organizations to study certain key characteristics of consumer behaviour (how many purchases were made over the last month and in which stores) and then make predictions about future behaviours. In the contemporary era, consumer profiling is automated and embedded within the processes of consumption. Its aim—through tracking patterns of consumption and continually monitoring the likes and dislikes we express in our choices about consumption—is to anticipate, cater to, and influence our future needs and wants.[23]

---

21 See, for example, Geoffrey C. Bowker and Susan Leigh Star, *Sorting Things Out: Classification and Its Consequences* (Cambridge, MA: MIT Press, 1999); Oscar Gandy, *The Panoptic Sort: A Political Economy of Personal Information* (Boulder: Westview Press, 1993); Jason Pridmore, "Consumer Surveillance: Context, Perspectives and Concerns in the Personal Information Economy," in *Routledge Handbook of Surveillance Studies*, ed. Kirstie Ball, Kevin Haggerty, and David Lyon, 321–29 (New York: Routledge, 2012).

22 Greg Elmer, *Profiling Machines: Mapping the Personal Information Economy* (Cambridge, MA: MIT Press, 2004), 5.

23 Elmer, *Profiling Machines*, 5–6.

Contemporary consumer profiling works, Elmer suggests, by seducing consumers into divulging their personal information, usually at points of purchase. Have you ever been asked, for example, for your AIR MILES card at the supermarket?[24] You accumulate points with each purchase, but in return you give LoyaltyOne Incorporated—the company that owns the AIR MILES program—valuable information about each purchase. Each time you use your AIR MILES card, you trigger an information flow that adds to the profile of you maintained by LoyaltyOne. By analyzing your consumption information and matching it with information about your location (your postal code, for instance), LoyaltyOne can sort you into a niche market. Are you a wealthy midtowner or a poor suburbanite? LoyaltyOne answers this question for retailers wishing to target their products to particular markets—if you're a wealthy midtowner, you might get advertising for gourmet macaroni and cheese; if you're a poor suburbanite, you might get advertising for last year's discount macaroni and cheese instead.

Drawing from marketing literature, Elmer argues that certain types of data have become integral to the way that consumer profiling works to identify, assess, and classify consumers. There are at least four key types of data coveted by the consumer profiling industry:

> First, geographic data encompass categories such as region, climate, population density, and market area. Examples of geographic data include telephone, area codes, zip codes, and Internet URLs and domain names. Second, demographic data tend to focus on personal information that is specific and unique to an individual. Examples of demographic data include age, sex, race, marital status, income, occupation, education, religion ... and nationality. Third, psychographic data attempt to address social aspects such as class, values, lifestyles, and personality. Finally consumer behaviour data refers to specific needs and desires, such as usage rate, brand loyalty, product knowledge, and attitude about specific products.[25]

Some of this data is publicly available, some you may divulge at various transaction points in the course of your consumer life, and some is imputed, or estimated, based on data that have already been obtained.

In order to organize and make sense of the different types of data that are collected, organizations rely on mundane as well as sophisticated profiling

---

24 Jason Pridmore, "Loyal Subjects? Consumer Surveillance in the Personal Information Economy" (PhD diss., Queen's University, Kingston, 2008).

25 Elmer, *Profiling Machines*, 79.

technologies.[26] You might think of your loyalty card as a comparatively mundane technology (although it is sophisticated enough in its own right—its unique identifier links you to the purchases you make), but this front-end profiling technology is supported by sophisticated back-end computer hardware and software technologies that enable organizations to construct detailed intelligence about consumers and markets. "Consumers may not be aware," Oscar Gandy observes, "of the many ways in which decision support systems supply the decisions, or the options, including prices that are set before them."[27] These profiling technologies scrutinize a broad data set to help make decisions about customer loyalty and the risk that unhappy customers will turn elsewhere for their consumer goods.

As Gandy argues, market-leading firms make use of their own data as well as data they purchase from specialized data mining companies, to figure out which markets to serve, which customers to cultivate, and which ones to ignore. They conduct experiments using the profiles they have built—simulations, or in Bogard's terms, surveillance in advance of surveillance—in order to segment their markets and maximize gain while minimizing risk in each market segment. The logical goal of this process is to individualize and personalize marketing. However, although consumer profiles may be individualized, "the fact is that most of the information in them is derived from data mining techniques that use theoretical and derived models as a basis for the classes and categories into which the individual is assigned."[28]

It is this process of imputation and estimation, of derivation and guesstimation, that implicates profiles, profiling technologies, and the surveillance they enable in stereotyping and the perpetuation of racist cultural representations. As Gandy argues, these interventions tend to automate discrimination. They rely on models that "reproduce the social, economic, and political disparities that are experienced as comparative and explicit disadvantage."[29] We shall now illustrate this process, which has been described as one of **cumulative disadvantage**,[30] with reference to examples from the financial, policing, international travel, and medical sectors.

---

26 Sami Coll, "Consumption as Biopower: Governing Bodies with Loyalty Cards," *Journal of Consumer Culture* 13, no. 3 (2013): 201–20.

27 Oscar Gandy, *Coming to Terms with Chance: Engaging Rational Discrimination and Cumulative Disadvantage* (Farnham: Ashgate, 2009), 81.

28 Ibid., 83.

29 Ibid., 78.

30 Rebecca Blank, Marilyn Dabady, and Constance Citro, eds., *Measuring Discrimination: Panel on Methods for Assessing Discrimination* (Washington: The National Academies Press, 2004); Oscar Gandy, "Quixotics Unite! Engaging the Pragmatists on Rational Discrimination," in ed. David Lyon, *Theorizing Surveillance: The Panopticon and Beyond* (Cullompton: Willan, 2006), 318–36.

What David Lyon calls **digital discrimination** is also a useful concept when it comes to understanding how profiles and profiling technologies come to reproduce inequalities. Digital discrimination is at play when, as Lyon puts it, "flows of personal data—abstracted information—are sifted and channeled in the process of risk assessment, to privilege some and disadvantage others, to accept some as legitimately present and to reject others."[31] While the concepts of cumulative disadvantage and digital discrimination nicely capture the automation of discrimination, our aim here is to emphasize that profiles and profiling technologies are implicated not merely in the reproduction of social, political, and economic disparities, but also that they enact stereotypes, sedimented cultural representations, and systemic racism.

The binary oppositions that Lyon outlines ("the privileged" and "the disadvantaged" and those who are "legitimately present" and "the rejected") speak to the ways in which tropes of representation secure power relations. As Stuart Hall demonstrates, binary oppositions and stereotyping secure power relations in that they operate in such a way that those "who are in any way significantly different from the majority—'them' rather than 'us'—are frequently exposed to this *binary* form of representation" and are "often required to be *both things at the same time.*"[32] Digital discrimination sees the symbolic power of stereotyping and binary opposition "digitized," enacting material effects on individuals and certain groups. Our hope is that through recognizing enactments of digital discrimination we can create a space to understand how we are differently implicated in these practices, and from this understanding be better able to form alliances that critically and collaboratively challenge stereotypical representations and social inequities.

Financial Profiling

In some cases entire neighbourhoods are profiled. Called *neighbourhood lifestyle segmentation* or *consumer segmentation*, this form of profiling is often done by way of postal codes and sees particular segments of a population, often consumers, subjected to interviewing, polling, product testing, and other forms of market research and information derived from census enumeration. From there they are categorized into segments within highly detailed consumer databases so that products and services can be marketed to them. In other words, consumers are made known by more than their postal code through a type of financial and geographical profiling (called *geodemographics*

---

31 David Lyon, "Technology vs. 'Terrorism': Circuits of City Surveillance Since September 11," *International Journal of Urban and Regional Research*, 27, 3, p. 674.

32 Stuart Hall, *Representation: Cultural Representation and Signifying Practices*. London: SAGE, 1997, p. 229.

and *psychographics* by those in the business of consumer analytics). By way of surveys and polling, this is the practice of segmenting groups by certain common attributes to predict and determine attitudes, transactional habits, and purchases. Environics Analytics, for example, has a database system called PRIZM C2 that neatly classifies Canadians into nearly 55,000 neighbourhoods and into 66 separate lifestyle segments or clusters, such as "Lunch at Tims," who are "high school-educated, blue-collar workers living in older homes and small apartment buildings," "Asian Up-and-Comers," "Money and Brains," "Park Bench Seniors," "Back Country Folks," and "Nouveau Riches" who "like other well-to-do Canadians—their average household income is $129,000—they travel abroad, shop at chi-chi chains like Holt Renfrew and own a range of investments." According to Environics Analytics "when your company links its customer database to PRIZM C2 segments or groups, the result is an accurate portrait of how your targeted consumers behave—whether they prefer luxury cars to subcompacts, tofu to tamales, or radio to podcasts."[33] Such customer profiling and data compilation marks a practice of trafficking in information where consumer profiles, or "lifestyle segments," and detailed transactional information from the use of consumer loyalty cards such as LoyaltyOne's AIR MILES Rewards Program (discussed above) to Shopper's Drug Mart's Optimum Card are sold, traded, rented, and used in targeted marketing. In other words, individuals are coded into particular lifestyle segments by way of information such as transactional habits derived, for example, from monitoring shopping or travel behaviours.

However, targeted marketing is not solely about using census and consumption data to code city spaces and those who live in them so that companies can successfully market tofu and tamales. Sometimes entire neighbourhoods, suburban enclaves, and city spaces are profiled for money lending, or what could be called *predatory financial services*. Since the 1980s, there has been a growth in high-cost financial services that target those with low incomes and few assets. These financial products and services include pawn shops, income tax refund loans, prepaid credit cards, cash-for-gold companies, and cheque-cashing and payday advance loan outlets.

Money Mart, for example, first opened in Edmonton, Alberta, in 1982 and now has over 450 locations across Canada. Money Mart was purchased by US-based Dollar Financial Corporation in 1996. A payday advance loan generally works like this: The borrower must provide proof of regular

---

33 Environics Analytics, *PRIZM CE Marketer's Handbook 2008*, http://www.tetrad.com/pub/ documents/prizmcemethodology.pdf (accessed April 15, 2012); Environics Analytics, *PRIZM C2*, www.environicsanalytics.ca/data/consumer-segmentation/prizmc2 (accessed April 15, 2012).

employment income, such as a pay stub; a working phone number and email address; proof of a working bank account, such as a blank cheque; and identification to prove that the borrower is over 18 years of age. With Money Mart, potential borrowers can apply online and are encouraged to feel secure in doing so, as the company's website states that the "payday loan application is secure, [so] you don't need to worry about the safety of your personal information online." Payday loans range from $120 to a maximum of $1,500, and Money Mart informs borrowers not to "feel obligated to receive the full amount for which you're qualified to borrow, you can always dial down the payday loan amount to just the cash you need." If the loan is approved, the money is either deposited in the borrower's account or received as cash at a payday lender branch. Daily interest is accrued and various processing fees are charged.

In Alberta the maximum borrowing costs for a $300 loan for 14 days is $69, with an annual percentage rate (APR) of 599.64%, according to Money Mart's website (www.moneymart.ca). The Ontario Payday Loans Act (2008) prevents payday loans in that province from being calculated at an annualized rate and sets a 62-day limit on the length of a loan. Federally, the payday loan industry's service charges are regulated by the *Criminal Code* of Canada under section 347.1, which "criminalizes the charging of usurious interest rates." Given these relatively high borrowing rates and lending fees, Money Mart has been subject to various class action lawsuits, including one filed in Ontario that reached a settlement in 2010 where that company was directed to pay $27.5 million in cash as well as other stipulations.[34] According to one study, the average payday loan customer in Ontario owes $23,579, excluding mortgages, to financial institutions. This same study found that 51 per cent of users of payday loan services did so because it is a "quick and easy process," while 18 per cent found the locations more convenient than that of mainstream banks, and 15 per cent reported having "no other alternative sources for borrowing."[35]

Cheque cashing is another popular product that these high-cost financial services companies offer. Users of cheque-cashing services pay a flat service fee plus a set percentage of the total value of the third-party cheque in order to cash that cheque. According to one 2006 survey of Canadian consumer attitudes and behaviour, 7 per cent had used a nonbank cheque-cashing service that year, with 31 per cent of those respondents using "this service to

---

34 Money Mart, *Notice of the Settlement of the Ontario Money Mart Class Action*, 2012, http://www
   .moneymart.ca/paydayloans.asp (accessed April 15, 2012).

35 Pollara, *Payday Loan Customer Survey*, http://www.cpla-acps.ca/english/mediastudies.php
   (accessed April 15, 2012).

cash a federal government cheque at a storefront cheque-cashing service, at least once last year"; this number represents "nearly half a million adult Canadians," according to this survey.[36] Avoiding service fees and other costs was part of the rationale for the introduction of debit cards to be issued to some Ontario Works income recipients rather than issuing cheques, since many recipients do not have bank accounts and need to use a cheque-cashing service to access their benefits. One report from the *Toronto Star* noted that over the course of a year these service charges would total $249 for an individual recipient.[37] With a prepaid debit card, users are said to no longer be easily identified as welfare clients and would use the card along with a PIN number for purchases anywhere MasterCard is accepted or to withdraw cash from an ATM. Some supporters of this City Services Benefit Card initiative have called it a "dignity card," with one City of Toronto councillor stating "I've been hearing people gripe for years—'People get a welfare cheque, and the first thing they do is go to the liquor store, the beer store.' Well, usually when I get my paycheque, one of the first things I do is go to the liquor store or beer store. You should have some enjoyment in life. I think it's a little draconian to start saying, 'You're on welfare, and this is exactly how you're going to spend the money we give you.'"[38]

While neighbourhood lifestyle segmentation and data derived from census enumeration can be used to target certain neighbourhoods as ripe for payday loan and cheque-cashing stores, mainstream banks and lending institutions have also been found to profile potential borrowers for financial services like subprime loans. This practice has led to a racialization of the home foreclosure crisis of the late-2000s in the United States, where discriminatory lending practices saw to it that Black and Latino homebuyers were saddled with risky, high-interest loans.[39]

According to a study by Jacob Rugh and Douglas Massey, subprime loans are considered "risky" because borrowers were often those who might not regularly qualify for traditional mortgage loans (due to poor credit scores, lack of assets, weak borrowing history, or other indicators of

36 Créatec, "Executive Summary," *General Survey on Consumers' Financial Awareness, Attitudes and Behaviour*, Conducted for the Financial Consumer Agency of Canada (FCAC) (Ottawa: FCAC), 4, http://www.fcac-acfc.gc.ca/Eng/resources/researchSurveys/Documents/FCAC_GenSurvExec_2006-eng.pdf (accessed April 19, 2014).

37 Councillor Paul Ainslie, quoted in Daniel Dale, "Debit Cards to Replace Welfare Cheques," *Toronto Star*, August 8, 2011, http://www.thestar.com/news/2011/08/08/debit_cards_to_replace_welfare_cheques (accessed April 15, 2012).

38 Ibid.

39 Joe Feagin, *Racist America: Roots, Current Realities, and Future Reparations* (New York: Routledge, 2010), 161.

riskiness) and who would be subject to higher interest rates and harsher penalties for default. In some cases certain borrowers who might qualify for lower loan rates were instead steered to higher-interest financial products. "Risky" borrowers were aggressively marketed to as their loans were later bundled and repackaged on the mortgage-backed securities market. Rugh and Massey found higher foreclosure rates in Black and Latino segregated neighbourhoods because these neighbourhoods were key locations for predatory lending services where, given the "legacy of redlining," these neigbourhoods "continue to be underserved by mainstream financial institutions."[40] *Redlining* is a practice that saw a denial of services by lending institutions, insurance companies, and other financial services by discriminating against racialized populations, particularly Black individuals in the United States beginning in the 1930s. It initially involved drawing red lines on maps that delineated areas where the privileged would be served and the disadvantaged would be underserved, separating, to use Lyon's terms, the "legitimately present" from "the rejected." According to Rugh and Massey, "the racialization of America's foreclosure crisis occurred because of a systematic failure to enforce basic civil rights laws in the United States," for example, Black borrowers receiving discriminatory treatment when attempting to procure financial lending services, or simply being denied service when entering a lending institution.[41] Rugh and Massey conclude that "discriminatory subprime lending is simply the latest in a long line of illegal practices that have been foisted on minorities in the United States."[42] So profiling, whether at the bank, on city streets, or at the airport, operates by segmenting particular populations by race, gender, class, or other categories of determination, often for discriminatory treatment and in ways that connect with extant inequities.

Airport Profiling

In 2009, Canadian rapper The Narcicyst (see Figure 10.4) released the music video for his track *P.H.A.T.W.A.* With this video, the Iraqi-born artist reflects on the security regimes and practices at the post-9/11 airport, extraordinary renditions,[43] and the ubiquitous orange jumpsuits and black hoods worn by

---

40 Jacob Rugh and Douglas Massey, "Racial Segregation and the American Foreclosure Crisis," *American Sociological Review* 75, no. 5 (2010): 630.

41 Ibid., 646.

42 Ibid.

43 Extraordinary renditions are the secret, extrajudicial, or forcible removal of a person to another country, often a country known to violate human rights and the due process of law.

Figure 10.4 Canadian rapper The Narcicyst

those held indefinitely at the Guantanamo Bay detention camp. The video begins with The Narcicyst and his travelling companion, a Black man, wondering which one of them will be harassed more at the airport's preboarding passenger screening zones. To this The Narcicyst states: "Obviously me, dog. You know Iraq is the new Black." In one scene, The Narcicyst sits in an interrogation room being questioned while his bags are searched by two agents, one with a badge that says FBI (which viewers later find out stands for Federal Bureau of Instigation) and who later tells The Narcicyst in Arabic that his interrogation was not "a racism thing" as he hands him a card that reads "U.S. Department of Arab Man Security." The interrogation centres on questions of The Narcicyst's "ethnicity" ("I know you're Canadian. What's your ethnicity?") while he raps: "at borders I'm sorted out from beardless cats that boarded the plane as I was boarding, then detained." With this video, The Narcicyst provides insight about racial profiling at the airport and he expresses, through sound and visual culture, the anxieties experienced by those "flying while brown."

The contemporary governance of travel, and in particular air travel, is marked by an ever-increasing accumulation of passenger data and file sharing of such data between government agencies and between nations, and in some cases the governance of movement is marked by traveller profiling through their purchase and travel patterns, national origin, or other markers.[44] From pre-enrolled passenger screening programs, to frequent flyer databases or the Advance Passenger Information System (APIS) and Passenger Name Record (PNR) databases that compile information on travellers' comings and goings, to "no-fly lists," travellers are profiled through their patterns. For example, in 2006, it was announced that the US Department of Homeland Security had been assigning "terror scores" or risk profiles through its Automated Targeting System to millions of travellers since 2002 based on methods of payment for flights (paying by cash or credit card, or last-minute purchases), gender, buying a one-way ticket, seating preferences, choice of halal meals, and other records. This example clearly illustrates how stereotypical attitudes can feed back into the creation and use of profiles, thus implicating this surveillance technology in the exacerbation of extant forms of discrimination, marginalization, and racism.

Profiling in Policing

> Policing is effected not only through territorial surveillance but also at the extraterritorial level of abstract knowledge of risk ...[45]

Another prominent domain in which profiles and profiling technologies structure relations between organizations and individuals is policing. This is plainly visible if we understand policing as an activity that is broader than patrolling the streets; that is, if we understand policing as connected at the level of knowledge with the risk management activities of numerous public- and private-sector organizations. Consider the policing of young drivers, for example. It is well known that insurance companies charge young drivers— especially young male drivers—higher rates. Insurance companies rationalize this form of age-based discrimination actuarially—that is, by deriving from an analysis of past patterns which categories of drivers have a higher probability of having an accident. Traffic policing is informed by and contributes to this actuarial knowledge. Police are aware that young male drivers are in a higher risk category than other drivers, so they may be more likely to notice the bad driving habits of young males than other drivers. And, by taking increased notice of these bad habits and stopping and charging young male drivers at a higher rate than other drivers, police contribute to the statistics that insurance companies use to create actuarially informed profiles of young male drivers.

---

44 Mark Salter, ed., *Politics at the Airport* (Minneapolis: University of Minnesota Press, 2008).

45 Richard Ericson and Kevin Haggerty, *Policing the Risk Society* (Toronto: University of Toronto Press, 1997), 5.

As the quotation by Ericson and Haggerty above suggests, police play a key role in gathering information about people. Moreover, by making this information available to other risk-managing organizations like insurance companies, they also play a key role in the production of knowledge about categories of people. They function, Ericson and Haggerty argue, "as an inspectorate that traces population movements in time and space, for example, through street-stop checks, registration of vice practitioners, special-event security, business and residential security reviews, vehicle registration systems, and driver licensing systems."[46] In the aggregate, they effectively help to risk-profile groups of people. As Ericson and Haggerty write:

> In the most routine aspects of their work—for example, reporting an accident, conducting a street-stop check or an employment screening check, and recording information about criminal suspects, victims, and informants—police officers register peoples' significant accomplishments and failures, credentials and demerits, routines and accidents.[47]

This routine surveillance work is structured in relation to the knowledge needs of other risk-managing organizations. Accordingly, police use categories like "age, race, gender, and ethnicity" to describe their observations and to build risk profiles of populations—this activity "forces people into specific institutional identities."[48]

One of the most notorious means of forcing people into specific institutional identities is racial profiling. **Racial profiling** has been defined by the Ontario Human Rights Commission as "any action undertaken for reasons of safety, security or public protection that relies on stereotypes about race, colour, ethnicity, ancestry, religion, or place of origin rather than on reasonable suspicion, to single out an individual for greater scrutiny or different treatment."[49] Numerous organizations—not just the police—undertake activities that are implicated in racial profiling. When the Ontario Human Rights Commission conducted an inquiry into the effects of racial profiling as experienced by those directly impacted, it encountered numerous examples:

- a law enforcement official assumes someone is more likely to have committed a crime because he is African Canadian;

---

46 Ibid., 7.
47 Ibid., 8.
48 Ibid.
49 Ontario Human Rights Commission (OHRC), *Paying the Price: The Human Cost of Racial Profiling* (Toronto: OHRC, 2003), 6.

- an employer wants a stricter security clearance for a Muslim employee after September 11;
- a criminal justice system official refuses bail to a Latin American person because of a belief that people from her country are violent.[50]

Summarizing the criminological literature, Scot Wortley and Julian Tanner indicate that racial profiling typically comes to light in policing through racial disparity in police stop-and-search practices, increased police patrols in minority neighbourhoods, and undercover activity that selectively targets ethnic groups.[51]

Although the definitions and scope of racial profiling in policing continue to be the subject of academic debate,[52] there is evidence that police engage, sometimes even unwittingly, in racial profiling.[53] Moreover, a range of social scientific research reports that individuals from marginalized communities have the experience and sense of being unfairly profiled, and therefore targeted, by police.[54] As this research indicates, racial profiling is experienced against the backdrop of existing social fissures and hierarchies. Its potential to worsen existing inequities is real, and surveillance practices that could be perceived of in terms of racial profiling pose serious challenges to the legitimacy of public organizations such as the police.

Racial profiling manifests linkages between stereotypes and systemic racism in two primary ways. At one level, when discretionary decisions enact stereotypical views of racial difference and suspicion, they conform with—and thereby support—systemic racism. For example, a 2010 study by the *Toronto Star* found that the Toronto Police Service stopped and documented (by way of filling out contact cards) Black males ages 15–24 at a rate 2.5 times higher than white males of the same age group. This study applied census data on

---

50 Ibid., 7.

51 Scot Wortley and Julian Tanner, "Data, Denials, and Confusion: The Racial Profiling Debate in Toronto," *Canadian Journal of Criminology and Criminal Justice* 45, no. 3 (2003): 369–70.

52 Vic Satzewich and William Shaffir, "Racism versus Professionalism: Claims and Counter-claims about Racial Profiling," *Canadian Journal of Criminology & Criminal Justice* 51, no. 2 (2009): 199–226; Frances Henry and Carol Tator, "Rejoinder to Satzewich and Shaffir on 'Racism versus Professionalism: Claims and Counter-claims about Racial Profiling,'" *Canadian Journal of Criminology and Criminal Justice* 53, no. 1 (2011): 65–74.

53 Mohammed Adam, "Former Kingston Police Chief Says Racial Study Has Its Merits," *Ottawa Citizen*, May 20, 2012.

54 Frances Henry and Carol Tator, *Racial Profiling: Challenging the Myth of a "Few Bad Apples"* (Toronto: University of Toronto Press, 2006); Karen Glover, *Racial Profiling: Research, Racism, and Resistance* (New York: Rowman & Littlefield, 2009); Scot Wortley and Julian Tanner, "Data, Denials, and Confusion: The Racial Profiling Debate in Toronto," *Canadian Journal of Criminology and Criminal Justice* 45, no. 3 (2003): 367–89.

the 74 police patrol zones in Toronto, finding "that blacks were documented at significantly higher rates than their overall census population by zone, and that in many zones, the same holds true for 'brown' people—mainly people of South Asian, Arab and West Asian backgrounds." The study also found that although Black people make up 8.4 per cent of the city's population, "they account for three times as many contact cards."[55] Discretionary decisions that support systemic racism can also be observed in decisions made by the Minister of Citizenship and Immigration to issue security certificates in order to detain or expel noncitizens who are deemed to be putting Canada at risk by having the potential to commit terrorist acts.[56]

At another level, to the extent these discretionary enactments of systemic racism are taken up by feedback loops—and counted as instances that validate the norms of systemic racism—they further cement and support the politics of representation that enables race-based discrimination, racism, and the de facto criminalization of racial difference.[57]

Profiling in Medicine

In our final example, profiling in a medical care context, we want to consider an instance in which the kind of sorting that profiling enables may have innocuous and even positive outcomes. Consider the example of atherosclerosis, as Annemarie Mol does in *The Body Multiple: Ontology in Medical Practice*. Atherosclerosis is, in biomedical terms, a condition of low blood pressure afflicting the lower limbs. Some would maintain that it has an objective and defining set of characteristics—it may be profiled according to its symptoms, like chest pains or numbness of the legs. Yet, as Mol argues, the characterization of atherosclerosis according to its symptoms is but one way of enacting the disease. It is, in fact, profiled according to different criteria depending on whether one is at home or in hospital, a patient or a doctor, a

---

55 Jim Rankin, "Race Matters: Blacks Documented by Police at High Rate," *Toronto Star*, February 6, 2010, http://www.thestar.com/news/crime/raceandcrime/2010/02/06/race_matters_blacks_documented_by_police_at_high_rate.html (accessed February 26, 2013).

56 Sherene Razack, *Casting Out: The Eviction of Muslims from Western Law & Politics* (Toronto: University of Toronto Press, 2008).

57 Scot Wortley and Julian Tanner, "Discrimination or 'Good' Policing? The Racial Profiling Debate in Canada," in Caroline Andrew, ed., *Our Diverse Cities*, 197–201 (Toronto: The Metropolis Project, 2004). http://canada.metropolis.net/research-policy/cities/publication/diverse_cite_magazine_e.pdf#page=198 (accessed March 4, 2013); Frances Henry and Carol Tator, *Racial Profiling in Toronto: Discourses of Domination, Mediation, and Opposition* (Toronto: Canadian Race Relations Foundation, 2005), http://crr.ca/divers-files/en/pub/rep/ePubRepRacProTor.pdf (accessed March 4, 2013); Henry and Tator, *Racial Profiling: Challenging the Myth of a "Few Bad Apples."*

laboratory technician or a surgeon. It is, in other words, profiled differently according to one's context and perspective. This difference of context and perspective is what makes atherosclerosis multiple. Yet in order for there to be a diagnosis of atherosclerosis, these different contexts and perspectives must be effectively coordinated according to the norm—the ideal that helps to determine what atherosclerosis ought to look like.

A diagnosis of atherosclerosis may lead to medical intervention that could prolong a patient's life. Yet, as Mol argues, the act of diagnosis is bound together with a normative judgment about what is healthy and what is not. This judgment differentiates some people, the deviants, from others, who are thereby taken to be standard. There is a lot of literature about the way in which this worked in the late nineteenth century. This was the period when women were marked as sickly deviants in contrast to the standard man, when Blacks acquired the status of unfit and invalid human exemplars falling below the standard set by whites, and when the category of the homosexual was invented to encompass people who were marked as developmental accidents failing to meet the maturity of heterosexuality. These various polarities, all feeding on the difference between the normal and the pathological, were linked together.[58]

Are there lessons to be learned from these historical examples? Certainly a continuity between the medical judgments of the nineteenth century and those of the twenty-first century is that in both eras profiles and classifications were informed by and used to create knowledge concerning what was normal and what was not. To what degree, however, does the medical determination of normalcy in the contemporary era—especially its shaping of and construction through surveillant profiles—enable governmentalities and the administration of diverse conduct? There is substantial social scientific literature on *medicalization*, or the transformation of social problems into medical ones.[59] In addition, sociologists and criminologists have been concerned about mapping the "medico-legal borderland," the conceptual space where actions are defined in terms of a hybrid of legal and medical principles.[60] These scholars have considered symmetries across—and connections between—the exercise of expert knowledge and authority in

---

58 Annemarie Mol, *The Body Multiple: Ontology in Medical Practice* (Durham: Duke University Press, 2003), 124.

59 See, for example, Peter Conrad, *The Medicalization of Society: On the Transformation of Human Conditions into Treatable Disorders* (Baltimore: The Johns Hopkins University Press, 2007).

60 Stefan Timmermans and Jonathan Gabe "Introduction: Connecting Criminology and Sociology of Health and Illness," *Sociology of Health & Illness* 24, no. 5 (2002): 501–16.

both medical and legal spheres. In studying the medico-legal borderland, it is apparent that problems once considered criminal are now viewed as amenable to medical treatment. Similarly, problems once viewed as medical are now criminalized. Foundational to the classification of problems within this borderland are the knowledges and signifying practices that rely on profiling.

And, as you have learned from considering profiling and profiling technologies in other sectors, the potential for such medical practices to interlock with existing stereotypical representations and systemic racism is real. Consider, for example, the way that persons identified as HIV seropositive are now increasingly subject to criminal prosecution in Canada for the non-disclosure of their serostatus—their "HIV positive" status—to sex partners.[61] This trend indicates that a medical condition is now, in key respects, being criminalized. And who among communities of individuals living with HIV are most subject to criminal prosecution? Analysis indicates that, to date, a majority of those prosecuted have been male defendants who are Black, African, and Caribbean.[62] This example suggests linkages between stereotypical representations, systemic racism, criminalization, medical monitoring, risk profiling, and surveillance, what Barry Adam and colleagues call a "striking case in the governmentality of health and disease."[63] By helping to constitute the range of what is believed to be normal (and by contrast what is viewed as abnormal), and by helping organizations and professionals to discriminate among normal and abnormal events, symptoms, behaviours, body types, and so on, medical profiling may, like the other kinds of profiling we have discussed, enable governmentalities and the administration of conduct. It is true that medical profiling may have positive outcomes, leading for example, to an early diagnosis and to interventions that may improve a person's health. However, analysts of surveillance need to be aware that the same kinds of profiling used to reach positive outcomes for some may also be used in ways that have negative outcomes for others.

---

61 Eric Mykhalovskiy, "The Problem of 'Significant Risk': Exploring the Public Health Impact of Criminalizing HIV Non-Disclosure," *Social Science & Medicine* 73, no. 5 (2011): 668–75.

62 Eric Mykhalovskiy and Glenn Betteridge, "Who? What? Where? When? And With What Consequences? An Analysis of Criminal Cases of HIV Non-Disclosure in Canada," *Canadian Journal of Law and Society* 27, no. 1 (2012): 31–53. See also Akim Adé Larcher and Alison Symington, *Criminals and Victims? The Impact of the Criminalization of HIV Non-Disclosure on African, Caribbean and Black Communities in Ontario* (Toronto: The African and Caribbean Council on HIV/AIDS in Ontario, 2010).

63 Barry Adam, Robb Travers, Richard Elliott, Ken English, and Patrice Corriveau, *How Criminalization Is Affecting People Living with HIV in Ontario* (Toronto: Ontario HIV Treatment Network, 2012), 1.

Conclusion

Our aim in this chapter has been to illustrate the relationship between contemporary surveillance, especially as effected through profiles and profiling technologies, and governmentality. Although surveillance is ubiquitous and plays a key role in the organization of contemporary life, not least in the management of our everyday transactions with organizations, it does have the potential to negatively impact people, especially those who are already marginalized in some way.

To illustrate this point, we have introduced the ideas of social control and governmentality, relating them to different understandings of the way that power functions. We have also suggested that surveillance, profiles, and profiling technologies can act as conduits of governmental power. In particular, we have focused on how profiling and profiling technologies can intersect with existing social hierarchies and inequities to perpetuate stereotypical representations, racism, and criminalization. We wanted especially to draw attention to how profiles and profiling technologies are informed by and help construct feedback loops and knowledge that has the potential to perpetuate inequities. To return to the story of Maher Arar, discussed at the beginning of this chapter, it is evident that stereotypes about Muslim and Arab Canadians were pervasively circulating among security forces (and the general population) in the aftermath of 9/11. These stereotypes were built into the profiles that security forces used to help identify the targets of their surveillance and investigation. In effect, they criminalized Muslim and Arab identities with disastrous consequences, as Arar's case illustrates. If there is a lesson to be learned from this terrible story, it is that surveillance, in spite of its ubiquity and centrality in contemporary life, can be wielded to dangerous ends.

Study Questions

1. What was your first encounter with a surveillance profile or technology today? Beginning from this encounter, make a list of all of your interactions with surveillance throughout the day. What doors have these interactions opened for you? What doors have they closed? How do you think the outcome of these interactions might differ if you were of differing race, age, sex, gender, ability, etc.?

2. Aboriginal peoples are overrepresented in Canadian prisons when compared to the non-Aboriginal population. Using the concept of cumulative disadvantage, describe some of the factors that may contribute to this inequity.

Exercise

Camera surveillance of public spaces has grown significantly over the past decade in Canada and in other countries around the world.[64] Can you think of a public space that you pass through as you go about your everyday affairs that is under camera surveillance? Visit this space with pen and paper in hand and count how many surveillance cameras appear to be in operation. Discuss with your peers the effect of these cameras. Do they make this public space safer? Canada's *Charter of Rights and Freedoms* describes the freedom of peaceful assembly and the freedom of association as fundamental freedoms. Do these cameras impinge upon your fundamental freedoms? Can we think of these cameras as profiling technologies?

Keywords

surveillance; profiles; profiling technologies; governmentality; social control; neoliberalism; cumulative disadvantage; digital discrimination, racial profiling

References

Adam, Barry, Robb Travers, Richard Elliott, Ken English, and Patrice Corriveau. *How Criminalization Is Affecting People Living with HIV in Ontario.* Toronto: Ontario HIV Treatment Network, 2012.

Adam, Mohammed. "Former Kingston Police Chief Says Racial Study Has Its Merits." *Ottawa Citizen,* May 20, 2012.

Arar Inquiry. *Report of the Events Relating to Maher Arar: Factual Background.* Vol. 1, *Commission of Inquiry into the Actions of Canadian Officials in Relation to Maher Arar.* Ottawa: Public Works and Government Services Canada, 2006.

Blank, Rebecca, Marilyn Dabady, and Constance Citro, eds. *Measuring Discrimination: Panel on Methods for Assessing Discrimination.* Washington: The National Academies Press, 2004.

Bogard, William. *The Simulation of Surveillance: Hypercontrol in Telematic Societies.* Cambridge: Cambridge University Press, 1996.

Bowker, Geoffrey C., and Susan Leigh Star. *Sorting Things Out: Classification and Its Consequences.* Cambridge, MA: MIT Press, 1999.

Coll, Sami. "Consumption as Biopower: Governing Bodies with Loyalty Cards." *Journal of Consumer Culture* 13, no. 3 (2013): 201–20. http://dx.doi.org/10.1177/1469540513480159.

Conrad, Peter. *The Medicalization of Society: On the Transformation of Human Conditions into Treatable Disorders.* Baltimore: The Johns Hopkins University Press, 2007.

---

64 Sean Hier, *Panoptic Dreams: Streetscape Video Surveillance in Canada* (Vancouver: UBC Press, 2010); Aaron Doyal, Randy Lippert and David Lyon, eds., *Eyes Everywhere: The Global Growth of Camera Surveillance* (New York: Routledge, 2011).

Créatec. "Executive Summary." *General Survey on Consumers' Financial Awareness, Attitudes and Behaviour*. Conducted for the Financial Consumer Agency of Canada (FCAC). Ottawa: FCAC. http://www.fcac-acfc.gc.ca/Eng/resources/researchSurveys/Documents/FCAC_GenSurvExec_2006-eng.pdf (accessed August 30, 2012).

Dale, Daniel. "Debit Cards to Replace Welfare Cheques." *Toronto Star*, August 8, 2011. http://www.thestar.com/news/gta/2011/08/08/debit_cards_to_replace_welfare_cheques.html (accessed April 15, 2012).

Doyal, Aaron, Randy Lippert, and David Lyon, eds. *Eyes Everywhere: The Global Growth of Camera Surveillance*. New York: Routledge, 2011.

Elmer, Greg. *Profiling Machines: Mapping the Personal Information Economy*. Cambridge, MA: MIT Press, 2004.

Environics Analytics. *PRIZM CE Marketer's Handbook*, 2008. www.tetrad.com/pub/documents/prizmcemethodology.pdf (accessed April 15, 2012).

Environics Analytics. *PRIZM C2*, 2012. www.environicsanalytics.ca/data/consumer-segmentation/prizmc2 (accessed April 15, 2012).

Ericson, Richard, and Kevin Haggerty. *Policing the Risk Society*. Toronto: University of Toronto Press, 1997.

Feagin, Joe. *Racist America: Roots, Current Realities, and Future Reparations*. New York: Routledge, 2010.

Foucault, Michel. *Psychiatric Power: Lectures at the Collège de France 1973–1974*. Edited by Arnold Davidson. New York: Picador, 2006.

Foucault, Michel. *Discipline and Punish: The Birth of the Prison*, translated by Alan Sheridan. New York: Vintage Books, 1995.

Foucault, Michel. "Governmentality." In *The Foucault Effect: Studies in Governmentality with Two Lectures by and an Interview with Michel Foucault*, edited by Graham Burchell, Colin Gordon, and Peter Miller, 87–104. Chicago: University of Chicago Press, 1991.

Gandy, Oscar. *The Panoptic Sort: A Political Economy of Personal Information*. Boulder: Westview Press, 1993.

Gandy, Oscar. "Quixotics Unite! Engaging the Pragmatists on Rational Discrimination." In *Theorizing Surveillance: The Panopticon and Beyond*, edited by David Lyon, 318–36. Cullompton: Willan, 2006.

Gandy, Oscar. *Coming to Terms with Chance: Engaging Rational Discrimination and Cumulative Disadvantge*. Farnham: Ashgate, 2009.

Gerth, Hans, and C. Wright Mills, eds. *From Max Weber: Essays in Sociology*. New York: Oxford University Press, 1958.

Glover, Karen. *Racial Profiling: Research, Racism, and Resistance*. New York: Rowman & Littlefield, 2009.

Haggerty, Kevin D. "Tear Down the Walls: On Demolishing the Panopticon." In *Theorizing Surveillance: The Panopticon and Beyond*, edited by David Lyon, 23–45. Cullompton: Willan, 2006.

Haggerty, Kevin, and Richard Ericson. "The Surveillant Assemblage." *British Journal of Sociology* 51, no. 4 (2000): 605–22. http://dx.doi.org/10.1080/00071310020015280.

Hali, Stuart. *Representation: Cultural Representation and Signifying Practices*. London: SAGE, 1997.

Henry, Frances, and Carol Tator. *Racial Profiling in Toronto: Discourses of Domination, Mediation, and Opposition*. Toronto: Canadian Race Relations Foundation, 2005. http://crr.ca/divers-files/en/pub/rep/ePubRepRacProTor.pdf (accessed March 4, 2013).

Henry, Frances, and Carol Tator. *Racial Profiling: Challenging the Myth of a "Few Bad Apples."* Toronto: University of Toronto Press, 2006.

Henry, Frances, and Carol Tator. "Rejoinder to Satzewich and Shaffir on 'Racism versus Professionalism: Claims and Counter-claims about Racial Profiling.'" *Canadian Journal of Criminology and Criminal Justice* 53, no. 1 (2011): 65–74. http://dx.doi.org/10.3138/cjccj.53.1.65.

Hier, Sean. *Panoptic Dreams: Streetscape Video Surveillance in Canada.* Vancouver: UBC Press, 2010.

Larcher, Akim Adé, and Alison Symington. *Criminals and Victims? The Impact of the Criminalization of HIV Non-Disclosure on African, Caribbean and Black Communities in Ontario.* Toronto: The African and Caribbean Council on HIV/AIDS in Ontario, 2010.

Lianos, Michalis. "Social Control after Foucault." *Surveillance & Society* 1, no. 3 (2003): 412–30.

Lyon, David. *Surveillance Society: Monitoring Everyday Life.* Buckingham: Open University Press, 2001.

Lyon, David. *Surveillance Studies: An Overview.* London: Polity Press, 2007.

Lyon, David. "Technology vs. 'Terrorism': Circuits of City Surveillance Since September 11," *International Journal of Urban and Regional Research,* 27, no. 3: 666–78.

Lyon, David, ed. *Theorizing Surveillance: The Panopticon and Beyond.* Cullompton: Willan, 2006.

Mol, Annemarie. *The Body Multiple: Ontology in Medical Practice.* Durham: Duke University Press, 2003. http://dx.doi.org/10.1215/9780822384151.

Money Mart. *Notice of the Settlement of the Ontario Money Mart Class Action.* http://www.moneymart.ca/paydayloans.asp (accessed April 15, 2012).

Mykhalovskiy, Eric. "The Problem of 'Significant Risk': Exploring the Public Health Impact of Criminalizing HIV Non-Disclosure." *Social Science & Medicine* 73, no. 5 (2011): 668–75. http://dx.doi.org/10.1016/j.socscimed.2011.06.051.

Mykhalovskiy, Eric, and Glenn Betteridge. "Who? What? Where? When? And With What Consequences? An Analysis of Criminal Cases of HIV Non-Disclosure in Canada." *Canadian Journal of Law and Society* 27, no. 1 (2012): 31–53. http://dx.doi.org/10.3138/cjls.27.1.031.

Ontario Human Rights Commission (OHRC). *Paying the Price: The Human Cost of Racial Profiling.* Toronto: OHRC, 2003.

Pollara. Payday Loan Customer Survey, 2007. http://www.cpla-acps.ca/english/mediastudies.php (accessed April 15, 2012).

Pridmore, Jason. "Loyal Subjects? Consumer Surveillance in the Personal Information Economy." PhD diss., Queen's University, Kingston, 2008.

Pridmore, Jason. "Consumer Surveillance: Context, Perspectives and Concerns in the Personal Information Economy." In *Routledge Handbook of Surveillance Studies,* edited by Kirstie Ball, Kevin Haggerty, and David Lyon, 321–29. New York: Routledge, 2012.

Rankin, Jim. "Race Matters: Blacks Documented by Police at High Rate." *Toronto Star,* February 6, 2010. http://www.thestar.com/news/crime/raceandcrime/2010/02/06/race_matters_blacks_documented_by_police_at_high_rate.html (accessed February 26, 2013).

Razack, Sherene. *Casting Out: The Eviction of Muslims from Western Law & Politics.* Toronto: University of Toronto Press, 2008.

Rose, Nikolas, and Peter Miller. "Political Power beyond the State: Problematics of Government." *British Journal of Sociology* 43, no. 2 (1992): 173–205. http://dx.doi.org/10.2307/591464.

Rose, Nikolas, Pat O'Malley, and Mariana Valverde. "Governmentality." *Annual Review of Law and Social Science* 2, no. 1 (2006): 83–104. http://dx.doi.org/10.1146/annurev.lawsocsci.2.081805.105900.

Ross, Edward. "Social Control." *American Journal of Sociology* 1, no. 5 (1896): 513–35. http://dx.doi.org/10.1086/210551.

Rugh, Jacob, and Douglas Massey. "Racial Segregation and the American Foreclosure Crisis." *American Sociological Review* 75, no. 5 (2010): 629–51. http://dx.doi.org/ 10.1177/0003122410380868.

Salter, Mark, ed. *Politics at the Airport*. Minneapolis: University of Minnesota Press, 2008.

Satzewich, Vic, and William Shaffir. "Racism versus Professionalism: Claims and Counter-claims about Racial Profiling." *Canadian Journal of Criminology and Criminal Justice* 51, no. 2 (2009): 199–226. http://dx.doi.org/10.3138/cjccj.51.2.199.

Snowden, Edward. "An Open Letter to the People of Brazil," *Folha de S.Paulo*, December 17, 2013, http://www1.folha.uol.com.br/internacional/en/world/2013/12/1386296 -an-open-letter-to-the-people-of-brazil.shtml (accessed December 17, 2013).

Timmermans, Stefan, and Jonathan Gabe. "Introduction: Connecting Criminology and Sociology of Health and Illness." *Sociology of Health & Illness* 24, no. 5 (2002): 501–16. http://dx.doi.org/10.1111/1467-9566.00306.

Weinberg, Darin. 2002. "Social Control." *Blackwell Encyclopedia of Sociology*, edited by George Ritzer. Blackwell Publishing: Blackwell Reference Online. http://www .blackwellreference.com/public (accessed May 2, 2012).

Wortley, Scot, and Julian Tanner. "Data, Denials, and Confusion: The Racial Profiling Debate in Toronto." *Canadian Journal of Criminology and Criminal Justice* 45, no. 3 (2003): 367–90. http://dx.doi.org/10.3138/cjccj.45.3.367.

Wortley, Scot, and Julian Tanner. "Discrimination or 'Good' Policing? The Racial Profiling Debate in Canada." In *Our Diverse Cities*, edited by Caroline Andrew, 197–201. Toronto: The Metropolis Project, 2004. http://canada.metropolis.net/research-policy/cities/ publication/diverse_cite_magazine_e.pdf#page=198 (accessed March 4, 2013).

eleven
Wanted by the Canada
Border Services Agency

ANNA PRATT

Introduction

In the summer of 2011, the then-familiar federal Canadian crime-fighting duo Immigration Minister Jason Kenney and Public Safety Minister Vic Toews announced the introduction of an FBI-style Most Wanted List as part of a public campaign by the Canada Border Services Agency (CBSA) to track down those who are the subject of a warrant for removal from Canada. This campaign, itself part of the larger CBSA Border Watch program, brought together two criminal law enforcement technologies and deployed them in the domain of immigration. In the manner of the most wanted lists now well known in the domain of criminal justice, the campaign publishes photographs of those "Wanted by the CBSA" for deportation on the Internet (see Figure 11.1), thus mobilizing a vigilant public already quite familiar with snitch lines in a range of public domains by calling upon them to phone in tips on the whereabouts of those wanted for deportation to a toll-free "Border Watch Line." The first Wanted by the CBSA List (the List) was published on the CBSA website in July 2011 and identified 30 suspected war criminals believed to be living in Canada. The second list, published in August 2011, identified 32 people wanted for deportation for reasons of serious criminality. In January 2012, the two lists were consolidated and expanded to also include those wanted for deportation for reasons of organized criminality and security.

The List includes a mug shot for each wanted individual, their name as well as any aliases, gender, date of birth, place of birth, last known address, identifying features, and a brief description of the reason why they are being sought for deportation.[1] The List is but one technology in an expansive,

---

1 On August 21, 2012, the List named 34 wanted individuals. On this day, six were wanted because "it has been determined that [they] have violated human or international rights under the Crimes Against Humanity and War Crimes Act or under International Law" (CBSA, Wanted by the CBSA website). One was wanted because "It has been determined that he is inadmissible to Canada on security grounds." Six were wanted because they "have been convicted of an offence outside of Canada that, if committed in Canada, would constitute a Canadian offence." One was wanted for reasons of organized criminality. Two were wanted for unspecified reasons of inadmissibility. The remaining 18 were wanted for reasons of serious criminality. Of the 34 named individuals, only one was female.

Figure 11.1 Wanted by the CBSA List webpage

heterogeneous, and well-established **immigration penality** that is enabled in large part by the varied intersections at the levels of discourse, authorities, and technologies that effectively blur the boundaries between the domains of criminal justice and immigration. This penality controls borders, polices noncitizens, identifies those who are dangerous, diseased, deceitful, or destitute and refuses them entry or casts them out.[2] It is made up of diverse and intersecting state and nonstate authorities, technologies, forms of knowledge, and regimes of rule. It includes a vast array of different state authorities,

2 Anna Pratt, "Immigration Penality and the Crime–Security Nexus: The Case of Tran Trong Nghi Nguyen," in *Canadian Criminal Justice Policy: A Contemporary Reader*, ed. Karim Ismaili, Jane Sprott, and Kim Varma (Oxford: Oxford University Press, 2012); Anna Pratt and Sara K. Thompson, "Chivalry, 'Race' and Discretion at the Canadian Border," *British Journal of Criminology* 48, no. 5 (2008): 620–40; Anna Pratt, *Securing Borders: Detention and Deportation in Canada* (Vancouver: UBC Press, 2005).

from public health to social welfare to criminal justice, immigration, border services, and security intelligence. In addition, nonstate authorities are also involved, including the private security companies that police detention centres, private airlines contracted for deportations, airline personnel enlisted in the policing of travellers, banks and bank tellers engaged in the policing of transnational organized crime and money laundering offences, legal aid that determines who will receive assistance for refugee claims, deportation appeals and detention review hearings and, as in the present example, private citizens and local communities mobilized and enlisted through most wanted lists and snitch line technologies in the identification and reporting of suspected criminal and security threats wanted for deportation.

However, when one considers that in 2008–09 (the most recent year for which removal statistics are available) the CBSA deported 13,249 people, and of these 1,855 were removed for reasons of criminality,[3] the number of individuals who are displayed on the Wanted by the CBSA List is negligible indeed.[4] And while from an enforcement perspective the List has not been without at least some success, the numbers are hardly overwhelming. In January 2012, the CBSA reported that between July 2011 and January 2012 they had received over 225 tips from the public, leading to 14 apprehensions and seven removals.[5]

While the enforcement effects of the List may be relatively limited and in some cases counterproductive (as I will discuss a little later), the CBSA List is nonetheless an effective and productive governing technology. The List participates not only in the policing of the border but in the very *making of* borders. Rather than a focus on borders as lines on a map that delineate a territory of nation-states, the process of *bordering* is here understood as an ongoing and artful accomplishment that is continuously and creatively constituted (performed, represented, and reproduced) at various sites.[6] Bordering takes place through the operations of the multiple and intersecting authorities, practices, technologies, forms of knowledge, and governing regimes that

---

3 Canada Border Services Agency, "Detentions and Removals Programs—Evaluation Study, Final Report," November 2010.

4 In fact, in November 2012 it was reported that the CBSA was having difficulty finding new names of so-called fugitives to include on the List, leading them to consider including individuals who are wanted for an admissibility hearing but who have not yet been ordered removed from Canada (Kim Mackrael, "Canada's Border Services Agency Looks to Widen the Scope of Its Most Wanted List," *Globe and Mail*, November 30, 2012).

5 Conservative Party of Canada, "Strengthening Community Safety and Our Immigration System," January 11, 2012.

6 Pratt, *Securing Borders*; Hille Koskela, "'Don't Mess with Texas!' Texas Virtual Border Watch Program and the (Botched) Politics of Responsibilization," *Crime, Media, Culture* 7, no. 1 (2011): 49–65; David Newman, "The Lines that Continue to Separate Us: Borders in Our 'Borderless' World," *Progress in Human Geography* 30, no. 2 (2006): 143–61.

make up the assemblage that is immigration penality. These include but are not limited to legal processes and the formal institutions of government. Bordering is not tied spatially to the perimeter of the nation but rather is performed and produced at diverse and dispersed sites both within and without the geopolitical nation-state. The Wanted by the CBSA List and its associated rationalizations, optics, artifacts, agents, and activities should therefore be understood not only in relation to its exclusionary, prohibitive, and coercive operations but also in terms of its enabling and productive effects. The List effectively produces and performs the border just as it is productive of dominant conceptions of the authority of a sovereign state, responsible citizenship, illegality, dangerous foreigners, and vigilant communities.[7]

This chapter explores the ways that the Wanted by the CBSA List and related developments represent the border as a thin blue line requiring constant vigilance to protect the safety and security of the population and the integrity of the Canadian immigration system and generous social programs. Operating in the shadow of the crime–security nexus,[8] a term I describe in detail in the next section, the bordering effects of the Wanted by the CBSA List rely centrally on the production of the dangerous and foreign criminal, regardless of how long they may have actually lived in Canada, in contradistinction to the law-abiding and hardworking citizen. This configuration of (dangerous) illegality versus (responsible) citizenship is given practical effect through the intersections between the domains of criminal justice, national security, and immigration at the levels of discourse, material technologies, and the specifics of law and policy. This chapter also brings to light the central influence of neoliberal preoccupations with fraud and "system abuse" and the mobilization of a vigilant, responsibilized citizenry in the reproduction of the national order of things, one spectacular deportation at a time.

What disappears from view in these representations are the complicated and specific individual situations at play. For this reason, in the second part of this chapter I take a close look at the deportation of Tran Trong Nghi

---

7 Another powerful example of border performance surfaced at the time I was writing this chapter. The federal Minister of Public Safety, Vic Toews, approved the filming of CBSA immigration raids and arrests at a construction site in Vancouver, British Columbia, in March 2013 by a reality TV show on Canadian border security called *Border Security*. While news of this government-sanctioned collaboration between the entertainment industry and border enforcement sparked widespread concern and criticism, there is no indication that the government is reconsidering. Minister Toews repeatedly defended his decision with reference to the costs of illegal immigration that are borne by Canadian taxpayers and law-abiding Canadians and the need to "send a message" about Canadian border security (Canadian Press, "TV Cameras Filming CBSA Immigration Raids for Reality Show Is Okay: Public Safety Minister Vic Toews," *National Post*, March 19, 2013).

8 Pratt, *Securing Borders*, 2005.

Nguyen, a man characterized by Minister Kenney as a "violent foreign criminal" who, like those included on the List, was deported because of the threefold threat he was deemed to pose to Canadian public safety, security, and the integrity of the immigration system. Tran's story sheds specific light on the more messy individual dimensions of the crime–security nexus that do not fit easily with the crude depictions of dangerous and threatening criminal foreigners that rationalize the Wanted by the CBSA List in the production of borders.

Blurring the Boundaries between the Domains of Immigration Enforcement and Crime Control

The publication of photos, names, and identifying information about those wanted by the police and the enlisting of citizens in the work of tracking them down is by now a familiar law enforcement technology, reminiscent of the days of sheriffs' wanted posters in the Wild West (see Figure 11.2).

Internet-based most wanted lists are now standard fare for most police forces across North America (see Figure 11.3); even the US Postal Inspection Service maintains an Internet-based most wanted list.

Figure 11.2 Butch Cassidy: Wanted "Dead or Alive" poster

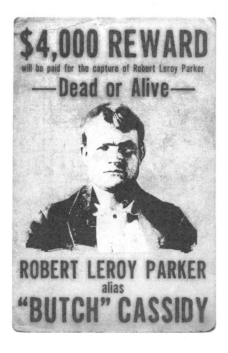

Figure 11.3 Internet-based most wanted lists from various agencies across North America: (1) FBI page for Osama Bin Laden, (2) US Marshals Service, (3) RCMP, and (4) Peel Regional Police

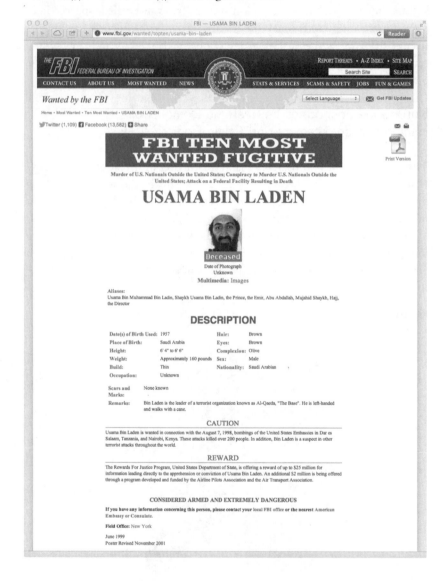

Figure 11.3 (Continued)

Figure 11.3 (Continued)

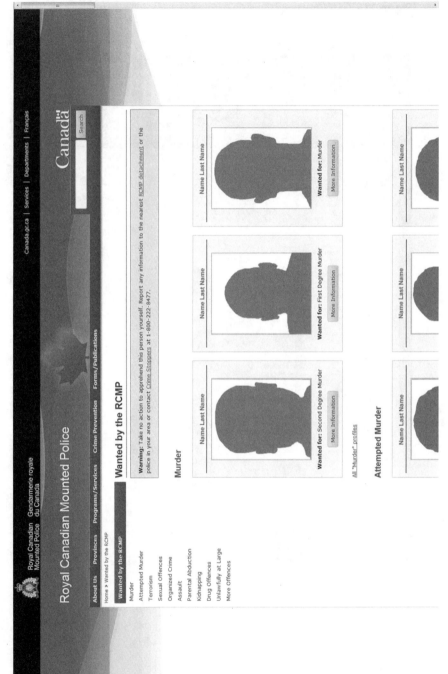

Figure 11.3 (Continued)

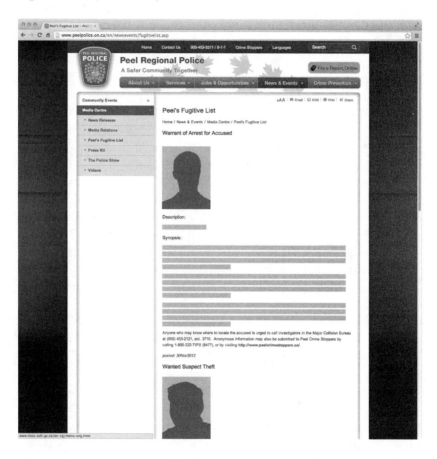

While in the United States this traditional law enforcement technology has been used in the context of immigration enforcement for some time,[9] its deployment is unprecedented in the context of Canadian immigration enforcement. It is thus unsurprising that the justification for the introduction of this technology is drawn not primarily from the traditional Canadian lexicon of immigration but rather is thoroughly embedded in the crime-fighting discourses of public safety and national security concerns that also fuel the federal Conservative government's national "get tough on crime" agenda. The discursive rationalizations that surround the Wanted

---

9 The US Department of Homeland Security maintains two 10 Most Wanted Lists: one for Enforcement and Removal Operations and one for Homeland Security Investigations. See http://www.ice.gov/most-wanted.

by the CBSA List repeatedly invoke the aims of public safety, security, and system integrity, and it appeals to responsible citizens and communities to be vigilant in the face of the dangerous threats posed by a mixed bag of foreign criminals. As explained by (then) Ministers Toews and Kenney in the news release announcing the consolidated Wanted by the CBSA List in January 2012,

> "Our Government will continue to be vigilant at our border, within our communities and around the world, keeping Canada a safe place to live," said Minister Toews. "Today's announcement is another example of how the Harper Government takes its obligation to safeguard public safety very seriously and is taking all necessary measures to ensure Canadians are protected. Canada's doors are not open to those who break the law or endanger the safety of our citizens … Our Government received a strong mandate to keep Canadians safe and secure. We remain committed to capturing and deporting dangerous foreign criminals who break our laws and abuse our generous immigration system," said Minister Kenney.[10]

The intersections between the domains of immigration and criminal justice are further evidenced not only by the deployment of a well-known criminal justice technology—the Most Wanted List—in the work of immigration enforcement, but also in the presentation of immigration enforcement as a key technology of Canadian crime control, national security, and public safety. Moreover, the guiding and ultimate policy objective of the List is to facilitate the detention and deportation of individuals deemed to be crime–security threats, two carceral and bodily sanctions that, as I have argued in detail elsewhere, are technologies deeply associated with the domain of criminal justice punishment.[11] The intersections between immigration enforcement, public safety, and crime control are further represented and reproduced through the regular pairing of Public Safety Minister Vic Toews and Immigration Minister Jason Kenney in a variety of carefully scripted and staged public appearances, press conferences, press releases, and photo ops relating to immigration enforcement (see Figure 11.4).

These intersections are widely represented as natural and self-evident. A recent example of just how embedded the intersections are between criminal

---

10 Canada Border Services Agency, "Government of Canada Enlists Help," News Release, July 21, 2011.

11 Anna Pratt, "Sovereign Power, Carceral Conditions and Penal Practices: Detention and Deportation in Canada," *Studies in Law, Politics and Society* 23 (2001): 45–78; Pratt, *Securing Borders*.

Figure 11.4 The crime-fighting duo: Public Safety Minister Vic Toews and Immigration Minister Jason Kenney[12]

justice and immigration was provided by Toronto Mayor Rob Ford who, after a number of fatal shootings in the city in the summer of 2012, proposed that the prime minister of Canada, Stephen Harper, should use Canada's federal immigration laws to ban individuals convicted of gun crimes from the City of Toronto:

> Anyone, I don't care if you're an immigrant or not, if you get caught with a gun, I want to find out the legalities of are you allowed to stay [in the City of Toronto] or are you not ... I'm sure it falls under some sort of immigration law, maybe it doesn't, but I'm going to find out through the prime minister what we can do.[13]

---

12 Readers may recall the publicity that surrounded the arrival of 492 Sri Lankan refugee claimants by boat on the coast of British Columbia in August 2010. Rather than being received and represented in the light of international human rights and refugee protection, these migrants were represented in the shadow of the crime–security nexus. This photo was taken at the refugees' widely publicized reception performed by Toews with Kenney at his side.

13 Don Peat, "Rob Ford Fails to Explain Proposal to Ban Gun Criminals from City," *Sun News*, July 20, 2012, http://www.sunnewsnetwork.ca/sunnews/politics/archives/2012/07/20120720 -144723.html, accessed July 2, 2014.

Further and flagrantly exploiting public fear and the blending of local crime problems with immigration enforcement, Immigration Minister Jason Kenney quickly tweeted his agreement that "foreign gangsters should be deported without delay," despite the complete lack of any information whatsoever that "foreign criminals" had been involved in any of the recent gun violence in Toronto. When pressed, Minister Kenney did clarify that of course Canadian citizens convicted of crimes could not be deprived of their mobility rights, and that in fact there was no information that "foreign criminals" were involved in the recent gun violence. Nonetheless, Minister Kenney did not miss the opportunity to plug his recently introduced immigration enforcement bill, the Faster Removal of Foreign Criminals Act, by drawing a general connection between the recent gun violence and the "broader" problem of foreign criminals, even in the absence of any specific connection to the incidents that had precipitated Ford's comments:

> But clearly, the recent rash of gun crime in Toronto is connected
> to criminal gang activity and we are aware that there have been
> foreign members, sometimes leading members of criminal
> gangs in Canada, able to recommit offences while delaying
> their deportation ... So, my comment was not in relation to
> any particular alleged criminal, it was in relation to the broader
> problem of gang crime which sometimes does involve foreign
> citizens who are delaying deportation from Canada and we
> shouldn't be squeamish about this.[14]

The close intersections of criminal justice and immigration indicated briefly here are of course neither a new development nor a novel observation. Scholars have by now well established the various connections that intertwine these two domains,[15] leading to the invention of catchy new

---

14 Canadian Press, "Kenney Links Toronto Gun Violence to 'Foreign Gangsters,'" *CTV News*, July 20, 2012.

15 See Anna Pratt and Mariana Valverde, "'From Deserving Victims to Masters of Confusion': Redefining Refugees in the 1990s," *Canadian Journal of Sociology* 27, no. 2 (2002): 135–61; Pratt, *Securing Borders*; Pratt, "Immigration Penality and the Crime–Security Nexus"; Michael Welch, *Detained: Immigration Laws and the Expanding INS Jail Complex* (Philadelphia: Temple University Press, 2002); Theresa Miller, "Blurring the Boundaries between Immigration and Crime Control after September 11th," *BC Third World Quarterly* 81 (2005): 81–123; Mary Bosworth, "Governing through Migration Control," *British Journal of Criminology* 48, no. 6 (2008): 703–19.

terminology—*crimmigration*.[16] The impact of security concerns on migration law and policy, the "securitization of migration," has also not gone unnoticed.[17] In both cases, the enabling effects of what I have called the crime–security nexus are centrally important.

The Crime–Security Nexus

According to CBSA officials, as of January 2012 the consolidated Most Wanted List "fully represents the CBSA's priorities for removals": war criminality, serious criminality, organized criminality, and security.[18] This consolidated list of largely unspecified criminality and security threats also neatly captures the heightened influence of the crime–security nexus in the governance of immigration penalty and border production. In Canada over the last 50 years, as human rights doctrine became more consequential and legal "rights talk" more established, explicitly racist, moralistic, and ideological grounds for exclusion were delegitimized. While certainly political enemies of the state have long been and continue to be the targets of detention and deportation, the grounds for exclusion based on criminal threats posed to the population have proliferated in Canada.[19]

The concept of the **crime–security nexus** refers more specifically to two simultaneous processes that are at play here. First is the way that certain forms of criminality have been reconceptualized and acted upon as threats to national security. Second, conversely, is the way that the conception of national security has been radically reconfigured and extended to include governmental concerns with public safety and the economy and to therefore encompass a host of "true" crimes that have been linked through the spectre of organized crime to national security, including violent street crimes, gun crimes, drug crimes, prostitution, and so on. In the past, while such forms of criminality may well have been linked to gangs or even to organized crime, they would not have been understood as threats to national security—a term previously reserved for threats posed to the political state by

---

16 Julie Stumpf, "The Crimmigration Crisis: Immigrants, Crime and Sovereign Power," *bepress Legal Series*. Working Paper 1635 (2006). http://law.bepress.com/expresso/eps/1635.

17 Didier Bigo, "Security and Immigration: Toward a Critique of the Governmentality of Unease," *Alternatives* 27 (2002): 63–92; Jef Huysmans, "The European Union and the Securitization of Migration," *Journal of Common Market Studies* 38, no. 5 (2000): 751–77; Anastassia Tsoukala and Ayse Ceyhan, "The Securitization of Migration in Western Societies: Ambivalent Discourses and Policies," *Alternatives* 5 (2002): 21–39.

18 CBSA, "Government of Canada Enlists Help of Canadians."

19 Pratt, *Securing Borders*.

subversion, treason, espionage, and sedition.[20] The powerful influence of the crime–security nexus is evidenced most dramatically by the unprecedented move in the mid-1990s to expand the working mandate of the Canadian Security Intelligence Agency (CSIS) to encompass crime and criminals as threats to national security. With the demise of traditional Cold War enemies and fears and in accordance with the increasing dominance of law and order concerns,[21] CSIS declared that organized and transnational crime now posed a monumental threat to "various aspects of Canadian national security, law and order, the integrity of government programs and institutions, and the economy."[22] CSIS explains this expansion by referencing the effects of globalization, which it argues has created a world "virtually devoid of national borders," providing vast opportunities for "members of highly sophisticated and organized criminal syndicates to pursue a complex web of lucrative legal and illegal activities world-wide."[23] The range of criminality included in the new operational mandate of CSIS is expansive:

> While still involved at the lower level with drug trafficking, prostitution, loansharking, illegal gambling and extortion [organized criminals] have expanded their activities to a quasi-corporate level where they are active in large-scale insurance fraud, the depletion of natural resources, environmental crime, migrant smuggling, bank fraud, gasoline tax fraud and corruption. In addition, their frequent use of money earned from their illegal ventures to fund legitimate ones allows them to launder money and earn even more profits. They apply many of their criminal tactics in these legal business operations, never hesitating to use violence or murder to get ahead.[24]

National security, previously understood in strict sovereign relation to the political state, now encompasses social and national concerns with "public

---

20 By the twenty-first century, immigration penalty in general and the practices of detention and deportation in particular had come to be governed through crime–security. What followed September 11, 2001 was a major refocusing on international terrorism in the context of a trend toward governing through crime that was already well entrenched (Jonathan Simon, "Governing through Crime," in *The Crime Conundrum: Essays on Criminal Justice*, ed. Lawrence M. Friedman and George Fisher, 171–89 [New York: Westview Press, 1997]). More recently, however, the surge of activity focused on international terrorism has subsided, and the focus on organized criminality has again come to the forefront, vitalized now by the more commonly taken-for-granted association between gangsters, organized crime, and therefore with national security.

21 For a detailed discussion of the historical lineage of the crime–security nexus in relation to Canadian immigration law and policy see Pratt, *Securing Borders*.

22 Canadian Security Intelligence Services, "Transnational Criminal Activity."

23 Ibid.

24 Ibid.

safety" and threats to the economic state: "In response to the rise of terrorism worldwide and the demise of the Cold War, CSIS has made public safety its first priority."[25]

The representation of organized crime as a threat to public safety and therefore to national security thus also signals the emergence of a new conception of "the state." The focus on ideological threats and national security that had been central throughout the Cold War years was consistent with a conception of the modern liberal state as a sovereign political institution. In contrast, the focus on criminal threats and national security constructs the state as primarily concerned with promoting the welfare of the population understood in terms of the security of property and the advancement of economic interests. This focus is thus consistent with processes of governmentalization, the emergence of the economic state, and neoliberal priorities including notably free market economics but also corollary concerns relating to "system integrity," fraud and "system abuse."

Neoliberalism, Fraud, and "System Abuse"

In addition to mobilizing the powerful logic of crime–security through the grouping of a variety of "most wanted" criminality and security threats and the linking of these threats with public safety and security, the Wanted by the CBSA List also deploys the powerful spectre of fraud, "system integrity," and "system abuse" that fuelled the neoliberal campaigns in the late 1990s and 2000s against bogus refugees and welfare cheats.[26] Neoliberalism is preoccupied with economic efficiency, good management, and system integrity. The spectre of fraud and its corollary—system abuse—represents a formidable threat to these touchstones of good neoliberal government—made all the worse when considered in relation to the already much-maligned distribution of administrative social benefits. It is therefore not surprising that the Wanted by the CBSA List has been repeatedly justified not only by reference to the threats posed by dangerous foreign criminals, but also by the associated and pressing need to "stop the abuse" and "protect the integrity" of "Canada's generous immigration system":

> Canadians gave our Government a strong mandate to help keep our streets and communities safe, while also working to maintain the integrity of our immigration system ... Our Conservative Government is taking action to identify wanted individuals and suspected criminals

---

25 Canadian Security Intelligence Services, "The CSIS Mandate," 2005.
26 Pratt and Valverde, "'From Deserving Victims to Masters of Confusion.'"

to stop their abuse of Canada's generous immigration system and help keep our streets and communities safe.[27]

Concerns about fraud and the unknown threats that lurk among us are particularly prominent in relation to those alleged war criminals on the Wanted by the CBSA List who may have gained entry to Canada by using fraudulent identity documents.

Fraudulent claims to state benefits, whether these take the form of the granting of refugee status, citizenship, or welfare, are particularly repugnant to neoliberal sensibilities, which are from the outset adverse to even legitimate claims to state benefits. Neoliberalism is understood here as not only an economic plan, but a moral campaign. The devaluation of most forms of dependency under neoliberal modes of rule is accompanied by the constitution and mobilization of the active, responsible, independent citizen—the kind of citizen who embraces their role in policing themselves and their communities as vigilant informants.

Vigilant Citizens for a Safe and Secure Nation

As captured by the title of the news release publicizing the first Wanted by the CBSA List in July 2011, "Government of Canada Enlists Help of Canadians to Enforce Canada's Immigration Laws," the CBSA List invokes not only a vigilant state but also mobilizes the participation of vigilant, responsible, and active citizens in the policing (and production) of borders. Taking its cue from Neighbourhood Watch programs and Crime Stoppers, the CBSA Border Watch Toll-Free Line exhorts ordinary community members to call in any "information about suspicious border activity," day or night, no matter how trivial and no matter whether the reported suspicions are "after the fact."[28] Tip lines and most wanted lists are key crime prevention and control technologies in neoliberal regimes of rule that favour governing "at a distance" through the participation of responsible, independent citizens in the policing of themselves, their communities, and their nation; as

---

27 Conservative Party, "Strengthening Community Safety."

28 While the information provided may be shared with the CBSA's national and international partners in security, the caller's anonymity and confidentiality is assured. While a reward is not guaranteed, it is offered as a possible outcome that is left to the discretion of the CBSA (Canada Border Services Agency, "Border Watch Toll-Free Line," http://www.cbsa-asfc.gc.ca/security-securite/bwl-lsf-eng.html, accessed April 19, 2014). For an interesting discussion of Crime Stoppers, see Randy Lippert, "Policing Property and Moral Risk through Promotions, Anonymization, and Rewards: Crime Stoppers Revisited," *Social and Legal Studies* 11 (2002): 475–502.

put by Hille Koskela, "the mentality of the neighbourhood watch—securing territory and defending 'yours' against the Others—is extended to the international level."[29] This enlisting of the participation of citizens in the bordering process in association with new forms of surveillance has been connected to the resurgence of what some are calling an informant culture[30] and a reconfiguration of citizenship in which "individuals are encouraged and assumed to positions previously held by authorities."[31] As explained by Koskela, in relation to the Texas Virtual Border Watch program:

> Theoretically, the program is a perfect example of synopticism: many watching few instead of few watching many (as in the Panopticon). The positions of the authorities and the public are structured in a new way. The public does the watching work and the authorities sort out the information.[32]

In the case of the CBSA List, the mobilization and participation of citizens to keep a watchful eye and report any suspicions to the hotline is continually encouraged by the CBSA, and special thanks are regularly offered to the responsible and hardworking citizens who have phoned in tips in the press releases issued about the List: "On behalf of the Government, I would like to thank all of the honest, hardworking Canadians who have called the tip line and whose help has been vital in capturing these foreign criminals and getting them off our streets. The results speak for themselves."[33]

This kind of voluntary vigilantism is consistent with the pervasive culture of fear and insecurity that has created heightened hostility, intolerance, and new forms of racism.[34] Indeed, the face of the border that is represented

---

29 Koskela, "'Don't Mess with Texas,'" 57.

30 Aaron Doyle, "An Alternative Current in Surveillance and Control: Broadcasting Surveillance Footage of Crimes," in *The New Politics of Surveillance and Visibility*, ed. Kevin Haggerty and Richard Ericson (Toronto: University of Toronto Press, 2006).

31 Koskela, "'Don't Mess with Texas,'" 56.

32 Ibid., 54. Koskela describes the rather extraordinary real-time Texas Virtual Border Watch program, in which citizens anywhere can log on to and observe live streaming video of the border between the United States and Mexico, fed through a network of webcams and sensors, and report any suspicious border crossing behaviour.

33 CBSA, "Government of Canada Enlists Help of Canadians."

34 Katja Franko Aas, "'Getting Ahead of the Game': Border Technologies and the Changing Space of Governance," in *Global Surveillance and Policing Borders: Borders, Security, Identity*, ed. Elia Zureik and Mark B. Salter (Cullumpton, UK: Willan, 2005); Alan Hunt, "Risk and Moralization in Everyday Life," in *Risk and Morality*, ed. Richard Ericson and Aaron Doyle (Toronto: University of Toronto Press, 2003); Hille Koskela, "Fear and Its Others," in *Handbook of Social Geography*, ed. Susan Smith, Rachel Pain, Sallie Marston, and John Paul Jones (London: Sage, 2012).

by the Wanted by the CBSA List is thoroughly racialized.[35] In response to criticisms that the List may be fuelling xenophobia and anti-immigrant sentiment, Minister Kenney declared:

> I think that's patently ridiculous. To the contrary, we've received nothing but a phenomenally positive response from new Canadians in general. And the evidence of that is most of the useful tips coming from the public are generated from cultural communities in which these people have been situated in Canada. So we thank members of those communities for their cooperation.[36]

Bordering and the Constitution of Communities

Kenney's dismissal of concerns about racism and xenophobia hinges upon what he describes as the active engagement and cooperation of "new Canadians" and "cultural communities" in the Border Watch campaign. This points again to the intersections between the domains of immigration enforcement and criminal justice, in this case through the application of the idea of "community policing" in the domain of immigration enforcement. The idea of community policing, whether at the level of local neighbourhoods or of nations, conjures up a vision of the forging and nurturing of mutually cooperative relationships between communities and the police in such a way as to reconfigure the relationship from one of hierarchy and alienation to one of mutual support and collaborative problem solving and policy design. Community policing works to constitute "the community," and it engages community members in the active and ongoing regulation of themselves and the community. It encourages the active involvement of community members in identifying and reporting not only criminal activities that have taken or are taking place, but also merely unfamiliar, suspicious, and risky elements that threaten the community and its members.

---

35 To provide a snapshot of the border, on August 21, 2012, of the 34 individuals displayed on the List three were from China, one was from Poland, three were from Mexico, two were from India, two were from Honduras, two were from Colombia, one was from the United States, four were from Jamaica, one was from Nigeria, one was from the Republic of Korea, one was from Sri Lanka, one was from Bangladesh, two were from Somalia, one was from Kosovo, one was from Guatemala, one was from Chile, one was from Hungary, two were from Iran, one was from Guyana, one was from St. Vincent and Grenadines, one was from Vietnam, and one was from Senegal. While nationality is not a straightforward marker of racialization, of the 34 individuals identified on August 21, 2012, as crime–security threats, only one was identifiably "white."

36 Stewart Bell, "Q&A: Immigration Minister Jason Kenney Speaks on the War Crimes Wanted List," *National Post*, July 28, 2012.

Victimization or potential victimization and associated fears and insecurity have become a new basis of active citizenship.[37] Through programs like Border Watch, the Wanted by the CBSA List, Crime Stoppers, Neighbourhood Watch and so on, the community is not merely acted upon, but is continuously constituted as a "vector for government." As put by Nikolas Rose, "Community is not simply the territory within which crime is to be controlled, it is itself a *means* of government." **Governing through community** involves the mobilization, enrolment, and deployment of its "vectors and forces" in "novel programmes and techniques which encourage and harness active processes of self-management and identity construction of personal ethics and collective allegiances."[38]

In place of social or collective risk management programs of welfare liberalism, individuals and smaller communities assume responsibility for their own risk management. This becomes part of their responsibility and identity as active citizens—what Pat O'Malley calls the "new prudentialism."[39] This contrasts with the dependent and passive citizenry that is said to be encouraged by welfare liberalism. As observed by Rose, "New modes of neighbourhood participation, local empowerment and engagement of residents in decisions over their own lives will, it is thought, re-activate self-motivation, self-responsibility and self-reliance in the form of active citizenship within a self-governing community."[40]

The crafting of the first Wanted by the CBSA List to target suspected war criminals is not so surprising, then, in light of these insights about the constitution and mobilization of local communities in policing activities. Widely held concerns in certain ethnic communities about the presence of both World War II and modern-day war criminals in Canada would surely add to the political popularity of the campaign and would presumably galvanize the support and participation of individuals and communities. Minister Toews, emphasizing community safety and the role of the public in this initiative, stressed that

> [W]e all have a part to play in making our communities safe, and today we are asking for Canadians' assistance ... In releasing

---

37 Alison Young, *Imagining Crime: Textual Outlaws and Criminal Conversations* (London: Sage, 1996).

38 Nikolas Rose, *Powers of Freedom: Reframing Political Thought* (Cambridge: Cambridge University Press, 1999), 176.

39 Pat O'Malley, "Risk, Power and Crime Prevention," *Economy and Society* 21, no. 3 (1992): 252–75; Pat O'Malley, "Risk and Responsibility," in *Foucault and Political Reason*, ed. Andrew Barry, Thomas Osborne, and Nikolas Rose, 189–208 (Chicago: University of Chicago Press, 1996).

40 Rose, *Powers of Freedom*, 249.

the names of individuals who are residing illegally in Canada and who are complicit in committing war crimes and crimes against humanity, it is our hope that new information will help our law-enforcement officials track them down and remove them from Canada.[41]

War Criminality, Fraud, and the Blurring of the Boundaries of Administration and Criminal Justice

The explicit foregrounding of war criminality as an enforcement priority in advance of the usual suspects—serious criminals, organized criminals, and national security threats—was indeed a novel, if politically strategic, approach. The List was devoted to the names and photographs of 30 individuals wanted because "It has been determined that they violated human or international rights under the Crimes Against Humanity and War Crimes Act or under International Law." On the surface, this initiative appears to introduce a welcome concern for international justice to the exclusionary justifications typically dominated by sovereign, domestic preoccupations with individual and gang criminality, national security, and public safety: the protection of international human rights and the prosecution of state crimes. Indeed, in announcing the List Ministers Kenney and Toews made particular reference to Canada's international reputation for its efforts to bring people suspected of war crimes or crimes against humanity to justice: "Canada is recognized around the world for its leadership in global efforts to hold persons suspected of, or complicit in, serious human rights abuses accountable for their crimes through cooperation with other countries and international tribunals."[42]

With considerable fanfare, and flanked as usual by his crime-fighting partner Immigration Minister Jason Kenney, Public Safety Minister Vic Toews explained that "For too long now, those who have complicity in such grievous crimes have managed to blend into a trusting and welcoming Canadian society." It was high time, according to the ministers, that anyone who has committed or been an accomplice to war crimes should be "rounded up and kicked out of Canada."[43] Immigration Minister Kenney explained further: "Our Government received a strong mandate from Canadians to maintain the integrity of our immigration system. Those who

---

41 CBSA, "Government of Canada Enlists Help of Canadians."
42 Ibid.
43 Louise Elliott, "Ottawa Names War Crimes Suspects in Canada," *CBC News*, July 21, 2011.

have been involved in war crimes or crimes against humanity will find no haven on our shores."[44]

However, this implied culpability cultivated by the government is misleading and again relies upon the blurring of the boundaries between criminal justice and the administration of immigration. This blurring is front and centre in Minister Kenney's response to concerns raised about privacy rights and the Wanted by the CBSA List:

> The notion that a foreigner who illegally enters Canada, has been found by our legal system to be involved in the worst kinds of crimes possible, such as war crimes and crimes against humanity, who is under a deportation order and a warrant—the notion that such an individual enjoys the same privacy rights as a law abiding Canadian citizen is bizarre in the extreme. And the fact that people are concerned about this just shows the kind of ideological process obsession that some people have that overrides any consideration for the public interest or the integrity of our immigration system.[45]

More accurately, the people on the first Wanted by the CBSA List had applied for refugee status in Canada but were found to be ineligible because the Immigration and Refugee Board (IRB) determined that they were inadmissible to Canada because there were reasonable grounds to suspect complicity in war crimes or crimes against humanity. This is not a finding of culpability in a criminal court—it is an *administrative* decision made by an *administrative* tribunal under the authority of *administrative* law (the Immigration and Refugee Protection Act, IRPA). As clearly explained in the CBSA's own report on Canada's program on crimes against humanity and war crimes, "It is important to note that an administrative investigation of a case is different from a criminal investigation."[46] Administrative

---

44 Ibid. It should be mentioned that because of the very broad inadmissibility provisions of the Immigration and Refugee Protection Act, the people named on the List as suspected war criminals may include those only very tangentially associated with a government that committed gross human rights abuses but who did not themselves have any direct association with war crimes. However, even notwithstanding the vagaries and elasticity of the definitions relating to complicity in war crimes and crimes against humanity, in light of these official claims members of the public would be forgiven for understanding that these individuals had in fact been found guilty of committing war crimes or of being directly complicit in war crimes in a domestic criminal court, the international criminal court, or an international tribunal.

45 Bell, "Q&A: Immigration Minister Jason Kenney Speaks."

46 Canada Border Services Agency, *12th Report on Canada's Program on Crimes Against Humanity and War Crimes*, 2008–2011.

remedies do not require probable grounds, but rather only *reasonable grounds to suspect* that the person may have committed or been complicit in war crimes or crimes against humanity. And this "determination" is itself governed by a much watered-down version of the rule of law, a "less than civil" standard of proof and much more relaxed rules of evidence than a criminal proceeding.[47]

This ambiguity surrounding the distinction between the administrative determination of criminal culpability, along with other largely legalistic concerns, quickly became the subject of forceful criticism from a variety of well-respected immigration lawyers and the Canadian Bar Association as well as a host of human rights advocacy groups including Amnesty International, the Canadian Council for Refugees, and the British Columbia Civil Liberties Association.[48] Less than one month after the publication of the first List, Amnesty International wrote an open letter to Ministers Toews and Kenney to express its concerns about the CBSA's Border Watch program. Amnesty International pointed out that the Wanted by the CBSA List does not even begin to live up to the principles of universal jurisdiction and international justice.[49] Rather than seeking simple deportation, these principles would oblige Canada to try to ensure that the individuals in question would be dealt with under criminal proceedings governed by the rule of law either in the person's home country, before an international court or tribunal or, if no such assurance is attained, then here in Canada. As echoed one month later in another statement released by Amnesty International and 15 other advocacy and human rights agencies, to simply deport people suspected of war crimes or crimes against humanity in no way assures that they will be held accountable and brought to justice, which is Canada's

---

47 Lorne Waldman, "Canada's Unwanted List," *The Lawyer's Weekly*, February 3, 2012.

48 Amnesty International has strongly encouraged the collaborative efforts of all governments to live up to their obligations with respect to human rights and international justice by bringing individuals who have committed war crimes, crimes against humanity, and other serious human rights violations to justice. It has been supportive of Canadian reforms over the past few decades that have enshrined the principle of universal jurisdiction for such crimes in the Canadian justice system through amendments to the Criminal Code in the late 1980s relating to torture and crimes against humanity and the passage of the War Crimes Act in 2000. Indeed, these are the reforms that earned Canada the international recognition that Ministers Toews and Kenney appealed to when announcing the List.

49 Amnesty International, "Amnesty International Canada Open Letter to Ministers Toews and Kenney about 'Wanted by the CBSA,' August 2, 2011, http://www.amnesty.ca/ news/news -item/amnesty-international-canada-open-letter-to-ministers-toews-and-kenney (accessed April 19, 2014).

international legal obligation. Deportation does nothing to ensure prosecution for war criminality.[50]

As alluded to at the start of this chapter, even from a strictly enforcement perspective the Wanted by the CBSA List is in some cases counterproductive. Rather than expedite deportations it may in fact hinder—perhaps even prevent—the deportation of targeted individuals. This is because Canada also has an obligation not to deport individuals to situations where they will face a serious risk of torture, extrajudicial execution, or enforced disappearance. The publication of the names, photographs, and details of those labelled as suspected war criminals raises not only privacy issues, but also the fact that this wide publicity may well result in increasing the risk they face if deported. Everyone facing removal from Canada receives a pre-removal risk assessment (PRRA). A positive PRRA means that the deportation cannot proceed unless there are exceptional circumstances. In fact, in advance of the release of the Wanted by the CBSA List, an internal CBSA briefing memo warned that the publication of the List "could effectively paint a target on their back and put them at risk of torture or human rights abuses."[51] The memo explained that the "release of this information would highlight a person's case to the public, potentially leading to the person being at risk when removed, potentially

---

50 As explained more specifically in this statement, the key principles that should guide Canadian policies on these matters include the following:
  • "The overarching goal and binding international obligation in such cases is to ensure that when there are credible allegations that an individual may have committed genocide, war crimes, crimes against humanity or other crimes under international law, all of which are subject to universal jurisdiction, the state in which the individual is present (Canada in this case) is obligated to ensure the allegations are promptly, thoroughly, independently and impartially investigated and that, if there is sufficient admissible evidence, the individual will be criminally charged and tried in keeping with international fair trial standards.
  • If it is not possible to extradite, surrender or otherwise transfer the individual to his or her home country, another country, or an international tribunal, Canada is obliged to launch criminal proceedings domestically.
  • No individual should ever be deported to a country where they face a serious risk of torture, 'disappearance,' extrajudicial execution, the death penalty, unfair trial or other human rights violations.
  • There should be care to ensure that the way cases of this nature are publicized does not infringe the principle of presumption of innocence, given that they have been dealt with through immigration proceedings, with a lower standard of proof and relaxed rules of evidence, rather than through the criminal justice system." (Amnesty International, "Amnesty International Canada's Response to Minister Jason Kenney's Open Letter about 30 'Wanted by the CBSA,'" August 10, 2011, http://www.amnesty.ca/news/news-item/response-wanted-by-the-cbsa [accessed April 19, 2014]).
51 Canadian Press, "'Most Wanted' List Could Raise Torture Risk, Agency Warned," *CBC News*, January 9, 2012.

leading to a positive Pre-removal Risk Assessment."[52] Interestingly, this memo also advised a "go slow" approach, starting with just five Toronto-based cases and publishing names in news releases only to assess the impact of the List, and in particular to test out possible Charter issues. Suggesting that the importance of the List does not rest strictly or even mostly on its enforcement value, the ministers totally ignored this advice. In fact, all of the criticisms have been summarily and resolutely dismissed. Minister Kenney's rebuke of Amnesty International's open letter was scornful and sarcastic. He dismissed all concerns about human rights and international justice as "poppycock" and justified the prioritizing of administrative deportation rather than criminal prosecution by referencing the "preeminent goal" of "defending Canada and upholding the integrity of our immigration system." Kenney scoffs at Amnesty's International's "ostentatious handwringing over the good name of war criminals and human rights violators" and rejects their "self-congratulatory moral preening." Instead, Minister Kenney declares that he is guided by "the common sense of the people and the law" who both want war criminals removed from Canada.[53]

Ministers Toews and Kenney make periodic announcements acclaiming the volume of calls from "hardworking Canadians" to the Border Watch hotline. The CBSA issues press releases announcing each new apprehension and removal, and the popular mainstream press faithfully broadcasts these successes. Minister Kenney's tweets regularly celebrate each new apprehension and removal, giving thanks to the members of the public who call the CBSA tip line to help "catch these bad guys" and encouraging his Twitter followers to "keep the tips coming!" (see Figure 11.5).

While the enforcement activity flowing from the CBSA List is relatively limited in terms of overall numbers, the List does an awful lot of productive work indeed. This technology, and the agents, artifacts, optics, and activity that surround it, work continually to perform and produce the border and the nation: the authoritative sovereign state, neoliberal regimes of rule, a vigilant public, the responsible citizen and community, the dangerous and fraudulent foreigner, and the desirable hardworking immigrant. The border is conceived as a high-risk zone that reaches deep into the fabric of Canadian society, requiring constant vigilance to protect the population and the integrity of the system from a host of foreign crime–security threats.

It is the targeting of suspected war criminals that has attracted most of the critical attention about the List, attention which has been largely

---

52 Ibid.

53 Jason Kenney, "Response to Open Letter from Amnesty International," August 9, 2011, http://www.jasonkenney.ca/news/an-open-letter-to-amnesty-international/ (accessed April 19, 2014).

Figure 11.5 Tweets from Citizenship and Immigration Minister Jason Kenney

concerned with the possibility that deportation from Canada will mean impunity from prosecution. This criticism has focused largely on the problems associated with resorting to an administrative immigration enforcement response (deportation) instead of a criminal justice one (prosecution) and the blurring of the boundaries between these two domains. Critics agree with the need to target war criminals, but they focus on the need for Canada to ensure accountability in accordance with international human rights obligations. Criticisms relating to the deportation of those convicted of serious crimes in Canada are not surprisingly much harder to find. As explained by Lorne Waldman, "The publication of a list of persons convicted [of criminal offences] in Canada and who are being sought for removal has not produced the same criticism. After all, these people have been given due process in Canada, were found guilty of serious offences and have failed to comply with their obligations under the immigration laws."[54]

Serious Criminality

However, even the deportation of those deemed serious criminals through the technology of the Wanted by the CBSA List and related enforcement initiatives raises important questions. In these instances, the production of the border often relies upon making even long-term permanent residents into "foreigners" and reducing complicated and diverse individual situations to sensational generalizations and sound bites about dangerous foreign criminals, public safety, system integrity, and responsible citizens. In June 2012, nearly a year after the introduction of the Wanted by the CBSA List, Jason Kenney announced the latest instalment of the crime–security nexus in the domain of immigration: Bill C-43, the Faster Removal of Foreign Criminals Act. At the news conference to announce the tabling of the new Bill, Minister Kenney explained that

> The Harper Government is committed to the safety and security of Canadians. This Bill is a strong expression of that commitment. Indeed, the changes proposed in this legislation will increase our ability to protect Canadians from criminal and security threats. At the same time, we are also strengthening our immigration program and facilitating entry for some low-risk visitors. These tough but fair measures will ensure that foreign criminals won't be allowed to endlessly abuse our generosity.[55]

According to Kenney, the legislation will preserve "the security of our borders and immigration system, and to protect the safety of Canadians" by closing "the loopholes that allow individuals found inadmissible to Canada to remain in the Country long after their welcome has worn out." Bill C-43 aims to do this in several ways:

- It would limit access to deportation appeal for those determined inadmissible to Canada for reasons of serious criminality, organized criminality, or war criminality.

---

54 Waldman, "Canada's Unwanted List."

55 Citizenship and Immigration Canada, "Speaking Notes for The Honourable Jason Kenney," (Ottawa: National Press Theatre, 2012), http://www.cic.gc.ca/english/department/media/speeches/2012/2012-06-20.asp (accessed April 19, 2014).

- It would remove the possibility of a humanitarian and compassionate review of their case that might allow them to stay in Canada.
- It would give the Minister of Citizenship and Immigration the discretionary power to deny resident status to foreign nationals "who raise public policy concerns."
- It would bar family members of those deemed inadmissible on these crime–security grounds from visiting Canada.
- It would increase penalties for giving false information in an immigration application.
- It would allow officials to compel immigration applicants to attend CSIS interviews.

Referencing the Wanted by the CBSA List, Minister Kenney emphasizes that under this new Bill foreign criminals would no longer "be allowed to endlessly abuse our generosity" and, he warns, "there are many examples of convicted criminals doing just that: Murderers, drug traffickers, fraudsters, child abusers, and thieves, some of whom were on most-wanted lists."[56]

The Making of "Jackie Tran"

But who are these "foreign criminals," beyond the fearful and vague branding? What is lost in the reduction of diverse circumstances to general and deeply moralized categories of the dangerous others? As an example of the kinds of convicted criminals who might have appeared on the CBSA List and for whom this legislation is targeted, Kenney describes an individual with a "long criminal record as a gangster and a major drug trafficker."[57] He refers to him by his nickname, Jackie Tran, evoking a racialized cultural icon perfectly suited for headlines in the very wide local and national press coverage that followed his case. While clearly a catchy nickname from the perspective of the cultural fluency of popular representations of gangsters and organized crime, Jackie Tran is not in fact this individual's real name. It is also inaccurate to describe him as someone with a "long criminal record as a gangster and a major drug trafficker."[58]

In the remainder of this chapter, I provide a few details about Tran Trong Nghi Nguyen and his case, and the racialized representations that transformed Tran from a long-term permanent resident of Canada into a

---

56 Ibid.
57 Ibid.
58 Ibid.

"violent foreign criminal" who "pose[d] a threat to the safety of Canadians and our communities."[59] Tran's story brings to light the many contours and complexities of individual cases that do not lend themselves to the simplistic dualisms and enforcement-oriented sound bites that justify the CBSA List and related crime–security enforcement developments like Bill C-43. Tran's case also demonstrates the powerful effects of the crime–security nexus and the intersection of the domains of criminal justice and immigration in the specific context of one young man. Tran Nguyen's case and ultimate deportation illustrate the local and individual dimensions of the production of borders through the operations of immigration penality in the shadow of the crime–security nexus.

Tran Trong Nghi Nguyen came to Canada from Vietnam with his mother in 1993 when he was just 11 years old. He became a permanent resident and lived in Calgary with his mother and nine-year-old sister. He left school in Grade 11 and found work as a skilled glasscutter. After his mother was disabled in a workplace injury, Tran became the sole income earner in the family and took on responsibility for the day-to-day demands of taking care of both his mother and his younger sister. In 2000, when Tran was 18 years old, he was convicted of two counts of trafficking in narcotics, and two years later he was convicted of an assault involving a fight with a co-worker. Tran served a conditional sentence of two years less a day in the community for the drug offences and received a fine for the assault charge. This is the extent of what Minister Kenney refers to as a "long criminal record as a gangster and a major drug trafficker."

Even though the provincial criminal court had proceeded summarily against Tran, deemed that he did not represent a danger to the public, and sentenced him to two years less a day to be served in the community, under the administrative regime of the IRPA Tran was deemed inadmissible to Canada on the basis of serious criminality and ordered deported.[60] Because Tran was sentenced to less than two years for these convictions, he retained the right to appeal his deportation to the Immigration Appeal Division

---

59 Public Safety Canada, "Public Safety Minister Toews and Citizenship and Immigration Minister Kenney Commend the CBSA on the Deportation of Jackie Tran," Press Release, March 5, 2010, http://www.reuters.com/article/2010/03/05/idUS166253+05-Mar-2010+MW20100305 (accessed April 19, 2014).

60 This category of inadmissibility was introduced by the IRPA in 2001 (s.36 (1)(a)). This provision applies in cases where the conviction for an offence is punishable by a maximum term of imprisonment of at least 10 years. It is not necessary that an individual actually receive a 10-year prison sentence, only that the offence with which he or she is charged—in this case trafficking in narcotics—could be punishable by a maximum term of 10 years or more.

(IAD) on issues of law and humanitarian and compassionate grounds.[61] In contrast to the representation that he "endlessly abused our generosity," Tran appealed deportation, as was his right under the law. And indeed, surely the "common sense" from which Minister Kenney seeks his guidance would also support this course of action in light of the compelling humanitarian and compassionate considerations raised by Tran's individual circumstances— considerations that were totally absent in the making of "Jackie Tran" as a dangerous foreigner.

The Enabling Effects of the Crime–Security Nexus

In the IAD decision that ultimately upheld the removal order against Tran, the crime–security nexus loomed very large. As discussed earlier, the crime–security nexus entailed the reconfiguration of the logic of national security to include everything from the run-of-the-mill, largely disorganized, violent, street-level criminality of youth gangs to highly organized, transnational criminal syndicates. It is this expansive understanding of organized crime and its association with transnational crime and national security that enabled the IAD's easy redefinition of a rather low-level, homegrown (and indeed unproven, either in the criminal courts or, as will be seen, even according to the IAD's own reasoning) threat like Tran into a serious criminal, a dangerous foreigner, and a national security threat.

Despite the failed attempts by the Calgary Police to charge and prosecute Tran for gang membership offences under the Criminal Code, the IAD determined in an administrative context that Tran was guilty of gang membership (in the absence of any criminal convictions) and then connected this form of organized criminality to national security. This indirect connection between Tran and national security essentially authorized the relative easy dismissal of the host of compelling and sympathetic humanitarian and compassionate dimensions of Tran's personal circumstances, dimensions that by definition should have been the tribunal's primary preoccupation (IRPA s.67 (1)(c).13).

---

61 The right of permanent residents, or "foreign nationals," to appeal a finding of inadmissibility for the reason of serious criminality is denied if there has been a conviction in Canada for a crime that was punished in Canada by a term of imprisonment of at least two years (IRPA, s. 64(2)). The absence of protection against deportation for permanent residents who may have virtually grown up in Canada indicates the spatial and temporal elasticity of the production of borders deep inside the Canadian nation through the targeting and deportation of those who are understood as "noncitizens" in strictly legal terms. A sentence of two years or more also makes refugee claimants ineligible to have their claim for refugee protection referred to the IRB for a hearing (IRPA, s.102 (2)(A)).

The IAD was utterly preoccupied with Tran's alleged association with a Calgary street gang called FK (Fresh Killers) and the implications of this association in light of the heightened focus on security that underpinned the writing of the IRPA. Quoting from the 2005 Supreme Court of Canada (SCC) *Medovarski* case, the IAD clearly articulates the conflation and prioritization of criminality and security concerns that governed their decision:

> The objectives as expressed in the IRPA indicate an intent to prioritize security. This objective is given effect by preventing the entry of applicants with criminal records, by removing applicants with such records from Canada, and by emphasizing the obligation of permanent residents to behave lawfully while in Canada ...Viewed collectively, the objectives of the IRPA and its provisions concerning permanent residents, communicates a strong desire to treat criminals and security threats less leniently than under the former Act.[62]

In this light, the IAD determined that Tran's association with the FK gang represented such a pressing threat to security that it heavily outweighed any humanitarian and compassionate factors raised by Tran's personal circumstances. Expert testimony that Tran was very unlikely to reoffend, the absence since 2002 of any convictions for any crimes endangering the public (despite sustained efforts by the Calgary Police), his expressions of remorse, and his demonstrated efforts at rehabilitation were all dismissed by the tribunal by reference to his imputed (untried and unproven in a court of law) association with FK and the elevation of security concerns under the IRPA. The tribunal acknowledged that Tran was well established in Canada, steadily employed, and the sole provider for his disabled mother and caregiver for his younger sister. Tran also carried out all household activities requiring manual effort and acted as an English translator for his mother in all her daily affairs, including dealings with the workers' compensation system and frequent medical visits. As noted in the decision, "The loss of his financial, emotional, physical, and language support would be very significant [as a result of deporting Tran]. There was minimal evidence to suggest a support network for Laura Tran outside of the appellant. The dependence of this disabled mother on her son is a significant factor which weighs in favour of the appellant."[63] The tribunal also accepted that Tran was a de facto parent

62 *Medovarski v. Canada*, 2005 SCC 51, para.10.
63 Immigration and Refugee Board, "Reasons and Decision: Removal Order," File No.VA4-01093, April 7, 2009, para. 38.

to his nine-year-old sister. He communicated with her teachers, schools, and doctors; he attended all her medical appointments, drove her to and from school, provided financial support for her, and took her to the movies, McDonald's, and the zoo. As the tribunal put it, he was the young girl's "lifeline to Canadian society."[64]

Rather than interpreting these connections in Tran's favour, however, the IAD held that Tran's sister (and his girlfriend) were "secondarily" in danger from those who might target Tran. In this very unusual twist, it was not even the danger posed by Tran himself that was of concern to the tribunal and that constituted a security threat so great as to disproportionately outweigh all of these humanitarian and compassionate considerations. Indeed, directly countering Minister Toews's characterization of Tran as a violent foreign criminal who posed a serious danger to public safety, the tribunal clearly stated that it did *not* believe that Tran posed any danger whatsoever to the public. Rather, in a peculiar use of terminology usually used to refer to illness and infection or natural disasters, the tribunal held that a "secondary danger" derived from the possibility that Tran might be victimized by others: "his mere presence in Canada creates a secondary danger."[65] This pronouncement on the "secondary danger" associated with Tran is particularly interesting when considered in relation to the links that have long been made between representations of disease and race in the context of immigration.[66]

Ultimately, the IAD concluded that the strong humanitarian and compassionate factors that weighed in favour of Tran—namely the severe effect of his removal on his family members—were "not so disproportionate as to outweigh the negative security interests which weigh against allowing the appeal."[67] In the shadow of the crime–security nexus and its constituent linkages with organized crime, and enabled by the much watered-down version of due process that applies in administrative settings, the tribunal "tried" Tran for his association with an organized criminal group and was able to connect the dots between Tran, street gangs in Calgary, organized crime, and national security in a way that the criminal justice system could not. The tribunal carefully set the case up as a matter of national security, used that construction to trump Tran's compelling

---

64 Ibid., para. 44.
65 Ibid., para. 42.
66 See, for example Mariana Valverde, *The Age of Light, Soap and Water: Moral Reform in English Canada 1885–1925* (Toronto: McClelland & Stewart, 1991).
67 IRB, "Reasons and Decision," para. 47.

humanitarian and compassionate grounds, and paved the way for Tran's deportation.

Tran's case received wide coverage and huge notoriety in the local Calgary press, and even some in the national media over the six years that it wove its way through the courts. This coverage dovetailed with the equally extensive press coverage of multiple shootings of and by suspected members of the two major street gangs in Calgary. Public fears and police frustration intensified as the Calgary Police Service seemed unable to put an end to the street violence and were frustrated in their attempts to prosecute suspected gang members, including Tran, in the criminal courts. This local panic merged with mounting national concerns framed by the crime–security nexus and the linked threats posed by dangerous foreign criminals and organized crime.[68] While most of those involved in street-level criminal activity in Calgary were citizens and therefore not removable, Tran's status as a permanent resident made him vulnerable to deportation even though he had lived in Canada with his family since he was a child. Immigration enforcement would ultimately succeed where criminal justice had failed. Tran's precarious citizenship status made him vulnerable to what is known as the "double punishment" of migrants convicted of crimes: Tran had already been punished by the criminal justice system for his prior offences, but was then doubly punished for these crimes when he was expelled from Canada.

Tran's case further suggests that the intersection between the domains of immigration and criminal justice offers new opportunities to police that were not previously possible. In the months leading up to Tran's deportation, a picture emerged of the sustained efforts of the local Calgary Police Service to target Tran: first through the collection of evidence to support conviction for gang membership offences and then, when this failed, through its repeated efforts to support his immigration detention and deportation through close monitoring of his release conditions and making submissions on the dangers he posed at his detention review

---

68 For coverage of the local Calgary panic surrounding gang violence, see for example, Nadia Moharib, "Gang War All about Revenge," *Calgary Sun*, February 27, 2009; Nadia Moharib, "Calgary Gang Ties Proving Deadly," *Calgary Sun*, January 15, 2009; *Calgary Herald*, "Justice System Blamed for Gang Violence," October 10, 2007; *Maclean's*, "Calls Made for More Resources on Gang Violence in Calgary," September 19, 2008; Jenna McMurray, "Young Children Joining Gangs," *Calgary Sun*, May 5, 2010. For a detailed review of the preoccupations at the national level with threats posed by dangerous foreign criminals associated with organized crime over the last few decades, see Pratt, *Securing Borders*; Wendy Chan, "Crime, Deportation and the Regulation of Immigrants in Canada," *Crime, Law and Social Change* 44, no. 2 (2005): 153–80.

hearings. When the Calgary Police gang taskforce failed in its efforts to charge and convict Tran through the criminal justice system, an officer who had been very active in targeting Tran then acted as the key expert witness in Tran's appeal of his removal order. The officer's testimony in the administrative context of the appeal ultimately served to clinch the case for Tran's deportation.

The resort to deportation as a solution to a criminal justice problem is not a new phenomenon. There are ample historical examples of the deportation of criminalized undesirables from Canada as a supplement—or even as an alternative—to criminal justice prosecution: from the deportation of "vagrants" during the Depression, to the deportation of immoral young women, to the deportation of communists and others who were thought to pose ideological threats to the political state, to the deportation of Chinese drug offenders in the past.[69] More recently, Canada deported Jamaican-born men deemed dangers to the public,[70] and as discussed earlier, Canada has opted to pursue civil avenues of deportation for suspected war criminals rather than prosecution in domestic criminal courts, the international criminal court or tribunal, or through the avenue of extradition.[71] In the pursuit of administrative as opposed to criminal proceedings, whether against suspected war criminals or against suspected street-level gang members like Tran, cumbersome procedural safeguards of criminal prosecution are sidestepped, making punitive action in the form of deportation more likely. In both instances, the heightened influence of the crime–security nexus is evident as is the degree of interchangeability

---

69 See Barbara Roberts, *Whence They Came: Deportation from Canada 1900–1935* (Ottawa: University of Ottawa Press, 1998); Valverde, *Age of Soap*; Donald Avery, *Dangerous Foreigners* (Toronto: McClelland & Stewart, 1979); Donald Avery, *Reluctant Host: Canada's Response to Immigrant Workers, 1896–1994* (Toronto: McClelland & Stewart, 1995); Catherine Carstairs, "Deporting 'Ah Sin' to Save the White Race: Moral Panic, Racialization and the Extension of Canadian Drug Laws in the 1920s," *Canadian Bulletin of Medical History* 16, no. 1 (1999): 65–88; Gary Kinsmen, *The Canadian War on Queers: National Security as Sexual Regulation* (Vancouver: UBC Press, 2009).

70 Pratt, *Securing Borders*.

71 Between 1987 and 1992, the government began four criminal proceedings against suspected war criminals in Canada, none of which resulted in criminal convictions. As a result, in 1995 the government announced a shift in focus from criminal prosecution to the civil avenues of denaturalization and deportation. This allows the government to take action against suspected war criminals in Canada without actually having to prove in a criminal court that the person in question is a "war criminal." Instead, under section 10 of the Citizenship Act, citizenship may be revoked if it can be proven that "they had entered Canada and/or obtained citizenship through misrepresentation, fraud, or the concealment of material facts" (Citizenship and Immigration Canada, "Canada's Program on Crimes against Humanity and War Crimes," 2005–06).

between administrative immigration proceedings and criminal proceedings, and between deportation and criminal punishment in the production of borders.

Producing the Border and the "National Order of Things" One Deportation at a Time

Tran was deported less for what he did than for what he represented. In the context of the larger political campaigns surrounding criminal migrants, organized crime, and national security, Tran's case quickly became emblematic of the scandal of dangerous foreign criminals and gangster violence. As put by his lawyer, Raj Sharma, Tran "had somehow become the public face of organized crime in Canada."[72] Even though he had lived in Canada since he was 11 years old, popular outrage focused on his constructed status as a foreigner who was taking advantage of an excessively permissive immigration system and a legal system overly preoccupied with due process and judicial review. Tran's efforts to stay in Canada legally with his dependent mother and sister enraged many. When Calgary Member of Parliament Art Hanger blasted federal laws for allowing Tran so many appeals by saying "You cut those avenues off and force them out of the country. Let's change the law," he was echoing the long-standing enforcement mentality that views legal rights as "impediments to removal" and forecasting the hard line to be taken five years later by Minister Kenney in his justifications for both the Wanted by the CBSA List and Bill C-53, the Faster Deportation of Foreign Criminals Act. Hanger added: "They don't deserve due process like all ordinary citizens of the nation. They've already violated the trust that was given to them when they came here, or allowed to come here."[73] Tran's case had come to represent for many all that is wrong with an immigration system that allows undeserving "violent foreign criminals" to delay their removal by taking advantage of legal appeals and rights.

By the time he was deported in 2010, Tran, who had lived in Canada since he was a child, who had three relatively minor and dated criminal convictions, and who had never been convicted under the Criminal Code of any offences specifically relating to gang membership, had become the poster boy for the gangster problem in Calgary and for the foreign criminal threat to

---

72 Raj Sharma, "In Defence of Jackie Tran," *Stewart, Sharma, Harsanyi Immigration Blog*, entry posted on June 28, 2009, http://immlawyer.blogs.com/my_weblog/2009/06/in-defence-of-jackie-tran.html.

73 *CBC News*, "Gang Member Freed Amid Deportation Fight," *The National*, October 22, 2008, http://www.cbc.ca/m/touch/canada/calgary/story/1.694593 (accessed April 19, 2014).

Canadian national security and public safety. As observed by his lawyer, the heightened fear of the public, stoked by the sensationalist media, resulted in Tran facing a frenzied outcry for his removal:

> As a former hearings officer and more recently an immigration lawyer, I have appeared in hundreds of immigration hearings and appeals. I know, from personal experience, that there are many permanent residents, inadmissible on criminal convictions far more serious than Tran's, that are allowed to stay in this country. It was clear however, that the deck was stacked against Tran because of this "persona."[74]

Tran's removal was upheld as a victory for a government deeply committed to the protection of the safety and security of its citizens. In yet another grand sovereign performance of the border, speaking to a throng of reporters on March 3, 2010, Vic Toews, flanked as usual by Jason Kenney, lauded the work of the CBSA in removing 27-year-old Tran Trong Nghi Nguyen to Vietnam. Minister Toews proclaimed:

> I would like to congratulate the CBSA officials who were instrumental in removing Tran Trong Nghia [sic] Nguyen (Jackie Tran) from our country. I am pleased this serious convicted criminal will no longer pose a threat to the safety of Canadians and our communities ... This deportation provides another example of the outstanding work by the CBSA to remove serious criminals from this country. I would like to commend the professionalism and dedication of the CBSA officers who carried out this removal. Protecting the safety and security of our citizens is the most serious responsibility of the Government of Canada.[75]

Conclusion

The expulsion of bodies from the nation in the noncriminal administrative context of immigration enforcement both demonstrates and reproduces the associations between the domains of immigration and criminal justice, between immigration and crime–security, between migrants and criminals,

---

74 Raj Sharma, "The Myth of Jackie Tran," *Stewart, Sharma, Harsanyi Immigration Blog*, entry posted on June 28, 2009, http://immlawyer.blogs.com/my_weblog/2010/03/the-myth-of-jackie-tran .html.
75 Public Safety Canada, "Public Safety Minister Toews and Citizenship and Immigration Minister Kenney Commend the CBSA on the Deportation of Tran Trong Nghia Nguyen."

as well as the coercive edge of sovereign power that permeates immigration penality. Discourses of national sovereignty continue to be dominant despite (or indeed because of) the growing recognition that global and transnational developments have increasingly unsettled the sovereignty of nation-states and the territorial borders that both constitute and are constituted by them. A global "intensification of interconnectedness"[76] has unsettled conventional constructions of the nation-state "as common territory and time"[77] and as the primary locus of citizenship.[78]

The Wanted by the CBSA List and the deportation of 27-year-old Tran Trong Nghi Nguyen to his country of origin must be understood in relation to this broader context. The last few decades have witnessed the proliferation of efforts by Western industrialized countries to secure their territorial borders against "undesirable" outsiders (who may be cast as such despite having lived for a long time "on the inside") through the intensification and expansion of diverse national and transnational technologies of interdiction, containment, and expulsion in the shadow of the crime–security nexus.[79] This flexing of sovereign muscle and reassertion of the authority of the nation-state to control its geopolitical borders against the migration of undesirable populations come at the same time that global

---

76 Jonathan Xavier Inda and Renato Rosaldo, "Introduction: A World in Motion," in *The Anthropology of Globalization: A Reader*, ed. Jonathan Xavier Inda and Renato Rosaldo, 1–12 (Massachusetts: Blackwell, 2002).

77 Jennifer Hyndman and Margaret Walton-Roberts, "Transnational Migration and Nation: Burmese Refugees in Vancouver," Unpublished Paper, December 4, 1998.

78 See, for example, Saskia Sassen, *Losing Control: Sovereignty in an Age of Globalization* (New York: Columbia University Press, 1996); Sakia Sassen, *Global Networks, Linked Cities* (London: Routledge, 2002); Engin Isin, ed., *Democracy, Citizenship and the Global City* (London: Routledge, 2000); James Holsten and Arjun Appadurai, "Cities and Citizenship," *Public Culture* 8, no. 2 (1996): 187–204.

79 There is an extensive literature that examines the proliferation of enforcement measures, the fortification of territorial borders, and processes of "securitization" in the European and North American contexts. See, for example, Peter Andreas, "The Escalation of U.S Immigration Control in the Post-NAFTA Era," *Political Science Quarterly* 113, no. 4 (1998): 591–615; Peter Andreas, "Borderless Economy, Barricaded Border," *NACLA Report on the Americas* 33, no. 3 (1999): 14–21; Peter Andreas and Thomas Snyder, *The Wall around the West: State Borders and Immigration Controls in North America and Europe* (Boulder: Rowman & Littlefield, 2000); Ruth Jamieson, Nigel South, and Ian Taylor, "Economic Liberalization and Cross-Border Crime: The North American Free Trade Area and Canada's Border with the U.S.A. Part 1," *International Journal of the Sociology of Law* 26, no. 2 (1998): 245–72; Peter Fitzgerald, "Repelling Borders," *New Statesman and Society* 8 (1995): 16–17; Steven Flynn, "Beyond Border Control," *Foreign Affairs* 79, no. 6 (2000): 57–68; Carol Nagengast, "Militarizing the Border Patrol," *NACLA Report on the Americas* 32, no. 3 (1998): 37–43; Josiah Heyman, "Why Interdiction? Immigration Control at the United States–Mexico Border," *Regional Studies* 33, no. 7 (1999): 619–30.

networks and flows of goods, capital, information, and cultural symbols have decentred the authority of the nation-state and unsettled its traditional geopolitical borders. This fortification of national borders and the intensification of efforts to reallocate "subjects to their proper sovereigns" continually perform the border and reconstitute the "national order of things,"[80] "sustain[ing] the image of a world divided into 'national' populations and territories, domiciled in terms of state membership."[81] As such, the Wanted by the CBSA List and the deportation of Tran Trong Nghi Nguyen must also be understood as technologies of Canadian citizenship that effectively shore up the distinctions between illegality and citizenship and which include the remaking of permanent residents of Canada into "foreigners."

The Wanted by the CBSA List and the deportation of Trang Tron Nghi Nguyen are thus not merely examples of prohibitive and exclusionary enforcement technologies at work, but are also important examples of productive and enabling technologies of governance. As I have sought to highlight, these processes rest upon and reproduce the conflation of the domains of criminal justice and immigration that is characteristic of contemporary Canadian immigration penality and is embedded in and fortified by the crime–security nexus. Both the List and the expulsion of Tran Trong Nghi Nguyen to Vietnam, his country of birth though not his home, are thus at the same time both single instances of the forceful and bodily reassertion of sovereign power and the national order of things through the representation, criminalization, and deportation of dangerous foreigners, as well as distinct entries in the larger story of the crime–security nexus and its influence not only on the enforcement practices of immigration penality, but on the simultaneous production of borders and the making of citizens.

Study Questions

1. Why should we be interested in the deportation of Tran Trong Nghi Nguyen?
2. In what ways is community policing consistent with neoliberalism?
3. In what ways do the domains of criminal justice and immigration intersect?

---

80 Lisa Malkki, "Refugees and Exile: From 'Refugee Studies' to the National Order Of Things," *Annual Review of Anthropology* 24 (1995): 495–523.
81 William Walters, "Deportation, Expulsion and the International Police of Aliens," *Citizenship Studies* 6, no. 3 (2002): 265–92.

Exercise

Drawing from recent news items, legal decisions, policy initiatives, and so on, provide and critically analyze a contemporary example that illuminates one or more of the following: (1) the blurring of the boundaries between immigration and criminal justice, (2) the crime–security nexus, and/or (3) neoliberal policing technologies.

Keywords

immigration penalty; crime–security nexus; governing through community

References

Aas, Katja Franko. "'Getting Ahead of the Game': Border Technologies and the Changing Space of Governance." In *Global Surveillance and Policing Borders: Borders, Security, Identity*, edited by Elia Zureik and Mark B. Salter. Cullumpton: Willan Publishing.

Amnesty International. "Amnesty International Canada's Open Letter to Ministers Toews and Kenney about 30 'Wanted by the CBSA.'" August 2, 2011. http://www.amnesty.ca/news/news-item/amnesty-international-canada-open-letter-to-ministers-toews-and-kenney (accessed April 19, 2014).

Amnesty International. "Amnesty International Canada's Response to Minister Jason Kenney's Open Letter about 30 'Wanted by the CBSA.'" August 10, 2011. http://www.amnesty.ca/news/news-item/response-wanted-by-the-cbsa (accessed April 19, 2014).

Andreas, Peter. "The Escalation of U.S Immigration Control in the Post-NAFTA Era." *Political Science Quarterly* 113, no. 4 (1998): 591–615. http://dx.doi.org/10.2307/2658246.

Andreas, Peter. "Borderless Economy, Barricaded Border." *NACLA Report on the Americas* 33, no. 3 (1999): 14–21.

Andreas, Peter, and Thomas Snyder. *The Wall around the West: State Borders and Immigration Controls in North America and Europe.* Boulder: Rowman & Littlefield, 2000.

Avery, D. *Dangerous Foreigners.* Toronto: McClelland & Stewart, 1979.

Avery, D. *Reluctant Host: Canada's Response to Immigrant Workers, 1896–1994.* Toronto: McClelland & Stewart, 1995.

Bell, Stewart. "Q&A: Immigration Minister Jason Kenney Speaks on the War Crimes Wanted List." *National Post*, July 28, 2011.

Bigo, Didier. "Security and Immigration: Toward a Critique of the Governmentality of Unease." *Alternatives* 27 (2002): 63–92.

Bosworth, Mary, and M. Guild. "Governing through Migration Control: Security and Citizenship in Britain." *British Journal of Criminology* 48, no. 6 (2008): 703–19. http://dx.doi.org/10.1093/bjc/azn059.

Calgary Herald. "Justice System Blamed for Gang Violence: Calgary's New Police Chief Says Lenient Sentences Are Crippling Efforts to Curb Growing Gang Violence in the City." October 10, 2007.

Canada Border Services Agency. "Border Watch Toll-Free Line." http://www.cbsa-asfc .gc.ca/security-securite/bwl-lsf-eng.html (accessed April 19, 2014).

Canada Border Services Agency. "Detentions and Removals Programs: Evaluation Study, Final Report." November 2010.

Canada Border Services Agency. "Government of Canada Enlists Help of Canadians to Enforce Canada's Immigration Laws: Government Will Not Tolerate War Criminals in Our Communities." News Release, July 21, 2011.

Canada Border Services Agency. *12th Report on Canada's Program on Crimes Against Humanity and War Crimes, 2008–2011.*

Canadian Press. "Most Wanted List Could Raise Torture Risk, Agency Warned." January 9, 2012.

Canadian Press. "Kenney Links Toronto Gun Violence to 'Foreign Gangsters.'" *CTV News*, July 20, 2012.

Canadian Press. "TV Cameras Filming CBSA Immigration Raids for Reality Show Is Okay: Pubic Safety Minister Vic Toews." *National Post*, March 19, 2013.

Canadian Security and Intelligence Service. "The CSIS Mandate." Backgrounder No. 1. Revised February 2005. www.skokos.com/files/EC-09-3033/Letters-Sent/csis/act/ _www.csis-scrs.gc.ca_nwsrm_bckgrndrs_bckgrndr01-eng.pdf.

Canadian Security and Intelligence Service. "Transnational Criminal Activity." https:// www.csis-scrs.gc.ca/prrts/trnsntnl/index-en.asp.

Carstairs, C. "Deporting 'Ah Sin' to Save the White Race: Moral Panic, Racialization and the Extension of Canadian Drug Laws in the 1920s." *Canadian Bulletin of Medical History* 16, no. 1 (1999): 65–88.

CBC News. "Gang Member Freed Amid Deportation Fight: Police Fear Gangster's Release Will Attract Rival Violence on Calgary Streets." *The National*, October 22, 2008, http://www.cbc.ca/m/touch/canada/calgary/story/1.694593 (accessed April 19, 2014).

Chan, Wendy. "Crime, Deportation and the Regulation of Immigrants in Canada." *Crime, Law, and Social Change* 44, no. 2 (2005): 153–80. http://dx.doi.org/10.1007/ s10611-005-9000-6.

Citizenship and Immigration Canada. "Canada's Program on Crimes against Humanity and War Crimes." 2005–06.

Citizenship and Immigration Canada. "Speaking Notes for The Honourable Jason Kenney." Ottawa: National Press Theatre, 2012. http://www.cic.gc.ca/english/department/ media/speeches/2012/2012-06-20.asp (accessed April 19, 2014).

Conservative Party of Canada. "Strengthening Community Safety and our Immigration System." News Release, January 11, 2012.

Doyle, Aaron. "An Alternative Current in Surveillance and Control: Broadcasting Surveillance Footage of Crimes." In *The New Politics of Surveillance and Visibility*, edited by K.D. Haggerty and R.V. Ericson. Toronto: University of Toronto Press, 2006.

Elliott, Louise. "Ottawa Names War Crimes Suspects in Canada." *CBC News*, July 21, 2011

Fitzgerald, P. "Repelling Borders." *New Statesman and Society* 8 (1995): 16–17.

Flynn, S.E. "Beyond Border Control." *Foreign Affairs* 79, no. 6 (2000): 57–68. http:// dx.doi.org/10.2307/20049967.

Heyman, Josiah. "Why Interdiction? Immigration Control at the United States–Mexico Border." *Regional Studies* 33, no. 7 (1999): 619–30. http://dx.doi.org/10.1080/ 00343409950078666.

Holsten, James, and Arjun Appadurai. "Cities and Citizenship." *Public Culture* 8, no. 2 (1996): 187–204. http://dx.doi.org/10.1215/08992363-8-2-187.

Hunt, Alan. "Risk and Moralization in Everyday Life." In *Risk and Morality*, edited by Richard Ericson and Aaron Doyle. Toronto: University of Toronto Press, 2003.

Huysmans, Jef. "The European Union and the Securitization of Migration." *Journal of Common Market Studies* 38, no. 5 (2000): 751–77. http://dx.doi.org/10.1111/1468-5965.00263.

Hyndman, Jennifer, and Margaret Walton-Roberts. "Transnational Migration and Nation: Burmese Refugees in Vancouver." Unpublished paper, December 1998.

Immigration and Refugee Board. "Reasons and Decision: Removal Order." File No. VA4-01093, April 7, 2009.

Inda, Jonathan Xavier, and Renato Rosaldo. "Introduction: A World in Motion." In *The Anthropology of Globalization: A Reader*, edited by J.X. Inda and R. Rosaldo, 1–12. Massachusetts: Blackwell, 2002.

Isin, Engin, ed. *Democracy, Citizenship and the Global City*. London: Routledge, 2000.

Jamieson, Ruth, Nigel South, and Ian Taylor. "Economic Liberalization and Cross-Border Crime: The North American Free Trade Area and Canada's Border with the U.S.A. Part 1." *International Journal of the Sociology of Law* 26, no. 2 (1998): 245–72. http://dx.doi.org/10.1006/ijsl.1998.0065.

Kenney, Jason. "Response to Open Letter from Amnesty International." August 9, 2011. http://www.jasonkenney.ca/news/an-open-letter-to-amnesty-international/ (accessed April 19, 2014).

Kinsmen, G. *The Canadian War on Queers: National Security as Sexual Regulation*. Vancouver: UBC Press, 2009.

Koskela, Hille. "'Don't Mess with Texas!' Texas Virtual Border Watch Program and the (Botched) Politics of Responsibilization." *Crime, Media, Culture* 7, no. 1 (2011): 49–65. http://dx.doi.org/10.1177/1741659010369957.

Koskela, Hille. "Fear and Its Others." In *Handbook of Social Geography*, edited by Susan Smith, Rachel Pain, Sallie Marston, and John Paul Jones. London: Sage, 2012.

Lippert, Randy. "Policing Property and Moral Risk through Promotions, Anonymization, and Rewards: Crime Stoppers Revisited." *Social & Legal Studies* 11, no. 4 (2002): 475–502. http://dx.doi.org/10.1177/0964663902011100401.

Maclean's. "Calls Made for More Resources on Gang Violence in Calgary." September 19, 2008.

Mackrael, Kim. "Canada's Border Services Agency Looks to Widen the Scope of Its Most Wanted List." *Globe and Mail*, November 30, 2012.

Malkki, L. "Refugees and Exile: From 'Refugee Studies' to the National Order of Things." *Annual Review of Anthropology* 24, no. 1 (1995): 495–523. http://dx.doi.org/10.1146/annurev.an.24.100195.002431.

McMurray, Jenna. "Young Children Joining Gangs." *Calgary Sun*, May 5, 2010.

Miller, Theresa. "Blurring the Boundaries between Immigration and Crime Control after September 11th." *BC Third World Quarterly* 81 (2005): 81–123.

Moharib, Nadia. "Calgary Gang Ties Proving Deadly." *Calgary Sun*, January 15, 2009.

Moharib, Nadia. "Calgary Gang War All about Revenge: Never-Ending Cycle of Violence Makes Organized Crime Life 'a Pretty Asinine Way to Live.'" *Calgary Sun*, February 27, 2009.

Nagengast, Carol "Militarizing the Border Patrol." *NACLA Report on the Americas* 32, no. 3 (1998): 37–43.

Newman, D. "The Lines that Continue to Separate Us: Borders in our 'Borderless' World." *Progress in Human Geography* 30, no. 2 (2006): 143–61. http://dx.doi.org/10.1191/0309132506ph599xx.

O'Malley, Pat. "Risk, Power and Crime Prevention." *Economy and Society* 21, no. 3 (1992): 252–75. http://dx.doi.org/10.1080/03085149200000013.

O'Malley, Pat. "Risk and Responsibility." In *Foucault and Political Reason*, edited by Andrew Barry, Thomas Osborne, and Nikolas Rose, 189–208. Chicago: University of Chicago Press, 1996.

Peat, Don. "Rob Ford Fails to Explain Proposal to Ban Gun Criminals from City." *Sun News*, July 20, 2012. http://www.sunnewsnetwork.ca/sunnews/politics/archives/2012/07/20120720-144723.html.

Pratt, Anna. "Immigration Penality and the Crime-Security Nexus: The Case of Tran Trong Nghi Nguyen." In *Canadian Criminal Justice Policy: A Contemporary Reader*, edited by Karim Ismaili, Jane Sprott, and Kim Varma. Oxford: Oxford University Press, 2012.

Pratt, Anna. *Securing Borders: Detention and Deportation in Canada.* Vancouver: UBC Press, 2005.

Pratt, Anna. "Sovereign Power, Carceral Conditions and Penal Practices: Detention and Deportation in Canada." *Studies in Law, Politics, and Society* 23 (2001): 45–78.

Pratt, Anna, and Sara K. Thompson. "Chivalry, 'Race' and Discretion at the Canadian Border." *British Journal of Criminology* 48, no. 5 (2008): 620–40. http://dx.doi.org/10.1093/bjc/azn048.

Pratt, Anna, and Mariana Valverde. "'From Deserving Victims to Masters of Confusion': Redefining Refugees in the 1990s." *Canadian Journal of Sociology* 27, no. 2 (2002): 135–61. http://dx.doi.org/10.2307/3341708.

Public Safety Canada. "Public Safety Minister Toews and Citizenship and Immigration Minister Kenney Commend the CBSA on the Deportation of Jackie Tran." Press Release, March 5, 2012. http://www.reuters.com/article/2010/03/05/idUS166253+05-Mar-2010+MW20100305 (accessed April 19, 2014).

Roberts, B. *Whence They Came: Deportation from Canada 1900–1935*. Ottawa: University of Ottawa Press, 1998.

Rose, N. *Powers of Freedom Reframing Political Thought*. Cambridge: Cambridge University Press, 1999. http://dx.doi.org/10.1017/CBO9780511488856.

Sassen, S. *Losing Control: Sovereignty in an Age of Globalization*. New York: Columbia University Press, 1996.

Sassen, S. *Global Networks, Linked Cities*. London: Routledge, 2002.

Sharma, Raj. "In Defence of Jackie Tran." *Stewart, Sharma, Harsanyi Immigration Blog.* Entry posted June 28, 2009. http://immlawyer.blogs.com/my_weblog/2009/06/in-defence-of-jackie-tran.html.

Sharma, Raj. "The Myth of Jackie Tran." *Stewart, Sharma, Harsanyi Immigration Blog.* Entry posted June 28, 2009. http://immlawyer.blogs.com/my_weblog/2010/03/the-myth-of-jackie-tran.html.

Simon, Jonathan. "Governing through Crime." In *The Crime Conundrum: Essays on Criminal Justice*, edited by Lawrence M. Friedman and George Fisher, 171–89. New York: Westview Press, 1997.

Stumpf, Julie. "The Crimmigration Crisis: Immigrants, Crime and Sovereign Power." *bepress Legal Series.* Working Paper 1635 (2006). http://law.bepress.com/expresso/eps/1635.

Tsoukala, A., and A. Ceyhan. "The Securitization of Migration in Western Societies: Ambivalent Discourses and Policies." *Alternatives* 27 (2002): 5.

Valverde, Mariana. *The Age of Light, Soap and Water: Moral Reform in English Canada 1885–1925.* Toronto: McClelland & Stewart, 1991.

Waldman, Lorne. "Canada's Unwanted List." *The Lawyer's Weekly*, February 3, 2012. http://www.lawyersweekly.ca/index.php?section=article&articleid=1587.

Walters, W. "Deportation, Expulsion and the International Police of Aliens." *Citizenship Studies* 6, no. 3 (2002): 265–92. http://dx.doi.org/10.1080/1362102022000011612.

Welch, Michael. *Detained: Immigration Laws and the Expanding INS Jail Complex.* Philadelphia: Temple University Press, 2002.

Young, Alison. *Imagining Crime: Textual Outlaws and Criminal Conversations.* London: Sage, 1996.

twelve

In the Name of Human Rights: Governing and Representing Non-Western Lives Post-9/11

MARCIA OLIVER

Introduction

Evidence of human suffering saturates our contemporary global order. A cursory glance at various news headlines within the last year reveals a long list of global injustices and, in particular, egregious violations of international human rights. These include, among others, genocide and crimes against humanity (like torture and systemic rape), crackdowns on political dissent, arbitrary and prolonged detention, military and police abuse of civilians, forced labour, sexual persecution and gender violence, religious repression and limits to free speech, and a long list of humanitarian crises, including famines, displacement, dire levels of poverty, and ecological disasters.

When faced with such continued violence and destruction throughout the world, how are we to make sense of and speak of international human rights? How does **globalization** change the way we think about crime and human rights violations? Or, more specifically, what challenges does globalization pose to our long-established ideas of the nation-state as the appropriate frame of reference and its citizens as the relevant subjects for justice? What are the norms that the human rights regime seeks to **universalize**? And what effects do these norms have on the diverse peoples and cultures around the globe? How are different nations, cultures, and populations represented and positioned within human rights discourse (e.g., superior/inferior, civilized/barbaric, saviour/victim), and how might the circulation of visual images of human suffering contribute to the different and hierarchical ways that the West and non-West are constructed and inform our understandings of the current world order?

This chapter will address many of these questions. It aims to challenge and expand our ideas about human rights, illuminating both the promises and limits of the international human rights regime. In many ways, human rights are indispensable to global justice practices that identify and challenge all those sites and practices that exclude millions of people around the globe from the protections that human rights ostensibly offer. Yet human rights are not simply emancipatory; their effects can also be regulatory and at times violent. This is because the human rights regime is premised on certain international norms about what it means to be human (and, it follows, not human or less-than-human) and therefore produces certain kinds of subjects, cultures, and ways of life in differential and hierarchical ways. Moreover, powerful transnational actors (such as international organizations, Euro-American governments, and multinational corporations) use human rights language in ways that obscure and mask imperialist practices that serve their geopolitical and economic interests. Following Costas Douzinas, we can understand this paradox the following way: "[R]ights help emancipate and protect people but they are also instruments of power used to discipline, exclude and dominate."[1] This does not mean that we should abandon the language of human rights, but nor should we adopt it wholeheartedly and without question. Rather, I want us to think critically about the language that we use (and the language that we hear others use) when talking about human rights and examine the multiple, often contradictory, and at times exclusionary effects of human rights discourse and practices on the lives, dignity, and diversity of peoples around the globe.

The first part of this chapter addresses the question of what human rights are by mapping their multiple meanings and historical influences and exploring how these have come to shape the post–World War II international human rights regime and our ideas about justice and the individual subject of human rights. Our task in this section is to develop an understanding of **human rights** as a cultural phenomenon that changes over time in response to various social, economic, and political influences.[2] Thus, the meanings we assign to human rights are not fixed or universal—they are shaped by multiple (and often competing) intellectual traditions and sociopolitical struggles that "have to be fought over and over again, justice won in new times and places by new generations and constituencies who give rights different local and temporal meanings."[3] The second part of this chapter examines some of the ways that scholars have approached the subject of human rights, highlighting the main differences between legalistic, normative, and discursive approaches. The third section applies the insights of one discursive approach

---

1 Costas Douzinas, *Human Rights and Empire: The Political Philosophy of Cosmopolitanism* (New York: Routledge, 2007), 113.

2 Sally Engle Merry, "Changing Rights, Changing Culture," in *Culture and Rights: Anthropological Perspectives*, ed. J. Cowan et al. (Cambridge: Cambridge University Press, 2001).

3 Sonia Corrêa, Rosalind Petchesky, and Richard Parker, *Sexuality, Health, and Human Rights* (Milton Park: Routledge, 2008), 162.

to human rights—known as governmentality (examined in Chapters One and Nine)—to examine the **normalizing power** and effects of the international human rights regime. In particular, we will ask questions about the dominant constructions of "violence" that are operative within the international human rights regime and critically examine the politics of representation that inform international interventions that lay claim to human rights, such as the US-led War on Terror or neoliberal development policies. In this section, we will interrogate conventional tropes of human suffering and human rights violations and ask questions about their implications for non-Western societies.

What Are Human Rights?

For centuries, numerous and conflicting political traditions have elaborated on different aspects of human rights and differed over which aspects of human rights had priority. Micheline Ishay's analysis of the origins of human rights illuminates the processes of historical continuity and change that have shaped the modern conception of the international human rights regime.[4] Although any question concerning the "origins" of human rights is inevitably the subject of much debate, the influence and dominance of the West over other civilizations is undeniable in the development of modern conceptions of human rights. Of particular importance was the **European Enlightenment**. As you read in Chapter Five, the European Enlightenment refers to a period in Europe during the seventeenth and eighteenth centuries that is characterized by a revolution in knowledge away from superstition or divine faith as the ultimate source of authority toward the application of reason and science. Described as the "Age of Reason," Enlightenment thinkers believed that reason and science would lead to steady human progress for the world by not only challenging religious oppression and the previously uncontested divine right of kings, but also in terms of furthering the recognition of (and respect for) individual human rights by states and bringing about a more peaceful world. Enlightenment thought therefore led the way for the development of liberal thought and new civil rights that were believed to reflect essential and inviolable truths about humanity or, more accurately, Euro-American "Man."

Although liberalism is a diverse political tradition that has taken root in different forms in different historical contexts, the classical or Enlightenment

---

4 Micheline Ishay, *The History of Human Rights: From Ancient Times to the Globalization Era* (Berkeley: University of California Press, 2004).

conception of liberal rights is based on individualism and freedom. These rights are widely regarded as **negative liberties**, which means they are an individual's right to be free *from* the intentional interference of others, and particularly from the state. Chief among these rights are the rights to life, liberty (such as freedom of religion and opinion), and property rights.[5]

Notwithstanding the significance of Enlightenment thought to modern conceptions of human rights, much critical scholarship has illustrated the exclusionary politics that lie at the heart of liberalism's promise of universal human rights. The classical liberal conception of human rights (and its assumptions of autonomy and reason) was not extended beyond the lives of Euro-America men: women, people of colour, propertyless men, children, and entire nations of colonized peoples were denied any rights to sovereignty and recognition of full humanity. Yet, Michel Foucault's oft-cited claim that "[w]here there is power, there is resistance"[6] helps us understand that the development of human rights is the history of many struggles and competing ideological projects that have been waged by those excluded from the overly individualistic Enlightenment conception of human rights. As Arjun Chowdhury reminds us, contrary to popular perception, human rights do not belong to states, nor are they entitlements for the state to give. Human rights were and continue to be fought for by political and social actors who contest injustice and the legitimacy of state power.[7]

One such struggle was rooted in the **socialist tradition**, a second important legacy of the human rights regime. With the continued expansion of industry and the development of the labour movement throughout the nineteenth century, growing numbers of disenfranchised people (like women and workers) challenged the classical liberal human rights focus on liberty by advocating for political and economic rights, including voting rights, improved working conditions (length of the workday), child welfare, and the rights to organize trade unions and to education. A second and equally important challenge that was waged against the Enlightenment conception of human rights came from nineteenth- and twentieth-century claims of

---

5 Ibid., 5. Of course, many of these rights, like the right to life, find roots in the world's ancient traditions and great religions, like Islam, Judaism, Christianity, Buddhism, Hinduism, and Confucianism. In other words, the idea of liberty was not born during the Enlightenment; "each great religion contains important humanistic elements that anticipated our modern conceptions of rights" (Ibid.). But rather than basing claims to freedom on revelation or religious devotion, Enlightenment liberalism appealed to universal reason as the basis for human rights.

6 Michel Foucault, *The History of Sexuality*, vol. 1, *An Introduction*, trans. Robert Hurley (New York: Vintage Books, 1990), 95.

7 Arjun Chowdhury, "'The Giver or the Recipient?' The Peculiar Ownership of Human Rights," *International Political Sociology* 5, no. 1 (2011): 35–51.

nationalism and self-determination, which today are most commonly associated with the cultural or group rights of indigenous populations and the postcolonial era.[8] This set of rights recognizes the need to protect cultures from forced assimilation and the homogenizing tendencies of globalization.

As the twentieth century gave rise to two world wars, so did efforts to promote human rights and world peace and security at the international level. In 1945, the United Nations Charter was adopted, followed by the proclamation of the **Universal Declaration of Human Rights (UDHR)** in 1948. The international human rights regime was born in response to the horrors of the Holocaust and the realization that a global check on state power was essential to avoid such horrors from happening again in the future.[9] The Declaration was drafted by an eight-member committee with diverse cultural backgrounds, philosophical commitments, and political loyalties (e.g., there was a Chinese-Confucian delegate, a French-Jewish scholar, a Lebanese-existentialist philosopher, and a Canadian law professor, among many others). Despite their cultural and political differences, these members all agreed on the importance of affirming universal respect for the inherent dignity and moral equality of all individuals everywhere, regardless of one's sex, race, nationality, religion, or other circumstances.

The Declaration incorporates many of the historical struggles and multiple meanings of human rights since the Enlightenment era. The first generation of civil rights is the most privileged and least controversial and thus enjoys a higher standing in global politics. They include the rights to life, liberty, and security of person; the right not to be subjected to cruel and inhumane treatment; the right to equality before the law; and the rights to mobility, nationality, religion, association, and voting (see articles 3–19 of the UDHR and the 1976 International Covenant on Civil and Political Rights). However, as we are now familiar, the notion of rights also includes the second generation of social and economic rights, which stretch well beyond liberalism's individualistic approach to human rights to promote the more socialist ideals concerning the rights of workers and the (re)distribution of wealth (see articles 20–26 of the UDHR and the 1976 International Covenant on Economic, Social and Cultural Rights). These include the right to a decent "standard of living adequate for the health and well-being of [one's] self and family, including food, clothing, housing and medical care and necessary social services, and the right to security in the event of unemployment, sickness, disability, widowhood, old age or other lack of livelihood

---

8 Ishay, *The History of Human Rights.*
9 Merry, "Changing Rights, Changing Culture."

Figure 12.1 Drafting Committee of the International Bill of Rights (Commission on Human Rights) in Lake Success, New York. Left to right: Dr. P.C. Chang, China; Henri Laugier, France; Mrs. Eleanor D. Roosevelt, USA; Prof. John P. Humphrey, Canada; Dr. Charles Malik, Lebanon; Prof. Vladimir M. Koretsky, USSR

in circumstances beyond [one's] control."[10] As we will learn below, social–economic rights are highly contested and marginalized within today's formal international and national human rights frameworks and practices.

The Declaration also entails the third generation of cultural or group rights, which embody principles of self-government and self-determination in matters relating to local affairs, respect for and equality of difference, and freedom from violence, forced assimilation, and destruction of cultural traditions

---

10 United Nations, *The Universal Declaration of Human Rights* (1948), Article 25, http://www.un.org/en/documents/udhr/index.shtml (accessed August 14, 2012).

and customs (see articles 27–28 of the UDHR and the 1976 International Covenant on Economic, Social and Cultural Rights).[11] Although the emergence of cultural rights can be traced to the early twentieth century, at the international level the doctrines of self-determination were further developed with critiques of **colonialism** in the 1950s and 1960s.[12] While these rights are undoubtedly important for safeguarding the collective rights of millions of indigenous peoples living in Africa, Asia, Europe, the Americas, and the Pacific, it is important to note that human rights claims made in the name of "cultural difference" demand critical scrutiny as they may be mobilized in national political rhetoric to prioritize group rights over individual rights, thereby making it much more difficult for marginalized populations to challenge oppressive power relations.

For instance, consider a recent example: In 2009, Uganda made international headlines when a Member of Parliament proposed the Anti-Homosexuality Bill, which would broaden the offence of homosexuality and impose harsh penalties for those who engage in and are deemed to "promote" same-sex relations. Many of the anti-gay positions that circulate throughout the country combine discourses of postcolonial nation-building and anti-colonialism to construct homosexuality as an abhorrent Western import that threatens to destroy Uganda's culture and "traditional" way of life. In characterizing homosexuality as "un-African" and attributing it to the white colonizer, political and religious elites give priority to claims of state sovereignty, cultural difference, and self-determination—the same claims that are protected by international human rights treaties. These claims construct the nation as purely heterosexual (perceived as under threat by progressive international forces) and serve to legitimate the exclusion of sexual minorities from global human rights protections, economic and social policy considerations, and access to essential social services and protections. For these reasons, claims to cultural difference demand critical attention because they often rely on a fixed and essentialized notion of culture that functions to maintain oppressive cultural practices, erase the diversity of a nation's people,

---

11 It must be noted, however, that in 1945 the colonial powers did not recognize colonized peoples as subjects with human rights. In fact, the illegitimacy of colonialism was only recognized in 1960 by a declaration that reaffirmed the UN's "faith in fundamental human rights, in the dignity and worth of the human person, the equal rights of men and women and of nations large and small" and proclaimed "the necessity of bringing to a speedy and unconditional end colonialism in all its forms and manifestations"; United Nations, *Declaration on the Granting of Independence to Colonial Countries and Peoples* (1960), http://www.un.org/en/decolonization/declaration.shtml (accessed April 21, 2014).

12 Merry, "Changing Rights, Changing Culture."

and authorize structural violence against marginalized groups.[13] To counter these claims, scholars, activists, and local people from around the world point to the multiple, contested, and changing meanings of culture across all time and space. As Desiree Lewis eloquently remarks, "invocations of static culture are fictions. Even the most seemingly pristine and unchanged cultural practices are affected by history, globalization, and social struggles."[14] The classical understanding of culture as a static shared system of beliefs and values is therefore rejected in favour of a new understanding of culture as "a process, developing and changing through actions and struggles over meaning."[15]

Box 12.1 The Universal Declaration of Human Rights, 1948

The General Assembly proclaims this Universal Declaration of Human Rights as a common standard of achievement for all peoples and all nations ...

Article 1 All human beings are born free and equal in dignity and rights. They are endowed with reason and conscience and should act towards one another in a spirit of brotherhood.

Article 2 Everyone is entitled to all the rights and freedoms set forth in this Declaration, without distinction of any kind, such as race, colour, sex, language, religion, political or other opinion, national or social origin, property, birth or other status. Furthermore, no distinction shall be made on the basis of the political, jurisdictional or international status of the country or territory to which a person belongs, whether it be independent, trust, non-self-governing or under any other limitation of sovereignty.

Article 3 Everyone has the right to life, liberty and security of person.

Article 4 No one shall be held in slavery or servitude; slavery and the slave trade shall be prohibited in all their forms.

Article 5 No one shall be subjected to torture or to cruel, inhuman or degrading treatment or punishment.

Article 6 Everyone has the right to recognition everywhere as a person before the law.

---

13 See Pheng Cheah, *Inhuman Conditions: On Cosmopolitanism and Human Rights* (Cambridge, MA: Harvard University Press, 2006).

14 Desiree Lewis, "Representing African Sexualities," in *African Sexualities: A Reader*, ed. S. Tamale (Cape Town: Pambazuka Press, 2011), 210.

15 Merry, "Changing Rights, Changing Culture," 39.

Article 7 All are equal before the law and are entitled without any discrimination to equal protection of the law.

Article 8 Everyone has the right to an effective remedy by the competent national tribunals for acts violating the fundamental rights granted him by the constitution or by law.

Article 9 No one shall be subjected to arbitrary arrest, detention or exile.

Article 10 Everyone is entitled in full equality to a fair and public hearing by an independent and impartial tribunal, in the determination of his rights and obligations and of any criminal charge against him.

Article 11 Everyone charged with a penal offence has the right to be presumed innocent until proved guilty according to law in a public trial at which he has had all the guarantees necessary for his defence.

Article 12 No one shall be subjected to arbitrary interference with his privacy, family, home or correspondence, nor to attacks upon his honour and reputation.

Article 13 Everyone has the right to freedom of movement and residence within the borders of each State. Everyone has the right to leave any country, including his own and to return to his country.

Article 14 Everyone has the right to seek and to enjoy in other countries asylum from persecution.

Article 15 Everyone has the right to a nationality. No one shall be arbitrarily deprived of his nationality nor denied the right to change his nationality.

Article 16 Men and women of full age, without any limitation due to race, nationality or religion, have the right to marry and to found a family.

Article 17 Every one has the right to own property alone as well as in association with others. No one shall be arbitrarily deprived of his property.

Article 18 Everyone has the right to freedom of thought, conscience and religion.

Article 19 Everyone has the right to freedom of opinion and expression.

Article 20 Everyone has the right to freedom of peaceful assembly and association.

Article 21 Everyone has the right to take part in the government of his country, directly or through freely chosen representatives.

Article 22 Everyone, as a member of society, has the right to social security and is entitled to realization, through national effort and international co-operation of the economic, social and cultural rights indispensable for his dignity and free development of his personality.

Article 23 Everyone has the right to work, to free choice of employment, to just and favourable conditions of work and to protection against unemployment; to equal pay for equal work; to form and join trade unions for the protection of his interests.

Article 24 Everyone has the right to rest and leisure, including reasonable limitation of working hours and periodic holidays with pay.

Article 25 Everyone has the right to a standard of living adequate for the health and well-being of himself and of his family, including food, clothing, housing, medical care, and the right to security in the event of ... lack of livelihood in circumstances beyond his control.

Article 26 Everyone has the right to education.

Article 27 Everyone has the right freely to participate in the cultural life of the community and to protection of the moral and material interests resulting from any scientific or artistic production of which he is the author.

Article 28 Everyone is entitled to a social and international order in which the rights and freedoms set forth in this Declaration can be fully realized.

We have just seen how human rights develop and change over time and the tensions that often arise between different types of human rights (e.g., cultural rights with self-determination, and civil rights with nondiscrimination and security of person). These tensions have led to much debate on the legitimacy of national and domestic law in light of a new conception of the international subject of human rights.[16] At the time when the foundational texts of human rights were created in the late eighteenth century (e.g., the French Declaration of the Rights of Man and of the Citizen in 1789, or the US Bill of Rights in 1791), the sovereign state was the sole authority that could grant recognition of and enforce such rights within its own territory. While this remains largely the case today,[17] the international human rights

---

16 Anna Yeatman, "Who Is the Subject of Human Rights?" *American Behavioural Scientist* 43, no. 9 (2000): 1498–1513.

17 Kate Nash, *The Cultural Politics of Human Rights: Comparing the US and UK* (Cambridge: Cambridge University Press, 2009).

regime and the salience of globalization have challenged the nation-state as independent of supranational forces and relations and the sole source of human rights. As Anna Yeatman observes, the post–World War II human rights corpus "represents a new set of positive demands of the governing authorities of states; namely, that they accord respect to the principle of human dignity not because the human beings in question are their subjects, their citizens, or their enemies, but because they are human beings."[18] The growing institutionalization of human rights throughout the world and the realization that human rights entail norms of global justice for *all* human beings has led some scholars to refer to global rights as *globalizing*.[19] This has also given way to a revised conceptualization of the "subject of rights" as no longer only a citizen of a nation but as an individual human being of the world. Thus, unlike national law, distinctions between citizens and noncitizens are not permitted in international law. Although this **cosmopolitan** notion of human rights is met with much resistance around the world, its moral force comes from the uncoupling of human rights from the doctrine of national sovereignty and the continuous transnational struggles that take place to expand the very meaning of human rights and make them more inclusive of all human beings.[20]

A recent illustration of the changing and contested meanings of international human rights is the emergence of a conception of women's sexual rights and its transplantation in different contexts around the world. Described as "the newest kid on the block in international debates about the meanings and practices of human rights, especially women's human rights,"[21] the emergent discourse of sexual rights is a key development in the international human rights corpus. For instance, the 1995 Beijing Platform for Action recognized women's rights to "have control over and decide freely and responsibly on matters related to their sexuality, including sexual and reproductive health, free of coercion, discrimination, and violence."[22]

---

18 Yeatman, "Who Is the Subject of Human Rights?" 1499.

19 See Alison Brysk, ed., *Globalization and Human Rights* (Berkeley: University of California Press, 2002).

20 Yeatman, "Who Is the Subject of Human Rights?"; Judith Butler, *Precarious Life: The Powers of Mourning and Violence* (London: Verso, 2004).

21 Rosalind Petchesky, "Sexual Rights: Inventing a Concept, Mapping an International Practice," in *Framing the Sexual Subject: The Politics of Gender, Sexuality, and Power*, ed. Richard Parker, Regina Maria Barbosa, and Peter Aggleton, 81–103 (Berkeley: University of California Press, 2000), 81.

22 Beijing Declaration and Platform for Action, 1995, para. 96, http://www.un.org/womenwatch/daw/beijing/pdf/BDPfA%20E.pdf (accessed April 21, 2014).

In many parts of the world, this new language of sexual rights is slowly changing how sexuality and crimes of sexual violence are perceived and understood by individuals, communities, governments, and international organizations.[23] For instance, it wasn't until the late 1990s that systemic rape in times of war was prosecuted as an international crime. Within the international legal system, the statutes and jurisprudence of the International Criminal Tribunal for Rwanda (1993) and the former Yugoslavia (1994), and the International Criminal Court (2002) recognize mass rape as a war crime and crime against humanity,[24] and in 2008 the United Nations Security Council voted unanimously to pass Resolution 1820, declaring rape and other forms of sexual violence as constituting a "tactic of war" constituting a crime against humanity. Thus, instead of viewing human rights in normative terms as a set of fixed universal principles or in **teleological** terms as leading to greater progress or civilization, we can view them more as an evolving body of ideas that are produced through continuous contestation and struggle over their meanings, interpretations, and institutionalization in specific historical and spatial contexts.

Approaches to Understanding Human Rights

International human rights have become the topic of widespread discussion and debate in recent years within scholarly, advocacy, and policymaking circles. Mark Goodale situates different understandings and approaches to human rights on a continuum that ranges from a more restricted legalistic understanding of human rights *as* positive law to a more expansive discursive approach that foregrounds social practices.[25] The legalistic approach to human rights refers to the juridical act of codifying and recognizing human rights as positive law, such as the body of international law that emerged in the aftermath of World War II with the passing of the Universal Declaration of Human Rights. Since then, numerous international and regional human rights conventions have been created, as well as mechanisms for their enforcement. The vast majority of the United Nations's 193 member states have

23 See Amy Lind, "Development, Global Governance, and Sexual Subjectivities," in *Development, Sexual Rights and Global Governance*, ed. Amy Lind (New York: Routledge, 2010); Barbara Klugman, "Sexual Rights in Southern Africa: A Beijing Discourse or a Strategic Necessity?" *Health and Human Rights* 4, no. 2 (2000): 144–73.

24 See Anne-Marie de Brouwer, *Supranational Criminal Prosecution of Sexual Violence: The ICC and the Practice of the ICTY and the ICTR* (Antwerp: Intersentia, 2005).

25 Mark Goodale, "Introduction: Locating Rights: Envisioning Law between the Global and the Local," in *The Practice of Human Rights: Tracking Law between the Global and the Local*, ed. M. Goodale and Sally Engle Merry (Cambridge: Cambridge University Press, 2007).

ratified the core international human rights treaties: 193 have ratified the Convention on the Rights of the Child; 187 have ratified the Convention on the Elimination of all Forms of Discrimination Against Women; 175 states have ratified the International Convention on the Elimination of All Forms of Racial Discrimination; 167 states have ratified the International Covenant on Civil and Political Rights; 160 have ratified the International Covenant on Economic, Social, and Cultural Rights; 151 have ratified the Convention Against Torture and Other Cruel, Inhuman or Degrading Treatment or Punishment; and 142 states have ratified the Convention on the Prevention and Punishment of the Crime of Genocide.[26] Several of these human rights treaties have been supplemented by optional protocols that specify additional human rights protections. There are also several other international human rights treaties that have been drafted and ratified by state parties, such as the Declaration on the Rights of Indigenous Peoples and the Convention on the Rights of Persons with Disabilities, as well as a number of regional human rights instruments in Africa, Europe, and the Americas.

With the expansion of international human rights law, diverse legal mechanisms and institutions have also been established in an attempt to enforce human rights protections and hold individuals criminally responsible and accountable for human rights violations. In addition to the 60-plus truth commissions or human rights trials that have been established by new or transitioning states, the early 1990s witnessed the creation of a number of international criminal tribunals by the UN Security Council, including the ad hoc International Criminal Tribunal for the former Yugoslavia and International Criminal Tribunal for Rwanda.[27] In 1998, with the adoption of the Rome Statute by 120 states, the international community moved to establish the International Criminal Court (ICC)—the first permanent international criminal court tasked with charging individuals for war crimes, crimes against humanity, and genocide. Finally, a number of hybrid domestic–international courts have been created, for instance in Sierra Leone, Cambodia, East Timor, and Lebanon. Scholars that approach human rights legalistically as international law generally agree that human rights "must be legislated, legally recognized, and codified before it can be taken seriously as part of the law of nations."[28]

---

26 United Nations Treaty Collection, https://treaties.un.org/Pages/Treaties.aspx?id=4&subid=A&lang=en (accessed February 13, 2013).

27 Alison Brysk and Arturo Jimenez, "The Globalization of Law: Implications for the Fulfillment of Human Rights," *Journal of Human Rights* 11, no. 1 (2012): 4–16.

28 Goodale, "Introduction," 6.

A second, middle position on Goodale's continuum is a somewhat more expansive approach to human rights that focuses on the various ways that the concept of human rights is itself normative—or in other words how human rights shape a certain idea of the individual and establishes certain norms and rules for behaviour while prohibiting others. These normative principles may be expressed through international human rights treaties, but they are not confined to them. Scholars that are concerned with the concept of human rights in terms of its norms and the production of certain individual and political subjects apply an approach to human rights that can be described as *analytical or conceptual normativism*. On this understanding, human rights are moral rights that are held by all individuals simply because they are human beings. They are rights shared equally by everyone regardless of distinctions based on sex, race, religion, nationality, and economic background. They are universal in content and they are **inalienable**, meaning they exist prior to any exercise of sovereign power and cannot be taken away. Human rights are also **indivisible**, which is to say that one cluster of human rights cannot dominate or be privileged over any other type of human rights. In other words, "it is an unacceptable assault upon one's dignity whether a person is forbidden to speak her mind, or to participate in political life, or is forced by hunger to beg for food, or is subjected to torture, or threatened with death."[29] This approach includes the work of moral and political philosophers, like Thomas Pogge, who argue that world poverty should be classified as a human rights violation insofar as the affluent countries in the global north have a negative duty not to harm the world's poor by imposing upon them a "global institutional order which is so designed that it foreseeably produces avoidable human rights deficits on a massive scale."[30]

The third and most expansive orientation to human rights moves beyond dominant understandings of human rights in terms of the study of formal legal instruments or normative principles by approaching human rights as **discourse**, or the organized systems of knowledge and social practices that regulate what can be said and done, what can be thought, and what is considered true or correct. Discursive approaches to human rights are broadly influenced by poststructuralist theory, which rejects structuralist ideas of social life (as shaped by stable, underlying structures or patterned arrangements that can be objectively known through science) and humanist notions of the individual (that there are universal, essential, and unchangeable truths

---

29 Ishay, *The History of Human Rights*, xix.
30 Thomas Pogge, "Introduction," in *Freedom from Poverty as a Human Right*, ed. T. Pogge (Oxford: Oxford University Press, 2007), 6.

about people, such as rationality or autonomy). Instead, they view human rights and its subjects as highly contested and produced through historical and social relations of knowledge/power.[31] While discursive approaches to human rights are internally diverse,[32] you may have already noted the influence of Michel Foucault as significant.

Foucault (and those influenced by his work) was often critical of humanism and the language of human rights. However, he also recognized the value of human rights to political struggle. In one of his most explicit political statements (made in 1981 at an international conference in Geneva and entitled "Confronting Governments: Human Rights"), Foucault affirmed the right and duty of the governed to resist abuses of power wherever they exist and to intervene in the world of international policy.[33] But he also argued (in his closing remarks in a 1976 lecture) that one should look "toward the possibility of a new form of right, one which must indeed be anti-disciplinarian, but at the same time liberated from the principle of sovereignty."[34] Although Foucault did not elaborate in detail on what he meant by this new form of right, it is reasonably clear that he was advocating for a notion of human rights that does not appeal to some universal and given human nature or that relies on the state and its juridical framework of the law for legitimacy. Moreover, rather than only focusing on international human rights in terms of law or state power, Foucault's work urges us to focus on the diverse range of sites and practices that exist outside the state and law, where social actors from all walks of life talk about, criticize, enact, and use human rights in its many forms toward numerous ends. This would include international organizations (like the United Nations) and the recent explosion of nongovernmental and humanitarian organizations throughout the world that respond to human suffering and gross violations of people's human rights. Other social actors who engage with human rights in diverse social contexts may include individuals mobilizing a protest movement, institutions designing campaigns to end violence against women (schools, health centres, nongovernmental

---

31 The concept of knowledge/power simply refers to their mutual constitution. In other words, the exercise of power leads to the production of new knowledge and, conversely, knowledge is part of the exercise of power.

32 Goodale, "Introduction."

33 Cited in Jessica Whyte, "Human Rights: Confronting Governments? Michel Foucault and the Right to Intervene," in *New Critical Legal Thinking: Law and the Political*, ed. Matthew Stone, Illan rua Wall, and Costas Douzinas (New York: Routledge, 2012).

34 Michel Foucault, "Two Lectures," in *Culture/Power/History: A Reader in Contemporary Social Theory*, ed. Nicholas B. Dirks, Geoff Eley, and Sherry B. Ortner (Princeton: Princeton University Press, 1994), 221.

organizations, and community-based organizations), states passing human rights legislation, or international organizations defining the standards of a "just" military intervention.

Some scholars influenced by Foucault's work on power have come to see human rights as constituting an important element of liberal governmentality and, in particular, "international governmentality."[35] Understood this way, human rights are part of the many, deliberate attempts of international governing institutions to direct and manage the actions of individuals, populations, and nation-states in "optimal" or "desired" ways and to regulate the conditions under which people's lives are lived. As Columbia University professor Samuel Moyn recently wrote in the *New York Times*: "Today, the issue of human rights is no longer just about limiting power in the global arena but also about how to deploy it."[36] However, as noted in previous chapters, Foucault's expanded concept of governmentality as "the conduct of conduct" refers not only to the regulatory and repressive effects of power, but also to power's productive and creative effects. For instance, the globalization of human rights can be seen not only to place limits on and regulate oppressive state practices, but also to transform and bring into being new political and economic systems, knowledges, identities, beliefs, and practices of governing that are predicated on the notion of freedom and, it follows, self-government. It is for this reason that governmentality scholars focus on liberalism as a dominant governmental regime: a "way of doing things" that is concerned with limiting state intervention on the one hand, and governing human behaviour through the production and management of freedom on the other.[37] Thus, liberalism requires—and indeed must produce—rational, self-governing subjects who are free to maximize socioeconomic opportunities and rewards. Moreover, with the rise and dominance of neoliberalism around the world, a wide range of governmental policies and programs have emerged that promote a particular neoliberal subjectivity: a self-regulating and entrepreneurial subject who is both able and motivated to provide for her own needs and those of her loved ones without state assistance or support. To be clear, human rights are not reducible to neoliberal governance, but they may be mobilized by governing authorities to bring about desired

---

35 Mitchell Dean, *Governmentality: Power and Rule in Modern Society* (London: Sage Publications, 2009), 247.

36 Samuel Moyn, "Human Rights, Not So Pure Anymore," *New York Times*, May 12, 2012, http:// www.nytimes.com/2012/05/13/opinion/sunday/human-rights-not-so-pure-anymore. html?pagewanted=all&_r=1& (accessed December 13, 2012).

37 Michel Foucault, "Governmentality," in *The Foucault Effect, Studies in Governmental Rationality*, ed. Graham Burchell, Colin Gordon, and Peter Miller (Chicago: University of Chicago Press, 1995).

subjectivities and individual conduct that aligns with free market activities and principles.

As you learned in Chapter Eight, governmental power is therefore intricately connected to processes of *normalization*—a form of social regulation that distinguishes "normal" from its opposite, "abnormal," and establishes a hierarchy that assigns greater value to those people, practices, and beliefs that conform to the standards of normality and ordinariness. Heteronormativity provides a good example. Consider the human rights claims that are made by lesbian and gay movements for same-sex marriage or partnership status. In what ways do these rights claims reinforce a certain model of "normal" intimacy or political subjectivity? Diane Richardson argues that these rights claims reinforce a particular model of citizenship that is associated with both heteronormativity and neoliberal governance.[38] For her, gay and lesbian rights claims to partnership status emphasize formal equality or sameness with the dominant group (heterosexuals). Thus, the "risks" that same-sex partnerships allegedly pose to society are minimized by constituting lesbians and gay men as "ordinary," "normal," and "responsible" citizens who share the same socioeconomic values and consumer-oriented lifestyles as heterosexuals. These claims not only imply shared interests and needs of all citizens (regardless of sexual, gender, class, or racialized differences), but they also privilege a specific form of "domestic" sexual coupledom that constitutes "other" forms of relationships as problematic and in need of control and serves as a basis for excluding such relationships from certain entitlements. This is what Judith Butler describes as the paradoxical function of the norm as being both socially integrative and "exclusionary or violent."[39] In the context of neoliberalism, it is possible to see "governments as motivated to introduce civil recognition of lesbian and gay relationships insofar as these are seen as a form of private welfare, providing economic interdependency and support."[40]

Discursive approaches to human rights are also informed by postcolonial theory. Postcolonial scholars have long identified international law (of which human rights is a part) as a key mechanism of governmental power that not only constitutes non-European subjects as Other, but also justifies their exclusion and subjugation. As we know from previous chapters, the "post" in *postcolonial* does not refer to the end of the colonial period, but rather to the continuation of past practices and effects of colonial rule

---

38 Diane Richardson, "Desiring Sameness? The Rise of a Neoliberal Politics of Normalisation," *Antipode* 37, no. 3 (2005): 515–35.

39 Judith Butler, *Undoing Gender* (New York: Routledge, 2004), 221.

40 Richardson, "Desiring Sameness?" 522.

in shaping the contemporary period. For Antony Anghie, the evolution of international law is best understood in terms of the problem of cultural difference, which is based on the colonial distinction between "civilized" European and "uncivilized" non-European cultures and peoples. This basic power dynamic underpins the history of international law; the formation of conventions, policies, doctrines, and jurisprudence designed "to bring the uncivilized/aberrant/violent/backward/oppressed into the realm of civilization, the universal order governed by (European) international law."[41] This narrative has been widely challenged by non-Western people, who question the equation of progress, modernity, and justice with Europe and show that the same view "ultimately served the colonial enterprise, justifying intervention in societies deemed primitive and backward."[42] For some postcolonial scholars, international human rights are part of the historical continuum of the European Enlightenment project "in which whites pose as the saviors of a benighted and savage non-European world."[43] As we will see below, contemporary imperialist interventions and humanitarian relief efforts continue to advise, constrain, and transform non-European countries and produce a wide range of texts and visual images (e.g., photography, film) that recycle Western (colonial) stereotypes and racialized tropes of human suffering in the global south.

The following section applies the theoretical insights of discursive approaches to human rights to explore some of the ways that human rights have been used to organize and justify a range of international interventions in non-Western countries. We will focus on the post-9/11 context, specifically the place of human rights in the US-led War on Terror. While it remains crucial to examine the various ways that social and political actors in local contexts give meaning to and use human rights to denounce global injustices and advocate for social change, for our purposes here we will apply our critical tools to examine the *effects* of human rights claims on regulating and representing non-Western lives—such as producing normative subjects and ways of life, reproducing colonial and Orientalist tropes of Western superiority and non-Western inferiority, and authorizing imperial practices that seek to regulate non-European populations and sustain unequal structures of power at local, national, and international levels.

---

41 Antony Anghie, "The Evolution of International Law: Colonial and Postcolonial Realities," *Third World Quarterly* 27 (2006): 742.

42 Ibid.

43 Makau Matua, *Human Rights: A Political and Cultural Critique* (Pennsylvania: University of Pennsylvania Press, 2002), 155.

Governing and Representing Non-Western Lives Post-9/11

More than a decade has passed since 9/11. Within this time, we have witnessed the United States declare war on terrorism as a global phenomenon and launch an aggressive and calculated military assault on Afghanistan and Iraq. We have seen the emergence of new government departments and laws across the globe that grant heads of state permanent expanded powers and give police and security forces new powers of investigation and detention. We have heard reports and seen evidence of torture, indefinite detention, and demeaning treatment of prisoners in US-run prisons. And many of us are likely familiar with the heightened surveillance practices at international borders that rely on risk-based discourses and tools to calculate, categorize, and sort "risky" from "nonrisky" subjects and the "criminals" from the "law-abiding" citizens.

We have watched US and European state officials abrogate international and national laws in the name of national security while simultaneously claiming global leadership in defending human rights around the world. This is especially the case concerning women's human rights and fighting gender oppression—as seen, for example, in George W. Bush's justification for invading Afghanistan in 2001 or in Laura Bush's speech to the nation just months after 9/11, where she claimed that "civilized people throughout the world are speaking out in horror" against the violence that the terrorists impose on women and children in Afghanistan and declared that "the fight against terrorism is also a fight for the rights and dignity of women."[44] The Associated Press photo in Figure 12.2 illustrates how women's human rights and racialized bodies can serve to legitimate Western imperialist and militaristic practices. The image shows an Afghan woman wearing a *burqa*—the iconic symbol of women's repression in much of Western public discourse—who encounters the promise of "freedom" on a city wall in the war-torn Herat province southwest of Kabul. She walks alone (an action Western audiences believe to be impossible under the Taliban) and the visual positioning of her body in the foreground against the backdrop of the word *freedom* suggests that she is empowered by the US military presence in Afghanistan.

The War on Terror can be analyzed as a global project of governance; it designs and employs numerous logics, strategies, and governing practices, some of them involving exceptional security measures, to govern and transform the "Arab" world. These governing strategies are predicated on the

---

44 Laura Bush, "Radio Address by Mrs. Bush," November 17, 2001, http://www.presidency.ucsb.edu/ws/?pid=24992 (accessed January 3, 2013).

Figure 12.2 The appropriation of women's bodies to legitimize US military action in Afghanistan

construction of two competing "worlds of globalization," described by Louise Amoore and Marieke de Goede as "one populated by legitimate and civilized groups whose normalized patterns of financial, leisure, or business behaviour are to be secured; and another populated by illegitimate and uncivilized persons whose suspicious patterns of behaviour are to be targeted and apprehended."[45] Whereas the former group comprises the "legitimate" and "well-behaving" subjects of human rights who are "deserving" of Western security and protection, the latter group entails the "undeserving" and "uncivilized" racialized others who are seen to be radically different from and the "enemy" of Western human rights and freedom.

At the very core of the US justification for the War on Terror is what feminists refer to as the "protection myth,"[46] which rehashes century-old

---

45 Louise Amoore and Marieke de Goede, "Introduction: Governing by Risk in the War on Terror," in *Risk and the War on Terror*, ed. Louise Amoore and Marieke de Goede (New York: Routledge, 2008), 13.

46 Katrina Lee-Koo, "'War on Terror'/'War on Women': Critical Feminist Perspectives," in *Security and the War on Terror*, ed. Alex Bellamy, Roland Bleiker, Sara Davies, and Richard Devetak (New York: Routledge, 2008).

Orientalist and colonial stereotypes of distant suffering and civilization. The master narrative entails the non-Western "uncivilized" state or culture (illiberal and authoritarian) that unleashes its tyranny on innocent, nonwhite and non-Western "victims" (powerless and helpless) who are to be rescued and made "free" by white saviours bearing Western values and practices (human rights).[47] This narrative has led postcolonial scholars to argue that human rights discourse is firmly entrenched in what Ratna Kapur calls "the tragedy of victimization rhetoric" or what Makau Matua describes in terms of a three-dimensional metaphor of the savage–victim–saviour.[48] These racialized and colonial-inspired scripts of human rights have become deeply embedded within Western consciousness with the mass production and distribution of visual images of human suffering of distant others, especially of nonwhite and non-Western women and children. For instance, in the aftermath of 9/11 one of the main international news stories focused on the plight of Afghan women. Consider the *TIME Magazine* cover published in August 2010. The cover features a photograph (taken by Jodi Bieber) of a young Afghan woman named Bibi Aisha, who was disfigured by her husband (a Taliban commander) as punishment for running away from his home. The iconic photo is accompanied by highly emotive text that reads "What Happens if We Leave Afghanistan." The absence of a question mark indicates an assertion: that such horrific crimes against women will increase if the US-led military intervention were to leave Afghanistan prematurely. Inside the magazine, we find an article that describes Aisha's story, as well as the stories of other Afghan women who have embraced the freedoms resulting from the US defeat of the Taliban, yet who continue to live in fear of a Taliban revival.[49] It is important to note, however, that Aisha's story did not quite fit the standardized morality tale of women victims and "barbaric" Taliban villains. Just months after the *TIME Magazine* publication, a report was released that linked Aisha's disfigurement to traditional Afghan male culture, specifically to a century-old tribal custom for settling disputes known as *baad*, where women and girls are given to a perceived victim of a crime as compensation.[50] Yet, despite this

---

47 Matua, *Human Rights*, 10–12.

48 Ratna Kapur, *Erotic Justice: Law and the New Politics of Postcolonialism* (London: The Glass House Press, 2005); Matua, *Human Rights*.

49 Aryn Baker, "Afghan Women and the Return of the Taliban," *TIME Magazine*, August 9, 2010, http://content.time.com/time/magazine/article/0,9171,2007407,00.html (accessed August 6, 2012).

50 Jonathan Steele, *Ghosts of Afghanistan: The Haunted Battleground* (Berkeley: Counterpoint Press, 2011); Human Rights Watch, "Afghanistan: Stop Women Being Given as Compensation," March 8, 2011, http://www.hrw.org/news/2011/03/08/afghanistan-stop-women-being-given-compensation (accessed November 6, 2013).

Figure 12.3 A young Afghan woman who was disfigured by her husband for running away from home

realization, the overly simplistic narrative of savage–victim–saviour remained firmly entrenched within the West's social imagery of Afghanistan and the US justification for the war against terror.

If we follow Edward Said's argument that "representations have purposes,"[51] we must ask what tasks are accomplished, what interests are served, and what knowledge is produced and distributed through visual representations of human suffering. With regard to the *TIME Magazine* cover photo, you might argue (as some critics have) that this kind of journalism represents what Mahmood Mamdani has called a "pornography of violence," in that it fixates "on the gory details, describing the worst of the atrocities in gruesome detail and chronicling the rise in their number."[52] You may see the magazine

51 Edward Said, *Orientalism* (New York: Pantheon Books, 1979), 273.

52 Mahmood Mamdani, *Saviors and Survivors: Darfur, Politics, and the War on Terror* (New York: Pantheon Books, 2009), 66.

cover as exploiting gender politics and violence against women to legitimate continued US military intervention in Afghanistan, or as perpetuating the false perception that war and Western secular values (freedom, democracy, human rights) will liberate Afghan women from the violent and misogynist practices of the Taliban regime (especially given recent evidence that suggests the War on Terror has dramatically worsened the situation for women and intensified the many physical and emotional insecurities that permeate their lives, such as sexual violence, poverty, beatings, and murder).[53] You may observe that the media coverage depicts Afghan women as "victims" of their culture, which following Kapur reproduces both "gender essentialism" and "cultural essentialism"—positioning the West as superior to and more tolerant/equal than the inferior/barbaric/uncivilized "Arab" world.[54] And many of you may take issue with the symbolic structure of the photo itself as it portrays the lone, disfigured woman as the passive, helpless, and generic or "pure" victim figure of Taliban rule. The portrayal of the lone, feminized "victim" serves a number of purposes: It reinforces a dominant discourse that views the world in terms of the clash of civilizations (Islam versus the West); it contributes to the widespread acceptance of the "protection myth" discussed above; and it decontextualizes violence against women from the historical and sociopolitical conditions that enable it to continue, such as the role of the United States in enabling this history and continuing to support current practices that violate women's human rights by fundamentalist Islamist groups, as well as US forces and military contractors.[55]

Some of you may also be questioning the relationship between the War on Terror and neoliberal globalization, especially since war's devastation creates the sociopolitical conditions that are ripe for international aid interventions. It has been widely recognized by US policymakers and their allies that "success" in Afghanistan will not be determined by military strength alone. Rather, counterinsurgency strategies revolve around building "an effective Afghan government" and "stronger governance at all levels—national, district, and provincial."[56] According to Senator Ted Kaufman, this requires

53 Lee-Koo, "'War on Terror'/'War on Women'"; Center for Human Rights and Global Justice, *A Decade Lost: Locating Gender in U.S. Counter-Terrorism* (New York: NYU School of Law, 2011); Madeleine Bunting, "Can the Spread of Women's Rights Ever Be Accompanied by War?" *The Guardian*, October 2, 2011, http://www.guardian.com/commentisfree/2011/oct/02/women-rights-afghanistan-war-west (accessed February 7, 2013).

54 Kapur, *Erotic Justice*, 99.

55 Corrêa, Petchesky, and Parker, *Sexuality, Health, and Human Rights*; Bunting, "Can the Spread of Women's Rights Ever Be Accompanied by War?"

56 Senator Ted Kaufman, "The Best Defense in Afghanistan Is Good Governance," *Huffington Post*, November 24, 2009, http://www.huffingtonpost.com/sen-ted-kaufman/best-defense-in-afghanist_b_369314.html (accessed February 13, 2013).

that President Karzai work with the United States and other international partners "to produce specific and measurable guidelines for combating corruption, improving government transparency and accountability, providing essential services, strengthening rule of law, tackling the drug trade, and improving economic conditions. Clear benchmarks must be set, and progress must be monitored to ensure compliance at every level."[57] For anyone who has taken an introductory course in international development, Kaufman's advice fits squarely within contemporary discourses and practices of international development that began to emerge in the mid-1990s in response to the growing realization that the market liberalization policies of the 1980s had intensified poverty, inequality, and conflict.

Faced with increased public pressure, Western donors and international organizations moved to embrace what has been described as a more "inclusive" neoliberal approach to development. This agenda continues to promote free market principles, but calls for an increased emphasis on building strong states and institutions via good governance mechanisms, civil society participation, poverty reduction plans, and human rights values.[58] The neoliberal reform policies of Western donors and international financial institutions like the International Monetary Fund and the World Bank have targeted not only the economies of developing countries, but also the political and social structures of third-world states. This involves promoting the virtues of good governance, the rule of law, and international human rights. Barry Hindess's recent work on international anti-corruption programs reveals a project of "large scale social engineering" that is mostly directed at developing countries and implemented under the heading of good governance.[59] Underlying these programs is a more extensive project that involves exporting a Western institutional framework for government to the non-Western world. Far from being a "neutral" project, these reforms embody both Western and neoliberal norms about how "good" government should operate. As Anghie explains, international governing institutions have attempted to use good governance and human rights law to further their neoliberal agendas rather than improving citizens' rights in any real way.[60] For some scholars, the current good governance and rights-based approach to development reflects a neoliberal mode of governing in that it promotes self-government, empowerment,

---

57 Ibid.

58 David Craig and Doug Porter, *Development Beyond Neoliberalism? Governance, Poverty Reduction and Political Economy* (New York: Routledge, 2006).

59 Barry Hindess, "Investigating International Anti-Corruption," *Third World Quarterly* 26 (2005): 1390.

60 Anghie, "The Evolution of International Law," 749.

and individual responsibility and seeks to regulate third-world citizens and nation-states through free market activities (liberalization, privatization) and principles (efficiency, productivity, cost effectiveness, accountability).[61] Although the use of military force in the War on Terror is an obvious example of US imperialism, it is equally important that we focus our attention on the less explicit and more mundane imperialism that is found in the economic and political reform packages of international institutions, which have accompanied the War on Terror and support its desire to transform Middle Eastern countries into freedom-loving "democratic" states.[62]

Discursive approaches to human rights are analytically valuable because they recognize the emancipatory features and potentials of human rights, while requiring that we critique the regulatory and normalizing effects that human rights have on people's lives. Moreover, they require that we ask questions about the forms of knowledge and social practices that are constitutive of the idea of human rights itself,[63] including why some norms of violence are prohibited and others are considered part of the "normal" and taken-for-granted social practices of the global order.[64] For instance, it is quite likely that all of us would agree that genocide, slavery, and other acts aimed at explicitly destroying human life and dignity are, without doubt, abhorrent acts of violence that violate human rights and are rightfully prohibited by international law. However, what if we were to use **structural violence** as our example? Unlike direct or explicit forms of violence, structural violence is almost always invisible, "concealed within the hegemony of ordinariness ... often part of taken-for-granted social practices, justified by ideas of racial inferiority, threats to security, or the need to control irresponsible people."[65] Structural violence is normalized within the current world order, embedded within the political, sociocultural, and economic arrangements that cause human injury and suffering on a global scale. Would you consider poverty, forced displacement, and famines in the global south as acts of violence committed by Western donors and international aid agencies, equal to the crimes of genocide or slavery? What about international trade rules that deny millions of people access to life-saving medicines, particularly for AIDS?

---

61 Tanya Basok and Suzan Ilcan, "In the Name of Human Rights: Global Organizations and Participating Citizens," *Citizenship Studies*, 10, no. 3 (2006): 309–28.

62 Anghie, "The Evolution of International Law."

63 Goodale, "Introduction."

64 Sally Engle Merry, "Introduction: States of Violence," in *The Practice of Human Rights: Tracking Law between the Global and the Local*, ed. Mark Goodale and Sally Engle Merry (Cambridge: Cambridge University Press, 2007).

65 Ibid., 43.

I imagine your responses to be much more varied and producing much more debate over the meanings of violence, human dignity and freedom, crimes against humanity, and responsibility. This is partly because the global corpus of human rights assigns primacy to civil–political rights and marginalizes social–economic rights. With the rise of neoliberal globalization, this is hardly surprising given that social–economic rights are widely believed to be an impetus to free market processes. As you continue to think more about international human rights, it is important to consider how and to what extent they can be used to advance the interests of marginalized peoples, to protect them from authoritarian and violent states, and as tools to resist the operations of imperialism and the more mundane and taken-for-granted normalizing practices that are authorized in the name of human rights.

Study Questions

1. In your own words, explain why it is important to think critically about human rights. Using an example from this chapter, explain what it means to say that human rights are paradoxical.
2. Compare and contrast the different approaches to studying human rights discussed in this chapter. How does a discursive approach challenge dominant assumptions about human rights?

Exercise

Choose a contemporary human rights campaign, such as Save Darfur, *Kony 2012*, or the UNHCR's "Dilemmas" campaign. Examine the different ways that the campaign visually represents human rights abuses and suffering. What knowledge is produced and distributed by the campaign, and for whom? In particular, how do these campaigns "frame" or represent non-Western cultures and populations, the perpetuators and victims of conflict, and the solutions that are needed to end the human suffering in question? In your study group, discuss the presence of neocolonial narratives and stereotypes of distant suffering and civilization, as well as their gendered and racialized dynamics.

Keywords

globalization; universalism; human rights; normalizing power; negative liberties; socialist tradition; Universal Declaration of Human Rights; teleological; inalienable rights; indivisible rights; discourse/discursive; governmentality; neoliberalism; normalization; heteronormativity; postcolonial theory; structural violence

References

Amoore, Louise, and Marieke de Goede. "Introduction: Governing by Risk in the War on Terror." In *Risk and the War on Terror*, edited by L. Amoore and M. de Goede, 5–20. New York: Routledge, 2008.

Anghie, Antony. "The Evolution of International Law: Colonial and Postcolonial Realities." *Third World Quarterly* 27, no. 5 (2006): 739–53. http://dx.doi.org/10.1080/01436590600780011.

Baker, Aryn. "Afghan Women and the Return of the Taliban." *TIME Magazine*, August 9, 2010. http://content.time.com/time/magazine/article/0,9171,2007407,00.html (accessed August 6, 2012).

Basok, Tanya, and Suzan Ilcan. "In the Name of Human Rights: Global Organizations and Participating Citizens." *Citizenship Studies* 10, no. 3 (2006): 309–27. http://dx.doi.org/10.1080/13621020600772099.

Beijing Declaration and Platform for Action. 1995. http://www.un.org/womenwatch/daw/beijing/pdf/BDPfA%20E.pdf (accessed April 21, 2014).

Brysk, Alison, and Arturo Jimenez. "The Globalization of Law: Implications for the Fulfillment of Human Rights." *Journal of Human Rights* 11, no. 1 (2012): 4–16. http://dx.doi.org/10.1080/14754835.2012.648147.

Brysk, Alison, ed. *Globalization and Human Rights*. Berkeley: University of California Press, 2002.

Bunting, Madeleine. "Can the Spread of Women's Rights Ever Be Accompanied by War? *The Guardian*, October 2, 2011. http://www.guardian.com/commentisfree/2011/oct/02/women-rights-afghanistan-war-west (accessed February 7, 2013).

Bush, Laura. "Radio Address by Mrs. Bush." November 17, 2001. http://www.presidency.ucsb.edu/ws/?pid=24992 (accessed January 3, 2013).

Butler, Judith. *Precarious Life: The Powers of Mourning and Violence*. London: Verso, 2004.

Butler, Judith. *Undoing Gender*. New York: Routledge, 2004.

Center for Human Rights and Global Justice. *A Decade Lost: Locating Gender in U.S. Counter-Terrorism*. New York: NYU School of Law, 2011.

Cheah, Pheng. *Inhuman Conditions: On Cosmopolitanism and Human Rights*. Cambridge, MA: Harvard University Press, 2006.

Chowdhury, Arjun. "'The Giver or the Recipient?': The Peculiar Ownership of Human Rights." *International Political Sociology* 5, no. 1 (2011): 35–51. http://dx.doi.org/10.1111/j.1749-5687.2011.00119.x.

Corrêa, Sonia, Rosalind Petchesky, and Richard Parker. *Sexuality, Health, and Human Rights*. Milton Park: Routledge, 2008.

Craig, David, and Doug Porter. *Development Beyond Neoliberalism? Governance, Poverty Reduction and Political Economy*. New York: Routledge, 2006.

Dean, Mitchell. *Governmentality: Power and Rule in Modern Society*. London: Sage Publications, 2009.

de Brouwer, Anne-Marie. *Supranational Criminal Prosecution of Sexual Violence: The ICC and the Practice of the ICTY and the ICTR*. Antwerp: Intersentia, 2005.

Douzinas, Costas. *Human Rights and Empire: The Political Philosophy of Cosmopolitanism*. New York: Routledge, 2007.

Foucault, Michel. "Governmentality." In *The Foucault Effect: Studies in Governmental Rationality*, edited by G. Burchell, C. Gordon, and P. Miller, 87–104. Chicago: University of Chicago Press, 1995.

Foucault, Michel. "Two Lectures." In *A Reader in Contemporary Social Theory*, edited by N. Dirks, G. Eley, and S. Ortner, 200–21. Princeton, NJ: Princeton University Press, 1994.

Foucault, Michel. *The History of Sexuality*. Vol. 1, *An Introduction*. Translated by Robert Hurley. New York: Vintage Books, 1990.

Goodale, Mark. "Introduction: Locating Rights: Envisioning Law between the Global and the Local." In *The Practice of Human Rights: Tracking Law between the Global and the Local*, edited by M. Goodale and S. Engle Merry, 1–38. Cambridge: Cambridge University Press, 2007. http://dx.doi.org/10.1017/CBO9780511819193.001.

Hindess, Barry. "Investigating International Anti-Corruption." *Third World Quarterly* 26, no. 8 (2005): 1389–98. http://dx.doi.org/10.1080/01436590500336864.

Human Rights Watch. "Afghanistan: Stop Women Being Given as Compensation." March 8, 2011. http://www.hrw.org/news/2011/03/08/afghanistan-stop-women -being-given-compensation (accessed November 6, 2013).

Ishay, Micheline. *The History of Human Rights: From Ancient Times to the Globalization Era*. Berkeley: University of California Press, 2004.

Kapur, Ratna. *Erotic Justice: Law and the New Politics of Postcolonialism*. London: The Glass House Press, 2005.

Kaufman, Ted. "The Best Defense in Afghanistan Is Good Governance." *Huffington Post*, November 24, 2009. http://www.huffingtonpost.com/sen-ted-kaufman/best-defense -in-afghanist_b_369314.html (accessed February 13, 2013).

Klugman, Barbara. "Sexual Rights in Southern Africa: A Beijing Discourse or a Strategic Necessity?" *Health and Human Rights* 4, no. 2 (2000): 144–73. http://dx.doi.org/ 10.2307/4065199.

Lee-Koo, Katrina. "'War on Terror'/'War on Women': Critical Feminist Perspectives." In *Security and the War on Terror*, edited by A. Bellamy, R. Bleiker, S. Davies, and R. Devetak, 42–54. New York: Routledge, 2008.

Lewis, Desiree. "Representing African Sexualities." In *African Sexualities: A Reader*, edited by S. Tamale, 119–216. Cape Town: Pambazuka Press, 2011.

Lind, Amy. "Development, Global Governance, and Sexual Subjectivities." In *Development, Sexual Rights and Global Governance*, edited by Amy Lind, 1–19. New York: Routledge, 2010.

Mamdani, Mahmood. *Saviors and Survivors: Darfur, Politics, and the War on Terror*. New York: Pantheon Books, 2009.

Matua, Makau. *Human Rights: A Political and Cultural Critique*. Pennsylvania: University of Pennsylvania Press, 2002.

Merry, Sally Engle. "Introduction: States of Violence." In *The Practice of Human Rights: Tracking Law between the Global and the Local*, edited by M. Goodale and S. Engle Merry, 41–48. Cambridge: Cambridge University Press, 2007. http://dx.doi.org/10.1017/ CBO9780511819193.002.

Merry, Sally Engle. "Changing Rights, Changing Culture." In *Culture and Rights: Anthropological Perspectives*, edited by J. Cowan, M-B, Dembour, and R. Wilson, 31–55. Cambridge: Cambridge University Press, 2001. http://dx.doi.org/10.1017/ CBO9780511804687.004.

Moyn, Samuel. "Human Rights, Not So Pure Anymore." *New York Times*, May 12, 2012. http://www.nytimes.com/2012/05/13/opinion/sunday/human-rights-not-so -pure-anymore.html?pagewanted=all&_r=1& (accessed December 13, 2012).

Nash, Kate. *The Cultural Politics of Human Rights: Comparing the US and UK*. Cambridge: Cambridge University Press, 2009. http://dx.doi.org/10.1017/CBO9780511576676.

Petchesky, Rosalind. "Sexual Rights: Inventing a Concept, Mapping an International Practice." In *Framing the Sexual Subject: The Politics of Gender, Sexuality, and Power*, edited by R. Parker, R. Barbosa, and P. Aggleton, 81–103. Berkeley: University of California Press, 2000.

Pogge, Thomas. "Introduction." In *Freedom from Poverty as a Human Right*, edited by T. Pogge, 1–10. Oxford: Oxford University Press, 2007.

Richardson, Diane. "Desiring Sameness? The Rise of a Neoliberal Politics of Normalisation." *Antipode* 37, no. 3 (2005): 515–35. http://dx.doi.org/10.1111/j.0066 -4812.2005.00509.x.

Said, Edward. *Orientalism*. New York: Pantheon Books, 1979.

Steele, Jonathan. *Ghosts of Afghanistan: The Haunted Battleground*. Berkeley: Counterpoint Press, 2011.

United Nations. UN Treaty Collection. https://treaties.un.org/Pages/Treaties.aspx?id= 4&subid=A&lang=en (accessed February 13, 2013).

United Nations. *Declaration on the Granting of Independence to Colonial Countries and Peoples*, 1960. http://www.un.org/en/decolonization/declaration.shtml (accessed April 21, 2014).

United Nations. Universal Declaration of Human Rights, 1948. http://www.un.org/en/ documents/udhr/index.shtml (accessed August 14, 2012).

Whyte, Jessica. "Human Rights: Confronting Governments? Michel Foucault and the Right to Intervene." In *New Critical Legal Thinking: Law and the Political*, edited by M. Stone, I. Rua Wall, and C. Douzinas, 11–31. New York: Routledge, 2012.

Yeatman, Anna. "Who Is the Subject of Human Rights?" *American Behavioral Scientist* 43, no. 9 (2000): 1498–1513. http://dx.doi.org/10.1177/00027640021956017.

thirteen
Where Are All the Corporate Criminals? Understanding Struggles to Criminalize Corporate Harm and Wrongdoing

STEVEN BITTLE

Introduction

As other chapters in this collection demonstrate, criminalization processes are highly ineffective at combating crime and seriously damaging for those caught-up in an increasingly punitive crime control web. In various and important ways these authors illustrate how contemporary representations of crime individualize complex social matters, treating the individual as the source of the problem and, in the process, punishing society's most marginalized peoples. By deconstructing the crime "problem," many of these authors also shed light on the ways in which dominant discourses of crime are based on the assumption that the decision to criminalize is natural or predetermined, therein obscuring the social construction of crime and its gendered, racialized, and class-based underpinnings.[1] The Canadian government's historically varied wars on crime provide stark examples of this law-and-order agenda in action, introducing legal and policy measures aimed at getting tough on so-called street thugs, drug dealers, illegal immigrants, and gang members; the dangerous criminals who, according to dominant voices, cause the most harm to society and as a result deserve harsh, new punishments (see especially Chapter Ten).

This chapter explores how representations of crime work very differently when applied (or more aptly, rarely applied) to society's most privileged individuals who own and control large, powerful, and increasingly multinational corporations. Despite political rhetoric warning us about the perils of street crimes, the reality is that corporate crimes cause more harm than all of society's "street criminals" combined.[2] On a global scale, corporations

---

1 Dorothy Chunn and Dany Lacombe, eds., *Law as a Gendering Practice* (Toronto: Oxford University Press, 2000); Elizabeth Comack, ed., *Locating Law: Race/Class/Gender Connections*, 2nd ed. (Halifax: Fernwood Publishing, 2000).

2 Susan C. Boyd, Dorothy E. Chunn, and Robert Menzies, eds., *[Ab]using Power: The Canadian Experience* (Halifax: Fernwood Publishing, 2001); Roy Coleman, Joe Sim, Steve Tombs, and David Whyte, "Introduction: State, Power Crime," in R. Coleman, J. Sim, S. Tombs, and D. Whyte, eds., *State Power Crime* (London: Sage Publications, 2009).

annually kill hundreds of thousands of workers, injuring millions more, through unsafe and illegal working conditions;[3] kill and sicken thousands of consumers by pushing unsafe pharmaceuticals and other dangerous products onto the marketplace;[4] damage and destroy the environment by illegally dumping toxic waste into watercourses and landfills and spewing harmful cocktails of pollutants into the atmosphere;[5] and steal millions of dollars through fraudulent accounting, price fixing, and illegal insider trading.[6] However, despite the frequency and seriousness of these offences we rarely treat them as harms worthy of criminal justice intervention. In fact, as Harry Glasbeek notes, "when corporate actors commit crimes they are rarely charged; if charged, they are rarely convicted; and if convicted, they are rarely punished severely."[7]

The differential treatment accorded **corporate crime** does not mean that corporate criminals enjoy absolute immunity from the law. The state will introduce new rules and regulations in response to serious corporate financial, environmental, and health and safety disasters.[8] At the same time, however, corporate actors will respond to these control efforts by employing their considerable political, cultural, and economic resources to resist the introduction of new laws (or water them down) and pursue strategies to minimize their impact when and if they are passed.[9] Although the outcome of these struggles are far from automatic—new laws do get implemented and *some* corporations and corporate actors are held accountable for their wrongdoing—there is little denying the history of powerful interests significantly shaping the state's attempts to discipline corporations and corporate actors. As such, efforts to legislate against corporate crime have

---

3 Steve Tombs and David Whyte, *Safety Crimes* (Cullompton: Willan, 2007).

4 David O. Friedrichs, *Trusted Criminals: White Collar Crime in Contemporary Society* (Belmont: Wadsworth Cengage Learning, 2010).

5 Frank Pearce and Steve Tombs, *Bhopal: Flowers at the Altar of Profit and Power* (North Somercotes: CrimeTalk Books, 2012).

6 Gregg Barak, "Financially Respectable Crimes of Wall Street," March 20, 2012, http://www .crimetalk.org.uk/index.php?option=com_content&view=article&id=720%3Afinancially -respectable-crimes-of-wall-street&catid=38&Itemid=41 (accessed April 21, 2014); Charles Ferguson, *Predator Nation: Corporate Criminals, Political Corruption and the Hijacking of America* (New York: Crown Business, 2012); Laureen Snider, "The Conundrum of Financial Regulation: Origins, Controversies, and Prospects," *Annual Review of Law and Social Science* 21 (2011): 1–17.

7 Harry Glasbeek, *Wealth by Stealth: Corporate Crime, Corporate Law, and the Perversion of Democracy* (Toronto: Between the Lines, 2002), 118.

8 John Braithwaite, *Markets in Vice, Markets in Virtue* (Annandale: Federation Press, 2005); Fiona Haines, *The Paradox of Regulation: What Regulation Can Achieve and What It Cannot* (Cheltenham: Edward Elgar, 2011); Fiona Haines and Adam Sutton, "The Engineer's Dilemma: A Sociological Perspective on Juridification and Regulation," *Crime, Law and Social Change* 39 (2003): 1–22.

9 Glasbeek, *Wealth by Stealth*; Laureen Snider, "Cooperative Models and Corporate Crime: Panacea or Cop-Out?" *Crime and Delinquency* 36, no. 2 (1990): 373–90.

rarely resulted in dramatic improvements in corporate responsibility and in most cases have supported rather than threatened corporate capitalism.[10]

In recent years the regulation of corporate wrongdoing has been front and centre as many Western capitalist states have turned to the criminal law in an attempt to address the many abuses of corporate power.[11] In Canada, for instance, the federal government introduced Criminal Code amendments in 2004 that criminalized the failure of "organizations" to ensure the safety of workers and the public.[12] Commonly referred to as the Westray Bill, the law followed the killing of 26 miners on May 9, 1992, in an underground explosion at the Westray Mine in Plymouth, Nova Scotia, a disaster caused by unsafe and illegal working conditions (see Figure 13.1).[13] The explosion was so intense that "it blew the top off the mine entrance, more than a mile above the blast centre."[14] The public inquiry launched by the provincial government to investigate how and why the miners died found the tragedy to be "foreseeable and preventable" and unearthed evidence that, prior to the explosion, management had received more than 50 warnings about workplace health and safety violations.[15] Among the inquiry report's 74 recommendations to improve workplace safety was that the federal government introduce corporate criminal liability legislation. This recommendation eventually led to the Westray Bill.[16] Legislation criminalizing the failure to ensure workplace safety was also introduced in Australia in 1995 (taking effect in 2000), and in 2007 the government of the United Kingdom enacted corporate manslaughter and homicide legislation.

---

10 Vicente Navarro, "The Limitations of Legitimation and Fordism and the Possibility for Socialist Reforms," *Rethinking Marxism* 4, no. 2 (1991): 27–60; Laureen Snider, "Towards a Political Economy of Reform, Regulation and Corporate Crime," *Law and Policy* 9, no. 1 (1987): 37–68; Steve Tombs, "Corporate Crime and New Organizational Forms," in *Corporate Crime: Contemporary Debates*, ed. F. Pearce and L. Snider (Toronto: University of Toronto Press, 1995).

11 Fiona Haines and Andy Hall, "The Law and Order Debate in OHS," *Journal of Occupational Health and Safety* 20, no. 3 (2004): 263–73; Snider, "The Conundrum of Financial Regulation."

12 Bill C-45, An Act to Amend the Criminal Code (criminal liability of organizations), Statutes of Canada: 2003, c. 21.

13 Eric Tucker and Harry Glasbeek, "Death by Consensus: The Westray Mine Story," *New Solutions* 3, no. 4 (1993): 14–41.

14 John McMullan, "Westray and After: Power, Truth and News Reporting of the Westray Mine Disaster," in *[Ab]Using Power: The Canadian Experience*, ed. S. Boyd, D.E. Chunn, and R. Menzies (Halifax: Fernwood Publishing, 2001), 135.

15 Glasbeek, *Wealth by Stealth*, 62.

16 To read more about the Westray disaster and its aftermath, see Steven Bittle, *Still Dying for a Living: Corporate Criminal Liability after the Westray Mine Disaster* (Vancouver: UBC Press, 2012); Glasbeek, *Wealth by Stealth*; Tucker and Glasbeek, "Death by Consensus"; McMullan, "Westray and After"; John McMullan, *News, Truth, and Crime: The Westray Disaster and Its Aftermath* (Halifax: Fernwood Publishing, 2005).

Figure 13.1 The Westray Mine disaster

Meanwhile, in 2002 the US government introduced the Enron-inspired Sarbanes-Oxley Act (SOX) in response to the bursting of the stock market bubble in 2000–01, a financial debacle that revealed many highly respected corporations were created and maintained through systematic corporate fraud. Enron, an energy company once considered the darling of the US economy, is one of several US companies in the early 2000s whose executives reported that their company was continuing to make profits when it was actually losing money at an alarming rate. Commonly referred to as a **pump-and-dump scheme**, illegal financial reporting allowed Enron's share value to rise despite its *actual* performance, making major shareholders, including company CEO Kenneth Lay and other senior executives, millionaires after they unloaded their stock before the company plummeted into bankruptcy.[17] SOX was meant to prevent future Enron's by increasing reporting requirements, penalties, and oversight over audits, financial reports, corporate counsel, senior executives, and boards of directors.[18] The Canadian government soon followed suit and enacted Bill C-13 (An Act to Amend the Criminal Code [capital markets fraud and evidence gathering]), criminalizing "improper insider trading," doubling penalties for "market manipulation," and creating the offence of "tipping," or insider trading.[19]

Together these legislative measures signalled the state's growing interest in corporate crime law reform. At the same time, however, despite official claims about the need to "get tough" on corporate criminals, there are few indications of a concerted effort to "crack down" on corporate crime. The Canadian context is instructive in this regard. Since the Westray Bill's enactment in 2004 there has been only a handful of charges, resulting in one conviction and two guilty pleas, and all of the cases thus far involve small companies where there are few difficulties establishing criminal responsibility.[20] In general, criminal justice officials appear unmotivated to investigate many of the approximately 1,000 annual workplace fatalities in Canada to determine whether they involve criminal negligence.[21] Canada's markets fraud legislation has suffered a similar fate, with the RCMP's Integrated Market Enforcement Team (IMET), the federal government's enforcement strategy to increase convictions for financial fraud, having produced few charges and even fewer convictions.[22] The acquittal of three senior Nortel executives from criminal fraud in January 2012 has raised further questions about the effectiveness of the IMET and Canada's markets fraud legislation. The three executives—Frank Dunn, Douglass Beatty, and Michael Gollogly—were accused of purposely misstating company accounts (an Enron-like scenario where they were accused of "cooking the books" to make the company look like it was performing better financially than it

17 Stephen Rosoff, Henry Pontell, and Robert Tillman, *Profit without Honor: White Collar Crime and the Looting of America*, 5th ed. (Upper Saddle River: Pearson, 2010).

18 Laureen Snider, "Accommodating Power: The Common Sense of Regulators," *Social & Legal Studies* 18, no. 2 (2009): 179–97.

19 Ibid.

20 Steven Bittle and Laureen Snider, "From Manslaughter to Preventable Accident: Shaping Corporate Criminal Liability," *Law and Policy* 28, no. 4 (2006): 470–96; Steven Bittle and Laureen Snider, "Moral Panics Deflected: The Failed Legislative Response to Canada's Safety Crimes and Markets Fraud Legislation," *Crime, Law and Social Change* 56 (2011): 373–87.

21 Bittle, *Still Dying for a Living*.

22 Snider, "Accommodating Power."

actually was) to trigger more than $12 million in bonus payments for themselves. The IMET had spent years investigating the case before charging the three accused in 2008, and Crown prosecutors spent countless hours scouring thousands of pages of evidence as part of a trial that lasted a year.[23] The outcome was disappointing for those who had hoped that a successful prosecution would send the message that the Canadian government was prepared to "get serious" about corporate fraud.[24]

The factors shaping the development and (lack of) enforcement of corporate crime laws are well documented in the corporate crime literature. These include, for example, the difficulties of applying traditional notions of *mens rea* to corporate offences, or the challenges of employing traditional notions of individualized guilt to crimes committed by large and complex organizations;[25] the ability of corporations to evade and resist new laws;[26] the poorly crafted corporate crime laws that make it difficult to charge and convict corporations and powerful corporate actors;[27] and the (in)capacity of underfunded and ill-equipped regulators or criminal justice officials to prosecute corporate criminals.[28] This chapter focuses on some of the ideologically based influences that counter efforts to discipline the modern corporation; the dominant social, political, and economic knowledge claims that help to isolate "these crimes from 'crime, law and order' agendas"[29] and ensure that the state's "authoritative interventions" remain highly asymmetrical—gazing down the social hierarchy, not up.[30] Instead of demonstrating how crime and criminals are socially manufactured, as is most often the case when new laws are introduced, this chapter will document what Courtney Davis refers to as the social construction of **moral *un-panics*** in relation to corporate harm and wrongdoing.[31] Despite the devastation caused by corporations, examples

23 See *CBC News*, "Three Former Nortel Executives Acquitted in Fraud Trial," January 14, 2013, http://www.cbc.ca/news/business/3-former-nortel-executives-acquitted-in-fraud-trial-1.829361; Jeff Gray, "After Nortel Verdict, RCMP's Fraud Unit Racks Up Dismal Conviction Record," *Globe and Mail*, http://www.theglobeandmail.com/report-on-business/industry-news/the-law-page/after-nortel-verdict-rcmps-fraud-unit-racks-up-dismal-conviction-record/article7344652/.

24 Gray, "After Nortel Verdict."

25 Bittle and Snider, "From Manslaughter to Preventable Accident"; Celia Wells, *Corporations and Criminal Responsibility* (Oxford: Clarendon, 2001).

26 Friedrichs, *Trusted Criminals*; Laureen Snider, *Bad Business: Corporate Crime in Canada* (Toronto: Nelson Canada, 1993).

27 Glasbeek, *Wealth by Stealth*; Snider, *Bad Business*.

28 Barak, "Financially Respectable Crimes of Wall Street"; Tombs and Whyte, *Safety Crimes*.

29 Tombs and Whyte, *Safety Crimes*, 69.

30 Coleman, Sims, Tombs, and Whyte, "Introduction," 4.

31 Courtney Davis, *Making Companies Safe: What Works?* (London: Centre for Corporate Accountability, 2004).

of which could easily fill the pages of this entire textbook, corporate harm and wrongdoing continue to be seen largely as aberrations, the unavoidable accidents that go along with the pursuit of profit.

This chapter outlines three factors that help to reinforce and reproduce the idea that corporate crimes are not "real" crimes. First, a commitment to neoliberal political and economic reasoning—the very conditions that helped generate the harms caused by corporations and subsequent demands for law reform—makes it difficult for states to punish corporations for their wrongful acts.[32] Second, the extant neoliberal regulatory context, which is supported and maintained by academic discourses, reinforces the belief that corporations are, for the most part, good and law abiding and that corporate actors who do run afoul of the law will respond to noncriminal regulations aimed at encouraging them to act in more socially responsible ways.[33] Finally, the state's efforts at disciplining the corporation are constrained by the structure of the limited liability corporation, an inherently criminogenic endeavour fixated on the accumulation of short-term profits.[34] In this respect, despite the introduction of new laws to deal with the abuse of corporate power, the corporation remains a "capitalist site"[35] that routinely produces serious social, economic, and environmental harms. At the same time, however, it would be erroneous to suggest that these influences are automatic or absolute. As we shall see, protest movements like Occupy Wall Street offer examples of grassroots resistances from below that challenge the abuse of corporate power and demand a more equitable distribution of wealth and resources in society.

What follows, then, invites us to reflect on how we think about corporate harm and wrongdoing differently than traditional crime. It asks us to take a step back from our day-to-day lives—to think analytically, as you are often challenged to do in university—to reflect on the factors that shape our thinking and influence our actions. In essence we need to deconstruct the way that we understand and as a result respond (or do not respond) to corporate crime in contemporary society. For instance, the way that we study crime in university shapes and is shaped by the society in which we live.[36] Courses in criminology historically have focused on crimes as they

---

32 Steve Tombs, "State-Corporate Symbiosis in the Production of Crime and Harm," *State Crime* 1, no. 2 (2012).

33 Tombs and Whyte, *Safety Crimes.*

34 Glasbeek, *Wealth by Stealth*; Harry Glasbeek, "The Corporation as a Legally Created Site of Irresponsibility," in *International Handbook of White-Collar and Corporate Crime*, ed. H.N. Pontell and G. Geis (New York: Springer, 2007).

35 Stephen A. Resnick and Richard D. Wolff, *Knowledge and Class: A Marxian Critique of Political Economy* (Chicago: University of Chicago Press, 1987), 229.

36 Colin Sumner, *The Sociology of Deviance: An Obituary* (Buckingham: Open University Press, 1994).

are defined officially by the state, such as youth crime, gangs, interpersonal violence, illegal drugs, organized crime, and so on. This observation is not meant to dismiss these subjects as unimportant or downplay the critical literature that you may have read in these areas, but simply to point out that corporate crime has been, and remains, a relatively marginal subject within the study of crime. As such, our preoccupation with traditional forms of crime helps to reinforce dominant beliefs about what crime is and what acts are deserving of criminal justice intervention. Another example is that our thoughts and beliefs about corporate crime are a product of our experiences living in a capitalist society. Take a look around your next lecture and observe how many students have the latest laptop or smartphone or are wearing the newest fashion trends. While many of us enjoy these luxuries, we rarely stop to ask if the corporation that made these products used child labour from a developing country, if they harmed the environment in the production process, or if they illegally conspired with other companies to inflate the item's purchase price. We are inundated with messages that corporations are a force of "good" in society (messages provided mostly by corporations themselves)—messages that overshadow the many and serious harms regularly committed by corporations.

Consistent with the chapter's focus on critically examining definitions of corporate crime, a key focus will be that language or discourse matters; they do not determine, but significantly shape our thinking and actions.[37] At the same time, however, we must recognize that discourses about corporate crime do not emerge in a vacuum, but instead are constitutive of (i.e., they shape and are shaped by) the broader context.[38] In this respect we need to situate the language used to describe corporate harm and wrongdoing within its social, political, and economic context. A key element of this involves determining what gives certain discourses their "truthfulness" or "appropriateness."[39] Why are certain discourses about corporate crime given more credence than others? Whose knowledge claims have legs[40] when it comes to defining the nature and scope of corporate crime and if or how we should respond through law?

Since this chapter is concerned with the **regulation** and control of corporate crime, it will focus particularly on the role of legal discourses in shaping our understanding of corporate wrongdoing. Law and the state play an

---

37 R. Ericson and Kevin D. Haggerty, *Policing the Risk Society* (Oxford: Claredon Press, 1997).

38 Tombs and Whyte, *Safety Crimes*.

39 Bernard McKenna, "Critical Discourse Studies: Where to from Here?" *Critical Discourse Studies* 1, no. 1 (2004): 9–39.

40 Laureen Snider, "The Sociology of Corporate Crime: An Obituary (or: Whose Knowledge Claims Have Legs?)" *Theoretical Criminology* 4, no. 2 (2000): 196–206.

important role in ordering relations of power in society.[41] It is, after all, decisions made within state relations that significantly influence which laws will be created and under which conditions they will be, or perhaps will not be, enforced. However, as we reflect on the development of legal discourses about corporate crime we need to keep in mind that law is not a "homogenous force" that determines social relations. That is, law's effects are not automatic or absolute; law is instead a powerful constraining and enabling practice that "plays a significant role in the process of governing life."[42] The point is that law is not simply a container of ideologies, capitalist or otherwise; as Kevyn Bonnycastle notes, it is "a site where particular ideologies are (re)produced."[43] We could also think of this in terms of law having a "distinctly social basis" in that it shapes and is shaped by the broader social context.[44]

Thinking about law's social underpinnings reminds us that law and legal struggles do not automatically or necessarily reproduce powerful interests.[45] Corporate crime law and its reform is therefore not a predetermined outcome; corporate power and influence is not absolute and the introduction of new laws to address corporate harm and wrongdoing is not impossible. If corporate power was omnipotent, then the state would never introduce corporate crime laws and corporations and senior corporate executives would never be held accountable for any of their harmful or illegal acts. Positing an all-powerful state that always or automatically supports corporate capitalism is therefore empirically incorrect as well as theoretically incomplete.[46] As Bob Jessop notes, the state is both "operationally autonomous" and "institutionally separate" from the capitalist system, which means there is no a priori guarantee that the state will either advance or challenge the interests of capitalism.[47]

Corporate Crime: Here Today, Gone Tomorrow

The first factor contouring the development and enforcement of corporate crime laws that we will examine is the neoliberal political and economic discourse that extols the virtues of the corporation while downplaying the

---

41 Brendy Cossman and Judy Fudge, *Privatization, Law and the Challenge to Feminism* (Toronto: University of Toronto Press, 2002).

42 Chunn and Lacombe, *Law as a Gendering Practice*, 14.

43 Kevyn Bonnycastle, "Rape Uncodified: Reconsidering Bill C-49 Amendments to Canadian Sexual Assault Laws," in *Law as a Gendering Practice*, ed. Dorothy Chunn and Dany Lacombe (Toronto: Oxford University Press, 2000), 65.

44 Comack, *Locating Law*, 11.

45 Bob Jessop, *The Future of the Capitalist State* (Cambridge: Polity Press, 2002).

46 Comack, *Locating Law*; Frank Pearce and Steve Tombs, *Toxic Capitalism: Corporate Crime and the Chemical Industry* (Toronto: Canadian Scholars' Press, 1999).

47 Jessop, *The Future of the Capitalist State*, 41.

harms that it causes. Over the past 40 years, Western capitalist states have witnessed an enormous increase in the power, influence, and profit-making capacities of the corporation.[48] The corporation started to increase its prominence in the early 1970s after fears of stagflation (high levels of inflation and unemployment) and growing global economic competition led many business leaders to raise questions about the viability of the Keynesian welfare state.[49] Keynesian economic principles, which emerged in the aftermath of the Great Depression of the 1930s, posited that the state needed to offset the downside of "capital's relentless drive to accumulate" by (at least theoretically) providing citizens with a suitable standard of living, or what was commonly referred to as the "universal social safety net."[50] However, with an end to the postwar worker shortage—propelled by a growing number of women working outside the home, an influx of new immigrants seeking employment, and increasingly global and technologically driven production processes—dominant corporate voices challenged Keynesian thinking and pushed for greater economic freedoms.[51] Fuelled by neoclassical economic reasoning, which argues for minimal state intervention in the free market economy, most Western capitalist governments responded by abandoning their welfare state ideals, reducing corporate taxes, and reconfiguring the regulatory environment in pro-business and market-friendly ways.[52] **Free market enterprise** was thus deemed to be the most effective and efficient means of generating and distributing economic benefits in society.[53]

Unfortunately, there were more than a few problems with neoliberal economic ideals.[54] Despite promises that everyone would benefit from the "free" market system (the so-called *trickle-down theory* that rich corporations would produce jobs and other economic benefits for society), the truth is that incomes rose and wealth increased only for the privileged few. What is particularly important to grasp for our understanding of the regulation of corporate crime is that neoliberal discourses paved the way for corporations to argue that

48 Glasbeek, *Wealth by Stealth*; Pearce and Tombs, *Toxic Capitalism*.
49 David Harvey, *The Enigma of Capital and the Crises of Capitalism* (New York: Oxford University Press, 2010); Steven A. Resnick and Richard Wolff, "The Economic Crisis: A Marxian Interpretation," *Rethinking Marxism: A Journal of Economics, Culture & Society* 22 (2010): 170–86.
50 Cossman and Fudge, *Privatization, Law and the Challenge to Feminism*.
51 R. Wolff, "In Capitalist Crisis, Rediscovering Marx," *Socialism and Democracy* 24, no. 3 (2010): 138–39.
52 Cossman and Fudge, *Privatization, Law and the Challenge to Feminism*.
53 Susanne Soederberg, *Corporate Power and Ownership in Contemporary Capitalism: The Politics of Resistance and Domination* (London: Routledge, 2010); Wolff, "In Capitalism Crisis, Rediscovering Marx."
54 See Harvey, *The Enigma of Capital and the Crises of Capitalism*; Resnick and Wolff, "The Economic Crisis"; Soederberg, *Corporate Power and Ownership in Contemporary Capitalism*.

criminal laws and government oversight were unnecessary given that market reputation was sufficient to keep corporations "honest"—nobody would want to conduct business with or work for a corporate deviant.[55] As a result, governments became increasingly disinterested with combating corporate harm and wrongdoing,[56] instead accepting that corporations were (and are) an inherent social and economic good.[57] Today, corporations occupy such a prominent role in society—providing us with much-needed employment (even if these are increasingly precarious and low-paying jobs) and the latest technological gadgets and athletic shoes—that it is difficult for us to think about them as criminals.

The priority accorded to corporate crime in recent decades has been very different than the state's "zero tolerance" approach toward street crimes.[58] In particular, while the state was busy cozying up to corporations, it was at the same time getting more and more punitive in response to street crimes.[59] However, it is important to understand that the state's admiration for corporations does not mean that it got completely out of the regulation business, but that it shifted its regulatory responsibilities in ways that benefited businesses and encouraged market "efficiency."[60] As Steve Tombs reminds us, it took a considerable amount of work by the state to create a pro-business regulatory environment and to create rules for corporations to self-regulate with minimal government interference.[61]

In the end, the ascendancy of neoliberal political and economic reasoning gave corporations the leeway to run their businesses in the most "efficient" possible way. In most cases this entailed extracting the maximum amount of labour for the minimum amount of pay, exploiting the burgeoning financial markets to the greatest extent possible, and externalizing all social and environmental costs.[62] Unfortunately, this "freedom" had an ominous downside, evidenced by a seemingly endless list of high-profile corporate

---

55 Joel Bakan, *The Corporation: The Pathological Pursuit of Profit and Power* (Toronto: Penguin Canada, 2004); R.H. Tillman, and M.L. Indergaard, *Pump and Dump: The Rancid Rules of the New Economy* (New Brunswick: Rutgers University Press, 2005); Snider, "The Sociology of Corporate Crime."

56 Frank Pearce and Laureen Snider, eds., *Corporate Crime: Contemporary Debates* (Toronto: University of Toronto Press, 1995).

57 Snider, "The Sociology of Corporate Crime."

58 John Braithwaite, "What's Wrong with the Sociology of Punishment?" *Theoretical Criminology* 7, no. 1 (2003): 5–28.

59 Cossman and Fudge, *Privatization, Law and the Challenge to Feminism*; Tombs and Whyte, *Safety Crimes*.

60 Cossman and Fudge, *Privatization, Law and the Challenge to Feminism*; Leo Panitch and Martijn Konings, "Myths of Neoliberal Deregulation," *New Left Review* 57 (2009): 67–83.

61 Tombs, "State-Corporate Symbiosis in the Production of Crime and Harm."

62 Bakan, *The Corporation*; Glasbeek, *Wealth by Stealth*.

debacles and disasters throughout the 1980s and 1990s. In addition to the aforementioned Westray disaster[63] and the "Enronitis" leading to the bursting of the technology stock market bubble in the early 2000s,[64] these harms include the explosion at the Union Carbide chemical plant in Bhopal, India, that immediately killed as many as 10,000 people;[65] the killing of more than 200 passengers and crew with the sinking of the sea ferry, the *Herald of Free Enterprise*, off the Belgian coast in 1987;[66] the systemic corporate frauds associated with the 2008 housing crisis in the United States and the resulting collapse of the global economy;[67] and the 2010 explosion at British Petroleum's Gulf of Mexico oil drilling platform, Deep Water Horizon, killing 11 workers and generating the largest oil spill in US history.[68] These disasters, among others, starkly revealed the limits of under-regulated global capitalism and produced calls for the state to do something about the growing abuse of corporate power.

Regardless if serious corporate harm and wrongdoing compelled legislators to contemplate law reform, any desire to discipline the corporation failed to erupt into the "war on crime" that we have witnessed in response to street crimes. Noteworthy is the state's contradictory position of having to legislate against corporate wrongdoing within a neoliberal context that represented (and still represents) a significant ideological pull or dominant common sense that downplays the seriousness of corporate crime and the need to intervene through law. Signs of the free market's hypnotic spell (governments have become extremely reliant on corporations to fuel the economy, provide voters with jobs, and hence to gain re-election) first emerged through the belief among legislators that law reform was only necessary to hold *some* corporations (primarily the "bad apples" or rogue corporations) accountable for their wrongful acts, as well as through arguments that any laws that were implemented should not treat corporations too harshly. Surely these offences are only a blip in capitalism's radar, dominant political and private-sector voices argued, so let's not get carried away by rushing into any law-and-order agendas. In Canada, for instance, it took more than 10 years after the Westray disaster and much political discussion and debate before Parliament introduced

---

63 Tucker and Glasbeek, "Death by Consensus."

64 Soederberg, *Corporate Power and Ownership in Contemporary Capitalism.*

65 Pearce and Tombs, *Bhopal*; Pearce and Tombs, *Toxic Capitalism.*

66 Tombs and Whyte, *Safety Crimes.*

67 Resnick and Wolff, "The Economic Crisis."

68 Vincenzo Ruggiero and Nigel South, "Critical Criminology and Crimes against the Environment," *Critical Criminology* 18 (2010): 245–50.

legal reforms. What is more, in contemplating the introduction of the Westray Bill, legislators questioned the wisdom of criminalizing corporations and cautioned against overly stringent laws that would impede the corporation's ability to accumulate profits.[69] Similar concerns with the smooth functioning of business also surfaced with Canada's markets fraud legislation, beginning with the federal government's promise to reserve the law's use for cases that "threaten the national interest in the integrity of capital markets."[70] And shortly after the law's introduction, regulators started to "rethink" their enforcement strategies, lamenting the difficulty of criminally prosecuting such complex cases.[71] While these dominant beliefs were far from absolute—that is, they did not determine the state's legislative efforts—they nevertheless signalled a reluctance to criminalize corporate wrongdoing.

It is hard to imagine legislators struggling with "cracking down" on gun crimes, drug dealers, or illegal immigrants. In this respect, the neoliberal commitment to minimal state intervention is buttressed by culturally rooted beliefs that conceptualize corporate offending differently than traditional street crimes. Media representations of crime aptly capture the different ways that we think about corporate crimes compared to street crimes. Although media do not determine how we, as a society, understand and respond to crime, it does importantly reflect dominant political and popular culture representations of crime.[72] While news about the latest bank robbery, home invasion, gang violence, drug bust, or mugging dominate media reporting, corporate offending receives considerably less attention, most typically in the context of stories about disasters like Westray or the Nortel scandal. Consider, for example, the different news headlines in Figure 13.2. Note how the headlines pertaining to street crimes employ sensationalistic language, while the descriptions of corporate offending suggest that something less ominous has occurred. Why do we so readily describe the offences committed by the most marginalized individuals in society in sensationalistic terms while largely ignoring the serious harms committed by powerful corporate actors? Why do rich, mostly white men who run major corporations get a "free pass" when it comes to being held accountable in the media for running corporations

---

69 Bittle and Snider, "From Manslaughter to Preventable Accident"; Bittle and Snider, "Moral Panics Deflected."

70 R. Mackay and M. Smith, "Bill C-13: An Act to Amend the Criminal Code (Capital Markets Fraud and Evidence-Gathering)" (Ottawa: Parliamentary Research Branch, Legislative summary, LS-468E, 2004), as quoted in Snider, "Accommodating Power," 184.

71 Snider, "Accommodating Power."

72 Richard Ericson, Patricia M. Baranek, and Janet B.L. Chan, *Representing Order: Crime, Law and Justice in the News Media* (Toronto: University of Toronto Press, 1991).

Figure 13.2 Examples of headlines about crime and corporate wrongdoing from Canadian newspapers

---

Homicide probe has town stunned
(Winnipeg Free Press, 21 January 2013: A3)

Woman slain in Etobicoke: One person in custody as police probe death of young female victim
(Toronto Star, 20 January 2013: A2)

Fatal stabbing a 'targeted' attack
(Calgary Herald 19 January 2013: B4)

Verdict a major setback for corporate fraud squad
(The Globe and Mail 15 January 2013: B5)

Top court will hear Enron appeal; Former CEO Jeff Skilling 'overwhelmed with joy'
(Edmonton Journal 14 October 2009: F3)

Coco Paving fined $212,505 in death
(The Windsor Star 18 January 2013: A3)

---

that seriously injure or kill workers or members of the public, destroy the environment, or steal millions of dollars?

A (re)commitment to neoliberal political and economic reasoning also followed the 2008 collapse of the global economy. This time the US government was confronted by the reality that some of the country's most "respected" financial institutions were built on systematic corruption and fraud—offences that resulted in the most significant economic downturn since the Great Depression.[73] However, despite the clear links between the crisis and risky and fraudulent securities transactions within the financial sector, the US government responded, not by "getting tough" on corporate crime, but by bailing out to the tune of $700 billion the very institutions responsible for the disaster.[74] What is more, as Gregg Barak notes, "some four years after the Wall Street debacle, no senior executives from any of the major financial institutions have been criminally charged, prosecuted or imprisoned for any types of securities fraud."[75]

The resulting global financial crisis has led most Western democratic governments, including Canada, to adopt a series of austerity measures aimed at "protecting" the economy, for which we can read guarding the role of corporations as the economy's primary wealth-generating mechanism.[76] As

73 Barak, "Financially Respectable Crimes of Wall Street"; Ferguson, *Predator Nation.*

74 Harvey, *The Enigma of Capital and the Crises of Capitalism*; Steve Tombs, "Foreword: The Struggle for Corporate Accountability," in *Still Dying for a Living: Corporate Criminal Liability after the Westray Mine Disaster*, S. Bittle (Vancouver: UBC Press, 2012).

75 Barak, "Financially Respectable Crimes of Wall Street."

76 Carlo Fanelli and Bryan Evans, eds., *Great Recession-Proof? Shattering the Myth of Canadian Exceptionalism* (Ottawa: Red Quill Books, 2013).

part of these measures states have cut spending across the board, including "costly" government regulatory programs and "unnecessary" bureaucratic interventions, leaving us, once again, in a period of "regulatory retreat."[77] What is particularly important for questions of regulating corporate harm and wrongdoing is that economic downturns are never conducive to "cracking down" on corporate crime,[78] with governments more concerned with (re)ensuring business-friendly climates than policing corporate wrongdoing. In this respect, the state's continued dependence on private enterprise raises questions about its desire and ability to discipline the corporation—whether there are "no-go areas"[79] for the capitalist state in holding corporations accountable.

Aren't (Noncriminal) Regulations Better Anyway?

A second and related factor that contours the development and enforcement of contemporary corporate crime laws is the neoliberal-inspired regulatory common sense that characterizes the policing of corporate crimes. Steve Tombs and Dave Whyte note that the history of corporate crime control is based on a "bifurcated model of criminal process," which entails attempts to *assimilate* corporate deviance into traditional criminal law by amending the mainstream criminal process to respond to corporate offenders, and efforts to *differentiate* corporate deviance from traditional crime by responding to it through a separate regulatory framework.[80] While legal reforms discussed in this chapter represent attempts to assimilate corporate deviance into the realm of criminal law, along with the challenges of doing so, in opposition stands the dominant model of responding to corporate wrongdoing that differentiates it from traditional crimes.[81] That is, corporate offences have been and continue to be dealt with primarily within a noncriminal regulatory framework.[82] Regulation generally relies on persuasion and education to ensure that organizations comply with particular rules, with punishment only as a last resort.[83]

---

77 Tombs, "Foreword: The Struggle for Corporate Accountability."

78 Gary Slapper and Steve Tombs, *Corporate Crime* (Essex: Pearson Education, 1999), 177.

79 Steve Tombs and David Whyte, "The State and Corporate Crime," in *State Power Crime*, ed. R. Coleman, J. Sim, S. Tombs, and D. Whyte (London: Sage Publications, 2009).

80 Tombs and Whyte, *Safety Crimes*, 110.

81 Ibid., 3.

82 Garry C. Gray, "The Regulation of Corporate Violations: Punishment, Compliance, and the Blurring of Responsibility," *British Journal of Criminology* 46, no. 5 (2006): 875–92.

83 Sally Simpson, *Corporate Crime, Law and Social Control* (Cambridge: Cambridge University Press, 2002), 93.

Regulatory offences are characterized as **inchoate offences** in that they focus on attempts rather than results.[84] This means that, unlike traditional crimes where the offender is charged with assault or robbery, for example, corporate offenders are most often charged with breaching a regulatory standard. For instance, Celia Wells notes how workplace deaths are rarely treated as homicides but instead as incomplete acts or attempts, such as the failure to provide safe working conditions. In the process, Wells argues, the language of regulation obscures the severity of injury and death in the workplace and reinforces the belief that they are "accidents," not crimes of violence.[85]

Since the early 1980s, within the context of neoliberalism, the dominant response to corporate offences has been regulation rooted in cooperation.[86] Cooperative or compliance strategies emphasize "persuasion and bargaining," or the idea that corporations need guidance and do not respond well to chastisement and deterrence.[87] This approach espouses **self-regulation** in that it trusts that corporations will "monitor and control their own compliance with the law under a minimalist regulatory framework."[88] Regulators cooperate with corporations to build consensus regarding the most effective ways to self-regulate, an approach that is based on the belief that, on the whole, individuals are "reasonable, of good faith, and motivated to heed advice."[89]

The advent of cooperative or compliance models of regulation have two important implications for our current discussion of the governance and control of corporate crime. First, recently developed corporate crime laws have been introduced against a backdrop of well-established noncriminal rules and regulations. In Canada, for instance, provincial regulations deal with occupational health and safety offences. This means that criminal law recently introduced to deal with corporate crime—the Westray Bill—has had to compete against a noncriminal structure and process, both practically from an enforcement viewpoint (it is most often easier to enforce noncriminal rules than undertake costly criminal prosecutions) and ideologically in terms of which mechanism constitutes the most appropriate and acceptable method for responding to corporate harm and wrongdoing. While provincial regulators are mandated to investigate and enforce noncriminal rules

---

84 Celia Wells, *Corporations and Criminal Responsibility* (Oxford: Clarendon, 1993), 6.

85 Ibid., 12.

86 Tombs and Whyte, *Safety Crimes*.

87 Slapper and Tombs, *Corporate Crime*, 165–69.

88 Tombs and Whyte, *Safety Crimes*, 166, fn. 14.

89 John Braithwaite, *Crime, Shame and Reintegration* (Cambridge: Cambridge University Press, 1989), 131.

and regulations, turning cases over to the police if they suspect that criminal liability is involved, Crown prosecutors and police are more accustomed to dealing with street crimes, not complex investigations of corporate crimes. This is the dominant common sense of criminal law and its enforcement— the "real" stuff of cops and robbers. As Harry Glasbeek notes, an inherent bias against criminalizing corporations and corporate actors "saturates the efforts of the police forces, prosecutorial offices, and policymaking institutions."[90] Within this context the regulatory status quo helps to reinforce the dominant belief that corporate offences are not "real" crimes; they are *mala prohibita* (wrong because prohibited), not *mala in se* (inherently evil and wrong).

Second, the ascendancy of self-regulation as it applies to corporate offences has spawned an industry of compliance scholars dedicated to understanding how best to apply these rules to the corporate realm.[91] In general, compliance scholars caution against using criminal law strategies against corporations and instead emphasize "persuasion and bargaining" to facilitate corporate compliance with the law.[92] Compliance scholars argue that strict legal enforcement produces "legalism," or assigning a uniform set of regulatory requirements when they are not always necessary;[93] that punishment instills resistance in corporate actors who become defensive and unresponsive to regulatory measures;[94] and that criminal law approaches are too costly (i.e., full enforcement is not practical) and are problematic in that the act must progress far enough along the causal chain of events to collect sufficient evidence for prosecution.[95] While there is no denying that compliance school scholars want to develop regulations that prevent corporate harm and wrongdoing, we should nevertheless ask ourselves if they take for granted the

90 Glasbeek, *Wealth by Stealth*, 149.
91 Eugene Bardach and Robert Kagan, *Going by the Book: The Problem of Regulatory Unreasonableness* (Philadelphia: Temple University Press, 1982); Keith Hawkins, *Environment and Enforcement: Regulation and the Social Definition of Pollution* (Oxford: Clarendon Press, 1984); Keith Hawkins, ed., *The Human Face of Law* (Oxford: Claredon Press, 1997); Keith Hawkins, *Law as a Last Resort: Prosecution Decision Making in a Regulatory Authority* (Oxford: Oxford University Press, 2002); Bridget Hutter, *The Reasonable Arm of the Law? The Law Enforcement Procedures of Environmental Health Officers* (Oxford: Claredon Press, 1988); Robert Kagan and John Scholz, "The Criminology of the Corporation and Regulatory Enforcement Strategies," in *Enforcing Regulation*, ed. K. Hawkins and J. Thomas (Boston: Kluwer-Hijhoff, 1984).
92 Slapper and Tombs, *Corporate Crime*, 165–69; Tombs and White, *Safety Crimes*, 166.
93 Bardach and Kagan, *Going by the Book*; Kagan and Scholz, "The Criminology of the Corporation and Regulatory Enforcement Strategies."
94 Kagan and Scholz, "The Criminology of the Corporation and Regulatory Enforcement Strategies," 73.
95 Snider, "Cooperative Models and Corporate Crime," 376.

ideologically based distinction between regulation and criminal law—that is, if by failing to question fully why corporate wrongdoing is dealt with through regulations instead of criminal law they reinforce the belief that corporate offending is different than "real" crime—and if they sufficiently question the neoliberal doctrine that underpins the existing regulatory context.

Critics of compliance scholars charge that, contrary to dominant claims that cooperative styles of regulation are flexible and consistent with market efficiency, in practice these strategies work predominantly to the advantage of powerful corporate interests.[96] In particular, corporations simply will not self-regulate in the absence of external pressures (evidenced by the corporate disasters outlined in this chapter) and corporate executives will falsify records to deceive regulators and corporations, agreeing to self-regulate only in symbolical terms and under limited conditions.[97] Critics also charge that the compliance school argument that strict enforcement does not work is hypothetical, since this style of enforcement has yet to occur in a sustained manner.[98] Compliance scholars are therefore criticized for confounding the way things are with the way things should or must be. As Frank Pearce and Steve Tombs argue, "their work is limited because *the legitimacy of a capitalist system and the illegitimacy of its being policed are in fact starting-points for their analysis.*"[99]

The profound harms caused by corporations over the past several decades do not exactly constitute a "ringing endorsement for compliance-oriented enforcement."[100] Nevertheless, the ideological dominance of status quo regulation, backed up by "credible" academic voices, remains strong. In fact, so ingrained is this belief that some corporate crime scholars continue to pledge support for cooperative models despite their self-admitted lack of empirical support. As Steve Tombs notes, this commitment to "realistic" forms of regulation is starkly illustrated in the comments by the editors of a recent special edition of *Criminology and Public Policy* dedicated to addressing the aftermath of the 2008 financial-sector collapse. In the face of all the

---

96 Charles Noble, "Regulating Work in a Capitalist Society," in *Corporate Crime: Contemporary Debates*, ed. F. Pearce and L. Snider (Toronto: University of Toronto Press, 1995), 271–72.

97 Garry C. Gray, "The Responsibilization Strategy of Health and Safety: Neo-liberalism and the Reconfiguration of Individual Responsibility for Risk," *British Journal of Criminology* 49 (2009): 326–42; John McMullan, *Beyond the Limits of the Law: Corporate Crime and Law and Order* (Halifax: Fernwood Publishing, 1992); Slapper and Tombs, *Corporate Crime*.

98 Tombs and Whyte, *Safety Crimes*, 156.

99 Frank Pearce and Steve Tombs, "Ideology Hegemony and Empiricism: Compliance Theories of Regulation," *British Journal of Criminology* 30 (1990): 429. Emphasis in original.

100 Slapper and Tombs, *Corporate Crime*, 189.

corporate harms that have occurred in recent decades, the editors do not question the regulatory status quo, but instead advocate for more of the same:

> There is currently a remarkably optimistic consensus in some
> academic quarters about how to reduce the harm caused by
> privileged predators. The heart of it lies in the presumed promise of
> pluralistic, cooperative approaches, and responsive regulation. These
> assumptions highlight the need for enhanced prevention, more
> diverse and more effective internal oversight and self-monitoring, and
> more efficient and effective external oversight. They have gained use
> throughout a variety of regulatory realms, many since their earliest,
> albeit embryonic, formulation nearly three decades ago ... They make
> sense theoretically, and we endorse them. We do so not because
> they have a record of demonstrable success but principally because
> sole or excessive reliance on state oversight and threat of criminal
> prosecution is difficult, costly, and uncertain. Still, we are mindful,
> as others should be, that the onset of the Great Recession occurred
> during and despite the tight embrace of self-regulation, pluralistic
> oversight, and notions of self-regulating markets by policy makers and
> many academicians.[101]

With this common sense firmly entrenched, it is not difficult to understand how criminal laws in this area have gained little traction. The question therefore becomes whether we should rethink dominant regulatory approaches to consider whether there is a role for criminal law strategies, both in terms of the symbolic import of naming corporate harm and wrongdoing and as a possible deterrent for future offending.

New Laws, Same Old Criminogenic Corporation

The final factor that casts a long shadow over the state's efforts to regulate corporate harm and wrongdoing is the legal structure and mandate of the modern corporation. As many critical corporate crime scholars argue, the modern corporation's incessant demand for profit maximization—corporations as amoral calculators—makes it inherently

---

101 Peter G. Grabosky and Neal Shover, "Forestalling the Next Epidemic of White-Collar Crime," *Criminology and Public Policy* 9, no. 3 (2010): 641–42; as quoted in Tombs, "Foreward," xii.

criminogenic.[102] For some observers these tendencies are prominently demonstrated through the corporation's evolution from being primarily a site of production (where things get made) to a vehicle fixated on generating maximal profits in the financial markets.[103] In many respect these criminogenic conditions are facilitated by the corporation's constitution as a "creature of statute" with its own "legal existence" that is separate from those who invest in it.[104] In essence it is a natural, independent person, regardless of whether one or more individuals own shares in the company.[105] A vital aspect of this arrangement is limited liability, whereby the primary risk for the individual investor is the money that he or she provides to the venture.[106]

Although the notion of limited liability was historically a privilege bestowed by the state—a structure from which corporations could serve the public interest—this privilege soon turned into an unassailable right once governments and investors realized the potential of corporations as a significant revenue-generating mechanism.[107] Despite some historical variations in its general purposes, the corporation's main motivation evolved into profit maximization for shareholders who invest in the limited liability corporation.[108] And while this does not mean that the corporation always or necessarily acts as an amoral calculator—that is, corporations can be constrained by law and, occasionally, by demands from society to act responsibly—we must also understand that the bottom line significantly informs decisions made by corporate boards of directors and senior executives.[109] This means that, for instance, decisions about how to run the corporation as efficiently as possible are not always congruent with ensuring worker safety, respecting the environment, or following legal financial practices. Meanwhile, the company's shareholders, a majority of whom are far removed from the corporation's

---

102 Glasbeek, *Wealth by Stealth*; Pearce and Tombs, *Toxic Capitalism*; Tombs and Whyte, *Safety Crimes*.

103 Glasbeek, *Wealth by Stealth*; Harry Glasbeek, "Enron and Its Aftermath: Can Reforms Restore Confidence?" in *Crime in the Corporation*, ed. A.I. Anand, J.A. Connidis, and W.F. Flannagan (Queen's Annual Business Law Symposium, Queen's University, Kingston, 2004); Roman Tomisac, "Corporate Collapse, Crime and Governance—Enron, Anderson and Beyond," *Australia Journal of Business Law* 14, no. 2 (2002): 183–201.

104 Robert Yalden, Janis Sarra, Paul Paton, Mark Gillen, Ronald Davis, and Mary Condon, *Business Organizations: Principles, Policies and Practice* (Toronto: Emond Montgomery Publications, 2008), 133.

105 Ibid., 135.

106 Snider, *Bad Business*.

107 Snider, *Bad Business*, 22; see also Bakan, *The Corporation*; Glasbeek, *Wealth by Stealth*.

108 Thomas Clarke, ed., *Theories of Corporate Governance: The Philosophical Foundations of Corporate Governance* (London: Routledge, 2004); Glasbeek, "Enron and Its Aftermath."

109 Pearce and Tombs, *Toxic Capitalism*.

inner workings, await the corporation's profits without the burden of worrying about the harms that the corporation might cause along the way.[110]

The limited liability corporation therefore represents a significant stumbling block for the state's efforts to discipline the corporation. In particular, despite recent efforts to introduce new criminal laws to confront the abuse of corporate power, the corporation remains a capitalist site that is fixated on pursuing (short-term) profits. In this respect, while corporate crime laws give the illusion of change—"let's crack down on these corporate miscreants!"—corporations can, for the most part, continue to operate with their best (economic) interests in mind. While this does not mean that we need to abandon efforts to hold corporations accountable for their harmful and illegal acts, including attempts to hold the individuals hiding behind the limited liability corporation criminally responsible for these offences,[111] it does remind us that there is much more to addressing the problem of corporate crime than what can be achieved through law reform.

Desperately required, therefore, is the capacity to think beyond the regulation of corporate crime as a technical problem—that is, how much regulation is required to discipline the corporation?—to examine the "broader socioeconomic realities of life in a capitalist system."[112] The (ongoing) inability or unwillingness of the state to discipline the corporation should be cause for concern, particularly given that corporations and senior corporate executives continue to commit crimes with little fear of being caught or punished.[113] Even more puzzling is that, regardless of the long list of corporate crimes committed over the past three decades (some of which are outlined in this chapter), and in the face of the most serious economic downturn since the Great Depression, the balance of power continues to favour neoliberal and global capitalist interests.[114] Faith in the "free" market has been tested and new laws enacted, but the near religious-like commitment to neoliberalism remains strong.

Corporate crime scholars Kate Burdis and Steve Tombs lament the loss of "truly transformative political ideals" within criminology, which they attribute to the discipline's preoccupation with crimes at the lower end of the social hierarchy (the so-called street criminals) and to the many corporate

---

110 Glasbeek, *Wealth by Stealth*; Glasbeek, "The Corporation as a Legally Created Site of Irresponsibility."

111 Glasbeek, *Wealth by Stealth*.

112 Snider, "Cooperative Models and Corporate Crime," 380.

113 Glenn Greenwald, *With Liberty and Justice for Some: How the Law Is Used to Destroy Equality and Protect the Powerful* (New York: Metropolitan Books, 2011).

114 Colin Crouch, *The Strange Non-Death of Neoliberalism* (Cambridge: Polity Press, 2011); Richard Dienst, *The Bonds of Debt: Borrowing Against the Common Good* (New York: Verso Books, 2011).

crime scholars who conceive the problem of corporate harm and wrong-doing in individualistic terms that can be addressed through improved regulation (e.g., the compliance scholarship discussed previously).[115] The authors argue that we need to escape this myopic thinking to embrace criminology's more radical and transformative roots—roots that have been largely ignored or forgotten.[116] In addition to pursuing reforms that can help protect individuals in society from the abuses of power, as with the struggles for corporate crime law reform discussed in this chapter, they advocate for broader social change. As Burdis and Tombs argue, "It is only if and when we can address the overhaul of the current form of economic organisation that the reduction of the deep cultural malaise and systematic violence inherent within contemporary capitalism becomes possible."[117]

The current economic crisis should invite us to consider whether capitalism itself has reached its limits—whether its time is up and that we need seriously to consider a different, more socially just and equitable way to organize society.[118] Until we're prepared to entertain this possibility and democratically discuss and debate the type of society that we want to live in, then the most we can expect is a series of reforms that may make capitalism "a little less socially and ecologically harmful,"[119] but leaves intact the very system that is the root of the problem. For inspiration we can look to various grassroots movements, or resistances from below, aimed at raising awareness about the abuse of corporate power or confronting the related and growing social and economic inequalities in society. The **Occupy Wall Street** movement (see Figure 13.3) is one example of this growing unrest, along with protests in opposition to the construction of oil pipelines across Canada and the United States and efforts in Canada by the labour/union movement to ensure the adequate enforcement of the Westray Bill. The Occupy Wall Street movement emerged following the 2008 global financial crisis, which was a crisis caused by systematic greed and financial fraud within the banking industry in the United States. Occupy protesters have expressed their frustration with the lack of accountability among the economic elite who were responsible for creating the greatest economic downturn since the Great Depression, and with the growing and massive social and economic

---

115 Kate Burdis and Steve Tombs, "After the Crisis: New Directions in Theorising Corporate and White-Collar Crime," in *New Directions in Criminological Theory*, ed. S. Hall and S. Winlow (London: Routledge, 2012), 276–77.

116 Ibid., 288.

117 Ibid., 289.

118 Ibid.; Resnick and Wolff, "The Economic Crisis"; Wolff, "In Capitalist Crisis, Rediscovering Marx."

119 Burdis and Tombs, "After the Crisis," 289.

Figure 13.3 Occupy Wall Street protests

inequality in which the richest 1 per cent of the population own and control the majority of society's wealth.[120] These examples of resistance importantly illustrate that our commitment to corporate capitalism is not absolute—that we are not all passive subjects who agree that the pursuit of profit, at almost any cost, is an inherent good.

Conclusion

This chapter has examined the ideologically based common sense that shapes the ways that we understand and respond to corporate harm and wrongdoing, particularly in terms of the state's efforts to develop and enforce criminal laws aimed at disciplining the modern corporation. In particular, dominant ideological commitments to neoliberal political and economic reasoning, along with related forms of regulation that are reinforced by academic perspectives, help to downplay the seriousness of corporate crime and funnel corporate offenders away from criminal justice processes. As a result, these offences remain isolated from "crime, law and order agendas."[121]

---

120 For example, see Richard Wolff, *Occupy the Economy: Challenging Capitalism* (San Francisco: City Lights, 2012).

121 Tombs and Whyte, *Safety Crimes*, 69.

Overall, the chapter does not paint a very flattering picture concerning the use of criminal law as a strategy for confronting the abuse of corporate power. However, while states rarely enact effective corporate crime laws, criminalization strategies nevertheless provide a discourse, or form of representation, to identify and "name" the harms caused by corporations—a valuable language for potentially deterring future offending. The continued dominance of neo-liberalsim does not mean that the state automatically reinforces and reproduces the interests of corporate capitalism.[122] New laws have been introduced, some corporations and corporate executives have been held accountable, and pressures continue to mount (e.g., the Occupy Wall Street movement) for corporations to be held accountable for their wrongdoing. At the same time, however, we must also recognize that criminal laws cannot address the underlying causes of corporate malfeasance. Therefore, we must also explore "truly transformative political ideals"[123] that, for example, challenge the priority accorded to the accumulation of wealth in modern capitalist society and the role of the corporation therein.

Study Questions

1. Why do criminalization strategies work differently when applied to corporate crimes compared to traditional "street" crimes?
2. As you learned in this chapter, critical scholars argue that the state has "relative autonomy" when it comes to the regulation and control of powerful capitalist interests. What does this mean? What does it tell us about the state's development and enforcement of corporate crime laws?
3. What are the pros and cons of using criminal law/punishment strategies in response to corporate crime? In your opinion, could punishment strategies be an effective means for combating corporate harm and wrongdoing?

Exercise

Search the Internet for a news story or article that deals with corporate harm and wrongdoing. For example, it could be a story about an environmental disaster, an incident in the workplace that seriously injured or killed a worker, or an opinion piece about insider trading or price fixing. How does the article or story describe the event? Does it refer to it as a criminal offence or

---

122 Pearce and Tombs, *Toxic Capitalism.*
123 Burdis and Tombs, "After the Crisis," 276.

a crime of violence? How does the language in the story compare to news reporting on traditional forms of crime? In your opinion, why are stories about corporate wrongdoing so different from reporting about street crimes?

Keywords

corporate crime; pump-and-dump scheme; *mens rea*; moral *un-panics*; regulation; free market enterprise; inchoate offences; self-regulation; criminogenic; Occupy Wall Street

References

Bakan, Joel. *The Corporation: The Pathological Pursuit of Profit and Power.* Toronto: Penguin Canada, 2004.

Barak, Gregg. "Financially Respectable Crimes of Wall Street." March 20, 2012. http://www.crimetalk.org.uk/index.php?option=com_content&view=article&id=720%3Afinancially-respectable-crimes-of-wall-street&catid=38&Itemid=41 (accessed April 21, 2014).

Bardach, Eugene, and Robert Kagan. *Going by the Book: The Problem of Regulatory Unreasonableness.* Philadelphia: Temple University Press, 1982.

Bittle, Steven. *Still Dying for a Living: Corporate Criminal Liability after the Westray Mine Disaster.* Vancouver: UBC Press, 2012.

Bittle, Steven, and Laureen Snider. "From Manslaughter to Preventable Accident: Shaping Corporate Criminal Liability." *Law & Policy* 28, no. 4 (October 2006): 470–96. http://dx.doi.org/10.1111/j.1467-9930.2006.00235.x.

Bittle, Steven, and Laureen. Snider. "Moral Panics Deflected: The Failed Legislative Response to Canada's Safety Crimes and Markets Fraud Legislation." *Crime, Law, and Social Change* 56, no. 4 (2011): 373–87. http://dx.doi.org/10.1007/s10611-011-9303-8.

Bonnycastle, Kevyn. "Rape Uncodified: Reconsidering Bill C-49 Amendments to Canadian Sexual Assault Laws." In *Law as a Gendering Practice,* edited by Dorothy Chunn and Dany Lacombe. Toronto: Oxford University Press, 2000.

Boyd, Susan C., Dorothy E. Chunn, and Robert Menzies, eds. *[Ab]using Power: The Canadian Experience.* Halifax: Fernwood Publishing, 2001.

Braithwaite, John. *Crime, Shame and Reintegration.* Cambridge: Cambridge University Press, 1989. http://dx.doi.org/10.1017/CBO9780511804618.

Braithwaite, John. "What's Wrong with the Sociology of Punishment?" *Theoretical Criminology* 7, no. 1 (2003): 5–28. http://dx.doi.org/10.1177/1362480603007001198.

Braithwaite, John. *Markets in Vice, Markets in Virtue.* Annandale: Federation Press, 2005.

Burdis, Kate, and Steve Tombs. "After the Crisis: New Directions in Theorising Corporate and White-Collar Crime." In *New Directions in Criminological Theory,* edited by S. Hall and S. Winlow. London: Routledge, 2012.

CBC News, "Three Former Nortel Executives Acquitted in Fraud Trial." January 14, 2013. http://www.cbc.ca/news/business/3-former-nortel-executives-acquitted-in-fraud-trial-1.829361.

Chunn, Dorothy, and Dany Lacombe, eds. *Law as a Gendering Practice.* Toronto: Oxford University Press, 2000.

Clarke, Thomas, ed. *Theories of Corporate Governance: The Philosophical Foundations of Corporate Governance*. London: Routledge, 2004.

Coleman, Roy, Joe Sim, Steve Tombs, and David Whyte. "Introduction: State, Power Crime." In *State Power Crime*, edited by R. Coleman, J. Sim, S. Tombs, and D. Whyte. London: Sage Publications, 2009. http://dx.doi.org/10.4135/9781446269527.n1.

Comack, Elizabeth, ed. *Locating Law: Race/Class/Gender Connections*. 2nd ed. Halifax: Fernwood Publishing, 2006.

Cossman, Brenda, and Judy Fudge. *Privatization, Law and the Challenge to Feminism*. Toronto: University of Toronto Press, 2002.

Crouch, Colin. *The Strange Non-Death of Neoliberalism*. Cambridge: Polity Press, 2011.

Davis, Courtney. *Making Companies Safe: What Works?* London: Centre for Corporate Accountability, 2004.

Dienst, Richard. *The Bonds of Debt: Borrowing Against the Common Good*. New York: Verso Books, 2011.

Ericson, Richard, Patricia Baranek, and Janet B.L. Chan. *Representing Order: Crime, Law and Justice in the News Media*. Toronto: University of Toronto Press, 1991.

Ericson, Richard, and Kevin D. Haggerty. *Policing the Risk Society*. Oxford: Claredon Press, 1997.

Fanelli, Carlo, and Bryan Evans, eds. *Great Recession-Proof? Shattering the Myth of Canadian Exceptionalism*. Ottawa: Red Quill Books, 2013.

Ferguson, Charles. *Predator Nation: Corporate Criminals, Political Corruption and the Hijacking of America*. New York: Crown Business, 2012.

Friedrichs, David O. *Trusted Criminals: White Collar Crime in Contemporary Society*. Belmont: Wadsworth Cengage Learning, 2010.

Glasbeek, Harry. *Wealth by Stealth: Corporate Crime, Corporate Law, and the Perversion of Democracy*. Toronto: Between the Lines, 2002.

Glasbeek, Harry. "Enron and Its Aftermath: Can Reforms Restore Confidence?" In *Crime in the Corporation*, edited by A.I. Anand, J.A. Connidis, and W.F. Flannagan. Queen's Annual Business Law Symposium, Queen's University, Kingston, 2004.

Glasbeek, Harry. "The Corporation as a Legally Created Site of Irresponsibility." In *International Handbook of White-Collar and Corporate Crime*, edited by H.N. Pontell and G. Geis, 248–78. New York: Springer, 2007. http://dx.doi.org/10.1007/978-0-387-34111-8_12.

Grabosky, Peter G., and Neal Shover. "Forestalling the Next Epidemic of White-Collar Crime." *Criminology & Public Policy* 9, no. 3 (2010): 641–54. http://dx.doi.org/10.1111/j.1745-9133.2010.00658.x.

Gray, Garry C. "The Regulation of Corporate Violations: Punishment, Compliance, and the Blurring of Responsibility." *British Journal of Criminology* 46, no. 5 (2006): 875–92. http://dx.doi.org/10.1093/bjc/azl005.

Gray, Garry C. "The Responsibilization Strategy of Health and Safety: Neo-liberalism and the Reconfiguration of Individual Responsibility for Risk." *British Journal of Criminology* 49, no. 3 (2009): 326–42. http://dx.doi.org/10.1093/bjc/azp004.

Gray, Jeff. "After Nortel Verdict, RCMP's Fraud Unit Racks Up Dismal Conviction Record." *Globe and Mail*. http://www.theglobeandmail.com/report-on-business/industry-news/the-law-page/after-nortel-verdict-rcmps-fraud-unit-racks-up-dismal-conviction-record/article7344652/.

Greenwald, Glenn. *With Liberty and Justice for Some: How the Law Is Used to Destroy Equality and Protect the Powerful*. New York: Metropolitan Books, 2011.

Haines, Fiona. *The Paradox of Regulation: What Regulation Can Achieve and What It Cannot*. Cheltenham: Edward Elgar, 2011. http://dx.doi.org/10.4337/9780857933157.

Haines, Fiona, and Andy Hall. "The Law and Order Debate in OHS." *Journal of Occupational Health and Safety* 20, no. 3 (2004): 263–73.

Haines, Fiona, and Adam Sutton. "The Engineer's Dilemma: A Sociological Perspective on Juridification and Regulation." *Crime, Law, and Social Change* 39, no. 1 (2003): 1–22. http://dx.doi.org/10.1023/A:1022499020874.

Harvey, David. *The Enigma of Capital and the Crises of Capitalism*. New York: Oxford University Press, 2010.

Hawkins, Keith. *Environment and Enforcement: Regulation and the Social Definition of Pollution*. Oxford: Clarendon Press, 1984. http://dx.doi.org/10.1093/acprof:oso/9780198275145.001.0001.

Hawkins, Keith, ed. *The Human Face of Law*. Oxford: Claredon Press, 1997.

Hawkins, Keith. *Law as a Last Resort: Prosecution Decision Making in a Regulatory Authority*. Oxford: Oxford University Press, 2002.

Hutter, Bridget. *The Reasonable Arm of the Law? The Law Enforcement Procedures of Environmental Health Officers*. Oxford: Claredon Press, 1988.

Jessop, Bob. *The Future of the Capitalist State*. Cambridge: Polity Press, 2002.

Kagan, Robert, and John Scholz. "The Criminology of the Corporation and Regulatory Enforcement Strategies." In *Enforcing Regulation*, edited by K. Hawkins and J. Thomas. Boston: Kluwer-Hijhoff, 1984.

McKenna, Bernard. "Critical Discourse Studies: Where to from Here?" *Critical Discourse Studies* 1, no. 1 (2004): 9–39. http://dx.doi.org/10.1080/17405900410001674498.

McMullan, John. *Beyond the Limits of the Law: Corporate Crime and Law and Order*. Halifax: Fernwood Publishing, 1992.

McMullan, John. "Westray and After: Power, Truth and News Reporting of the Westray Mine Disaster." In *[Ab]Using Power: The Canadian Experience*, edited by S. Boyd, D.E. Chunn, and R. Menzies. Halifax: Fernwood Publishing, 2001.

McMullan, John. *News, Truth, and Crime: The Westray Disaster and Its Aftermath*. Halifax: Fernwood Publishing, 2005.

Navarro, Vicente. "The Limitations of Legitimation and Fordism and the Possibility for Socialist Reforms." *Rethinking Marxism* 4, no. 2 (1991): 27–60. http://dx.doi.org/10.1080/08935699108657962.

Noble, Charles. "Regulating Work in a Capitalist Society." In *Corporate Crime: Contemporary Debates*, edited by F. Pearce and L. Snider. Toronto: University of Toronto Press, 1995.

Panitch, Leo, and Martijn Konings. "Myths of Neoliberal Deregulation." *New Left Review* 57 (2009): 67–83.

Pearce, Frank, and Laureen Snider, eds. *Corporate Crime: Contemporary Debates*. Toronto: University of Toronto Press, 1995.

Pearce, Frank, and Steve Tombs. "Ideology Hegemony and Empiricism: Compliance Theories of Regulation." *British Journal of Criminology* 30 (1990): 423–43.

Pearce, Frank, and Steve Tombs. *Toxic Capitalism: Corporate Crime and the Chemical Industry*. Toronto: Canadian Scholars' Press, 1999.

Pearce, Frank, and Steve Tombs. *Bhopal: Flowers at the Altar of Profit and Power*. North Somercotes: CrimeTalk Books, 2012.

Resnick, Stephen A., and Richard D. Wolff. *Knowledge and Class: A Marxian Critique of Political Economy*. Chicago: University of Chicago Press, 1987.

Resnick, Stephen A., and Richard D. Wolff. "The Economic Crisis: A Marxian Interpretation." *Rethinking Marxism: A Journal of Economics, Culture & Society* 22 (2010): 170–86.

Rosoff, Stephen, Henry Pontell, and Robert Tillman. *Profit without Honor: White Collar Crime and the Looting of America*. 5th ed. Upper Saddle River: Pearson, 2010.

Ruggiero, Vincenzo, and Nigel South. "Critical Criminology and Crimes against the Environment." *Critical Criminology* 18, no. 4 (2010): 245–50. http://dx.doi.org/10.1007/s10612-010-9121-9.

Simpson, Sally. *Corporate Crime, Law and Social Control.* Cambridge: Cambridge University Press, 2002. http://dx.doi.org/10.1017/CBO9780511606281.

Slapper, Gary, and Steve Tombs. *Corporate Crime.* Essex: Pearson Education, 1999.

Snider, Laureen. "Towards a Political Economy of Reform, Regulation and Corporate Crime." *Law and Policy* 9 no. 1 (1987): 37–68.

Snider, Laureen. "Cooperative Models and Corporate Crime: Panacea or Cop-Out?" *Crime and Delinquency* 36, no. 2 (1990): 373–90.

Snider, Laureen. *Bad Business: Corporate Crime in Canada.* Toronto: Nelson Canada, 1993.

Snider, Laureen. "The Sociology of Corporate Crime: An Obituary (or: Whose Knowledge Claims Have Legs?)" *Theoretical Criminology* 4, no. 2 (2000): 196–206.

Snider, Laureen. "Accommodating Power: The Common Sense of Regulators." *Social & Legal Studies* 18, no. 2 (2009): 179–97. http://dx.doi.org/10.1177/0964663909103634.

Snider, Laureen. "The Conundrum of Financial Regulation: Origins, Controversies, and Prospects." *Annual Review of Law and Social Science* 21, no. July (2011): 1–17.

Soederberg, Susanne. *Corporate Power and Ownership in Contemporary Capitalism: The Politics of Resistance and Domination.* London: Routledge, 2010.

Sumner, Colin. *The Sociology of Deviance: An Obituary.* Buckingham: Open University Press, 1994.

Tillman, R.H., and M.L. Indergaard. *Pump and Dump: The Rancid Rules of the New Economy.* New Brunswick: Rutgers University Press, 2005.

Tombs, Steve. "Corporate Crime and New Organizational Forms." In *Corporate Crime: Contemporary Debates,* edited by F. Pearce and L. Snider. Toronto: University of Toronto Press, 1995.

Tombs, Steve. "State-Corporate Symbiosis in the Production of Crime and Harm," *State Crime* 1, no. 2 (2012): 170–95.

Tombs, Steve. "Foreword: The Struggle for Corporate Accountability." In *Still Dying for a Living: Corporate Criminal Liability after the Westray Mine Disaster,* S. Bittle. Vancouver: UBC Press, 2012.

Tombs, Steve, and David Whyte. *Safety Crimes.* Cullompton: Willan, 2007.

Tombs, Steve, and David Whyte. "The State and Corporate Crime." In *State Power Crime,* edited by R. Coleman, J. Sim, S. Tombs, and D. Whyte. London: Sage Publications, 2009. http://dx.doi.org/10.4135/9781446269527.n8.

Tomisac, Roman. "Corporate Collapse, Crime and Governance—Enron, Anderson and Beyond." *Australia Journal of Business Law* 14 (2002): 183.

Tucker, Eric, and Harry Glasbeek. "Death by Consensus: The Westray Mine Story." *New Solutions* 3, no. 4 (1993): 14–41.

Wells, Celia. *Corporations and Criminal Responsibility.* Oxford: Clarendon, 1993.

Wells, Celia. *Corporations and Criminal Responsibility.* 2nd ed. Oxford: Clarendon, 2001. http://dx.doi.org/10.1093/acprof:oso/9780198267935.001.0001.

Wolff, Richard. "In Capitalist Crisis, Rediscovering Marx." *Socialism and Democracy* 24, no. 3 (2010): 130–46.

Wolff, Richard. *Occupy the Economy: Challenging Capitalism.* San Francisco: City Lights, 2012.

Yalden, Robert, Janis Sarra, Paul Paton. Ronald Davis, Mark Gillen, and Mary Condon. *Business Organizations: Principles, Policies and Practice.* Toronto: Emond Montgomery Publications, 2008.

fourteen

Social Movements and Critical Resistance: Policing Colonial Capitalist Order

TIA DAFNOS

"The history of all hitherto existing society is the history of class struggles."
(Karl Marx and Friedrich Engels, 1848, *The Communist Manifesto*)

"Where there is power, there is resistance."
(Michel Foucault, 1978, *History of Sexuality*, Volume 1)

Introduction

The study of the policing of resistance, dissent, and the relationship between them is important for understanding the social, political, and economic changes that shape our lives. Paraphrasing Marx and Engels, human history is made through struggles—social conflict drives changes to the structures and relations of our societies. For Foucault, resistance is inherent in the exercise of power. Both statements are based on an understanding of power and resistance as **dialectical**, meaning that resistance and "power," or domination, are not independent of each other but are mutually constitutive. The struggles characterizing exercises of power are continuous, which produce the social changes of human history.

As an institutionalized exercise of power, modern policing has been shaped by resistance since its emergence in the nineteenth century. In the last few decades, there has been a significant expansion of police powers. This has occurred through developments such as the loosening of legal restrictions on investigative powers, the broadening of organizational mandates to include "national security," technological developments enhancing surveillance capabilities and increasing the range of less-than-lethal weapon options available, and the adoption of intelligence-led policing frameworks. This expansion of police powers has arguably been most evident in the criminalization of dissent. Social movements have historically relied on forms of protest as strategies of resistance, action, and change. The policing of dissent, therefore, reveals the social, political, and economic relations of nation-states. As Michel Foucault suggests, resistance makes power relations

Figure 14.1 G20 Summit protests, Toronto, June 26, 2010

visible, and through analyses of acts of resistance we can gain insights into how power works.[1]

When we think about the policing of dissent in Canada today, we generally think of "mega-events" like the global justice protests at the 1997 APEC summit in Vancouver, the 2001 summit of the Americas in Quebec City, or the 2010 G20 summit in Toronto (Figure 14.1). The policing of indigenous peoples' protests, however, are often left out of the picture—except in certain high-profile cases—despite the pervasiveness of these struggles in Canada. These events and how they are policed, have been and continue to be crucial in shaping the social, political and economic relations of the Canadian settler state and its institutions of governance.

The first part of this chapter addresses the significance of policing dissent and resistance, which is commonly associated with "public order policing." We begin by problematizing the conventional definition of "public order policing" and the concepts of "order" and "policing" as social–political constructions that both shape and are shaped by forms of dissent and resistance. The second objective is to examine the historical emergence of the modern

---

1 Michel Foucault, "The Subject and Power," in *Power: Essential Works of Foucault 1954–1984*, vol. 3, ed. James D. Faubion (New York: The New Press, 2000).

Anglo-American police institution and the significance of its role in producing "order" through class and colonial power relations. Third, we focus on militarization and negotiation, which are two important trends in public order policing that have significant implications on the expression of dissent in the context of neoliberal democracy. These two trends are sometimes viewed as being contradictory; however, their complementarity emerges through the constituting of a binary representation of "good protester"/"bad protester" based on discourses of responsibilization, security, citizenship, and rights. These representations have both symbolic and material implications, which are made clear in the case of indigenous resistance.

In the second part of the chapter, we turn more specifically to how these policing trends are put into practice in relation to indigenous peoples' activism. This presents a "colonial paradox" because of the fundamental struggles relating to land, self-determination, and rights. The final objective of this chapter is to examine how these policing dynamics manifest in a recent concrete example. This case study example focuses on the reforms adopted by the Ontario Provincial Police (OPP) after the reclamation at Ipperwash and the shooting death of Dudley George. We will look at how these reforms were applied in response to the 2006 reclamation action at Kanonhstaton (Douglas Creek Estates) near Caledonia, Ontario. In the specificity of this case study, we can identify how contemporary public order policing secures the settler state and global capitalism.

What Is Public Order Policing?

Public order policing refers to the tasks associated with policing potentially disruptive gatherings in public spaces. This can include a wide range of activities, including protests and demonstrations, labour disputes, large cultural events, parades, or sporting event celebrations. Within most contemporary police forces, public order policing is treated as a specialized function, which is reflected in the establishment of specially designated units (e.g., public order units) that are employed in these exceptional circumstances.

Another way to understand public order policing is in a much broader and more literal sense—as policing that aims to maintain or produce public order in society. This definition encompasses the spectrum of police activities from directing traffic to investigating deaths. All of these activities revolve around the enforcement of law as a way of ensuring that people follow the "rules" and, thus, maintain order in society. The narrowness of the conventional definition of public order policing as a specialized function prevents us from seeing this broader role of policing in general. Rather than thinking of the policing of protests as exceptional circumstances, it is more useful to locate it on a continuum, with everyday order at one end and large-scale "mega-events" on the other. With this framework, establishing "public order" is understood as the essence of policing. We might thus think about public order policing as a form of social regulation.

Policing Beyond "the Police"

One way that we can see how central this order-maintenance role is to the police is to understand the police—as a specific formal institution—as merely one specific manifestation of the *practice* of policing. The concept of policing includes forms of regulation or governance that are carried out by a range of actors and entities, and refers to practices concerned with the ongoing monitoring or maintenance of conduct or situations according to certain norms or standards. The work of Michel Foucault, discussed in Chapter One, and governmentality scholars[2] have contributed to an understanding of policing as an activity that can produce or shape behaviours, rather than being strictly repressive, which tends to be our common understanding of policing. This *constitutive* characteristic of policing is evident in the historical origins of the concept.

The term *police* derives from the Greek root word *polis*, meaning "city-state." The emergence of the concept of "police" is intertwined with urbanization and referred to the management of every aspect of city life by state authorities to ensure the well-being of the urban population. This preventative project included the management of things such as sewers, public health, the grain trade, roads and transportation—all aimed at ensuring order. Gradually, the concept of "police" became more narrowly associated with a specific formal institution in the nineteenth century.[3] This police institution is unique because it is invested with the state's monopoly on the use of violence. The police therefore can legitimately exercise coercive power to produce public order, which distinguishes it from the policing practices carried out by other organizations and institutions in society.

It is important to problematize what is meant by the central concept of "public order." First, it assumes a social consensus that "order" is natural and a universal good that everyone shares as a common interest. *Disorder*

---

2 See, for example, Pasquale Pasquino, "Theatrum Politicum: The Genealogy of Capital—Police and the State of Prosperity," in *The Foucault Effect: Studies in Governmentality*, ed. Graham Burchell, Colin Gordon, and Peter Miller (Chicago: University of Chicago Press, 1991).

3 Mark Neocleous, *The Fabrication of Social Order: A Critical Theory of Police Power* (London: Pluto Press, 2000); Michel Foucault, *Security, Territory, Population: Lectures at the Collège de France 1977–1978* (New York: Picador, 2007); George Rigakos, *A General Police System: Political Economy and Security in the Age of Enlightenment* (Ottawa: Red Quill Books, 2009).

is therefore undesirable, and the state's ability to use force via the police to ensure order is viewed as necessary and legitimate. Working from a critical framework, however, we need to ask, "What does order entail? Whose order is this? Where does it come from?"

Order is a political–social construct that is grounded in a historical context. As such, the meaning of order is fluid and changes across time and space. The fact that order must be constantly imposed or produced through policing is evidence that it is being resisted and opposed—there is *conflict* rather than consensus of interests. This challenges the hegemonic understanding of order as natural, universal, and static. Adopting a critical perspective of this concept has implications for our understanding of policing and the assumption that the policing of dissent is an occasional and specialized task of modern police forces. Rather, the production and maintenance of specific social, political, and economic orders that reflect particular interests is a crucial function of the modern police.

History of (Public Order) Policing

The first Anglo-American professional public police force that is the model for police forces today in Canada, other British colonies, and the United States, was the Metropolitan Police (the "Met") of London, England. Conceived of by Sir Robert Peel, the Met was established in 1829 and consisted of full-time public employees who were accountable to the government and the courts. The new police were presented as being an impartial, objective force whose responsibility was to the law. Before the Met, policing was carried out in various decentralized forms such as local constabularies and community watch systems. What changed to make a new form of policing necessary?

Explanations for why and how the modern police institution came to be established can be categorized into three main schools or approaches: orthodox, radical, and historical. All three perspectives identify the emergence of the police as a direct response to the social changes created by the Industrial Revolution, which led to mass migrations of landless people to urban centres. Where these three approaches differ is in how they explain the order-production task of the police.

According to the orthodox or conventional explanation, urbanization led to growing social disorder, characterized by frequent riots and increased criminal activity.[4] The existing constable and watch systems were unable to

---

4 Michael Banton, *The Policeman in the Community* (London: Tavistock, 1964); Eric H. Monkkonen, "History of Urban Police," in *Modern Policing*, ed. Michael Tonry and Norval Morris (Chicago: University of Chicago Press, 1992).

deal with these conditions, which led to the establishment of the state-based formal police organization. In this view, a pre-existing ideal or normal state of order had been disrupted by social changes brought about by urbanization. Modern policing is therefore concerned with the reimposition and maintenance of a consensual and natural order. This perspective is reflected in the description of policing as "*keeping* the peace."

For radical or revisionist scholars drawing on a conflict–Marxist framework, the main reason for the establishment of the modern police was to deal with the contradictions of the emerging capitalist system that gave rise to class conflict.[5] Their role was to control class struggle and protect private property, which would facilitate capitalist accumulation. According to this perspective, there is no consensual order—rather, policing involves the imposition of a *hierarchical class-based order* amid social conflict, serving the interests of a new capitalist class.

The third explanatory approach consists of historical studies. Scholars such as Mike Brogden, Robert Sigler, David King, and Greg Marquis emphasize that modern policing emerged as an important institution in the formation of nation-states and imperial expansion.[6] While producing order in the home country, the modern police also served as a "softer" or "friendly" alternative to military forces in colonial contexts. Using a range of strategies, police were the front line in controlling indigenous populations while protecting and creating order among settlers, colonial institutions, and capitalist enterprises. In this perspective, policing is concerned with the imposition and production of *colonial* order, facilitating capitalist accumulation and territorial expansion on a global scale.

While informed by different theoretical frameworks and scopes of inquiry, these three approaches are not mutually exclusive. At the root of the emergence of the modern Anglo–American police was the problem of changing social relations and conditions arising from industrialization and urbanization. While orthodox accounts focus on this immediate and

---

5 Sidney Harring, "Policing a Class Society: The Expansion of the Urban Police in the Late Nineteenth and Early Twentieth Centuries," in *Crime and Capitalism: Readings in Marxist Criminology*, ed. David Greenberg (Philadelphia: Temple University Press, 1993); Steven Spitzer, "The Political Economy of Policing," in *Crime and Capitalism: Readings in Marxist Criminology*, ed. David Greenberg (Philadelphia: Temple University Press, 1993); Neocleous, *The Fabrication of Social Order*.

6 Mike Brogden, "An Act to Colonise the Internal Lands of the Island: Empires and the Origins of the Professional Police," *International Journal of the Sociology of Law* 15, no. 2 (1987): 179; Robert T. Sigler and David J. King, "Colonial Policing and the Control of Movements for Independence," *Policing and Society* 3, no. 1 (1992): 13; Greg Marquis, "The 'Irish Model' and Nineteenth Century Canadian Policing," *Journal of Imperial and Commonwealth History* 25, no. 2 (1997): 193.

localized level, the radical perspective explains the factors underlying urban "disorder" as stemming from newly emerging power relations in the transition from feudalism to capitalism. The historical analyses situate these processes within a global context of modern nation-state formation, imperialism, and colonialism.

Producing a Capitalist Colonial Order

Bringing these perspectives together allows us to understand the police institution as historically integral to establishing capitalist colonial order. In particular, the police played an important role in the eighteenth-century formation of two key interconnected features of **industrial capitalism**: **private property** and **wage labour**.

The private ownership of property is a defining feature of capitalism and has been facilitated by law and its enforcement. With the privatization of land came the disappearance of "the commons" and customary practices whereby people could obtain sustenance from the land for survival. For example, if you needed firewood, you could go out and cut what you needed. With privatization of property, the same actions would now be considered theft and trespassing. Ownership gives owners legal control over their property, including the right to use it as they please and to exclude others from it.

The wage labour system characterizes the mode of production in capitalist society in which there is a small number of people who own the means of production, secured through private ownership (i.e., wealth, land, access to resources, tools, and machinery) but need others to put these means to use and produce goods. People without the means of production must "sell" their labour power to the owners in exchange for monetary wages. One consequence of the privatization of property was to criminalize means of sustenance outside of formal wage labour. If you needed firewood but did not own land from which you could cut down your own trees, you would have to purchase firewood from someone that did own it—and thus you needed money.

In addition to the creation of private property laws, lawmakers enforced **vagrancy laws** in the nineteenth century, which criminalized "idleness" of those who are physically capable of work but do not engage in wage labour. At the same time, living or making money in ways outside of wage labour was also criminalized. Over time, this criminalization process, buttressed by moral discourses about disciplined work ethic, served to normalize wage labour as the only legitimate form of work, and therefore of survival. These processes have produced a distinction between the respectable "working class" and the morally inferior "criminal class." Included in the criminal class are those who refuse or resist this system of labour in various forms—surviving by engaging in now-criminalized activities that may once have been normal as customary practices, but also through engaging in active opposition and dissent in the form of protests or "rioting."

Imperialism and the Production of Order in Canada

It is important to situate the localized emergence of industrial capitalism in the context of imperialism, which was driven in large part by the expansionist tendencies of capitalism. As local markets for mass produced goods became saturated and resources were used up, there was a need to expand. Colonies provided new markets as well as natural resources.

As in other British colonies such as Ireland and India, the police institution, alongside the military, was a key component of the colonial apparatus necessary for securing the interests of capitalist enterprises and nation-states in colonies. Urban police forces modelled on the Met were established in Upper and Lower Canada largely between the 1830s and 1870s, spurred directly by the need to deal with the threat to order posed by "problem populations" such as workers and "rebellious French peasants."[7] In the expansion and formation of the Canadian state, rural forces, including the **North West Mounted Police (NWMP)**, the OPP, and a BC mounted troop, were established to protect new industries (particularly the railways and mining) as well as to deal with indigenous uprisings.[8] The NWMP in particular played an active role in the colonial settlement of the west by protecting land surveyors and settlers while they parcelled up and occupied the land, while controlling the so-called Indian problem. While using force was always an option, the police also engaged in practices aimed at obtaining control through forms of negotiation. In part this was because the police forces were significantly outnumbered by the indigenous population. The expropriation of land was therefore accomplished primarily through colonial legal mechanisms such as the **Indian Act, 1867** and treaty agreements that were often made on unequal grounds.[9]

---

7 Marquis, "The 'Irish Model,'" 194; see also Allan Greer, "The Birth of the Police in Canada," in *Colonial Leviathan: State Formation in Nineteenth Century Canada*, ed. Allan Greer and Ian Radford (Toronto: University of Toronto Press, 1992).

8 Todd Gordon, *Cops, Crime and Capitalism: The Law and Order Agenda in Canada* (Halifax: Fernwood Publishing, 2006).

9 Bonita Lawrence, *"Real" Indians and Others: Mixed-Blood Urban Native Peoples and Indigenous Nationhood* (Vancouver: UBC Press, 2004).

According to the imperial legal doctrine of *terra nullius*, land not owned or under sovereign control of a state was free for taking by corporations, states, and settlers who could establish their ownership by occupying it. This goes hand in hand with privatization of property. A key role for the military and police, therefore, was the removal or displacement of indigenous peoples from their land. This included their segregation on **reserves** and exclusion from the now-secured private and Crown property, which disrupted traditional means of subsistence.

The police institution was merely one part of the colonial project of assimilation, working together with the Department of Indian Affairs and church and missionary groups, which were often given responsibility for running **residential schools**. Together these institutions, backed by the authority of law, worked to produce colonial order by segregating indigenous peoples so that they could be "civilized" and integrated into the colonial capitalist order of the settler state. These assimilationist techniques can be seen as forms of disciplinary power aimed at pacifying and neutralizing threats of indigenous resistance.[10]

It is important to emphasize that throughout the history of Canada as a settler state, indigenous peoples have engaged in resistance against the appropriation of land, segregation, assimilationist mechanisms, and colonial violence through a number of strategies, ranging from armed conflict to the continuation of customary and traditional practices outlawed by the settler state. In turn, this forced the police and Indian Affairs to adapt their own practices of regulation.

The Policing of Dissent in the Late Twentieth Century

As this brief historical overview demonstrates, the common sense notion of "order" as a consensus-based universal ideal or good is a politicized construct that produces certain relations of power. As Sherene Razack emphasizes, this ordering is not just about placing certain racialized, gendered, and sexualized bodies in specific geographical or physical spaces like reserves, but also locating them socially, politically, and economically. Those who are "out of place" spatially and symbolically are viewed as threats to the social order and must be put (back) in their place.[11] Modern policing

---

10 Lawrence, *"Real" Indians and Others*; Kevin Smith, *Liberalism, Surveillance, and Resistance: Indigenous Communities in Western Canada, 1877–1927* (Edmonton: AU Press, 2009).

11 Sherene Razack, "Gendered Racial Violence and Spatialized Justice: The Murder of Pamela George," in *Race, Space and the Law: Unmapping a White Settler Society*, ed. Sherene Razack (Toronto: Between the Lines, 2002).

regulates spaces and people in ways that maintain particular social, moral, political, and economic relations that are constantly being contested by those resisting the imposition of this order. Explicit challenges to the status quo posed by overt resistance and protest come to be framed as "disorder," crime, or national security threats.

Integral to the symbiotic development of modern nation-states and capitalism since the nineteenth century was **liberalism**, a political and economic philosophy centred on the freedom and equality of individuals and the pursuit of self-interests. Enabling this freedom and independence is participation in the free market.[12] This ideology underlies the normalization of wage labour and private property and was reflected in nineteenth-century vagrancy laws. Central to liberalism is the recognition of individual rights—including that of private property. In the late twentieth century, Western nation-states began to formally enshrine rights and freedoms in policy and legislation, thereby protecting individuals from state power. In Canada, the 1982 constitutional entrenchment of rights in the **Canadian Charter of Rights and Freedoms** provided protection for civil and political rights, including section 2, which guarantees the "fundamental freedoms" of "conscience," "thought, belief, opinion and expression," "peaceful assembly," and "association." The protection of rights resonates with notions of "civilized" liberal society and is one way of distinguishing a nation-state from others. Because the freedom of expression is a critical hallmark of liberal democracy, Willem De Lint and Alan Hall note that the policing of dissent is an important symbolic indicator of how democratic a state is.[13] A state that violently suppresses dissent (and lacks formal protection of rights) is anti-democratic, authoritarian, or fascist. Conversely, the enshrining of rights signifies the status of a nation-state as a liberal democracy and, thus, as engaging in practices favourable to the expansion of global markets.

Social movements played an important role in the struggle for formal protection of rights and freedoms. At the same time, this legal codification is an institutional factor that now shapes the dynamics of political contention. The importance of rights and their protection underlies two developments in policing and conceptions of public order, which revolve around representations of "good" citizenship in liberal democratic society.

---

12 Neocleous, *The Fabrication of Social Order.*

13 Willem de Lint and Alan Hall, *Intelligent Control: Policing Labour in Canada* (Toronto: University of Toronto Press, 2009).

The Shift from Escalated Force to Negotiated Management

The first significant development in Anglo-American policing in the late twentieth century coincides directly with the formalized protection of rights in the 1980s. This is what is described as a shift from **escalated force** to **negotiated management**. These two "models" of public order policing are often positioned as opposites. The primary goal of the police under an escalated force model is to protect individuals and property that are targeted by protesters. The aim of police is to quell contention as quickly as possible, which often entails the use of highly coercive and violent tactics to overwhelm and suppress the threat. This approach reflects a highly polarized conception of dissent whereby the protesters are positioned as directly challenging and threatening the stability and security of the state, leading to highly confrontational encounters between police and protesters.[14]

Escalated force was most visible in the policing of civil rights/Black freedom and anti-war movements during the 1960s and 1970s in the United States and Britain. Repressive police actions were criticized as contributing to an escalation of violence between protesters and police, leading to serious physical harm and sometimes deaths.[15] While conflict did not occur in Canada at the same intensity of scale or level of violence, the geographical and political proximity of these events did have an influence.[16] This was a period of growing organized militancy by indigenous peoples, which in light of events in the United States and Britain raised fears of potential violence in Canada.[17] The shift away from escalated force occurred somewhat later in Canada than it did in the United States and Britain, but followed a similar pattern. A key factor was criticism of police conduct at the 1997 APEC summit in Vancouver, which led to a formal inquiry.[18] Out of this experience, the RCMP officially adopted a measured response framework, which reflects

14 John McPhail and John McCarthy, "Protest Mobilization, Protest Repression, and their Interaction," in *Repression and Mobilization*, ed. Christian Davenport, Hank Johnston, and Carol Muller (Minneapolis: University of Minnesota Press, 2005).

15 Donatella Della Porta and Herbert Reiter, eds., *Policing Protests: The Control of Mass Demonstrations in Western Democracies* (Minneapolis: University of Minnesota Press, 1998); McPhail and McCarthy, "Protest Mobilization"; David Waddington, *Policing Public Disorder: Theory and Practice* (Cullompton: Willan, 2007).

16 de Lint and Hall, *Intelligent Control*.

17 Donald Purich, *Our Land: Native Rights in Canada* (Toronto: James Lorimer, 1986).

18 Wesley Pue, *Pepper in Our Eyes: The APEC Affair* (Vancouver: UBC Press, 2000); Richard Ericson and Aaron Doyle, "Globalization and the Policing of Protest: The Case of APEC 1997," *British Journal of Sociology* 50, no. 4 (1999): 589.

the principles of a negotiated management approach as adopted in other countries. This had effects on other police forces, and measured response is now the norm among police in Canada.[19]

In contrast to escalated force, the negotiated management/measured response model emphasizes the protection of civil rights. To avoid the escalatory dynamic, the measured response approach aims to avoid the use of force unless necessary, thus reflecting a higher degree of tolerance for disruption and even violations of the law. Central to this model is the creation of ongoing opportunities for communication between the police and protesters with the stated aim of facilitating expressions of dissent while minimizing harm to those involved and those potentially affected, such as bystanders. One defining feature of negotiated management is the establishment of designated units for this specific purpose, such as the Community Relations Group (CRG) that was established for the 2010 G8/G20 Summits in Huntsville and Toronto.[20] In the outreach material from the CRG, we can see that the language of rights is prominent in the description of the unit's mandate to "facilitate peaceful and lawful protests":

> *The Canadian Charter of Rights underscores the right of individuals to peacefully express their opinions and views.* The G8-G20 ISU [Integrated Security Unit] upholds this right and balances the demonstrators' lawful right to free speech and our duty to ensure the safety and security of residents, businesses and their property as well as visitors to Canada. *Through its Community Relations Group (CRG), the ISU and its partners are reaching out to protest groups to facilitate peaceful and lawful protests* during the Summits.
>
> The CRG and its partners *encourage open dialogue* with any potential protest organizers *to deescalate tensions* and ensure that any potential protests are carried out *peacefully and within the limits of lawful advocacy, protest and dissent.* The CRG is also responsible for reaching out and consulting with the communities and businesses that may be impacted by security measures during the Summits.[21]

---

19 Sidney Linden, *Report of the Ipperwash Inquiry*, May 31, 2007, http://www.attorneygeneral.jus .gov.on.ca/inquiries/ipperwash/report/index.html.

20 McPhail and McCarthy, "Protest Mobilization."

21 G8-G20 Integrated Security Unit, *G8-G20 Summits Integrated Security Unit Backgrounder* (2010), 2. Emphasis added.

The Militarization Trend

In a seeming contradiction to the "softening" of policing represented by negotiated management/measured response is a second key trend in contemporary policing: an ongoing militarization, or "hardening," of police organizations and practices. Militarization of policing describes a process by which police forces increasingly come to adopt features associated with the military and engage in more integrated exercises and operations with the armed forces.

The increased interlinkages between police and military organizations have been evident in the growing frequency of joint training exercises as well as a blurring of jurisdictions. This blurring stems from the expansion of police responsibilities to include national security, which is reflected in changes to formal mandates as well as the establishment of specialized units. In Canada and the United States, the events of September 11, 2001, were important catalysts to this expanded jurisdiction. Facilitating this widened scope are legislative changes that have broadened police investigative powers by loosening restrictions.[22]

Arguably the most visible manifestation of militarization is the normalization of **police paramilitary units (PPUs)** (e.g., SWAT, Emergency Response Teams).[23] The formal adoption of PPUs in Canada occurred in preparation for the 1976 Summer Olympic Games in Montreal, and they were tasked specifically with responding to hostage and terrorism incidents. Since then, the normalization of PPUs is evident; almost every police force in Canada employing more than 100 officers now has at least one such unit.[24] The mandates of PPUs have expanded to include search and rescue, intelligence gathering, "high-risk" arrests or raids, as well as public order events such as protests. PPUs are specially trained in militaristic tactics as well as the use of specialized technologies.

A key feature of militarization has been the crossover and adoption of military technologies by police forces, including lethal and less-than-lethal weapons, protective equipment, armoured vehicles, information

---

22 Chris Murphy, "'Securitizing' Canadian Policing: A New Policing Paradigm for the Post 9/11 Security State," *Canadian Journal of Sociology* 32, no. 4 (2007): 451.

23 Peter B. Kraska, "Militarization and Policing—Its Relevance to 21st Century Police," *Policing* 14 (2007): 501; Christian Parenti, *Lockdown America: Police and Prisons in the Age of Crisis* (New York: Verso, 2009).

24 Ontario Provincial Police, *OPP Public Order Units: A Comparison of 1995 to 2006*, submission to the Ipperwash Inquiry, July 17, 2006, http://www.attorneygeneral.jus.gov.on.ca/inquiries/ipperwash/policy_part/projects/pdf/Tab5_OPPPublicOrderUnitsAComparisonof1995to2006.pdf (accessed April 22, 2014); de Lint and Hall, *Intelligent Control*.

technologies, and investigative/surveillance technologies.[25] The technological enhancement of investigative techniques meshes with the implementation of **intelligence-led policing (ILP)** as an overarching framework for policing. Reflecting the adoption of a national security orientation, ILP emphasizes the gathering and use of intelligence to guide operations. It has a preventative and pre-emptive orientation, which is contrasted to traditional reactive and responsive policing.[26] Covert operations such as surveillance, infiltration, and the cultivation of informants are part of the ILP repertoire aimed at developing intelligence.

To operationalize ILP, there has been a greater formalization of command-and-control structures. While police organizations are already hierarchical, decision making at the strategic, tactical, and operational levels has been more clearly delineated.[27] This is particularly evident in the context of public order policing.

The coercive implications of militarization seem to be at odds with the "soft" policing of negotiated management. Rather than a contradiction, scholars have variously described the relationship between these two trends as an "iron fist in a velvet glove,"[28] a "carrot and stick" approach,[29] and as a "two-track" strategy[30]—militarization and the potential use of force underlies the initial soft touch of a negotiation-based framework.

Responsibilization and Negotiation

As changes in the organization and practices of policing are reflective and constitutive of the changing social, political, and economic order, it

---

25 Peter Manning "Information Technologies and the Police," in *Modern Policing*, ed. Michael Tonry and Norval Morris (Chicago: University of Chicago Press, 1992); Kevin Haggerty and Richard Ericson, "The Military Technostructures of Policing," in *Militarizing the American Criminal Justice System: The Changing Roles of the Armed Forces and the Police*, ed. Peter B. Kraska (Boston: Northwestern University Press, 2001); de Lint and Hall, *Intelligent Control.*

26 Peter Gill, *Rounding up the Usual Suspects? Developments in Contemporary Law Enforcement Intelligence* (Aldershot: Ashgate Publishing, 2000); Nina Cope, "Intelligence Led Policing or Policing Led Intelligence?" *British Journal of Criminology* 44, no. 2 (2004): 188; de Lint and Hall, *Intelligent Control.*

27 Tony Jefferson, "Pondering Paramilitarism: A Question of Standpoints?" *British Journal of Criminology* 33, no. 3 (1993): 374; P.A.J. Waddington "The Case against Paramilitary Policing Considered," *British Journal of Criminology* 33, no. 3 (1993): 353; Alex S. Vitale "From Negotiated Management to Command and Control: How the New York Police Department Polices Protests," *Policing and Society* 15, no. 3 (2005): 283.

28 Gary Marx, "Some Reflections on the Democratic Policing of Demonstrations," in *Policing Protests: The Control of Mass Demonstrations in Western Democracies*, ed. Donatella Della Porta and Herbert Reiter (Minneapolis: University of Minnesota Press, 1998).

29 Waddington, *Policing Public Disorder.*

30 de Lint and Hall, *Intelligent Control.*

is important to situate the "iron fist in the velvet glove" in the globalizing of neoliberalism and the discourse of human rights since the 1980s. *Neoliberalism* refers to social restructuring characterized by the shrinking of the welfare state in favour of creating conditions beneficial to market expansion. **Responsibilization** can be understood as a technique of governance by which individuals are made responsible for their behaviour and their circumstances. As the state increasingly sheds responsibility for helping people deal with circumstances emerging from social and economic conditions by limiting and reducing programs such as unemployment insurance, welfare, and health care, individuals become responsible for being in these situations and getting out of them.

Negotiated management purports to uphold and respect rights; however, the caveat is that the exercise of these rights must occur in a specific manner that is defined by the state—via the police—that emphasizes the responsibilization of protesters. First, protesters must communicate their intentions with police prior to events and actively cooperate with them in planning. Second, there is a *downloading* or *devolution* of social regulation to protesters who will police themselves and others to remain within the realm of acceptable behaviour. While the rhetoric of negotiated management appears to place police and protesters on even ground, the police clearly have significant leverage in their power to enforce the law, which is always backed up by the threat of force. The monopoly on legitimate violence has not been relinquished. As such, it has been argued that negotiated management has actually increased or enhanced police discretion—a key source of power.[31] For example, the requirement that protesters obtain permits to occupy public space is an important mechanism by which police can either prevent protests or impose conditions on and control them.

"Good" and "Bad" Protesters

As many scholars argue, the "negotiation" process is informed by and shapes distinctions between "good" and "bad" protesters.[32] "Good" protesters are

31 Della Porta and Reiter, *Policing Protests*; Marx, "Some Reflections on the Democratic Policing of Demonstrations."

32 Donatella Della Porta, "Police Knowledge and Protest Policing: Some Reflections on the Italian Case," in *Policing Protests: The Control of Mass Demonstrations in Western Democracies,* ed. Donatella Della Porta and Herbert Reiter (Minneapolis: University of Minnesota Press, 1998); P.A.J. Waddington, "Controlling Protest in Contemporary Historical and Comparative Perspective," in *Policing Protests: The Control of Mass Demonstrations in Western Democracies,* ed. Donatella Della Porta and Herbert Reiter (Minneapolis: University of Minnesota Press, 1998); Mike King and David Waddington, "The Policing of Transnational Protest in Canada," in *The Policing of Transnational Protest,* ed. Donatella Della Porta, Abbey Peterson, and Herbert Reiter (Aldershot: Ashgate Publishing, 2006); Waddington, *Policing Public Disorder.*

those who are known to police, participate in negotiations, have goals that are clearly defined and concrete, use predictable and institutionalized tactics, and engage in self-policing during public actions. In contrast, "bad" protesters engage in "transgressive contention" with goals that seem highly abstract or radical. Reflecting the concern with unpredictability—and therefore increased risk—"bad" protesters are those who are either not well known to police or are known to employ innovative tactics aimed at circumventing police control and causing disruption. Their failure to participate in negotiation is perceived as a challenge to authority.[33] Importantly, this categorization is informed by the degree to which the social subjectivities or identities of protesters are institutionalized in the dominant social, political, and economic structures of society, which is further shaped by age, race, and class.[34] This classification of protesters as "good" and "bad" is both informed by and constructs the binary of citizen/noncitizen, with significant implications for how police respond to resistance and protest.

The failure to exercise rights "properly" as a "good" liberal citizen has material and symbolic effects. When the bad protester refuses or fails to cooperate, or steps out of bounds of an agreement with police, this provides a rationale for deployment of overt and covert militaristic policing to find out what the plans are (since the protesters are not telling them) and to deal with the risks posed by unanticipated disruptive actions. This legitimizes the use of measures like wiretaps, surveillance, infiltration, pre-emptive arrests, cultivating informants, or deploying lethal or less-than-lethal weapons. Bad protesters are positioned as outside of—and therefore a threat to—the consensual social order of the nation-state. As the perception of protesters as "bad" is also very much informed by social locations, those at the margins of the social, political, and economic order are more susceptible to these coercive tactics, furthering their exclusion through representations as "criminals" or "national security threats."

The Chilling Effect?

Tony Jefferson has been a prominent critic of militarization in the policing of dissent. He argues that the militaristic culture, equipment, and training of public order units foster a perception of protesters as "enemies," which could fuel anticipation among officers for a potential "battle" thus increasing the potential for violence. Jefferson also raises concerns about the normalization

---

33 John A. Noakes, Brian V. Klocke, and Patrick F. Gillham, "Whose Streets? Police and Protester Struggles over Space in Washington, DC, 29–30 September 2001," *Policing and Society* 15, no. 3 (2005): 235; Waddington, *Policing Public Disorder*.

34 Waddington, *Policing Public Disorder*.

of intelligence-gathering activities that are highly intrusive and violate privacy.[35] In the context of the expanded national security mandate of policing, critics have raised concerns about **net-widening** and rights violations as domestic "crime" issues are represented as threats to national security. In the case of protest the use of information-gathering or pre-emptive disruption tactics is highly problematic if no actual violation of the law has occurred and there is a legitimate right to protest. However, such practices are increasingly rationalized through **security discourse** as necessary to protect "our" liberty.[36] For example, surveillance, infiltration, and pre-emptive arrests of activists were significant parts of the policing operations for the 2010 Winter Olympic Games in Vancouver and the G20 Summit in Toronto.[37]

Gary Marx cautions that the "iron fist" that animates the "velvet glove of negotiated management" can have a chilling effect on expressions of dissent in two ways. First is the potential co-option or **institutionalization** of dissent.[38] Institutionalization is a process through which practices or activities become part of a dominant normative order that is taken for granted as legitimate, which may be reflected in law, customs, or common sense assumptions.[39] One example of institutionalization is the practice of filling out a form notifying the local police of protest plans. The format of these forms often resembles a contract, placing responsibility on the person completing the form to adhere to what is reported.

Through institutionalization, dissent becomes embedded within the dominant structures of the state rather than transforming social relations and structures. One indication of this is what Gary Marx refers to as the "ritualization" of protest—protest happens, but it is largely symbolic or scripted to follow accepted conventions. The effect is that while reinforcing the image of a state as a liberal democracy where people are free

---

35 Tony Jefferson, "Beyond Paramilitarism," *British Journal of Criminology* 27 (1987): 47; Jefferson, "Pondering Paramilitarism."

36 Mark Neocleous, *Critique of Security* (Montreal: McGill-Queen's University Press, 2008).

37 See *CBC News*, "RCMP Using Intimidation to Silence Olympic Protest, Group Says," June 24, 2009, http://www.cbc.ca/news/canada/british-columbia/rcmp-using-intimidation-to-silence -olympic-protest-group-says-1.775023; Tim Groves, "Living among Us: Activists Speak Out on Police Infiltration," *Briarpatch*, July 1, 2011, http://briarpatchmagazine.com/articles/view/ living-among-us; Tim Groves and Zach Dubinsky, "G20 Case Reveals 'Largest Ever' Police Spy Operation," *CBC News*, November 11, 2011, http://www.cbc.ca/news/canada/g20 -case-reveals-largest-ever-police-spy-operation-1.1054582; Jeffrey Monaghan and Kevin Walby, "Making up 'Terror Identities': Security Intelligence, Canada's Integrated Threat Assessment Centre and Social Movement Suppression," *Policing and Society* 22, no. 2 (2012).

38 Marx, "Some Reflections," 255.

39 Richard Scott and John Meyer, *Institutional Environments and Organization: Structural Complexity and Individualism* (Thousand Oaks: Sage, 1994).

to express dissent, there is little "potency" in the protest as a means of effecting social change. In other words, protest poses less of a threat to the state and existing power relations. The second related chilling effect is the *silencing* of dissent. Being aware of the potential for police to use tactics such as surveillance, infiltration, pre-emptive arrest, or violence, people may be less willing to engage in disruptive public protest out of fear of the potential consequences.[40]

The complementarity of the iron fist in the velvet glove in relation to producing capitalist colonial order is most evident in the context of indigenous peoples' protest. This stems from the nature of the issues and claims at the heart of protests and reclamations, which exposes the contradictions of policing and rights. Indigenous peoples' protests are most often based on direct contention with the Canadian state. This creates a paradoxical situation that predisposes indigenous peoples to being classified as "bad" protesters and more significantly as *internal* threats to national security.

Colonial Paradox for Indigenous Peoples' Resistance

As noted in Chapter Three, since the arrival of colonizing settlers indigenous resistance to colonialism has been expressed in many different ways. In light of the systemic colonial violence perpetrated against indigenous peoples, it is important to recognize that instances of armed and violent resistance against the Canadian settler state have been rare.[41] As Augie Fleras and Jean Elliot note, instances of violence have been largely defensive in response to aggressive actions of the state and settlers.[42] The form that resistance takes both shapes and is shaped by social, political, and economic formations, including the strategies of governance adopted by the state. In the late 1960s, indigenous resistance in Canada took a more visible and militant tone. This period of mobilization was part of a global rise in anti-colonial struggles, including the Red Power movement in the United States. Since then, direct actions such as blockades and land reclamations have become more common and widespread, in addition to legal challenges in relation to treaty rights and land claims.

---

40 Marx, "Some Reflections."

41 Augie Fleras and Jean Leonard Elliot, *Unequal Relations: An Introduction to Race and Ethnic Dynamics in Canada*, 4th ed. (Toronto: Prentice Hall, 2003); Linden, *Report of the Ipperwash Inquiry*; Smith, *Liberalism, Surveillance and Resistance*.

42 Fleras and Elliot, *Unequal Relations*.

"Legitimate" Avenues of Social Change

What are the legitimate or conventional liberal democratic channels people are expected to turn to if we seek to make changes in society or to have wrongs addressed? In a liberal democratic society with constitutionally embedded rights, "legitimate" avenues of voicing dissent and having grievances addressed include participation in the *political* system (by voting, communicating with elected representatives, or running for office), turning to the *judiciary* to enforce the rule of law (and thus uphold rights), and exercising one's freedoms of political dissent in public spaces. In the latter case, one must go through or come into contact with the *police*.

The paradox should be evident. In a liberal democratic society, "good citizens" are expected to express dissent or grievance through the political, legal, judicial, and police institutions. For indigenous peoples, these are the colonial institutions imposed by the very state whose legitimacy is being challenged and from which they have historically been and continue to be systemically excluded.

Reflecting the dialectic nature of resistance and the imposition of order, significant gains have been made by indigenous peoples through these institutions, such as the constitutional recognition of **Aboriginal and treaty rights** and the settlement of some land claims. The removal of Indian Act prohibitions on political activities in the 1960s was crucial to mobilizations in relation to the content of the Canadian Constitution. In turn, the formal protection of Aboriginal and treaty rights now provides a basis for legal challenges. Although limited, the funding available for researching land claims is crucial to bringing these claims forward. Yet, as Taiaiake Alfred and Jeff Corntassel emphasize, these legal processes have inherent "logical inconsistencies" because they are colonial institutions.[43] The formal land claims process established in 1973 is a prime example, because the state is both the negotiator and the defendant against indigenous challenges.[44] Between 1970 and 2006, 1,337 claims had been filed and only 275 resolved. On average, it takes 20 years to resolve a claim, which has created a significant backlog.[45]

---

43 Taiaiake Alfred and Jeff Corntassel, "Being Indigenous: Resurgences Against Contemporary Colonialism," *Government and Opposition* 40, no. 4 (2005): 612.

44 The land claims process is administered by Aboriginal Affairs and Northern Development Canada (formerly known as Indian and Northern Affairs Canada), presented as a negotiation-based alterative to court challenges for addressing grievances. There are two types of claims: Comprehensive claims are a form of contemporary treaty-making with groups whose land is not covered by existing treaties or other legal arrangements. Specific claims concern grievances regarding the state's obligations to First Nations as set out in existing treaties or other agreements.

45 Todd Gordon, *Imperialist Canada* (Winnipeg: Arbeiter Ring Publishing, 2010).

Paradox of Negotiated Management

Direct action protest methods such as blockades and reclamations are often options of last resort in light of the limitations of political and judicial channels. This puts indigenous peoples into a space of interaction with the police, an institution that has been directly involved in their displacement, dispossession, and repression. Through historical practices of overpolicing and underprotection, there is a deeply embedded lack of trust in police–indigenous relations. Yet under negotiated management, trust is crucial in enabling cooperation between protesters and police. As with the land claims process, there is a contradiction here too: as agents of the state with a mandate of maintaining order, police play a dual role in the "negotiation" process. Indigenous peoples are structurally situated to be framed as "bad" protesters because of the state's inherent interest in maintaining sovereignty and the social order, which are directly challenged by self-determination struggles for the fulfillment of Aboriginal and treaty rights and protection of land.

Under negotiated management, the police task is to balance the "right" to protest with other rights, such as the protection of property and of bystanders not to be harmed. Aboriginal and treaty rights are based on recognizing the existence of indigenous societies prior to settler arrival and therefore are *not derived from the settler state*. The struggle to have these rights upheld reflects a conflict between the dominant liberal regime of *individual rights* versus the *collective* or group nature of Aboriginal and treaty rights. The claim to these rights is based on indigenousity, which relies on an assertion of identity category of difference that challenges the dominant liberal discourse of universality, equality, and guarantees of individual rights.

Land is at the root of indigenous self-determination, and has been systematically expropriated through colonialism in establishing settler-state sovereignty; land is therefore at the centre of Aboriginal and treaty rights, as well as title claims. Claims regarding land include assertions that land was never voluntarily ceded to the Crown, that treaties apparently ceding land were illegitimate, or that the Crown has consistently failed to fulfill its obligations set out in treaties or has actively violated their terms. Contestations over land—whether through legal or direct actions—threaten capitalist production and the state's economic productivity by, for example, disrupting the interests of natural resource extraction, infrastructure projects, or commercial building projects. This conflict reflects a deeper struggle over the means of production and human subsistence. Land appropriated by the Crown has been developed and often sold to private individuals and corporations, all of which have derived material benefit.

The privatization of land creates another paradox for the application of negotiated management to indigenous protests. One of the characteristics of public order policing is the requirement for protesters to obtain permits to hold their event in a public space. This option does not exist in the context of private property, as property rights, which include the right to exclude, are a cherished component of liberalism. In particular, reclamation actions (often to prevent and protect the land from exploitation) are often criminalized as trespass on private property. Consequently, the "right" to protest that is supposed to be facilitated by police is nullified by the supremacy of private property rights. Indigenous peoples' resistance is therefore channelled toward criminalization and being treated as threats to national security.

Divide and Rule

One consequence of this colonial paradox is to "divide and rule" by differentiating between indigenous peoples who choose to cooperate with the police and those who do not. While this is certainly a concern with any group engaging in protest, "divide and rule" is a historically grounded colonial strategy. It is another form of state practice, such as the imposition of band council systems by the Canadian government in place of traditional indigenous forms of governance, that create divisions among members of indigenous communities and organizations. Through representational and material practices, "divide and rule" contributes to fragmentation that threatens solidarity and the potential for mass mobilization. These practices draw on and reproduce racist colonial discourse and representations of indigenous peoples as the "uncivilized other" whose use of direct actions is juxtaposed against the legitimate "civilized" means of the courts or political system, which are perceived as neutral and objective in a liberal democracy. Consequently, those who engage in disruptive direct actions are often "labelled defiant or *unreasonable*"[46] and are discursively constructed as "militants," "extremists," or "splinter groups" in police, government, and mainstream media discourse.[47]

---

46 Fleras and Elliott, *Unequal Relations*, 199. Emphasis added.

47 Jennifer Adese, "Constructing the Aboriginal Terrorist: Depictions of Aboriginal Protests, the Caledonia Reclamation, and Canadian Neoliberalization," in *Engaging Terror. A Critical and Interdisciplinary Approach*, ed. M. Vardalos, G.K. Letts, H.M. Teixeira, A. Karzai, and J. Haig (Boca Raton: Brown Walker Press, 2009); Tia Dafnos, "Beyond the Blue Line: Researching the Policing of Aboriginal Activism Using ATI," in *Brokering Access: Politics, Power and Freedom of Information in Canada*, ed. Mike Larsen and Kevin Walby (Vancouver: UBC Press, 2012).

Figure 14.2 Private Patrick Cloutier face to face with Brad Larocque: This image, captured during the Oka crisis at Kanesatake (Oka, Quebec) in 1990, has become an iconic image of the "native warrior."

Interfacing with racist stereotypes, these discursive constructs have come to be symbolized by the image of the indigenous warrior at the barricades; masked, dressed in fatigues, and carrying the Mohawk warrior flag (see Figure 14.2). As Taiaiake Alfred and Lana Lowe emphasize, the cultural and ethical foundations for warriors in many indigenous societies are based on a commitment to maintaining peace and defending land and indigenousity. However, the English-language translation of "warrior" connotes militarism and violence, invoking dominant representations based on racial stereotypes of both the "Noble Savage" and the "bloodthirsty renegade."[48]

Rather than being limited to specific individuals or groups, as a form of racialization these characterizations tend to be generalized to all indigenous peoples as perpetual *potential* "militants."[49] Thus, not only do these representations foster divisions among indigenous peoples, they reproduce the binary of the (white) Canadian settler and the native Other. Emma LaRoque

---

48 Taiaiake Alfred and Lana Lowe, *Warrior Societies in Contemporary Indigenous Communities,* submission to the Ipperwash Inquiry, 2005, 23, http://www.attorneygeneral.jus.gov.on.ca/inquiries/ipperwash/policy_part/research/pdf/Alfred_and_Lowe.pdf.

49 Adese, "Constructing the Aboriginal Terrorist."

has shown how the representation of indigenous peoples as "savages" has pervaded colonial literature in a "civ/sav dichotomy," reinforcing the superiority of "civilized" white colonial settlers.[50] As Rita Dhamoon and Yasmeen Abu-Laban argue, the construct of the indigenous "barbarian" is positioned as *foreign* or external to the Canadian nation-state.[51] The risk posed by this racialized colonial version of the "bad protester" represents not just a threat to public order but to national security. Symbolically, these constructions of criminality, signifying risk and threat, *depoliticize* and *delegitimize* acts of political resistance and instead cast them as acts of crime and terrorism. Materially, these representations provide a rationale for coercive militaristic policing practices.

Indigenous protests are, as Willem de Lint states, inherently "high stakes" events for police and the state because they directly challenge the legitimacy of state sovereignty while also challenging the hegemonic ideals of liberal democracy reflected in discourses of rights and citizenship, and in negotiated management.[52] Examining the dynamics of resistance and policing in indigenous struggles can be revealing of the kind of colonial capitalist order being produced through policing.

Case Study: Policing Indigenous Resistance in Ontario

Ipperwash and the Death of Dudley George

In relation to public order policing, the Ipperwash reclamation was highly significant because it was the first time that an indigenous person had been killed by police in a reclamation action in Canada. The events at Ipperwash also led to the formal adoption of a negotiated management approach by the OPP and had effects on police forces across Canada.

In 1993, members of the Stony Point First Nation engaged in a reclamation action of CFB Ipperwash after years of inaction by the federal government to address their claims.[53] The reclamation was largely peaceful until Labour Day 1995 when the action expanded to Ipperwash Provincial

---

50 Emma LaRoque, *When the Other Is Me: Native Resistance Discourse, 1850–1990* (Winnipeg: University of Manitoba Press, 2010).

51 Rita Dhamoon and Yasmeen Abu-Laban, "Dangerous (Internal) Foreigners and Nation-building: The Case of Canada," *International Political Science Review* 30, no. 2 (2009): 163.

52 Willem de Lint, *Public Order Policing in Canada: An Analysis of Operations in Recent High Stakes Events*, submission to the Ipperwash Inquiry, 2004, http://www.attorneygeneral.jus.gov.on.ca/inquiries/ipperwash/policy_part/research/pdf/deLint.pdf.

53 In 1942, the contested land had been appropriated by the federal government to be used as a military base during World War II, with the promise of return afterwards.

Park, which the OPP had anticipated and prepared for. Two days later, Anthony "Dudley" George was killed by a sniper from the OPP's Tactics and Rescue Unit.[54] Eight years later, the provincial government launched a public inquiry into the OPP's conduct at Ipperwash and the events that led to the shooting of Dudley George. The inquiry mandate included examining political interference in police operations and the OPP's conduct and approach to indigenous peoples' protests and reclamations in general. The inquiry ended in August 2006 and the final reports were released in May 2007.

Post-Ipperwash OPP Reforms

In the 11 years between the Ipperwash reclamation and the conclusion of the inquiry, the OPP engaged in significant reorganization and policy development relating to its public order policing approach and improving the force's relationship with indigenous communities. These new policy and structural reforms reflect both militarization and the adoption of a negotiated management approach.

The most obvious element of militarization is the adoption of an intelligence-led policing framework. In the context of public order policing, this is evident in the emphasis on pre-emptive and preventative strategies based on intelligence, and the adoption of a formal command-and-control structure for public order events. Directly inspired by the "Gold," "Silver," and "Bronze" model used in Britain, this practice institutes a formalized division and hierarchy of decision making.[55]

Alongside these reforms are those that resonate with a negotiated management approach and the building of relationships with the communities being policed. This includes changes to training programs to incorporate "native awareness" education, as well as training in gradual use-of-force models. There is an emphasis on improving regular contact with communities to build relationships but also in the specific context of conflict. Central to building the relationships sought through the new frameworks were the

---

54 Peter Edwards, *One Dead Indian: The Premier, the Police, and the Ipperwash Crisis* (Toronto: McClelland & Stewart, 2003).

55 Gold, Silver, and Bronze refer to three levels of command: The Gold commander is responsible for strategic decision making, which informs the tactical decisions of the Silver commander. Making operational decisions on the ground is the Bronze commander, who takes direction from the Gold and Silver levels. The activation of Gold and Silver command depends on the seriousness and scope of the event at issue.

Aboriginal Relations Teams (ART).[56] ARTs were composed of indigenous OPP officers who maintained an ongoing relationship with indigenous communities with the goal of building trust. The idea is that this trust would allow for negotiations around emergent issues to avoid future "escalation."[57] ARTs were responsible for being aware of issues or conflicts within communities, particularly those that could lead to "critical incidents." In the event of a critical incident, ART officers act as liaisons to facilitate two-way communication of the interests and intentions of both the police and protesters to each other. According to the OPP, ART officers are supposed to "remain neutral throughout a major incident" and not engage in intelligence gathering or enforcement.[58]

These reforms are implemented under *A Framework for Police Preparedness for Aboriginal Critical Incidents*, which establishes guidelines for the OPP approach to critical incidents based on principles of negotiated management. These principles are to adopt flexibility in the resolution of conflict and in managing crisis, to engage in "accommodation and mutual respect of differences, positions and interests of the involved Aboriginal community and the OPP," and to use "strategies that minimize the use of force to the fullest extent possible."[59] Coupled with the introduction of ARTs, the *Framework* appears to be fully consistent with the spirit of negotiated management and a commitment to minimizing police use of force. But how does this fit with the militarization of the OPP through ILP and command and control? This becomes clear from the definition of a *critical incident*:

> [Any incident] where the source of conflict may stem from assertions associated with Aboriginal or treaty rights, e.g. colour of right, a demonstration in support of a land claim, a blockade of a transportation route, an occupation of local government buildings, municipal premises, provincial/federal premises or First Nations buildings.[60]

---

56 In 2009, ARTs merged with the OPP's Major Events Liaison Teams (also introduced after Ipperwash) to form Provincial Liaison Teams.

57 Ontario Provincial Police, *A Framework for Police Preparedness for Aboriginal Critical Incidents*, submission to the Ipperwash Inquiry, 2006, http://www.attorneygeneral.jus.gov.on.ca/ inquiries/ipperwash/policy_part/projects/pdf/OPP_Appendix_E_Framework_for_Police _Preparedness.pdf.

58 Ontario Provincial Police, *Aboriginal Initiatives: Building Respectful Relationships*, submission to the Ipperwash Inquiry, July 17, 2006, 24–25, http://www.attorneygeneral.jus.gov.on.ca/inquiries/ ipperwash/policy_part/projects/pdf/Tab2_OPPAboriginalInitiativesBuildingRespectful Relationships.pdf.

59 OPP, *A Framework for Police Preparedness*, 2.

60 Ibid.

What does this definition tell us? Essentially any incident that is a form of protest or resistance or merely *involves* indigenous peoples is a "critical incident." This designation has important implications. The assessment of an event as a critical incident leads to activation of the OPP's integrated response protocol used for high-risk situations. This protocol includes the implementation of the command-and-control response and the activation of the paramilitary Emergency Response Teams (ERT) and Tactics and Rescue Units (TRU), which are specially trained for "high-risk" situations and are equipped with militaristic protective equipment and weapons.[61]

Evident in this new policy direction of the OPP is an assumption that all indigenous protests are "high risk," which means that the negotiated management goals of the *Framework* are to be operationalized with a precautionary or preventative militaristic response. This is not anything new—as discussed, policing in Canada has always been directly concerned with indigenous peoples' threat to colonial order. What is different is that the OPP's *Framework* formalizes this policing response and in so doing, provides legitimacy for any potential use of coercive tactics or force "as necessary" due to "bad" protesters who fail to fully cooperate.

Reforms in Practice: Six Nations of Grand River and Kanonhstaton/Douglas Creek Estates

In 2006, a group of people from the Six Nations of Grand River moved onto an area of land, Kanonhstaton, which was slated for a housing development known as Douglas Creek Estates near Caledonia, Ontario. Occurring prior to the conclusion of the Ipperwash Inquiry, this reclamation was the first major test of the OPP's new *Framework* combining a negotiated management approach with militaristic innovations.

There is a long history of struggle by the Haudenosaunee of Six Nations that preceded the reclamation action, reflecting the ineffectiveness of "legitimate" channels for resolution.[62] Despite being the subject of an outstanding land claim filed in 1987, construction of the housing development by Henco Industries was in progress when protesters reclaimed the site on

---

61 Ontario Provincial Police, *OPP Emergency Response Services: A Comparison of 1995 to 2006,* submission to the Ipperwash Inquiry, July 17, 2006, 49, http://www.attorneygeneral.jus.gov .on.ca/inquiries/ipperwash/policy_part/projects/pdf/Tab4_OPPEmergencyResponseServices AComparisonof1995to2006.pdf.

62 Laura DeVries, *Conflict in Caledonia: Aboriginal Land Rights and the Rule of Law* (Vancouver: UBC Press, 2011).

Figure 14.3 Six Nations of the Grand River reclamation, Kanonhstaton (Douglas Creek Estates), 2006

February 28, 2006. Exercising its private property rights, on March 3, 2006, Henco obtained an injunction against the protesters to force them to leave. By March 17, 2006, three injunctions had been ordered and all were ignored, leading to a finding of contempt by the presiding judge. Protesters were given five days to leave the site before warrants would be issued. After the five days, a criminal contempt charge was added to the existing civil charge and the OPP were instructed by the judge to enforce the warrants and remove the protesters from the site. Reflecting their new approach, the OPP did not enforce the warrants, seeking to avoid unnecessary escalation. However, at 4:30 in the morning on April 20, OPP ERT members conducted a raid on the site and arrested 16 people. Following the raid, protesters re-established blockades and a large number of supporters arrived at the site. On April 22, an agreement was reached between Six Nations representatives and the Canadian and Ontario governments to resume negotiations. In June 2006, the Ontario government purchased the land from Henco.

Throughout the reclamation, there has been conflict involving non-indigenous residents of Caledonia targeting Six Nations as well as the government and the OPP for a perceived "double standard" in not enforcing the law against the indigenous activists. As of November 2013, the land claim remains in the negotiation process.

The OPP framed their response to the reclamation as a success of their new *Framework*. While the April 20 raid appeared to be a clear and sudden escalation from the apparently flexible approach that had prevailed until then, it reflects how negotiated management and militarization work together. The raid had highly militaristic features as an aggressive action carried out by ERT members in full protective gear in the early morning hours, allowing for the element of surprise. In addition to firearms, ERT members carried and used batons, tasers, tear gas, and pepper spray on protesters. According to the OPP's public statements, officers used only the minimum force necessary. The raid itself was deemed necessary because of an assessment of increased risk by the OPP—the details of which were never made public. In this we can see how the militaristic raid was discursively legitimized through (1) the responsibilization of protesters, (2) the centrality of intelligence, and (3) the frame of national security.

First, despite the emphasis on their active negotiation and communication in the periods prior to and following the raid, the implication is that there was a failure on the part of protesters to be open and cooperative with the police. Therefore, the police had to resort to a raid to address a risk created by the protesters. Second, there is the question of how the police became aware of this apparent threat. This is because during communications and negotiation, there was also ongoing covert and overt intelligence-gathering operations, which were documented by protesters and the media and have emerged through the release of police records.[63] Finally, the ambiguity and vagueness of the OPP's statements about the nature of the immediate threat—which has not been revealed—speaks to the dominance of security discourse and positioning of Aboriginal peoples as perpetual threats to the settler nation-state. This discourse allows for reduced transparency of police decisions and justifies the "pre-emptive" intelligence operations and the militaristic raid. Together, these police actions and discursive strategies contributed to what Jennifer Adese describes as the construction of the generalized "Aboriginal terrorist" propagated in media representations of the reclamation.[64]

Conclusion

The policing of the Kanonhstaton/Douglas Creek Estates reclamation demonstrates how negotiated management and militarization, as specific developments in public order policing, work together with dominant liberal

---

63 Dafnos, "Beyond the Blue Line."
64 Adese, "Constructing the Aboriginal Terrorist."

discourses of responsibilization and individual rights to continue producing a colonial social, political, and economic order in the settler state. In this process, the underlying issue of the land struggle is overshadowed by policing activities and the dominant representations of protests and reclamations as radical or extreme actions that are inconsistent with "civilized" institutionalized forms of dissent in liberal democracies. Through constructions of "good" citizens and "bad" or *non*citizens, this policing is informed by and maintains the inherent conflict of legal and governance structures that predispose indigenous peoples to being criminalized for not complying with colonial order—the colonial paradox of resistance.

What are the implications of contemporary policing practices for anticolonial struggles and other forms of dissent? While there are significant concerns about the potential chilling effects of the "iron first in the velvet glove," we have the examples of indigenous struggles that have not been institutionalized, ritualized or silenced despite being most impacted by repressive policing practices. Power exists as a dialectical relationship characterized by material and ideological struggles; social transformation, including decolonization, requires that we start by challenging common sense representations of indigenous and other collective resistance as criminal or national security threats.

Study Questions

1. Identify the historical continuities in policing practices from the nineteenth century to the contemporary context.
2. What is the significance of discourses of rights, responsibility, democracy, and citizenship to policing and protest?
3. What is the "paradox" of policing indigenous resistance in Canada? What does this reveal about law and criminalization?

Exercise

Select an example of a recent protest, strike, demonstration, or reclamation action. Examine how this event/conflict was covered in the mainstream media. Drawing on at least three different mainstream media sources (e.g., text-based articles, video, and images), identify the dominant discourses evident in the media descriptions of the event and the people or groups involved. How are the various participants (protesters, supporters/allies, police, targets/opponents of the protest, bystanders) represented? How do participants in these sources represent themselves and their actions? What are the similarities and differences in how the protesters, the police, and the media represent the issues and actions? How do race, colonialism, age, class, and gender shape these representations, and what are the implications for constructions of threat or danger?

Keywords

public order policing; industrial capitalism; private property; wage labour; Indian Act, 1867; liberalism; Canadian Charter of Rights and Freedoms; escalated force; negotiated management; police paramilitary units (PPUs); intelligence-led policing; responsibilization; security discourse; institutionalization; Aboriginal and treaty rights

References

Adese, Jennifer. "Constructing the Aboriginal Terrorist: Depictions of Aboriginal Protests, the Caledonia Reclamation, and Canadian Neoliberalization." In *Engaging Terror. A Critical and Interdisciplinary Approach*, edited by M. Vardalos, G.K. Letts, H.M. Teixeira, A. Karzai, and J. Haig, 275–285. Boca Raton: Brown Walker Press, 2009.

Alfred, Taiaiake, and Jeff Corntassel. "Being Indigenous: Resurgences against Contemporary Colonialism." *Government and Opposition* 40, no. 4 (2005): 597–614. http://dx.doi.org/10.1111/j.1477-7053.2005.00166.x.

Alfred, Taiaiake, and Lana Lowe. *Warrior Societies in Contemporary Indigenous Communities*. Submission to the Ipperwash Inquiry. 2005. http://www.attorneygeneral.jus.gov.on.ca/inquiries/ipperwash/policy_part/research/pdf/Alfred_and_Lowe.pdf.

Banton, Michael. *The Policeman in the Community*. London: Tavistock, 1964.

Brogden, Mike. "An Act to Colonise the Internal Lands of the Island: Empires and the Origins of the Professional Police." *International Journal of the Sociology of Law* 15, no. 2 (1987): 179–208.

CBC News. "RCMP Using Intimidation to Silence Olympic Protest, Group Says." June 24, 2009. http://www.cbc.ca/news/canada/british-columbia/rcmp-using-intimidation-to-silence-olympic-protest-group-says-1.775023.

Cope, Nina. "Intelligence Led Policing or Policing Led Intelligence? Integrating Volume Crime Analysis into Policing." *British Journal of Criminology* 44, no. 2 (2004): 188–203. http://dx.doi.org/10.1093/bjc/44.2.188.

Dafnos, Tia. "Beyond the Blue Line: Researching the Policing of Aboriginal Activism Using ATI." In *Brokering Access: Politics, Power and Freedom of Information in Canada*, edited by Mike Larsen and Kevin Walby, 209–33. Vancouver: UBC Press, 2012.

de Lint, Willem. *Public Order Policing in Canada: An Analysis of Operations in Recent High Stakes Events*. Submission to the Ipperwash Inquiry. 2004. http://www.attorneygeneral.jus.gov.on.ca/inquiries/ipperwash/policy_part/research/pdf/deLint.pdf.

de Lint, Willem, and Alan Hall. *Intelligent Control: Policing Labour in Canada*. Toronto: University of Toronto Press, 2009.

Della Porta, Donatella. "Police Knowledge and Protest Policing: Some Reflections on the Italian Case." In *Policing Protests: The Control of Mass Demonstrations in Western Democracies*, edited by Donatella Della Porta and Herbert Reiter, 228–52. Minneapolis: University of Minnesota Press, 1998.

Della Porta, Donatella, and Herbert Reiter, eds. *Policing Protests: The Control of Mass Demonstrations in Western Democracies.* Minneapolis: University of Minnesota Press, 1998.

DeVries, Laura. *Conflict in Caledonia: Aboriginal Land Rights and the Rule of Law.* Vancouver: UBC Press, 2011.

Dhamoon, Rita, and Yasmeen Abu-Laban. "Dangerous (Internal) Foreigners and Nation-building: The Case of Canada." *International Political Science Review* 30, no. 2 (2009): 163–83. http://dx.doi.org/10.1177/0192512109102435.

Edwards, Peter. *One Dead Indian: The Premier, the Police, and the Ipperwash Crisis.* Toronto: McClelland & Stewart, 2003.

Ericson, Richard, and Aaron Doyle. "Globalization and the Policing of Protest: The Case of APEC 1997." *British Journal of Sociology* 50, no. 4 (1999): 589–608. http://dx.doi.org/10.1111/j.1468-4446.1999.00589.x.

Fleras, Augie, and Jean Leonard Elliott. *Unequal Relations: An Introduction to Race and Ethnic Dynamics in Canada.* 4th ed. Toronto: Prentice Hall, 2003.

Foucault, Michel. "The Subject and Power." In *Power: Essential Works of Foucault 1954–1984,* vol. 3, edited by James D. Faubion, 326–48. New York: The New Press, 2000.

Foucault, Michel. *Security, Territory, Population: Lectures at the Collège de France 1977–1978.* New York: Picador, 2007. http://dx.doi.org/10.1057/9780230245075.

G8-G20 Integrated Security Unit. *G8-G20 Summits Integrated Security Unit Backgrounder.* 2010.

Gill, Peter. *Rounding up the Usual Suspects? Developments in Contemporary Law Enforcement Intelligence.* Aldershot: Ashgate Publishing, 2000.

Gordon, Todd. *Cops, Crime and Capitalism: The Law and Order Agenda in Canada.* Halifax: Fernwood Publishing, 2006.

Gordon, Todd. *Imperialist Canada.* Winnipeg: Arbeiter Ring Publishing, 2010.

Greer, Allan. "The Birth of the Police in Canada." In *Colonial Leviathan: State Formation in Nineteenth Century Canada,* edited by Allan Greer and Ian Radford, 17–49. Toronto: University of Toronto Press, 1992.

Groves, Tim. "Living among Us: Activists Speak Out on Police Infiltration." *Briarpatch,* July 1, 2011. http://briarpatchmagazine.com/articles/view/living-among-us.

Groves, Tim, and Zach Dubinsky. "G20 Case Reveals 'Largest Ever' Police Spy Operation." *CBC News.* November 11, 2011. http://www.cbc.ca/news/canada/g20-case-reveals-largest-ever-police-spy-operation-1.1054582. http://www.cbc.ca/news/canada/story/2011/11/22/g20-police-operation.html.

Haggerty, Kevin, and Richard Ericson. "The Military Technostructures of Policing." In *Militarizing the American Criminal Justice System: The Changing Roles of the Armed Forces and the Police,* edited by Peter B. Kraska, 43–65. Boston: Northwestern University Press, 2001.

Harring, Sidney L. "Policing a Class Society: The Expansion of the Urban Police in the Late Nineteenth and Early Twentieth Centuries." In *Crime and Capitalism: Readings in Marxist Criminology,* edited by David Greenberg, 546–67. Philadelphia: Temple University Press, 1993.

Jefferson, Tony. "Beyond Paramilitarism." *British Journal of Criminology* 27 (1987): 47–53.

Jefferson, Tony. "Pondering Paramilitarism: A Question of Standpoints?" *British Journal of Criminology* 33, no. 3 (1993): 374–81.

King, Mike, and David Waddington. "The Policing of Transnational Protest in Canada." In *The Policing of Transnational Protest,* edited by Donatella Della Porta, Abbey Peterson, and Herbert Reiter. Aldershot: Ashgate Publishing, 2006.

Kraska, Peter B. "Militarization and Policing—Its Relevance to 21st Century Police." *Policing* 14, no. 4 (2007): 501–13. http://dx.doi.org/10.1093/police/pamo65.

LaRoque, Emma. *When the Other Is Me: Native Resistance Discourse, 1850–1990.* Winnipeg: University of Manitoba Press, 2010.

Lawrence, Bonita. *"Real" Indians and Others: Mixed-Blood Urban Native Peoples and Indigenous Nationhood.* Vancouver: UBC Press, 2004.

Linden, Sidney. *Report of the Ipperwash Inquiry.* May 31, 2007, http://www.attorneygeneral.jus.gov.on.ca/inquiries/ipperwash/report/index.html.

Manning, Peter. "Information Technologies and the Police." In *Modern Policing*, edited by Michael Tonry and Norval Morris, 349–98. Chicago: University of Chicago Press, 1992.

Marquis, Greg. "The 'Irish Model' and Nineteenth Century Canadian Policing." *Journal of Imperial and Commonwealth History* 25, no. 2 (1997): 193–218. http://dx.doi.org/10.1080/03086539708582998.

Marx, Gary. "Some Reflections on the Democratic Policing of Demonstrations." In *Policing Protests: The Control of Mass Demonstrations in Western Democracies*, edited by Donatella Della Porta and Herbert Reiter, 253–70. Minneapolis: University of Minnesota Press, 1998.

McPhail, Clark, and John McCarthy. "Protest Mobilization, Protest Repression, and Their Interaction." In *Repression and Mobilization*, edited by Christian Davenport, Hank Johnston, and Carol Muller, 3–32. Minneapolis: University of Minnesota Press, 2005.

Monaghan, Jeffrey, and Kevin Walby. "Making up 'Terror Identities': Security Intelligence, Canada's Integrated Threat Assessment Centre and Social Movement Suppression." *Policing and Society* (2011). http://www.tandfonline.com/doi/abs/10.1080/10439463.2011.605131.

Monkkonen, Eric H. "History of Urban Police." In *Modern Policing*, edited by Michael Tonry and Norval Morris, 547–80. Chicago: University of Chicago Press, 1992.

Murphy, Chris. "'Securitizing' Canadian Policing: A New Policing Paradigm for the Post 9/11 Security State?" *Canadian Journal of Sociology* 32, no. 4 (2007): 449–77. http://dx.doi.org/10.2307/20460665.

Neocleous, Mark. *The Fabrication of Social Order: A Critical Theory of Police Power.* London: Pluto Press, 2000.

Neocleous, Mark. *Critique of Security.* Montreal: McGill-Queen's University Press, 2008. http://dx.doi.org/10.3366/edinburgh/9780748633289.001.0001.

Noakes, John A., Brian V. Klocke, and Patrick F. Gillham. "Whose Streets? Police and Protester Struggles over Space in Washington, DC, 29–30 September 2001." *Policing and Society* 15, no. 3 (2005): 235–54. http://dx.doi.org/10.1080/10439460500168576.

Ontario Provincial Police [OPP]. *A Framework for Police Preparedness for Aboriginal Critical Incidents.* Submission to the Ipperwash Inquiry. 2006. http://www.attorneygeneral.jus.gov.on.ca/inquiries/ipperwash/policy_part/projects/pdf/OPP_Appendix_E_Framework_for_Police_Preparedness.pdf.

Ontario Provincial Police [OPP]. *Aboriginal Initiatives: Building Respectful Relationships.* Submission to the Ipperwash Inquiry. July 17, 2006. http://www.attorneygeneral.jus.gov.on.ca/inquiries/ipperwash/policy_part/projects/pdf/Tab2_OPPAboriginalInitiativesBuildingRespectfulRelationships.pdf.

Ontario Provincial Police [OPP]. *OPP Emergency Response Services: A Comparison of 1995 to 2006.* Submission to the Ipperwash Inquiry. July 17, 2006. http://www.attorneygeneral.jus.gov.on.ca/inquiries/ipperwash/policy_part/projects/pdf/Tab4_OPPEmergencyResponseServicesAComparisonof1995to2006.pdf.

Ontario Provincial Police [OPP]. *OPP Public Order Units: A Comparison of 1995 to 2006.* Submission to the Ipperwash Inquiry. July 17, 2006. http://www.attorneygeneral .jus.gov.on.ca/inquiries/ipperwash/policy_part/projects/pdf/Tab5_OPPPublic OrderUnitsAComparisonof1995to2006.pdf.

Parenti, Christian. *Lockdown America: Police and Prisons in the Age of Crisis.* New York: Verso, 2009.

Pasquino, Pasquale. "Theatrum Politicum: The Genealogy of Capital—Police and the State of Prosperity." In *The Foucault Effect: Studies in Governmentality,* edited by Graham Burchell, Colin Gordon, and Peter Miller, 105–18. Chicago: University of Chicago Press, 1991.

Pue, Wesley. *Pepper in Our Eyes: The APEC Affair.* Vancouver: UBC Press, 2000.

Purich, Donald. *Our Land: Native Rights in Canada.* Toronto: James Lorimer, 1986.

Razack, Sherene. "Gendered Racial Violence and Spatialized Justice: The Murder of Pamela George." In *Race, Space and the Law: Unmapping a White Settler Society,* edited by Sherene Razack, 121–56. Toronto: Between the Lines, 2002.

Rigakos, George, ed. *A General Police System: Political Economy and Security in the Age of Enlightenment.* Ottawa: Red Quill Books, 2009.

Scott, Richard, and John Meyer. *Institutional Environments and Organization: Structural Complexity and Individualism.* Thousand Oaks: Sage, 1994.

Sigler, Robert T., and David J. King. "Colonial Policing and the Control of Movements for Independence." *Policing and Society* 3, no. 1 (1992): 13–22. http://dx.doi.org/ 10.1080/10439463.1992.9964654.

Smith, Kevin. *Liberalism, Surveillance, and Resistance: Indigenous Communities in Western Canada, 1877–1927.* Edmonton: AU Press, 2009.

Spitzer, Steven. "The Political Economy of Policing." In *Crime and Capitalism: Readings in Marxist Criminology,* edited by David Greenberg, 568–94. Philadelphia: Temple University Press, 1993.

Vitale, Alex S. "From Negotiated Management to Command and Control: How the New York Police Department Polices Protests." *Policing and Society* 15, no. 3 (2005): 283–304. http://dx.doi.org/10.1080/10439460500168592.

Waddington, David P. *Policing Public Disorder: Theory and Practice.* Devon: Willan, 2007.

Waddington, P.A.J. "The Case against Paramilitary Policing Considered." *British Journal of Criminology* 33, no. 3 (1993): 353–73.

Waddington, P.A.J. "Controlling Protest in Contemporary Historical and Comparative Perspective." In *Policing Protests: The Control of Mass Demonstrations in Western Democracies,* edited by Donatella Della Porta and Herbert Reiter, 117–142. Minneapolis: University of Minnesota Press, 1998.

Conclusion: Representation, Regulation, and Resistance

DEBORAH BROCK

Thinking Beyond Crime

A key objective of this text has been to disrupt commonsensical, naturalized, and universalized assumptions about crime and criminality. You should have grasped by now that *crime* is a dynamic concept that changes over time; it is a social construct. Emphasizing the relative character of crime (that something might be defined as a crime in one context but not in another) does not imply that crime is, at best, neutral social phenomena and, at worst, meaningless. On the contrary, throughout this book we have worked with particular theoretical and methodological tools inspired by Michel Foucault to demonstrate that crime and criminality are not natural and inevitable, but socially understood and determined within the context of historical and prevailing power relations.[1]

In Part One of this text, we aimed to provide you with a theoretical and methodological grounding from which to frame the chapters that follow. We noted that while Foucault-inspired analysis is commonly associated with poststructuralism, this book aimed to provide a materially grounded and historically contextualized analysis—that is to say, an analysis grounded in the conditions in which people live, struggle, make choices, resist, and change; an analysis premised on the notion that "regulation" is not a set of abstract rules and laws hanging over the heads of people, but rather something that is internalized, embodied, and lived; an analysis that insists that history matters.

Similarly, *government* is much more than a political apparatus—it is a way of shaping conduct, regulating what people actually believe and do. Government, then, is not removed from the self but is found in the government of self and others. All of this should lead us to question what we understand as "truth" and "fact," particularly (for our purposes here) in how

---

1 Our point here is not to suggest that one theory or theorist "fits all," but to acknowledge and appreciate some of the tools, however roughly hewn, that Foucault's investigations have made available to us, often through their elaboration by subsequent scholars.

we come to understand crime and criminality. Moreover, we have seen how regulation is typically more subtle, and therefore difficult to detect, than the blunt forces of social control. This points to the dangerousness in contemporary flows of power and governance that Foucault addressed directly in his work: Governance is harder to see and so more difficult to resist.[2]

The Politics of Representation

Our foregrounding of the politics of representation throughout this text is not intended to suggest that crime is a myth, although it is possible to suggest that some people's fear of crime might outweigh the likelihood of their victimization. Rather, our objective has been for you to develop the skills to understand the ways in which representations of crime can serve to detract from and obscure some of the very real underlying issues. The critical thinking skills you have been developing should lead you to ask important questions about the nature and content of knowledge production, so that you question where particular knowledges or truths come from and ask whose interests are being served. You should be able to make the connections between knowledge production and the circulation of power, and understand that representational practices have both symbolic value and material effects. This, we believe, is crucial for understanding the production of the social inequalities that are at the core of the making and meaning of crime and criminalization.

Another key theorist in this textbook—Stuart Hall—finds that power and ideology can serve to "fix" meaning by attributing particular attributes and intentions to groups and individuals (e.g., through racial stereotypes). But meaning can never finally be fixed—it can be contested and changed. By revealing and contesting the practices of representation, we make the production of new kinds of knowledge possible.[3] We establish some of the crucial conditions for resistance and change.

Through the work of Stuart Hall, which has appeared frequently throughout this book, we can also better understand the uses of theory and theorists in providing a toolkit for an engaged social and intellectual life. Hall's corpus of scholarship has refused and transcended distinctions between materialist and poststructuralist scholarship. It has analytically foregrounded practices of racialization in systems of political rule. It has shown that discourses are part of the constitution of material life, but that without

---

2 Michel Foucault, *The History of Sexuality*, vol. 1, *An Introduction* (New York: Random House, 1978).
3 Stuart Hall, *Representation and the Media* (Video) (London: Open University, 1997).

material life discourses have no meaning. It has been put to use to explain how power and knowledge intersect in processes of representation, criminalization, and regulation.

The Uses of Intersectional Analysis

In Part Two of this text we began to explore how people, as individuals and as members of populations, become entangled with law and governance. Using concepts such as *intersectionality*, *conjunctural analysis*, *mutual constitution*, and *interdependency* to examine complex social processes, both historical and contemporary, we found that social relations of race, class, gender, and sexuality are interrelated and interdependent. Each chapter in Part Two highlighted a particular dimension for social investigation, drawing attention to the ways in which race, gender, sexuality, and class feature in the politics of representation and in social processes of criminalization. Each chapter advanced our intersectional approach by insisting on the multidimensional character of subjectivity and on the importance of social location and experience. Exploring how race, gender, sexuality, and class are produced in relation to one another in specific contexts, we began to understand the complexities of power relations behind the constitution of law, crime, and criminalization. Perhaps we also began to learn how to ask good analytic questions of our own regarding how the social bases of inequality are produced and sustained in relation to criminalization.

Part Three drew upon these analytic bases to explore some of the core emerging issues in criminology and sociolegal studies today: the surveillance society, the rise of the national security state, human rights in international contexts, unfettered neoliberal corporate power, and the policing of social movements. We broadened our analytic framework further through making the connection between the global and the local. We began to see how studies of criminalization, representation, and regulation are able to show how the often mundane and taken-for-granted features of our everyday lives (such as showing your passport at a national border) are enmeshed in broader relations of surveillance, national security, immigration control, the concentration of wealth and movement of capital, the territorial claims of white settler states, and so on. This should cause us to think critically about the meaning of *human rights* and how peoples and nations are positioned differently in relation to human rights claims. Finally, we explored the politics of dissent and resistance in some of its historical and contemporary variants so that we can gain a better appreciation of what contestation can look like and some of the forces that attempt to contain it.

What Has Been Learned, and What Do We Do with This Knowledge?

A significant number of students enrolled in the sociology and criminology courses in which this text is being used will have specific career objectives in mind following completion of their degree program. Employment within the criminal justice system, work in social welfare, and work in public policy and administration are several directions that might be pursued. Numerous more students will have taken the course out of general interest rather than because they have specific career objectives in mind. Both groups of students are equally important for our objectives in producing this book. We hope that students who are set on a career trajectory in a related area will take with them a critical analysis of the social context for crime and criminalization. We hope that they will challenge themselves and others when confronted by stereotypes, victim blaming, pathologization, and other means of placing blame and responsibility on individual actors or the social groups they have been associated with. Individuals should in most cases be held accountable for their actions, but not without first holding accountable the social context for those actions, and not without first understanding and rethinking what we ourselves bring to the framing and interpretation of those bodies and those actions. We hope too that students who pursue careers in criminal justice–related areas will seek to reform, if not abolish, those institutions and practices that perpetuate social inequalities.

For students who have read this book out of general interest, our hope is that you will now be better positioned to engage in social analysis and critique and to understand the complexities of regulation. We trust that you have gained an appreciation of the ways in which you are enmeshed in relations of power linked to broader social institutions and processes. You will be better positioned to act upon this knowledge in your everyday lives, from challenging representations of crime and criminality that crop up in conversation to more intentional and active participation in social movements. We have signaled periodically throughout the text how social movements figure in the practices of social change. The women's movement; anti-racist, anti-poverty, and anti-globalization organizing; and indigenous peoples' struggles against colonial rule are just some of the expressions of people's resistance to the violence and oppression that they experience in their daily lives and that they witness in the lives of others. Systems of criminalization, policing, and containment figure significantly in this violence and oppression.

Regardless of your future direction, if we have been at all successful in achieving our objectives for this text you will continue to draw on these critical thinking and learning skills in questioning taken-for-granted, every-day conditions, ideas, and actions and insist on change within and beyond practices of criminalization, representation, and regulation. This textbook was premised on the belief that critical sociologists and other researchers have a role and a responsibility for contributing to a politics of resistance and change. This is what we write for.

Glossary

Aboriginal and treaty rights Rights identified in section 35 of the *Constitution Act, 1982*. Aboriginal rights refer to distinctive cultural practices, traditions, and customs of Aboriginal societies that predate settler contact and derive from prior occupancy of the land. Treaty rights refer to the rights set out in treaties created between Aboriginal societies and the Crown.

archaeological method A mode of analysis developed by Michel Foucault that analyzes discourse in the context of its social, historical, and political emergence.

Asian American Refers to Americans of Asian descent. In the US Census Bureau, for example, the category of "Asians" refers to a person having origins in any of the original peoples of the Far East, Southeast Asia, or the Indian subcontinent. It includes people who indicated their race(s) as "Asian" or reported entries such as "Chinese," "Filipino," "Indian," "Vietnamese," "Korean," "Japanese," and "Other Asian." Activists coined the term "Asian American" in the 1960s as an alternative to the term "Oriental" because the latter term is considered derogatory.

assemblage A concept recognizing that political activism and solidarity movements do not need to be established through a shared identity or identity politics. An assemblage is temporary, ongoing, and unpredictable. Assemblages are not based on concrete or stable identity formations. The concept enables us to consider wider possibilities for the politics of resistance in relation to the representation and regulation of crime and criminality.

binary Dual, made up of a pair or two parts, divided in two, as in the common division of humans into females and males. Binary categories are often dichotomous (e.g., male/female, Black/white), assuming absolute differences across groups, and little to no overlap between them.

biopolitics According to Michel Foucault, the style of government that regulates and governs subjects through biopower. Central to this project of biopolitics is the need for authorities to know a population: If a population can be studied and measured, it can then be acted upon and changed. By producing a particular category of knowable people, a range of strategies and programs can be created in which individuals can work on themselves to improve their health and well-being.

biopower A term coined by Michel Foucault to refer to a form of power aimed at managing populations. Biopower was a new form of power that arose in the eighteenth century with the shift from hereditary, monarchical rule to elected liberal democracies and the growth of the nation-state. Biopower is meant to account for the ways in which forms of discipline and governance *require* the establishment and assessment of specific groups of people *as populations*. For Foucault, biopower is a technique used to manage people as groups by extending control over both the physical and political bodies of a population. Biopower acts on the population in a preventative fashion (a power to "make live") and attempts to intervene upon the vital characteristics of human existence in the name of individual or collective life or health. Under this system of rule, individuals are trained to see themselves as biological beings and encouraged to engage in practices of the self to optimize their life chances.

black box In science and engineering, a black box is a device, system, or object for which only the input and output are specified, while the internal mechanisms are unknown or hidden from view. Once a science is accepted as legitimate or a technology is deemed perfected, they become "black boxes" because the science or technology is no longer questioned or scrutinized. Scholars in the field of *science and technology studies (STS)* aim to challenge the taken-for-granted status of these devices, systems, or objects by "opening up the black box" of science and technology and revealing their inner workings. The aim is to show how various social, political, historical, and cultural factors influence and shape the content of science and technology.

Black studies An interdisciplinary area of academic research that emerged in the United States in the late 1960s to address the exclusion of Black students and faculty from the university, as well as the racism embedded in much of the curriculum. One key aspect of this racism was the exclusion of Black experience and perspective in multiple fields. Black studies thus addresses this issue by centralizing Black writers, scholars, experiences, and perspectives in such disciplines as history, philosophy, politics, religion, literature, sociology, and anthropology.

broken window theory A criminological theory associating the absence of social and legal responses to minor offences and signs of disorder in a neighbourhood (a broken window, for example) to serious criminality.

Canadian Charter of Rights and Freedoms A part of the Canadian Constitution that sets out the rights and freedoms associated with a democratic society. The rights and freedoms are not absolute and can be limited under section 1 of the Charter if justified as reasonable in a free and democratic society. Section 2 identifies fundamental freedoms associated with the expression of dissent.

capital In Bourdieu's sociology, capital refers to "usable resources and powers" possessed by each individual. Bourdieu identifies three forms of capital: social, economic, and cultural. Symbolic capital refers to the relative importance of the three forms of capital in a society.

chivalry thesis The idea that women receive lenient treatment by criminal justice officials simply because they are women. This theory implicitly assumes that criminal justice officials are male and act to protect women because of their assumed inherent weaknesses.

colonialism A political project that extends a nation's sovereignty over territory beyond its borders by the establishment of either settler colonies or administrative dependencies in which indigenous populations are directly ruled, displaced, and murdered. Colonizers generally dominate resources, labour, and markets and also impose legal, sociocultural, and linguistic structures on subject populations. Colonial expansion and wealth extraction were part of empire-building, but in later stages coincided with the development of capitalism and the nation-state.

common sense The values and norms of the ruling class that have been accepted as universal by most members of society. Common sense knowledge and values are integral to *hegemony*.

conjunctural analysis A nuanced analysis of the nature of representations and media images that asks questions such as, what are the economic, political, and cultural forces of a given time and place? What are the implications for the social organization of race, class, gender, sexualities, age, religion, nation, citizenship, and dis/ability? This mode of analysis helps us locate the production conditions of a film or other cultural product (i.e., when, why, and how it was made).

conservative analysis of crime An example of a conservative analysis of crime is that it may locate the crisis or "problem of masculinity" in modern Western societies like the United States and Canada as a breakdown of the heterosexual nuclear family unit. The solution to the problem is to restore modern "family values" through state legislation to ensure normative, hetero-patriarchal gender roles and regimes.

corporate crime Offences committed within a corporation that are punishable by administrative, civil, or criminal law and which are meant to benefit the organization. These crimes can be the result of deliberate decisions or negligent actions by individuals or groups within a corporation. Corporate crimes are distinct from organizational crimes in which an individual in an organization commits a crime solely for their own benefit.

cosmopolitanism A form of social solidarity that recognizes human difference through an ethics of global coexistence and shared community. Cosmopolitanism is a politics of human difference that connects local political and social struggles with global struggles.

couch-surfing A temporary mode of lodging that involves staying on acquaintances' couches.

crime–security nexus Refers to two simultaneous processes. First is the way that certain forms of criminality have been reconceptualized and acted upon as threats to national security. Second, conversely, is the way that the conception of national security has been radically reconfigured and extended to include governmental concerns with public safety and the economy and to therefore encompass a host of "true" crimes that have been linked through the spectre of organized crime to national security, including violent street crimes, gun crimes, drug crimes, prostitution, and so on.

criminal anthropology The field of study that examines the supposed connections between criminal behaviour and the personality or physical features of the offender. Criminal anthropology is most commonly associated with Cesare Lombroso and the Italian School of criminology of the late nineteenth century. These scholars believed that criminals were born with certain physiological deficiencies that could be seen on one's body, which set them apart from "normal" individuals. They also assumed that the root causes of crime were found primarily inside the individual and not within one's environment or social conditions.

criminogenic The conditions that create a propensity toward criminal activity; also refers to an argument made by critical corporate crime scholars that the very structure of the modern corporation, particularly that its *raison d'être* is the accumulation of the maximum amount of profit in the shortest time possible, creates pressures or incentives to break the law to achieve the organization's goals.

crisis of masculinity During the late 1990s, debates about a so-called crisis of masculinity emerged in popular discourses of Europe and North America. It refers to the sentiment of men who felt emasculated by second-wave feminism, which gained momentum in the late 1960s. Rather than pinpointing changes to the global economy and the industrial manufacturing sector that occurred after World War II, some men blamed women for taking away their social and economic status, thereby posing a threat to traditional forms of male power and authority.

critical race theory An interdisciplinary theoretical approach and field of study that examines race and processes of racialization in social, legal, political, cultural, and economic processes.

cultivation theory George Gerbner's theory that television watching cultivates viewers' perceptions of social reality based on the representations and narratives found onscreen.

cultural studies An interdisciplinary area of academic research that draws on both the social sciences and the humanities to analyze texts and the everyday practices of cultural life.

cumulative disadvantage The process of accumulating disadvantages over time. As Oscar Gandy notes, the concept "helps to explain how racial effect can be produced within a society that may have in fact experienced a decline in the level of animus or negative racial intent as the motivation behind critical choices that have been made" (2009, 12).

dark figure of crime The amount of crime that goes unreported or undiscovered by police. Because official crime statistics are based on crimes reported by police, the dark figure of crime calls into question the ability of official crime statistics to accurately measure the actual amount of crime that is happening in a given community.

deviance A traditional criminological term that refers to the definition and regulation of difference through identifying, naming, and judging behaviours, identities, ideas, appearances, and so on as violations of social norms, rules, or laws.

dialectical A process of knowledge production through which the interaction of opposing forces or claims produces "truth." Rejecting the philosophical idealism of this concept, *dialectical materialism*, as articulated by Marx and Engels, is grounded in the material activities reflecting struggles between classes. These activities are the basis of human history and the shaping of social conditions.

digital discrimination The computer-mediated processes and practices that sort people and objects into different categories for diverse purposes—including management and control—with the consequent effect of marginalizing some while privileging others.

disciplinary power A modality of power, described by Michel Foucault, which regulates subjects through the organization of space, time, activities, and behaviours and is enforced through systems of surveillance. Disciplinary power aims to regulate the behaviour and conduct of individuals in a given society through the use of systems of surveillance and regulation. These systems are accomplished through the organization of social spaces and the regulation of individual activity and behaviour.

disciplinary society A society composed of forms of disciplinary power.

discourse The organized systems of knowledge and social practices that produce a particular version of reality. Discourses regulate what can be said and done, what can be thought, and what is considered true or correct. They provide the frameworks that people use to give meaning to and interpret the everyday world. Discourses are knowledge systems built on clusters of ideas and representations that structure how one should evaluate the subject under study and often suppress alternative ways of making sense of an issue.

discursive formation The analysis of particular bodies of knowledge (e.g., sociology, criminology as a body of knowledge) and the ways in which these bodies of knowledge produce particular kinds of "truths" taken as social fact.

escalated force A model of Anglo-American public order policing aimed at quelling disruption as quickly as possible, often using overt coercive tactics. It was most visible during the 1960s and 1970s in the United States and Britain, where this model was criticized as fuelling an escalation of violence between police and protesters/targets leading to serious physical harm.

essentialism The belief that people or things have an underlying and unchanging "essence." An essentialist approach or idea treats human behaviours as if they are rooted in some in-born, unchanging essence. Essentialism leads to statements and assumptions about "women" and "men" as if everyone within a category is the same as each other because they share some fixed, universal inner quality. It describes any statement that attempts to close off the possibility of changing human characteristics. The term *essentialism* is often used when human behaviour is explained through biological or scientific explanations and social or cultural forces are ignored.

Ethnocentric The belief in one's own cultural or ethnic superiority over another cultural group.

Eurocentric A perspective that prioritizes European philosophies and practices to the harm or exclusion of non-European worldviews. It is deeply rooted in racist and colonialist processes and usually assumes superiority to non-European ways of knowing.

European Enlightenment A historical period in Europe during the seventeenth and eighteenth centuries that is characterized by a revolution in knowledge away from superstition or divine faith as the ultimate source of authority toward the application of reason and science in understanding and shaping the social world.

expert knowledge The gaze of the expert who attempts to define who people are without direct input from those under observation. It expresses relations of power in which those at the centre can define and categorize social and material life.

extralegal factors The range of considerations that can come into play to affect legal outcomes, such as moral assessments of an accused's sexual behaviours, racial identity, religious affiliation, and other social relations.

familialization An ideology of family life advancing a so-called traditional set of values, expectations, and organization upon which people are expected to emulate as a model for their own lives.

feminism An approach and social movement with multiple and often conflicting viewpoints. At its most basic, feminism problematizes the social construction of gender hierarchies. Feminism involves a commitment to challenge sociopolitical hierarchies that place males, or the traits we associate with males (i.e., masculinity), in a position of dominance over females, or the traits associated with females (i.e., femininity).

feminist analysis of crime An analysis that challenges the exclusion of an analysis of gender in criminological analysis. A feminist analysis of crime often relies on experiential knowledge and the notion of intersectionality as analytic tools in examining the wider historical, political, and social context, while recognizing the ways in which the interlocking systems of race, gender, sexuality, and class simultaneously structure processes of criminalization.

free market enterprise A commitment to *laissez-faire* economic principles that purports free market actors (primarily corporations) are naturally inclined to produce quality goods and services at the most appropriate prices and with little oversight by the state.

gender A term referring to differences between women and men and the social meanings and differential power relations that accrue from the biological differences between being male and being female. Critical gender theorists believe that the social meanings given to gender shape our understanding of anatomical sex differences rather than the other way around, which is the assumed relationship in more conventional analyses.

genderqueer A term used to describe the idea that the two-gender system sets limits on the range of potential gender identities. It offers the possibility of seeing gender as fluid rather than fixed. The term can also refer to disruptions of the sex–gender system, where the assumption is that your anatomical "sex" determines or predicts your social "gender." Being genderqueer can therefore mean presenting yourself socially in a way that is dominantly seen as incongruent with your sex. A person who is genderqueer has a gender identity that is neither man nor woman, is between or beyond genders, or is some combination of genders. This identity is usually related to or in reaction to a binary gender system. Some individuals who identify with this term also consider themselves to be transgendered, while others do not.

genealogical method A historical approach developed by Foucault to examine the circumstances, particularly power relations, that have produced current "truths." Genealogy starts with the present, not to affirm or deny it but to interrogate it, asking how the present has come to be constituted as it is and how we create ourselves according to or against those truths. Foucault developed this approach to interrogate the production of discourses, knowledge, and objects and the meanings associated with them. Foucault used this method to avoid making universal claims, for example, that there is such a thing as "truth" or "human nature." Instead, he undertook an analysis of how we come to believe in universal claims, seeking to discover how particular discourses come to be regarded as "truth."

genealogy A word used by Michel Foucault to describe a way of undertaking historical analysis. A genealogical method is often described as "a history of the present" (rather than accounts of the past) in the sense that the approach examines contemporary social phenomena in relation to the histories on which they depend. A genealogy eschews attempts at totalizing narratives of history and focuses instead on the ways that discourses link ideas, narratives, and events together to produce what appear to be coherent historical stories. A genealogy is interested in examining ideas that are accepted as "truths" in a given society and in a given historical period.

globalization The intensification, expansion, and compression of economic, cultural, and political interconnections throughout the world. Globalization also involves processes of deterritorialization, where territory or geography become less relevant to human relations (aided by information technology, for example). Globalization is not a neutral process and often produces new patterns of inequality.

governing through community Involves the mobilization, enrolment, and deployment of its "vectors and forces" in "novel programmes and techniques which encourage and harness active processes of self-management and identity construction of personal ethics and collective allegiances" (Nikolas Rose, *Powers of Freedom: Reframing Political Thought*, 1999, 176).

governmentality A term coined by Michel Foucault to describe how the process and practice of governing can become a state of mind. As articulated by Foucault, governmentality is the "art of government" (i.e., how governance is accomplished) and is based on the "conduct of conduct" (i.e., how certain behaviours are brought about and any attempt to shape or guide behaviour with specific goals in mind). Governmentality scholars after Foucault have developed this concept in the specific context of neoliberal society. Foucault suggested that not only do governments regulate populations explicitly through laws, police enforcement, and military threats, but that governance works most effectively when it is naturalized, internalized, and reproduced.

governmental power For Foucault, contemporary Western power can be a positive, creative force originating from everywhere and possessed by no one. It is not simply a top-down expression of social control that is used by some groups and individuals over others.

habitus In Bourdieu's sociology, refers to a series of predispositions that result from social conditioning and that produce affinities. These predispositions are habitual and patterned, shaping our thought and behaviour. They develop from our social position and our membership in particular social fields (e.g., religious, cultural, intellectual, or educational locations, networks, and relationships).

hegemonic masculinity A term created by masculinities scholar R.W. Connell that refers to normative, dominant, or hegemonic forms of masculinity. Some of the characteristics associated with hegemonic masculinity include being middle or upper class, able-bodied, white, straight/ heterosexual, English speaking, university educated, and Anglo-Saxon.

hegemony A concept developed by Antonio Gramsci describing a power relation characterized by consent rather than coercion. Hegemony is secured through political and ideological struggle in which the interests of the ruling class are accepted as the universal interest of all classes. More recently, the definition has been broadened to include the process through which ruling groups maintain their dominance by convincing those whom they dominate that they share the same values and interests as the ruling group. These beliefs are not simply imposed upon less powerful groups; rather, through cultural practices, consent is created. Hegemony implies that the consent of the populace to the prevailing order is continually being manufactured and thus is open to contestation and resistance.

heteronormative patriotism A performance of racialized hetero-masculinity that displaces queerness and deviance onto the bodies and subjectivities of pathologized, inhuman terrorist "others" while simultaneously producing normative, white, and sometimes homosexual Western citizen subjects.

heteronormativity A set of ideas that views heterosexuality as the normal and natural expression of sexuality. Heteronormative discourses organize categories of gender and sexual identity into hierarchical binaries, which situates "man" as the opposite of (and superior to) "woman," and "heterosexual" as the opposite of (and superior to) "homosexual." Heteronormativity works in multiple ways, marginalizing and excluding a diverse range of gendered and sexual identities that do not fit within heterosexual norms.

heterosexual Sexual attraction to a person of the "opposite" sex and gender. Derived from the binary sex–gender system, which assumes that men and women are fundamentally different and that heterosexuality is the natural and normal condition. The term emerged in the late 1800s in medical discussions of sexual perversion, including sexual acts that were not directed at reproduction. Only in the twentieth century did it acquire its current meaning.

historical materialism A term drawn from the work of Karl Marx and Friedrich Engels that refers to the Marxian interpretation that social change is primarily determined by economic factors.

historicization An understanding of history as a process rather than a set of facts; to render a narrative as historical.

homonationalism The incorporation of LGBTQ individuals into nationalist and patriotic projects in defence of the nation.

homonormativity The adoption of heteronormative values and beliefs by LGBTQ individuals to assimilate and achieve acceptance.

homosexual Denotes sexual attraction to a person of the same sex and gender (the opposite of *heterosexual*). Derived from the binary sex–gender system, which assumes that men and women are opposites of one another. First used in the mid-nineteenth century to describe people who are psychologically of the "opposite" sex. By the nineteenth century, it was used to describe same-sex desire as abnormal and pathological. More recently, it has been supplanted by terms such as gay, lesbian, and queer.

human rights Principles for human behaviour, generally formally established by national and international law. Human rights are premised on certain international norms about what it means to be human, and therefore produces certain kinds of subjects, cultures, and ways of life in differential and hierarchical ways.

identification A process through which a person adopts the characteristics of another person, including aspects of that person's identity, desires, and fears.

identity politics A range of political activity and theorizing founded on the shared experiences of injustice of members of certain social groups with the aim to secure political freedom and self-determination. Members of that specific marginalized group assert or reclaim their distinctiveness in ways that challenge systems of oppression and domination.

ideology A belief system or philosophical stance that legitimates a sociopolitical system or economic structure. In Marxist theory, ideology refers to a set of conscious and unconscious ideas about the world that are presented and accepted as neutral, natural, and universal and have the effect of legitimizing the social order.

immigration penalty The vast array of different state and nonstate authorities, technologies, forms of knowledge, and regimes of rule that control borders and police noncitizens.

imperialism The economic and political processes of extending the dominance of an empire, nation, or metropolitan centre over foreign entities, or of acquiring and holding colonies and dependences through diplomatic or imperialist means.

inalienable rights Human rights that exist prior to any exercise of sovereign power and that cannot be taken away.

inchoate offences A legal term referring to crimes that are incomplete or have not yet been committed. In the context of corporate crime, it refers to offences for which a company is charged with failing to fulfill a legal obligation as opposed to the outcome of an offence.

Indian Act, 1867 An amalgamation of various pieces of federal legislation aimed at the assimilation and governance of Aboriginal peoples. Through the Indian Act the federal government governs and administers to reserve communities and status Indians (whose status is defined under the Act).

indigenous populations Peoples that have survived colonization, conquest, occupation, settlement, and destruction. They have distinct historical, sovereign, cultural, and enduring relationships to the territories and natural resources in the dominant societies in which they live.

indivisible rights The idea that one cluster of human rights cannot dominate or be privileged over any other type of human rights.

industrial capitalism A period in the emergence of capitalism in the nineteenth century during which economic production became characterized by the mechanization of the production process. This enabled the mass production of goods by fewer workers.

intelligence-led policing (ILP) A framework for policing based on a preventative and pre-emptive orientation. The intelligence process is central to ILP and consists of six stages through which raw information is turned into intelligence: prioritization, collection, collation, analysis, dissemination, and evaluation. Police operations and planning are supposed to be guided by intelligence products.

institutionalization A process through which practices or activities become part of a dominant normative order that is taken for granted as legitimate. Expressed in law, customs, or common sense assumptions.

intersectionality A method of analysis that recognizes that individuals occupy and embody multiple social locations, subject positions, and identities. It makes central how individuals embody and live a range of social locations and subject positions, including race, class, gender, sexualities, age, religion, citizenship, dis/ability, and so on. In this way, it explains why not all people react in exactly the same way to the same media or representation, since we are differently located.

knowledge Foucault advanced the idea that in contemporary forms of governance, knowledge and power are co-constitutive and linked together in a circular manner so that they incite one another.

language For cultural critics, refers to any communicative system, encompassing not only written and spoken words, but also imagery, fashion, music, body gestures, advertisements, and so on.

liberal feminism Characterized by the belief that women themselves have the power to achieve equality. Liberal feminists believe that the reform of social institutions such as law and education are the key to changing the status of women. This will open up more avenues for women to prove themselves as equal to men. Social reform rather than radical social change will provide sufficient remedy.

liberalism A way of knowing and organizing social relations based on the ideals of liberty and equality, which privileges the subject as autonomous and rational.

liminal An intermediate, threshold, or ambiguous state in ways of knowing and being.

lumpenproletariat In Marx's theory, refers to a fraction of the working class left out by capitalist economies and unlikely to engage in the revolutionary class struggle.

Manichean A dualistic view of the world. The word is derived from a spiritual practice (Manichaeism) that promoted a doctrine of struggle between good and evil.

Marxist Politics or perspectives related to the political theory and philosophy of Karl Marx (1818–1883), a historian and social theorist whose highly influential work provided a radical critique of capitalism and class relations. Marxists tend to make sense of social relations and inequality in terms of class divisions and economic processes. Private ownership and control of the means of production is understood as a linchpin for the exploitation and oppression of working-class people.

masculinities A relatively recent concept in Western history that refers to the social construction of gender, particularly what it means to be a "man." The concept is pluralized to acknowledge that there are multiple forms of masculinity as it relates to other performances of identity, including race, class, gender, sexuality, nation, dis/ability, and age.

masculinization thesis An assumption that because of the women's movement women are becoming more like men, as evidenced through their presumed increased involvement in crime. This thesis also implicitly assumes that crime is linked to masculinity and that women who appear less feminine are more likely to be criminals.

mens rea A legal term that refers to the offender's state of mind at the time of the offence.

model minority A cultural myth or stereotype that claims all Asian Americans are hardworking, smart, and the most successfully assimilated racial group in dominant American society.

monsterization The process by which certain people accused of crimes are demonized and dehumanized. Lombroso and Ferrero described female offenders as "monsters" because they were "doubly exceptional" as both criminals and women.

moral panic A phrase introduced by the sociologist Stanley Cohen to refer to the reaction by a group of people to the perception that another group or culture (most often a minority group or a subculture) is dangerous or deviant and is therefore a social threat.

moral regulation An approach that seeks to link various forms of regulatory activity (including, but not limited to, legal regulation) as always organized by moral imperatives aimed toward the production of "good" subjects.

moral un-panics The systemic lack of concern demonstrated by the capitalist state when forced to confront the considerable harms caused by powerful social actors. This response differs considerably from the moral panics that frequently follow the commission of traditional street crimes.

mythopoetic men's movement Attempts to liberate men from the constraints of the modern world, which keeps them from being in touch with their true masculine nature. Leaders of the movement believe that modernization results in the feminization of men and the loss of true masculinity. The movement emphasizes homosocial rites of passage that secure and sustain the indestructible hardness of manhood.

the nation An imaginary space through which subjects (or social, rather than legal, citizens) are produced. The concept is distinguishable from "the state" (or the formal institutions of government, such as the law). It is linked to notions such as "character," "ethical subjectivity," and "respectability."

negative liberty The freedom from obstacles, barriers, or interference by other persons or the state. Generally, a negative definition of liberty supports placing strong limitations on state action.

negotiated management A model of Anglo-American public order policing that emphasizes the protection of civil rights and the minimization of the use of force. There is a higher tolerance for disruption and use of discretion in enforcing the law. This model emerged in response to critiques of the escalated force approach. In Canada, this model is known as "measured response."

neoliberalism A particular formation of government in which market forces, rather than a social collective, are taken as dominant and preferred forms of governing. Derived from a political philosophy that originated with the rise of conservative governments in Britain, the United States, and Canada during the mid-1970s, neoliberalism accomplished the reorganization of capitalist states and social life around the idea of markets as the most efficient and moral mechanisms for allocating social goods and shaping individual and collective behaviour. Neoliberal policies result in and legitimize upward redistribution of wealth. Although neoliberal philosophy decries government "interference" in the economy, neoliberal governments take an active role in negotiating the frameworks for global trade and financial activity, protecting private property, and converting public assets into private, for-profit businesses.

net-widening A process through which the range of phenomena or people targeted for forms of social regulation is expanded.

normalization A term used by Foucault to denote the way in which a particular version of things takes on the appeal as standard, true, or "normal." Normalization has become a popular theoretical tool for identifying the arbitrariness of assigning "normal" status to many things most of us take for granted. Foucault believed that normalization is the most effective means of social regulation in contemporary Western societies.

normalizing power Compares, differentiates, creates a hierarchy, homogenizes, and excludes. It is therefore also a dividing practice, because it clearly involves the making of value-laden distinctions between people.

normative femininity Also referred to as *emphasized femininity* (to place it in relationship with hegemonic masculinity), normative femininity is the idealized set of expectations about what it means to be feminine in any given time and place. Normative femininity is intimately linked to heterosexuality, whiteness, and middle-class values.

norms Indicates social expectations about attitudes, beliefs, and values.

North West Mounted Police (NWMP) A paramilitary police force established in 1873 to police the newly acquired territories of Rupert's Land, sold to the Dominion of Canada by the Hudson's Bay Company. In 1920, the NWMP merged with the Dominion Police to form the Royal Canadian Mounted Police (RCMP).

Occupy Wall Street A grassroots social movement that emerged following the 2008 global financial crisis to protest the lack of accountability among the economic elite responsible for the crisis and the related massive social and economic inequalities in society.

Orientalism The way in which the "Orient" is constructed by the West in an attempt to control and claim authority over Eastern cultures that are typically characterized as backwards, inferior, and uncivilized.

Other A process of exclusion through which certain groups of people are considered different and inferior. Othering simultaneously secures the otherer's own social position.

panopticon A new form of prison designed by Jeremy Bentham (1748–1832) that placed guard posts at the centre of a circular structure so that guards located in a central tower could observe the activities of inmates without themselves being seen. Inmates were compelled to modify their behaviour because they could not know when they were being observed. The panopticon would not only constrain the bodies of the prisoners, but also affect their minds since they had to assume constant surveillance. Foucault adapted the model of the panopticon to illustrate the growth and effects of the disciplinary society. Foucault argued that we could understand many modern organizations (schools, hospitals, factories, etc.) as operating in panoptic fashion.

patriarchy A system in which social, economic, and political privilege and entitlement is conferred upon men regardless of the presence or absence of privilege in other areas of men's lives and regardless of if or how they act upon that privilege.

people of colour A political category and umbrella term that became widely used in the 1980s and 1990s and was coined by US civil rights and Canadian anti-racist activists. It refers to nonwhite people or people not of predominantly European ancestry and is often used to convey a sense of unity and shared experience of racism among nonwhite persons.

police paramilitary units (PPUs) Specialized police units trained in militaristic tactics and the use of lethal and less-than-lethal weapons.

politics of representation The ways in which power is associated with the construction of images and meanings. In order to analyze the politics of representation, we need to consider questions like, Where do images come from? Who produces images? How is meaning circumscribed in representation? Who is silenced in the production of images? This concept relies on cultural studies theorist Stuart Hall's idea that (1) all representations are produced through relations of power, (2) the purpose of power and the ambition of ideology are to fix a particular meaning to a specific set of images, and (3) representation is a site of contestation and struggle.

positivism A school of thought that is premised on the belief in an external reality that exists independently from human beings—that is, independently of our own subjective experiences of it—that can be objectively studied and observed. This reality operates according to its own set of natural laws that create stability and order. For positivists, the primary goal of research is to uncover these general truths about the world and the underlying laws that govern them. This is achieved through quantitative research and the gathering and analysis of aggregated data.

positivist approach The belief that empirical methods of analysis will reveal reliable and value-free facts about the social world. From a positivist perspective, scientific knowledge, including social scientific knowledge, can be universal and neutral.

postcolonial studies An interdisciplinary field of study that focuses on the historical, political, economic, cultural, legal, and social effects of colonialism. Although the "post" in postcolonialism carries the connotation of *after* colonialism, postcolonial theory provides a critical scholarly approach that examines the history, legacy, and continuation of European colonial rule throughout the world.

postmodern As a philosophical stance, postmodernism rejects the notion that truth and knowledge can be stable, fixed, and objective. Standing in opposition to grand and essentialist narratives of history and social phenomena, postmodernists instead focus on analysis that is partial, contingent, and deconstructive.

poststructuralism A concept that rejects the notion that society and human behaviour are structured into coherent and predictable patterns. Instead, poststructuralism focuses on the contingency and instability of meaning and seeks out gaps, lapses, and contradictions within a given discourse or practice. Poststructuralism is a philosophical movement and theory that postulates that meaning is never fixed, and as such is closely related to postmodernism.

power Foucault's definition of power involves recognizing power as productive rather than repressive and negative; he offers a positive theory of power. See *governmental power* and *sovereign power*.

private property Tangibles (such as land or objects) and intangibles (such as intellectual products) over which individuals assert exclusive use, protected by legal mechanisms of ownership.

profile A representation of a phenomenon that is distilled down to what are believed to be its key characteristics, or a description of a person based on the aggregation of discrete pieces of information thought to pertain to that person. Thus, we can say that profiles are used to define the key characteristics of a class of phenomena ("criminal behaviours," for example), as well as the individuals who are thought to exhibit some or all of those characteristics.

profiling technologies Tools or artifacts that help maintain and manage profiles. This definition is limited in the sense that it strips from these artifacts the larger relational, organizational, social, and cultural settings in which they are embedded. To understand how these larger settings make meaning for profiling technologies and how they are used, it is more helpful to explain profiling technologies as material artifacts that are embedded within—and that facilitate—systems of profiling and surveillance. They help automate, routinize, and instrumentalize information through the collection, diagnosis, and treatment of data related to the demographic and psychological characteristics of the subjects under surveillance.

projects of the self How governance shapes personal identity and how we come to know ourselves, wish to be known by others, and engage in becoming a particular kind of person.

prudentialism A term defined by Pat O'Malley as a form of self-governance that is linked to the risk society, in which individuals take care to manage their own risks rather than look to a social collective to ensure their well-being.

public order policing The tasks associated with policing potentially disruptive gatherings in public spaces. In a much broader and more literal sense, it is policing that aims to maintain or produce public order in society.

pump-and-dump scheme A type of securities fraud whereby an individual or individuals artificially manipulate share prices in a company. The offenders then sell their shares at an inflated price, leaving investors who were duped into buying shares in the company owning worthless stocks once it is discovered that the company is not profitable.

queer An umbrella term that includes the categories of lesbian, gay, bisexual, and transgendered people. The term also conveys the belief that sexual identities and desires are not determined by nature—that is, they are socially constructed concepts and practices that change over time and place. The term also contests any fixed, binary, oppositional understanding of gender and sexuality to remind us that identity and sexuality are fluid constructs.

race A socially constructed classification of individuals based on real or imagined physical characteristics. Race is not biologically determined, nor an objective social or political fact, but a consequence of power relations that has been used to define and reinforce the unequal relations between dominant and subordinate groups.

racialization A process produced through sociopolitical, legal, economic, and cultural formations and meanings. Racialization signifies and emphasizes the processes through which ideas about race are constructed.

racial profiling Defined by the Ontario Human Rights Commission as "any action undertaken for reasons of safety, security or public protection that relies on stereotypes about race, colour, ethnicity, ancestry, religion, or place of origin rather than on reasonable suspicion, to single out an individual for greater scrutiny or different treatment."

racism The social, political, cultural, and economic expression of forms of racialization.

rape culture The social, political, and discursive messages that suggest that rape is permissible and that women are responsible for the violence that occurs against them.

recidivism The act of repeating an undesirable behaviour after one has experienced negative consequences or treatment for that behaviour. In criminology, the topic of recidivism is often studied within the context of punishment by examining the likelihood that an offender will reoffend after being punished through a criminal sanction, such as a term of incarceration.

regulation All of the ways in which certain attitudes and behaviours are accepted as normal, right, and proper, or are punished for their transgressions and refusals. Regulation can take place discursively (in language, dictums, advice, and advertising), bodily (through physical punishment), or officially (through legal processes, incarceration, and violence). A more narrow definition is a legal restriction imposed by the state on an individual or an organization that is subject to a penalty if not followed or respected. Examples include regulations relating to operating a motor vehicle and workplace health and safety standards.

relational An analysis that establishes the meaning of one belief or thing in relation to another belief or thing so that they become constituent of one another.

relations of power The equal or unequal distribution of power in a given society.

reserves Portions of land designated under the Indian Act and through treaties for the exclusive use by an Aboriginal band. The land is held "in trust" for the band by the federal government.

residential schools A system established by the federal government and administered by churches aimed at assimilating Aboriginal children through the eradication of Aboriginal identity. Children were forcibly removed from their communities and placed in residential schools and often subjected to physical and sexual violence and abuse. The last residential school in Canada closed in 1996.

responsibilization A process associated with (neo)liberalism through which individuals are made responsible/accountable for their behaviours and circumstances and for managing their everyday risks, including the risk of crime.

risk A particular discourse that has emerged alongside neoliberalism through which events like crime are imagined. Risks are sets of probabilities that require management through responsible self-care and through the production of knowledge (risk knowledge) that focuses on individuals for responsible risk management.

science and technology studies (STS) An interdisciplinary field that explores the creation, development, and consequences of science and technology within their cultural, historical, and social contexts. STS scholars examine how various social, political, and cultural factors influence the shape of science and technology and how these, in turn, affect society, politics, and culture.

scientific method The process by which scientists, collectively and over time, endeavour to construct an accurate and objective representation of the world in which reality speaks for itself. The scientific method consists of systematic observation, measurement, and experimentation, and the formulation, testing, and modification of theories and hypotheses.

second-wave feminism A term commonly used to refer to the political movement of the late 1960s and early 1970s in Europe and North America that had the goals of raising consciousness about sexism and patriarchy, legalizing abortion and birth control, and attaining equal rights and sexual liberation for women.

security discourse A way of knowing and of organizing social relations that privileges the security of the nation-state and its citizens, which are understood as being free from risk, threat, or danger.

self-governance The ways in which the prevailing social, political, and economic ethos informs and shapes subjectivity and action. A more narrow definition of self-governance is a form of regulation that allows the corporation to self-monitor rules that are created by the state. In this scenario the state typically cooperates with corporations to ensure adherence to the law, intervening with formal punishments only as a last resort.

semiotics The study of communication through signs. The origin of semiotics lies with Swiss linguist Ferdinand de Saussure (1857–1913), who investigated the nature of language as a system of signs. From this perspective, basically *anything* can be a sign (a word, an image, an odour, a flavour, a texture, a musical note, etc.) so long as it expresses an idea or conveys information and refers to something other than itself.

settler colonialism A racial project that is dependent on the usurpation of land and the legal, administrative, cultural, and bureaucratic governance of indigenous populations.

sex A term that is commonly used in two ways in the West: (1) to refer to the label of female or male assigned to bodies on the basis of supposedly binary genital and reproductive differences. A person's sex is often assumed to be biologically based or naturally occurring; (2) to refer to erotic practices. Since the late nineteenth century, sex acts have come to be seen as the basis of sexual identity and are linked to who a person is rather than just what a person does or desires.

sexual citizenship A set of claims about sexual rights and responsibilities that bind the individual to the nation-state. The meanings of these rights and responsibilities are highly contested, as is the idea that one's loyalty to the nation-state should be continually demonstrated.

sexual exceptionalism A position advanced by Western liberal democratic countries where the support of sexual freedoms (for women and gays) has become a hallmark of a nation's superiority and is mobilized in diplomacy, policy, and military tactics to advance a nation's interests.

sexual identity The process, in practice since the late nineteenth century, of regarding sexual practices as a principle means of knowing who a person is and how he or she is to be treated on the basis of that identity.

sexuality The representation and social meaning attributed to sexual practices and identities.

signified The idea or concept of a sign to which the *signifier* refers.

signifier The form of the semiotic sign, as distinct from its conceptual meaning or idea, the *signified*.

signifying practices Meaning-making behaviours that constitute the interconnected relationship between creation and reception. In this way, the consumer of the text plays just as vital a role as the designer of the text in the production of meaning.

social class Marx defined social classes as collective entities constituted by the economic relationship between those who own the means of production (capitalists/bourgeoisie) and those who own the labour power (workers/proletariat) with specific economically oriented class interests and consciousness. Bourdieu defined social classes as individuals "who, by virtue of the fact that they occupy similar positions in social space ... are subjected to similar conditions of existence and condition factors and, as a result, are endowed with similar dispositions, which prompt them to develop similar practices."

social construction The idea that what we understand as reality is constructed by, or socially made, through our shared culture. As such, social constructionists attempt to identify the historically and culturally specific character of social beliefs and practices.

social control The social structures and belief systems that may function to dominate and constrain the actions of individuals and collectivities.

socialist tradition A political, economic, and intellectual movement that originated in the eighteenth century in opposition to the negative effects of industrialization and capitalism. Socialist ideals include support for some form of collective ownership and distribution of wealth, democratic processes, and a society based on principles of human welfare and social justice.

social regulation The ways in which the beliefs and practices of people, individually and as members of specific populations, are infused with power relations which shape our will, our interests (in a word, our subjectivity), as well as our actions.

sovereign power Power exercised by the sovereign or ruler for direct political rule. It can also include other asymmetrical relationships (e.g., patriarchal power) where power is held over groups and individuals that is negative and prohibitive—for the purpose of social control. Foucault believed that governmental power has overtaken sovereign power in contemporary Western societies.

squeegeeing An activity consisting of wiping someone's car windshield in exchange for money.

the state The set of political institutions that encompasses governments and their agencies (the police, military, courts, legislature, public service). The state is a political and administrative apparatus that claims legitimacy to manage or rule the affairs of a geographical and political territory. Within capitalist economic systems, it is fundamentally a capitalist state. It ultimately works in the interest of preserving a particular economic order that benefits foremost the owners of economic wealth. The modern state carried forward some of the features of sovereign power, particularly through its juridical authority.

stereotypes Attempts to "fix" meanings associated with particular bodies and populations, according to Stuart Hall. Stereotypes typically narrow the meanings in which these bodies and populations can be understood, thereby naturalizing them and limiting how they can be understood.

stereotyping A representation or knowledge claim that characterizes a social identity to a fixed and limited set of characteristics.

stranger danger The idea that violence against women is perpetrated by strangers, usually in public spaces. This is in sharp contrast to the statistical realities, which tell us that over 80 per cent of all sexual assaults against women and girls are committed by someone they know, usually intimately.

structural violence The systematic yet often invisible ways that social structures or arrangements harm or cause injury to individuals and populations.

445

subject creation In Foucault's theory, refers to the processes including the production of knowledge and the use of techniques and technologies of power through which human beings are made into subjects.

subordinate masculinity Marginalized, deviant, or outlaw forms of masculinities that tend to be the inverse of hegemonic masculinities; for instance, gay, queer, nonheterosexual, nonwhite, immigrant, working class, non-English speaking, non-Protestant, or disabled.

surplus value The value produced by workers in excess of the costs related to their labour, including their salaries, and which is then left to be appropriated by the capitalists.

surveillance According to the *Oxford English Dictionary* (OED), denotes a watch or guard kept over a person, especially over a suspected person or prisoner. It also signifies spying, supervision and, less commonly, supervision for the purpose of direction or control. In addition to these meanings, surveillance has come, in contemporary parlance, to refer to a host of technical devices used in military, police, or government surveillance. To broaden out this dictionary definition, surveillance may also be characterized in terms of power relations; that is, it can function as a means of power, shaping social relations in given settings.

taxonomy A system of classification.

teleological The assumption that events occur in a particular way because there is a larger purpose, goal, or end point that must be achieved.

terra nullius A legal doctrine central to imperialism that justifies the acquisition of land by settler occupation on the premise that it is uninhabited and does not belong to anyone. The presence of indigenous peoples was dismissed on the basis that they did not *own* the land.

transgender An umbrella term used to describe the various categories of people who do not fit into the binary gender system. This includes cross-dressers; transvestites; female and male impersonators; drag kings; drag queens; non, pre-, and postoperative transsexuals; and those whose perceived gender or anatomical sex may conflict with their gender expression.

trope A common metaphor or overused theme or device (e.g., a cliché) in literature, films, or other forms of popular culture.

truth-claims Foucault's term for denoting that "truth" is socially and historically produced and is never far from a contestation over meaning.

truth regime A dominant system of knowledge that attempts to establish the limits of what is knowable and possible.

Uniform Crime Reporting (UCR) Survey An instrument designed to measure the incidence of crime and its characteristics in a particular jurisdiction. UCR data reflect reported crime that has been substantiated by police and include the number of criminal incidences, the clearance status of those incidents, and persons-charged information. Since the UCR Survey only collects information on crimes that come to the attention of the police, the data do not contain a count of all crime.

Universal Declaration of Human Rights (UDHR) A declaration adopted by the United Nations General Assembly on December 10, 1948, in response to the horrors of the Holocaust and the realization that a global check on state power was essential to avoid such horrors from happening again in the future. The UDHR represents the first global expression of human rights to which all human beings, regardless of sex, race, nationality, religion, or other circumstances, are entitled.

universalism A modern Western political philosophy or doctrine claiming that there are universal facts or unchanging "truths" about the world that can be discovered through scientific reason and experimentation.

vagrancy laws Legal mechanisms that target those without visible means of conventional sustenance or lodging who are considered able to work. While primarily associated with the nineteenth century, contemporary legislation prohibiting panhandling, busking, street vending, squeegeeing, sex work, and sleeping in public spaces are forms of vagrancy law.

wage labour A system characterizing the capitalist mode of production in which people expend their labour power (work) in exchange for monetary wages.

whiggish view of history An approach that sees historical events as occurring in a relatively seamless line of progression toward an enlightened end.

yellow peril The imagined danger of Asian populations to Western civilization arising from the expansion of the power and influence of Asian nations. In contemporary times, it is used to describe the threat to Western living standards from the influx of Asian labourers willing to work for low wages.

Contributors

Steven Bittle is an Assistant Professor in the Department of Criminology at the University of Ottawa. His main research interests focus on corporate crime and corporate criminal liability. His publications include (with L. Snider) "Moral Panics Deflected: The Failed Legislative Response to Canada's Safety Crimes and Market Fraud Legislation," *Crime, Law and Social Change* 56, no. 4 (2011): 373–87; (with L. Snider) "The Challenges of Regulating Powerful Economic Actors," in *European Developments in Corporate Criminal Liability*, eds. J. Gobert and A.M. Pascal (Routledge, 2011); "Corporate Crime and the Neo-Liberal State," in *Theorizing Justice Interdisciplining the Divide: A Reader*, eds., K. Gorkoff and R. Jochelson (Fernwood Publishing, forthcoming); and *Still Dying for a Living: Shaping Corporate Criminal Liability in After the Westray Mine Disaster* (UBC Press: forthcoming).

Deborah Brock is an Associate Professor in the Department of Sociology at York University. Her research and teaching address social, moral, and sexual regulation. Her publications include *Power and Everyday Practices* (co-edited with Rebecca Raby and Mark Thomas) (Nelson, 2011); *Making Work, Making Trouble: The Social Regulation of Sexual Labour* (University of Toronto Press, 2009, 1998); and *Making Normal: Social Regulation in Canada* (Nelson, 2003).

Simone Browne is an Assistant Professor of Sociology at the University of Texas at Austin. She is the author of numerous publications about race, surveillance, and border control. Her work can be found in *Cultural Studies, Citizenship Studies*, and *Critical Sociology*, among other scholarly journals. She is a contributor to the forthcoming *Routledge Handbook of Surveillance Studies*. Her book-length study of surveillance and Black mobilities is in progress.

Tia Dafnos is a PhD candidate in the Sociology program at York University. Her research interests include racialization and racism in policing practices, intelligence-led policing, the criminalization of dissent, and research methodologies. The current focus of her research is the criminalization and policing of Aboriginal peoples' activism in Canada in the context of neoliberal discourses of democracy and human rights. She is co-editor with Alan

Bourke and Markus Kip of the volume *Lumpen-City: Discourses of Marginality/ Marginalizing Discourses* (Red Quill Books, 2011). The volume includes her chapter contribution "Shifting the Gaze Upwards: Researching the Police as an Institution of Power." Her forthcoming book chapter "Beyond the Blue Line: Researching the Policing of Aboriginal Activism Using ATI" will appear in *Brokering Access: Politics, Power and Freedom of Information in Canada* (edited by Mike Larsen and Kevin Walby, UBC Press).

Martin French is a SSHRC Postdoctoral Fellow with the Department of Sociology at Queen's University. Dr. French's book-length manuscript in preparation, *Viropolitics: HIV Testing and the Criminalization of Disease*, examines how circuits of information traverse and connect the institutions of law and science. His publications include "Woven of War-Time Fabrics: The Globalization of Public Health Surveillance," *Surveillance & Society* 6, no. 2 (2009): 101–15; and "In the Shadow of Canada's Camps," *Social & Legal Studies* 16, no. 1 (2007): 49–69.

Amanda Glasbeek is an Associate Professor in the Department of Social Science at York University, where she is also appointed to the Graduate Faculty in Socio-Legal Studies and Women's Studies. Specializing in feminist criminology, her publications include "An Avalanche of Tragedy: Modern Girls and the Murder of Mrs. Mick," *International Review of Victimology* 19, no. 1 (2013): 7–22; "Apprehensive Wives and Intimidated Mothers: Women, Fear of Crime, and the Criminalization of Poverty in Toronto," in *Poverty, Regulation and Social Justice: Readings on the Criminalization of Poverty*, ed. D. Crocker and V. Johnson, 123–38 (Fernwood Publishing, 2010); *Feminized Justice: The Toronto Women's Court, 1913–34* (UBC Press, 2009); and *Moral Regulation and Governance in Canada* (CSPI, 2006). She is currently working on a SSHRC-funded project (with E. van der Meulen) on diverse women's relationships to public video surveillance in Toronto.

Ummni Khan is an Associate Professor at Carleton University. She has earned a BA from Concordia University, an MA from York University, an LLB from Osgoode Hall Law School, an LLM from the University of Michigan, and an SJD from the University of Toronto. Her research focuses on analyzing the interpenetration of cultural constructions, criminological theories, and legal regulations of sexuality. Her publications include "Prostituted Girls and the Grown-up Gaze," *Global Studies of Childhood* 1, no. 4 (2011); "Running in(to) the Family: 8 Short Stories about Sex Workers, Clients, Husbands, and Wives," *American University Journal of Gender, Social Policy & the Law* 19, no. 2 (2011): 495–528; "Putting a Dominatrix in Her

Place," *Canadian Journal of Women and the Law* 21, no. 1 (2009): 143–76; and "A Woman's Right to be Spanked: Testing the Limits of Tolerance of S/M in the Socio-Legal Imaginary," *Law & Sexuality: A Review of Lesbian, Gay, Bisexual and Transgender Legal Issues* 18, no. 1 (2009): 79–120. Her book, *Vicarious Kinks: S/M in the Socio-Legal Imaginary* (2014) has just been released by the University of Toronto Press.

Ruthann Lee has a PhD in Sociology from York University. She is an Assistant Professor of Cultural Studies at the University of British Columbia (Okanagan Campus). Her research interests are in the areas of gender and women's studies, cultural studies, critical criminology, transnational feminism, queer, Native, anti-colonial, and transgender theory. Her work is published in *Women and Environments, Canadian Woman Studies*, and *Pimps, Wimps, Thugs and Gentlemen: Essays on Media Images of Masculinity* (McFarland Publishers, 2009). Ruthann has also worked as a community educator and video artist.

Michael Mopas is an Assistant Professor in the Department of Sociology & Anthropology at Carleton University. He specializes in the area of science, technology, and law. His past research has looked at the regulation of the Internet and representations of forensics in popular culture. He is currently working on a SSHRC-funded project that examines the place of sound in law. The study explores the ways in which judges hear and make sense of auditory evidence presented at trial and documents the work of audio forensic experts in making, interpreting, and rendering them audible. His publications include (with Sarah Turnbull) "Negotiating a Way In: Access to Information and Socio-Legal Research," *Canadian Journal of Law and Society* 26 (2011): 585–90; (with Dawn Moore) "Talking Heads and Bleeding Hearts: Public Criminology, Emotions and Newsmaking," *Critical Criminology* 20, no. 2 (2012): 183–96; and "Examining the 'CSI Effect' through an ANT Lens," *Crime, Media, Culture* 3, no. 1 (2007): 110–17.

Carmela Murdocca is an Associate Professor in the Department of Sociology at York University, where she is also appointed to the Graduate Faculty in Socio-Legal Studies and Social and Political Thought. Her research focuses on the sociology of law, race, and gender with an emphasis on historical injustice and social marginalization. Her work has appeared in *Law and Social Inquiry, Social and Legal Studies*, the *Australian Feminist Law Journal*, and the *Canadian Journal of Law and Society*. Her most recent book is entitled *To Right Historical Wrongs: Race, Gender and Sentencing in Canada* (Vancouver: University of British Columbia Press, 2013).

Marcia Oliver is an Assistant Professor in Law and Society at Wilfrid Laurier University. Her research interests are in the areas of international development, global governance, sexuality and gender, and inequality and justice. She is the author of "The US President's Emergency Plan for AIDS Relief: Gendering the Intersections of Neoconservatism and Neo-liberalism," *International Feminist Journal of Politics* 14, no. 2 (2012): 226–46; and (with S. Ilcan and D. O'Connor) "Spaces of Governance: Gender and Public Sector Restructuring in Canada," *Gender, Place and Culture* 14, no. 1 (2007): 75–92.

Anna Pratt is an Associate Professor of Criminology at York University. Her interests encompass policing and punishment; law, administration and discretion; borders, risk, and security; and national inclusions/exclusions as they relate to immigrants and refugees in Canada. Her research has focused on the intersections of criminal justice and immigration and refugee domains that culminate in detention and deportation (*Securing Borders: Detention and Deportation in Canada* [UBC Press, 2005]). Her current major study is a SSHRC-funded investigation into the culture, organization, and knowledges that shape the policing of borders in Canada.

Marie-Eve Sylvestre is Director of Graduate Studies and Associate Professor at the Faculty of Law of the University of Ottawa where she teaches criminal law and punishment and legal theory from critical and multidisciplinary perspectives. Her research interests include the intersection between law and poverty, the criminalization of social conflicts, and the regulation and control of public spaces. She is the author of two award-winning articles published respectively in the *McGill Law Journal* ("Rethinking Criminal Responsibility for Poor Offenders: Choice, Monstrosity and the Logic of Practice"—2011 Canadian Association of Law Teachers Scholarly Paper Award), and in the *Canadian Journal of Law and Society* ("Le droit est aussi une question de visibilité: occupation des espaces publics et parcours judiciaries des personnes itinérantes à Montréal et à Ottawa"—2011 Paper Competition Award of the Quebec Bar Foundation). Her recent work has also been published in *Urban Geography* and *Policing and Society*.

Index

453